DATE DUE

DEMCO 38 296

LIBIDINAL CURRENTS

Libidinal Currents

SEXUALITY AND THE SHAPING OF MODERNISM

Joseph Allen Boone

THE UNIVERSITY OF CHICAGO PRESS
CHICAGO AND LONDON

Joseph Allen Boone is professor of English at the University of
Southern California. He is the author of *Tradition Counter Tradition:
Love and the Form of Fiction* and coeditor of *Engendering Men: The
Question of Male Feminist Criticism.*

The University of Chicago Press, Chicago 60637
The University of Chicago Press, Ltd., London
© 1998 by The University of Chicago
All rights reserved. Published 1998
Printed in the United States of America

07 06 05 04 03 02 01 00 99 98   1 2 3 4 5

ISBN: 0-226-06466-2 (cloth)
      0-226-06467-0 (paper)

Library of Congress Cataloging-in-Publication Data

Boone, Joseph Allen.
    Libidinal currents: sexuality and the shaping of modernism /
Joseph Allen Boone.
        p.   cm.
    Includes bibliographical references and index.
    ISBN 0-226-06466-2 (alk. paper).—ISBN 0-226-06467-0
(pbk.: alk. paper)
    1. Sex in literature.   2. Modernism (Literature)   3. Literature,
Modern—19th century—History and criticism.   4. Literature,
Modern—20th century—History and criticism.   I. Title.
PN56.S5B66 1997
809'.933538—dc21   97-30717
                                                  CIP

⊗ The paper used in this publication meets the minimum require-
ments of the American National Standard for Information Sciences—
Permanence of Paper for Printed Library Materials, ANSI Z39.48-
1984.

in memory of
THEODORE ALLEN (1961–1992) *and* WALTER HUGHES (1960–1995)

discerning readers of issues of sexuality and narrative
who should have lived to write the books
that would have superseded those of their teachers

The Press gratefully acknowledges the generous contributions of the Hyder E. Rollins Fund and Fred N. Robinson Publication Fund of the Department of English and American Literature at Harvard University, and funding from the College Award for Excellence awarded this project by the Office of the Dean of Research, College of Letters, Arts, and Sciences, at the University of Southern California, toward the publication of this book.

Portions of this book grew out of earlier versions of the following articles and essays: a version of chapter 1 appeared as "Depolicing *Villette:* Surveillance, Invisibility, and the Female Erotics of 'Heretic Narrative,'" *Novel: A Forum on Fiction* 26, no. 1 (1992) copyright NOVEL Corp. © 1992; part of chapter 3 as "Staging Sexuality: Repression, Representation, and 'Interior' States in *Ulysses*," in *Joyce: The Return of the Repressed,* ed. Susan Stanford Friedman (Cornell University Press, 1993) © 1993 by Cornell University and used by permission of the publisher; part of chapter 4 as "Queer Sites in Modernism: Harlem/The Left Bank/Greenwich Village," in *The Geography of Identity,* ed. Patricia Yaeger (University of Michigan Press, 1996); parts of chapter 5 as "Creation by the Father's Fiat: Paternal Narrative, Sexual Anxiety, and the Deauthorizing Designs of *Absalom, Absalom!*" in *Refiguring the Father: New Feminist Readings of Patriarchy,* ed. Patricia S. Yaeger and Beth Kowaleski-Wallace (Southern Illinois Press, 1989), © 1989 by the Board of Trustees, Southern Illinois University, and as "Of Fathers, Daughters, and Theorists of Narrative Desire: At the Crossroads of Myth and Psychoanalysis in *The Man Who Loved Children*," *Contemporary Literature* 31 (Winter 1990) © 1990, by permission of the University of Wisconsin Press; part of chapter 6 as "Mappings of Male Desire in Durrell's *Alexandria Quartet*," *South Atlantic Quarterly* 88 (Winter 1989).

The following images have been reproduced as part of the chapter openings. Introduction: Annie Liebowitz, photograph from the "White Oak Project, Florida" (1990), James Danziger Gallery. Chapter 1: Edvard Munch, "The Cry," 1895, © 1997 The Munch Museum / The Munch-Ellingsen Group / Artists Rights Society (ARS), New York. Black and white photograph © 1996, The Art Institute of Chicago. All rights reserved. Chapter 2: Dana Gibson, untitled drawing (1890s). Chapter 3: Alen MacWeeney, "The Studio Mantlepiece, Charleston," plate 22 in MacWeeney's and Sue Allison's *Bloomsbury Reflections* (New York: W. W. Norton, 1990). Chapter 4: Brassaï, "Couple at the Homosexual Ball" (1931), © copyright Mme. Gilberte Brassaï, MOMA collection. Smithsonian Institution Photo No. 69.232.1. Chapter 5: Unattributed photo of "Hitler and Mussolini with Sculpture by Josef Thorak" (1938), from the Institute of Contemporary History and Wiener Library Limited. Chapter 6: Jane Ray, "Egypt" (1988). First published by Roger la Borde © 1988.

The author is grateful to all these presses, institutions, and individuals for permission to reprint and reproduce materials.

CONTENTS

ACKNOWLEDGMENTS

If the genesis of this book could be traced back to a single event, it would probably be that moment in graduate school when I nervously presented one of my professors, Joseph Wiesenfarth, with a gargantuan outline for the dissertation I was hoping to get permission to write under his direction. He took one long hard look at the table of contents, his eyebrows arching in a way that did little to allay my anxieties. Then, firmly drawing a line midway through the document, he tactfully suggested—in an understate-ment that I can only now fully appreciate—that I save "the rest . . . for, well, later."

It was advice well heeded, since the first half of that outline provided more than enough material for what became not only my dissertation but my first book, and since "the rest"—which in that outline reached from the 1920s to the 1960s—served as the impetus for what has finally emerged as *Libidinal Currents*. Now, sitting down to write these acknowl-edgments, I find that I want to salute not just the people who have sup-ported this project but to acknowledge the very process that has led to its composition. And a significant part of this process lies in the contrast be-tween the evolution of the present book and that of its predecessor. The strength of the earlier book lay in the clarity of its argument (once those extra chapters in the initial proposal were eliminated), which bestowed on the entire project a logic and a structure that seemed "right" from the be-ginning. Only when I began casting about for a second project did I realize that ideas for books do not always emerge full-blown, with ready-made arguments and outlines. I had initially assumed I could return to the de-ferred half of that original table of contents and, with a few substitutions of terms (namely, "sexuality" and "modernist narrative" for "love" and the "nineteenth-century plot"), produce a serviceable thesis. It didn't take me long, however, to discover that no such neatly symmetrical formulas lay at hand, or were even desirable, in writing about the unruly interimplications of sexuality and psychology in modernist fiction. Indeed, *Libidinal Cur-*

rents turned out to be a project whose ends were never predictable and whose thesis only emerged piecemeal through the long and exploratory process of composing its many component parts. Such a method of creation seems only too appropriate, I can now see, in a book concerned with the unruly and unpredictable effects of the polymorphous perverse, not only on human sexuality and the formation of the human subject, but also on modernist experiments to represent states of consciousness and libidinal desire.

Likewise, as in writing about such deviously slippery currents of desire, I now find it much more difficult to group into clearly differentiated categories the various debts, both personal and intellectual, accumulated in the long process of composing this book: the boundaries between friends, mentors, colleagues, students, and intimates have proved as shifting as the sexual subject matters I have written about. But one debt stands out clearly, and that is to the numerous students I have taught in several seminars, first at Harvard and then at the University of Southern California, in which I tested out many of the materials that eventually found a place in this book; in these seminars I have repeatedly experienced the thrill that comes when scholarship emerges from teaching, as well as a new and deepened respect for the process of collaboration that precedes and underlies the act of individual composition. Something of this debt can be gleaned from the number of students whose papers are cited in the following pages (several of whom, undergraduates then, are literature professors now): among them, Deirdre d'Albertis, Elizabeth Young, Carla Mazzio, David Wingrove, Ruthanna Hooke, Moira Wallace, Eleanor Drey, Erin Carlston, Carolyn Cowie, Elizabeth Traynor, Michele Whelan. That eight of these students were participants in the very first seminar I taught on this topic, back in 1985, is a powerful testament to the excellence and inspiration of that entire group, which I gratefully salute here.

Among the others whose support and encouragement have been inestimable are the circles of friends I associate with three geographical areas. First, those friends and colleagues I fondly associate with the eight years I lived in New England, however dispersed many of us may now be: Dale Wall, Jonathan Strong, Morgan Mead, Patricia Herrington, Judith and Bill Holt, Deborah Nord, Laura Doyle, Kathryne Lindberg, Patricia Yaeger, Marilyn Reizbaum, Joe Litvak and Lee Edelman, Ben Boone and Alice Daniel, Marjorie Garber, Jack Yeager and Timothy Cook, Gail Finney, Marianne Hirsch, Michael Cooper and Nancy Bauer. Second, a cadre of New York friends whose roots go back twenty years: Robert Vorlicky, Ken Corbett, Michael Cunningham, Ellen Bialo, Elaine Tannenbaum, Joseph Wittreich, Tom Healy, Deborah Holmes. Third, those friends and colleagues I now associate with California: Dale Wall (again), David Román, Marjorie Becker, Tania Modleski, Nancy Vickers, Hilary Schor, Teresa McKenna, Vincent Cheng, Richard Ide, Leo Braudy, Moshe Sluhovsky, Alice

ACKNOWLEDGMENTS

Gambrell, Jim Kincaid, Ron Gottesman, Maeera Schreiber, David St. John, Molly Bendall, Larry Ryan, Tom Young. Then there has been the support offered by those friends and relations who don't happen to fit any of these geographical categories but to whom my appreciation is just as heartfelt: Susan Friedman, Susan Winnett, Juliet Fleming, Debra Shostak, Joseph Wiesenfarth, Vincent Newton, Lisa Strauss, Elaine Showalter, Catharine Stimpson, David Boger, Andrea Musher, Eve Sedgwick, Margaret Homans, Betsy Draine, John Boone, Harry and Beth Boone, my parents, the Wall family.

Special thanks go to those individuals who read portions of this manuscript along the way, providing the incisive commentary that has made it a better book, or who generously shared their research with me. Among these, I am especially indebted to Patsy Yaeger, Laura Doyle, Susan Friedman, David Román, and Susan Winnett, all of whom read and commented on multiple chapters of the project; I am also grateful for the comments on individual sections offered by Deborah Nord, Nancy Paxton, Bob Vorlicky, Hilary Schor, Jonathan Strong, Peter Manning, Robert Kiely, Jay Watson, Kathryne Lindberg, Karen Lawrence, Richard Pearce, and David Blackmore. The copious notes at the end of this book signal another debt: to the indefatigable research assistants who have helped on this project—Ami Regier in particular, but also Jennifer Kennedy, Cindy Sarver, Marya McFadden, and Don Solomon. This book would never have been completed without the release-time from teaching made possible by a 1990–91 Senior Grant from the American Council of Learned Societies, which, in tandem with a fellowship from the Humanities Institute at the University of California-Davis, made it possible for me to spend my first year at USC on leave; in addition, two travel grants administered by the ACLS allowed me to present aspects of this work at international conferences. Two very generous subvention grants from Harvard and USC have abetted the physical production of this book. And, last, but not least, thanks to my editor at Chicago, Alan Thomas, for continuing to believe in and support this project to its completion.

It should be clear from the anecdote with which these acknowledgments began, as well as the mention of the contributions that various students have made to this project, that acts of pedagogy form the unifying thread in this account of scholarly and personal debts. Likewise, the special bonds to which the process of academic mentoring sometimes gives rise underlie this book's dedication. If one function of the acknowledgments that traditionally appear at the beginning of a scholarly work is to enact a public expression of gratitude and obligation, as part of a ritual that recognizes the authority of others in helping to bring a project to fruition, a dedicatory statement pays tribute to something or someone more; it commemorates, through the affixing of a name or names to the book, a relation that transcends specific debts and inspires, as *Webster's* reminds me, a "devotion"—

be its source in a person, a cause, or a moment that transcends space and time—that is hardly distinguishable from vocation. Those who knew the two young men to whom I dedicate this book will understand my impulse to memorialize their names here: among the first graduate students I taught at Harvard in the 1980s, Walter Hughes and Theodore Allen were exceptional individuals whose immense potential as scholars, teachers, and role models was cut short by illnesses caused by AIDS. Walter died during his assistant professorship, and Ted while completing his Ph.D. It is above all as a teacher—and here I mean that relation in its strongest sense—that I feel the impact of their deaths. Language is supposedly our special gift as scholar-writers, but for such losses, words aren't really adequate. A dedicatory statement can do no more than gesture to the silence that exists in the space where their voices, along with mine, should be speaking.

Modernity's Fictions of Sexuality

DEFINITIONS / PARAMETERS / DESIRES

Modernity lives on the experience of rebelling
against all that is normative.
—Jürgen Habermas[1]

Fiction plays on the stratification of meaning: it narrates one thing
in order to tell something else; it delineates itself in a language from
which it continuously draws effects of meaning that cannot
be circumscribed or checked.
—Michel de Certeau[2]

Sexuality rests between things. . . . Its variety makes it
intrinsically ambiguous.
—Muriel Dimen[3]

Most of us would probably agree that sexuality and narrative are overpowering components of both the lives we lead and the fictions we
create. However, just what "overpowering" means in the context of modernity remains open to question. Michel Foucault's *The History of Sexuality*
has schooled contemporary intellectuals into an awareness of the extent to
which sexuality is a function of power, of the institutional forces and
modes of knowledge that regulate desire through the proliferation of the
discourses that produce us as sexual subjects. Likewise, D. A. Miller's *The
Novel and the Police,* applying Foucault's insights to the dynamics of textual
power, has underlined for a new generation of literary critics the degree to
which the power that narrative fiction holds over its readers is a product of
the novel's enmeshment in systems of disciplinary control that make the
genre an agent of those ideological forces that its romance plots so often
censure.[4]

Yet as is true with all stories, the prevailing critical wisdom that holds
sexuality and narrative to be the strong arm of ineffable but inescapable
operations of power remains only a single perspective. For there is a sense
in which both the act of sex and the art of fiction are not only *overpowering*
but expressions of absolute *powerlessness,* enacting the intense human desire
to let go—to be released, to yield to an "other" (a lover, a text) that ceases
to remain other in the imaginary intercourse that is constitutive of sexual

and fictional exchanges alike. Nor should surrender to otherness on these terms be confused with masochistic submission to a greater power, as the psychologist Emmanuel Ghent has recently argued.[5] Difficult as our disciplinary culture makes it to conceptualize acts of surrender that are not acts of submission, I want to suggest that the longing to yield to a space in which subject meets subject in terms other than those accruing to the rhetoric of power—whether expressed in the interchanges that form the substance of sexual fantasy or fictional narrative—is not an exercise in self-deluded mysticism or nostalgic transcendentalism. Rather, as soon as such intersubjective desires enter the imagination, they take on a phenomenological reality, becoming a materially embodied (which is to say a real) component of the individual's emotional, psychic, and somatic life. And this reality belies the myth of power's hegemony as, in fact, a myth. Likewise, our sometimes easy acquiescence to the critical doctrine that power is totalizing and inescapable may also be a "fiction," its mythic stature one of the most effective strategies by which hegemony (no less than its critics) seeks to convince its subjects of the inevitability of a monolithic system—be it the disciplinary forces of social control or critical theory—whose strictures may be everywhere felt but are not therefore necessarily encompassing.[6]

The more skeptical among my readers may have noted that the contrast made between power in the first paragraph above and powerlessness in the second hinges on an unmarked transition from *sexuality* to *sex,* from the word typically signifying the realm of instinct to one denoting a physical act, as if both were the same, or as if the substitution of one term for the other made no significant difference.[7] But the unstable slippage between these terms is part of my point. Not only is it difficult, if not impossible, to pin the word *sex* and its cognates down without an explicit context, but the nature of sexuality itself remains radically indeterminate, or, according to Freud in the *Three Essays,* the "weak spot" in the "process of human cultural development"—it is the most unstable, least self-evident feature of the constituted personality, comprising a psychological borderline that both holds the constituted self together (via the workings of the Oedipus complex, according to Freud) and threatens its dissolution into chaos.[8] Hence the cautionary note sounded in the introductory epigraph by the psychologist Muriel Dimen, who reminds us that "sexuality rests between things, it borders psyche and society, culture and nature, conscious and unconscious, self and other. Its variety makes it intrinsically ambiguous." This sentiment is echoed in the introduction to the landmark essay collection *Powers of Desire: The Politics of Sexuality,* where the editors, having scrupulously detailed the social construction of modern sexuality, nonetheless conclude that "sexuality is, at the moment, a comparatively open subject in a world of domination, despite the forces seeking to close the conversation down." As the double meanings of the phrase, "at the moment," so well capture, when the historical moment undergoes change, so too do conceptions and experiences of sexuality. Despite the regulatory pressures that threaten to subdue sexual feelings and expressions, they continue to emerge in new, unpredictable forms that reveal their subversive "power" to incite and shape desire.[9] "At the moment," even in the moment of this writing, sexuality remains "between things," escaping rigid categorization even as categories devised to contain its energies proliferate.

Something of the same sense of the "in between" accrues to the novel, given its status as a relatively recently invented genre that is notoriously impure, assembled from the flotsam and jetsam of various literary forms. In Bakhtin's influential definition, the novel is a heteroglossic compilation of multiple voices and competing social discourses held in dialogic suspension, such that no one ideological viewpoint dominates the text. While we need to be wary of romanticizing the novel as an unalloyed expression of autonomy, as well as avoid being seduced by its self-reinforcing promulgation of the myth of its freedom from constraints, it remains a fact that the novel, both as a dialogical form and as a collection of heterogeneous voices, perspectives, and discourses, not only frequently violates established boundaries (of decorum, of genre, of subject matters high and low) but remains more open-ended, more plastic, less susceptible to rigid categorization than many other forms of literary and social discourse.[10] The incompleteness, instability, and contemporaneity that Bakhtin attributes to the novel as a "genre-in-the-making" evoke equally well Freud's argument that sexuality is *by definition* variable, precisely because it is neither a complete nor a ready-made thing in itself, but rather a mutable, mobile field of drives "constructed in the process" of its unfolding.[11] As Freud's and Bakhtin's observations both illustrate, phenomena that from one point of view can be seen as instruments of totalizing power become, from another, the wildcards that deconstruct those very efforts to totalize their effects— and this variability suggests the need for a mode of criticism that can make room for both perspectives at once.

Keeping both these views in mind, *Libidinal Currents* undertakes to investigate the impingement of issues of sexuality, psychology, and narrative on the evolution of cultural and literary modernity, particularly in the first half of the twentieth century. It is no news that, on the level of content, sexuality has played an important role in shaping the reputation and reception of modern fiction—a fact to which the suppression of sexually scandalous fictions by Chopin, Lawrence, Joyce, Radclyffe Hall, Henry Miller, and others bears testimony. But surprisingly little has been written about the complex interrelations of these modern "fictions of sexuality" either to the erotics of narrative that, as Peter Brooks has perhaps most comprehensively demonstrated, shape the desires and trajectories of fiction, or to the psychosexual and libidinal energies that, since the advent of turn-of-the-century sexological and psychoanalytic discourses, have come to be seen as constitutive of human subjectivity. In pursuing the theoretical implications of these intersections of sex, psychology, and narrative, this book focuses in particular on those novelistic fictions whose attempts to construct new forms to evoke the flux of consciousness and the erotics of mental activity also invite a reexamination of the literary and sexual politics of modernism.

The following introduction consists of four parts. The first, "Modernism and the 'Fiction' of Interiority," examines the theoretical implications of the novelistic turn to interior representation for modernism in particular and modernist studies in general. The next section, "Working Propositions: Both Sides of the Colon," recasts these theoretical considerations in an autobiographical light, as I recount the evolution of this project's conceptual structure by reviewing, among other shifts in emphasis, the changes in title (and the particularly volatile transformations of subtitle) it has undergone over the years. The personal nature of these reflections sets the tone for the third section, "'Farewell to Angria': In Defense of Close(ly Felt) Reading," which ponders the efficacy and politics of this book's methodological reliance on and allegiance to close textual reading in an epoch of criticism that increasingly values broadly cultural over narrowly literary exegesis. The fourth and final section, "The Shape of Things to Come," returns to more familiar terrain as I preview the chapter-by-chapter organization that underlies the book's focus on the libidinal politics that have contributed, in often radical ways, to the shaping and reshaping of modernist narrative.

Modernism and the "Fiction" of Interiority

The novelistic endeavor to shift attention from externally rendered reality to the realm of the interior that exists beyond direct representation is a hallmark of that body of formally experimental fiction most often subsumed under the rubrics of *modernism* and *stream-of-consciousness* narration. Both terms, however, merit some consideration because of the misperceptions that have often accompanied their application in literary studies. In the first case, the origins, agendas, and ownership of modernism have been fiercely contested in recent years by scholars who have either attempted to expand the term's boundaries or who have decided to dismiss the label altogether because of the elitist affiliations, reactionary politics, and limited vision that have been associated with its practice. In the second case, the concept of stream-of-consciousness narrative has been so loosely and often poorly applied to any number of extremely divergent attempts to represent states of interiority that the nomenclature tends to lose meaning altogether.[12]

An initial goal of this project, then, will be to move beyond the imprecision of such a term as *stream of consciousness* by interrogating the specific techniques and strategies whereby something like "consciousness" and something like a "stream" of libidinally charged thoughts, images, desires, and repressions associated with the psyche are insinuated into the trajectories of an array of more or less experimental fictional narratives engaged in exploring the inner life or, in Virginia Woolf's words, "the dark places of psychology."[13] Such fictions of interiority and sexuality, I argue, include not only those well-known examples of high modernist bravado that simulate the moment-by-moment unfolding of associative thought (as in Molly's interior monologue at the end of *Ulysses*), but a range of other less obviously experimental novels ranging from Kate Chopin's *The Awakening* to Christina Stead's *The Man Who Loved Children,* texts whose ostensibly realistic formats are nonetheless subtly, and profoundly, infused with the rhythms and reverberations that evoke the power of libidinal activity and unconscious desire to shape not only human subjectivity but external "reality."[14] In turn I will be suggesting that the effort to expand our knowledge of the techniques and the range of narrative modes used to represent such states of interiority can intervene significantly in current debates about what "counts" as a "modernist" work of fiction.

Reconsidering what counts, however, merits a brief review of what others have meant by modernism. The generally accepted perception of the aesthetic movement spawned in the wake of Marx, Freud, Darwin, the First World War, Einsteinian relativity, and existentialist philosophy invokes modernist art as that which "responds to the scenario of our chaos," including the "linguistic chaos that ensues when public notions of language have been discredited and when all realities have become subjective fictions."[15] In attempting to depict the radical subjectivity of perception and the relativity of meaning in a world without order or certainty, modernist aesthetics enacts, as Elizabeth Hirsh has put it, "a revolution in, of, or against representation per se," and it embodies the larger "crisis-in-narrative" that critics like Alice Jardine see as the defining characteristic of the era of modernity itself.[16] On the textual level, this revolution against modes of representation that take for granted the transparency of either language or reality has been associated with a number of formal innovations, especially in regard to the "high modernists" of the 1920s and 1930s. These include the use of multiple perspectives, fragmented structures, nonlinear chronology, paratactic juxtaposition, associative rather than logical sequences of thought, superimposed images or events to achieve the sensation of temporal and spatial simultaneity, narrative indirection, incompleteness, and self-reflexive commentary. On the thematic level, the modernist revolt against traditional realism has been associated with subjective states, the relativity of meaning, the evanescence of the temporal, an emphasis on technique, speed, and motion, and a fascination with such icons of modernity as the city, the machine, and the factory. Those texts that most closely approximate these characteristics—think, for example, of "The Wasteland"—present themselves, in Roland Barthes's definition, as a bricolage of "quotations drawn from the innumerable centers of culture," creating a "multi-dimensional space in which a variety of writings . . . blend and clash."[17]

Despite this nod to the multivalent, discordant elements comprising modernist aesthetics, it remains a critical commonplace that the modernist artist's response to the fragmentation and alienation associated with early-twentieth-century life was to valorize his (or perhaps her) unifying vision as the ultimate authority capable of bestowing meaning on the randomness, the flux, of an otherwise meaningless, decentered universe. From the perspective of postmodernity, however, such a reification of the autonomy of the artist and such a totalizing of the artwork as a complete, self-sufficient world dangerously perpetuates a western metaphysics of centered meaning. As David Bennett explains, "inexhaustible semantic complexity"—the characteristic signature of the inaccessible modernist text—"is not only compatible with, but integral to, the modernist conception of art as a compensatory 'autonomous' realm of subjective experience."[18] That is, the supposedly antitraditionalist difficulty of the modernist artifact can also work to support a very traditional metaphysics of textual coherence, however complexly figured, and a conservative politics of individual autonomy, however fragmented.

No doubt this theory of modernism's limitations holds true for the scholar who has primarily approached the period through the accepted canon of high modernism—in particular, Eliot, Pound, Yeats, and Joyce—and those earlier critics—say, Wilson, Trilling, and Kenner—who sought to make sense of this canon through the lens of the New Critical practice instituted by Eliot. But to those readers who have approached the period primarily through its prose fiction, I suggest, modernism has never seemed to fetishize "totality" or uphold the "autonomy" of the artifact to the extent that others have charged. Approaching the various experimental endeavors in fiction written in the first several decades of the twentieth century outside the framework and mythopoetics of Eliot, or Pound, or Stevens not only calls into question the assumption that all modernist texts share the impulse to totalize chaos, as David Harvey puts it,[19] but also radically changes the contours of what looks like or goes under the name of modernist writing. Rather, the narrative modernism(s) familiar to students of the novel have always seemed presciently aware, before contemporary theory was around to tell us as much, of the destabilization inherent in all modes of representation; consequently, the manipulations of language, time, and space in such novels have ultimately seemed less an attempt to totalize chaos than to impart a vision of complexity and irresoluteness that more closely resembles Bakhtin's definition of the genre as a necessarily incomplete, indeterminate artifact. Moreover, for those modern fictions intent on exploring, to repeat Woolf, "the dark places of psychology" newly opened to representation by psychoanalysis, the narrative acts of exposing the repressions and ruptures that subtend consciousness and of evoking the polymorphous play of anarchic desires that compose the libido have resulted in fictional texts that necessarily challenge unitary conceptions of narrative along with those of coherent identity or fixed sexuality. The shift in worldview occasioned by the Freudian revolution, that is, cannot be separated from the modernist revolution in art. More specifically, I will suggest that in mapping the instability and variability of psychosexual impulses and in tracking the dispersive, wayward trajectories that the libido etches in the subconscious, such modern fictions of sexuality have produced what I will be calling a poetics and politics of the perverse. The psychological and textual "perversities" that have ensued from such representations, as we shall see, have created a spectrum of modern narratives that are anything but totalizing or hegemonic, either in their aesthetic impulses, their deviant narrative energies, or their ideological positioning *vis-à-vis* the new sexological and psychoanalytic discourses arising simultaneously with the formation of the modernist movement in art and culture.

This is not to imply that such deviations from the norm are never problematic, or that they are automatically more effective in combating structures of power and social control; indeed the caution that the editors of *Powers of Desire* express about the paradoxical nature of sexual discourse applies equally to modern sexual fictions: "To advance the cause of sexual freedom . . . may paradoxically tighten the grip of the system." Similarly, Jonathan Dollimore warns that "the same instability that destabilizes [an oppressive category] can become a force of repression much more than a force of liberation."[20] The key here, however, lies in the discursive expression that the narrative act "advanc[ing] the cause of sexual freedom" or "liberation" takes; not all modes of speaking sex are equivalent, and the perverse narrative energies characterizing many of the sexual fictions in which I am interested, by virtue of the libidinal currents they are willing to explore, are less invested in destabilization for the sake of liberation *from,* than in destabilization as a mode of liberation *into*—into realms of unknown, untapped desires that have no necessary end.

Having now sketched a preliminary framework for examining the techniques developed to represent interior states and the sexual-aesthetic politics invested in such endeavors, I want to turn to a set of assumptions built into the language of interiority upon which these modernist texts freely draw. These are assumptions that have come under attack in some of the most significant recent theorizations of sexuality and gender. I have already twice cited Woolf's claim that the task of the modern writer lies in exploring "the dark places of psychology"; in an analogous formulation that could easily be used to gloss the novelistic mission outlined by Woolf, Freud speaks of the psychoanalyst's task as that of "bringing to light what human beings keep hidden within them," of "making conscious"—which is to say, bringing into the realm of articulation and hence representation—"the most hidden recesses of the mind."[21] Tellingly, these two statements reveal a shared reliance on metaphors of depth, of digging beneath the "surface" of consciousness to uncover an "inside" where the psyche exists—whence the implied binaries of dark/light, hidden/visible, and depth/surface, which together work to enforce the boundaries separating interior and exterior, a division which subtends, as poststructuralist critics have argued, the fictions of centered truth and coherent identity against which deconstructive theory has positioned itself. In response, Michel Foucault attempts to rewrite Freud's language of *internalization,* which locates the sexual drives at the core of human subjectivity as its hidden "truth," by positing instead a rhetoric of *inscription* or *implantation,* which shifts the emphasis to the process by which externally circulating discourses, including those of psychology and sexuality, write themselves *onto* human subjects, implanting the very scripts by which we recognize ourselves as sexual subjects.[22] Judith Butler has pressed Foucault's theory of discursive power further to demonstrate how assumptions of "interiority"—the "dark places" and "hidden recesses" that are the shared objects of modernist fiction and Freudian psychology—are *effects* of the sexual and gender ideologies whose power lies in their ability to posit as "natural" or "innate" social constructions that are in fact enacted upon the body. From this "surface," their performance is then introjected by the subject as originating *cause,* as essence or truth of being.[23]

In face of such trenchant criticisms of the assumptions underlying the language of interiority, it is necessary to question the efficacy not only of modernism's investment in representing interior states but also of my use of these terms to probe the interimplications of sexuality, psychology, and narrative in the making of modern culture. I address these questions in more detail in chapter 3, but here I would like to make two basic points. First, it should be noted that the poststructuralist gesture of exposing interiority as a discursive fiction is not necessarily the same as denying the existence of the psyche or its operations; likewise, while some Freudian concepts, such as the Oedipus complex, exemplify the social constructions that abet the illusion of a centered, contained self, other Freudian concepts devised to evoke psychic interiority—the libido, the polymorphous perverse, the unconscious—provide poststructuralist criticism with the very tools it needs for theorizing the ongoing destabilization, dissemination, and indeterminacy of all human identity. Second, as critics begin to acknowledge a range of alternative and adjacent modernist practices extending beyond the parameters that have traditionally defined the field, it becomes less clear that the novelistic explorations of states of subjectivity and sexuality included in this study narrowly subscribe to an *a priori* doctrine of interiority. Even though many of the texts taken up in my chapters uphold certain humanist ideals of a coherent self—it would be misleading to suggest otherwise—by and large their perverse narrative trajectories repeatedly demonstrate the complexities and complications whereby the negotiations of desire that make up both the subject and the subject's worldview dissolve distinctions of "inner" and "outer"—and, along with them, the normalizing sexual categories that, as Butler has shown, this binary maintains. Evoking internalization as inscription, and vice versa, the errant narrative energies that give shape to many of these fictions of sexuality show how surface and depth alike are continually inundated by those psychosexual currents that provide a meeting point between individual subjectivity and social formations. Such fictions suggest the need for a non-totalizing theory of sexuality and narrativity that can accommodate both Freud's polymorphously perverse instincts and Foucault's polymorphously proliferating discourses, without making one the adversary—or worse, the negation—of the other.[24] For theory that seeks conclusively to subsume its critics may only be a classic instance, writ large, of Lacanian misrecognition, in which part of our critical egos have yet to evolve beyond entrapment in the mirror-stage; assuming that our reflection in the other is, or should be, part of an extension of ourselves, we make criticism an object of conquest, rather than creating a space where subjects may encounter one another in relationships that are critical without becoming adversarial.[25]

Working Propositions: Both Sides of the Colon

Jessica Benjamin's call upon critics to entertain a "transitional space in theory" where "competing ideas [may be] entertained simultaneously"[26] is not unrelated to the impulse that led me, in presenting a section of this book at a faculty seminar some years ago, to begin by sharing with the seminar members a list of the various titles and subtitles that at one time or another I had taken up, modified, and discarded in my search for that ineffable combination of words that best summed up my authorial and scholarly intentions. I wasn't simply confessing to an inability to pin down my subject matter—however many doubts I may have had along the way—but working from the intuition that there might be some heuristic value both for my audience and myself in laying bare the uncertain process of evolution, the missteps, the starts and stops, through which any book project proceeds. This exercise proved both gratifying and instructive, in no small part because it created between this particular critic and his audience a relationship in which both participants were called upon to read each other "in the desire of the other," acknowledging the materiality of our relation as critics and subjects. "As the text calls out its need to 'enter into a relationship with someone,'" Isobel Armstrong writes, "the answering need to understand accepts the displacement understanding requires."[27] Now, looking back at the list of titles and subtitles I presented that day from the vantage point of a completed manuscript, I realize something else: the use value of many of these tags and phrases in outlining the various themes and topoi—or what I call "working propositions"—that, while perhaps no longer providing the dominant note, nonetheless flow throughout and lend support to the main argument of this book. If the image of subterranean, intermingling, and diverging "currents" is a particularly evocative metaphor, as Freud discovered, for describing the libidinal energies subtending consciousness, the same trope also usefully glosses the undertow of ideas from which this project emerged. What follows, then, is an annotated list of six such subcurrents or "working propositions" that retrospectively map out my thinking on this project as it evolved over the years and began to assume a shape and meanings little suspected in its earliest stages of development.

WORKING PROPOSITION #1: CRISES OF AUTHORITY AND ANXIETY IN MODERNIST NARRATIVE

However unwieldy, variations on this phrase served as title or subtitle throughout several versions of the manuscript (with, as whim would have it, the word *modernist* sometimes being replaced by *modern,* and *narrative* by *novel*). What the title pinpointed were the parallel crises in sexual and textual authority occasioned among many modernists by the opening up to novelistic representation of the psychosexual and spatial dimensions of subjectivity. The dynamics of *narrative* authority that complicate, indeed become implicated in, the *sexual* subjects of the novels I investigate has remained a constant in this study. For this book suggests that the crises of narrative authority that have come to be seen as endemic to modern fiction must also be evaluated in light of the specifically sexual anxieties to which the fictional exploration of interior consciousness and subconscious desire gives voice. Conversely, the representation of sexual authority within these texts—particularly in regard to issues of female agency—frequently precipitates a degree of *textual* anxiety that has most often been viewed as symptomatic of the crisis-in-narrative brought about by the delegitimation of modernity's masterplots. Such interplay between textual and sexual manifestations of authority and anxiety is relevant, as well, to the sphere of lived experience where, as Jonathan Dollimore puts it, "an endless displacement of social crisis and conflict into sexuality" continually problematizes, and textualizes, both the sexual and social.[28] While my analyses make frequent reference to the terms *authority* and *anxiety,* I want to underline the metaphoricity of speaking of any text's authority, or for that matter, its manifestations of anxiety. Critics have sometimes tended to use these terms unproblematically, as if they weren't figures of speech but descriptions of tangible textual attributes, and this has had the effect of obscuring what are in fact the indeterminate relations of author to text, and of text to reader. Note, for example, the different meanings that the term *authority* can assume: the critic may be an "authority" on a particular subject matter; an author may attempt to impose "authority" (or, in poststructuralist wordplay "author-ity") upon his or her subject matter by authorizing certain themes, behaviors, and ideas and deauthorizing others; the term *narrative authority* may signal the textual processes by which techniques such as sequencing and point of view frame or limit the reader's reception; ideologies that are translated into textual practices may stem from "authoritarian" impulses to master textual as well as human subjects. But none of these manifestations of authority (and the same goes for the term *anxiety*), while often passing under the same name, are identical, and care must be taken to remember that the utility of such terms resides in their metaphoric status.

WORKING PROPOSITION #2: THE PSYCHOLOGY OF SEX AND SELF IN MODERN FICTION

This proposition served as the title of a course I first taught in 1985, in which I assigned many of the novels (and much of the theory) that eventually worked their way into this book, and it became the title of the first abstract of the project I wrote in order to enter various fellowship competitions. As regards this title's legibility, I probably should have seen the writing on the wall when one of the anonymous reviewers for the National Endowment for the Humanities (NEH) singled out the phrase "the psychology of sex and self" as a deplorably "predictable" example of recent jargonistic trends in literary criticism. Despite this discouraging note, I stubbornly held on to this formulation for some time, in part because it seemed to tie together into an interestingly causal relationship the three areas of interest—identity, sexuality, psychology—that had first engaged my attention in the seminar. If anything, I soon discovered that the interrelations implied by the wording of the title were less jargon-ridden than theoretically naive, as the influx of studies on sexuality and desire stemming from Lacanian, French feminist, and Foucauldian perspectives flooded the literary scene of the latter 1980s and worked their way into my syllabus. The result was an increased awareness of "self" and "sex" as socially constructed categories and cultural fictions, which led to my putting these terms in quotation marks when I revised the course's title and adopted it as the subtitle for the book project now beginning to take shape under the (still-vague) rubric "Sexuality, Narrative, and Modernity: The Psychology of 'Sex' and 'Self' in Modern Fiction."

Looking back at these early abstracts from today's vantage point, I am most forcibly struck by memories, first, of the degree to which I then felt theoretically obligated to account for Lacanian psychoanalysis, especially in a study whose subtitle foregrounded "psychology," and second, the degree to which I felt it incumbent to use the project's opening chapter to defend psychoanalysis—and Freudian concepts such as instinct, desire, and the unconscious—against the antipsychiatric, anti-essentializing biases of Foucault's discursive and new historicist emphases. To serve these ends, I originally conceived an introductory chapter that would put Lacanian and Foucauldian methodologies into a dialogic "cross-fire" by reading their theories against two provocative narratives of indeterminate sexuality, *Herculine Barbin, Being the Recently Discovered Memoirs of a Nineteenth-Century Hermaphrodite* (1868) and Angela Carter's *The Passion of New Eve* (1977). Because *Herculine Barbin* seemed the perfect candidate for a Foucauldian reading—especially given Foucault's introduction to the memoir and Herculine's obsessive concern with the religious-medical-legal authorities responding to her/his predicament—I wanted to read this narrative from a Lacanian perspective of desire in language, metonymic slippage, and lack. Likewise, because of Angela Carter's knowing deployment of concepts that readily lent themselves to Lacanian and French feminist interpretations, including the originating trauma of sexual difference (parodied in the scene in which the male misogynist Evelyn surgically becomes the new Eve at the hands of a knife-bearing Amazon named Mother), I intended to read it through the filter of a Foucauldian historicist perspective. This deliberate reading of both texts against the theoretical grain, I reasoned, would have the added benefit of providing conceptual and historical bookends for the project's focus on modernity, marking its trajectory from the mid-nineteenth century to the present day.

But I gradually realized that, however enticing the texts at hand, beginning the book on this note was problematic on several levels. First, the effect of putting a spotlight on Lacan at the very beginning imposed on the project an explanatory narrative of origins of precisely the sort against which a Foucauldian understanding of sexuality works. Likewise, such a beginning committed me to attend throughout to Lacanian tropes—desire in language, the question of sexual difference, the Phallus/phallus, imaginary and symbolic registers—that threatened to sidetrack my analyses from the perverse narrative energies and modernist modes of representation that really interested me—energies and modes whose psychological dimensions, I increasingly became convinced, were best served in this project by a return to and (feminist) revision of Freud, without the *necessary* mediation of Lacanian theory. Second, I came to realize that staging a confrontation between Lacan and Foucault only reified a mode of oppositional criticism in which a victor must emerge: as if the real drama were in the battle of critics, rather than in the ideas that their theories, if taken into account simultaneously, might more usefully produce. So, despite my affection for those ten or so pages I completed on *Herculine Barbin* and *New Eve,* they now rest in a file marked "could have beens," caught in a state of desire that, as Lacan would have it, once had an origin but now has no end.

WORKING PROPOSITION #3: TOWARD A POETICS
AND POLITICS OF THE PERVERSE

I have already noted that the act of putting the dispersive energies of the psyche into writing often summons forth a welter of errant narrative desires and deviating narrative trajectories that suggest the appropriateness of theorizing a "poetics and politics of the perverse" as an analytic model for this project. Definitional support for such a model lies in Freud's early, brilliant postulation of the polymorphous perverse that characterizes infantile sexuality. Rather than consisting of one unified or even dominant drive, the sexual instinct consists, as Freud writes in *Three Essays,* of infinitely dispersive component parts whose autoerotically cathected objects and aims, such as they are, are contingent, replaceable, and partial.[29] A *poetics* of the perverse would look for formations analogous to the polymorphous perverse on the linguistic, stylistic, and structural levels of the text; a *politics* of the perverse would go one step further and advocate the necessity of reclaiming the perverse as a viable model for an adult erotics, not simply as a description of a developmental stage in infantile sexuality that is superseded by oedipally directed desires (a paradigm which renders any adult manifestations of polymorphous sexuality a deviation from the adult norm, a disruptive "return" of what even Freud pejoratively calls the "perversions"). Such an affirmative politics of the perverse, ironically, would find its justification in Freud's early theory of polymorphous perversity, which suggests that the perversions constitute the *original* form and expression of sexuality, from which all other expressions (such as object-directed drives) are themselves the "perversion." As Teresa de Lauretis notes, it is entirely possible to read Freud's theory of the psyche and sexual drives from an angle of vision in which "the 'normal' is conceived only by approximation . . . while perversion and neurosis . . . are the actual forms and contents of sexuality."[30] De Lauretis is one of several prominent theorists who have recently reappropriated the Freudian concept of perversity for a feminist/queer hermeneutics and politics, and while her overall aim is to create a less prejudicial model for understanding psychoanalytic and cultural formations of lesbian sexuality, the implications of her work for the entire range of adult erotic practice and fantasy are enormously thought-provoking.[31] Another important critic who has made perversion a touchstone for a wide-ranging analysis of sexual dissidence and a "radical sexual politics" is Jonathan Dollimore, who turns to the history of the word *perversion* before Freud to historicize the contradictory doubleness of a concept that originated not in opposition to some hypothesized "normativity" but "*internally to* just those ['natural'] things it threatens. . . . The clear implication is that civilization actually depends on that which is usually thought to be incompatible with it."[32]

While my chapters draw on such revisionary conceptions of the perverse where they seem useful, I have opted not to make my formulation of the "poetics and politics of the perverse" an all-encompassing catch-phrase to describe this project's analysis of modernity's fictions of sexuality for three reasons: (1) in part because of the widely divergent aesthetic and sexual-political responses that the modern exploration of the "dark places of psychology" and its libidinal currents inspires; (2) in part because, however careful one is with terminology, the word *perversity* comes freighted with a history of deprecatory meanings that makes it all too easy to slip between understandings of perversity as a celebration of polymorphous sexuality, perversion as the result of imperfect repression or sublimation, and perversion as a social category of disapprobation; and (3) in part because the term begs the difficulty, as Foucault's methodology demonstrates, of separating the discourses that name perversion in order to produce the modern pervert from discourses of innate sexuality that, in positing perversion as the norm of the sexual instincts, nonetheless participate in what remains a discursive construction of perversity. Thus my working proposition remains a gesture *"toward* a poetics and politics of the perverse." My sympathies, nonetheless, are with the endeavors of critics such as de Lauretis who make perversity a hermeneutic both for reenvisioning human sexuality's potential and for analyzing literary and cultural texts—especially since, as Freud has also shown, the sexual instincts, however much they originate in bodily sensation, "can be known only by [their] representation or 'psychical representative,'" in the form of those fantasies that mediate the representations of the mind and the imposition of cultural scripts.[33]

WORKING PROPOSITION #4: QUEER SITES IN MODERNISM

Those libidinal and textual emanations that look "perverse" from one theoretical perspective often appear, with a slight shift of vision, "queer" from another. "Queer Sites in Modernism" names what has become the subject matter of chapter 4, in which I take up the gay and protogay production of an alternative modernist practice that encodes many of the precepts of contemporary queer theory. In addition, it will soon become apparent that, despite the primarily heterosexual focus of the novels analyzed in the surrounding chapters, issues of same-sex eroticism and same-sex desire tend to crop up anywhere and everywhere. These sightings include the heady eroticism among women that triggers Edna Pontellier's autoerotic self-discovery (chapter 2), underlies Dora's deepest repressions (chapter 2), and defines Clarissa Dalloway's memory of the most perfect moment in her life (chapter 3); the sublimated homoeroticism that can only find an expression in racial and fratricidal violence in *Absalom, Absalom!* (chapter 5); and the scapegoating of homosexuality in the colonial narratives of Durrell and Lessing (chapter 6). On the one hand, this persistence of homosexual themes might suggest to some readers that I am actually writing—or perhaps *should* be writing—a study of gay desire as it has permeated and reshaped the contours of modern fiction in the wake of Freud, but that I have "closeted" this subject matter within a broader consideration of sexuality. My response, however, is that, as a study of the libidinal currents, both sexual and textual, to which the modernist attempt to represent interiority gives rise, this book is, foremost, an interrogation of sexuality in *all* its "betweenness"—"Sexuality rests between things," as Dimen says—and therefore it is not only a study of homosexuality for the same reason it is not only a study of heterosexuality. As regards object-choice, one of Freud's most incisive points in the *Three Essays*—which still has the power to startle in a culture that often feels compelled to speak otherwise—is the simple fact that, from the psychoanalytic point of view, the "sexual interest felt by men for women is also a problem that needs elucidating, and not a self-evident fact" (12). So, too, from the literary and cultural critical points of view: any elucidation of the *problem* of heterosexual relations—the overt contents of the majority of these fictions of sexuality—is not only necessary, but is also necessarily an analysis of homosexuality as heterosexuality's inevitable other,[34] and, by extension, of all the component instincts, chameleon desires, embedded identities, and fantasies that make up the vastly complex realm of sexuality in general.

On the other hand, it is no structural coincidence that chapter 4—the longest in the book—stands at its center, from which point its queer excesses and energies self-consciously permeate outwards, retrospectively and prospectively shading the readings in the chapters surrounding it. For the overtly alternative, contentious modernist practice that chapter 4 links to gay and protogay urban formations demands a reenvisioning of the modernist enterprise as a whole, forcing us to see within canonical modernism traces of queer alterity that shed new light on the obsessive marking of inside/out, the theatricalized play of and on surfaces, and the imagery of psychic depths that compose the cartographies of modernist textuality mapped by the surrounding chapters. And, if viewed from the perspective of a poststructuralist enterprise that has deconstructed "centers" as the illusory repository of unifying or universal truths that pass as normative, the act of inscribing a resolutely non-normative, queerly decentered "center" in a book on the vagaries of psychosexuality and its fictional representations seems a felicitous gesture, one that goes hand in hand with the forementioned poetics and politics of the perverse to which the book in its entirety subscribes.

WORKING PROPOSITION #5: THE RETURN OF
THE (TEXTUALLY) REPRESSED

Although its phrasing expresses one of the repeated concerns running throughout *Libidinal Currents,* these words, I confess, are not mine, but are borrowed from the title of an anthology on Joyce edited by Susan Stanford Friedman. In the introduction to this essay collection, as well as in a work in progress, Friedman draws on Shoshana Felman's psychoanalytic theory of reading as a transferential scene and on Fredric Jameson's conception of the political unconscious to make an argument for the presence of a psycho-political "textual unconscious" in literary examples of modernism.[35] This textual unconscious is composed of the unresolved "complexes" that form the repressed of the text but that become "manifest" or accessible in the process of reading and interpretation. The great value of Friedman's formulation is that it creates a methodology for reading politics into modernism without falling into the trap of arguing for a "good" subversive modernism (conceived as oppositional, marginal, and most often female) and a "bad" high modernism (conceived as hegemonic, canonical, and most often male)—a simplistic binary that has been one negative effect of the otherwise salutary debates about modernism that have helped revitalize the field.[36] But whereas Friedman's methodology for uncovering the "unconscious" of the text is to locate the repressed or disguised layers of story that exist, palimpsest-like, in drafts, early versions, and later revisions of the same story, I tend to read the text's repressed content more locally, in those instances within the narrative proper in which otherwise censored matter "returns" to reveal the contradictions, the ambivalences, either stemming from the psychosexual forces dictating its representations of interiority or inciting its narrative desires and structure. Such returns of the repressed, because of the anxieties they engender, are integrally related to the dynamics of authorial mastery and anxiety that, as summarized in my first working proposition, run throughout and disturb all these texts.

WORKING PROPOSITION #6: EVADING EVE'S SECOND AXIOM

The forerunner of several of the most important advances in literary studies of the past decade, Eve Kosofsky Sedgwick again helped inaugurate a new critical field when, in the second of the several axioms that begin *Epistemology of the Closet*, she advocated a conceptual as well as strategic disarticulation of the analysis of gender (the sex/gender system) from that of sexuality (orientation). Following the lead of Gayle Rubin's "Thinking Sex," which challenges the notion that "feminism is or should be the privileged site of a theory of sexuality," Sedgwick argues that while the oppressions wrought by the sex/gender system are the proper focus of feminist studies, the development of sexuality as "an alternative analytic axis" is a "particularly urgent project for gay/lesbian and antihomophobic inquiry."[37] As a tactic for jump-starting a theory of same-sex desire freed from the heterocentrism that almost automatically attaches to considerations of the binaristic structure of gender, the value of Sedgwick's call to arms was immediately apparent, and indeed it has helped create as well as energize the field now known as queer theory. Despite these virtues, however, I've never been entirely comfortable with this disentangling of the axes of sexuality and gender—or, correlatively, with Rubin's and Sedgwick's segregation of the tasks of gay theory and feminist theory. For one thing, this division of labors underestimates the degree to which feminist inquiry has been willing to engage seriously the realm of the sexual; for another, in making the proper object of feminist critique "the coarser stigmata of gender difference," as Sedgwick puts it,[38] such a division of labor not only creates a binary but institutes a hierarchy based on refinement (that which is less "coarse") and appeal. For gay theory not only gets to claim the sexy subject—sexuality—but also gets to play the sexier role of politically incorrect renegade—all of which dispensations reinforce the stereotype of the Hardcore Feminist as She Who Is Always Serious ("politically correct," forever engaged in battles against the oppressor) and no fun (antisex if not sexless).[39] But, more important among my hesitations, it has always been as difficult for me to conceive of a theoretical paradigm of sexuality that doesn't constantly call upon and have recourse to issues of gender (which can signify more than the analysis of inequities, oppression, and heterocentric binaries) as it has been for most feminist scholars to interrogate paradigms of gender without making sexuality some part of their formulation.

Casting a helpful light on this impasse, the psychotherapist Ken Corbett has recently argued that critics influenced by theories of social construction and poststructuralism have often shied away from linking categories of gender to those of sexuality because of the dangerously punitive stereotypes that have historically emerged from the collapse of sexuality into gender. However, the real danger, Corbett maintains, is less the collapse of these categories than the limited understanding of gender that has accompanied such views, for, as he shows in great detail, "analysts, beginning with Freud, have repeatedly restricted the possibilities of gender to the conventional heterosexual masculine/feminine binary." Using the example of the "girlyboy" factor in the development of "homosexual boyhood"—a topic that simply doesn't exist within standard psychoanalytic discourse—to demonstrate the complex interimplications of gender and sexuality in the formation of sexual and social identity, Corbett concludes that "queer hope and resistance [need not be] radically divorced from what may be developmental aspects of gender [as well as] sexuality." The key phrase that echoes throughout Corbett's study, and one which this study of sexuality also attempts to honor, is the concept, borrowed from Judith Butler's *Bodies That Matter*, of "complex *inter*implications," as opposed to unidirectional, causal "implications." Such a concept not only acknowledges the multilinearity of the "psychological process that is born of gender's and sexuality's intertwining,"[40] but also serves as a blueprint for a mode of critical inquiry that neither totalizes its or the other's theories, nor evades its own complex interimplications with the subjects—and objects—it attempts to interpret and revise.

So, how, from this welter of potential titles, designations, axioms, and tags, did the title *Libidinal Currents* emerge triumphant? During the writing of this project I found myself increasingly turning to the adjective *libidinal* because it encompassed both the sexual and psychological dimensions of the modernist fictions I was analyzing. The *OED* defines *libido,* which derives from the Latin for "lust," as a psychic energy that can be associated with either "the sexual instinct" (hence the "lust" at its root) or with those more general "instinctive mental desires and drives" that are *not* expressly sexual. The examples given in the entry, moreover, make it clear that the term has been used to designate unconscious as well as conscious desires, and that it has been associated with infantile polymorphousness (Freud, Jung) as well as with those unruly, undirected energies characterizing adolescence (Erikson, Mead). For some psychologists the libido is characterized as violent and brutal—animal "lust," as it were, denuded of conscience or morality—while for Freud, ever the sentimentalist in spite of his mask of scientific objectivity and general pessimism, the libido also describes those emotions "which have to do with all that may be comprised under the word 'love.'" And, intriguingly, by 1953 the *OED* cites the emergence of the phrase "political libido": the term that originally referred to infantile drives is now seen to have manifest social (or political) effects, governing the adult's relationship to community as well as the community's collective psychology. Given this wealth of meaning, *libidinal* thus emerged as an eminently useful tool for describing the myriad interpenetrations of the psychological and sexual, the conscious and unconscious, the psychosexual and psychopolitical, the anarchic and erotic, invested in the modernist enterprise of exploring and representing subjectivity.[41] These psychological and modernist imperatives also relate to the title's second term, *currents,* which connotes continuous flow; movement that is progressive yet not contained by prescribed trajectories; changeability and instability; sudden perspectival shifts between surface and depth; and a temporal present (as in "current" affairs) that, in its unfolding, simultaneously becomes indistinguishable from the past. In turn, *currents* evokes the fluidity and flux that modernist writing simultaneously associates with mental activity, unconscious desire, and objective reality, and that it raises to an aesthetic principle in its experimental narrative flows and representational forms.

The phrase "libidinal currents," then, describes the shapes of sexuality and subjectivity that these modernist texts evoke, as well as the shapes that compose the narrative erotics of their telling: hence the subtitle, *Sexuality and the Shaping of Modernism*.[42] Here, though, is one shift in focus that deserves mention. Where earlier versions foregrounded the concept of *modernity*, this subtitle uses the more historically specific and literary term *modernism*. This substitution reflects my growing confidence that once canonical understandings of modernism are thrown into question and reshaped to include the less obvious, alternative, or oppositional modes of narrative provocation occurring throughout the first half of this century, it more accurately serves to mark this book's exploration of psychological and libidinal currents than modernity.[43] In some ways, I attempt to have it both ways by beginning this book with Charlotte Brontë's *Villette* (1853). For on the one hand, its psychosexual currents seem a quintessential expression of the forces of *modernity* that emerged during Brontë's lifetime; on the other hand, this novel strikes me as an equally quintessential expression of *modernist* writing "before its time," presciently avant-garde in its creation of a deviantly elliptical narrative to convey the impingements of sexuality, representation, and psychology on the constitution of the modern subject. But I'm jumping ahead of myself, for I now want to offer some theoretical speculations on the methods this project employs, and I will do so by making another Brontë document, "Farewell to Angria," the springboard for this discussion.

"Farewell to Angria": In Defense of Close(ly Felt) Reading

> Let us never cease from thinking—what is this 'civilization' in which we find ourselves? What are these ceremonies and why should we take part in them?
> —Virginia Woolf, *Three Guineas*[44]

There is a phrase in Tillie Olsen's "Tell Me a Riddle," describing a mother with a newborn child "lost in the maze of the long, the lovely drunkenness,"[45] that periodically returns to haunt me, but never with such frequency as when I find myself, exhausted to a state of near-delirium and collapse, so enmeshed in the long mazes and intricacies of writing that I lose all sense of time, and sometimes place, forcing myself to push through the exhaustion into a kind of hyperactive intensity that borders, perversely, on ecstasy. In drawing on Olsen's wording to describe this uncanny sensation, I realize I skirt the danger of participating in a history of writers who have appropriated images of female reproduction to legitimate their attempts at writerly production,[46] but I hope I escape the worst of this implication since my interest in Olsen's figure is less in the "birthing" of a text than in the idea of those "long lovely mazes" that, as a literary trace, have reverberated in my subconscious since first reading "Tell Me a Riddle" twenty-some years ago. Not only does the image speak to the total immersion that accompanies the process of composition; it beautifully evokes for me the very process, as a reader of fiction, of threading one's way through the mazes of plot and counterplot in those long, lovely novelistic fictions whose enticements, mysteries, and eventual rewards encourage that willing suspension of disbelief, that delirious process of surrender into otherness, that I attempt to describe at the beginning of this introduction and that has been a lifelong "passion." Or, better, a lifelong "passionate fiction"— to borrow de Lauretis's term in *Practices of Love*—that allows for the imaginative experience of an intersubjective space that can also become, from the vantage point of reader-turned-critic, the charged site of those "complex interimplications," as Corbett and Butler put it, that evince the multivalent "powers" of the fictions of both sexuality and narrative.

To speak of "the long, the lovely drunkenness" of reading and interpreting fiction, however, is also to beg the question of the material practice, the mode of inquiry, that underlies the local scenes of interpretation making up this book's six chapters. Whereas the goal of the preceding sections has been to set out the argument, theoretical positions, and methodologies that have gone into the making of *Libidinal Currents,* in this section I want to consider the implications of the habit of close reading that, for all this book's theoretical framings, make up the vast proportion of its material substance, heft, and, in more than one sense, weightiness. The idea of using this introduction to stage some sort of defense of "the long read"— if only to make sense to myself of the pleasures, both professional and psychological, to which the formalist impulse to expend enormous amounts of energy and time spinning out intricate webs of analysis that no one except myself may have the patience or desire to read—has been on my mind for some time. But it has assumed particular urgency in the past few years as the rise of cultural studies has made me question, first, whether there is a legitimate place in the humanities for extended close analysis, however theoretically informed or beautifully executed, and, second (even if there is a need still to be served by such practice), whether it stands any chance of surviving in a contemporary milieu in which the phenomena of information overload, sound bytes, and the snapshot image, among others, demonstrate our culture's increasing incapacity for, if not outright intolerance of, *any* kind of analysis (think of the brevity allotted prime-time news items) that necessitates closely maintained attention to the ever-more-complex minutiae that make up our world. These questions have been exacerbated in my case by the knowledge that my most recent work—a book project on orientalist erotics—is moving in an increasingly interdisciplinary, synthesizing, and broadly cultural rather than exclusively literary mode that leaves less and less room for the extended analysis and lingering formalism of the sort in which this book indulges and delights. That is, I find myself wondering, at times, whether in bringing this project, conceived and written over many years, to a close I have merely been postponing my belated recognition of its obsolescence in the face of prevailing critical currents, whether I have in fact been writing an end—my end—to the critical practice that I have known best, loved, but must now leave behind: writing my version, you see, of Charlotte Brontë's "Farewell to Angria."

Brontë's "Farewell" seems to me to provide a particularly apt allegory for the shift in critical modes I am describing, seeing that I launch this book's series of textual readings with an extended analysis of Brontë's valedictory novel, *Villette*, that transforms Lucy Snowe into an emblem for the errant textual practice that novelistic representations of the darker places of psychology seem prone to producing. As Brontë aficionados know, "Farewell to Angria" (1839) is a private statement that Brontë, aged 23, wrote to mark her resolve to leave behind the voluminous juvenilia of her youth and embark upon an adult novel-writing career. In this poignant document, Brontë attempts to coax herself into abjuring, Prospero-like, the fantastical kingdom of Angria that she and her siblings created in childhood and continued imaginatively to inhabit in their writings ever since, experiencing in Angria a world more real, more vivid, more passionate, than any external order of being. Yet even as Brontë speaks of the need, even desire, for change, she expresses an intense longing to hold on, a bit longer, to that visionary kingdom to which she has hitherto ceded all powers of control. "But we must change, for the eye is tired of the picture so oft recurring and now so familiar," Brontë writes in one breath, only immediately to beg a temporary postponement before quitting "that burning climate where we have sojourned too long—its skies aflame—the glow of sunset . . . always upon it." No wonder, then, that the somber if not quite convincing statement of renunciation with which she ends the document—"the mind would cease from excitement and turn now to a cooler region where the dawn breaks grey and sober, and the coming day for a time at least is subdued by clouds"—is mitigated by the passion of telling that has preceded it:

> Yet do not urge me too fast, reader: it is not easy to dismiss from my imagination the images which have filled it so long; they were my friends and my intimate acquaintances, and I could with little labour describe to you the faces, the voices, the actions, of those who peopled my thoughts by day, and not seldom stole strangely even into my dreams by night. When I depart from these I feel almost as if I stood on the threshold of a home and were bidding farewell to its inmates.

No mean "close reader" of the world of her creation, remembering and reveling in all its particulars, Brontë thus performs a "Farewell" that holds an especially resonant note for *this* close reader, who, also, feels as if he may be standing (with many other literary critics) on a threshold, at century's end, between a "burning clime where we have sojourned too long" and the prospects of "a distant country where every face [is] unknown and the character of all the population an enigma it would take much study to comprehend and much talent to expound."[47] There are not a few ironies, however, in the identification I've forged with Brontë here, first, since one might as easily say I am leaving behind the "grey reality," the boring familiarity, of extended readings of entire narratives for the much more exciting "burning clime" and "distant land" of cultural and postcolonial studies, and, second, since the fantastical kingdom to which Brontë is bidding farewell, Angria, is an example *par excellence* of the orientalizing erotic imagination (albeit one filtered through the fervor of adolescent hormonal rage) that my next project seeks to analyze.

And what of the deadlock that I perceive between this burgeoning field of cultural studies—which I like many others see as offering literary studies, increasingly dismissed as too narrow and elitist, a new lease on life—and my penchant for the close, long read, for the exacting textual exegesis of entire narratives, that critics could easily enough charge is a Romantic nostalgia for a mode of knowledge that, in the press of postmodernity, has already passed? The critic who has given me the most helpful purchase to date on the issues at stake in this quandary is Joseph Litvak, who in a new book in progress makes an unapologetic argument for the *usefulness* of narrative "as an analytic strategy, despite, or rather because of, the countless postmodern techniques of disjunction and disorientation that would seem to have rendered it obsolete." Despite its immense significance in reconnecting academic practice to the world of the everyday, the rise of cultural studies, Litvak suggests, has contributed to the general postmodern tendency to distrust narrativity (and by extension the novel) because of its historical association with and complicity in reproducing the master narratives by which dominant culture has enforced its often restrictive ideologies. The era of the postmodern, some might argue, literally has *no time* for sustained narrative pleasures. That is, cultural studies tends to focus less on the micro-processes of sequence and succession that compose narrative and more on illustrative moments that can be lifted from the text and, regardless of context, be combined with other evidentiary materials to form a multilayered, heteroglossic account of macro-cultural formations. The most serious foe of narrative, however, is not cultural studies itself, despite the piecemeal dismantling of the trajectories built into narrative form that necessarily accompanies such a practice. Rather, the most formidable opponent of the long *durée* is a postmodern culture at large in which the rapidity and multidirectionality with which information floods daily experience leaves little time for honing processes of thought or interpretation that depend on the gradual unfolding, over time and space, of carefully sustained webs of explication—precisely those processes that constitute both the art of storytelling and the act of reading for the plot. Or, as Litvak sums up this specific cultural moment, narrative dilation (as well as its corollary, I would add, the long read) "by definition offends against the rule of a culture (our own) in which intelligence is coming to mean nothing more than knowingness, and in which power and privilege increasingly belong to those busy people who best affect a bored impatience with the excesses of time-consuming, self-indulgent storytelling."[48]

If Litvak argues convincingly for the continuing *need* to practice the art of sustained narrative readings in order to counteract the deintellectualizing tendencies of contemporary culture, I find another spirited defense of close reading, and of the "ardent" experience it involves, in Eve Sedgwick's ruminations on the psychological determinants of (her) queer reading practices in *Tendencies.* Sedgwick speaks (in words that, in this case, could be Brontë's in "Farewell to Angria") of how, in childhood, "a kind of formalism, a visceral near-identification with the writing I cared for, at the level of sentence structure, metrical pattern, rhyme, was one way of trying to appropriate what seemed the numinous and resistant power of the chosen objects." Such a habit of attaching to mystifying and impenetrable textual worlds, treasured for their sheer difference from the cultural "codes most readily available to us," and of learning to read between the lines for alternative codes, was, in Sedgwick's evocation, "a prime resource for survival. We needed for there to be sites where the meanings didn't line up tidily with each other, and we learned to invest those sites with fascination and love." Sedgwick concludes that for herself this investment in close reading as an act of survival and love was anything but a coolly impersonal, outmoded formalist exercise: "quite to the contrary: the need I brought to books and poems was hardly to be circumscribed, and I felt I knew I would have to struggle to wrest from them sustaining news of the world, ideas, myself, and (in various senses) my kind."[49] "My kind," I think, extends Sedgwick's felt passion for the literary text to all those disenfranchised readers for whom fiction, as Michel de Certeau puts it in the passage excerpted as the second of the epigraphs to this introduction, "narrates one thing in order to tell something else," limning "itself in a language from which it continuously draws effects of meaning that cannot be circumscribed or checked." This, too, is the power that Bakhtin ascribes to the novel, as well as the power of those experimental, daring fictions of sexuality that also exist "between" the lines or demand to be read against the grain of conscious desire, but that, once tapped by the "ardent" seeker, create passional "effects of meaning that cannot be circumscribed or checked."

This view of the "numinous and resistant power" of textual objects whose secret knowledge of alternative worlds can only be disclosed by struggle and dogged persistence—that is, by reading closely—brings to my mind, specifically, the case of modernist fiction, whose difficulty, impenetrability, and obliqueness has raised serious questions about the aesthetic politics of a literary elitism that necessarily excludes large populations of would-be readers—even some of Sedgwick's ardently queer readers—and whose exclusivity becomes a self-justifying reason for its canonical enshrinement as "high art." On the one hand, the fact that such obscure writing came into being at the same time as the New Criticism— an interpretive method dedicated to the discovery of the underlying unity drawing the artwork's many complex parts into a meaningful whole—returns us to the problematic status of close reading when practiced only for its own sake, or in the name of an ideal of literary "autonomy" meant to hold the encroaching masses at bay while promoting an isolationist dream of individual "freedom."[50] Nor can the question of the potential elitism of the deliberately difficult text be avoided in many of the convoluted modernist fictions considered in this study. On the other hand, not all textual difficulty is necessarily "bad," as Lee Edelman reminds his readers in a different but related context. Offering a trenchant defense of his use of "difficult" critical jargon in *Homographesis,* Edelman notes that proponents of political activism often automatically decry the language of academic theory for being too specialized, too abstract, to serve the political needs of the real world and engage concrete social issues. In counterpoint to such arguments, Edelman suggests that "the fiction of a common language that can speak a universally available truth" is in fact precisely *the* "fantasy on which the structures of dominance anatomized throughout this volume rest." And, indeed, Edelman's entire project goes far in demonstrating that only the most exacting, and at times highly specialized, analysis of those rhetorical tropes whose mundaneness often allows them to pass unobserved holds any hope for effective resistance: to free ourselves from the often invisible grip of power or ideology, we need first to see—which is to say *read,* and read closely and well—the discursive strategies that imprison us within their prescribed meanings. Only then can we begin to unravel the regulatory logic by which more visibly oppressive social institutions keep us in "our place"—which is to say, the place that has been discursively assigned to or textually inscribed upon us. Nowhere is this more true than in the realms of subjectivity and sexuality, where the "fiction of a common language" shared by everyone, easily accessible to all, is in fact more likely to work in the service of the demagogue or the reactionary proponent of social control than is true of the uncommonly multiple, specialized languages of the maligned "intelligentsia." Likewise modernist fiction has the potential—which it is up to us to realize—to hone our skills in a politics of resistance by forcing us, through the necessarily involved readings that such texts invite, to sharpen our analytical ability to spot (and thereby slip through) the loopholes invisibly marking the logic of hegemonically legislated discourses.[51]

Instead, then, of seeing cultural criticism and close reading at odds, one might say that the goal of the latter, if construed more broadly than the traditionally conceived formalist enterprise of upholding the autonomy and superior unity of the art work, speaks quite directly to the work that the study of culture, at its best, attempts to achieve through "thick description." For the practice of reading a form of narrative such as the novel closely and then committing that reading to writing, drawing upon the novel's language in an act that continuously interweaves critical voice and textual evidence to reconstruct, in the critic's prose, the novelist's construction of the novel, ultimately disentangles and makes available for a more public hearing the *plurality* of voices already present in the fiction but often hidden between the lines. This, of course, is also the goal of a cultural criticism inspired by the example of contemporary ethnography and anthropology. "Cultural poetics," muses James Clifford, makes possible "an interplay of voices, of positioned utterances," and it "obliges writers to find diverse ways of rendering negotiated realities as multisubjective, power-laden, and incongruent . . . [for] 'culture' is always relational, an inscription of communicative processes that exist, historically, *between* subjects in relations of power." Clifford himself makes the link between such a practice of cultural criticism and the reading of fictional narrative when he lauds Bakhtin's theory of the novel for demonstrating the "dialogical processes [that] proliferate in any complexly represented discursive space"— be it an ethnography or a novel—where "many voices clamor for expression."[52] The novel-critic's dilatory habit of reading for the plot, then, becomes a useful, perhaps even necessary, preparation for reading the simultaneously microcosmic and macrocosmic cultural narratives that, as Clifford's wording denotes, exist—like sexuality, like fiction—in the spaces "between."

Hence one might reverse the usual critique of close reading by saying— and here I follow Isobel Armstrong's lead in her provocative essay—that "arguably, close reading has never been close enough." In fact, the New Criticism's practice of close reading might more accurately be called "distance reading," Armstrong maintains, because its allegiance to a Kantian separation of thought and feeling dismisses the emotion or affect that is also an integral but undervalued part of the analytical reading experience. Truly close reading demands that we give our selves over to the "closeness" of the relationship that texts elicit in readers, acknowledging the affective dimensions of reading that are not caught up in a reading for mastery but that seek an understanding of what it means to occupy, however temporarily, the place of the other as part of oneself. This affective aspect of the thought-making process shares affinities with Sedgwick's description of "ardent reading" as the fervent search between the lines for meaning as if one's survival and future well-being depended on it. "A refusal to consent to closeness," Armstrong concludes, "may produce a traumatized reading," and this trauma repeats itself in the hierarchizing tendency of many readers to interpret texts as others to be mastered, and of many critics to treat critical interchange as a field for displays of one-upmanship.[53]

In light of these hypotheses, perhaps one might speculate that *Libidinal Currents,* rather than signifying a farewell to "that burning clime" of a habit long practiced, even longer loved, also signals the (welcome) return of the lessons learned from such reading, in a revitalized form that might engage with renewed perspicuity the shape of things to come, both in culture and criticism.

The Shape of Things to Come

It's about time I step back from millennial predictions of "the shape of things to come," along with questions of whether academic criticism as we know it will survive into that future, in order to address the more modest but immediate question of the shape of things to come in the book at hand. The chapters that follow have been designed to unfold on several simultaneous levels. Most obviously they chart a historical progression that reaches from Brontë's 1853 novel through post–World War II fiction, with the primary focus falling on the period from 1899 through 1950. Within this historical sweep can also be traced a three-phase literary progression through what might loosely be called protomodernist, high modernist, and late modernist modes of writing—terms that indicate the relative degree of linguistic and formal experimentation characterizing such efforts, with the high modernist innovations of the 1920s and 1930s signaling the most aggressively experimental or linguistically revolutionary of these phases. By no means simply a literary and cultural history, however, *Libidinal Currents* is structured around a series of thematic and narrative tropes that take their cue from various psychological and psychosexual paradigms or important moments in the theorization of psychoanalysis and sexuality. Each of the groupings of sexual fictions that make up these chapters, moreover, is framed by various contemporary theoretical texts in an effort to tease out the chapter's historically and psychologically specific contexts. More all-encompassing than any of these structuring devices, however, the unifying subject that resounds at the center of this book and that provides its methodological coherence is the sustained emphasis on sexuality—even though we will see that sexuality itself continually changes shape from chapter to chapter, text to text, in tandem with its equally transforming contexts. Within this psycho-political topography, these myriad representations of sexuality provide the meeting place for a rendezvous, as it were, among the psychological, sociological, metaphysical, historical, and aesthetic concerns that contribute to this rereading of modernism.

In at least two senses, chapter 1, "Policing and Depolicing the Theory of the Novel: Repression, Transgression, and the Erotics of 'Heretic Narrative' in 'Victorian' Fiction," is an exception to the inclusiveness that characterizes the other chapters, for it examines a single fictional narrative, and a nineteenth-century novel at that. Here I suggest that Brontë's *Villette* forms a precursor text in which can be located, in embryonic form, many of the issues of sexuality and narrative that dominate experimental fiction written in the first half of the twentieth century. As already suggested, one reason for using *Villette* to launch my arguments is that it serves as a near-perfect illustration of the newly emergent disciplinary society based on surveillance and the ferreting out of each other's innermost secrets that Foucault associates with the beginnings of the culture of modernity. Given these emphases, the novel provides an excellent departure for contesting recent theories of the novel that tend to view all novelistic discourse as a disguised form of social regulation, and theories of narrative desire that interrogate the gendered coordinates of plot and story. Examining *Villette* within this larger theoretical framework allows me to stage an encounter among Foucauldian, Freudian, and feminist theories of oppression and repression and, simultaneously, to query the limits and possibilities of novelistic form, both in its realist and modernist manifestations. Concurrently, my reading positions *Villette* as a *proto*modernist novel in its manipulation of narrative form, its use of a duplicitous narrative voice, its interrogation of the existentially alienated self, its "diagnosis" of the psychosocial origins of female hysteria, and, finally, its dreamlike exploration of the libidinal currents set into motion by the dialectic of repression and expression. In creating a self-proclaimed "heretic narrative" that transgresses the boundaries of Victorian societal mores and realist fiction, Brontë's first-person narrator, Lucy Snowe, becomes my self-conscious figure for the subversive narrating impulses—call them perverse, hysterical, queer, modernist, revolutionary—that proliferate in twentieth-century experimental fictions of sexuality probing the depths of the psyche.

Chapter 2, "Channeling the Floods of Desire: Women, Water, and the Plot of Sexual Awakening in Turn-of-the-Century Narrative," focuses on the conceptual shift from a "Victorian" to "modern" understanding of repression and desire. I argue that this shift involves the convergence of three elements: a specific moment in the history of sexuality; the rise of Freudian psychoanalysis; and the development of incipiently modernist fictional techniques of narration. This intersection of the sexual, the psychological, and the aesthetic is particularly pronounced in the plot of female erotic awakening that proliferates around the turn of the century, a plot format that makes hitherto unrepresentable female sexuality the privileged representation of the libidinal forces that motivate *all* human sexuality. I focus on three such awakening plots—Kate Chopin's *The Awakening,* D. H. Lawrence's *The Virgin and the Gipsy,* and Freud's *Dora*—as emblems of this transitional moment in the history of modernism, psychology, and sexuality. The chapter positions these attempts to "authorize" female sexuality within a theoretical framework bracketed, on the one side, by Freudian attempts to construct an oedipal story of female development, and, on the other, by the efforts of Klaus Theweleit (greatly influenced by the antioedipal theory of Gilles Deleuze and Félix Guattari) to unravel the links in the male imagination among women, hydraulic models of sexuality, and the desirous floods that threaten to overrun masculine ego boundaries. Reading Chopin against Lawrence, and both against the backdrop of Freud's casebook "fiction" of female sexuality, highlights one of this book's central concerns: the anxieties of sexual and textual authority that ensue once the protean currents of libidinal desire are put into writing, particularly for the author who attempts to channel these threateningly mutable floods into normative scripts of masculinity and femininity.

Chapter 3, "Modernist Theaters of the Mind I: Staging Sexuality in the Flux of Consciousness," turns to the more radical break with formal realism evident in high modernist representations of the temporal-spatial flux of conscious and unconscious mental activity. To the degree that such representations acknowledge the instability and variety of the psychosexual forces associated with the worlds of the interior, as well as the ruptures and repressions that both constitute and threaten to dissolve human subjectivity, these landmark formal experiments challenge preexisting conceptions of "identity," "sexuality," and "narrative" as unitary entities. In particular, I focus on how the return of the sexually and textually repressed functions as the underlying mechanism of psychological representation and the stimulus of narrative desire in two of the century's most widely recognized examples of modernism, James Joyce's *Ulysses* and Virginia Woolf's *Mrs. Dalloway*. Drawing on Julia Kristeva's and Judith Butler's critiques of the assumptions and language of interiority that foster the myths of self-coherence and of natural sexuality, the chapter suggests that Joyce's and Woolf's fictions resist these myths by creating simulacrums of interiority whose stylistic self-reflexivity calls into question the distinction between "interior" and "exterior" upon which the western metaphysics of the insular self rests. Not only do these novels dramatize the degree to which the principles of flux and indeterminacy associated with the inner domain of consciousness are equally true of external reality, therefore inundating both "surface" and "depth" with multiple and proliferating desires, but they also drive home the point that, even in the innermost spaces of psychosexual fantasy, the mind remains a *theater*, a stage on which modernity's fictions of sexuality are continually enacted and performed. Butler's theory of the performativity of sexuality and gender in particular provides a lens through which to evaluate the theatricalization of polymorphous sexuality that, in both novels, contributes to their rebellion against normativity.

While continuing to investigate this theatricalized representation of consciousness and sexuality, chapter 4, "Theaters of the Mind II: Queer Sites in Modernism: Harlem / The Left Bank / Greenwich Village in the 1920s and 1930s," takes up the diverse modernist practices originating within nonmainstream, mainly homosexual subcultures of the 1920s and 1930s, arguing that the literally and figuratively perverse fictions of sexuality they produced cannot be separated from the uniquely twentieth-century urban topographies that these sexual subcultures inhabited and represented. Among such renegade modernist endeavors, this chapter focuses on four examples: Bruce Nugent's stream-of-consciousness narrative of a black protagonist's "coming out" in jazz-age Harlem in "Smoke, Lilies, and Jade," Djuna Barnes's surreally baroque psychodrama of the world of the "invert" on Paris's Left Bank in *Nightwood,* Charles Henri Ford and Parker Tyler's avant-garde prose montage evoking the polymorphous circulation of desires and bodies in the primarily gay male enclave of Greenwich Village in *The Young and Evil,* and Blair Niles's narrative of the multiple cross-identifications engendered by the bond that unites a straight woman and gay man when their paths cross in the "safe" space that Harlem's nightworld forms in *Strange Brother.* In arguing for the profound influence of the modern metropolis on the creation of subcultural formations powerful enough to resist socializing norms, I draw on a number of cultural and urban theorists, ranging from Georg Simmel and Raymond Williams to Michel de Certeau, to suggest an alternative to Foucault's reading of the metropolis as the bastion of totalizing power. Because the dissident, most often homosexual, communities amassing in the hidden enclaves in the urban landscape are notoriously fluid in sexual expression, and because they manifest any number of affiliations across multiple categories of difference and oppression—including, among others, race and gender—I also draw extensively on queer theory to explain the subversive potential (and ultimate failure) of the historical moment reflected in these literary texts. Simultaneously, I argue that the multidirectional circuitry of the city grid, coupled with the anonymity and alienation enforced by modern city life, abets the creation of a deliberately perverse narrative erotics in these texts that seriously challenges the heterosexualizing and oedipal trajectories of traditional fiction.

This desire to escape the imperative of oedipal narrative becomes a sustained inquiry in chapter 5, "Under the Shadow of Fascism: Oedipus, Sexual Anxiety, and the Deauthorizing Designs of Paternal Narrative," in which I examine the assumed ubiquity of oedipal patterns both in western narrative and in much critical theory that takes the paternal plot as a given ("Doesn't every narrative lead back to Oedipus?" Barthes asks).[54] The chapter interrogates these assumptions by examining two examples of modernist gothic written in the late 1930s, William Faulkner's *Absalom, Absalom!* and Christina Stead's *The Man Who Loved Children,* both of which literalize the paradigmatic "plot of the father" by telling the story of fathers who are monomaniacally obsessed with creating family texts designed to reflect their omnipotence back to them. These discussions are framed by the theoretical contexts provided, on the one hand, by Peter Brooks's influential reading of the Freudian masterplot of sons rebelling against fathers, and, on the other, by Teresa de Lauretis's equally influential feminist argument that fictional narrative is an inevitably gendered form in which only men can serve, like Oedipus, as questing subjects. To the contrary, the argument that emerges from a reading of these two novels suggests that even the most authoritarian oedipal masterplots prove to be self-subverting, doomed to replay the anxieties of paternal authority that return in the form of the very elements (maternity, female sexuality, racial difference, homoeroticism) that the father's plot is designed to eliminate. Moreover, the universality of oedipal narrative is also called into question by the historical contexts that give rise to such fictions—such as the rise of European fascism in the 1930s, with its rhetoric of fatherland and the Führer—suggesting that the father's plot may in fact express cultural and fictional anxieties of authority that are less transhistorical than many theorists have assumed.

Chapter 6, "Fragmented Selves, Mythic Descents, and Third World Geographies: Fifties' Writing Gone Mad," examines the postwar anxieties of masculinity and femininity that come to a head in the "sex wars" of the late fifties and that are reflected in the struggle of two late modernist novelists, Doris Lessing and Lawrence Durrell, to represent the relativity of artistic and personal vision in a world of increasing fragmentation and chaos. The dispersion of chronological plot over time and space (measurable in Lessing's multiple notebooks and Durrell's multiple volumes) becomes a narrative equivalent of the crises of inner splitting that confront their protagonists, in both cases blocked writers and frustrated sexual subjects whose only hope of sexual, mental, and textual recovery lies in archetypically Jungian descents into an underworld of libidinal perversity, madness, and otherness. Fascinatingly, in both novels these interior confrontations with one's own alien otherness, the dark demon within, are projected outwards, first onto racially "foreign" geographies—Egypt in the *Alexandria Quartet* and Africa in *The Golden Notebook*—and, second, onto the homosexual figures to whom these colonial landscapes give expression, figures who eventually become scapegoats sacrificed to the anxieties of masculinity and femininity that beset the sexual and textual quests of both protagonists. I suggest that contemporary postcolonial and queer theories allow us to look anew at these two novels, which stand at the end of a long line of modernist experiments in representing states of interiority. From this vantage point, these novels seem less "period pieces" than evidence of the continuing pressures of a postwar sexual ideology whose habits of scapegoating politicized, sexualized, and racialized others continue to disturb western culture at the end of the twentieth century.

This, then, is the shape of the libidinal currents traced in this book. In making this subject my focus, I have attempted to contribute to three distinct debates being waged in current cultural and literary theory: first, this project attempts to make an intervention in studies of sexuality by creating a more flexible theoretical model that makes room both for Freud's polymorphously perverse instincts and for Foucault's polymorphously proliferating discourses without forcing a choice between them; second, this book participates in the ongoing debate over modernism by tracking modernism's evolution through simultaneously transforming historical, thematic, and formal vectors, thereby countering the frequent tendency to isolate modernism and oppose it to postmodernism and contemporary theory; and, third, it challenges universalizing paradigms of narrative by historicizing the always varying shapes and functions that modern experimental narrative has assumed, especially in relation to issues of sexuality and psychosexuality. No doubt, as in Freud's theory of the component instincts, there are myriad other paths that I could have followed; no doubt, too, the sequence I have constructed performs its own "channeling" of desires, creating a master narrative that disguises itself as transgressive criticism. But I also trust that there are enough disturbing energies in the sexual fictions I have chosen to narrate, and in the narratives that make up these sexual fictions, to spill over the edges of the borders that I have imposed and to honor the spirit of perversity that has motivated the poetics and politics of this project. No better place to begin to explore that element of the perverse, I submit, than in Lucy Snowe's deliberately perverse narration, in a novel that not only vies with Joyce's *Ulysses* in the sheer complexity of its interlocking, self-referential systems of imagery, symbols, and motifs, but also forms a veritable sexual and psychological minefield in the canon of nineteenth-century fiction, exploding the verities of Victorian realism and morality, along with their agencies of social control and surveillance.

As critics who are wont to turn their interpretations into acts of discipline and surveillance, then, *Villette* serves us professional notice, warning, as we venture forward into its perverse currents, to watch out lest—*as is inevitable*—we lose our footing and drown in its floods of impassioned and frustrated desire. The real risk, as we shall now see, is that in losing Lucy as the object of our critical gaze, we may surrender to *her* powers— powers ultimately less interested in policing us than in creating a long and lovely maze of libidinally charged narrative in which she may find herself as we lose ourselves. And, in our ecstatic surrender to her otherness, we may also find she is no longer "other" to us, that we, too, in our deepest fantasies, have always been Lucy Snowe.

CHAPTER ONE

Policing and Depolicing the Theory of the Novel

REPRESSION, TRANSGRESSION, AND
THE EROTICS OF "HERETIC NARRATIVE"
IN "VICTORIAN" FICTION

Charlotte Brontë, Villette
·····

Villette reads like one long meditation on a prison break.
—Kate Millett, *Sexual Politics*[1]

Unbroken always is this blank: alike entire and unexplained.
—Charlotte Brontë, *Villette*[2]

Distinguishing literary periods is both a necessary and futile task. The evolution in literary criticism of such mutually exclusive categories as "realist" and "modernist," along with their common equivalents "Victorian" and "modern," in order to differentiate nineteenth-century from twentieth-century fiction at once makes intuitive sense and creates an unnecessarily wide gulf between fictional modes and periods. This, however, is a gulf that a nineteenth-century novel like Charlotte Brontë's *Villette* (1853) usefully tends to upset. Indeed, this chapter will locate many of the "modern" issues of sexuality and "modernist" ones of narrative that occupy the rest of this book in this "Victorian" precursor text. For the following pages argue that the unconventionally elliptical form of *Villette*'s "heretic narrative" (as the novel's first-person protagonist Lucy Snowe calls her story) at once disguises and discloses a transgressive fiction of sexuality that bears many of the markers of cultural and literary modernity that chapters 2 through 6 pursue in a series of experimental twentieth-century narratives. Perhaps as much as any other novel taken up in this study, *Villette* manifests an almost gleefully perverse narrative erotics that anticipates the attempts of its modern and modernist successors to convey in fictional form those elusive psychosexual and libidinal currents that, since the advent of turn-of-the-century sexological theory and psychoanalytic discourse, have increasingly come to be seen as constitutive of human subjectivity. As such, Brontë's covert fiction of sexuality, I suggest, deserves to be considered a pivotal (proto)modernist fiction of interiority.

Simultaneously, precisely because *Villette* conceptually bridges, and thus makes all the more apparent, the dominant (as well as covert) concerns of both nineteenth-and twentieth-century fiction, I will make the following discussion of Brontë's text the launching point for a larger inquiry into the genre of the novel and its relation to ideological formations of sexuality. In particular, I want to pose, by means of *Villette*'s example, two challenges: first, to recent novelistic studies, indebted to Foucault's analysis of the rise of an increasingly disciplinary society in the nineteenth century, that tend to view novelistic discourse as a disguised form of social regulation and supervision (a stance propounded in D. A. Miller's *The Novel and the Police*); and, second, to theories of narrative, usually influenced by psychological or mythic paradigms, that tend to view all novelistic structures as repetitions of the same transhistorical masterplot (versions of which can be found in the work of Peter Brooks and early Teresa de Lauretis). In contrast, the perverse twists and turns whereby Brontë's Lucy Snowe creates an interior narrative of personal—and, I argue, autoerotic—desire that attempts to elude the various agents of surveillance and incarceration (including prying readers) suggests material modes of novelistic representation that resist and sometimes subvert the disciplinary mechanisms of nascent modern society and the prescriptions of a yet-to-be instituted psychoanalytic discourse.

Such a reading of novelistic resistance and difference, as noted in my introduction, points the way to theorizing a poetics and politics of the textually perverse at work in modern fiction. In the wonderfully ambiguous statement heading this chapter, Kate Millett writes that "*Villette* reads like one long meditation on a prison break." Are we meant to understand Millett's insight as a confirmation of the policing function of the novel as genre—that is, one can only dream of escaping it? Or does her statement suggest that novels sometimes not only break away from the constraints of *social* discourses, but also break through assumptions about *literary* discourse? Given the totalizing theories of fiction based on the former assumption, the question of the novel's relation to power (and ideologies of power) raises vital issues with important implications for the narratives of subjectivity and sexuality continuing to shape twentieth-century cultures of modernity. These are questions that the indirections of *Villette,* I want to argue, are craftily designed to help us see anew.

To facilitate this slantwise vision, the following pages first demonstrate what a reading of the novel based on the premises of Foucault and Miller might look like. Then, having illustrated how a paradigm of discipline seems to pervade and regulate every nuance of the novel's and Lucy's consciousness, the chapter gradually throws its argument into reverse, revealing the incompleteness of this paradigm by mapping the complexities of

Lucy's psychic disguises, textual strategies, and covert desires onto it. The complications that ensue from this layered reading, I suggest, have implications that extend beyond this single text and illuminate an undercurrent of possibilities that critics of the genre of fictional prose narrative might do well to reclaim. If *Villette*'s quirky perverseness is an exception to the (ostensible) rule of "Victorian" fiction, it is nonetheless an exception that brings into clearer focus the wayward impulses, the libidinal currents, that underlie and inspire modernity's fictions of sexuality in twentieth-century writing.

Protomodernism and Psychological Narrative

Before turning to the commentary that *Villette* provides on these larger debates, I would like to outline some ways in which this novel's representation of interiority bears so dramatically on what I am calling its protomodernist poetics. A caveat, however, is first in order. In suggesting a link between this novel's investment in depicting psychological states and the experimental irregularities of its form, I do not mean to imply that novels must be experimental or nonrealistic to register interior states of mind. As Dorrit Cohn has demonstrated in *Transparent Minds,* fictional modes of representing consciousness are by no means new to the twentieth century, nor is realistic technique inimical to the representation of psychology; indeed, some of the greatest novels of the nineteenth-century realist tradition are deeply, probingly, psychological (one need only think of George Eliot, Dostoyevsky, Flaubert).[3] What sets *Villette*—as well as the fictions taken up in the following chapters—apart is the sense that the traditional techniques for establishing interiority within the domain of novelistic verisimilitude—for example, quoted monologue, first-person narration, and indirect free discourse—ultimately fall short of articulating the darker reaches of desire, anxiety, and repression to which the dreamlike narrative of *Villette* attempts to give expression. To convert these psychosexual currents into narratable story necessitates, as Brontë's author-surrogate Lucy discovers, a "heretic narrative": one that dissents from, that refuses to conform to, traditional belief systems, whether they be doctrines of church, self, or literary form.

And this perverse veering away from the norm is something that *Villette* executes with a passion, creating a quintessentially unstable fiction in which the representation of consciousness is deeply interimplicated with its sexual subtexts and its narrative self-reflexivity. This instability pervades the narrating presence of Brontë's protagonist, whose highly interiorized, first-person voice, evoking the rhythms of her deep-seated depression, confers upon the novel its immediate feel of psychological depth and claustrophobic intensity. Wildly swinging between extremes of passionate emotion and chilly reserve, Lucy Snowe speaks and writes in a language that is, paradoxically, intimately confessional *and* stubbornly unforthcoming, her retrospective narration withholding information and fomenting ambiguities in the very act of professing to tell the "true" story of her life. Brontë enhances the illusion of psychological depth conveyed by the simple device of fictional autobiography, moreover, by punctuating Lucy's narrative with a series of gaps and lacunae that, as we shall see, become signs of the repressed within the protagonist's psyche. "Unbroken always is this blank: alike entire and unexplained," cryptically explains Lucy of the "stilly pause[s]" (348) that intrude not only into her solitary life but into the autobiographical narrative she writes. The ebb and flow of Lucy's first-person voice, with its erratic starts and stops, conveys the meandering workings of consciousness, of the mind in process, particularly in its overdetermined interplay of conscious thought and unconscious desire.

On the thematic level, the psychic disturbances incurred by such repression become manifest in Lucy's symptomatically hysterical behavior, which reaches a climax in the nervous breakdown she has when, left alone during the long summer vacation at the foreign school where she has found employment, she imagines herself a "maniac or an idiot" gone "mad from solitary confinement" (356) and in desperation seeks relief in confession—all the ingredients of a classic Freudian case study. On the formal level, this feverish psychic activity finds a narrative correlative in the novel's many psychodramatic set pieces that serve as projections of extreme mental states and imbue the narrative with its heightened, often dreamlike, ambience. On the level of genre, as well, Brontë's incorporation of aspects of gothic narrative—particularly the legend of the nun's ghost and the use of doubles—becomes an index of the erotic deprivation, emotional duress, and fantasy life that Lucy's first-person voice attempts, only half-successfully, to conceal. The narrative exploration of these subliminal states continues in the several surreal scenes that seem to plunge Lucy into the realm of the dreaming unconscious and the underworld of mythic quest. Consider, for instance, the event of Lucy's night-sea journey across the English channel to the defamiliarizing realm of total otherness represented by Labassecour ("All this was very un-English," Lucy will observe shortly, "truly I was in a foreign land" [132]). Completely disoriented as she disembarks into this unknown world under the cover of night, she is immediately waylaid by male assailants whose pursuit causes her to stray from the city's main thoroughfare and lose herself in a labyrinth of narrow backstreets that uncannily mirror the image of the collateral channels that Freud uses to describe the component instincts—a route of indirection that brings Lucy, tellingly, to the threshold of the unknown: the door of the reputedly haunted pensionnat that becomes her new home. Finally, the psychological intensity of Brontë's narrative is manifested in the sadomasochistic struggle between the impulse to dominate and the impulse to submit in love that pushes the novel's eroticism far beyond that of comparable Victorian fictions.

The various strategies Brontë employs to create a narrative in which Lucy's mental life takes precedence over external reality contribute to a radical reenvisioning of subjectivity that, as will be explored, is as radically decentered, as unmoored from the commonplaces of a stable or coherent identity, as is the narrative form itself. The text's elliptical movement, gap-filled trajectory, indefinite beginnings and inconclusive endings, dreamlike sequences, disorienting spatial and temporal schemes, undermining of readerly expectations of narrative authority, and privileging in Lucy of an "antihero" who is so determined to remain behind the scenes that she nearly succeeds in erasing herself from the plot of which she is the central subject—all these formal strategies and choices create a novel that is presciently modernist in its ambitions, even as it masqueraded, to its Victorian reading public, as a realistic, if gothically inflected, fictional autobiography.

While the above paragraphs have begun to suggest a few of the ways in which the psychological forces of repression and desire are given expression through the novel's elliptical modes of narration, they have yet to pinpoint the intersection of Brontë's psychological and narrative concerns with the latent sexuality that vibrates beneath the surface of the text, suffusing scene after scene with an erotic energy that just, by the skin of its teeth, escapes explicit articulation. Because sex in *Villette* is so volatilely suffused with issues of power and control, and because this power is not merely psychological in origin but also imposed and enforced through social institutions and discourses, we need to attend to the intersections that exist between Brontë's representation of the psychodynamics of sexuality and the regulatory mechanisms of societal power theorized by Foucault. And from a consideration of Foucault's diagnosis of the rise of disciplinary modes of social governance as *the* signature of modernity, we will find it but a short step to a reconsideration of recent theories of the novel that suggest that the genre is therefore inevitably the policing agent of cultural norms.

The Novelistic Panopticon

If ever there were a novel filled with spying eyes, knowing looks, and significant glances, it is *Villette*. Such characteristics are also familiar to readers of Foucault; both the foreign city and the text that share the imaginary name "Villette" manifest the crucial earmarks of the modern disciplinary society that Foucault sets forth in his monumental study *Discipline and Punish: The Birth of the Prison* (1975). The single most important means by which the modern "democratic" state emerging in early-nineteenth-century Europe maintained its power over its subjects, Foucault argues, was not by sovereign rule (as in the reign of the eighteenth-century monarch or despot) but by making each of its citizens an agent of surveillance and regulation: as our gazes police each other, we internalize its laws and become our own policing agents. Such a system appears fully operative in the world of interspersed and intercepted glances in *Villette,* a fact that is ironically brought home, as it were, by Brontë's need to displace its operations to a "foreign" and "very un-English" realm.

Tellingly, a scene occurs near the end of the novel that provides a textbook gloss on one of Foucault's key symbols of disciplinary power: that of the Panopticon, or central watchtower, originally designed by Jeremy Bentham for use in contemporary penitentiaries, from which the victim of incarceration is subjected to an anonymous field of constant supervision: "He is seen," Foucault writes, "but he does not see; he is the object of information, never a subject in communication."[4] In Brontë's version of this topos, Lucy Snowe is strolling in the enclosed garden of Mme. Beck's pensionnat with M. Paul Emanuel, a teacher at the adjoining boys' academy, when the latter makes a confession that works to confirm our suspicion that surveillance is ubiquitous and inescapable in Villette. Asserting in his typically irascible manner that the reticent Lucy needs "watching, and watching over," M. Paul proudly reveals that he has taken this "duty" upon his own shoulders in the most literal manner possible. "I watch you and [the] others pretty closely, pretty constantly, nearer and oftener than you or they think," he boasts, then points to a window overlooking the garden that serves as his covert "post of observation," which he identifies as "a room I have hired, nominally for a study—virtually for a post of observation. There I sit and read for hours together. . . . My book is this garden; its contents are human nature—female human nature. I know you by heart. Ah! I know you well" (453). As we will shortly discover, M. Paul's post of observation is only one of many forms that Bentham's Panopticon takes in *Villette.* Moreover, as the example of M. Paul demonstrates, this is a transaction in which the spy, when not busily prying into everybody else's secrets, openly confesses his own: making sure that those spied upon *know* that the spying eye has penetrated their inmost secrets becomes a perverse way of consolidating and displaying one's superior powers. In such an economy, knowledge counts for everything, as M. Paul's sigh of satisfaction—"I know you by heart. Ah! I know you well"—aptly but chillingly acknowledges.

The presence of such mechanisms of supervision, and the complicitous circuit of surveillance and voyeuristic delight it encourages, raises the related question of how invested this novel—and every novel as a series of textual operations—might also be in analogous modes of regulation. This question, as earlier indicated, is central to D. A. Miller's influential study, *The Novel and the Police,* which draws upon Foucault's theories to argue for the complete entanglement of the novel in the disciplinary measures it represents.[5] Consider the passage above: here we are, after all, looking down from the privileged position of reader-observer and spying upon the private conversation of Lucy and Paul, as Paul confesses *his* spying activities to Lucy. And yet we only occupy our "superior" vantage point by the good graces of Lucy, whose revelations and reticences as first-person narrator, themselves regulated by Brontë, in turn regulate *our* field of knowledge. Our privileged position outside and above the text, it turns out, is simultaneously the circumscribed space of our imprisonment within an even more encompassing system of textual constraints. The novel as genre, Miller argues, depends on and is in fact defined by the totalizing effects of such reversible circles of confinement and circumscription. This policing function is most obviously demonstrable in omniscient narrations which presuppose "a fully panoptic view of the world [they] plac[e] under surveillance"; but it is equally present, Miller notes, in first-person narration, where the confessing voice of the "secret subject," by disclosing the always already "open secrets" of his inner privacy and enclosing them within the pages of a book, guarantees his subjection within the prison of his very telling (23, 200–7).

Before exploring how deeply this economy of spied and spied-upon infiltrates the thematic and textual codes of novelistic fiction, I want to return to the above scene in *Villette* and make a perhaps obvious but nonetheless crucial point about the gendered nature of the surveillance it records. For if the object of M. Paul's study is, as he claims, "*human* nature," it is, as his immediately following qualification betrays, quite pointedly "*female* human nature" that he gazes upon in the closed recesses of Mme. Beck's garden. A psychosexual dynamics of erotic domination hence insinuates itself into M. Paul's description of the "female" secrets disclosed by "yonder . . . magic lattice" (454); this garden is a space to be penetrated, if not by M. Paul's phallic spyglass, which he self-importantly reveals he is in the habit of using, then by his secret forays into the garden itself. For as he taunts Lucy, "The garden itself is open to me": he alone possesses the key to a hidden door at its bottom, by means of which he can "come and go at pleasure" (455). Probing spyglasses, master keys, magic lattices, bottom doors—the sexualized and anatomical tenor of M. Paul's metaphors emphasize the fact that the circulation of power in the disciplinary world sketched by Foucault and adapted by Miller is not genderless but is the product of a social system whose phallocentric biases originate in conceptions of sexual difference. To the degree, then, that M. Paul's statements force us to question the continuities and discontinuities between modes of social surveillance theorized by Foucault and the scopic gaze that Freud links to the psychosexual development of men, they also suggest that psychoanalytically inflected and gender-conscious inquiries—while certainly not inimical to theoretical models of narrative indebted to Foucault—might have something more to say about the applicability of his insights concerning discursive social formations to novelistic formulations.[6]

The implications of this conflation of disciplinary and erotic gazes, of textual and sexual modes of authority, are only underlined when we consider Lucy Snowe's position, not only as a subject of discipline but as a woman who writes, in light of the literary metaphor of the book that M. Paul uses to describe the female objects of his study: "My book is this garden; its contents . . . female human nature." Yet if this female geographical space is *his* "book" by virtue of his gaze, what is the status of the text that Lucy herself is writing and that we are reading? Are there ways in which Brontë casts Lucy's narration of her search for fulfillment so that it dodges the circuit of surveillance and countersurveillance that constructs her world? Or is Lucy's narrative doomed to police itself when others' possessive gazes fail? What might either outcome imply about a novelistic poetics and politics of the perverse, not only for nineteenth-century fiction like *Villette* but for modernist mappings of desire written in the wake of the revolution occasioned by Freudian psychoanalysis? These are some of the questions the following pages address, first by detailing Brontë's representation of the effects of disciplinary power on Lucy's psychology, and then by tracing the maneuvers whereby she shrouds Lucy's inner quest and interiorized narration in a cloak of invisibility that allows Lucy to pursue, beneath her roles as actor and narrator, an erotic and autoerotic voyage of self-discovery. Entering a libidinal terrain rarely trespassed in Victorian fiction, Brontë's text opens onto unpoliced pains and pleasures that encourage a critical reconsideration of theories of the novelistic Panopticon and that invite, as the rest of this book demonstrates, a rereading of the dynamics of anxiety and authority underlying the modernist imperative to explore the darker places of psychology and sexuality.

Lucy under Lock and Key

A Foucauldain reading of *Villette* might well begin with Lucy's modest occupation as a teacher, for one of the more provocative claims of *Discipline and Punish* is that the regulatory principles of the modern penitentiary were rapidly assimilated by a wide variety of early-nineteenth-century social institutions, not the least of which were schools. And from the moment that Lucy takes up residence first as governess and then as teacher in Mme. Beck's Pensionnat de Demoiselles, she is beset by the sense that this is a house filled with spying eyes and walls with ears. As Lucy sardonically comments after observing her employer secretly search her personal belongings,

> Madame had her own system for managing and regulating this mass of machinery, and a very pretty system it was. . . . 'Surveillance,' 'espionage,'—

these were her watch-words. . . . She was sick, she would declare, of the means she had to use, but use them she must; and after discoursing, often with dignity and delicacy to me, she would move away on her 'souliers de silence,' and glide ghost-like through the house watching and spying everywhere, peering through every key-hole, listening behind every door. (135–36)

As Mme. Beck's "ghost-like" surveillance suggests, she consolidates her power by becoming an all-seeing presence that is everywhere at once but seen by no one, not unlike Bentham's model of the Panopticon—or the pose of the all-seeing narrator of traditional third-person narration. Thus it comes as no surprise to learn that Mme. Beck, like M. Paul, also occupies a "summit of observation" above the pensionnat's garden, from which "open window" no "transaction" below is said to escape her watchful eye (182).

As a hyperactive site of disciplinary power, the school on the secluded Rue Fossette might first seem an exception to the rule—it is, after all, only a girls' school. But Mme. Beck's establishment, the text immediately implies, is a microcosm of the state itself, embodying in the person of its director the methods by which the larger social order maintains its power. Lucy is being only half-facetious when she declares that Mme. Beck "ought to have [ruled] a nation: she should have been the leader of a turbulent legislative assembly. . . . In her own single person she could have comprised the duties of a first minister and a superintendent of police" (137). And Mme. Beck, like any good superintendent of the police, commands a legion of subalterns to carry out her dirty work. "As Madame . . . ruled by espionage, she of course had her staff of spies," Lucy reports, a staff which allows Madame to remain the ever-unruffled, amiable mistress of the situation, lodged at the center of her information-gathering bureaucracy, "plotting and counterplotting, spying and receiving the reports of spies all day" (136, 135).

If the similarity between Mme. Beck's pensionnat and the modern police state is cinched by Lucy's reference to her mistress as "a little Buonaparte" (213), it is also true that Mme. Beck is not the only Napoleon in the world of *Villette.* Her kinsman and most valued schoolmaster, M. Paul, is another agent of disciplinary control whose "love of power" and "eager grasp after supremacy" has, according to Lucy, "points of resemblance to Napoleon Bonaparte" (438, 436). M. Paul ostensibly epitomizes a more legitimate face of discipline, that of the worthy judge whose "unerring penetration of instinct," "questioning eyes," and "ruthless researches" (423–24) are instruments of moral efficacy. It is ironic, then, that this champion of truth, while busily stripping away others' "florid veilings" of deceit (423), not only elects to censor Lucy's reading, but also attempts to prohibit her observation of unveiled female bodies in the museum episode. Such actions indicate that M. Paul's exercise of authority is not so disinterested after all; for him, as for Mme. Beck, knowledge is a means of power and control. Hence the man whom Lucy calls her "self-elected judge" (386) turns out to be an incorrigible spy, one whose Jesuitical training, Lucy jests, has prepared him all too well to make good his avowed intention to "[keep] his eye on me" (387).[7]

The reader soon learns that the individual skills of M. Paul and Mme. Beck are subject to a yet greater supervisory agency: that of the Catholic Church, which keeps the budding friendship of the heretic Lucy and its faithful son M. Paul "under the surveillance of a sleepless eye" (503). For the "*magic* lattice" through which M. Paul admits he spies on the enclosed garden of the pensionnat is subtly refigured by Brontë as "that *mystic* lattice," the "sliding panel of the confessional," through which the Church probes M. Paul's conscience and infuses his mind with the injunction to self-discipline and repression (454, 503; emphases added). Nor is this exercise of unseen power restricted to the privacy of the confessional booth, as the Protestant Lucy learns when she goes to confession in a moment of despair and is afterwards followed into the streets by her confessor, Père Silas, who "esteem[s] it a Christian duty" (258) to ferret out the details of Lucy's identity: detection undertaken in the name of "spiritual" discipline knows no bounds.[8]

The appropriateness of reading *Villette* as an illustration of the modern disciplinary society theorized in *Discipline and Punish* and applied to the genre of prose fiction in *The Novel and the Police* is seemingly reaffirmed by the fact that Lucy, beset as she is by this world of incessant surveillance, doesn't refrain from using its techniques when they work in her behalf. Indeed, several episodes reveal the keenly and quietly observant Lucy to be as gifted a spy as Mme. Beck. A paradigmatic instance occurs on Lucy's first night in Villette, when she discovers her new employer rifling through her possessions. Lucy feigns sleep less out of fear of being detected, however, than in order to outspy her observer. The pleasure that Lucy takes in remaining the unseen observer of Mme. Beck's activities on this and subsequent occasions—"I will not deny that it was with a secret glee I watched her" (186)—underlines the degree to which Beck functions not only as Lucy's foil but as her psychological double, revealing a more actively scheming underside to Lucy's reticent public demeanor.[9] Moreover, like Mme. Beck, Lucy occupies her own less spacious Panopticon in the form of the children's nursery—"my watch-tower," she calls it, "[from] whence I . . . made my observations" (138). And it is precisely within these quarters that the handsome young physician called in to attend to Mme. Beck's children, Dr. John, increasingly becomes the object of Lucy's not disinterested surveillance, as her phrasing over the course of three exemplary pages betrays. "Indeed, when you looked well at him . . . ," she first comments upon surveying his comely appearance, ostensibly to explain the attraction he exerts on Mme. Beck. Within sentences, however, the fiction of Mme. Beck's mediating eye has dropped out altogether ("I noticed," Lucy says, then, "I noticed more" [160]); and as Dr. John's visits to the school accelerate, we find Lucy lamely protesting her equally stepped-up surveillance: "It was not perhaps my business to observe the mystery of his bearing . . . but, placed as I was, I could hardly help it. He laid himself open to my observation" (162). In Brontë's psychodramatic rendition of the "very un-English" and "foreign land" (132) of *Villette,* cold-minded surveillance reveals its other face as warm-blooded voyeurism, epitomized in the eroticized gaze theorized by Freud and recently the subject of much ground-breaking feminist criticism.[10]

As the examples of Mme. Beck, M. Paul, and Lucy make clear, the quintessential instrument of surveillance in the world of this novel is the sometimes disciplinary, sometimes eroticized gaze: eyes are everywhere— even in Lucy's private garden, where "the eyes of the flowers" have "gained vision" (183). The complexity of interpretation generated by this network of covert and caught glances is epitomized in the concert episode of chapter 20, an event to which Lucy has been escorted by Dr. John and his mother. While the singers and musicians assemble on stage, a second drama unfolds in the royal box in the balcony above Lucy, where she reads the mute "spectacle" of the king's melancholia engraved on his brow (291); Dr. John, meanwhile, witnesses yet another psychologically and erotically damaging "spectacle" when he catches Ginevra Fanshawe, the current object of his adoration, ridiculing his mother from afar (294). One is not quite sure where the stage ends or the audience begins in this pyschodramatic theater of intercepted gazes, which is indeed Brontë's point; *anyone* is liable to become the unwitting spectacle to another's observation in this world of blurring boundaries, where eroticized and disciplinary gazes collide.[11] This potential volatility and interchangeability is, as we have seen, a hallmark of the disciplinary society envisioned by Foucault; by making everyone agents of a mobile, diffuse power that circulates among a plurality of "subsidiary authorities," this system creates subjects who, in Foucault's words, assume responsibility for their own subjection; held captive by the ideal of a larger but unseen policing power, we become our own best jailers, internalizing the command to repress our desires, lest we become (yet more) oppressed, in the name of "stable" identity (*Discipline* 21, 202–3).

Hence, complementing surveillance as a mode of social control is the ever-present threat of imprisonment or incarceration. This danger is manifested throughout *Villette* in a series of images of stifling enclosure, ranging from rooms to burial plots, that mark Lucy's negotiation of the competing paths of desire and duty, of expression and repression. Domestic incarceration, for instance, becomes more than a figure of speech when M. Paul locks Lucy in the attic of the pensionnat to study for her role in the school play. Notably, this garret prison provides the setting both for Lucy's first sighting of the ghostly nun rumored to haunt the school and for her subsequent hysterical outbreak. Incarceration—in the form of interment—is also the "moral" of the nun's story, whose unnamed transgressions have resulted, according to legend, in her being "buried alive" in the school's garden "for some sin against her vow" (172). The inference that these must be sexual crimes vividly serves to remind Lucy of the necessity of containing her own wayward and perhaps "sinful" desires—hence her decision to bury her treasured letters from Dr. John on the spot where the nun was interred. The most that can be hoped of this never-realized love, Lucy muses in yet another image of physical and psychological containment, is that Dr. John still maintains a little closet marked Lucy's Room in the "goodly mansion" of his heart; as for herself, she confesses, "I kept a place for him, too—a place of which I never took the measure. . . . All my life long I carried it folded in the hollow of my hand" (555).[12]

This figurative act of sexual self-repression—whereby we become our own best disciplinarians—attests, like all these images of enclosure, to the introjected marks of the prison that, as the consequence of continual deprivation and loss, have been etched into Lucy's psyche since childhood. Yet, paradoxically, these same images also bespeak the intense desire to maintain a private space, an inner sanctum of self, untouched by the external world that imprisons the individual in its rules and regulations. This tension between incarceration and inwardness is central to Miller's thesis in *The Novel and the Police.* Miller argues that the entire if covert project of the nineteenth-century novel is to confirm the bourgeois reader in his or her identity as a free "liberal subject"[13] and that the novel does this by creating for the reader the *illusion* of a sheltered or private space, an outside or "elsewhere" to the all-encompassing operations of institutionalized power. In fact, the novel's obsession with policing the boundaries between good and evil, inside and outside, mind and body, the domestic and the carcereal, the psychological and the social, is precisely a strategy to imply that there *is* an alternative realm—the reader's bourgeois-liberal realm— free of the police and the criminal sphere they patrol. The catch in this ideological gambit, Miller argues, is that the privileged, psychologically inflected "categories of the individual, the inward, [and] the domestic" only recreate with ever-discrete ploys those disciplinary powers they claim to disavow; likewise, "*the very practice of novelistic representation*"—the emphasis is Miller's—itself merely "reinvent[s]" the "policing powers" it pretends to censure (ixxx–x, 5, 63, 16–18, 82, 20).

Deferring for the moment the question of whether "the very practice of . . . representation" in the novel is as unitary or panoptic as Miller's formula implies, it is nonetheless clear that his theory raises serious questions about Lucy's attempt to maintain any kind of private space hidden from the world's knowledge and free from the constraints of power—if only a place "folded in the hollow of my hand." Such a theory also calls into question Lucy's attempt, both as subject of her narrative and as its author, to construct an identity or adopt a pose resistant to the social pressures that surround and define her as a woman, particularly one who is unmarried, plain, and unprotected in the world. To say as much, however, is to make explicit what the preceding images of enclosure, imprisonment, and containment have thus far only implied: that issues of sexuality, repression, and identity create an especially coercive psychological and social bind for the female subject in a disciplinary society where power is also patriarchal, invested with an erotics whose purpose is to ensure the subjection of women.

Undercover Operations

To begin, then, to unravel the ways in which Lucy's sex affects her position in a society based on supervisory discipline, I would like to turn to her psychological investment in remaining as invisible as she can in this world of innumerable eyes, and then to her participation as first-person narrator in recreating, insofar as words make possible, this invisibility on the level of narrative structure. Without doubt, Lucy's favorite position in social situations is to remain the unnoted but all-seeing observer, seeking out vantage points "whence unobserved I could observe" (211). Is this simply an attempt to retain the power of the panoptic gaze for herself, or does Lucy's willed invisibility simultaneously serve other functions? An answer, I suggest, is implicit in the response Lucy makes to Ginevra Fanshawe's consternated query, "Who *are* you, Miss Snowe? . . . But *are* you anybody?" "Who am I indeed? Perhaps a personage in disguise," Lucy teasingly replies (392–94), at once supplying an answer to the question of her identity, but one that defers direct "meaning." Likewise, Lucy deliberately figures herself as a "cypher" (445), a seeming nonentity not worth the bother of one's attention, an in-significance that does not signify. But this very figure, as Karen Lawrence has noted, is itself a disguise, a covering, one that allows Lucy to "pass"—queer subject that she is—unimpeded before a world of exacting judges.[14] For Lucy's most characteristic feature, as she readily admits, is a "staid manner" which she likens to a "cloak and hood of hodden gray; since under its favour I had been enabled to achieve with impunity, and even approbation, deeds that if attempted with an excited and unsettled air would in some minds have stamped me as a dreamer and zealot" (104). Just as Lucy hides the zealous dreams firing her inner life from disapproving judges, she also disguises her physical being, constantly representing herself as "a mere shadowy spot on a field of light" costumed in a "gown of shadow" (200).

One effect of this self-effacing performance, ironically, is to heighten the existential solitude, the dreary sense of "solitary confinement" (356), that has pervaded Lucy's inward life from its earliest years. Thus Lucy envisions herself forever "thinking . . . my own thoughts, living my own life in my own still, shadow-world" (185). But inhabiting a "shadow-world," even if one of one's own making, necessarily incurs a certain psychological cost; to retreat behind a mask of invisibility and coolness is to court the dangers of masochistic self-negation (not only to *become* the shadow that is one's mask, but to revel in it) and self-deception (to mistake the mask for reality). Invisibility, even as a defense against the imprisoning gazes of others, can thus become another kind of prison, a self-imposed life-sentence. To become so enclosed within oneself, to repress all outward manifestations of feelings, is to risk the stasis of nonlife, of the plotless existence that Lucy seems to have embraced as her fate at the opening of the novel. The neurotic disassociation or self-splitting that ensues from such a willed separation of "inner" and "outer" selves marks the younger Lucy's first naming of herself in the text (which, true to Foucauldian paradigm, takes the form of a plea before a hypothesized jury) as she declares, "I, Lucy Snowe, plead guiltless of an overheated . . . imagination" (69). This is a claim, however, that the reader soon realizes could not be further from the truth. It is, indeed, the lack of an outlet for the "burning clime"[15] of imagination and feeling that Lucy bottles up within herself that precipitates her nervous breakdown when left alone during the summer school vacation.

Yet, as Brontë proceeds to demonstrate, this willed invisibility, this veneer of imperturbability, is not only symptomatic of neurosis. It also heralds a strategic psychic mechanism designed to shelter Lucy from greater oppression and discrimination, more generally as one who has faced tremendous loss and unspoken pain but more specifically as a woman whose physical appearance has already rendered her "invisible" in the eyes of most men—an appearance, Lucy wryly comments, inciting "just that degree of notice . . . given to unobtrusive articles of furniture, chairs of ordinary joiner's work, and carpets of no striking pattern" (162). To lack a "striking pattern," however, is not to be without designs altogether. Rather, as Lucy's strategically assumed invisibility attests, her "cloak and hood of hodden gray" is part of a design, one that provides her with a mode of psychic survival while affording her some unexpected, even pleasurable, benefits: "In quarters where we can never be rightfully known, we take pleasure, I think, in being consummately ignored" (164). And, indeed, beneath her shadowy demeanor Lucy bides her time, waiting to know and "be rightfully known," which means not only to see but also to be seen: to become, in psychoanalytic terms, a human subject that recognizes and is recognized by others in a world of coexisting subjects. But until Lucy chooses that moment, subterfuge serves her cause best.

In a defiant proclamation of her right to privacy and the integrity of her interior life, Lucy declares, toward the novel's end, that "who[ever] wills, may keep his own counsel—be his own secret's sovereign . . . my whole inner life . . . was still mine only" (545). While one might question—precisely on the grounds that Miller has sketched out—Lucy's assumption of the coherence of an inner life, a natural self, that is her own possession ("mine only"), her statement nonetheless usefully suggests the strategic doubleness embedded in her first-person narrative, which "keeps its own counsel," its privacy, at the same time, paradoxically, that it publicly documents in writing the materials of her "inner life." Tantalizingly, her language also echoes an earlier statement she makes in defending her decision to withhold from her godmother the inner trials that have led to her nervous collapse: "So the half-drowned life-boatman keeps his own counsel and spins no yarns" (254). One can hardly imagine a clearer enunciation of the mechanisms of self-repression. But while it is true that Lucy never reveals to her concerned friends—or her readers—the long-buried childhood traumas that underlie her adult fears of isolation and deprivation, it is not true that the "half-drowned" survivor that is Lucy "spins no yarns." Rather, as Karen Lawrence has suggested, Lucy turns to self-articulation in writing precisely in order to counter being "misread" in person and hence to control, in this medium at least, how one signifies.[16] For Lucy tells her tale so that it also signifies *differently*, and the result is an indirect and circuitous narrative trajectory that creates, in the face of apparent subjection, an unprecedented degree of authorial freedom for its subject. As such, *Villette* participates in the creation of a poetics of the textually perverse that foreshadows its modernist incarnations.

Lucy's narration, to say the least, is self-consciously, perversely devious from the onset, beginning with her initial perverse strategy of displacing herself, as subject of her narrative, from its center. By focusing on Paulina, the newcomer to the Bretton household, as if she were the novel's true subject, the narrating Lucy in effect goes "under cover," remaining as inscrutable as possible. Then, in a move typical of this elliptical narrative, the shift at the beginning of chapter 4 reveals that the entire Bretton episode has been a kind of false start, a narrative feint, and the novel begins again, this time with Lucy at its center. But as the well-known metaphor of the "shipwreck" that Lucy employs to explain her loss of family in this passage illustrates, this beginning is just as duplicitous in its way as the Bretton episode was, employing a metaphorical figure—"picture me . . . as a bark slumbering through halcyon weather" (94)—to cover over the blank of eight years that Brontë leaves forever unexplained. In this spectacular instance of textual repression that, indeed, is flaunted as such, we are denied knowledge of what really happened, who Lucy's kindred were, whether she had always been an orphan before becoming (in a subtle continuation of the shipwreck metaphor) the "half-drowned" survivor who chooses, in regard to her origins, to spin "no yarns" (254).

These uncertain narrative beginnings give rise to two related, equally destabilizing narrative functions or strategies. First, this radical lack of narrative origins, of an "original" home, inaugurates Lucy's quest into the un-

known, a journey for which there is no necessary end, no teleological finality, no prospect of a happy return to stasis: temporally, spatially, and
psychologically, Lucy's trajectory anticipates that of the expatriate modern
artist in exile from family, country, even language. Following her original
displacement *to* Bretton—already a movement away *from* home—Lucy
moves farther and farther into uncharted realms, on existential and geographical grounds: first to London, then, by means of her night-sea journey, to the European kingdom of Labassecour and its capital city, Villette.
Encountering otherness out of necessity as a traveler in foreign lands and
daring the forbidden become hallmarks of Lucy's physical and psychic
quest: she constantly depicts herself as "venturing out of what I looked on
as my natural habits" (222), venturing beyond limits and into the "allées
défendues" (174) of the world—and, we might add, into the "allées défendues" or forbidden channels of the unconscious. In the process, the
"uncertain future" (117) that has always faced Lucy as a "placeless person"
(103) also becomes an effect of narrative's radical "placelessness," as it
traces a trajectory whose direction repeatedly swerves out of the reader's
grasp, frustrating one's ability to pinpoint its present location or predict its
evolution and outcome.

Second, this existential and textual uncertainty is mirrored in the forementioned gaps and lacunae, "the stilly pause[s]" of textual repression, that
self-reflexively disrupt the linearity of Lucy's retrospective telling. These
"unbroken" blanks remain, as noted in this chapter's second epigraph,
"alike entire and unexplained" (348). The narrative's most infamous reticence involves Lucy's suppression of her knowledge of Dr. John's identity
as her childhood companion Graham Bretton, an omission that forces the
reader to assume the position of Dr. John himself, who has also been also
left in the dark. "To *say* anything on the subject, to *hint* at my discovery,
had not suited my habits of thought, or assimilated with my system of
feeling," Lucy states, "I . . . preferred to keep the matter to myself. I liked
entering his presence covered with a cloud he had not seen through" (248).
Lucy's calculated wording recalls the issues of disguise and sight, silence
and speaking, that are intrinsic to a disciplinary order, but with a critical
difference. For by means of her gesture of simultaneous withholding and
disclosure, Lucy not only eludes Dr. John's judgment; she also double-
crosses those policing readers who would prefer to categorize, compart-
mentalize, and fix her identity within the realm of the knowable. We are
forced, uncomfortably, to admit that Lucy's confessional first-person does
not confess *all*.[17]

In fact, if Lucy's narrative confesses any truths, they are perversely unorthodox ones. The indirect, elliptical strategies that she uses to unfold
her story inscribe what she labels a "heretic narrative" (235), a dissenting
narrative that defies the authorizing agencies that would discipline this
non-believer's life and normalize her telling of it. Significantly, Lucy uses

this phrase as she looks back on her experience of confession and contemplates the consequence had she accepted Père Silas's invitation to return for further instruction in the "true faith": "Did I, do you suppose, reader, contemplate venturing again within that worthy priest's reach? . . . the probabilities are that had I visited Numero 10, Rue des Mages, at the hour and day appointed, I might just now, *instead of writing this heretic narrative*, be counting my beads in the cell of a certain Carmelite convent on the Boulevard of Crécy in Villette" (235; emphasis added). At this moment Lucy explicitly defines her entire writerly enterprise as *transgressive*. For in writing her life Lucy continues to confess, but in contradistinction to her confessor's orthodox desires, confesses (to anyone who will hear) a heretic narrative. And however elliptical, or disjointed, or perverse Lucy's narrative might *appear*, it nonetheless clearly speaks her refusal to be silenced, to let her story "venture" forth only to die within the mute walls of a conventual cell—a specifically female form of incarceration.

Lucy's unorthodox psychological and narrative stratagems—her silences, her disguises, her willful misconstructions; in sum, her undercover operations—are thus crucially related to the artistic questions of female representation and self-representation that face her as a woman and a writer, and, by extension, Brontë as Lucy's creator. For Lucy, the question becomes one of how to represent the female as subject without risking her immediate objectification by the privileged male gaze, that ubiquitous instrument of surveillance and control in a patriarchal society. The "Cleopatra" and "Vashti" chapters offer linked but contrasting perspectives on this problem.[18] If Lucy dismisses the nude painting of Cleopatra she views in the museum episode as a blatantly unrealistic male representation of female flesh put on display for all viewers, she recognizes in the riveting stage performance of the fiery actress Vashti an audacious attempt at female self-representation, one in which Vashti deliberately usurps the gaze by displaying a transgressive "spectacle" of female desire and "disclos[ing] power like a deep, swollen, winter river, thundering in cataract" (341). The risk of such openly defiant self-representation, however, is to incur the sobering reactions of the Dr. Johns of the world. "He judged her as a woman, not an artist" (342), Lucy intuitively gleans. And although Lucy too holds ambivalent feelings about Vashti's flouting of convention, her immediate comment is that this night has been "marked in my book of life . . . with a deep-red cross" (342). Lucy's metaphor underlines, I want to suggest, the degree to which the writing of her *own* text—"my book of life"—simultaneously encodes and discloses, through its double-cross of narrative indirection, an equally turbulent, unmeasured, flood of erotic passion. In this double-cross, the issues of sexuality, psychology, and narrative central to this study intersect to unleash the libidinal currents that serve as the motivation, the narrative desire, inspiring Lucy's courageously defiant, deliberately deviant, presciently modernist act of writing.

Emotional Bondage; or, the Chains of Love

As part of Lucy's attempt to represent herself as the desiring subject of her heretic narrative, her story insistently raises the question of her desire for others. In attempting to evade the regulatory mechanisms of a social system and moral code that police female passion, however, Lucy also risks never being loved, of remaining invisible to those whom she loves. The following pages turn to the unconventional ways in which Brontë uses Lucy's two affairs of the heart to dramatize, in an especially condensed form, the problematics of surveillance and detection, power and hierarchy, incarceration and freedom, and self and other that traverse the represented world of this novel and circumscribe its field of erotic play.

Lucy's hidden passion for Dr. John Bretton reveals itself, as already noted, in her meticulous observation of his every movement. Her gaze, however, remains powerless as long as *he* does not recognize her; it is his vision that holds power in Villette's world. Hence his manly knowledge becomes at once the source of his sexual attractiveness to Lucy, as well as a disturbing sign of the inherent inequality in their relationship. "I often felt amazed at his perfect knowledge of Villette," Lucy marvels as he takes her about town, "a knowledge not merely confined to its open streets, but penetrating to all its galleries, salons, and cabinets: of every door which shut in an object worth seeing . . . he seemed to possess the [magical] 'Open! Sesame'" (273). The phallic connotations of this commanding (and, one might add, looking ahead to chapter 6, thoroughly orientalized) potency become even more apparent in one of the novel's most libidinally charged passages, a meditation in which Lucy uses allegorical language to evoke the quickening effect that Dr. John's sunny rays have on "the starved hollow" that evokes her sexuality:

> Conceive a dell, deep-hollowed in forest secrecy; it lies in dimness and mist: its turf is dank, its herbage pale and humid. A storm or an axe makes a wide gap amongst the oak-trees; the breeze sweeps in; the sun looks down; the sad, cold dell, becomes a deep cup of lustre; high summer pours her blue glory and her golden light out of that beauteous sky, which till now the starved hollow never saw. (334)

Yet because Dr. John is blind to Lucy's passion, never seeing in her anything more than "a being inoffensive as a shadow" (403), she can only participate in his desires vicariously, as the intermediary who facilitates *his* affairs of the heart. Hence it is a sign of Lucy's emerging psychological stability, of her growing capacity to be an active subject in the plot of her own desire, when she refuses his seductive appeal that she serve the office of go-between in his courtship of Paulina Home, as she has previously, and painfully, served in his flirtation with Ginevra Fanshawe. "'No, *I could not*,'" she replies with "an inward courage, warm and resistant" (403–4).

In turn, when Paulina attempts to draw Lucy into a triangular relation with herself and her now-declared lover by asking Lucy how Dr. John appears to her eyes, Lucy refuses the gambit, answering in charged language, "*I never see him.* I looked at him twice or thrice about a year ago, before he recognized me, and then I shut my eyes." As Polly presses Lucy for a further explanation, Lucy reiterates, "I mean that I value vision, and dread being struck stone blind" (520). Significantly, it is Lucy who now *chooses* "not to see" Dr. John's castrating gaze (in this reversal of the Medusa myth), whereas previously Dr. John has *failed* to see her. That the symbolic culmination of this subplot returns to the disempowering properties of the male gaze only underlines its importance in maintaining the psychosexual and gendered dynamics of control in the society in which Lucy lives.

Emancipated from one romantic obsession, Lucy moves into an increasingly erotic alignment with her fellow teacher, M. Paul. This character's chauvinism and love of power have given many critics and readers pause; does Lucy simply install a domestic version of the police in her life by falling in love with this beady-eyed despot? As M. Paul's surveillance of Mme. Beck's garden of feminine flowers has already indicated, this man penetrates secret spaces with a violent sexual energy that even exceeds Dr. John's magical skill in springing open the hidden doors of Villette's society. "As usual he broke upon us like a clap of thunder," Lucy routinely reports of M. Paul's Zeus-like entrance into the girls' schoolroom, "with his vehement burst of latch and panel" (317). Just as M. Paul holds sway over the entire female pensionnat, so too he continually insinuates himself into Lucy's most private spaces, her desk included, in the most sexually suggestive manner possible. "Now I knew, and had long known," Lucy confides, "that that hand of M. Emanuel's was on intimate terms with my desk; that it raised and lowered the lid, ransacked and arranged the contents, almost as familiarly as my own" (430)—and the tell-tale evidence of his ransacking is none other than the scent left by his phallic cigars. What is a blatant attempt to police Lucy's privacy, however, also has another side: Paul invades Lucy's desk to leave her the books and pamphlets that arouse as they validate her intellectual ambition. And it is this intellectual reciprocity that ultimately differentiates Lucy's relation with Paul from that with Dr. John, leading to an imagistic reversal that transforms Lucy into the force who penetrates M. Paul's private sanctums: "His mind was indeed my library," Lucy says, "and whenever it was opened to me, I entered bliss" (472). It is now Paul who is "open" to Lucy's entrance, he who serves as static threshold or portal through which her active quest for knowledge leads.

The psychological role M. Paul plays in goading Lucy's "ambitious wishes" (440) for intellectual advancement retroactively explains many of his other acts of seeming tyranny: under the guise of impatience and irascibility, he seeks to stimulate Lucy into an active realization of her own powers. Good intentions do not explain away M. Paul's often inexcusable paternalism, but they do point to a simultaneous level of signification at work not only in his complex psyche but also in Brontë's narrative design. For example, it is M. Paul's demand that Lucy act in the school play that, in spite of its aura of sexual violation ("the doors burst open . . . two eyes . . . hungrily dived into me") and carcereal enforcement (literally imprisoning the reluctant understudy in the attic till she learns her part), results in Lucy's awakening to her potential as a literally and figuratively *acting* subject: "I acted to please myself. . . . A keen relish for dramatic expression had revealed itself as part of my nature" (211). And despite her protestation afterward that she has locked this performative desire away, the fact is that "dramatic expression" and "relish," in the most positive sense, come to define her subsequent encounters with M. Paul. She proves herself the consummate actress in deliberately tempting his outbreaks; her vaunted coolness, formerly the sign of her emotional alienation, increasingly serves the task of erotic play: "I had a certain pleasure in keeping cool, and working him up" (277).

In addition, M. Paul's fiery temper complements the inner "fire," the burning clime within, that he alone among Lucy's acquaintances perceives beneath her calm exterior. "I know you!" he says after her performance in the school play, "I watched you. . . . What fire shot into the glance! Not mere light, but flame" (226). Hence, although the disconcerting gaze that Paul levels at Lucy seems all too frequently a gross violation of her privacy, one product of his surveillance, paradoxically, *is to free the light in her own eyes*—"What fire shot into the glance!" With these words, Brontë recasts the so-called male gaze as this female subject's self-empowering property. Lucy's reappropriation of the gaze triggers another key imagistic reversal, as, having just bested M. Paul in one of their verbal bouts, she thinks to herself, "You are well habituated to be passed by as a shadow in Life's sunshine; it is a new thing to see one testily lifting his hand *to screen his eyes*, because you tease him with *an obtrusive ray*" (421; emphases added).

It is crucial to emphasize that these imagistic reversals—whereby Lucy becomes the penetrator of Paul, her "coolness" a form of intimate love-play rather than alienation, and the "rays" of her gaze blinding—do not simply attest to her usurpation of the "male" position. Rather, they participate in the unsettling of categories and oppositions that runs throughout the text and that is inherent in its elliptical mode of narration. And these continual slippages in signification illustrate one way in which the diffusion of power into multiple conduits in the Foucauldian schema may also countermand that very system—in this case, by making possible a multifaceted mode of signifying, and hence of being, that, gradually embraced by Lucy, gives her the psychological space and inner strength to avert male objectification. This destabilizing tendency is present everywhere, even, tellingly, in the garden scene earlier cited as a textbook example of Foucauldian social discipline. For the view from M. Paul's covert "post of observation" above the girls' garden in fact uncovers a spectacle that overturns the hierarchy of seer/seen he is attempting to impose on the sexes: what he sees are Mme. Beck's charges acting not "like" girls but rather even "the most reserved . . . romp[ing] like boys" (454). Similarly, his secret forays into the garden via the agency of his key—ostensibly a sign of his phallic superiority—involve both a descent from his tower *and* the traversing of a sexual divide that effectually strips him of his masculinist claim to distanced authority. Once on Lucy's turf, that is, he must walk side by side with her, and thus the hierarchy of high/low is also overturned: it is Lucy who, in condemning his spying activity, now maintains a "*high* insular presence," M. Paul complains, and he whose ravings have plummeted him to the level of "a *third-rate* London actor" (455; emphases added).

Having preserved her "insular presence" in the face of M. Paul's on-slaughts, and having recuperated, at least partially, the powers of activity and sight through their reciprocal exchanges, it is appropriate, finally, that Lucy likewise finds her voice through dialogue with her newly declared lover in chapter 36: "That night M. Paul and I talked seriously and closely. . . . I could talk my own way—the way M. Paul was used to—and of which he could follow the meanderings and fill the hiatus, and pardon the strange stammerings, strange to him no longer" (513). Lucy's description of her speech—meandering, stammering, full of hiatuses—calls to mind the elliptical, perverse, heretical methods by which she inscribes her subjectivity into her written text. If M. Paul has become an adept reader of Lucy's verbal text, it thus is not because, as in the case of his earlier comment, "My book is this garden," he has insidiously penetrated it, but because his and Lucy's dialogic interchange of ideas has made possible an analogous interpenetration of dialogic selves. Lucy presents herself to be read, finally, by one who will not misinterpret her (in)significance, nor overlook her (in)visibility.

This is not to say that imbalance disappears entirely from M. Paul and Lucy's love relationship. Despite the partial truth in Paul's declaration that "we are alike—there is affinity" (457), there remain between the lovers irreducible differences, especially those involving power and submission in love—and these are differences that, given prevailing gender constructions, Brontë if not Lucy seems to find insurmountable. However much the understanding established by Lucy and M. Paul points to a new model of reciprocal adult love that simultaneously acknowledges the complexity and contradictions inherent in all passion, Brontë draws back from testing this intersubjective ideal in the "real" world of middle-class marriage, as her choice to end the novel with M. Paul's apparent drowning at sea so powerfully attests. But while the bonds of heterosexual love remain, for

Brontë, potentially incarcerating, this does not necessarily mean that the woman who remains unmarried is doomed to a life without eroticism, one in which no libidinal currents flow. For the prison of nonsexuality assigned to the single or chaste Victorian woman is not the fate of Lucy Snowe; the "deep-red cross" marked in her "book of life" covertly reveals something rather different and more dangerous: an inner life imbued with erotic potential and autoerotic pleasure. Crosses represent, among many other things, the point at which paths not only intersect but allow for a complete about-face, and the following pages, in keeping with this talismanic sign-post, will execute the reversal towards which this chapter (like Lucy's narrative) has been building all along, showing what happens when a poetics and politics of the perverse is mapped onto and over the carceral plots that have driven Lucy undercover rather than under lock and key.

Out of Bounds

The dramatic growth in mental health that ensues from Lucy's relationship with M. Paul is, as often noted, part of the larger emergence from repression that her story charts.[19] I have already noted how Lucy's psychological trajectory is imagistically represented as a continual venturing forward into the unknown. This ceaseless movement, echoed in the narrative's deviating structure, is accompanied by "heretic" expressions of yearning for liberty, for freedom from the constraints of a society that, as shown above, attempts to enforce Lucy's subjection. Inscribing this desire to become an actively questing subject and independent agent into her narrative, Lucy, I will now propose, writes into her "book of life" an interior voyage of libidinal self-discovery that displaces, if not dismantles, the incarcerating erotics of its courtship plots and reconfigures sexual desire as Lucy's, rather than men's, imaginative property.[20] While total autonomy, or "freedom of self," as Miller and numerous other poststructuralist critics remind us, remains an impossible bourgeois myth, Lucy's imaginative participation in fantasies of (auto)eroticism nonetheless creates within *this* writing subject an existential interiority and an ontological space that, if not entirely free of the police, is neither quite a prison. In face of the dark, ever equivocal but immensely moving portrait of depression, deprivation, and rage that makes this novel so uncompromisingly modern in its worldview, these pages advance a deliberately euphoric reading of its final chapters, in order to draw attention to an overlooked dimension—one that anticipates modernist attempts to represent the libidinal dynamics increasingly understood, after Freud, to constitute human subjectivity in all its precariousness—to Brontë's scripting of the resolve with which Lucy faces her solitude after M. Paul's death

This covert dimension of Lucy's erotic quest is the focus of the intensely psychodramatic events that form the emotional climax of the novel, as she embarks on a revelatory midnight voyage into the city's park during its annual masked celebration of liberation from foreign invasion. Imbued with a *Walpurgisnacht* atmosphere that is both carnivalesque in a Bakhtinian sense of the word (in which the world of normative behavior has been turned upside down) and dreamlike in a Freudian sense (as if the polymorphous perverse has sprung loose), this episode foreshadows the psychodramatic voyages into the underworld of unconscious desire examined in Joyce's nighttown, Barnes's nightwood, and Durrell's Carnival in chapters 3, 4, and 6 respectively. Brontë's representation of Lucy's analogous descent is composed of two stages that blur the boundaries between reality and dream: first as Lucy imagines herself journeying to the park, then as she actually ventures forth under the cover of darkness. Stimulated into heightened mental activity by an opiate that Mme. Beck has administered in hopes, ironically, of putting her employee to sleep, the drugged Lucy hallucinates a vision whose psychosexual contours are stunning in their clarity. Initially, under the spell of the moonlight shining in her bedroom window, she imagines the revelries in the park; then, with feverish intensity her mind fixates on a huge, circular, stone basin lying among its alleys: "*that basin I knew,* and beside which I had often stood—deep-set in the tree-shadows, brimming with cool water, clear, with a green, leafy, rushy bed" (547; emphasis added). As Brontë's evocative language suggests, the circular basin with which Lucy is on intimate terms becomes an encoded emblem of her sexuality, and as such it becomes the secret object of the libidinal energies that are now surfacing from layers of repression. Its representation also echoes the image of the marshy forest dell, "deep-hollowed in forest secrecy" (334), that Lucy has earlier associated with her unfulfilled sexuality. Now, however—and this is the crucial difference—Lucy does not wait for a phallic "storm or axe" to cut the swathe that will admit the sun's "golden light." Disavowing the penetrative imagery of male conquest and insemination, she resolves in her fantasy to seek out the basin herself: she becomes the actor in her own imaginative quest, searching out her own autoerotic desire. Thinking that the park must be locked at this hour, she wonders if she can force an entry on her own, at which point she remembers—as Brontë conspicuously phrases it—"a gap in the paling . . . a narrow irregular aperture" through which a "*man could not have made his way . . . but I thought I might:* I fancied I would like to try, and once within, at this hour the whole park *would be mine*—the moonlight, midnight park!" (547; emphases added). The symbolic landscape through which the hallucinating Lucy imagines traveling is *herself,* a topography of the female body that (in contrast to the girls' garden behind the pensionnat) no man occupies.

The psychosexual intensity with which Lucy imagines this scene is maintained in the account of the actual voyage to the park that follows as she sneaks out of the pensionnat and discovers the festival-in-progress. Her "vague aim" remains to find the stone basin, with its clear depth and mossy lining:

> Of that coolness and verdure I thought, with the passionate thirst of unconscious fever. Amidst the glare, and hurry, and throng, and noise, I still secretly and chiefly longed to come on that circular mirror of crystal, and surprise the moon glassing therein her pearly font. (551)

In that "circular mirror" that is also her sexuality, where Lucy will see her own reflection, gaze to gaze, she also imagines seeing the reflected moon—which Brontë's novels repeatedly associate with female sexuality—a "glassing moon" whose "pearly font" replaces the ray of the invasive masculine sun envisioned in the earlier image of the hollowed-out forest dell. Previously, Lucy has lamented that "the orb" of her single life is "not to be so rounded," that for her "the crescent-phase must suffice" (451). Now, on the brink of autoerotic realization, that image is totally rewritten; for the reader has already been apprised that the "glassing" moon imagined here as blending with Lucy's reflection is *supremely full* this night, "in an element deep and splendid" (547).

In establishing Lucy as the desiring subject of her own autoerotic quest, this episode also begs a reconsideration of critical theories relating sexual difference to narrative's deep or mythic structures. In a widely influential chapter in *Alice Doesn't,* Teresa de Lauretis locates a paradigm for all narrative desire in the Oedipus myth, which leads her to hypothesize that the position of the questing hero, the subject who motivates the transformations that create narrative movement, is always, symbolically and morphologically, male. Because of "the inherent maleness of all narrative movement," de Lauretis despairs, female desire can never be represented as the moving force, the motor, of narrative; the female protagonist's story will always remain a question of *his*—the man's—desire. *Villette,* I suggest, calls this theory into question.[21] Not only in Lucy's imagined quest for that "rushy basin," that circular mirror, that will quench her "passionate thirst," but in her "heretic" role as narrator, she defiantly becomes *the* questing hero, *the* desiring actor, who also becomes the motive force, the subject in both senses of the word, of her own narrative and its quest for meaning.

What happens as Lucy ventures into the spectacular realm of the festival reigning throughout the park confirms this sense of new-found agency and subjectivity. For the climax of Lucy's emotional crisis occurs not when she detects M. Paul and his youthful charge, Justine Marie, in what she mistakenly assumes is a romantic tryst, but seconds later when she *refuses* to be an onlooker to her own pain and renounces the roles of spy and voyeur with the defiant statement, "I *would* not look" (566; Brontë's italics here create a parallel to Lucy's earlier epiphany regarding Dr. John, "*I never see him*"). Upon returning to the pensionnat, she confronts for a final time the nun's ghost, this time laid out upon her very bed. Literally ripping the veil from *this* illusion, she discovers the hoax that has been played on her:

> I defied spectra. In a moment, without exclamation, I had rushed on the haunted couch; nothing leaped out, or sprang, or stirred; all the movement was mine, so was all the life, the reality, the substance, the force. . . . I tore her up—the incubus! . . . And down she fell—down all round me—down in shreds and fragments—and I trod upon her. (569)

*Dis*embodying the artifice of the nun, this false mirror of her sexuality, Lucy in effect *embodies* herself, taking as her province "life," "reality," "substance," and "force." Laying to rest the ghostly machinery of dead, repressive desire, she becomes the quintessential acting subject: "all . . . movement was mine."

The vast difference between the perversely non-normative textual erotics of Lucy's story and those of conventional romantic fiction is only confirmed by *Villette*'s ambiguous ending, in which, as I have already noted, M. Paul's return to Lucy is forestalled indefinitely by his apparent drowning at sea. Brontë's metaphoric language of storm and shipwreck circles us back to chapter 4's equally ambiguous use of the same imagery to launch Lucy's venture into the unknown; the uncertain grounds from which this narrative has arisen are thus mirrored in the radical uncertainty of its ending. As such, *Villette* also rewrites the oedipal structure of classic nineteenth-century fictions organized around the search for the proper ending that will return the plot to the original quiescence from which it arose.[22] In contrast, there *has never been* a quiescent beginning for Lucy, for whom homeless "origins" have been vexed from the start. The ending she writes to her narrative only continues this process of disturbance by frustrating the normative reader's desire for the quiescence of closure, for a final detection and supervision of meaning.

As part of its effort to evade the constraints associated with a disciplinary worldview and novelistic order, then, *Villette* proposes an alternative textual and sexual economy, one in which "pleasure" and "narrative desire" stand in a markedly different relation to its questing subject and the subject of her quest. That difference has already been figured in Lucy's choice of a transgressively "heretic narrative" over the plotlessness of a life spent wordlessly counting her beads in a Carmelite cell. The image of counting beads—coupled with that of the controlling gaze—returns toward the end of *Villette* to provide yet one more striking instance of the gulf separating conventional narrative structures and Lucy's quite unconventional strategies for writing her female subjectivity into being. This occurs when Père Silas attempts to drive a wedge between Lucy and M. Paul by telling Lucy an admonitory tale, "quite a little romantic narrative" (484), about the prior commitments that supposedly make it impossible for Paul to marry. As Lucy summarizes her encounter with Père Silas, what initially seem to be only artless little incidents, "a handful of loose beads," suddenly "drop pendant in a long string," a perfect rosary of intent, when "threaded" by the glance she catches from Père Silas's "quick-shot and crafty" gaze: "I caught that glance, despite its veiled character; the momentary gleam shot a meaning which struck me" (486). The metaphoric "clasp" that holds this "monastic necklace" (486) together, Lucy now discerns, is none other than M. Paul, since the covert end or aim of Père Silas's narrative design is to warn Lucy away from him.

Crucially, however, this is the very clasp, the traditional closural knot, ultimately missing from *Lucy's* heretic narrative, which ends with M. Paul's *absence,* and the result, significantly, is that Lucy's narrative "unstrings" the authoritarian, paternal logic of what Susan Winnett has described as the oedipal "masterplot that wants to tell us in advance where it is that we may take our pleasures and what must inevitably come of them."[23] The unpredictabilities and perverse pleasures of Lucy's heretic narrative, rather, engender the construction of a resolutely independent female subject whose mental and autoerotic health—as opposed to her depressive anxieties—depends, finally, on her refusal to be pinned down, either by possessive men or by prying readers. This is not to say that Lucy is "free" of the prison—that is, of all those forces, social, psychological, rhetorical, that seek to curtail her desires—but that the very act of refusal, emboldened by her mobility, creates an alternative mode of subjectivity in which terms like *freedom* and *imprisonment* come less to designate an absolute boundary than an ever-shifting series of contiguous relations. Continually swerving out of our grasp just when we think we have her, Lucy thus weaves a space both within and outside her text that becomes definitive of her very being; as such she anticipates Teresa de Lauretis's description, in work published since *Alice Doesn't,* of the contemporary feminist subject-position: "The subject I see emerging from current writings and debates within feminism is one that is at the same time *inside and outside* the ideology of gender, and conscious of being so, conscious of the twofold pull of that division, that doubled vision."[24] Ever-changing, elusive, provisionally autonomous—Lucy constructs within her narrative a mobile self that escapes confinement by the authorities of (social and novelistic) discipline epitomized in Père Silas, a self that refuses those conventional (social and novelistic) images of Victorian womanhood which would render her only an object and not a subject, and, most stunningly, a self that rewrites the regulatory devices of traditional narrative form by *seeing through,* as it were, the ruse of the panoptic male gaze that threads them together.

Emancipatory Possibilities in the Novel

With Lucy's heretic subversiveness as subject and narrator in mind, I would like to return to Miller's *The Novel and the Police* and take one last look at its Foucauldian reading of the genre of prose fiction. In making this return the final stage of my argument, I am aware of certain ironies: first, that I may seem to be creating a circular narrative of oedipal origins and returns of precisely the type that, I have been arguing, the erotics of Lucy's desires and Brontë's text displaces; second, that this return to novelistic theory via *Villette* may seem to reduce "Lucy"—or, more precisely, questions about female subjectivity—to the position of inconsequential third in a triangulated relation between male critics without whom Lucy, no doubt, can happily exist. My hope, however, is that these final pages result in something less pernicious. Precisely by returning to theories of imprisonment after having looked at the specific twist *Villette*'s example gives them, I hope to create a space in which Lucy—a manipulator of language and not unaccomplished literary theorist in her own right—emerges with the last word. This is the "Lucy," I maintain, who from a position of self-empowered authority writes in advance those perverse fictions of sexuality and fictions of interiority that have since become a hallmark of experimental modernist practice.

The nineteenth-century novel, Miller argues, depends on the *subjection* of the subject, whose subjectivity depends on a "game of secrecy"—a game whereby the self's "defining inwardness," precisely the interiority the subject thinks has been kept inviolate or secret, is actually always already in the hands of the police (220, 200). Yet Lucy's defining interiority, it strikes me, participates in a rather different "game of secrecy," one in which the police must also learn to play by *her* rules. Foremost, the narrative strategies whereby her voice never fully discloses or confesses itself maintain for Lucy a conditional freedom—epitomized in her mobility of being—and (in de Lauretis's phrase) a "doubled vision" that together are constitutive of both her subjectivity and her desires. At the same time, these deviant, deviating narrative strategies inscribe a shifting self that we can only come to "read" and "know" in a way that is radically nonappropriative: the reader who intuits *why* Brontë has created a fictional heroine whose identity is rooted in continual deferral or postponement of meaning is automatically disbarred from becoming a trustworthy agent of the novelistic police.

Likewise, I suggest there is a subtle but important distinction to be maintained between Miller's definition of the illusory "place elsewhere," or private space, occupied by the so-called liberal subject and "the elsewhere of meaning" that Lucy, no conventional subject, inhabits.[25] First of all—and this is a measure of Brontë's perspective as a woman who has suffered privation and sexual oppression first hand—*Villette* never assumes an unconditional "outside" to, or total escape from, ideology, as do the primarily male-authored texts discussed by Miller. If Miller's quintessential subject knows himself "only when he forgets or disavows his functional implication in a system of carcereal restraints" (x), Brontë's Lucy never forgets those branding marks, even in assuming the position of narrator of her life story. Second, Miller's equation of this "elsewhere" or "outside" with the so-called domestic realm of the home, however true of many nineteenth-century fictions, has little to do with the ontological realities of the private spaces nurtured within Lucy's narrative: privacy is not reducible to conventional domesticity in this novel. For the trajectory of her experience, beginning with her radical dislocation from any sense of home as "origin," has always been *away from* domestic convention; that realm is left for the Dr. Johns and Paulina *Homes* of the world to police and populate, in happy if insipid matrimony. Rather, the existential realm that Lucy comes to occupy might best be symbolized in her actual dwelling place at novel's end, the school/residence that M. Paul bequeaths her before sailing away: this is a space that is at once public *and* private, a space that fulfills Lucy's professional ambitions *and* that she comes to claim as her true and most happy home. It is a space, in effect, that disenables the very language of "in" and "out" upon which the power and binaristic hierarchies of a male-dominated disciplinary order depend.

Hence, for all the verve with which Miller elucidates the infinitely complex workings of disciplinary constraints and surveillance in our fictional and social lives, he seems to deny the same rich complexity and indeterminacy to the categories of the individual, the inward, and the private against which he positions the agents of the law. Collapsing these values—the individual, the inward, the private—into a monolithic one-dimensionality, rather, effectively insures their infiltration by the novelistic police. One result, then, of bringing a text like Brontë's to bear on Foucauldian-based analysis is to illuminate the degree to which a narrative poetics like Miller's may occasionally engage in its own kind of policing—a policing of the subversive potentialities of fiction, no less than of the polymorphous unpredictabilities of the libido, that ends up reinforcing the very binaries of public and private, in and out, that his argument sets out to deconstruct.

I do not mean to deny the immense impress of ideology on the form and content of the nineteenth-century novel or its twentieth-century successors. Nor do I mean to imply that Lucy Snowe or Charlotte Brontë can ever entirely escape society's rules or the internalization of its maxims. But I would suggest that the heteroglossic voices that, as Bakhtin has shown, comprise fictional narrative mean that the novel, relative to other modes of discourse, may create a space—however minimal, compromised, or "imaginary"—for dissent, self-interrogation, and subversive dialogue with those supposedly totalizing systems of power that inculcate the values of a disciplinary social order.[26] In our excitement at discovering the Foucauldian prisons lurking in so much novelistic discourse, we ought not lose sight of this dialogical dimension of fiction. The way in which Brontë's narrating Lucy strings together—or, more properly, unstrings—the narrative of her desires, creating a text that continually swerves out of our control, creating a message that, for its time and place, is indeed heretic, creating a self that remains seen and unseen, attests, to use Patricia Yaeger's term, to the emancipatory potential embedded in the very work that Brontë's perversely brilliant, experimental textual strategies undertake to *do*.[27] If Lucy can outwit the police—if only as a life-long, text-long effort—we reader-critics owe it to her to continue the work of depolicing *Villette* by reconceptualizing, in our theories of narrative, the unorthodox possibilities of a "heretic" novelistic enterprise that we, however well trained in the arts of academic discipline, can never entirely encompass or subdue.

For all these reasons, then, Lucy Snowe becomes this book's privileged figure for the excessive, aberrant, daunting, destabilizing tendencies that the following chapters locate in several canonical and noncanonical modernist fictions of sexuality and interiority, fictions in which the ghostlike trace of Lucy keeps reappearing, in various avatars, to unsettle our assumptions about narrative, sexuality, subjectivity, and criticism itself: the Lucy who undergoes, in advance of the fact, the turn-of-the-century plot of female sexual awakening traced in chapter 2; Lucy the modernist novelist who, like Joyce and Woolf in chapter 3, uses theatricality to plumb the interior depths of the psyche; the deviously perverse Lucy who "queers" narrative linearity and urban space by making the city grid she inhabits a site of pleasure and resistance to the norm, foreshadowing the queer modernisms of chapter 4; the orphaned Lucy who, like the de-sired sons, daughters, and servants of chapter 5, outmaneuvers the dictatorial imperatives of paternal fiat; and Lucy the displaced traveler and ethnographer for whom the "un-English" psychogeography of Villette, like the foreign terrains in chapter 6, becomes the backdrop for an encounter with the dark other that dwells within and haunts the Anglo-European self. As these many figurations suggest, in this book, at least, "Lucy Snowe," insubstantial and shadowy though she purports to be, indeed emerges with the last word.

CHAPTER TWO

Channeling the Floods of Desire

Kate Chopin, The Awakening
• • • • •

D. H. Lawrence, The Virgin and the Gipsy
• • • • •

Sigmund Freud, Dora: An Analysis of a Case of Hysteria
• • • • •

> One wishes the Flood might come, to sweep away the
> festering excess of ugly-spirited people.
> —D. H. Lawrence, *Collected Letters*[1]

> Risen in a
> welter of waters
> . . . born in a
> tidal wave of the father's overthrow
> —Muriel Rukeyser, "The Birth of Venus"[2]

> Woman. As easy stop the sea.
> —Leopold Bloom in James Joyce, *Ulysses*[3]

Lucy Snowe's erotic pleasure—which, as the analysis of Charlotte
Brontë's *Villette* in chapter 1 has demonstrated, is considerable—depends upon her scrupulously cloaking from public view and narrative representation her interior wishes, dreams, and desires. But if Lucy chooses
invisibility for herself, what she calls "[her] book of life" is forever
"marked," as we have seen, by the "indelible" image of her opposite: the
actress Vashti, a woman who both enacts and embodies, in full public view,
her sexuality. Searching for a metaphoric equivalent to describe this spectacle of unleashed female desire, Lucy writes of the "disclosed power"—an
interesting choice of words in light of the previous chapter's inquiry into
the dynamics of power and vision—of Vashti's performance as a "deep,
swollen, winter river, thundering in cataract, and bearing the soul, like a

leaf, on the steep and steely sweep of its descent" (341). Not coincidentally, this image of female passion as a "thundering" flood—which Luce Irigaray relates to a mechanics of fluids neglected by masculinist science[4]—turns up repeatedly in narratives of female sexual awakening that emerge with an explicitness worthy of Vashti at the beginning of the twentieth century. Such narratives form the focus of this chapter, which proposes to examine the anxieties of authority, the crises of modernity, that these hitherto taboo representations of female desire engender in an era marked by new psychoanalytic, sociological, and literary readings of sexuality as the secret key to and inner truth of identity.

But why water? To bridge the temporal gap between Lucy's reticent narrative and these early modernist texts, it may be helpful to consider an often-cited metaphor in Freud's *Three Essays on the Theory of Sexuality:* his characterization of the libido as a powerful "stream" that always threatens to spill over into unsuspected "collateral channels" when its "main bed has become blocked" (36). As Freud notes elsewhere, the sheer proximity of these collateral tributaries to "what is . . . called normal sexual life" attests to the fragility of the "boundaries" that both culture and the ego impose on the erotogenic multiplicity of the sexual instinct in order to distinguish the so-called normal from the abnormal. The primary "culture-work" of ego formation, Freud concludes, is the redirecting of libidinal flux into appropriate channels, a task he compares to the draining of the Zuider Zee: "Where id was, the ego shall be."[5] Likewise, throughout the *Three Essays* Freud repeatedly refers to the "mental dams" that the ego erects to "impede the course of the sexual instinct" and "restrict its flow" (44, 43). Libidinal desire, it is clear, tends to flow over and needs to be curbed.

These watery tributaries—along with the barriers that attempt to contain them—figure prominently in the symbolic geographies of Kate Chopin's *The Awakening* (1899) and D. H. Lawrence's *The Virgin and the Gipsy* (1930), two fables of female sexual emergence that this chapter examines in conjunction with Freud's *Dora* (1905). The climactic event of Lawrence's posthumous novella, for example, occurs when an "ancient" underground tunnel—"unsuspected, undreamed of"—collapses beneath an immense reservoir and causes its dam to burst. The flood that ensues not only sweeps away the repressive world of the rectory that blocks Yvette Saywell's erotic awakening, but also unleashes "the flood [that] was in her soul" and thus sets the scene for her sexual rescue by Lawrence's Gipsy-savior.[6]

Likewise, in Chopin's novel Edna Pontellier's doctor attempts to arrest what he sees as her dangerous drift toward adultery by narrating an admonitory tale that draws on a similar nexus of images: "He told the old, ever new and curious story of the waning of a woman's love, seeking *strange, new channels,* only to return to *its legitimate source* after days of fierce unrest."[7] And in the *Analysis of a Case of Hysteria* popularly known as *Dora,* Freud, taking as his cue the words *wet* and *water* that figure prominently in his patient's dreams, reminds the reader that sex, as even the virginal Dora subconsciously knows, "makes things wet," unleashes a flow (90).

Appearances to the contrary, it is not my intention to focus solely on the water imagery that links these texts. Rather, I've cited this pattern to anticipate some of the theoretical implications that inhere in the way all three of these stories of female erotic awakening and repression comment upon, intersect with, and illuminate each other's sexual, and ultimately textual, assumptions. I want to suggest that these crosscurrents have everything to do with the degree to which the incipiently modernist strategies of these narratives coalesce conceptually with a moment in the history of sexuality that simultaneously becomes a moment in the history of psychoanalysis.

The most obvious sign of this juncture of aesthetic, sexual, and psychological discourses is the fact that the vehicle chosen to represent the subconscious drives and desires subtending all identity in these texts is specifically that of awakening female sexuality. Just how and why the scenario of woman's desire comes to occupy this privileged space in the early twentieth century is a vexed question in cultural, literary, and psychoanalytic criticism. Among various attempts to address this issue, the hypothesis that Klaus Theweleit offers in the first volume of his eclectically monumental study of the psychosocial roots of German fascism, *Male Fantasies: Women, Floods, Bodies, History*, is especially intriguing. While Theweleit's focus on the evolution of Hitler's SS troops from the volunteer armies, or Freikorps, active in the interwar period is quite different from my own, the links he proposes between political oppression, modernity, and the sexual politics dominating the western history of heterosexual relationships have proved especially relevant to three interrelated aspects of this chapter's inquiry: first, the modern cultural fantasy of female sexuality *as* desire; second, the anxieties of authority subtending that fantasy; and third, the impact for literary modernism of the narrative shapes assumed by that fantasy.

Also pertinent is the language that Theweleit uncovers in the private and public writings of the Freikorps that form the core of his evidence. These "male fantasies," as Theweleit dubs them, reveal a remarkably monolithic representation of female sexuality as a surging ocean or an inundating deluge that provokes men's fears of dissolution and, by extension, the breakdown of (in the telling words of one Freikorps writer) the "ancient dam of traditional state authority"[8] in the face of anarchic libidinal desire. This terror of engulfment is most vividly realized in the propagandistic representation of working-class women as a "red flood" overrunning the Aryan fatherland, an equivalence which comes to justify the brutal violence used by the soldier male—Theweleit's term—to suppress proletarian unrest: one red tide (spilled blood) counters another (bolshevism) in fascism's effort to contain or "dam up" the threat simultaneously equated with communism, female sexuality, and the unconscious (63–84, 183–96).

What the soldier male really fears and thus projects onto women, Theweleit suggests, is the eruption not so much of female libidinal energies but of those pent up in *himself*—all that which "has hitherto been forbidden, buried beneath the surface" (231). "Desire does not 'want' revolution," Gilles Deleuze and Félix Guattari have argued in *Anti-Oedipus,* because it "is revolutionary in its own right."[9] The soldier male reacts to this terrifying possibility, Theweleit evocatively argues, by standing firm, asserting his discrete identity, his fixed boundaries, through "a kind of sustained erection of [the] whole body" (244). In effect, he transforms his corporeal boundaries into a *dam* to hold back the floods threatening him both from inside and outside. Hence, as Theweleit notes, the only movements in which he is allowed to engage are military parades or formations. For troops, moving as "one man," symbolically convert "feminine" streams into "masculine" columns (429) and thereby erect yet one more phallic barrier against living floods.

Theweleit's hypothesis that the long-standing metaphoric association of women with floods covertly expresses the male fear of the dissolution of his bodily and ego boundaries shares significant points of contiguity with Luce Irigaray's comments in her nearly contemporaneous essay, "The 'Mechanics' of Fluids." Irigaray begins by noting that in scientific discourse "the properties of fluids have been abandoned to the feminine" because water as a "physical reality . . . resist[s] adequate symbolization."[10] She then attempts to transform this gender-based neglect into a rallying cry for a feminist epistemology that draws its rhetoric and metaphors from water's properties—its diffuseness, instability, turbulence, viscousness, fluctuation, permeability. These are properties that Irigaray claims a rationalist, masculinist science privileging solid over fluid mechanics has ignored because of the cultural association of these same characteristics with women's fickle nature and ungovernable sexuality. More recently, N. Katherine Hayles has attempted to give the feminist implications of Irigaray's largely poetic invocation of fluid mechanics a more scientific basis. Hayles's essay, "Gender Encoding in Fluid Mechanics: Masculine Channels and Feminine Flows," makes the important point that the properties assigned to fluids do not have "simple or unified gender identifications": if the properties of turbulence, complexity, nonlinearity, and duplicity attributed to water in scientific discourse are associated with femaleness, those of "steady flow," "manly laminar flow," and straightforwardness are associated with men (note Theweleit's image of fascist soldiers marching as a solid stream). At work in this differentiation, Hayles argues, is the influence of the conservation principle within the developing science of thermodynamics, which in imposing "limits on how much flow can be achieved, . . . also insure[s] that excessive flows will not get out of hand." Such principles are in turn "reinforced by the construction of male bodily experience [specifically of ejaculation] that makes conservation laws seem, if not obvious, at least intuitively sound."[11] This conclusion supports Irigaray's claim that one of the goals of traditional psychoanalysis, for which the primacy of the phallus is a central tenet, has been to find ways to appropriate the dangerously fluid properties associated with women by converting them into more safely containable masculine attributes of "flow"—a "takeover" that facilitates the symbolic transformation of "fluid to solid," which Irigaray claims to be the psychoanalytic project's "object of desire" (113).

The masculine dread of such female-associated flux, however, also contains its inverse: the secret desire to *break through* the dams that the ego has imposed on the libido and gain access to hitherto restricted territories of pleasure. Here, again, both Theweleit's and Irigaray's analyses become relevant to the focus of this chapter, for historically it is *women's* sexuality that has come to stand as symbol both of this forbidden geography and this subversive desire, as Theweleit's exhaustive survey of the literary representations coupling female eroticism and desirous floods throughout four centuries of western history convincingly attests. But why this specifically *literary* fascination with women and/as transgressive floods? Theweleit argues that ever since the Enlightenment's remapping of desire's streams as the flow of capital, protest against the colonization of the body and against the limitations mapped over its pleasures has increasingly become the province of male poets and novelists, whose literary representations of women's bodies have served as these men's displaced arena for fantasies of opening up new possibilities of desire and for fantasies of expanding bodily boundaries—a process that Theweleit, following Deleuze and Guattari, terms "deterritorialization."[12] In stark contrast to these utopic fantasies, Theweleit reminds us that the actual experience of heterosexual relations in post-Enlightenment western modernity has increasingly served, rather, as the grounds for "massive reterritorializations" of desire and the body—that process whereby dominant social forces mobilize "to prevent the new productive possibilities from becoming new human freedoms" (299, 264).

In one sense, it is the liberation of these constrained floods of libidinal and bodily desire—along with the freeing of female sexuality from the romanticization of past literary representations—that forms the overt goal of the paradigmatic plot of female sexual awakening that dominates early-twentieth-century writing. As *Villette* attests, the Victorian "reterritorialization" of women's bodies in the name of bourgeois propriety and property placed formidable obstructions in the way of overtly expressing female desire. For all Brontë's daring in articulating a single woman's sexual feelings, Lucy Snowe's eroticism, despite the degree to which it reverberates in the gaps and reticences of her elliptical narrative, only attains *representable* form in veiled symbols and allegorical set pieces. This feint, however subversive in its own right, leaves unchallenged the dominant ideology of femininity espoused, to cite only one example, by Dr. William Action in a medical guide contemporaneous with *Villette:* "I should say that the majority of women (happily for them) are not very much troubled with sexual feeling of any kind. . . . As a general rule, a modest woman seldom desires any sexual gratification for herself."[13] It is precisely the breaking of this myth that creates the conceptual zone bridging what are popularly thought of as "Victorian" and "modern" eras, and it is within this zone that Freud, Chopin, and Lawrence locate their sexually explicit texts. The impulse that leads Kate Chopin, on artistic grounds, to avow that the modern writer's subject must be human psychology "stripped of the veil with which ethical and conventional standards have [hitherto] draped it" is not unrelated to the impulse leading Freud, on scientific grounds, to justify the explicitness of the "sexual questions" he asks Dora by comparing his task to that of the gynecologist who "does not hesitate to make [his female patients] submit to uncovering every possible part of their body" (65).[14]

Unveiling the female subject, however, is not without its liabilities, as the contrasting libidinal politics of Chopin and Freud's texts indicate; frankness in writing about female sexuality is no guarantee that the dams of repressive tradition will be broken—or, more to the point, that the waters that flow upon their breaking will give birth to anything other than traditionally restrictive iconographies of "Woman." Three statements of caution are thus in order. First, even when plots centered on a woman's erotic awakening have as their goal the reclamation of female sexuality *for* the female subject, her sexuality inevitably risks becoming the object of the narrative project itself, with the reader positioned as voyeuristic onlooker to the spectacle of female desire. Second, as in any erotic narrative, fictional or nonfictional, narrative authority often reconstitutes itself as an implicit sexual authority: specifically at issue is the conflict between the represented female subject of awakening and the authorial power to circumscribe, legitimize, or politicize that subject's response through the manipulation of her representation. Too easily, that is, the sexuality of the subject may become the subject of a statement about sexuality.[15] Third, Michel Foucault's writings, despite certain limitations noted in chapter 1, forcefully remind us that the production of "new" sexual discourses—of which the liberatory fiction of female awakening is exemplary—are nonetheless expressions of power. Hence even the taboo-defying plot of awakening, in producing discourses on sexuality, may serve as implicit means of reterritorialization or control—"control not through denial or prohibition," Jeffrey Weeks explains, "but through 'production,' through imposing a grid of definition on the possibilities of the body."[16]

Mention of Foucault also calls to mind the specific, indeed privileged, construction of sexuality emerging around the turn of the century, that symbolic (if not temporally precise) boundary—between "Victorian" and "modern," "old" and "new"—upon which the paradigmatic plots of female awakening that I will be investigating self-consciously pivot.[17] For only in the modern era has sexuality, as Foucault emphasizes, come to be seen as the supreme "secret, the omnipotent cause, the hidden meaning" of our being, or, as Weeks puts it, the "privileged site in which the truth of ourselves is to be found."[18] And this conceptual shift of sexuality from the periphery to the center of human identity has proved, until recent post-structuralist critiques, absolutely pivotal to twentieth-century sexual epistemology and its metaphysics of the self.[19] Indeed, this quintessentially modern formulation of sex as the wellspring of human subjectivity gives the taboo-defying plot of sexual awakening its very reason for being. For to the extent that sex has come to signify the central but hidden *essence* of one's nature, it follows that the instinctual drives, the pent-up floods of libidinal desire, are forces which must be *released,* as it were, from their interior and anterior captivity before any "awakening" can occur as conscious event—a release that, as the word *awakening* itself implies, ushers sexuality from the twilight of unconsciousness and into the light of day, the realm of erotic realization. This figurative movement from darkness to light is repeated time and again in these narratives of sexual emergence. Thus, in Lawrence's sexual fable, Yvette's erotic awakening involves becoming conscious of the "dark, tremulous, potent secret of her virginity" buried deep "inside . . . [her] secret female self" that the Gipsy's scopic gaze can alone penetrate and validate (84); in Chopin's narrative, Robert's "glance penetrate[s] to the sleeping places of [Edna's] soul and awaken[s] them" (156); and Freud likens his psychoanalytic project to the archeological one of "bringing to the light of day after their long burial" the "priceless though mutilated relics" of Dora's long-repressed sexuality (27).

Such a movement from inside to outside, across the bar of repression, thus not only replicates the trajectory traced by the plot of female erotic awakening but manifests the characteristics of the Freudian drive-reduction model of sexuality, in which repression is responsible for "the blocking or redirecting of sexual energy" that otherwise seeks release and flow.[20] The representation of desire as that which flows along a horizontal axis (in/out) may also be represented, as we have already seen in the imagery of Freikorps, along a vertical axis; the threatening eruption into view of that which lies "buried below the surface" encodes a hydraulic model of libidinal release that similarly posits a "truth" of self and sex that lies deep within, awaiting translation to "higher"—that is, "awakened"—consciousness. In the process of their assimilation into psychoanalytic and popular discourses, these directional signposts—in/out, up/down—thus become much more than convenient metaphors; they become ways of *knowing* sexuality, of situating sexual desire in relation to its less and more conscious manifestations.

As such terms also begin to indicate, the turn-of-the-century sexological discourses responsible for these hydraulic and drive-oriented models existed in close proximity to an emergent psychoanalytic discourse that, in devising spatial models to differentiate among hypothesized strata of psychic activity, reached its apogee in Freud's theorization of the unconscious and the radically split status of human subjectivity. The modernity of both Chopin and Lawrence's fables of sexual awakening, I will be arguing, lies in their intuitive understanding of this fundamental division in human identity and its relation to sexual desire. While, as we shall see, their sexual politics greatly differ, both writers acknowledge, in unprecedented fashion, the power of unconscious desire shaping the erotic awakenings of their female protagonists. The authorial goal of rendering the difference *within* identity created by the unconscious is captured perfectly at the end of *The Awakening* as the emotionally distraught Edna walks along the beach: "But she knew a way to elude them. She was not thinking of these things as she walked down to the beach" (175). Not even sutured by a semicolon to simulate some unstated strand of continuity between "knowing" and "not thinking," the seeming contradiction embraced by these two sentences is forced into simultaneous existence on the syntactical plane.

If this recognition of divided consciousness is one mark of the modernity of these texts, even more so are the textual strategies that Chopin and Lawrence—as well as Freud—devise to evoke the undertow of libidinal activity, the stirrings of desire as it comes into and fades out of the consciousness of their female protagonists. While these writers do not attempt the more radical linguistic approximations of states of consciousness taken up in the following chapters, their methods do look forward to the experimental techniques developed by such self-consciously modernist writers as Joyce and Woolf. Working within the parameters of third-person realist narrative, Chopin and Lawrence present sequences of seemingly "real" events that turn out to be connected less by the linearity of cause and effect than by a process of association that approximates what we now call Freudian dream-logic: external events thus repeatedly become indices, when not projections, of interior states. Similarly, both novels make use of an intensely imagistic lyricism, rooted in rhythmic repetitions and echoic effects, to suggest the atemporal flux of libidinal activity. In turn, the subtle detachment from the assumptions of formal realism effected by these fables of sexual awakening prepare the reader for the detachment from ego constraints that forms the primary stage of the erotic journeys of Chopin and Lawrence's protagonists; for to become active sexual subjects, Edna and Yvette must first passively yield to the drift of desire, allow themselves to be borne along its turbulent currents and away from the strictures of conscience or morality.

Freud demands something of the same giving over, or ceding of control, from his patient Dora, in order to induce the process of association that will bring to the surface of consciousness the repressed memory of a sexual initiation that, according to his deductions, has already occurred. A psychoanalytic case study, *Dora* is not a "fiction" in the generic sense that *The*

Awakening and *The Virgin and the Gipsy* are. But to the degree that Freud must assemble his psychological profile from necessarily partial clues and subjective surmises, a "fictional" personality emerges from his pages, bearing indeed a fictional name, since Dora is the pseudonym given the real-life Ida Bauer. And, for Freud, Dora's resistance to easy interpretation—a trait she shares with Lucy Snowe—occasions a crisis in narrative authority, played out as a struggle for mastery of her words, that perhaps makes more explicit than fiction itself the coercive narrative dynamics at work in novelistic plots of female awakening. These anxieties of authority and control, furthermore, are integrally related to the modernity of Freud's text. As a *reader* of Dora's hysteria, Freud confronts a fragmented text that, like modernist fiction, defers as much as it begs interpretation; and in his simultaneous role as *author* of this case history, Freud finds himself engaged in an equally modernist enterprise. That is, in order to represent the psychic processes whereby "what is missing" or repressed in Dora's history emerges "piecemeal" (Freud's term) from analysis and randomly across time, he is forced to experiment with unconventional methods of narration: the splintering of chronological development; the multiplication of techniques for rendering Dora's verbal testimony; the use of free association not simply as a clinical but as a narrative method; and the exploitation of language's radical instability and substitutive construction (as in the technique of the "switch-word").

If it is fair to say that the breakdown of unitary modes of representation that has come to be seen as definitive of high modernist technique is related, in these three transitional texts, to their probings into the psychology of sexuality and the divided self, it is also true that the narrative anxieties occasioned by the attempt to authorize female desire cannot be extricated from the historically specific anxieties, the sometimes opposing social and psychological demands, that stand in the way of fulfillment for the protagonists of these plots. Most notably, the *psychological* injunction to give oneself over to a state of passive drift in order to facilitate the emergence of desire—a process repeated in the narrative drift characterizing these texts—coexists uneasily with the turn-of-the-century *social* imperative that equates such passivity with traditional norms of "femininity." Likewise, in terms of the evolving psychological-medical discourses of the early century, the sexually "awakened" woman is repeatedly subjected to the discursive and specular mode of sociomedical control that Foucault identifies as the "hysterization" of the female body:[21] hence the diagnosis of hysterical repression used to classify—and to some degree contain—the effects of Dora's adolescent exposure to male sexuality; or the charge of "depravity" and threat of incarceration (in "a criminal-lunacy asylum," no less!) with which Yvette's father attempts to curtail her sexual attraction to the Gipsy (133); or the willful blindness whereby Edna's husband reads her transformation into a creature "palpitant with the forces of life" (123) as a "morbid condition" (122) in need of the family physician's surveillance.

Despite such similarities, the different developmental states embodied by these three women—Dora as "traumatized adolescent," Yvette as "archetypal virgin," and Edna as "married woman"—at once complicate and broaden the narrative possibilities signified by the rubric "the plot of female sexual awakening." This diversity, in fact, is one source of the power of this plot format as an early-twentieth-century aesthetic device and cultural phenomenon. At first glance, it might seem logical to order my analyses of these three texts accordingly, tracing in chronological sequence the stages of female awakening that these stories inscribe: girl, virgin, sexually mature woman. Such an ordering logic, however, invites precisely the same set of problems involved in the teleological reading of femininity to which Freud's attempt to theorize female development in his "Femininity" and "Female Sexuality" essays falls prey. Rather than replicate this culturally overdetermined script, I have opted for another mode of organization, one that takes its cue from the imagery of floods and dams, collateral channels and armored bodies, with which I opened this chapter, and one that methodologically plays a Freudian hermeneutics of desire, repression, and oedipalized femininity against the more radical theorization of desire-as-flow that Theweleit develops from the work of Deleuze and Guattari. Since the deployment of such imagery by both male and female writers raises questions about the gendered nature of the attempt to authorize, speak for, and write female desire, I begin with the floods of eros to which a female author's representation of the "impassioned, newly awakened being" (94) of her heroine gives vent in *The Awakening*. Then, following Theweleit's hypothesis that men's fantasies of women's sexuality encode a narcissistic terror of engulfment, of the dissolution of bodily and psychic boundaries, I trace the threat that Chopin's fantasy of female desire set free to drift comes to signify in the creative and speculative imaginations, respectively, of Lawrence and Freud, whose texts, as "male fantasies" of female sexual liberation, attempt to "master" or dam up the flood that their plots simultaneously attempt to release. In the process, we will perhaps become more able to assess the contention of Deleuze and Guattari, noted earlier, that "desire does not 'want' revolution; it is revolutionary in its own right." In turn, the very word *revolution* may suggest why the realm of the political—which an application of Theweleit necessarily invokes—may not be totally out of place in plotting the textual and psychosexual transactions linking Creole sensuality, Laurentian phallicism, and Viennese hysteria in early-twentieth-century narratives—narratives whose authority depends on giving voice to hitherto censored expressions of female sexuality while negotiating the cultural and psychological anxieties to which the topos of unboundaried female desire is, for a multiplicity of reasons, irrevocably attached.

KATE CHOPIN, *THE AWAKENING*
SWIMMING INTO THE UNKNOWN

"She's making it devilishly uncomfortable for me," he went on nervously. "She's got some sort of notion in her head regarding the eternal rights of women; and—you understand—we meet in the morning at the breakfast table."

. . . "Pontellier," said the Doctor, after a moment's reflection, "let your wife alone for a while. . . . Woman . . . is a very peculiar and delicate organism. . . . It would require an inspired psychologist to deal successfully with them."

—Kate Chopin, *The Awakening* (117–19)

Hers is the realm of the unconscious, the subjective, of receptivity and reverie.
—Wendy Martin on Edna Pontellier[22]

I would like to begin my discussion of Kate Chopin's *The Awakening* (1899) by recalling an image in Theweleit 's *Male Fantasies*—the "body armor" of the soldier male, worn to protect himself from female floods. If, as the first epigraph above intimates, Edna Pontellier's female subjectivity and eroticism seem circumscribed on the one hand by the sexual politics of marriage that her husband espouses and on the other by theories of "inspired psychologist[s]" regarding the "delicate" sex that Doctor Mandelet espouses, it is also true that late-nineteenth-century American constructions of manhood were in turn circumscribed by the fear of those desirous floods increasingly identified with the *political* "rights of women."[23] In Chopin's text, the most graphic example of authoritarian misogyny surrounding itself with protective body armor is none other than Edna's visiting father, a Southern patriarch whose advocacy of absolute male rule in marriage is rumored to have "coerced his own wife into the grave" (125). This American version of Theweleit's soldier male exhibits a self-control variously described as "fixed," "rigid and unflinching," and "stiff," all aspects of the "military bearing" he learned as a colonel in the Confederate army (120–21). Such hyperbolic masculinity, however, is undercut by one ironically telling detail, filtered through his daughter's viewpoint: the Colonel, as he still insists on being called, wears "his coats padded, which gave a fictitious breadth and depth to his shoulders and chest" (120). His psychic armor may be impenetrable, but his pose of masculinity is only that—a pose, a fiction. The second appearance in the text of the accoutrements of male body armor occurs when Adèle Ratignolle presses upon Edna a sewing pattern of night-drawers for her youngest son. A "marvel of construction, fashioned to enclose a baby's body so effectively that only two small eyes might look out from the garment, like an Eskimo's," this "impervious" garment not only resists the penetrating reaches of "treacherous drafts" and "deadly cold" (51–52), but surreptitiously prevents infantile masturbation, enforcing the freezing up rather than expenditure of polymorphous pleasure. The one body part it doesn't constrict, tellingly, is the boy's eyes, thereby encouraging the development of his scopic gaze.

Reaching from Edna's male progenitor to her male progeny, such imagery might seem to gesture toward a dynastic plot of male succession as the deep structure of *The Awakening*—a plot, that is, in which Edna, no matter her individually awakened eroticism, occupies woman's traditional position as the intermediary between men, the child-bearer linking male generations who is herself expendable, replaceable. The narrative sequencing of these two textual moments, however, points to a quite different set of priorities, for Edna is neither deceived nor awed but rather amused by these manifestations of male body armor. She is "glad to be rid" of her father when he departs "with his padded shoulders" (124–25). Likewise, she only pretends to take an interest in Adèle's patterns; "quite at rest" concerning her boys' clothing needs, she finds of more immediate concern the new, vague desires agitating her psyche.

For Chopin's narrative, of course, focuses on a woman's inner awakening to her sexuality, and, in vivid contrast to the above examples of efforts to insulate the male body, the story of Edna's psychosexual development traces an opposing and ongoing process of *divestiture*. "Daily casting aside that fictitious self which we assume like a garment with which to appear before the world" (108), Edna successively loosens herself from social and psychological constraints—literally shedding her clothing during the Chênière idyll, abandoning her Tuesdays at home, moving out of her husband's house.[24] And as Edna strips down to the essentials, loosening the restraints that have hitherto confined her, Chopin depicts her simultaneous entrance into a world of fluidity associated both with her nascent sexuality and with the gulf setting that provides a watery backdrop to these erotic stirrings. In this plot of awakening, divestiture and water work hand in hand to limn the trajectory of Edna's psychological development. "The water must be delicious; it will not hurt you. Come" (56), Robert enticingly invites Edna at the Grand Isle sea resort where the text opens, and the immediate, liberating consequence of the momentous night when Edna learns to swim is her feeling of "being borne away from [those] anchorage[s] which had held her fast," and consequently of being left "free to drift whithersoever she chose" (81). Likewise, upon her return to New Orleans, Edna increasingly immerses herself in "the deeper undercurrents of life" (151), while progressively "casting off" (135) those outer forms that interfere with her exploration of the libidinal underside of consciousness.

The dream of oceanic freedom, however, can also become a nightmare of constriction, of fluidity frozen in time and space. The dangers, both real and psychological, of Edna's revolutionary desire "to swim far out, where no other woman had swum before" (73) can be glimpsed in Freud's recounting of a dream uncannily evocative of Edna's experience: "One of my patients told me that she had had her favorite dream again the night before, and that it always recurred in the same form: she had dreamed of swimming in the blue sea, of joyfully parting the waves. . . . [But] on one occasion . . . she was swimming in a frozen sea, and surrounded by icebergs" (*Dora*, 112). Indeed, this dialectic between fluidity and paralysis becomes the signature of Edna's tragic life as well as Chopin's narrative format.[25] It also becomes, in light of much feminist theory, one of the text's most telling inscriptions of the interimplication of gender and sexuality in a woman's story. For the imagistic and narrative fluidity or diffuseness that, on a formal plane, mirrors Edna's awakening desires and physical mobility evokes not only the myriad currents that her eroticism follows, but, less positively, the multiple ambiguities that ultimately entrap her in a pattern of eroticized indecision. Given the conflict of psychological and social imperatives set into motion by Edna's contradictory status as a female subject of desire in a genre, and a society, that usually recognizes women as objects, Chopin represents her protagonist's inner awakening as fundamentally split, ambivalent, and insoluble, just as she ends the narrative not in a resolution—or a revolution—but in an impasse.[26] In order to investigate how far Chopin is willing to go to authorize, in all senses of the word, female desire in a culture hostile to its expression, the following pages begin with a paradigmatic instance of awakening, then relate it, first, to the text's innovative formal techniques and, second, to the erotics and autoerotics that inscribe Edna's immersion in the worlds of the senses and sex(es).

Libidinal Flows

It is telling that an early reviewer could dismiss *The Awakening* as part of "the overworked field of sex fiction" and overlook its formal advances.[27] For, in fact, Chopin's attempt to evoke the complexities of her protagonist's psychological and existential predicament issues in a series of formal innovations that build on the protomodernism of *Villette* and anticipate, more than has been generally acknowledged, her high modernist successors.[28] To contextualize these innovations and their relation to Chopin's depiction of Edna's interior world of desire, I find it useful to begin with the trope of awakening announced in the novel's title. The text's very first report of a literal awakening from sleep inaugurates a two-staged sequence of metaphoric awakenings that form a microcosm of the novel's larger representational goals. In section 3 (the text is composed of short, lyrical sections rather than chapters), Edna is roused from sleep by her husband Léonce Pontellier, who returns to their summer cottage on Grand Isle in a state of intoxication and uncharacteristic talkativeness. What this abrupt external awakening initiates is the beginning of Edna's internal awakening to her secondary status as, in Mr. Pontellier's perspective, "the sole object of his existence" (48)—a sentimental cliché that, in superficially elevating Edna to a position of eminence, really means that Edna's wifely function as "sole object" is to attend to "*his* existence," regardless of whether he remembers to attend to hers. Wounded by his drowsy wife's inattention, Mr. Pontellier avenges himself by accusing Edna of being a negligent mother—a clear displacement of his feeling of being denied a proper wife's attentions. At this point Edna's only psychic defense is to remain silent and refuse to continue the debate on Leonce's terms, which, however, is also to *be* silenced: "She said nothing, and refused to answer her husband when he questioned her" (48). Like Lucy Snowe, Edna has yet to learn that becoming an acting subject means learning to articulate oneself through words.

As if it were an unconscious supplement to Edna's voicelessness, another voice—"the everlasting voice of the sea" (49)—immediately enters the scene to inaugurate a second phase in this awakening sequence. For as soon as Mr. Pontellier falls asleep, Edna—now "thoroughly awake" (48)— leaves the bedroom and goes outside. And here, under the influence of the sea's "mournful lullaby" (49)—an image that, as in Whitman, equates the ocean with maternity and, as in Kristeva, with the semiotic register of language—Edna's dawning sense of social oppression leads to a corresponding outburst of the repressed, of the unconscious made manifest in an unquenchable deluge of tears that traverses the nominal boundary separating inner and outer, depth and surface, oceanic interior and the surrounding sea:

> The tears came so fast to Mrs. Pontellier's eyes that the damp sleeve of her *peignoir* no longer served to dry them. . . . She could not have told why she was crying. . . . An indescribable oppression, which seemed to generate in some unfamiliar part of her consciousness, filled her whole being with a vague anguish. It was like a shadow, like a mist passing across her soul's summer day. It was strange and unfamiliar. (49)

"Could not have told why," "indescribable," "vague," "like a shadow," "like a mist," "strange and unfamiliar": all these word-choices attempt to articulate a level of mental activity that is still inarticulate, slowly emerging from that "unfamiliar part of . . . consciousness" that Freud was in the same decade identifying as the unconscious, the seat of repression. But while Edna may not yet have words for these "strange and unfamiliar" feelings tentatively groping toward consciousness, Chopin's writing of the scene renders the repressed visible. For the sobbing Edna is represented at this moment in a pose of total sensuous materiality: one uplifted arm holding the back of her chair, its sleeve slipping to her bare shoulder, her "steaming and wet" face is thrust into the fleshy crook of her arm, where she goes "on crying . . . not caring any longer to dry her face, her eyes, her arms" (49). No shadow-ghost like Lucy Snowe, Edna's sheer physical presence, all "firm, round" flesh amidst this flood of wetness, evinces the truth of Foucault's insight that sexuality always makes itself discursively present, even when it is assumed to be suppressed by cultural prohibition. For it is precisely Edna's erotic body, her material sensuousness, that is achieving expression here.

In line with turn-of-the-century sexology, Chopin sees this unacknowledged sensuality as the key to Edna's most authentic, natural self.[29] To awaken as a sexual being, Edna must—as in giving vent to the flow of her tears—progressively let go of the ego constraints that bind her in order for her libidinal desires to surface and enter into erotic engagement with her environment. Hence the successive scenes trace the steps whereby Edna cuts herself adrift from social sanctions and allows herself mentally and physically to wander "idly, aimlessly, unthinking and unguided" (61).[30] Within pages of the episode of the midnight cry, Chopin repeats this sense of the repressed libido welling up from within, coming into the light of day, as Edna begins to sense and resist her attraction to her constant companion on Grand Isle, Robert Lebrun: "A certain light was beginning to dawn dimly within her,—the light which, showing the way, forbids it. . . . It moved her to dreams, to thoughtfulness, to the shadowy anguish which had overcome her the midnight when she had abandoned herself to tears." Everything up to this point suggests that this dawning but forbidden "light" has to do with the stirring of erotic feelings for Robert. Yet in the following sentence, the authorial voice delivers an unexpected twist: "In short, Mrs. Pontellier was beginning to realize her position in the universe as a human being" (57). With this one phrase, the narrative's protofeminist impulse—like the "rights of women" (118) that Mr. Pontellier fears have tainted Edna's mind—meshes with a specifically American version of Romantic transcendentalism and political self-determination; in Chopin's rewriting of female desire, to awaken erotically as a woman is simultaneously to awaken to one's existential position in the universe.[31] This revelation is registered on the narrative plane as the text shifts into a lyrical paean, delivered in the present tense, to the sea. At once an external agent of nature spurring Edna's bodily and spiritual awakening, the gulf ocean simultaneously becomes a figure for the floods of the unconscious, the currents of repressed eroticism, beginning to surface from deep within her psyche:

> The voice of the sea is seductive; never ceasing, whispering, clamoring, murmuring, inviting the soul to wander for a spell in the abysses of solitude; to lose itself in mazes of inward contemplation.
> The voice of the sea speaks to the soul. The touch of the sea is sensuous, enfolding the body in its soft, close embrace. (57)

In this intensely lyrical passage, Chopin deploys with consummate artistry the historical association of women and water traced by Theweleit and reclaimed by Irigaray. In doing so she condenses a series of inseparable issues—from sensual gratification to existential solitude—that impinge upon, and radically complicate, any woman's quest for erotic agency and satisfaction in turn-of-the-century America.

Narrative Drifts

The prose-poetry achieved in this sixth section of *The Awakening* is significant for more than its psychosexual and philosophical import. Veering from the overlay of indirect free discourse and narrative omniscience of the prior sentences, its lyrical repetitions disrupt the illusion of verisimilitude and augur the textual and stylistic innovations to follow. To be sure, Chopin's narration never breaks from a third-person point of view, but it manipulates the possibilities of what Dorrit Cohn calls psycho-narration in order to simulate those libidinal currents that underlie Edna's awakening process but have not reached conscious verbalization.[32] This effect is often achieved by strategically arranging episodes, sequences, and images according to an associative rather than causal logic, so that externalized action—the objective plot—bears the imprint of interior, subjective states of mind, unsettling attempts to treat the novel's plot in only mimetic terms. For example, in the lyrical "voice of the sea" passage quoted above, the wording used to describe the sea's call to the soul to "wander" and "lose" itself "in mazes of inward contemplation" repeats, almost verbatim, a prior description of the way Edna's eyes focus on objects "as if lost in some inward maze of contemplation" (46). The figurative evocation of the (real) ocean's seductive call in section 6 thus becomes an extension of a condition of being *already* identified as *interior* to Edna. Moreover, these "inward mazes" of the mind reappear in yet another guise only a page later, in the form of the mazelike sandy paths along which Edna and Adèle walk to the beach in section 7. In a remarkable turn of imagistic and narrative association, Chopin's poetic evocation of the sea as an emblem of subconscious desire (section 6) comes to anticipate the plot's record of "real" actions (the walk of section 7), illustrating, as Freud would also show, the degree to which the world of the unconscious subtends and shapes conscious life.

An even more dramatic example of this narrative tendency to blur the realms of reality and thought via metaphor occurs a few scenes later, the night that Mlle. Reisz's piano-playing arouses "the very passions themselves" within Edna's "soul, swaying it, lashing it, as the waves daily beat upon her splendid body" (72). Within sentences, the watery content of the third-person simile ("as the waves . . .") *becomes* "reality": Mlle. Reisz's listeners go outside to bathe in the moonlit gulf, where the waves now literally beat on Edna's body as she learns to swim for the first time. In a daring reversal of the novelistic logic of cause and effect, the third-person description of a psychosexual state (Edna's electric reaction to the music) seems actually to create action on the level of story—an action, moreover, described in the language of dissolving boundaries and dream, of nonverisimilitude. This dreamlike swimming sequence thus serves as a kind of textual projection of the unconscious, expressing Edna's heightened emotional and sexual state as she undergoes the "first-felt throbbings of desire" (77). In the process, the forwarding of plot comes to depend as much on the moment-to-moment process of associative drift reflective of the protagonist's subjective states as on the linear logic of traditional realistic plotting. Having once broached the realm of dream, the narrative, it would seem, can no longer free itself from the spell of libidinal desire.

Examples of this associative movement abound, creating a text in which the usual fictional boundaries distinguishing the "real" and "unreal" continually dissolve. Listening to music, for instance, Edna conjures up the image of "a demure lady stroking a cat" (71); much later in the text, Robert comes across Edna in a secluded outdoor cafe stroking a cat as she reads a book (164)—an authorial image whose potent autoeroticism also blurs the distinction between the sexual (stroking a cat) and textual (reading a book).[33] Image again foreshadows actual event as, in this scene, Robert takes it upon himself to tell Edna the ending of the book she is reading "to save her the trouble *of wading through it*" (166; emphasis added); his metaphor is ironically realized as Edna literally wades into the gulf at the end of *Chopin's* book, undoing Robert's act of authorial usurpation by scripting her own ending.

The strategies whereby Chopin's narrative structure imitates the freely associative and image-making activities of consciousness are closely allied to her manipulation of narrative viewpoint, especially in creating rapid shifts in focalization; moving freely and without warning among authorial third person, indirect free discourse, and objective narration, Chopin renders the boundaries separating fictional text, authorial voice, character viewpoint, and reader unusually fluid and permeable. A representative example involves Edna and Adèle's escape to the beach in section 7. Under the seductive influence of the sea and her friend, Edna begins to confess aloud her feeling of drifting aimlessly. Edna's recollections are initially recorded as direct quotations ("Let me see . . . perhaps I can retrace my thoughts . . ." [60]), but as she continues to speak to Adèle, the narrative focus shifts, first to omniscient third-person summary, then to a limited third-person narration of Edna's perceptions of her early infatuations. The structure of the sequence and the use of indirect free discourse leads the reader to assume that all this information is being spoken by Edna to Adèle. But this assumption is abruptly modified as the authorial voice equivocally interjects, "Edna did not reveal so much as all this to Madame Ratignolle that summer day" (63). This destabilization of viewpoint occurs repeatedly throughout the text, creating a polyphonic layering of perspectives and voices that intensifies the novel's illusion of fluid movement.

Such rapid, often unsignaled, slippages in focalization also tend to dissolve the boundaries between, on the one hand, the narrator and her subject, and, on the other, the narrator and her reader. In a move that reverses the process whereby descriptive images of interiority occurring on the narrative plane become actions on the level of plot, the third-person authorial description of Mlle. Reisz's "disposition to trample upon the rights of others" (70) is echoed word for word by Edna's first-person voice at the end of the novel to refer to herself, Edna (171); as Edna impossibly parrots her creator's language, the ontologically distinct categories of author and character blur. Analogously, when we read that the piano music arousing Edna's passions is none other than a Chopin Impromptu, or when the third-person voice tells the reader that Adèle is "the fair lady of *our* dreams" (51; emphasis added), the boundary between author and reader begins to waver, leaving us uncertain of where we stand in relation to the narrated material. This lack of grounding is only intensified by Chopin's frequent recourse to a hypothetical, questioning mode of narration that flaunts the uncertainty of its own position: "There may have been—there must have been—influences . . . this might have furnished a link. Who can tell . . . ?" (57).[34]

The way in which all these narrative strategies evoke states of interiority—ranging from the structural arrangement of images and episodes to discourage transparent verisimilitude to the blurring of boundaries between reader, text, and subject matter—not only exemplify Chopin's protomodernist sympathies, but also call to mind contemporary theories of women's writing. For more than a decade, various feminist critics—largely inspired either by Nancy Chodorow's psychoanalytic reinterpretation of the importance of the preoedipal bond for infant girls or Julia Kristeva's theorization of the semiotic as the maternal linguistic register—have been suggesting the importance of the mother-daughter bond to women's less rigidly differentiated sense of ego boundaries and its textual manifestations in women's writing. According to Judith Kegan Gardiner, the blurring of the distinction between inner and outer realms on the level of plot, and the intermingling of modes of discourse and types of subgenres on the formal plane—textual strategies I have been highlighting in *The Awakening*—frequently occur in female fictions of development, and Gardiner attributes these characteristics to the more fluid, relational sense of identity that emerges from the daughter's never-completed differentiation from the mother. Less from this object-relations perspective than from a Lacanian-influenced feminist framework, Irigaray, as noted at the beginning of this chapter, has returned to the science of hydraulics to champion "fluidity" as a trope that distinguishes female erotogenic multiplicity from the unitary model of male desire rooted in phallic sexuality; more recently, Susan Stanford Friedman has theorized a complex model of relational or fluid identity, originating in feminist psychoanalytic and materialist discourse, as a way out of the persistent reduction of differences to binary systems of logic in cultural narratives of sexuality and race.[35]

Chodorow's revisionary paradigm has also provided many feminist literary critics with an explanation of the importance that female bonding and relationality assume in much women's fiction that, like Chopin's text, is concerned with issues of individual autonomy and erotic agency. And, indeed, female bonds are indispensable to the libidinal plot and politics of *The Awakening:* to put it simply, women are the most important agents, none barred, in Edna's awakening. Until recently, it has been a commonplace of Chopin criticism that Robert Lebrun and Alcée Arobin trigger Edna's sexual awakening, and that her two female friends, Adèle Ratignolle and Mlle. Reisz, allegorize the mutually exclusive options—patriarchal marriage or a loveless career—that face Edna as a woman.[36] Adèle and Reisz, however, are not simply cardboard figures, representing opposing "types" of womanhood, but figures whose *structural* functions in Chopin's narrative are in fact more alike than opposed. Without the subconscious influence they exert on Edna—an influence far more potent than the heterosexual attractions of Robert or Arobin—there would be, simply put, no plot of *female* sexual awakening for us to read, or for Chopin to attempt to authorize, as I will now attempt to show.

Autoerotic Awakenings in the Company of Women

Edna's relationships with Adèle Ratignolle and Mlle. Reisz are established in the opening sequences of *The Awakening,* which take place, as Sandra Gilbert puts it, in the "no-man's-land" of the "female colony" of Grand Isle.[37] A "border" territory off the Louisiana coast where prosperous wives vacation with their children and servants while their husbands disappear to the mainland, the setting is particularly conducive to fostering intense emotional relations among women. Framed by this setting, Adèle is introduced as precisely that which Edna is said *not* to be—an archetypal "mother-woman" exuding every "womanly grace and charm" to the point of stereotypicality. As the narrator ironically puts it, "There were no words to describe her save the old ones that have served so often to picture the bygone heroine of romance." The text, however, almost immediately opens up a space between this near-parodic representation of untouchable femininity and Adèle's sensual *immediacy:* the sheer force of her presence— "There was nothing subtle or hidden about her charms; her beauty was all there, flaming and apparent" (51)—deconstructs the spirituality that her angelic maternity is taken to signify. And this sensuous materiality serves importantly as the agency that first stimulates Edna—in another image of divestiture—to "loosen a little the mantle of reserve that had always enveloped her" and explore her latent eroticism. Indeed, she is "first attracted" not by Adèle's personality or values but by her "excessive physical charm."

For Edna, as the authorial narrative voice confides, has "a sensuous suscep-tibility to beauty" that, in the case of her "attraction" to Adèle, issues in a "subtle bond . . . we might as well call love" (57–58).

The intensity of the feelings unlocked by Edna's attraction to this "sen-suous Madonna" (55)[38] facilitates the first significant turn in her psycho-sexual awakening, which is registered in the scene in section 7 where the two women go to the beach alone. With her gaze, significantly, "at rest upon the sea" (59), Edna begins to loosen her tongue as well as her "mantle of reserve" (57) in response to Adèle's innocent question, "Of what are you thinking?" (60). What follows uncannily resembles a psychoanalytic encounter, as Edna, attempting to "retrace [her] thoughts" for Adèle, un-leashes a stream of hitherto repressed associations in a process of self-analysis that allows her, first, to articulate her vague feelings of being adrift and, next, "len[ding] herself readily" to the physicality of Adèle's "gentle caress" (61), to confess the story of her past infatuations and suppressed erotic desires.[39] So moved to confession by Adèle's maternal and material presence, Edna becomes, for the first time in the recorded narrative, a *speaking subject:* "She was flushed . . . with the sound of her own voice. . . . It muddled her like wine, or like a first breath of freedom" (63). Tellingly, it is also in this scene that the narrator finally refers to Edna by her given name, rather than as "Mrs. Pontellier": only in the eroticized company of another woman does Edna cease to be her husband's possession and begin to speak for herself, as a woman with unanswered desires and a separate identity, and as a woman whose awakening has the potential either to "muddle" her perception or to grant her a new sense of "freedom."

Edna's friendship with Mademoiselle Reisz traces an equally eroticized movement from repression to self-expression. The pivotal scene capturing this erotic intimacy occurs in section 9 when Mlle. Reisz plays the piano for Edna. Far from being the sexless creature her fellow vacationers assume her to be, the unmarried, homely pianist quite literally has at her fingertips the power to bring Edna to the brink of orgasm, or so Chopin's depiction of Edna's electric reaction to Mlle. Reisz's piano playing intimates: "The very passions themselves were aroused within her soul, swaying it, lashing it. . . . She trembled, she was choking, and the tears blinded her" (72). If piano music—a Chopin Impromptu, no less—becomes the instrument of mediation joining Edna and Mlle. Reisz in this highly eroticized scene, later the piano will drop out of the picture altogether as the latter woman takes Edna's hand "between her strong wiry fingers" and, "executing a sort of double theme upon the back and palm" (114), performs a kind of body-music, a tactile *écriture féminine,* on Edna's warm flesh.[40]

Adapting current lesbian diacritical discourse, one might say that Edna in such moments plays the femme to Reisz's butch number. In her relations with the feminine Adèle, in contrast, it is Edna who plays the more re-served, masculine role—the narrator deliberately sets her "long, clean, and symmetrical" lines off against Adèle's "more feminine and matronly figure" (58). That Reisz illustrates the new turn-of-the-century type of the sapphic or lesbian, barely able to repress her crush on Edna, seems clear from a contemporary vantage point; hence the scene where Reisz watches Edna bathe in the ocean, "rav[ing] much over her appearance in her bathing suit" (99), as well as her admission to Edna that she is "a foolish, old woman whom you have captivated" (116). To be sure, Edna's interactions with both Adèle and Mlle. Reisz assume much more ambivalent under tones when they transpire outside the protected female space of Grand Isle. Nonetheless, as the narrative structure of the novel attests, these bonds expose the omnipresence of sexuality that is *already* present in Edna's life, long before she becomes actively involved with Robert or Arobin: in Chopin's lexicon, awakened sexual desire is not automatically subsumed under the rubric of compulsory heterosexuality.

To the degree that Adèle and Reisz serve as mirroring others in whom Edna may begin to recognize aspects of her own sexuality as a woman, these bonds also bring to the surface Edna's latent autoeroticism: in this text, as in *Villette*, the story of repressed female sexuality becomes a story of the autoerotic recovery of the colonized female body. Perhaps the most evocative among the text's many representations of Edna's autoeroticism occurs during the Chênière interlude, as, in more imagery of divestiture, Edna prepares for a nap. "Loosen[ing] her clothes, removing the greater part of them," she quite literally awakens to her body as she begins to "observ[e] closely, as if it were something she saw for the first time, the fine, firm quality and texture of her flesh" (84). "Female sexuality finds autonomous satisfaction," notes Jean Wyatt of this moment, and "autonomous satisfaction" is an apt expression for Edna's "awakening sensuousness" (131).[41] Such autoeroticism also functions as an extension of Edna's extraordinarily physical connection to the natural world, from the sensuous fluidity of Grand Isle to the hidden nooks she seeks out in New Orleans where she can be "one with the sunlight, the color, the odors, the luxuriant warmth of some perfect Southern day" (109). In this and similar textual moments, the terrain of eros appears radically deterritorialized, the mapping of its pleasures at least temporarily unlimited. Concurrently, Chopin represents Edna's surfacing eroticism as diffuse, heterogeneous, and capable of attaching to multiple sources of stimulation; her desires may extend toward *various* objects but, like the component instincts, are not *object-specific*. A perfect example of Edna's ability to take her pleasures randomly and diffusely occurs in section 35, when, coming down to breakfast "only half dressed," she receives a series of letters—a "delicious printed scrawl" from her son Raoul, a businesslike note from her husband, a love letter from Arobin—all of which she reads with equal pleasure, for as the narrative democratically notes, "All these letters were pleasing to her" (162).[42] This diffusion of desire into multiple channels even pervades

Chopin's representation of Edna's eventual affair with Arobin in the latter part of the novel. For it is impossible to pinpoint the precise moment in the narrative in which sexual consummation occurs: just as one textual site is not privileged over another, neither is "sex" a necessarily singular experience for Edna.

What, then, does such non-goal-specific eroticism have to do with the definitions of female psychosexuality emerging at the turn of the century? In the secondary version of oedipal triangulation that Freud postulated to talk about female development, the daughter only attains sexual maturity through the double displacement of an originally incestuous desire—first for the mother, then for the father, the latter stage occurring as she marries a man (often modeled on the father) who assumes the father's place as object of legitimate desire.[43] One is hard-pressed to find much of a traditional female oedipal pattern in *The Awakening*, however, beyond the narrator's coy declaration that "we need seek no further for the motives" leading Edna to marry Léonce Pontellier than her father's "violent opposition" (62). The fact is that neither marriage nor fathers have much of an impact on Edna's emerging sexuality. Rather, the hitherto repressed erotic current to which the novel gives expression illustrates a modality of desire that resembles the model proposed by Deleuze and Guattari in their Marxist refutation of Freud's theory of incestuous desire as the universal basis of repression. Desire, they write in *Anti-Oedipus,* overflows the oedipal boundaries altogether: "Flows ooze, they traverse the triangle, breaking apart its vertices."[44] Likewise, in its syncretic ability to achieve pleasure from multiple stimuli, Edna's sexuality epitomizes Deleuze and Guattari's concept of the body as a "desiring-machine" that "does not require whole persons" but obtains pleasurable discharge by knowing part-objects, achieving a series of satisfactions through transitory connections between parts of itself and parts of other objects in relationships that are protean and changing—a description that holds true for Chopin's fluid, associative mode of narrative as well as for the randomness of Edna's autoerotic "flows."[45]

Freud's fallacy, according to Deleuze and Guattari, is to implicate this purely productive libidinal energy in an oedipal structure of incest and castration. This structure is not intrinsic to desire itself, they argue, but originates in social mechanisms of repression—mechanisms originating in the bourgeois redirection of desire into the flow of capital.[46] And, indeed, the distance between the desiring streams unleashed by Edna's awakening from repression and the oedipal structures largely absent from Chopin's representation of Edna's psychic life seem to substantiate this critique, as does the text's implicit linking of father/husband figures to the burgeoning capitalism of the American Gilded Age. It is no coincidence, after all, that Thorstein Veblen's *The Theory of the Leisure Class* was published the same year as *The Awakening.* For if Edna's father, as a land-owning Southern patriarch, represents a mode of postwar economic viability now on the wane, the entrepreneurial Léonce Pontellier, who is absent in New York tying up a "big scheme" (119) during the most critical moments of Edna's awakening, represents modern American capitalism's shift toward corporate monopoly, a further narrowing of desire's streams; in terms that could have been taken verbatim from Veblen's text, he internalizes Edna's material worth to him as "a valuable piece of personal property" (44).[47]

Viewed within the psychoanalytic framework supplied by Deleuze and Guattari, Edna's erotic heterogeneity cannot therefore be reduced to a so-called regressive return to archaic, polymorphous, infantile desire. Rather, her eroticism signals a *productive* desirous energy that traverses the line between the imaginary and the symbolic, the regressive and progressive, the individual and intersubjective, redefining the possibilities of an *adult* sexual economy of the polymorphously perverse—and, as such, *The Awakening* contributes significantly to the (proto)modernist poetics and politics of the perverse theorized in the previous chapter. For the randomness and heterogeneity of Edna's desires stand as a challenge to the politics of sexuality practiced in her society and, more specifically, to the political and economic institutions that depend upon a channeling of female desire into the trajectory of patriarchal marriage. Paradoxically, though, as politically revolutionary as these desires are, Edna herself remains largely unconscious of the class and racial hierarchies that underwrite her process of awakening and that form the "textually repressed" of *The Awakening*. As Veblen's analysis of the middle-class wife's commodity function in late-century American capitalism makes clear, only a well-to-do woman like Edna would have the unencumbered time to "drift" toward an inner awakening without the worry of material concerns. Edna's leisured awakening is not only made possible by her husband's enterprising capitalism—part of the same system, ironically, that oppresses her—but by the racial caste system prevailing in Louisiana. That is, the autoerotic "decolonization" of Edna's body that occurs as she sheds the encumbrances of marriage and recovers her "latent sensuality" (163) depends, ironically, on the colonization of others. If Edna appears to accept without question the many, usually unnamed, black and mulatto servants who maintain the domestic duties (including caretaking of the children) that she deliberately neglects as part of her rebellion against *female* servitude, the text self-consciously underlines the mute, shadowy presence of all the subalterns whose contrasting servitude makes Edna's self-discovery possible.[48]

Just how a sensuality that, like Edna's, is not particularly object-specific may be misunderstood by psychoanalytic readings based on traditional oedipal paradigms is graphically illustrated in Cynthia Griffin Wolff's widely anthologized dissection of *The Awakening*. Wolff argues that all of Edna's gestures toward sexual emancipation and independence are in fact *infantile regressions,* precisely because her desires are not genitally oriented toward men. Thus, of Edna's exploration of her body on Chênière, Wolff writes, "Powerfully sensuous as this scene is, we would be hard put to find *genital significance* here"; she adds that Edna's "libidinal energies have been arrested at a *pre-genital level*," and finally states that the only alternative to her "inner turmoil" would be a *"genuine genital relationship* . . . a significant attachment with a *real man*."[49] Wolff, however, is only able to argue that Edna is attempting to escape mature sexuality because she (like many Freudian-influenced psychoanalytic literary critics of the 1950s–1960s) assumes that an adult woman's sexuality is properly expressed in heterosexual coitus rather than in randomly autoerotic pleasures. Such a line of reasoning constitutes, in Deleuze and Guattari's terminology, a "reterritorialization" of the female body par excellence. Not only does it subscribe to a teleology of female development that assumes one appropriate "aim" (heterosexual) and "object" (male) to an identity rooted in phallic lack; Wolff's argument that the culmination of this "regressive" pattern can *only* be a desire to return to the mother's womb—hence explaining Edna's final suicidal swim into the ocean—expresses a similar Freudian bias that assumes the maternal only functions as an object of desire in the realm of the pre-oedipal, rather than, as Chodorow demonstrates, manifesting itself as a sustaining if ambivalent model of identification and relationship throughout adult women's lives and bonds.

If, as I have been arguing, Edna's awakening to her sexual nature is largely facilitated by her bonds with women and her intersubjective connection with the sensual world at large, it is now time to query what happens to thwart that awakening when she attempts to engage in "genital relationship[s]" with those "real m[e]n" that patriarchy, psychoanalysis, and some literary critics have touted as the *sine qua non* of adult female sexuality.

Stranded at Sea; or, the Impossible Fiction of Romantic Passion

Sex and men are ingredients that, to risk understatement, combine uneasily in Edna's erotic experience. Léonce Pontellier complains to Doctor Mandelet that Edna's new-found notions of independence—which he attributes to talk about the "rights of women"—have deprived him of a *husband's* rights, that is, of sexual intercourse: "and—you understand—we meet at morning at the breakfast table" (118). But Léonce's perspective is only half the picture, since Edna actively attempts to establish erotic relationships with men other than her husband, only to have these attempts prove equally frustrating. The problem, I suggest, is an extension of two competing claims at work in Edna's awakening from its outset. To emancipate herself from oppressive social constructions of gender, Edna needs to assert a more *active* control over her individual life, to become an acting subject who, in rebelling against her social identity as "Mrs. Pontellier," is strong enough to resolve "never again to belong to another than herself" (135). But to awaken sexually, Edna must relinquish ego controls—the will-to-power that makes active social rebellion possible—and drift passively along the currents of subconscious, often irrational, impulse (hence the various images of loosening and drifting that punctuate her awakening). In effect Edna's sexual emancipation requires two contradictory modes of rebellion—simultaneously taking control and letting go—neither of which is feasible for a woman of Edna's position and class, given turn-of-the-century standards of female behavior. The great irony is that Edna's sensuousness escapes overt comment or condemnation as long as it finds socially *invisible* expression in autoerotic pleasure or in the company of women; but when her roused sexuality seeks outlets in *visibly* amorous relationships with Robert Lebrun and Alcée Arobin, her awakening is sundered by irreconcilable ambiguities.

These two men—not unlike the two women, Adèle and Mlle. Reisz, whose initials they share—turn out to serve interestingly parallel plot functions, despite their overtly contrasting personalities. In representing Edna's bond with Robert, Chopin stresses the physical similarities and shared tastes that align the two in a type of eroticized siblingship; tellingly, the boyish Robert Lebrun is much more at home among the female population of Grand Isle than he is among other men.[50] While the relationship at first seems to repeat Robert's penchant for focusing his chaste attentions on a different married woman every summer—a pattern so familiar to those who know him that no one even thinks twice about it—his chivalric companionship comes to mean much more to Edna, precisely because the nonthreatening tenor of his intimacy provides her with a safe context within which to begin to acknowledge the erotic feelings surfacing in her consciousness. Thus, Wolff misses the point when she scoffs at Robert and Edna's relationship as an example of "pre-genital avoidance"; it is, in fact, the very *lack* of heterosexual "genital" pressure that transforms their intimacy into the means for Edna's exploration of her previously repressed erotic feelings.

Once Robert leaves for South America, however, his structural role in the plot shifts dramatically. True to the courtly myth of adulterous passionate love, distance breeds desire. In the process, desire is constructed *as* absence; fetishizing the impossibility of establishing more than a fleeting or clandestine attachment, the lover self-destructively begins to long for that which is absent precisely because it *is* impossible to realize. Something similar happens to Edna's feelings for Robert, and vice versa, once they are separated geographically. Projecting onto Robert a fantasy-role that he cannot fulfill in reality, Edna becomes increasingly possessed by a metaphysical "longing" for "the presence of [a] beloved one" who now only exists in the imagination. In falling victim to this highly literary construction of desire, not only is Edna assailed with "hopelessness" and "a sense of the unattainable" (145), but, as Patricia Yaeger has written, she "falsifies the diversity of her awakening consciousness" by narrowing the course of her erotic trajectory to fit "the *romantic stories* she is told . . . and comes to tell herself."[51]

This particular formulation of never-realized desire depends, as René Girard has shown, on triangulated structures—one never loves an other directly but through the mediation of a third party.[52] And, fascinatingly, in Edna and Robert's case it is Mlle. Reisz who serves as the go-between whetting Edna's desires for Robert. If, in earlier scenes, Mlle. Reisz has served as an independent agent in Edna's autoerotic awakening, now she plays a much more ambiguous and complicitous role, one indicative, perhaps, of her own thwarted desires for Edna. Notably, she not only gives Edna Robert's letters to read but *names* Robert's "love" for him in his place ("It is because he loves you, poor fool" [135]). In addition to playing the Chopin music that has previously brought Edna to autoerotic awareness, Mlle. Reisz now performs, in a grand irony, themes from Wagner's adaptation of the Tristan and Isolde myth, *the* paradigmatic plot of impossible, because adulterous, desire.

In Edna's subsequent affair with Alcée Arobin, desire again assumes a triangulated and ultimately self-defeating form. For at the same time that Edna's infatuation with the still-absent Robert becomes the stimulus for her attraction to the seductively available Arobin, she subconsciously allows her idealized love of Robert to cover over, or excuse, her sexual responsiveness to the latter man. Thus, immediately following the scene in which Arobin's animal presence begins to work on her "like a narcotic" (132), Edna confesses "for the first time" her love for Robert (136); the very evening of this admission, she receives from Arobin "the first kiss of her life to which her nature had really responded" (139). It is hard to imagine a more triangulated example of desire than the one illustrated by this series of rapidly juxtaposed scenes. Moreover, even as Arobin's kiss—"a flaming torch that kindled desire"(139)—sets the stage for the final phase of her sexual exploration, Edna feels "a dull pang of regret because it was not the kiss of love which had inflamed her, because it was not love which had held this cup of life to her lips" (139). Internalizing an either/or logic (either love or sex) in the affair that follows, Edna eventually yields to a sense of disillusionment and the conviction that in experiencing the ecstasy of sexual abandon she has also "abandoned herself" (162) to a perpetual series of unsatisfactory love affairs ("To-day it is Arobin; tomorrow it will be some one else" [175]). Edna's attempt at exerting sexual agency thus dead-ends in the critical confusion that ensues in her mind when she fails to distinguish adequately between the validity of the passions brought into being by the awakening of her "latent sensuality" (163) and the inherited cultural and literary fiction of passion as "'life's delirium'" (107)—a phrase that even Chopin puts in quotation marks. All that Edna has read, watched, and experienced seems to argue that "delirious" passion is self-defeating, impossible to realize in the "real" world: hence, why not drift aimlessly, indifferently, she reasons, convincing herself to accept with fatalism and "a dull pang of regret" the inevitability of thwarted desire.

The tragedy of *The Awakening*, then, is that the more Edna engages in heterosexual relationships, the more she increasingly confuses her emergent sensuality and this literary mythology of doomed love. The results of her internalization of this inevitably frustrating construction of desire as a longing that can never be satisfied are at least threefold. First, Edna falls into a prolonged mental depression in the latter segments of the novel, as a mood of overwhelming "indifference" leads her to excuse all her actions, once she enters into the affair with Arobin, as the whim of "fate."[53] Second, in internalizing her society's myth of grand passion as impossible longing, Edna dangerously begins to eroticize indecision itself. Third, Edna relinquishes her hard-won status as a speaking subject as her ability to articulate these various contradictions falters. This loss of voice is painfully illustrated in her final dialogue with Doctor Mandelet, hours before committing suicide: "She felt that her speech was voicing the incoherency of her thoughts, and stopped abruptly. . . . 'Oh! I don't know what I'm saying, Doctor. Good night. Don't blame me for anything'" (171–72). By novel's end, Edna is left stranded in an impasse of subjectivity, suspended between mutually exclusive poles, some of which her society has constructed and some of which she constructs herself— suspended, that is, between formulations of desire as only love or only sex, between autoerotic self-awareness and fictions of consuming passion, between the dictates of will and the press of instinct, between active rebellion and passive ineffectuality. None of these oppositions are equal, or even necessarily stable, and in their constant shifting, Edna finds herself, literally and figuratively speaking, at sea.

These slippages between undecidable oppositions also mark the two climactic events that precipitate Edna's final despondency and suicidal swim. The first, her long-deferred reunion with the returned Robert, is structured around a series of contradictory valences. On the one hand, because Edna takes charge of her erotic destiny by initiating the lovemaking, the scene represents the apex of her quest for sexual autonomy; in a reversal of the Sleeping Beauty myth, it is the woman whose "voluptuous" kiss "penetrate[s]" the man's "whole being" (166) and who first declares "I love you" (168). In asserting herself, Edna also attempts to place herself outside the chain of male exchanges that define woman's place in patriarchal culture. Thus she chides Robert, "I am no longer one of Mr. Pontellier's possessions to dispose of or not. I give myself where I choose. If he were to say, 'Here, Robert, take her and be happy; she is yours,' I should laugh at you both" (167). On the other hand, this manifesto of self-possession is rendered suspect by all the triangulated exchanges between men into which she has already inserted herself and through which her desires for men have been constructed.[54] Simultaneously, Edna attempts to insert Robert into the illusive myth of all-consuming passion. Her plea—"We shall be everything to each other. Nothing else in the world is of any consequence" (168)— articulates perfectly the self-destructive logic of the Continental love-myth she has internalized, in which "love" has become the ultimate escape from reality and avoidance of self-determination. Under the sway of this fiction, Edna also falsifies the terms of her initial awakening by naming Robert as sole "author" of her growth and by relegating herself to the grammatical position of object of his desire: "It was *you* who awoke *me* last summer out of a life-long, stupid dream" (168; emphases added). Yet, as we have seen, it was not just Robert but Adèle and Mlle. Reisz who pivotally triggered Edna' first erotic feelings. Ironically, the sexual currents set into motion by these female bonds have become the textually repressed, the unspoken, in a story that began as an awakening *from* repression.

Edna's declaration of love to Robert is interrupted by the second event precipitating the novel's denouement: the psychodramatically surreal scene in which Edna is summoned to Adèle's bedside as her friend gives birth. This dreamlike "scene of torture" provides yet another example of the duplicitous slidings of this narrative, as the beneficent maternal side of Adèle that encouraged Edna's confessions on the beach transforms into the castrated/castrating mother who, as an agent of patriarchy, reminds Edna of the cultural mandate that the latter has been attempting to repress: namely, that female reproductive biology is destiny. Before the force of Adèle's parting shot—"Think of the children, Edna! Oh, think of the children"— Edna is literally left "speechless" (170), no longer the acting subject who voices her desires. To the contrary, upon returning home she finds not Robert but his farewell note, which, standing in for *his* voice, speaks *to* her, *against* her desire: "Good-by, because I love you" (172). Earlier, Edna has predicted that the walls of Robert's reserve cannot "hold against" the flood of "her own passion"; now, ironically, it is precisely his moral and mental dams that prove "insurmountable" and Edna who is left without words, "never uttering a sound" throughout an all-night vigil in which a cloud of "despondency" descends that "never lift[s]" (162, 164, 175).[55]

It is in this conquered state of mind that Edna returns to Grand Isle in the final section, a divided subject no longer able to articulate her confused desires or reason her way out of the social and psychological strictures impeding her development. Thwarted on the personal plane by Robert's desertion and on the social by the vivid reminder of motherhood invoked by Adèle, Edna yields to a state of unthinking drift that, in yet another example of the text's unstable terms, transforms what was previously a *willed* surrender to passivity (to facilitate the emergence of desire) into a state of utter *lack* of will (a tendency that has always been latent in Edna). Given the confusions engendered by these unstable shiftings, Edna's final act— her suicidal swim—is less a conscious decision than a subconscious response to the impasse in which she finds—or, more aptly, no longer finds—herself.

To a degree, these confusions also attest to the authorial anxieties in Chopin, herself caught between the irresolvable choices—life or death—imposed by the plot's trajectory. Hence, like the text's other shiftings, Edna's suicide suggests multiple readings. Most obviously, it is clear that Edna has negatively internalized her society's restrictive views of women's sexuality; she sees herself as a fallen woman whose unlocked desires, like the libidinal floods in Theweleit's analysis, are now insatiable, portending a life of endless, unhappy affairs. On another level, however, there are ways in which Edna's act of suicide seems a celebratory final awakening and rebirth. Significantly, Edna composes her suicide scene, making it her own artistic representation as she steps into the scenario that she has previously imagined while listening to music—replacing, moreover, the solitary naked man she then imagined with her own female body as, in one last liberatory gesture of divestiture, she "cast[s]" her "unpleasant, prickling garments from her" and stands "naked in the open air" (175). Death as such becomes a spiritual triumph over and defiant refusal of society's prohibitions, recalling the protofeminist implications of the midnight swimming episode. Moreover, as the sea "enfold[s]" Edna's naked body in its "soft, close embrace" (176), death is also eroticized, reaffirming Edna's material sensuousness and thwarted desire for autoerotic subjectivity. The scene replays, as it were, the erotic drowning figuratively enacted in Edna's orgasmic reaction to Mlle. Reisz's piano playing the evening of her triumphant swim: "she trembled, she was choking, and the tears blinded her" (72). And if Edna feels like "some new-born creature" (175) as she walks into the ocean, its enveloping waters—the primordial origin of life—take the place of the sensuous mother whom Adèle has just attempted to eclipse, the mother who affirms the heterogenous fluidity of identity that the phallocentric order attempts to regulate with mental dams.

The signs of personal or spiritual triumph that inhere in Edna's suicide, however, coexist with ambiguous traces of the illusory constructs of passion that have threatened throughout to transform her libidinal quest into a vague desire for the ineffable. For example, from Cynthia Griffin Wolff's Freudian perspective, Edna's final swim is proof of an ultimately regressive, narcissistic desire to return to the womb, to the impossible bliss of "oceanic" preoedipality. Likewise, Edna's final actions can be read as a late-century manifestation of the archetypal Romantic (and usually male) quest pattern, in which the solipsistic thrust of the hero toward transcendence inevitably leads to the oneness of oblivion; the disturbing implication of such a reading is that Edna, in entering heterosexual relationships, has internalized a male model of identity and ego-formation that subverts the earlier heterogeneity of her libidinal energies. Just as unsettling are the traces of illusory desire that infiltrate Edna's final moments of consciousness. Prominent among the sensory images that occur as her memory returns to the green Kentucky meadow of her childhood in her final moments of consciousness is that of the spurred cavalry officer, the very first of her impossible infatuations: "The spurs of the cavalry officer clanged as he walked across the porch. There was the hum of bees, and the musky odor of pinks filled the air" (176).

Thus a dialogue of multiple voices and conflicting aims makes up the narrative of Edna's suicide. Not only do the final pages of text resonate with multiple, ambiguous valences; so, too, on a sheerly formal level, an intricate system of subliminal echoes and cross-references constitutes the words we read: in a lyrical return of the textually repressed, significant images, phrases, and even entire sentences from previous scenes inundate the final paragraphs, creating a verbal flood of complex textures and plural sonorities that, as Yaeger notes, move the novel into a "heterogeneous zone" that challenges orthodox modes of seeing and categorizing events and objects.[56] By simultaneously inscribing this multiplicity—of voices, echoes, images, textual references—into her text on the levels of content and form, Chopin, as much as possible, holds her authority as "author" of Edna's awakening in abeyance and resists the temptation to impose a final meaning, an ultimate statement about female sexuality, onto the sexual trajectory of her female protagonist. "Truth," as Chopin laconically commented in one of her few published aesthetic pronouncements, "rests upon a shifting basis and is apt to be kaleidoscopic."[57] Likewise, Chopin's narrative admirably manages to capture the rhythm of impasse in which Edna has been stranded among multiple and competing truth claims without violating Edna's integrity as a fictional subject. In effect Chopin refuses to write desire as an appropriation of the other.

At the same time, the plurality of voices and the open-ended rhythm of impasse that characterize the ending evoke the rhythm of the polymorphous sexuality to which Edna's awakening initially gives expression: a shifting, merging, objectless desire that threatens to flood over, eradicate, the boundaries by which *fin-de-siècle* American patriarchy attempts to contain and hierarchize differences. Mirroring Edna's manifold desires in its textual multiplicity, Chopin's innovative narrative thus becomes its own autoerotic culmination *and* continuation at this point, and in the phenomenological weave of consciousness that holds author, protagonist, and reader in an indeterminate fluidity of intersubjective relation, the text transforms its potential anxieties about narrative authority into something more tangibly, sensually, intimately productive: we are touched, the text touches us.

The productive disturbances wrought by this tactile movement across boundaries are beautifully allegorized when Edna momentarily becomes, like Chopin, an author, telling her two sons a bedtime story that, "instead of soothing . . . excited them, and added to their *wakefulness*"; they are left "speculating about the conclusion of the tale which their mother promised to finish the following night" (92; emphasis added). So Chopin's open-ended narrative leaves her readers: awakened to disturbing realities, suspended without answers, hypothesizing beyond the pages of the text. The plot of female sexual awakening that issues from Chopin's imagination may frustrate some contemporary readers who wish that the text could end—despite *fin-de-siècle* improbability—in the emergence of a speaking female subject for whom "the rights of women" and "newly awakened" passion might coexist. But through the constant ebb and flow of its lyrical narration, the very *texture* of Chopin's discourse on the reading and writing of female sexuality forcefully articulates the material and fantasmatic strictures that, in all their modernity, thwart women's desires, even as this plot of sexual awakening speaks, in multiple and shifting languages, of a range of possibilities that suicide fails to silence.

D. H. LAWRENCE, *THE VIRGIN AND THE GIPSY*
"LISTEN FOR THE VOICE OF THE WATER"

Long ago we watched in frightened anticipation when Freud set out on his adventure into the hinterland of human consciousness. He was seeking for the unknown sources of the mysterious stream of consciousness. . . . Oh stream of hell which undermined my adolescence! I felt it streaming through my brain . . . encircling my established mind . . . bubbl[ing] up in the cerebellum. . . . Horrid stream! Whence did it come, and whither was it bound? The stream of consciousness!
—D. H. Lawrence, "Psychoanalysis and the Unconscious"[58]

The subject of Lawrence's fable of sexual initiation—or perhaps more properly its object—is Yvette Saywell, the "virgin" of its title. But the text opens with the legend of another woman's sexual awakening. "When the Vicar's wife went off with a young and penniless young man," the first sentence declares of Yvette's mother Cynthia, "the scandal knew no bounds" (3). I like to think that the vignette of "She-who-was-Cynthia" (so she comes to be known in her absence) provides an alternative to the ending of *The Awakening:* here is the married woman who, instead of committing suicide, escapes, leaving behind two daughters rather than the two sons whose "little lives" precipitate Edna's final despair. Cynthia's sexuality, moreover, is figured in images of fluidity evocative of *The Awakening.* Precisely because she is a "flow of life," her sexuality unleashes a scandal that—mirroring her transgressive energy—knows "no bounds" (8, 3). Such fantasies of unruly "flow," as Theweleit makes clear, are rooted in men's anxieties about loss of control—over themselves, over women. In face of the "danger of instability" (9) that such floods presage, the stony world of the

Rectory in which Yvette grows up erects a "stubborn fence of unison"—a dam of seeming consensus—to fend off the immoral "outer world" (12) where wayward desires dangerously proliferate. This familial barricade, then, becomes an emblem of the degree of repression Yvette must overcome in order to awaken that "hidden part of herself which she denied" (118): her secret sexual self.

On one level, the fact that Cynthia, unlike Edna, is allowed to succeed in her rebellion against marital norms is a measure of the historical changes differentiating the late 1890s setting of *The Awakening* from the more permissive 1920s milieu providing the backdrop to Lawrence's sexual psychodrama. On another level, however, the staging of awakening in both these narratives suggestively points to the psychodramatic and structural continuities, rather than differences, that situate both these fictions of female sexuality within a shared imaginary geography of desire overlapping Victorian and modern periods.[59] Within this symbolic terrain Lawrence stages an allegory of sexual awakening that echoes Chopin's on several levels. Drawing on metaphors we have already encountered in *The Awakening,* Lawrence opens his narrative by likening Yvette to a young sloop seemingly "slipping from the harbour, into the wide seas of life," but in fact "moving from one chain anchorage to another" (16)—that which appears fluid movement is in reality another form of confinement. To reverse this process, Yvette must undergo the same breaking loose from moorings as Edna Pontellier, the same freeing from ego controls, in order to encourage libidinal desire to surface from its hidden depths.[60] The "mesmerised states" (46) into which Yvette repeatedly lapses in this coming-of-age fable thus become markers of these subliminal tides overtaking rational thought. Such mental and erotic currents are mirrored on the formal plane by a series of techniques that echo the incipiently modernist strategies developed in *The Awakening;* for the ultimate effect of the imagistic lyricism, impressionism, and noncausal structural rhythms shared by both narratives is to suggest the random drift of thought and the even less conscious flux of desire.[61]

Despite these similarities, exactly *how* Lawrence chooses to tell the story of a woman's sexual awakening, and the crises of authority and anxiety that his choices occasion, profoundly distinguish his effort from Chopin's. Perhaps the most intriguing difference can be traced to Lawrence's handling of the topos of water that, for both narratives, implies a politics of female desire. On the overt level, the fluidity evoked in Lawrence's fiction signifies the freeing of female sexuality from moral constraints, as it does for Chopin. Hence the old Gypsy woman's prophecy that Yvette must "listen for the voice of the water" (146) in order to realize her desires is literally and metaphorically fulfilled when the climactic flooding of the river Papple unleashes a correspondingly figurative flood in Yvette's psyche: "She was barely conscious: as if the flood was in her soul" (155). But on a less overt level, Lawrence effects a partial, ambiguous relocation of these floods, so that they come to exist, as we shall see, within the body armor of masculinity itself. This maneuver not only bespeaks Lawrence's personal uneasiness about that "mysterious" and "horrid stream" that he accuses Freud's "adventure into the hinterland of human consciousness" of having uncovered in his adolescent psyche (see the epigraph above). Precisely because of the literary and psychoanalytic association of those "hinterlands" of unconscious flows with femaleness, Lawrence's strategic displacement and redirecting of "feminine" floods of desire in this text also reveal an anxiety about female sexual agency that he feels threatens men's textual and sexual authority. Indeed, if at the end of *The Virgin and the Gipsy* the flood's destruction of the repressive world of the rectory has not necessarily launched the now-awakened Yvette onto the "wide seas of life" (16) as promised in the opening pages, this may be partly because the very structure of Lawrence's version of the plot of female sexual awakening conceals more "chain anchorages" than one.

Mythopoetic Form and Psychosexual Representation

In generic terms, *The Virgin and the Gipsy* is an allegory of sexuality and psychosexual awakening that operates as much on a mythopoetic as on a realistic level. In a manner befitting such allegorical and mythic shadings, its thematic structure hinges on a very clear-cut opposition, established from the opening pages, between the repressive world of the Rectory and the "free-born" self (136) that lies dormant in Yvette, awaiting release. If the Rectory is variously described as "dank," "sordid," "stuffy," "unclean" (16)—words repeated so often within single paragraphs that they assume a surreal effect—Yvette's spirit is associated with the outdoors, mobility, sunshine, nature. As long as Yvette remains physically and psychologically imprisoned within the walls of the Rectory, where the act of throwing open a window to admit "a breath of fresh air" (22) becomes grounds for serious reprimand, she also remains, in the narrator's phrase, "shut up . . . inside [herself]" (16), suffering from an "intolerable irritation" originating "deep inside" (19)—an irritation for which, like Edna's first inchoate stirrings of dissatisfaction during her midnight vigil, Yvette has no explanation or language. Not surprisingly, Yvette meets the Gypsy in the bracing air of the outdoors, and to the degree that the two are imagistically joined on the same side in a struggle against the values and morality of the Rectory, the narrative valorizes their transgressive union as the triumph of Nature—and of the "natural"—over the unclean, unnatural, and degenerate lives of the English middle-class: "She was conscious of her gipsy, as she sat there musing in the sun . . . she felt intensely that *that* was home for her: the gipsy camp, the fire, the stool, the man with the hammer, the old crone . . . everything was natural to her, her home, as if she had been born there" (151–52).

But this rather unsubtle dialectic—pitting Victorian repression against healing Nature—is displaced by a second, more subtle polarity as the story progresses: namely, the sexual, and even epistemological, opposition intimated by the title's copulative "and." For in the case of the dance of attraction that escalates between unknowing "virgin" and knowing "Gipsy," the imagery initially used to valorize *both* Yvette and the Gypsy on the same side of the divide ("Yes, if she belonged to any side . . . it was his" [143]) comes to pit the Gypsy's elemental superiority, as a pure force of nature, against the overly civilized, sexually neurotic Yvette. In this latter formulation, that is, the opposition between freedom and repression has taken on specifically gendered, hierarchical connotations. The message that emerges from the slippage between these two sets of oppositions—the dynamics of which create the text's driving desire—is simple: Yvette's awakening must be ignited by a dark, masculine other external to herself. Just as autoerotic self-discovery is not an option in this text, woman's empowerment depends first on submission to her male superior.

I will return to the power dynamics—and the gendered valences—encoded in both of these dialectics, but first I would like to turn to the ways in which this structural thematic is heightened by a series of formal strategies designed to give expression to the libidinal and psychosexual currents subtending Yvette's awakening. On one level, as my terms have already begun to indicate, beneath its apparent realism this text unfolds as an allegorical fiction: Lawrence imbues his narrative of female awakening with a mythopoetic quality that reduces his characters to universal types in a timeless drama of sexual attraction and desire. Thus we have the nameless, shadowlike Gypsy, who primarily looms as a psychic embodiment of eros and manifests an uncanny likeness to countless other darkly phallic Laurentian gods. Likewise Yvette's individuality is subsumed in her archetypal function as the Virgin. The descriptive fetishizing of her "young, tender face" (39), "soft, vague waywardness" (49), and "soft, virgin, heedless candour" (88) reduces her to one essence—the "dark, tremulous, potent secret of her virginity" (84).[62] Even though both Yvette and the Gypsy are assigned character traits that make them interesting, even unpredictable, individuals in their own right, the primary effect of the text's mythic format is to diffuse their personalities onto the archetypal level, where their representative value as universal Man and Woman overshadows their individuality. As a result, the novella assumes the aura of a fairy tale, its plot suffused with a timeless, dreamlike quality.[63]

If one function of *The Virgin and the Gipsy*'s mythopoetic structure is to give representable form to a level of instinctual response that exists just below the threshold of active consciousness—hence the emphasis on characters as psychic archetypes—Lawrence simultaneously attempts to evoke the impingement of libidinal desire on mental activity through the sequencing of narrative events according to associative rather than strictly causal patterns. The result, as in *The Awakening,* is that the narrated plane of reality often appears to be a projection of subconscious drives or forces. For example, Yvette's erotic fantasy as she lies in bed and imagines herself caressed by the "naked insinuation of desire" in the Gypsy's "bold eyes" (63) becomes reality in the immediately following chapter, when the Gypsy shows up at the door of the Rectory and gazes upon her with a "naked suggestion of desire" that echoes not only the content but the very language of her daydream (80); no wonder the third-person narrator says of the Gypsy's magical appearance, "It was like something seen in a sleep" (77). The ultimate example of reality taking its cue from subliminal impulses is the climactic flooding of the river Papple, which echoes the metaphoric floods of desire already raging within Yvette's subconscious.

While such structural arrangements subtly evoke the associative processes characteristic of interior states, Lawrence's use of lyrical repetition in individual passages forms a more immediate attempt to capture the processes of instinctual motivation in third-person prose. In such narrative moments the litanic repetition, with slight variations, of key words or phrases creates units of lulling prose-poetry that, if only on the syntactical level, "stop time" by momentarily halting the temporal progression of plot. Such plays with the temporal and spatial dimensions of narrative in order to suggest states of interiority point to Lawrence's modernist affinities. A paradigmatic example occurs during Yvette's return to the Gypsy camp in chapter 6. On a *conscious* level, as the narrator takes pains to inform us, Yvette has not been thinking of the Gypsy at all as the Friday of her visit approaches (95), while on a *subconscious* level she is preparing to give herself sexually to the Gypsy. Arriving at the camp, Yvette is handed a cup of steaming coffee by the Gypsy—a purely realistic novelistic detail that serves as the springboard plummeting Yvette into a state of suspended consciousness. Yvette's trancelike condition, in turn, is registered on the narrative plane by the text's shift from a mimetic to lyric mode in which the rhythmic repetition of images and phrases halts the narrative's forward momentum, simulating a sense of time's momentary suspension as libidinal desires well forth from the subconscious:

> Vaguely, as in a dream, she received from him the cup of coffee. She *was aware* only of his silent figure. . . . Her will had departed from her limbs, he had power over her: his shadow was on her.
>
> And he, as he blew his hot coffee, *was aware* of one thing only, the mysterious fruit of her virginity, her perfect tenderness in the body.
>
> At length he put down his coffee-cup by the fire, then looked round at her. Her hair fell across her face, as she tried to sip from the hot cup. On her face was that *tender look of sleep,* which *a nodding flower* has when it is *full out,* like *a mysterious early flower,* she was *full out,* like *a snowdrop* which

spreads its three white wings in a flight into the *waking sleep* of its brief blossoming. The *waking sleep* of her *full-opened* virginity, entranced like *a snowdrop* in the sunshine, was upon her.

The gipsy, *supremely aware* of her, waited for her like the substance of a shadow, as shadow waits and is there. (101–102; emphases added)

What we have here is an intensely psychodramatic representation of that moment in the dance of mutual attraction when instinct assumes precedence over thought, and consciousness of time simply dissolves. The graphically gendered dynamics of this heightened moment—first, Yvette's subliminal "awareness" of *her* abdication of "will" in face of the Gypsy's "power over her," and then his subliminal "awareness" of the receptive virginity that awaits *his* taking—are linguistically conveyed in the parallel construction of these sentences ("she was aware only . . ."; "he . . . was aware of one thing only"). With the sentence of the next paragraph that begins, "On her face was that tender look of sleep," Lawrence undertakes to represent the intrusion of the unconscious—which he calls blood-consciousness[64]—into Yvette's waking life, as the rhythmic variations on waking/sleeping ("that tender look of sleep . . . waking sleep . . . waking sleep") and flower similes ("like a mysterious early flower . . . like a snowdrop . . . like a snowdrop") evoke the sway of libidinal desire as it nudges Yvette toward sexual receptivity ("full out . . . full out . . . full-opened virginity"). Incantatory passages like this abound, creating textual spaces that temporarily halt the plot's forward momentum, rendering palpable the process of desire emerging from states of repression.

The "waking sleep" that Yvette experiences in this passage is reminiscent as well of the general "vagueness" with which she moves through life, barely conscious of her surroundings—"like walking in one of those autumn mists," the narrator comments, "when . . . you don't quite know where you are" (82–83). Indeed, Yvette's "straying, absentminded detachment from things" is read by the men attracted to her precisely as a signifier of her "peculiar virgin tenderness" (122), that is to say, her readiness for sexual initiation. Lawrence thus suggests that the subject of awakening must to some degree give herself over to the drift of unconscious desire, allow herself to float "detach[ed] . . . from things" (122), in order to facilitate the emergence of eros from years of repression and denial. But while *The Awakening*, which dramatizes a similar state of drifting, shows how such passive yielding almost inevitably comes into jarring conflict with social structures for the female subject, placing Edna outside the pale, the trajectory of Lawrence's novella creates an *alignment* between the psychological injunction to abdicate rational control and Yvette's successful emergence as a sexually mature woman within her social world.

To determine more precisely the implications of and ironies created by the sexual politics underlying these aesthetic and formal choices, we need to look more closely at the dynamics of power encoded in two closely interlinked structuring patterns running throughout the text: first, the slippages between the forementioned sets of oppositions—the Rectory versus Nature, Yvette versus the Gipsy—that propel the narrative's trajectory of desire; and second, the elements of Freudian family romance—particularly, of oedipal triangulation—that reinforce these oppositions. Indeed, despite Lawrence's overt rejection of Freud, his obsessive replaying of aspects of oedipal conflict, when read in the context of the alternative models of desire offered by Deleuze and Guattari, may begin to clarify the crises of authority, the anxieties of narration, that complicate Lawrence's desire to authorize female sexuality as a subject worthy of "modern" fiction.

The "Family Romance" and the Devouring Mother

The two structuring patterns that I have just mentioned intersect most obviously in the world of the Rectory. In the first instance Yvette's home symbolizes the falsities that oppose the realm of natural passion, and in the second it provides the site in which the "family romance" of the Saywells unfolds across two generations. As earlier noted, in Lawrence's social vision the Rectory represents all that is wrong with the standards of Victorian morality that have persisted into early-twentieth-century middle-class life. It is worth pausing to ask who, among its inhabitants, serves as the real foe of progress here. Although Yvette's oedipally structured conflict with her father might seem to indicate that the Rector—as the titular head of the household—is a likely candidate, it is significant that from its beginning the narrative identifies as "the central figure in the house" (5) and as Yvette's "great rival" (9) not the Rector but his mother. Known as the Mater, this "cunning" old body rules her family by virtue of what Lawrence calls "the static inertia of her unsavory power" (29). This power masks itself as mother-love but is as obdurate and unmoving as the stone-walled house in which she sanctimoniously rules. Her physical senses failing—she is nearly deaf and half blind—the Mater epitomizes all that is unsensual; "sitting in her ancient obesity" and "'rift[ing]' in gross physical complacency" (23–24), this grotesque relic is associated with rank materiality, mat(t)er in its most chthonic, nonproductive state. As such, Lawrence's Mater—as her name also implies—forms a debased version of the archetypal Magna Mater of ancient religions. Simultaneously the Mater serves as the instrument of Lawrence's sociopolitical critique, for her physical description parodies that of Queen Victoria, the most beloved middle-class symbol of nineteenth-century maternity and female rule: hence the constant references to the Mater "reign[ing]" over the household (20), "enthroned" in her chair (28), and sporting a look of "horrible majesty" (23) that, from lace cap to pendulous jowls to bulging stomach, twit countless portraits of this icon of Victorian feminine authority.

And it is precisely the Mater's combination of female rule and maternity that Lawrence's narrative finds so threatening. For the Mater's goal is to coerce the "family [into becoming] her own extended ego" (12), a status she achieves by becoming the "devouring mother" incarnate, greedily consuming the lives of her offspring.[65] The awful power of mother-love to thwart the individuation of one's progeny is most graphically represented in the case of Yvette's weak-willed father. By playing up to the Rector's "skulking self-love" (7) and by using flattery to reduce him to a state of infantile dependence after his wife Cynthia's desertion, the Mater binds her son to her greater will, thereby insuring her own domination within the household hierarchy. Such a dynamic points to the elements of unresolved oedipal conflict pervading the Rectory. For the power dynamic of mother and son depends on the virtual erasure of the Mater's husband (the narrative makes only a single reference to the deceased Pater, referring to his function as the Mater's bed-warmer for 54 years). For the son, the result is, at least on one level, a realization of the male child's oedipal fantasy: the Rector has symbolically done away with the father and taken his place in the mother's affections, but at the price of never resolving his oedipal complex (he remains locked in a stage of infantile dependency). However, in Lawrence's recasting of the Oedipus myth, it is perhaps even more pointedly the mother who realizes her oedipal desire: to rid herself of the inadequate husband and secure her son's love forever.[66] By forcing the Rector into the self-emasculating position of serving as *her* phallus in the world, the instrument of her "unsavoury power" (29), the Mater completes her unnatural usurpation of the male's rightful position in the family.

All this talk of devouring and castrating one's progeny reveals a not-so-latent anxiety about female sexuality underlying Lawrence's representation of the Mater, one that complicates the narrative's ostensible endorsement of Yvette's sexual awakening. This anxiety becomes explicit in an image that occurs at the end of chapter 2, in which the Mater is likened to an "old toad" that waits outside a beehive, and "with a demonish lightning-like snap of its pursed jaws, caught every bee as it came out to launch into the air, swallowed them one after the other, as if to consume the whole hive-full, into its aged, bulging, purse-like wrinkledness" (30). An image of *vagina dentatis,* this unflattering portrait encodes a specifically male fear of losing authority before the all-powerful mother. For the Mater's most heinous transgression against the natural order, Lawrence stresses, is "seeking forever her own female power" (11), a power which depends on the willful castration of all patriarchy's potential "sons." Within the logic of Lawrence's sexual fable, the devouring mother must be destroyed, then, her destructive "female power" replaced by the affirmative "dark, complete power" (102) residing in the Gypsy, the phallic god incarnate.

If the Mater as devouring mother brings into focus the repressive, life-denying connotations of the Rectory that the Gypsy's life-giving potency is erected to supplant, it is interesting to consider the role that maternity plays in the second generation of oedipal triangulation at work within the Rectory—one with implications for the structural oppositions giving momentum to the text's awakening plot. In this triangle—in which the emphasis falls on the daughter Yvette's struggle for individuation—the role of paternal authority, first of all, is occupied by the Rector, who in this position recuperates some of the male authority he has abdicated as emasculated mama's boy in the first-generational instance of triangulation. The role of mother, meanwhile, is diachronically split between Cynthia, Yvette's biological mother, and the Mater, who stands in for Cynthia in her absence. Within Yvette's subconscious, She-Who-Was-Cynthia functions, therefore, as what Freud called the "phallic mother," the all-powerful, beneficent maternal imago that precedes the female child's discovery of the mother's castration or lack. Once lost, this imago is forever idealized and mourned; and, indeed, Cynthia is represented in her daughter's memory as a bright glow of sunshine, a ray of hope and freedom. Given the Freudian contours of the female developmental pattern emerging from Lawrence's text, it is also appropriate that the all-powerful phallic mother quite literally be replaced by the devouring/castrating mother.[67] For the Mater, as a negative maternal imago, serves to remind her granddaughters (as Adèle reminds Edna) of their own lack, at the same time that she threatens Yvette and Lucille with the further castration—infantilization and sexual frigidity—that she has already visited upon her own offspring (which, in addition to the docile Rector, include the colorless, live-at-home bachelor Fred and spinster Cissie, a caricature of angry sexual frustration).

A telling structural parallel emerges in comparing the triangles formed by the first and second generations of Saywells: just as the erasure of one parent, the Pater, has facilitated the incestuous bonding of mother and son in the first, so the absence of another parent, Cynthia, opens the way to the incestuous intensity of Yvette's struggle with her father in the second. In each, that is, it is the *absence* of the same-sex parent that creates the gap in the triangle that eases the way for the emergence of incestuous desires that, notably, are *heterosexually* rather than homoerotically oriented. Here Lawrence's delineation of the erotics of family life, despite his professed objections to Freud, anticipates in significant aspects Freud's explanation of the female oedipal complex in "Female Sexuality" (1931) and "Femininity" (1933), lectures published in the years immediately following the posthumous appearance of *The Virgin and the Gipsy*. As noted earlier in this chapter, Freud suggests that the girl's developmental trajectory not only includes a change of aim (from "phallic"—i.e., clitoral—to vaginal excitation), but also a change in primary love object (from mother to father). With this latter shift in parental allegiances, the mother figure now becomes the girl's hated antagonist (recall that the Mater is said to be Yvette's "great rival"), whose place the child will attempt to take in the father's affections ("Femininity," 107). These shifts hinge, ultimately, on the girl's acceptance of her daughterly lack under the Law of the Father ("Perhaps we haven't really *got* any sex" [118], Yvette and Lucille will concur). Whether Yvette feels "incestuous desire" for the Rector or whether a more complex dynamic is being played out in their relationship is a question to which I will return; but what is clear is that in the claustrophobic psychodrama being enacted within the Rectory, Yvette is caught in an oedipal struggle upon which her future sexual development—its expression or repression—seems to hinge.

The Gypsy's Speculum

So how does the Gypsy, the outsider par excellence, fit into this Freudian family romance? How is the power struggle waged between Yvette and her father, as the agent of her repression, transformed or displaced into the sexual combat between Yvette and the Gypsy, as the agent of her revitalization? Freud argues that "normal" femininity can only be achieved when the daughter shifts her impossible (because taboo) desire for the father to a male other outside the family, one who thus functions as a father-substitute and a means of legitimate sexual fulfillment. While at first glance it may seem ill-advised to describe the Gypsy—who seems so antithetical to everything the Rector stands for—as a father-substitute, Lawrence makes it resoundingly clear that the source of Yvette's overpowering attraction to the Gypsy is his complete otherness. As racial other, the Gypsy's dark foreignness stands opposed to Yvette's bland Englishness; as social and class other, he is a self-proclaimed "pariah" who wages eternal war on the educated bourgeoisie to which Yvette belongs; as the ·personification of carnal knowledge, the holder of the keys to Yvette's own self-knowledge, he is her sexual other; in his figuration as Yvette's shadow-self (the phrase "his shadow was upon her" echoes throughout the text), he represents the other within, her psychological other. The effect of all this otherness is to rewrite the text's initial opposition between the natural and the repressive, which has imagistically *joined* Yvette and the Gypsy against the forces of the Rectory, into an *opposition between* the would-be lovers, in which terms like *nature, freedom,* and *outsidership* accrue to the male figure, while the female comes to epitomize the very values against which she has earlier rebelled—society, England, refinement, sexual and emotional sterility. In the process, a polarity founded on socially constructed values is textually reformulated as an elemental sexual polarity.

As the values assigned these polarities also suggest, the Gypsy has become not just Yvette's opposite but more specifically her superior in power. This superiority, indeed, provides the final charge to her attraction to the Gypsy, since in Lawrence's sexual epistemology, otherness and power together create female heterosexual desire. Thus Yvette will marvel upon her first view of the Gypsy, "Of all the men that she had ever seen, this one was the only one who was stronger than she was, in her own kind of strength" (48). Such a statement enacts the slippage between sets of opposition that I have been talking about; it aligns Yvette and the Gypsy on one side of the fence (sharing "her own kind of strength"), at the same time that it enforces a hierarchical distinction ("stronger than she") upon which the sexual and gendered dynamics of their attraction hinge. The elemental *maleness* of the Gypsy's power and strength, moreover, is emphasized in Lawrence's representation of his visual gaze and the mesmerizing effect it has on Yvette when she becomes its object. During their first encounter, his "full, conceited, impudent black eyes" transfix and "transfus[e]" Yvette with their seminal force, inciting an immediate physical reaction—"Yvette felt it, felt it in her knees" (43)—that soon washes over her entire body and, in terms evocative of Theweleit's *Male Fantasies,* brings the proverbial floods of desire repressed within Yvette to her bodily surface: "He looked at Yvette as he passed, staring her full in the eyes. . . . The surface of her body seemed to turn to water" (47). The mastery encoded in the Gypsy's gaze is even more blatantly stated upon her second visit to the Gypsy camp: "He looked into her eyes . . . with that naked insinuation of desire which acted on her like a spell, and robbed her of her will. . . . She wanted someone, or something to have power over her" (80, 82). The Gypsy's invasive gaze has become a powerful tool of persuasion.

Now, within Lawrence's sexual metaphysics, a loss of will usually denotes a positive event for both men and women, and, as Edna's experience in *The Awakening* also dramatizes, a temporary relinquishing of ego control forms a necessary stage in any person's sexual awakening, in order to encourage the emergence of libidinal desire from layers of repression. But Yvette's powerlessness only parades as a universal human precondition to sexual initiation. For the "transfusing" and "insinuating" power of the penetrative gaze that "robs" her of her will and that is represented as "shoot[ing] her in some vital, undiscovered place, unerring" (90), is figured in bluntly phallic terms, which in turn codes her submission as feminine and her sexuality as solely receptive. In this light, the curious simile that Lawrence uses to express Yvette's admiration of the Gypsy's "fine, quick hips, *alert as eyes*" (90; emphasis added) makes absolute sense on the psychological level, where alert eyes and erect penis stand in metonymic relationship to one another; this is a man who indeed "shoots" from the hip, as it were, and his visual/sexual aim is "unerring" in its ability to penetrate to "the dark, tremulous, potent secret of . . . virginity" (84) that is figured as lying within Yvette, awaiting discovery and release: "It was some hidden part of herself which she denied, that part which mysteriously and unconfessedly responded to him" (118). In such textual moments, the language of feminine "secrets" and "hidden" interiors dovetails with the early-twentieth-century belief, in the fields of both psychology and sexology, in "interiority" as the site of the true self, in sexuality as the key to identity, and in a hydraulics of containment and release regulating the operation of psychic and libidinal "fluids" alike.

The gender imbalances underlying Lawrence's narrative of female sexual awakening can also be measured in the irony that this secret interior realm remains an "undiscovered place" (90) to its possessor; without the Gypsy's penetrative power of (in)sight, Yvette would remain in the dark about her own "dark, tremulous, potent secret." It is fascinating, then, to discover that in Yvette's erotic reveries about the Gypsy, the memory of his transfusing gaze quite literally serves the function of a speculum, providing the (phallic) mirror that allows her to view her sexuality "from inside" for the first time. "She had been looked upon," the indirect free discourse reports of her memory of his gaze, "not from the outside, but from the inside, from her secret female self" (84). Yvette's revelatory feeling of being seen from the inside by the Gypsy is rendered all the more dramatic by the fact that at this very moment she is playing "dress up" before an actual mirror where *her* gaze is fixed on her costumed reflection (82). The female look, that is, is arrested on the surface, just as female development is often viewed, in psychoanalytic terms, as arrested at the narcissistic stage (for an instructive contrast, one might consider Lucy Snowe's disavowal of her mirror image in the pink dress, in the Vashti chapter of *Villette*). The Gypsy, however, as the narrative emphasizes, sees *right through* Yvette's "pretty face and . . . pretty ways" (84) to the "real" sensual self beneath the reflection. This contrast in ways of looking (male scopophilia versus female narcissism) vividly illustrates, fifty years in advance, Luce Irigaray's theory of the specular logic by which phallocentric culture maintains its dominance. The speculum, which might be a means of revealing woman to herself, becomes, in the scopophilic logic of western cultural narratives, a substitute phallus which implants within women an *image* of feminine sexuality that phallocentric culture needs women to "see" there, in to order to serve as men's inverse images ("not-men") rather than as "women."[68] The cumulative effect of Yvette's realization of the Gypsy's specular (in)-sight, then, is to secure her utter submission to his spell, which reinforces female masochism as part of the machinery of heterosexual desire. Indeed, Jessica Benjamin's definition of the female masochist's "search for recognition of the self by an other who alone is powerful enough to bestow this recognition" forms a disconcertingly accurate description of Yvette's ready submission to the Gypsy.[69]

One alternative to the specular logic that reduces women to "not-men" would be for women to serve as each other's mirrors—to put the speculum, metaphorically speaking, into the hands of women, where it would cease to be a phallic instrument of domination and become a means of self-discovery. Something like this happens in *The Awakening*, where Edna's sexual awakening *begins* with other women, triggering a level of sexual confirmation that comes from within and precedes her heterosexual entanglements. In contrast, despite the fact that *The Virgin and the Gipsy* begins as a tale of two sisters, implying a story of twinned female self-discovery, Lawrence gradually removes Lucille from the sphere of action in which Yvette's awakening takes place.[70] This shift in focalization, depriving Yvette of her one female confidant and mirroring self, makes it easier for Lawrence to represent Yvette's blossoming eroticism, her "natural" sexuality, as other-directed rather than self-directed. For Yvette's awakening is significantly void of the autoeroticism so crucial to Edna's and Lucy Snowe's erotic quests; one only need compare the intense autoerotics of Lucy's hallucinatory, drugged quest through the female geography of the park at night or Edna's "luxurious" (84) exploration of her body as she stretches out in bed at Chênière to the one depiction of what parades as female autoerotic pleasure in *The Virgin and the Gipsy*. At first glance, chapter 4's description of Yvette lying in bed while thinking sexual thoughts might seem comparable to the Chênière episode.[71] Yet, while Lawrence's wording seems to connote the pleasures of masturbation— Yvette "quiver[s] suddenly," feels "as if a drug had cast her in a new, molten mould," lies "prone and powerless," then "stir[s] luxuriously" as she feels a "release" of energy in "her limbs"—it is surely telling that the source of Yvette's stimulation specifically has to do with her memory of the Gypsy's "big, bold eyes upon her" and the "naked insinuation of desire" they hold (63). Lawrence represents Yvette's autoerotic pleasure of the moment, that is, as dependent on her memory the Gypsy's active, naked gaze "insinuat[-ing]" itself into her interior spaces (of memory, of body).

Yvette has as much a right to use a fantasy of penetration to attain masturbatory pleasure as anyone else, of course, but the fact that Lawrence seems intent on inscribing even Yvette's private fantasies with an other-directed rather than a self-directed mode of satisfaction echoes certain disturbing ideological assumptions in Freudian theories of female development. The "Femininity" essay, as already noted, argues that the girl's successful resolution of her oedipal complex involves not only a change in object of desire (from mother to father) but also a shift in aim (from clitoral excitation to "the truly feminine vagina" [104]). Just as the former transition guarantees heterosexual identity as the outcome of "normal" female development, the latter implicitly valorizes heterosexual intercourse—consisting of the active (or "insinuating") presence of the male partner and the passive (or "prone") receptivity of the woman—as the *sine qua non* of female sexual satisfaction. Freud's description of the psychological effects on the girl of this change in erotogenic zone betrays the fact that what is actually at stake in his theory is less the "truth" of "femininity" than masculine anxieties about which sex has claim to activity: "Along with the abandonment of clitoral masturbation, *a certain amount of activity is renounced.* Passivity now has the upper hand. . . . You can see that a wave of development like this, which clears the phallic [i.e., clitoral] activity out of the way, smooths the ground for femininity" (113; emphasis added).

As we shall see, the "wave" that makes way for true "femininity" will make an interesting return at the end of *The Virgin and the Gipsy*, in the form of the flood that flattens the Rectory. And what Lawrence's narrative, when read in tandem with Freud's, makes perfectly clear is that renouncing "a certain amount of activity" is the *precondition* of Yvette's sexual awakening; only by first submitting to the Gypsy's superior power will her "feminine" desires, her "true" inner nature, be set free. Thus, while the overt message of Lawrence's sexual fable is that salvation comes from aligning oneself with natural forces, the binary oppositions and Freudian dynamics shaping its trajectory reveal a more covert ideological message—namely, that natural force, first embodied in man, is necessary to awaken the latent floods of sexuality in woman. The assertion that feminine "passivity" somehow holds "the upper hand" in this scenario of awakening only re-articulates the structural sleight-of-hand whereby the *fact* of powerlessness—surely the Gypsy's primary effect on Yvette—is touted as a *fantasy* of empowerment.

Between Men

So, given the immense attraction between Yvette and the Gypsy, and given her recognition of his "dark, complete power" (102) over her, what does it finally take to unite the two, and why does it take so long? The answer to both questions lies in Yvette's tortured relationship with her father, which further complicates the gendered power dynamics underlying her awakening. For Yvette's desires are not only directed *towards* the Gypsy but *against* the Rector: in the process the Rector becomes, ironically, the ultimate agent of Yvette's awakening, propelling her into the Gypsy's waiting arms. Two identically structured, highly psychodramatic sequences illuminate this truth. Each involves a brutalizing encounter between father and daughter that assumes classically incestuous overtones, and each, ironically, awakens Yvette more emphatically than ever to her passion for the Gypsy and, hence, to her true "femininity."

The first of these two devastating confrontations occurs in chapter 4, when the Rector discovers that Yvette has borrowed money from Aunt Cissy's charity fund. The effect of his "sneering" put-downs is to leave Yvette feeling "crushed and deflowered," as if her "whole flesh" has been "defiled" (57). Psychologically, as Lawrence's word choices imply, Yvette has undergone a kind of rape. However, the sense of debasement that ensues ("I am nothing" [55]) is transformed into a nascent awakening to "the other sanctity of herself" (58), a recognition of self-worth that fills her heart "with repugnance, against the Rectory," as her consciousness aligns this "other sanctity" with the freedom of Gypsy life. Moving from Gypsies in general to one in particular, Yvette's mental associations provoke her most conscious articulation of sexual desire ever, in the erotic revery I have already noted:

> And the gipsy man himself! Yvette quivered suddenly. . . . The absolutely naked insinuation of desire [in his eyes] made her lie prone and powerless in the bed, as if a drug had cast her in a new, molten mould. . . . The thought of the gipsy had released the life of her limbs, and crystallized in her heart the hate of the rectory: so that now she felt potent, instead of impotent. (63)

Not only does this passage enact the central ambiguity in the text's representation of female sexual awakening and rebirth—namely, that to become "potent," to have one's limbs filled with life, woman must first "lie prone and powerless"—but it also suggests the intimate psychological link between Yvette's hatred of the Rectory and her nascent desire for the Gypsy: the two emotions symbiotically feed upon each other.

The process of repudiating the father for a substitutive object of desire is even more explicitly represented in the grotesquely surreal confrontation that occurs in chapter 8, when the snarling Rector denounces Yvette's friendship with the "immoral" Eastwoods as a sign that she too will "go the way" of her mother Cynthia (134). But, ironically, at the very moment that the Rector is accusing Yvette of depravities that she "had best curb, and quickly, if you don't intend to finish in a criminal-lunacy asylum" (133), the narrative reveals that "somewhere in his mind he was thinking unspeakable depravities about his daughter" (132). The desire to curb Yvette's sexuality, then, turns out to be a displacement of his own barely "curbed" sexual thoughts *about* Yvette. Yvette's initial reaction to her father's threats, as in the earlier sequence, is first to feel as if her entire sense of self has been crushed; this feeling, however, is again superseded by an outright expression of physical desire *for* the Gypsy that articulates itself as a rejection of the father: "She wanted, now to be held against the slender fine-shaped breast of the gipsy. . . . She wanted to be confirmed *by him, against her father*" (137; emphasis added). The father, ironically, has completed his daughter's awakening into the very sexual consciousness he has attempted to suppress.[72]

There is, however, one salient difference between these otherwise structurally parallel sequences, a difference that highlights the excessive narrative stratagems to which Lawrence must resort in order to lend an aura of inevitability to the text's climactic event—the Gypsy's timely rescue of Yvette from the sudden flood that, to borrow Freud's words, "smooths the ground for femininity" by mowing down the repressive world of the Rectory. At the conclusion of both these sequences, Yvette's erotic fantasies of the Gypsy are followed by his literal appearance at the Rectory's doorway, as if in answer to her dreams; both times he delivers a summons that Yvette visit him at the Gypsy encampment. The first time, she indeed goes, and her entrance into his wagon on the pretense of washing her hands—just as his "dark" will is "bathing" and "washing" over her (102)—is interrupted on the threshold by the arrival of the Eastwoods, in an extreme instance of sexual/textual interruptus. The second time, however, she *doesn't* go, despite her wish to do so. Instead, as Lawrence informs us in the first lines of the fateful chapter 9, "Yvette did not keep her promise. . . . She had a curious reluctance always, towards taking action, or making any real move of her own. She always wanted someone else to make a move for her" (149).

Always, I am tempted to ask? True, throughout Yvette has been characterized by a certain drifting, unthinking vagueness, and the effect of her encounters with the Gypsy is to rob her of her active will. But it is equally true that, up to this point in the text, she has kept herself in fairly constant motion, literally and psychologically speaking (note her constant bike rides and car trips, as well as the initiatives she takes in her rebellions against the family). Hence her supposed "curious reluctance" to move or take action at the opening of chapter 9 seems an overstatement, one which, in breaking the above pattern, ultimately attests to the extreme narrative manipulation necessary in order to create a situation at this point in the plot in which Yvette *has* to be rescued by external powers, rather than taking her cure into, as it were, her own hands (a double entendre that is all too appropriate in light of Freud's devaluation of clitoral masturbatory satisfaction). Her desire to have "*someone else* make a move for her," that is, becomes a pretext for *Lawrence's* desire to make that "move" and disguise it as her own wish. It is at this point in the narrative that Lawrence's textual authority decisively becomes an expression of sexual authority as well: by channeling the potential flux of Yvette's desire to fit the patriarchal fantasy of inert helplessness, he effectively silences Yvette as a speaking subject, making her the subject of his own statement about female sexuality. Consequently, on the same page he describes Yvette wandering in the Rectory garden by the swollen river "too lazy, too lazy" to do anything except drift in a half-conscious, "half dreamy" (149) state, vaguely "expecting something" (150).

That "something" arrives with a double emphasis, as the roaring flood and the Gypsy burst onto the scene in as nearly simultaneous timing as can be achieved in prose: the breaking-down of the dams of repression and advent of the sexual savior come in one package, setting loose the floodgates of libidinal desire that signal the advent of the final stage in Yvette's awakening. Just how the narrative incorporates—or fails to incorporate—these potentially unruly floods of desire within the restrictively Freudian contours of Yvette's emergent "femininity" lies at the heart of the authorial anxieties underpinning Lawrence's version of the plot of female sexual awakening and speaks to the sexual/textual politics inscribed within it.

Feminine Floodgates, Phallic Fountains

"Listen for the voice of the water," Yvette has been warned by the old Gypsy woman, along with the admonition, "Be braver in your body" (146). This double-hinged prophecy anticipates the highly charged climax toward which the novel's whole trajectory has been moving: the flood as sexual union, sexual union as flooding. That we have now entered the realm of psychodrama is signaled by the "state of unconsciousness" (158), "the blind unconscious frenzy" (159), and the "ghastly sickness like a dream" (156) that overtake Yvette. For as so often happens in this novella—and a mark of its modernism—the workings of the subconscious are projected outward onto external occurrences, so that the very tenor of events such as the flooding of the river Papple becomes an index of deeper psychosexual realities.

In light of this psychodramatic geography, then, it is highly suggestive that the cause of the flood is the breaking of an upriver dam whose structure has been "undermin[ed]" by the collapse of an underground Roman mine hidden beneath the reservoir (173). The dams that Theweleit associates with the channeling mechanisms of the male ego, and that Lawrence's text more specifically associates with the strictures of Victorian and Christian morality, are thus sabotaged by an "unsuspected, undreamed of" conduit that evokes the "collateral channels" of Freud's *Three Essays* into which the libido overflows when its main channel is blocked. In addition, the "ancient" status of this underground tunnel suggests that the desirous floods released upon the breakdown of sexual repression originate deep within the psyche, in its most archaic (hence "ancient" and even "undreamed of") recesses. This realm of instinctual desire comprises what Lawrence calls "blood-consciousness," or the innermost core of human existence: "Here," Lawrence writes elsewhere in imagery well suited to the apocalyptic tenor of his sexual fable, "is the world of living dark waters, where the fire is quenched in watery creation."[73] Thus the flooding of the Papple becomes the reader's signal that Yvette has finally entered the libidinal realm of blood-consciousness, a world of fluid instinct in which the universal drama of sexual attraction and initiation can take place without external impediment.

The libidinal drives surfacing within Yvette's psyche are, Freud would argue, themselves without sex or gender: "There is only one libido, which serves both the masculine and feminine sexual functions. To it itself we cannot assign any sex" ("Femininity" 116). But as a matter of fact, the language Lawrence uses to describe both the flood and the "world of living dark waters" stirring within Yvette is not only sexually charged, but takes on explicitly gendered connotations. This should not be too surprising, given the overdetermined status of images of water, floods, dams, and channels in psychological, sexological, and scientific discourses since the turn of the century. Indeed, given Theweleit's account of men's obsessive association of water with female sexuality throughout western representation, the libidinal world of "watery creation" summoned into being at the end of *The Virgin and the Gipsy* might seem particularly "female": not only has Yvette's body previously turned "liquid" under the influence of the Gypsy's gaze and her fate been linked by the old Gypsy woman to the "voice of the water," but the flooding of the River Papple—its own name suggestive of maternal nurturance—is explicitly associated with Yvette's interiority, which the narrative has already made synonymous with "the dark, tremulous, potent secret of her virginity": "The flood was in her soul" (155), Lawrence writes, even as the actual flood literally sweeps her off her feet.

From another angle of vision, however, the female floods of desire set in motion by Yvette's release from repression evoke an opposing set of associations that recall the male anxieties underlying the historical association of women with engulfing floods in the first place. For the "swollen . . . mass" (150) of the river, surging forth as one tremendous "roaring *cliff* of water" and "advancing like a *wall*" (155; emphases added), also evokes the ejaculatory force of male orgasm, and hence suggests the phallic power embodied in the Gypsy. And the latter's simultaneous arrival on the scene makes his presence analogous to that of the flood; the flood-as-tidal-wave, after all, is the "masculine" force that penetrates the dams of repressed virginity while maintaining its own wall-like solidity, its male armor.[74] Even the engineering feats (reservoir dams, underground tunnels) whose collapse eventually cause the flood echo those male-based hydraulic and evacuatory models of the sexual drive emerging in late nineteenth-century sexological and medical discourses, in which sexuality is understood as an instinctual compulsion that must, on the analogy of spermatic flow, ultimately erupt to the surface after a buildup of sufficient internal pressure.

What thus appears to be Lawrence's covert redirection of female libidinal energies into a male evacuatory model calls to mind Luce Irigaray's admonition, in "The 'Mechanics' of Fluids," that in traditional psychoanalytic understandings of female sexuality, "the object of desire itself . . . would be the transformation of fluid to solid," sealing "the triumph of rationality" (113) over the flux and uncertainty associated with women. The narrative's tricky "masculinizing" of its representations of awakening "feminine" desire also begins to explain some of the macabre events that the arrival of the flood precipitates. First, as the Gypsy pulls the half-conscious Yvette through the swirling waters of the garden and into the already flooding Rectory to seek the safety of its upper floors, they pass the surreal sight of the dethroned Mater bobbing down the hallway, her "one old purple hand . . . showing the glint of a wedding ring" (158) as it futilely claws at the banister of the stairs they are ascending just before she sinks into the rising waters. Symbolically, this crossing of paths renders Yvette's impending sexual initiation, her "ascent" (up the stairs) to normative femininity, structurally dependent on the Mater's deathly descent into the waters. Given that this event marks a crucial rite of passage in Yvette's movement to adult femininity, it is telling that this gleefully sadistic killing off of the Mater invokes a psychological paradigm—differentiation from the devouring mother at any cost—that is generally more descriptive of male than female ego development.[75]

Second, this imposition of male paradigms onto the event of female awakening pervades the site of sexual initiation itself, Yvette's bedroom, which will resist the raging chaos of the floods *not* because it is an assigned "feminine" space but because, as the Gypsy excitedly boasts, its chimney, "like a tower," "will stand" (160). With the introduction of this image, the narrative executes a telling shift in male signifiers, from the flood as ejaculatory flow to the upright chimney as phallus, a shift which uncannily actualizes the "transformation of fluid to solid" that Irigaray posits as the covert goal of the phallic sexual economy. And with this shift in signifiers, the flood reverts to its prior "feminine" associations as flux or chaos over which the male principle, now embodied in the erect and stationary chimney, can reign.

Like these shifting signifiers, the Gypsy himself becomes Lawrence's strategic embodiment of the reterritorialization of "feminine" flux within the male principle. For the Gypsy is liquidity in motion: the narrative constantly returns to his fluid, supple movements, the sum of his "loose-bodied" poses (38), "limber" legs (43), "loping" and "flexible" hips (48), "flexible" lips (80), and "flexible loins" (81). Yet this fluidity is encased within the Gypsy's rigid body armor, manifested both on the physical plane (in his taut, muscular body) and on the psychological (in his obdurate pride; in the "harden[ing]" that is the effect of his "ha[ving] been through the war" [111]). These dual valences continue in the climactic flooding scene, where he gets to act both the part of ejaculatory flood which breaks down hymenal dams and that of erect chimney that withstands the destructive floods of female sexuality. Now, insofar as male power and hierarchy are concerned, the depiction of the Gypsy as the ideal incorporation of *both* fluidity and rigidity allows Lawrence to eat his cake and have it too. For, crucially, the representation of the Gypsy's incorporation of fluidity within phallicity works to allay male anxieties about female sexuality as uncontainable and voracious by containing it within the male principle itself.

An illuminating gloss on the Gypsy's symbolic function as a container of fluidity exists in one of Lawrence's letters, where he describes his libidinal drives as the "complete, all-containing surge of which I am the fountain, and of which the well-head is my loins."[76] Lawrence's desires may flow, but their mobility is figured in terms of a "complete, all-containing surge" that serves to channel or "contain" that flow into one "complete," uninterrupted movement. And in accord with contemporary hydraulic/ejaculatory models of male sexual expenditure, the indisputable origin of this fluidity is figured as the phallus ("well-head is my loins"), from which the discrete male ego, or the "I am," erupts with volcanic force, but with its boundaries intact ("complete, all-containing"). This self-generating economy of male subject-formation serves, then, as a prophylaxis against self-engulfment or dissolution, achieved through its appropriation of the mechanics of fluidity traditionally associated with women.

Which brings us, finally, to the scene that transpires when, having attained her room at the top of the Rectory, the Gypsy and Yvette shed their wet clothes and crawl, shivering, into bed. As with the phallic-but-flowing flood and liquid-but-rigid Gypsy, this scene strategically enacts a harnessing of "dangerous" female flux in service of a model of male sexuality. For, when in response to Yvette's moan, "Warm me! . . . Warm me! I shall die of shivering" (164), the "semi-conscious" Gypsy takes her in his "vice-like grip," his body is represented as being at once all in motion, "rippling" with electric "currents" that writhe around Yvette like tentacles, *and* the solid bedrock that steadies them both, a "rigid" mass of "muscles" which, significantly, becomes the "*only stable point* in [Yvette's] consciousness" (164–65; emphases added), like the chimney that stands erect above the floodwaters. But rather than this muscular rigidity only serving, as Theweleit postulates, as body armor with which to ward off all desire, the Gypsy's firmness becomes the stabilizing center *around which* female flux or desire can productively, if secondarily, organize itself. Likewise, inversely, female flux (Yvette's wet, quivering body) is surrounded, circumscribed by the Gypsy's "clasp like a vice." Both center and circumference determining the flow and boundaries of female desire, the Gypsy thus meets the threat of female floods with what Theweleit calls "a kind of sustained erection of [the] whole body" (244). Given the psychodramatic level on which these actions are unfolding, the long-standing critical debate about whether the Virgin and Gipsy have "sex" becomes a moot point. For insofar as the Gypsy's entire body has come to stand in for/as his phallus, he doesn't need literally to "penetrate" Yvette for the plot of her awakening to have its desired effect: that is, her ascension to femininity and her place within a phallic order whose power resides in its ability to regulate or channel female sexuality to its own specular advantage.[77]

Reveling in the Masquerade of Femininity; or, Mission Accomplished

Yvette thus completes the final rite in her passage to adulthood, but we may well ask to what end, given the cryptic "day after" denouement that follows. While the repressive Victorian world of the Rectory may have been swept away by the force of natural desire, the question of whether that society's conventions have so entirely disappeared lingers. Indeed, at the beginning of the novella's last chapter, Yvette awakens (this time quite literally) from her "world's-end night" (170) to find not only that the Gypsy has disappeared from her side but that a policeman has taken his place in her bedroom; the representative of "social law" has replaced that of "natural law," demonstrating the degree to which both are two faces of the same phallocentric desire.[78] Meanwhile, Yvette's awakening to her "natural" sexuality ironically leads back into the realm of the "social": gendered role-playing. Deciding that she will "keep the gipsy a secret from [her father]" (171), Yvette "[weeps] away into her hanky" (172) and then, having descended the ladder from her bedroom window, she "appropriately faint[s]," as if on cue, into her father's waiting arms (173). In so doing, Yvette self-consciously assumes the masquerade of femininity, as well as accepts the *fiction* of paternal authority that she has already internally disavowed, in order to get what she wants. Such dissimulation, even more ironically, is a lesson culled from her father's example: "He would always play up to appearances. She would do the same. She too would play up to appearances" (138). Hence the end of Yvette's awakening, her ascension to what Freud calls normative femininity, is indoctrination not into femininity as a "natural" state but rather into the empowerment that lies in an embrace of its very constructedness: under its guise she can experience sexual release *and* maintain her outward respectability, or as she has earlier put it, have her fling, then give in and get married: "So a woman could eat her cake and have her bread and butter" (144).

The cavalier offhandedness of such an assertion might seem to be cause for not a little male anxiety, given the expendability of male partners that it implies (a disturbing possibility to which, as we will see in the next chapter, Joyce's Molly Bloom also gives voice). But such fears are allayed by the fact that both the cake and the bread and butter, as it were, attest to the indispensability of men to female sexual pleasure and hence uphold the primacy of phallic sexuality. Likewise, any power that Yvette now exploits through her "feminine" role-playing occurs within a specular logic that already defines femininity as the mirror image of masculine desire and women as "not-men." Within the schema proposed by Lawrence's reworking of the plot of female awakening, coming under the sway of the Gypsy's magnetic gaze, yielding to the drift of desire, has clearly *facilitated* rather than *hindered* Yvette's successful emergence as a fulfilled, "normal" woman, even if she must maintain her knowledge of that fulfillment as a "secret" within herself. Appropriately, what the narrative has previously fetishized as the "secret" of Yvette's blossoming virginity is now replaced by the "secret" of sexual knowledge ("she would keep the gipsy a secret") that has been incorporated into the inmost recesses of her consciousness as, in Judith Butler's terms, an anterior truth of being. Hence, also, the inevitability of the Gypsy's disappearance; he is no longer really needed, for what he represents is now lodged inside, where both "identity" and "sexuality" are also said to reside.

Given the Gypsy's disappearance, the argument might be made that all along Yvette has been acting in her own best interests, using the Gypsy to realize her erotic fantasies, then discarding him when he's served the function of having facilitated her awakening. Such "use," however, should not be mistaken as female agency in excess of the patriarchal inscription of femininity. Rather, to the extent that the Gypsy might be seen, in such terms, as Yvette's discardable penis-toy, or dildo, bringing her satisfaction on her own terms, his status is that of a fetish, one which operates precisely to "save" Yvette from assuming a phallic female identity that, within the scope of Freud's schema in "Femininity," would necessarily countermand her emergent, normative womanhood. That is, through the Gypsy's position as her (female) fetish, Yvette can simultaneously avow and disavow her supposed castration (precisely the function Freud assigns the fetish), thus acceding to femininity-as-lack on the one hand without succumbing either to neurosis or sexual "frigidity" on the other. Through the process of awakening to her true "nature," to "natural" sexuality, a perfect woman has, ironically, *been made.*[79]

Moreover, this possible scripting of the phallic Gypsy as fetish-object only underlines the fact that sexual initiation for Yvette necessarily comes from outside: female arousal cannot occur without an other, whether in the form of the actual Gypsy's corporeal presence or nature's flood or Yvette's own imaginary projections of the Gypsy-as-fetish or, as we earlier noted, the Gypsy-as-speculum. The autoerotic sufficiency temporarily experienced by Edna and the heterogeneity of desires that flood Chopin's text are out of the question here, for the very structure imposed on the narrative of Yvette's awakening allows her no possibility of desires that are not other-oriented. In so scripting Yvette's fate, Lawrence perpetuates an age-old myth of female sexuality that is dependent on maleness as its first term, and he wields his textual authority, ultimately, to make this the only story that the awakening of the female subject can exemplify.

Such a politics makes sense, then, of the curious ending of the text: the Gypsy's letter to Yvette, alerting her of his safety and whereabouts, which ends with his very English and unforeign signature, Joe Boswell: "And only then she realized that he had a name" (175). With this generic move from myth to realism (the Gypsy proposes meeting Yvette some day at the cattle fair!), it is Joe Boswell who is allowed to exit the world of the text, while Yvette now rather contentedly remains fixed within her social context. And the fact that the text's very last word is Boswell's name, not Yvette's, provides an ironic signature to this narrative of supposedly female sexual awakening—a signature alerting us, graphically, to the phallocentrically erected channels of desire in whose name and authority this fable has been constructed, itself a dam to more threatening floods. "And she wept gallons" (173), we learn of Yvette upon her descent from her bedroom the morning after the flood, her copious tears (signifying relief at her rescue or grief at the Gypsy's departure?) amplifying those of her sister Lucille and Aunt Cissie: the threatening torrents of female passion have now become, as is only proper in the social world she has rejoined, the signifier of the successful masquerade of femininity itself.

SIGMUND FREUD, *DORA*
(FREUD'S) WET DREAMS

My powers of interpretation had run dry that day; I let her go on talking.
—Sigmund Freud in *Dora* (76–77)

Dora shares several points of contiguity with the awakening narratives of Chopin and Lawrence. First, the ghost of Freud makes a brief but telling appearance in *The Awakening*, when Mr. Pontellier, worried that his wife may be "growing a little unbalanced mentally" (108), seeks out the advice of the family physician. As we have seen, Dr. Mandelet cautions against interference, warning that "it would require an inspired psychologist to deal successfully" with the "sensitive and highly organised" (119) nervous constitution of a woman like Edna. The fact is, of course, that in the same twelve-month span as *The Awakening*'s 1899 composition, one such "inspired psychologist," working in Vienna, was concurrently occupied in theorizing the "peculiar" pathology of hysteria in women—the issue of which was the innovative case study *An Analysis of a Case of Hysteria*, popularly known as *Dora* (written 1901, published 1905). Quite literally located on the cusp of the transition from Victorian to modern culture, this text would help insure the emergence of Freudian psychoanalysis as *the* mode of conceptualizing modernity's discourses of sexuality, as well as its fictions of interiority, in the new century.

Second, as in *The Virgin and the Gipsy*, Freud's text presents its readers with a "virgin" who needs to be awakened to her sexuality in order to become a healthy, "normal" woman—but with a difference. For if Lawrence's novella builds steadily toward the climactic union of Yvette and the Gypsy, Freud's analysis hinges on the assumption that his patient's awakening has already occurred but lies buried under layers of repression that conceal her long-standing love for Herr K., a family friend, and, as a result of his sexual advances, the "sexuality which was already present in her" (108). Therefore Freud's psychoanalytic task, recapitulated in the narrative structure of the case study, is to dig backwards in time, to excavate the traces of that earlier, thwarted sexual awakening in order to prove that Herr K.'s interest in Dora is what "really *woke you up* out of your sleep" (90; emphasis added). Freud's goal is to integrate Dora into society by restoring her to psychological health; as in *The Virgin and the Gipsy,* the assumption is that the social and psychological *can* be brought into productive alignment, that female desire need no longer be disavowed in a more enlightened age. Yet, despite its intentions, the narrative that recounts Dora's experience of erotic initiation and repression ends up dramatizing the same uneasy impasse between social and psychological imperatives that confronts Edna at the end of *The Awakening.* For in fact the social structures that circumscribe Dora are not only beyond her control but may well be the primary source of her psychoneuroses. Thus Freud's "inspired" attempt both to authorize and to channel the "flow" of female desire in this pivotal document in the history of sexuality presents a revealing gloss on the reading and writing of female desire, and in the process it illuminates the anxieties of authority underlying many modernist fictions of sexuality, including Lawrence's and Chopin's. Simply put, the assumptions and contradictions embedded in this case study cannot be separated from the obsessive attempt to represent the plot of female awakening as *the* plot of "modern sexuality" in early twentieth-century writing and thought.

The tension between the authorial impulse to liberate hitherto censored female sexuality and the potential threat to textual authority that such an enterprise engenders is apparent from the very opening of Freud's study, where it is translated into a contest between his incessant worries about controlling the flow of information (especially protecting it from the prurience of "unauthorized readers" [23]) and his desire to release the libidinal flow that Dora's traumatic experiences have blocked, a current that only the torrent of her uncensored words in the therapeutic encounter can set streaming again; indeed, up to the very end of Dora's sessions, Freud declares that "the material for the analysis *had not yet run dry*" (141; emphasis added). Freud's articulation of this tension between the control and flow of information, I want to suggest, participates in the discourse of female floods that this chapter has found to be integral to early-twentieth-century plots of female awakening. For throughout *Dora,* water is not only a marker of desire (and the anxieties such floods engender) but intimately linked to and interspersed with leitmotifs of awakening that form the text's residual plot. For example, the most recent sexual overtures of Herr K.—the immediate cause of the "psychic trauma" (42) triggering Dora's latest outbreak of hysteria, according to Freud—transpired on a walk along the shore of an Alpine lake resort (a watery setting that recalls that of Grand Isle in *The Awakening*). The incident by the lake triggers Dora's repressed memories of a literal awakening that occurred later the same day: being roused from an afternoon nap to find Herr K. looming over her bed, asserting that he will not be locked out of a room in his own house. This disturbing memory has surfaced upon Dora's recounting to Freud a dream that contains two more instances linking water and awakening—first, being woken by her father standing over her bed (as Herr K. has in real life) because the house is on fire; second, "[waking] up" again once safely outside (81). Fire, as Freud proceeds to demonstrate, implies its opposite, *water:* the material for this dream stems from her father's habit in previous years of waking the young girl in the middle of the night to break her of the habit of "making her bed wet" (109). And sex, as Dora intuits even as a child, involves wetness; not only does bedwetting, according to Freud, have "no more likely cause than masturbation" (92), but the female mentors in Dora's life ooze unwelcome liquids in the form of infections, discharges, and catarrhs associated with their real and imagined connections with men. Water, sexuality, and awakening are thus highly overdetermined terms in the treacherous psychic terrain that Dora must negotiate en route to so-called "normal" womanhood.

These watery scenarios of (thwarted) sexual awakening also bring into play a number of issues raised in the earlier sections of this chapter. First Dora's situation, no less than Edna's and Yvette's, graphically illustrates the necessity of articulation, of speaking for oneself rather than being spoken for, in order to become an actively desiring subject. It is no coincidence that one of Dora's earliest hysterical symptoms is aphasia, a loss of voice; or that the trauma she has repressed finds expression in the alternative language of her hysterized body, whose symptoms "speak" that which the mind has rendered unconscious; or that any hope of recovery that Freud posits for Dora depends on what has come to be known as "the talking cure." Second, Freud's vested interest in reading and interpreting the verbal texts to which Dora gives expression points to another crucial topos linking this narrative with Lawrence's and Chopin's fictions—the potential conflict between expressions of authorial mastery and the female subject of the awakening plot. As we shall see, the specific narrative techniques by which Freud establishes his authority at Dora's expense provide a symptomatic illustration of textual control becoming a cover for those sexual anxieties to which the male contemplation of the floods of female desire gives rise.

On a more general level, these anxieties point to another issue that these and many other modernist narratives hold in common: the representational risks involved in endeavoring, as Freud explains his task, to "mak[e] conscious the most hidden recesses of the mind" and "[bring] to light what human beings keep hidden within them[selves]" (96). For the attempt to find modes of representing the inner life, of plumbing the unconscious and giving voice to the sexual secrets "hidden within," ties Freud's narrative experiments in the genre of the case study to the protomodernist imaginings of many novelists who were experimenting with nonrealist modes in the early decades of the twentieth century, as Steven Marcus has shown.[80] Representing the psychosexual components of subjectivity, whether in the name of science or art, is already to lay oneself open to the anxieties attendant upon encountering an unruly flux of subconscious impulses whose movement one can neither predict nor ever fully control. And when those libidinal and erotic energies are projected onto the figure of the "modern" liberated woman, as in the turn-of-the-century plot of female awakening, the gendered politics and representational poetics that ensue threaten a revolution in phallocratic norms that makes the channeling of those wayward desires all the more an anxious imperative in culture's scripting of the relation between the sexes.

Buried Secrets, Hidden Histories

To read *Dora* as a variation on the female plot of sexual awakening is to be reminded of the links that Freudian psychoanalysis posits among hysteria, repression, and sexuality. Hysteria, according to Freud, is a neurotic condition in which the (generally female) patient suffers a series of somatic symptoms for which there are no immediate physical explanations. These symptoms, rather, are expressions of concealed desires, wishes, and thoughts that because of their traumatic or frightening nature have been repressed to the unconscious, from which site they seek an indirect means of expression through "hysterical" bodily reactions such as those causing Dora's father to bring his daughter, "who had . . . grown unmistakably neurotic," to Freud for "psychotherapeutic treatment" (34). For Freud it is a dictum that the traumas causing hysteria are sexual in origin, often emanating from childhood. To help the hysteric recover and work through her repressed memories, the analyst must make the unconscious conscious, make representable those psychic processes internal to but hidden from the subject.[81]

Throughout his *Analysis of a Case of Hysteria,* Freud repeatedly draws upon two geographical metaphors, one involving archeology and the other riverbeds, to evoke the seat of these mysterious, unseen psychic forces. The former is introduced in his "Prefatory Remarks," where Freud notes that he "start[s] out with whatever surface [the patient's] unconscious happens to be presenting . . . at the moment," then likens his task of making sense of the random associations that emerge "piecemeal" to the efforts of "those discoverers whose good fortune it is to bring to the light of day after their long burial the priceless though mutilated relics of antiquity" (27). Inscribed in this metaphoric movement from the "surface" provided by words and bodies to buried depths and thence back up to "the light of day" is an implicit understanding that what lies *within* also lies *below* the "surface" of consciousness, an anterior sexual "truth" of being of which the surface inscriptions that Freud reads are an after-effect. The vertical plumbing of the psyche to recover these "priceless though mutilated relics of antiquity" is also in keeping with the hydraulic models of libidinal release promoted in turn-of-the-century sexological discourse: that which lies hidden below will eventually force its way upward and outward. But because of the masking effects of hysterical repression, the originating trauma of hysteria can never be fully recovered or seamlessly represented; like the priceless relics unearthed by the archeologist, it exists in shards, to be pieced together into a comprehensible whole by the superior talents of the psychoanalyst. "I have restored what is missing," Freud explains in a well-known passage, "taking the best models known to me from other analyses; but like a conscientious archeologist I have not omitted to mention in each case where the authentic parts end and my constructions begin" (27). The authorial task of piecing together from these *broken* fragments "an intelligible, consistent, and *unbroken* case history" (32; emphasis added) capable of "restor[ing]" Dora to mental well-being thus entails an act of creative fiat that, despite Freud's distinction between "authentic parts" and "constructions," problematizes the very enterprise of knowing and recording the secret, the essence, the key, that is presumed to lie within and to define his patient's sexuality.

The fragmented condition of this buried truth of self is mirrored in the image that Freud introduces a few pages later—that of a river current splintered into multiple tributaries and paths—to describe the effects of repression on Dora's initial narration of "the whole story" of her illness: "This first account may be compared to an unnavigable river whose stream is at one moment choked by masses of rock and at another divided and lost among the shallows and sandbacks" (30). Here, the river current serves as a metaphor to explain the deviations from the straight course that would convey a coherent life story. Similarly, the language of rivers and tributaries reappears many pages later as a figure for the "unconscious perverse activities" (68) of the libido. Imagine, Freud proposes, as he attempts to explain the reactivation of the "undifferentiated sexual pre-disposition of the child" (67) in adult victims of hysteria, that "a stream of water which meets with an obstacle in the river-bed is dammed up and flows back into old channels which had formerly seemed fated to run dry" (68). This imagery is identical to that which Freud uses in *Three Essays,* cited at the beginning of this chapter, to evoke the erotogenic multiplicity (and, I might add, the modernist structuration) of the nonlinear, atemporal realm of the libido; desire always threatens to overflow and needs to be curbed by the "narrow lines," the regulated channels, that both culture and the ego impose on adult sexuality "as the standard of normality" (67). In Dora's case, Freud deduces that the "development of normal sexuality" (68) was arrested four years ago when the then-fourteen-year-old girl was accosted without warning by Herr K., the family friend, in his deserted factory. Dora's suppression of this traumatic event from her consciousness causes her repressed libidinal desires—as in the riverbed analogy—to flow back into those "old channels" represented by the so-called infantile perversions: hence, Freud argues, the revival of her oedipal love for her father to mask the feelings aroused by Herr K.'s kisses and embrace.

While Freud introduces these archeological and river metaphors in an attempt to produce an image of the invisible play of the unconscious forces, the layers of repression, in Dora's psyche, both figures also betray the extent to which the world *within* Dora is also prey to constructions *external* to herself, whether in the form of the psychoanalyst's own "constructions" ("I have restored what is missing . . .") or in the form of those "imposed . . . standard[s] of normality" whereby adult sexuality is channeled within extremely "narrow lines" (67). The most cursory look at Dora's immediate family structure also makes clear the impact of the realm of the social on the psychosexual, revealing a world that is *already* dysfunctional, as prone to neurosis, deception, and morbidity as the Rector's family in *The Virgin and the Gipsy*.[82] Indeed, for every Saywell there is an analogue in Dora's family; in both texts, the bourgeois myth of family happiness is exposed as a cover-up for much darker oedipal compromises. The "dominating figure" in Dora's "family circle" (33), according to the family portrait that Freud introduces at the beginning of the case study, is the young girl's intelligent, successful father. Underlying his "shrewdness" and "perspicacity" (40, 38), however, Freud, like Dora, detects a "strain of falseness" (50, 131), resembling the "false note" sounded by the Rector in Lawrence's text. And if, as Freud states, Dora owes her intellectual precocity to her father, this man's health history indicates a less happy resemblance between them: suffering a series of illnesses ranging from tuberculosis and syphilis to "confusional attack[s]," "slight mental disturbances," and suicidal depression, Dora's upright father provides a perfect model for her own symptomology. Neuroses also plague Dora's aunt and uncle on her father's side: the aunt suffers a "severe form of psychoneurosis" that leads to her death from anorexia (compare to the eating disorders of Aunt Cissie) while the uncle (like Yvette's unmarried Uncle Fred) is a "hypochondriacal bachelor" (33–34). Intriguingly, the one relative that Freud has not met firsthand is Dora's mother. Never directly represented in the case study, she thus occupies a position analogous to that of the offstage She-Who-Was-Cynthia in Lawrence's text. What Freud learns of Dora's mother from hearsay, however, convinces him that she too is a victim of neurosis, leading to his diagnosis of her cleaning obsession as "housewife's psychosis" (34).[83] Rounding out this "family portrait" are two proxy members who participate in its dysfunction in more ways than one: Herr K., whose love-making assault on Dora—first at the factory, then at the lake—has triggered her most recent disturbances, and his wife, Frau K., introduced into the household as the father's nurse and suspected lover, whose nervous disorders have obliged her "to spend months at a sanatorium" (49). Within this emotionally and libidinally charged environment, Dora holds no monopoly on the neuroses that produce hysteria.[84]

But the external circumstance that has the most damaging effect on Dora's psychological well-being involves the double plot of adultery and sexual intrigue—or, as Claire Kahane calls it, the "melodrama of sexual politics riddled with illness and infidelity"[85]—that the girl uncovers within this network of family and friends. For "sharp-sighted" Dora begins to suspect not only that her father and Frau K. have been carrying on an illicit affair for years, but that she has been "handed over to Herr K." by her father "as the price of his tolerating the relations between her father and his wife" (50). And, indeed, everyone willfully chooses to ignore Herr K.'s increasingly inappropriate attentions to the adolescent Dora—sending her flowers every day for a year, buying her expensive gifts, shadowing her in the street. To Dora's mind, it is clear that she has become "an object of barter" (50) between men, one whose position enacts the classic position of women in Gayle Rubin's formulation of the systemic male bonding that sustains the power of patriarchy. Steven Marcus has eloquently summarized the effects of such a revelation on an adolescent psyche, especially once Frau K. adds her betrayal to that of Dora's father by asserting that Dora must have fantasized Herr K.'s proposition at the lake:

> The three adults to whom [Dora] was closest, whom she loved the most in the world, were apparently conspiring—separately, in tandem, or in concert—to deny her the reality of her experience. They were conspiring to deny Dora her reality and reality itself. This betrayal touched on matters that might easily unhinge the mind of a young person; for the three adults were not betraying Dora's love and trust alone, they were betraying the structure of [her] actual world.[86]

In a profound sense, then, the "sicknesses" pervading the realm of the social that constitutes Dora's known world precede and shape her psychological state. Freud's tendency, however, is to keep looking for additional levels of denial and repression to uncover in Dora, a tack which places the onus of her morbid condition on the unstable structure of her individual psyche rather than on the "structure of the actual world" circumscribing her actions, and this focus allows Freud to evade confronting head-on the ideological assumptions underlying a phallocentrically organized social order that allows men like Herr K. and Dora's father to believe in sexual privilege as their natural right.[87]

The Proliferating Phallus: From Textual to Sexual Mastery

Such assumptions of male privilege, moreover, factor significantly into the anxieties of authority, both textual and sexual, that return to haunt Freud's reading and writing of female desire. For, as a number of feminist critics have shown, Freud participates in the chain of male exchanges of women that support networks of male power. We have seen how Dora feels she has been "handed over to Herr K." (50) by her father as part of their gentleman's agreement; the fact that Freud uses identical wording to describe her father's delivery of her to him for treatment—"he handed her over to me" (34)—reveals Freud's unconscious enmeshment in the same system of male exchange. And this transaction between client and doctor is a business arrangement charged with power, given the fact that, five years before, Dora's father had been Freud's client, recommended to Freud by none other than Herr K. Freud's authority to "cure" Dora, moreover, depends on a prior chain of authorizations. "Only her father's authority," Freud notes, has been powerful enough to induce Dora "to come to me at all" (37), and the father places his daughter in Freud's hands with an admonition rife with ambiguities: "Please try and bring her to reason" (42). Restore my daughter to mental health, he overtly seems to be pleading, but the context of his statement implies a more self-serving wish—that Freud convince Dora that her suspicion of his affair with Frau K. is "unreasonable," the fantasy of a sick girl.

Freud is savvy enough to see through and ignore the latter ploy, but he remains blind to his own ideological conformity with many of the patriarchal assumptions he shares with Dora's father. Examples of these blind spots, punctuating the case study at every turn, reinforce Freud's interpretive and textual authority over Dora's story of thwarted sexual awakening: the assumption that a fourteen-year-old girl accosted by a sexually aroused man twice her age should feel erotic pleasure instead of fear and disgust; the overidentification that allows Freud to cast Herr K. as Prince Charming to Dora's Sleeping Beauty with honorable intentions; the erasure of the influence of Dora's mother on her daughter's psychosexual development.[88]

The most stunning reminder, however, of Freud's ideologically imposed blinders involves his overevaluation of male sexuality and consequent neglect of nonphallic expressions of desire. Indeed, at three pivotal points he hinges his interpretation on the existence of penises/phalluses that may only exist in his imagination. First, in his analysis of the factory incident in which the fourteen-year-old Dora is accosted by Herr K.—her original sexual "awakening"—Freud introduces as the surprise twist, the narrative climax of the sequence, his deduction that Herr K. has an erection: "I have formed in my own mind the following reconstruction. . . . I believe that during the man's passionate embrace she felt not merely his kiss upon her lips but also the pressure of his erect member against her body" (45). Freud's very rhetoric—"formed in my own mind," "reconstruction," "I believe"—signals that he is beginning to fantasize, like any fiction writer, his own story, and in the process he fails to make the critical distinction between "authentic parts" and his "own constructions" that he has earlier assured the reader he will not hesitate to point out.[89] The effect of this clision is that Herr K.'s fantasized "erect member" becomes *the* explanatory "truth," amazingly, upon which the rest of the analysis pivots: Dora's sexual refusal begets neurotic frigidity, which in turn manifests itself in sexual hysteria. That within a page Freud repeats three times the claim that a "healthy" girl would have reacted to Herr K.'s embrace with pleasure forms a striking instance of the repetition compulsion at work; the overzealousness with which Freud asserts and reasserts his opinion attests not only to a high degree of anxiety about female sexuality yet to be worked through, but to his unexamined assumptions about what a frightened adolescent girl's sexual response might be.[90]

The second pivotal instance in which Freud conjures forth a phallus occurs in the elaborate chain of reasoning by which he deduces that Dora's repressed feelings for Herr K. have reactivated her infantile, incestuous desires for her father. Freud concludes that her nervous cough and gagging reflex is the result of having fantasized herself in Frau K.'s position during oral intercourse with her father (the latter's impotence has led to Dora's admission that she believes oral-genital contact is the couple's sole means of gratification). It is clear, of course, that Freud is imagining an act of *fellatio,* but given the impotence of Dora's father it is far more likely— as critics since Lacan have noted—that the act in question is *cunnilingus,* and Frau K. is therefore on the receiving rather than giving end.[91] Again, Freud's automatic tendency to think of sex in phallic terms leads to a blatant misreading that ignores female pleasure as a sexual possibility. A third example of phallic sexuality serving as a linchpin in the analysis occurs at the end of the lengthy interpretation of Dora's first dream, where Freud argues in quick succession that Dora's unadmitted love for Herr K. has revived her oedipal love for her father, summoned forth her homosexual love for Frau K., and surfaced, at this very moment, in the transferential desire for a kiss from Freud himself—at which point Freud proudly claims that "everything" in his narrative now "*fits together* very satisfactorily" (92; emphasis added). But what clue allows Freud to insert his presence into Dora's psychic life as its ultimate "love-object" and as its narrative knot? None other than his cigar-smoking habit, the smell of which has triggered Dora's memories of Herr K.'s kiss at the factory. And a cigar, as all readers of the *Interpretation of Dreams* (and, indeed, Brontë's *Villette*) know, is never only a cigar.

The link that this passage establishes between Freud's interpolation of himself into Dora's fantasy life as a "sexual player" and his simultaneous proclamation that all pieces in *his* story now fit perfectly together powerfully underlines the process by which the textual mastery Freud exerts as reader and author of Dora's confession becomes indistinguishable from sexual mastery. This uneasy conflation of the sexual and textual typifies the often cited gynecological metaphor that Freud introduces early on to defend his determination to discuss "sexual questions . . . with all possible frankness" by claiming for himself the "rights of the gynaecologist" (23). But when this analogy recurs later in the analysis, that which is meant to ward off prurience becomes prurient in its own right: "A gynaecologist, after all, under the same conditions, does not hesitate to make [his female patients] submit to uncovering every possible part of their body" (65). Not only does this statement posit the male psychoanalyst as the agent who disrobes female bodies and the naked female patient as the one who necessarily "submit[s]," but the psychoanalytic encounter itself has been cast as a vaginal penetration of the woman, since Freud's analogy renders her genitals (the object of the gynecological examination) as the metaphoric equivalent of her psyche (into which the therapist probes). Psychoanalysis thus fills the symbolically "male" role of "dominator" whose task (like the Gypsy's in Lawrence's fable) it is to delve into Dora's most private recesses, forcing a reawakening to the natural sexuality that has temporarily been repressed or hidden. And, in a presciently Foucauldian move, the discursive implantation that Freud's analogy achieves helps to insure that the "secret of self"—the core and wellspring of being—will hereafter be seen as the "secret of sex." The discomforting implications of the gynecologist/psychoanalyst equation are only exacerbated by the wordplay that follows: "I call bodily organs and processes by their technical names, and I tell these to the patient. . . . *J'appelle un chat un chat.*" (65). The coy lasciviousness implicit in Freud's association of "bodily organs" with the French word for cat—a slang term for female genitalia—casts doubt on the simultaneous claim to scientific objectivity: directness is replaced with the indirection of another language, and frankness with a punning sexual euphemism.

The sexism of such textual moments not withstanding, they seem less indicative of an erotic attraction to Dora than of the thrill of detection, the rush of power, that interpreting and "fill[ing] in" (32) the broken narrative of the hysteric gives Freud. Yet the erotics of interpretation that exhilarate Freud never free themselves of sexual connotations that retrospectively cast suspicion on the intellectual endeavor itself. Hence even the straightforward, heartfelt declaration that Freud makes at the end of the case history—"sexuality is the key to the problem of the psychoneuroses. . . . No one who disdains the key will ever be able to unlock the door" (136)—is undercut by his joking reference, in an earlier footnote, to keys as phallic symbols: "It is well known, too, what sort of key effects the opening [of female genitalia] in such a case" (84). Such humor becomes even more disconcerting when placed beside Freud's announcement to Wilhelm Fleiss that his new patient (Ida Bauer) is "a girl of eighteen" whose "case has opened smoothly to my collection of picklocks"[92]—a case, moreover, that Freud avows in his "Prefatory Remarks" is *not* "a *roman à clef* designed for . . . private delectation" (23). Not only do these allusions equate the solution to solving the psychoneuroses with a Freudian phallic symbol, but they make that phallus/key/clef the defining tool of the psychoanalytic method itself.

If at times Freud's textual authority thus blurs indiscriminately into a kind of sexual authority, the narrative techniques and strategies he uses to establish authorial control both over his patient's story and the reader's reception of that narrative also attest to the politics of sexuality embedded in his narrative poetics. On the most basic level, Freud asserts mastery over his general audience through the use of highly technical scientific language; unless the reader opts to spend all day in a dictionary, Freud's command of words lends his interpretation instant credibility and, with it, authority. Likewise the case study's elaborate chains of logical reasoning perform— as in the best detective fiction—an intellectual seduction of its readers; we are so caught up in following each stage of ratiocination that we forget to consider alternate possibilities. The traditional third-person novelistic privileges that Freud assumes also become a potent method of establishing authority over the reader. In the name of clarity and cohesiveness he claims *the privilege of occasional elision,* expecting (and often winning) acquiescence to his superior judgment. Conversely, Freud also claims *the right of exacting mimesis,* no matter how confusing or unbelievable the details, if it better suits his aims, since "in the world of reality, which I am trying to depict here, a complication of motives. . . is the rule" (77). This dual privilege of telling all in the name of "truth" while selectively editing for the sake of coherence gives Freud incredible leeway in shaping the reader's reception of his own reading of Dora's hysteria.[93]

The textual mastery Freud establishes over subject matter and reader is most dramatically illustrated, however, like that of any master novelist, in his manipulation of narrative structure to give the case study a form that will support the ideological as well as "poetic" meanings he wishes it to convey. We are alerted to the importance of narrative sequence in consolidating Freud's authority when, having just explained his method of composition, he off-handedly adds that he has altered nothing "except in several places *the order in which* the explanations are given; and this has been done for the sake of presenting the case in a more connected form" (24; emphasis added). A revealing example of such "alteration" in the name of "a more connected form" occurs in Freud's reconstruction of the factory episode. Freud first reports Herr K.'s sudden embrace and kiss of the young girl, then Dora's mysterious disgust rather than excitement, and finally the presence of Herr K.'s erection. I have already noted how the latter revelation is part of Freud's hypothetical (hence perhaps fictional) "reconstruction" of the scene, and how it strategically positions phallic sexuality as the climax and hidden key of the episode. But perhaps even more revealing is how it almost certainly *reverses* the actual temporal sequence of events. For Herr K.'s erection, if indeed he has one, has probably been incited by his embrace of Dora *and thus would precede rather than follow her disgust,* the latter of which might more properly be seen as episode's climactic event: embrace/erection/disgust. This ordering, however, would suggest an entirely different reading of the scene than the one Freud offers, for it would place the onus for Dora's hysteria on the sexual threat embodied in Herr K.'s seductive machinations and remind us that Dora is a defenseless adolescent girl. By replacing a reading more sympathetic to Dora with one that valorizes Herr K.'s virile display, Freud's manipulation of narrative sequence fosters a very particular ideological meaning about what he considers normal male and female sexuality.

An equally uneasy manifestation of authorial fiat involves Freud's linguistic appropriation of Dora's story, gradually subsuming her speaking voice into his own narration. Claire Kahane notes that "as brilliant as Freud was in constructing a narrative of Dora's desire, he essentially represented his own."[94] First, his hypotheses about how the unconscious makes itself heard in the face of repression justify his tactic of converting each of Dora's negatives into an affirmative. "[It] soon begins to appear," he confidently generalizes, that "'No' signifies the desired 'Yes'" (76). Yet as the telltale adjective "desired" betrays, these reversals serve the *analyst's* desire foremost, allowing him to reconstruct Dora's language of refusal (of Herr K.'s advances, of Freud's persistence in believing she is secretly in love with Herr K.) to fit a script whose meaning or "coherence" has already been determined. Second, Freud's theory of the switch-word allows him to reverbalize Dora's entire sentences, quite literally bringing them under his control. Hence in regard to the bracelet that Dora's father gives his wife to appease her, Freud admonishes Dora, "You would have been glad to accept what your mother had rejected. Now let us just put 'give' instead of 'accept' and 'withhold' instead of 'reject.' Then it means . . ." (87). The "let us" is more than a bit disingenuous, not merely because Freud is the one creating the substitutions, but because the words being replaced ("accept"/"reject") are *also* Freud's. The passage is thus rigged from beginning to end to support Freud's interpretation—namely, that Dora has revived an incestuous desire for her father to cover her actual "temptation . . . to yield" to Herr K. (88).

By so divesting Dora's language of her expressed intentions and investing them with his own, Freud accomplishes two tasks simultaneously: he proves his intellectual and interpretive superiority, and he effectively silences Dora as the subject of her own discourse—the fate of Edna and Yvette as well. In fact Freud gives himself the proverbial last word, as in a frenzy of masterful interpretation he simply takes over the final session, declaring in a climactic act of fiat that "you have not even got the right to assert . . ." as he denies Dora's version of events and transforms Herr K.'s sexual advances at the lake resort into an honorable proposal of marriage that "would have been *the only solution* for all the parties involved"—a rather dubious claim in light of all the further complications, including two divorces, such a solution would entail (130; emphasis added). Although he concludes the case study by reiterating his belief that "the patient . . . always provide[s] the text" (138), this final session demonstrates, to the contrary, the efforts Freud takes to foist onto Dora's "text" the marriage plot in which he, the psychoanalyst, desperately needs to believe.

Authority's Anxieties and the Lesbian Threat

This desperation becomes a clue to the anxieties both concealed and engendered by such excessive displays of authority—anxieties that tap, among other things, into the dialogic nature of the psychoanalytic encounter. Because Dora *does,* in the first instance, "provid[e] the text," the analyst, however brilliant an interpreter, is not sole author of the scene, and this reality triggers Freud's uneasiness that his interpretation has not completely solved the "task of guessing and filling in" the mystery that "the analysis offers . . . in the shape only of hints and allusions" (58). The result is that Freud's narration of the sessions increasingly stages a battle for mastery of the "text" that is doubly Dora/*Dora.* And Freud rightly senses in Dora a "sharp-sighted" sleuth whose talent in "suspect[ing] . . . hidden connection[s]" and "unearth[ing]" (49–50) clues rivals her therapist's ratiocinative skills. It is also telling that the most recent "serious" exercise of her "intellectual precocity" (34) has involved "attending lectures for women" (38). This protofeminism, coupled with her "very independent judgement" and habit of "laugh[ing] at the efforts of doctors" (37), underlines the degree to which Dora's deviation from turn-of-the-century standards of femininity increases the apprehensions upsetting Freud's quest for textual and medical authority.

The gendered and sexually charged valences of this struggle come together with particular force in a session reported near the middle of the case study, as Freud's process of association leads him to link Dora's "deviance" with the metaphors of floods and libidinal flow associated, as we have seen, with unchanneled female sexuality. On this occasion, the somewhat chagrined Freud reports that, whereas Dora opens the session with several comments, "My powers of interpretation had run dry that day; [so] I let her go on talking" (76–77). Immediately eye-catching here is the formulation ("run dry") that Freud gives his own silence, for it highlights a paradox intrinsic to his conception of his psychoanalytic mission: how to speak in as "dry and direct" (65) a manner as possible, maintaining one's scientific objectivity, without running dry, being left with nothing to say, or, conversely, being overrun—as in the present case—by another's verbal flood of associations. Freud's immediate solution is to let Dora go on talking until her associations reveal information "which I did not neglect *to use against her*" (77; emphasis added). In turning Dora's words, her text, into weapons "against her[self]" in order to allay his own anxieties at having nothing to say, Freud transforms the session into an arena of combat. Using Theweleit's terminology, one might say that Freud's method functions as a prophylaxis or body armor designed to ward off the floods that momentarily threaten to engulf and hence diminish his official storytelling power.

Nor is my metaphor of floods in the last sentence mere hyperbole. For Dora's flood of words immediately releases another kind of flood within Freud's train of thought. In a remarkable example of free association, Freud jumps from his account of this session to a digression in the next paragraph on the "homosexual current" set flowing by Dora's psychoneuroses: not only has the repression of her (presumed) love of Herr K. reactivated her incestuous love of her father, but it has also awakened, Freud now reveals, a desire "which had [Frau K.] as its *object*—a feeling, that is, which could only be based upon an affection on Dora's part for one of her own sex" (77).[95] Explaining that adolescent homosexual feelings are often a typical precursor of adult heterosexuality, Freud once again likens the libido to a stream of water to make his point: "Thenceforward, in favourable circumstances, the homosexual current of feeling often runs completely dry. But if a girl is not happy in her love for a man, the current is often set flowing again by the libido in later years" (77–78). In other words, those archaic or collateral channels of the polymorphous perverse associated with "unconscious perverse activities" that "had formerly seemed fated to run dry" ten pages earlier (68) have been reactivated by the overflow that sexual repression creates in the main (e.g., heterosexual) waterway. Reinforcing the teleological assumptions involved in positing homosexuality as an adolescent resurgence of polymorphous desires that "in favorable circumstances" are channeled into normative heterosexuality, Freud's phrase describing what causes the homosexual current to flow again—a girl "not happy in her love for a man"—betrays most clearly the anxiety that motors Freud's subconscious linking of his own "dried up" interpretive powers, Dora's flood of words, and, now, this wave of same-sex feeling. For what Freud finds most threatening are expressions of an active female desire that doesn't depend on male objects—and here the story of Dora intersects with the expressions of autonomous pleasure and autoerotic self-expression glimpsed in Lucy Snowe's quest to the park and Edna's awakening on Grand Isle.

This threat reveals a central irony in Freud's enterprise: his self-professed goal is to awaken and bring to the surface the flow of female desires that it is *also* psychoanalysis's task to regulate, to rechannel into conformity with normative definitions of femininity as the complementary other of phallic sexuality. Part of the therapeutic mission, then, is not only to free feminine currents but to construct the dams necessary to regulate such potentially unruly flow. Yet erecting one dike only serves to raise the phantom of another dyke, as it were; for to the degree that Freud reads female autoeroticism as excluding the male principle and therefore as antimale, he reads these desirous floods as homoerotic—hence his diagnosis of the "homosexual current of feeling" that has *failed* to "run completely dry" in this passage, at the very instant that his own interpretive prowess has indeed "run dry" (77).

The next occurrence of the river metaphor cinches the fact that the (sexual) anxieties aroused by Freud's temporary failure of (textual) authority are less about lesbianism per se than about *any and all* expressions of self-sufficient female desire, for which homosexuality has become Freud's catch-all metaphor. Having just uncovered evidence of the "masturbatory satisfaction" Dora experienced as a child, Freud speaks of the period of guilty abstinence and onset of hysterical symptoms that often follow childhood autoeroticism, until "another and more normal kind of satisfaction" is found in "marriage and normal sexual intercourse." However, Freud warns, "if the satisfaction afforded in marriage is again removed . . . then the libido flows back into its old channel" (97–98). Semantically, the libidinal "flow" identified in this passage—signifying a return to masturbation that augurs the return of hysterical symptoms—is exactly the same as the "current" (78) associated with female homosexuality. And either sexuality—autoerotic or homoerotic—is defined as antithetical to the "satisfaction" that women (should) attain in intercourse with men. Regulating the flow of female sexuality is the only guarantee that phallic sexuality has of its indispensability.

Dream-Texts of Desire

The specter of female autoeroticism that provokes these anxieties of authority, I suggest, inspires the two dreams that Dora reports in therapy and that Freud spends nearly half of the case study analyzing. Whatever one thinks of Freud's conclusions, his interpretations of these dreams are *tours de force* in which he adroitly shifts among multiple layers of time, keeps simultaneous strands of conjecture in play, and chases down rapidly unfolding associations that reach far beyond the dreams' contents. Not surprisingly, perhaps, the readings produced by Freud support a vision of female oedipal struggle, in which the girl's incestuous desire must yield to that of a suitable father-substitute in order to guarantee adult psychosexual health. But in so focusing on the father-daughter struggle, Freud remains completely silent on the subtexts of female *autoerotic* awakening that envelop both dreams; such silences protect Freud from confronting more directly the anxieties that propel him to frenzied extremes in attempting to master these same dream-texts.

Even a cursory review of Dora's two dreams reveals a powerful fantasy of female desire freed from either male control or heterosexual necessity. In the first dream, which Dora has for three nights in a row after Herr K.'s advances at the lake, she is awakened by her father because the house is on fire, then hurries outside where she wakes again—events which, to Freud, express Dora's wish that her father would protect her from the desire to yield to Herr K. Intriguingly, the dream not only begins and ends with moments of physical awakening but triggers a series of memories of a more remote, distinctly female, erotic awakening. Almost immediately Freud fixes on one detail of the dream, the jewel-case that the father refuses to let the mother stop to save. If the phrase "jewel-case" is common slang, as Freud asserts, for "the female genitals" (87) and Dora's mother the possessor of the case of which Dora dreams, then the iconography of the dream maps out a highly specific female anatomy and context (even Freud concurs with Dora that "the mystery" of the dream "turns upon your mother" [87], whose influence he otherwise discounts[96]). Within this female geography, the dream hints of a realm of autonomous female sexuality and fluid pleasures, as evinced in Freud's ingenious unearthing (under the assumption that "fire" must imply its opposite, "water") of the event allowing Dora to substitute her father for Herr K. in the dream. For, as we have seen, Freud surmises that Dora's father "used to wake her up long ago . . . to prevent her from making her bed wet" (109)—and not only does the girl already intuit that amorous activity also "makes things wet" (90), but she herself engages in one such activity, since childhood bedwetting, according to Freud, "has no more likely cause than masturbation" (92). Implicit in this autoerotic activity is the clitoral stimulation that Freud posits girls must eventually renounce on the path to normative femininity.

Thus, in waking his daughter to prevent her bedwetting, Dora's father comes to function within her unconscious as an agent *prohibiting* autoerotic pleasure; no wonder that in Dora's dream he declares "I refuse to let my children go to destruction" ("as a result of masturbation," Freud finishes the sentence [112]). In Dora's psyche, moreover, the guilt and anxiety that attach to and replace her masturbatory activity have to do with yet another childhood waking experience: overhearing the sound of her father's labored breathing emanating from the adjacent bedroom during sexual intercourse. Aware that her father, who suffers from shortness of breath owing to his tubercular condition, should not overexert himself, Dora fears for his mortality, and this association of sex and death incites her subconscious fear that she too may have dangerously overexerted herself in masturbating—hence the shortness of breath and dyspnoea that overtake her in the intensified form of hysterical symptoms.

Tellingly, Freud seizes control of the revelation of Dora's childhood masturbatory desires by positioning it as *the* secret residing in "the most hidden recesses of [her] mind," one that only his superior analytic skill can "bring to light" (96). Pointing out the symptomatic act whereby Dora reveals her masturbatory secret—fingering the aperture of her reticule—Freud declares that "he [who] has eyes to see and ears to hear may convince himself that no mortal can keep a secret. If his lips are silent, he chatters with his finger-tips; betrayal oozes out of him at every pore" (96). By means of this rhetorical power play, the masturbating girl becomes the mere "mortal" who "oozes" secrets and "chatters with [her] finger-tips," while Freud wields the panoptic power of the all-seeing, all-hearing, self-ordained judge of human nature. Given that Dora's "secret" is represented as "oozing" out of her, it is worth noting that Freud also seeks to control the autoerotic implications of Dora's dream by converting the fluids hitherto associated with female sexuality to phallocentric ends. This move is reminiscent of Lawrence's similar strategy in *The Virgin and the Gipsy*. For Freud's interpretation transforms the wetness that Dora subconsciously associates with both sex and masturbatory release into a *masculine* characteristic: namely, her father's gift to his wife of pearl "drop" earrings, which come to signify, in Freud's reading of Dora's hysteria, the spermatic (i.e., male) flow from which women must protect themselves. In contrast, "wetness" for women becomes not the flow of natural desire but the sign of the contagion that may result from their exposure to the venereal disease from which men suffer. In light of this reappropriation of female floods as male property, it is no wonder that at the conclusion of his analysis of this dream, Freud's associations lead him, as if by accident, from Dora's internalization of the father's taboo against masturbation to Freud's story of another female patient—cited in my discussion of *The Awakening*—who dreams that she finds herself swimming in a frozen sea: better female frigidity than female floods.

In the second dream Dora reports that she is wandering through a strange town, and then upon receiving word from her mother that her father has died, she finds herself entering a "thick wood" (114) in search of the train station; she arrives at home to find that the others are already at the cemetery, and, in an addendum to the dream that Dora later recalls, she goes upstairs to her room and calmly begins reading a book that lies on her writing table (120). For Freud, this dream clearly signifies a fantasy of oedipal revenge against the father, in which Dora punishes him for failing to protect her from sexual menace. But it just as strikingly encodes a deoedipalizing plot that traces an autoerotic quest—recalling *Villette's* trajectory—of specifically female discovery. Like Lucy Snowe at the beginning of Brontë's novel, Dora finds herself wandering in an unknown city, and, like Lucy's midnight quest to seek out the rushy basin in the moonlit park, Dora's solo journey through the thick wood (she declines the offer of a man to serve as her guide) is rife with sexual connotations, particularly given the etymological links Freud discerns between the train station that is her immediate goal and the female nymphae or labia.[97] The latter association, moreover, originates in a painting Dora has observed the day before at the Successionist Exhibition, in which nymphs cavort in the background of a thickly wooded scene. Such details seem to point to a singularly autoerotic experience: Dora's dreaming unconscious is allowing her to explore *her own anatomy* in symbolic form (so, too, with Lucy Snowe's hallucinatory fantasy that she will enter the park through "a gap in the paling," a "narrow, irregular aperture," through which a "man could not have made his way" [547]). However, in a telling example of Freud's own repressive mechanisms, he denies the dream's autoeroticism by declaring that the persona traveling through this female geography must be a male figure, for only through the perspective of a man's gaze would it "have been appropriate for the goal to have been the possession of a woman, *of herself*" (116–17; emphasis added). The implication is that it is inappropriate not only for a woman to possess another woman, but for a woman to seek "possession . . . of herself," to find or fantasize erotic fulfillment that excludes the male principle.

Freud inadvertently provides another clue to this dream's female libidinal erotics when he links its opening image of wandering alone in a strange city to Dora's visit to Dresden. Having chosen to go alone to its famous art museum, she spends two hours before its Sistine Madonna, "rapt in silent admiration" (116; again Lucy Snowe's observation of the paintings of women in the museum chapter of *Villette* comes to mind). When Freud asks Dora what so captivates her about the painting, she has no "clear answer" beyond the enigmatic words, "The Madonna" (116). Freud attempts to argue that the painting's maternal subject relates to childbirth fantasies that Dora has entertained after rebuking Herr K. at the lake. To Freud the painting thus becomes one more piece of evidence that "in your unconscious you . . . regretted the upshot of the scene" (125). In pressing Herr K.'s case, however, Freud not only overlooks the obvious appeal that a virgin birth—eliminating the necessity of the male partner—might have for a young woman who senses she is a sexual pawn of men, but he also remains blind to the desire for an idealized mother-daughter bond that Dora's rapt admiration of this maternal figure may signal.[98] Dora's actual mother, after all, plays as pivotal a role in this dream as in the first, writing the letter that informs her daughter she can now return home "if you like" because the father has died; such signs of communication between mother and daughter (which run throughout the case study but go unnoted by Freud) imply an at least fantasized network of female exchanges to which men may be extraneous.[99] Similarly, Dora's fascination with an idealized maternal object may also signify the girl's longing for the safety she associates with a homosocial world of female love and friendship. In this respect Dora's admiration of the Sistine Madonna recalls Edna's fascination with Adèle, a "sensuous Madonna" whose physical beauty and emotional intimacy temporarily provide Chopin's protagonist with the haven she needs in order to awaken from sexual repression, and it anticipates the pattern of covert female homosocial relations theorized at greater length in chapter 5.

The addendum that Dora brings to the dream—in which she calmly begins to read the book laid out on her writing table instead of going to her father's funeral—also hints at an alternative narrative of female eros unfolding within the symbolic terrain of the dream. Freud attempts to incorporate the book into his predetermined plot—Dora's secret love for Herr K.—by identifying it as the sexual encyclopedia from which he assumes Dora has garnered her knowledge of the facts of life. But, given its placement on Dora's writing table, it is also possible to see the book as the hidden text of Dora's desire, the heretical counternarrative to the "secret and possibly sexual meaning of the clinical picture" (123) that Freud is so intent on producing. Such a subversive text, like Lucy Snowe's heretical "book of her life" marked with a red cross, must be kept from others' eyes in order to avert its being appropriated into a normalizing narrative of female maturation. Significantly, in the dream, Dora chooses *not* to join the mourners at the father's burial—in effect refusing to participate in the narrative "death" seen as endemic to oedipal plotting—in order to begin reading, an activity that extends the emphasis on the textualization of female sexuality already created by the two paintings underlying the dream's formation (the Successionist painting, the Sistine Madonna). With a Scheherazade-like circularity, this reading/writing activity signals no immediate "end" or "death" to the dream's autoerotic subtexts or to the subversive authority invested in Dora's ability to create her own narratives—it is, after all, *her* "writing-table" at which she sits in the dream.

Dueling Authors

These telltale signs of Dora's covert authority and authorship only incite Freud's increasingly no-holds-barred attempt to master both his subject and the text of her hysteria. In their continuing war of words, it has become increasingly important to Freud that *he* have the last word, and thus he ends the penultimate session with so violent a reiteration of his thesis— "So you see that your love for Herr K. . . . has persisted down to the present day"—that Dora is finally rendered silent: "—And Dora disputed the fact no longer" (125). The abrupt rupture signified by the dash that Freud inserts between his spoken demand and what he takes to be Dora's capitulation indicates the violence that is occurring both in the session and on the level of its textual inscription. In response to Dora's announcement that she is breaking off the therapy in the next and final session, Freud again commandeers the moment, converting the talking cure in a desperate act of authorial fiat exercised to allay his mounting fears that his subject may be slipping from his control. "*Now I know* your motive," he decrees in a barrage of bullying words that engulf the session, and then declares, "You *have not even got the right* to assert that [a marriage proposal from Herr K.] was out of the question. . . . After all, you *did not let him finish* his speech." This, ironically, is the very "crime" that Freud, by not letting Dora insert a word edgewise, is making sure won't happen to himself. Without a break he boldly continues to implant within Dora his version of truth as *her* truth, in a proleptically Foucauldian assertion of knowledge-as-power: "And I think *that is why*. . . . So it *must have been*. . . . You *will* agree. . . . *I know now*" (128–30; emphases added). One can almost sense Freud's simultaneous glee (at "knowing") and anxiety (the fear that he does not know enough, or that Dora knows more than she tells) as he in effect becomes author by default of this case study's version of female sexual repression. His words may pour forth in a flood, but their logic forms a wall, a dam, through which Dora's voice can no longer break. "He was caught in words," Wilhelm Reich wrote of Freud, "He was caught in words."[100]

At the same time, however, the very urgency of Freud's authorial attempt to control Dora and her story contains the deconstructive seeds that doom his project to unravel of its own accord. It is no coincidence, for instance, that all four characteristics that Freud identifies as traits of the hysteric's narrative can be found in his own text, dangerously eroding the boundaries that supposedly separate the doctor's enlightened "scientific" discourse from the fabrications of the self-involved patient.[101] Similarly, Freud's ability to control the text that Dora provides is thrown into question by the simple fact that *it takes two* to create a psychoanalytic encounter. Freud's masterful interpretation, after all, hinges in a parasitic fashion on Dora's continuing returns to his office and her ongoing revelations; he cannot afford to "shut her up" entirely, for his livelihood depends on her presence. This necessary interdependence of analyst and analysand has even further implications for the anxieties of authority that riddle Freud's attempt to fit Dora into a preconceived plot of female awakening and desire. For the therapeutic encounter is built not only of the free flow of associations that occur to Dora but of those free associations to which Freud also gives voice as he lapses into and out of Dora's "mind" and his own thoughts. The constant combination, splitting asunder, and recombination of the multiple associations arising from *both* participants, forming chains of provisional meaning that both lead to and dissolve in the face of successive connections, evoke Deleuze and Guattari's redefinition of desire as the continuous flow created among partial objects as they connect and reconnect in ever-new patterns. In a profound sense, then, the desires engendered by and within the psychoanalytic dialogue always, inevitably, escape the authority of any one participant's "final word."

More specifically, the authority of Freud's interpretation is undermined by the element in Dora's psychosexual makeup that he claims to have discovered too late: the strength of her lesbian feelings. This disclaimer, which occurs in a footnote at the very end of the text, is a bit disingenuous given the much earlier discussion of the "homosexual current of feeling" reactivated in victims of hysteria whose "normal" sexual outlets have been blocked (77–78). That "homosexual current," however, was generalized as a temporary recurrence of the "*normal* germs of perversion" that exist in everyone—in other words, the polymorphous perverse of infantile desire.

In contrast, the "homosexual (gynaecophilic) love" that Freud *now* claims is "the strongest unconscious current in her mental life" but that he admits he "failed to discover in time" (142) threatens to invalidate Freud's interpretation at its very core. For if this lesbian desire is truly "the strongest" of Dora's adult erotic cathexes, not merely a reaction to sexual trauma, an acknowledgment of its place in her psychosexual history would topple the entire edifice of thwarted heterosexual love that Freud has constructed around his patient and Herr K. The narrative terms whereby Freud chooses to convey to the reader this new lesbian subtext, this alternative "love plot," is most revealing of all, for he relegates his commentary to three long footnotes placed at the end of the case study—footnotes that simultaneously introduce the subject of lesbianism and exclude it from the main body of text. This potentially incendiary information is further marginalized by the fact that the first two notes deal primarily with other issues, merely making asides to Dora's "deep-rooted homosexual love for Frau K." (126) at their conclusion; only the third note—three pages from the end of the case study—directly addresses lesbianism, declaring its "omission" to be the major "fault" of the case (142).[102] Most strikingly, while the footnote makes the reader privy to this lesbian subtext, this information, as the note admits, has been withheld all along from Dora herself. The "secret" of lesbianism that Freud keeps to himself—in yet one more authorial power play—allows him to maintain *his* fantasy that the "secret" harbored by Dora is her unadmitted love for Herr K. and her wish to have succumbed to his sexual advances. In designating who receives this contraband knowledge, as well as in creating heterosexual and homosexual plots whose separation is reinforced on the level of narrative structure (the body of the text versus the subordinated footnote), Freud might be accused of writing a schizophrenic text whose embedded incoherences expose its conflicting narrative desires.[103]

The authority of the case study is also impugned by the role that transference plays in blurring the boundaries supposedly separating analyst and analysand. "I did not succeed in mastering the transference in good time," Freud admits in regard to Dora's projection of negative feelings onto him, a failure that he deems responsible for her decision to break off the analysis "prematurely" (140). Even here, the anxiety Freud feels at his oversight is expressed as a failure of authority, and hence as a failure to direct the memories, revelations, and associations flooding Dora's subconscious into a more useful channel. "But I . . . [thought] I had ample time before me, since . . . the material for the analysis had not yet run dry. In this way the transference took me unawares" (141). If the transference reveals Freud's authority to be less than total by "taking him unawares," his claim to mastery is even more seriously called into question by the effects of countertransference: those desires, values, and assumptions that the analyst unconsciously projects onto the patient, making objectivity, and with it a coherent, unified vision, an impossible goal. We have seen the undiagnosed countertransference at work throughout the analysis, particularly in the way Freud begins to insert his own fantasies, even his own words, into Dora's narrative, in order to impose a culturally overdetermined script of normative femininity onto her experience of sexual awakening. But because of the undetected presence of this countertransference, Freud is unable to give himself the critical distance to be objective, which in turn calls his "superior" interpretive ability into question. And with this loss of objectivity, yet another of the masculine boundaries or dams supposedly protecting the analyst from the vertiginous floods of unchecked female desire gives way, subjecting Freud to a wave of sexual anxieties that ironically only bind him more closely to, rather than helping him separate from, his clinical and textual subject matter, Dora's sexual hysteria.

Nothing more forcefully demonstrates the crisis of sexual and textual authority that such anxieties breed than the upshot of the analysis. In what turns out to be the final session on New Year's Eve of 1900—all too fateful a date for a text located on the cusp of modernity—Freud succeeds in having (and speaking) "the last word," but Dora turns the silence imposed on her voice into her own last word by terminating the analysis, breaking off Freud's ongoing interpretation as he has broken off the possibility of her reply. In doing so, she revives her earlier "refusal" of Herr K. as a refusal to participate any longer in Freud's plot of her awakening and repression. "And—came no more" (130), Freud writes of Dora's leavetaking, his insertion of the dash mid-sentence repeating on the textual level the psychological violence that her departure represents for Freud, who is left in an impasse of unresolved countertransference, psychologically unable to let Dora go. Freud's one recourse is to attempt to write Dora out of his system—an endeavor he undertakes with a vengeance, completing a draft of the case study in a record three weeks.[104] If Dora refuses to submit to his interpretive authority in person, he at least can be assured of her acquiescence on paper, as the subject of his text.

Through the agency of writing, moreover, Freud is even able to turn the humiliation of her leavetaking to his benefit. For he presents their last session as a story of female vengeance, in which *he* becomes Dora's final victim, the last in the series of various men—the cruelly rebuffed Herr K., the heartsick father—she has maligned. Once again, Freud has inserted himself into Dora's "story" as a major character: its tragic hero. Hence the self-pitying statement that immediately follows his labeling Dora's announcement that she is quitting therapy as "an unmistakeable act of vengeance": "No one who, like me, conjures up the most evil of those half-tamed demons that inhabit the human breast and seeks to wrestle with them, can come through the struggle unscathed" (131). In a supreme gesture of authorial fiat, *his* battle-wounds, not Dora's sufferings, become the focus of the case study's ending. Such self-aggrandizement underlines the anxieties that remain in play despite—or because of—the attempt to wrest narrative agency from Dora in order to authorize psychoanalysis's official story of female desire. Obsessively revising the completed manuscript for another five years, Freud's inability to let go of the case study—despite his spontaneous composition of the first draft—implies that his subject cannot be written out of his psyche as easily as he thought: having penetrated his male armor, Dora now resides, ghostlike, *within.* In a profound irony, the phantasm of Dora has become the Foucauldian "truth" of being, the sexual "secret," that defines *Freud's* interiority.[105]

Given the ongoing struggle for mastery that has precipitated the impasse in which Freud ultimately finds himself, it is perhaps inevitable that Dora returns to him fifteen months later (on another unbelievably ironic date, April Fools' Day), "to finish her story and to ask for help once more" (143). It is perhaps equally inevitable that Freud makes Dora pay for her perceived act of vengeance against him by saying no; converting what was previously *her* refusal into *his* negative, he declines to take her request for help seriously (after all, it *is* April Fools' Day) and instead promises to *forgive* Dora "for having *deprived me* of the satisfaction of affording . . . a far more radical cure" (144; emphasis added). Why would the ever-curious Freud decline the chance, this once, of hearing more? Perhaps because he no longer *needs* to hear Dora "finish her story," since he has already made it his own creative property. Having worked so long to make her story mesh with his own conclusions, he needn't hear new revelations that might untie the fragile knot he has begun to solve on paper. As he says at one point in the text, "everything fits together satisfactorily," and the satisfaction afforded by his expenditure of narrative desire in drafting the case study may compensate for the satisfaction that he claims Dora has denied him in breaking off the therapy.

Where then does this leave Dora, who, after all, has provided the occasion for Freud's masterful text? Caught, one may imagine, like her "master," in a state of subjective impasse. But the impasse in which Dora finds herself, unlike Freud's, is also existential, and it poses no clear or comforting escapes or alternatives. Rather, paralleling Edna's predicament at the end of *The Awakening,* Dora is left suspended between impossibly conflicting societal claims and psychosexual imperatives; and these conflicting demands in turn mirror the contradiction embedded at the heart of Freudian psychoanalysis, a contradiction that is made manifest in the imagery of flowing currents and streams in the case study. On the one hand, the flux of water represents for Freud the dispersive, heterogeneous, autonomous force of the libidinal currents that have been blocked by sexual trauma and need to be set flowing again before Dora can experience sexual reawakening. On the other hand, the desire that Freud seeks to free within Dora in order to restore her to mental and sexual health is also, ironically, precisely the threatening force that both psychoanalytic and societal codes seek to curb, to channel into culturally sanctioned conduits. Within emerging Freudian psychoanalytic discourse, these regulatory conduits shape the path to the normative vaginal "femininity" that assures phallic "masculinity" of its indispensability. Within *fin de siècle* sociomoral codes, these conduits uphold those sexual standards of male dominance/female submission that society sometimes tacitly condones (as in Freud's fantasy that a marriage between Dora and Herr K. would solve everyone's problems), sometimes pretends to ignore (as in Herr K.'s pursuit of Dora), and sometimes self-righteously condemns (the more likely outcome had Herr K. "had his way" with Dora at the lake[106]).

In none of these possible scenarios of sexual initiation does Dora stand to win; each serves only to exacerbate the very tensions and reinforce the silences that leave her in an unresolved impasse of subjectivity, divided within herself and between competing claims. In the process the dams, embankments, and other feats of engineering that appear in tandem with Freud's imagery of libidinal flow not only come to symbolize a means of regulating Dora's sexuality to make it conform to narrowly conceived, socially legislated dictates of gender, but they also tellingly function as analogues of the prophylactic protection the male ego seeks in order to stave off the threat of dissolution that, as Theweleit so forcefully reminds us, feminine floods portend in the phallocratic cultural imagination. These defensive masculine barriers provide an interesting clue to Freud's final comments on the case study, as he attempts, in the name of psychology and science, to justify the failure to deliver a "far more radical cure" (144) for Dora's hysteria. "In spite of every theoretical interest and of every endeavor to be of assistance as a physician," Freud writes, "I keep the fact in mind that *there must be some limits set* to the extent to which psychological influence may be used, and I respect as one of these limits the patient's own will and understanding" (131; emphasis added). In a sleight of hand that follows a typically Freudian logic (whereby a reproach against another conceals a self-reproach), Freud makes Dora responsible for the "limits" that in fact *he himself is imposing,* limits that curtail the flood of revelations that his "psychological influence" has, ironically, set into motion. For implicit in the psychoanalytic—as well as modernist—agenda of penetrating the depths of another's psyche, of "bringing to light" that which lies hidden within (even as such evacuatory gestures implant the "sexual secrets" that are then taken to define the essence and truth of one's being) is the possibility of an immersion in otherness that may begin to call into question the very boundaries of self and other.

Whether such immersion in the other is to be seen as a threat or a promise, the source of anxiety or a "far more radical cure," forms the dilemma that propels the sexual and textual crises of authority that, for Freud, as well as for Chopin and Lawrence, the *fin de siècle* plot of female sexual awakening serves to catalyze and embody. It also forms the challenge embraced by subsequent modernist writers devising far more experimental and self-conscious formats to probe the psychology of sex and self. This anticipation of the high modernist response to the challenges posed by Freudian psychology—the subject of the following chapter—should not, however, diminish our perception of the advances made on both thematic and formal levels by the numerous plots of female sexual awakening emerging in the first decades of the twentieth century.[107] By focusing on the liberation of the hitherto constrained floods of female libidinal desire, novels like *The Awakening* and *The Virgin and the Gipsy* (as well as nonfiction like *Dora*) not only helped break the taboo on the representation of women's sexuality, freeing it from the romanticization of prior literary tradition, but by embodying these libidinal currents in the imagistic, associative, and lyrical structures of their awakening fables, Chopin and Lawrence helped pave the way for those experiments in fictional form that even more directly disavowed traditional verisimilitude in order to record the profound reality of the mind's conscious and unconscious rhythms.

As this chapter has shown, the attempt to "authorize" female desire in the protomodernist plot of sexual awakening persistently raises questions of authority—and of crises in authority—that have long been seen as definitive characteristics of high modernism, the byproducts of modernity's delegitimation of its master-narratives of progress in the wake of Darwin, Marx, and Freud. But as this chapter has also illustrated, in those texts that make the emancipation of women's eroticism their subject, these anxieties of narrative authority cannot be separated from the sexual anxieties to which the representation of the floods of female desire give rise—anxieties that, tellingly, are linked to the female protagonist's process of awakening to *autoerotic* desires whose pleasures are potentially random, multiple, and directionless. Because desire detached from specific aims or objects exceeds, in Deleuze and Guattari's formulation, the oedipally imposed limits that restrict women's sexual fulfillment to male needs, the portent of female autoeroticism that stands outside this phallic economy poses the greatest imaginable threat to masculine identity and male power. Anti-oedipal desire, to repeat Deleuze and Guattari's injunction, doesn't "demand" or even need to "demand" revolution because it is *already* "revolutionary in its own right"—an observation that seems all the more relevant when the libidinal floods in question are women's desires freed of male demand. Even when the desiring female subject—for example, Edna in *The Awakening*—remains largely unaware of the political stakes and class privileges that make her sexual rebellion possible, her awakening desires remain "revolutionary in [their] own right," charged with a libidinal politics that outlasts either her eventual misprision of her "awakening sensuousness" (131) for cultural myths of romantic yearning or her final yielding to despair.

The "revolutionary" potential of these early-twentieth-century fables of awakened sexuality, however, is ultimately limited by a formal feature that is intrinsic both to the trajectory of the awakening plot and to the belief system these works share with turn-of-the-century sexological and psychological discourses. For Chopin, Freud, and Lawrence are products of their day to the extent that they accept without question the assumption that there exists at the core of every individual a natural sexual force that not only predates the repressive mechanisms of conscience or societal prohibition, but whose expression would liberate our most *authentic* selves; this innate force of nature, as the structure of the awakening story repeatedly demonstrates, only awaits uncovering (as in Chopin's plot of divestiture), release from constraint (as in Lawrence's breaking of the dams of morality), or (in Freud's terms) "bring[ing] to the light of day" (27). To the degree, then, that these writers accept what is in fact a late-nineteenth-century discursive formulation of sexuality as, in Foucault's words, "a primitive, natural, and living energy welling up from below"[108] that provides the secret key to one's essential identity, they overlook the possibility that such a conception—like the notion of interiority on which it depends—may also be a construction, a *fiction* of sexuality that disguises itself as a truth of being. Despite their acutely perceptive and often radical questioning of the taboos and constraints placed on desire, these narratives of sexual awakening ultimately misrecognize, one might say, the "secret of self" that Freudian psychology attempts to excavate for the "secret of sex" that Foucault evacuates as a historical construction, creating in the process an impasse that necessarily limits the "radical cure" (*Dora,* 144)—sexually or novelistically speaking—that the awakening plot can achieve.

In the following chapter, we will see what happens when the novelistic attempt to represent states of consciousness and to fathom the recesses of subjectivity (1) results in the suspicion that the notion of interiority may itself be a fiction, and (2) calls into question the boundaries presumed to separate self and other, deeds and desire, signifiers and signifieds. In immersing their texts, and their protagonists, in the profound otherness that exists both within consciousness and beyond the perceived borders of the self, such modernist experimenters create stunningly original fictions in which the power of sexuality to make and unmake the self revolutionizes the parameters of twentieth-century fiction, proffering "a far more radical cure" than hitherto imagined to the question of *what* as well as *how* the genre of the novel can mean in a changing world-order.

CHAPTER THREE

Modernist Theaters of the Mind I

James Joyce, Ulysses
·····

Virginia Woolf, Mrs. Dalloway
·····

Nothing exists outside of us except a state of mind.
—Peter Walsh dreaming, in Virginia Woolf, *Mrs. Dalloway*[1]

It's always flowing in a stream, never the same,
which in the stream of life we trace.
—Bloom walking by the Liffey, in James Joyce, *Ulysses*[2]

Means something, language of flow.
—Bloom musing, in James Joyce, *Ulysses* (216)

Both Chopin's *The Awakening* and Lawrence's *The Virgin and the Gipsy* manifest a keen interest in the magnetic pull of the subliminal and libidinal on the waking life of their protagonists, as the previous chapter has made clear. But for all their advances beyond the constraints of traditional fictional realism, these narratives still approach the world of interior reality indirectly and impressionistically, through a combination of textual strategies that at times makes quotidian reality seem dreamlike, even surreal, but that does so without forfeiting a primary commitment to "the waking life" of their characters and its linear exposition in "real" time. Indeed, the very format of the awakening plot depends, as the word *awakening* implies, on the protagonist's temporal as well as psychological progress from one state to another (from sleep to awakening, from repression to revelation) through a sequence of causally linked events that owes as much to the trajectory of the nineteenth-century bildungsroman (with its archetypal movement from ignorance to knowledge) as to the experiments in registering states of consciousness that were emerging under the aegis of high modernism.

Just what sets these modernist visions apart is the subject of Virginia

Woolf's epoch-defining essay "Modern Fiction." Originally conceived as a defense of Joyce's *Ulysses*—whose lack of even the remotest resemblance to previous English fiction was sending shock-waves throughout the literary world as it appeared serially in the *Little Review*—"Modern Fiction" sounds the rallying call for a new fiction to mirror a new era's understanding of reality. "Look within," Virginia Woolf famously directs her contemporaries in a passage that spells out the radical shift in vision separating her novelistic aims from those of her Edwardian and Victorian forebears: "Let us record the atoms as they fall upon the mind in the order in which they fall . . . let us trace the pattern, however disconnected and incoherent in appearance, which each sight or incident scores on the consciousness." Beginning with the supposition that the most meaningful "reality" no longer resides in the seemingly objective or the faithful rendering of surfaces but exists "within," wrapped in a subjective haze of consciousness, subliminal thoughts, and inchoate desires, Woolf argues that in order to relay this realm of conscious and unconscious impulse in all its indeterminacy, atemporality, and randomness, the modern writer of fiction has to reject the external signposts—the "series of gig-lamps symmetrically arranged"—of mimetic realism and linear plotting.[3] The innovations summoned forth by such a departure from the dominant novelistic tradition helped solidify the twentieth-century revolution in art and culture that now goes by the name of "high modernism." Reconceptualizing the parameters of fictional representation, such modernist experiments dramatically redefined the novel by the unprecedented attention they paid to the intangible psychosexual forces associated with interiority—those dimly perceived, often preverbal, desires and drives that, in the wake of Freud's postulation of the fundamentally split human subject, were increasingly understood to suffuse all aspects of existence, giving shape to identity even while threatening its continual subversion.

The importance of this connection between formal experimentation and psychological representation was not lost on modernism's detractors. Georg Lukács, for example, argued that modernism's "'experimental' stylistic distortion," a practice he condemned as elitist and solipsistic, was the logical outcome of the movement's uncritical embrace of the "psychopathology" of modern consciousness (and, in his view, its abandonment of history and the tradition of fictional realism).[4] While Lukács maintains that the modernist emphasis on the alienated psyche has dangerously separated form from content by elevating "stylistic distortion" over themes of social responsibility, his wording nonetheless betrays a very specific link between experimental form and thematic content at work in the modernist text, one which, if stripped of the pejorative connotations of "distortion" and "pathology," reveals a commitment to "reality" and to a politics of representation as engaged as his own. After all, as Bertolt Brecht restated the problem in his passionate defense of the political efficacy of avant-garde art, "New problems appear and demand new methods. Reality changes," and "in order to represent it, modes of representation must also change."[5]

The following pages attempt to unfold these complicated, and sometimes contradictory, representational poetics and politics by investigating how issues of sexuality, psychology, and narrative impinge upon each other in the "psychopathological" endeavor to represent the flux of consciousness and the erotics of mental activity in modernist narrative form. It does so by taking as its test cases two of the most notoriously experimental practitioners of canonical modernism, James Joyce and Virginia Woolf. Their attempts to approximate "interior," often nonverbal, states of being in *Ulysses* (1922) and *Mrs. Dalloway* (1925)—texts that both fulfill Woolf's directive to "examine an ordinary mind on an ordinary day" ("Modern Fiction," 106)—pose an unparalleled challenge to unitary conceptions of identity, sexuality, and narrative. And that challenge, as we shall see, gives rise to a threat—not, as Lukács would have it, to social reality or the practice of realism per se, but to a sociocultural *construction* of reality as "pathological" in its constraints as the so-called "anti-realist" modernism that Lukács fears.

Woolf's privileging of the inner life as "the proper stuff of fiction" in "Modern Fiction" (110) finds expression throughout the 1920s in imagistic patterns that initially seem identical to the directional signposts (up/down, surface/depth, light/dark) associated with the awakening plot in chapter 2. Thus Woolf notes, in the phrase that I have already cited, that "for the moderns"—writers such as herself engaged in rethinking the novel—"the point of interest . . . lies very likely in the *dark places* of psychology" (108; emphasis added). A contemporary reviewer, having asserted that Woolf's "art is that of the psychologist," echoes her words when he singles out as her greatest achievement the searing "light" her imagination sheds on "things which have long been latent in the *dark places* of consciousness, [but] hitherto unrealized by any power of explicit speech."[6] Comparable images pervade Woolf's ruminations on *Ulysses*. In an unpublished notebook she commends Joyce's "desire to be more psychological," foregrounding "*inner* thought" and adding just enough of "the little scatter of life *on top* to keep you in touch with reality."[7] In print she praises his courageous dismissal of those narrative "signposts which for generations have served to support the imagination of a reader when called upon to imagine what he can neither touch nor see," in favor of new techniques that reveal "the flickerings of that *innermost* flame which flashes its messages through the brain" ("Modern Fiction," 107). Woolf's insights into Joyce's quintessentially modernist effort to evoke mental processes are corroborated, albeit in more melodramatic language, by Joyce himself. Arthur Power remembers Joyce declaring that the "modern theme" of literature concerns "the *subterranean* forces, those *hidden* tides which govern everything and run humanity *counter to the apparent flood:* those poisonous subtleties which envelop the soul, the *ascending* fumes of sex."[8] Interviewed in 1922 by Djuna Barnes—whose modernist contribution to this dialogue will be examined in the next chapter—Joyce states his goals in *Ulysses* in similarly psychological terms: "I have recorded, simultaneously, what a man says, sees, thinks, and what such seeing, thinking, saying does, to what you Freudians call the subconscious."[9]

From one perspective, the imagery of surface and depth that recurs in these passages might seem to confirm a set of unquestioned assumptions about the psyche and its organization that runs throughout both the psychoanalytic and popular discourses of the 1920s (assumptions in which, following *Webster's*, "consciousness" consists of "the *upper* level" of mental life, while the "subconscious" indicates those mental activities "just *below* the threshold of consciousness"). Describing the psyche's topography in structural terms is meant, of course, to make comprehensible those qualities that one "can neither touch nor see" through recourse to visual and spatial analogies. A less obvious but nonetheless potent ideological effect of demarcating such hierarchical boundaries *within* the human subject, however, is to lend support to those boundaries distinguishing "interior" from "exterior," or self from other, that are intrinsic to Anglo-European conceptions of the coherence and fixity of the self. The descending vertical movement implicit in such metaphors recalls, as well, the hydraulic or drive-reduction model of repression/release embedded in turn-of-the-century sexological discourse, a model invoked, as chapter 2 illustrated, by the language of channels, dams, and flows typifying the paradigmatic plot of female sexual awakening. This model, as we have also seen, privileges a sexual "truth" of being, buried within and definitive of the self, that awaits translation upwards to the light of day. Such a notion of sex as a hidden key to being, a secret essence that explains everything, dovetails with the logocentricism and metaphysics of presence that underlies the post-Enlightenment ethos of individualism.

Metaphors of dark "subterranean" places and "ascending" fumes of sex not withstanding, I will be making the case that the representations of interiority created by Joyce and Woolf do not simply recapitulate, only perhaps in a more sophisticated version, a traditional hydraulics of desire or metaphysics of coherent identity. To the contrary, Joyce's and Woolf's creation of a spatial dimension within narrative expressive of the atemporal, nonchronological, associative processes of mental and libidinal activity is a radical articulation of modernity precisely because of the *complexity* of their shared understanding of the divided constitution of the human subject—a subject split by repression (or, in Joyce's words, "those hidden tides . . . run[ning] humanity counter to the apparent flood")[10] and constituted in and by language, itself the site of division and rupture, as Lacan has emphasized. In self-consciously harnessing both the power and slip-

periness of language—and of the desire in language—to express the dilemmas and impossible desires of the radically split, never internally coherent
self, Joyce and Woolf, in differing styles and sometimes with differing intentions, construct fictive illusions of interiority that call into question not
only the distinction between "interior" and "exterior" on which humanist
assumptions of identity depend, but also the metaphoric efficacy of the
binary division between psychological surface and depth, between upper
and lower compartments of the mind, often unquestioningly used to distinguish more or less conscious mental activity from subconscious or repressed energies—those so-called hidden tides that, to repeat Joyce's claim,
"govern everything."

If Freud's theory of the unconscious has been the most original contribution of psychoanalysis to modernity, a related fundamental Freudian insight is that repression, which splits the subject and creates desire, is never
complete but must always work against a continuous straining or "pressure
in the direction of . . . conscious[ness]." To this intrapsychic phenomenon
Freud gives the name "the return of the repressed."[11] Part of Joyce's and
Woolf's achievement is to dramatize the way in which repressed, unconscious energies continually permeate the flux of consciousness and the flux
of human existence, inundating both "surface" and "depth," as it were,
with multiple and proliferating desires. Identity remains irrevocably divided, both within and against itself, but the grounds of that division are
always shifting, never constant. Within the textual worlds that Woolf and
Joyce create, then, "desire" does not take the form of one libidinal release
or "eruption" welling up to the surface from below, nor is it predicated on
one climactic breaking of the dams of repression (as in *The Virgin and
the Gipsy*). Rather, the psychosexual and discursive desires to which these
modernist texts give expression are characterized by a fluidity and free play
that already saturates all levels of "reality": the protagonists of *Ulysses* and
Mrs. Dalloway inhabit "inner" and "outer" worlds *both* of which exist in
perpetual states of flux and indeterminacy.[12]

Not all critics, however, see the modernist attempt to evoke the inner
life as heralding so complete a break from traditional conceptions of the
internal fixity or coherence of the self. In a fascinating note to an essay in
Desire in Language, Julia Kristeva argues that "what is persistently being
called 'interior monologue' . . . in texts that pretend to reconstitute the so-
called physical reality of 'verbal flux'" is modern civilization's last-gasp
effort to preserve, under the guise of something new and daring, a traditional norm of identity in the form of "organized chaos" and "transcendence." That is, despite the depiction of the inner world in "verbal flux,"
the very format of interior monologue serves as a kind of *container* that
bestows order and hence transcendent meaning on the random chaos it
frames. For Kristeva, this is a "limited literary effect" rather than an avant-
garde one, still operating within the realist premise that the "self" can

somehow be captured in narrative (if only as organized chaos). This "fiction of an internal voice," however, can no longer be legitimately maintained in the face of "the discovery of the split within the subject"—that which Kristeva labels "Freud's 'Copernican' revolution" in theorizing subjectivity. While I agree with Kristeva that Freud's theorization of the split within subjectivity (and its Lacanian extensions) spells "an end to the fiction" of interiority insofar as this "revolution" posits the subject's *radical exteriority in relation to, and within, language,"* I want to argue that the novelistic attempts by Joyce and Woolf to represent the erotics of mental activity also recognize "interiority" to be a kind of linguistic after-effect, the refraction of a series of surfaces, signs, masks, and roles that call into question the assumed distinction between "interior" and "exterior," "self" and "other." Both writers strategically exploit what Kristeva dismisses as a "limited literary effect" to address the "radical exteriority of the self in relation to . . . language" that, in Kristeva's view, the "fiction of an internal voice" threatens to erase, and in the process they challenge normative conceptions of the boundaries understood to circumscribe and define identity and sexuality, no less than narrative.[13]

Such a description of the modernist challenge to notions of internal fixity or, in poststructuralist parlance, self-identical being forcefully calls to mind the important work of Judith Butler. Stressing that we must ask why and "for what reasons . . . the trope of interiority and the disjunctive binary of inner/outer [has] taken hold" in modern western culture and philosophy, Butler demonstrates how the regulatory norms of sexuality and gender depend upon the construction and subsequent policing of an imagined boundary between inside and outside—located on the skin, the body's "surface"—precisely in order to maintain the fantasy of the self's interior coherence: "'Inner' and 'outer' constitute a binary distinction that stabilizes and consolidates the coherent subject." The myth of such self-integrity in turn maintains the "illusion of an interior and organizing gender core, an illusion discursively maintained for the purposes of the regulation of sexuality." But, as Butler makes vividly clear, the gendered and sexual prescriptions that culture teaches us to read as inviolable essences of being, as central or core truths emanating from within the self, are *effects* rather than *causes,* cultural enactments performatively produced *on* the body through various discursive codes that only give the illusion of substance or depth. In other words, what we too often take to be manifestations of an originary "hidden depth" are actually culturally inscribed effects—transmitted through and by words, acts, gestures, looks—that performatively "constitut[e] the appearance of [their] own interior fixity."[14]

Butler's insights into identity as a continuous performance enacted on the surface of the body, and into the relation of that performance to the social regulation of sexuality, become extremely useful in measuring the implications of Joyce's and Woolf's libidinal politics in their literary inter-

rogations of the psychosexual energies encompassing individual consciousness. For, without wishing to overstate the parallels, I see at work in their
fictions an incipiently Butlerian understanding that identity and sexuality
are part of an unending masquerade, a donning and divestiture of words,
roles, and masks whose surfaces repeatedly gesture toward an interior essence that can only be hypothesized retrospectively. Even within the most
interiorized spaces of psychosexual fantasy depicted in *Ulysses* and *Mrs.
Dalloway*, the mind remains a theater upon whose representational stage,
as it were, modernity's fictions of sexuality are continually being enacted.
While neither Joyce nor Woolf would deny the existence of an "inner reality" to human subjectivity, the linguistic and stylistic self-reflexivity that
characterizes their textual performances reveals an intuitive understanding
that any written approximation of the psyche's energies and desires must
necessarily remain imbricated in a performative play of linguistic surfaces
and exteriors whose ontological status is always in the process of being
constructed by the very culture that reads them. As such, Woolf's and
Joyce's literary *fictions* of interiority become a critique of the cultural fiction
of interiority that shores up the boundaries of self and sex deemed necessary to maintain the status quo.

The magnitude of the undertaking to break down traditional definitions of narrative, sexuality, and identity creates in both texts a fair share
of the anxieties of authority whose sexual and textual manifestations in the
plot of sexual awakening were examined in chapter 2: "liberating" the text
or the sexual subject from traditional expectations or values, setting oneself
up as the harbinger of the change that defines modernity, always entails a
certain defensive posturing and consequent anxiety.[15] Questions of authorial mastery and/or anxiety in modernist writing and their relation to a
politics of representation are also a by-product of the sheer difficulty, the
often deliberate inaccessibility, of the texts of high modernism. It is not
necessary to repeat in detail here the familiar argument that the impulse to
bring order out of the fragmentation and alienation associated with early-
twentieth-century life resulted in the modernist artist's valorization of his
or her subjective yet nonetheless supposedly unifying vision as the ultimate
authority capable of bestowing meaning on random flux and chaos. I suggest, however, that a more complex understanding is needed of, among
other things, the performative dimensions of such manifestations of creative fiat and ego—ranging from Joyce's verbal exhibitionism in *Ulysses*
to Woolf's pose of self-erasure in *Mrs. Dalloway*—in order to assess the
complicated, and sometimes contradictory, ways in which textual representations of psychosexuality and interiority are mediated by issues of
(modernist) narrative authority and anxiety. The struggle for meaning that
these texts self-consciously stage, moreover, entailing the reader's constant
engagement in the production of "significance" from ambiguity, opacity,
and indeterminacy, in effect yields to the reader a surrogate authority that

further complicates any simplistic interpretation of the modernist impulse as a disguised will to power. Finally, I hope to show that the textual anxiety or unease that the thematizing of repression and unconscious desire at times unlocks in Joyce's and Woolf's explorations of the psyche is not only produced by their psychosexual subject matter but also issues from, to use Susan Stanford Friedman's formulation, the "textual unconscious" of their novels—the unresolved contradictions or "complexes" that exist as the text's repressed and that become "manifest" only in the transferential process of reading and interpretation, always unraveling the text's claims to authority.[16]

Speaking of transferential readings, one of those fascinating nuggets of literary history is the fact that Woolf was engaged, as her diary shows, in reading, ruminating about, and resisting Joyce's marvel of modernist technique, *Ulysses,* at the very time she was conceiving her own uniquely modernist version of a June day in the life of a middle-aged protagonist who, like Joyce's Leopold Bloom, is well past the threshold of "sexual awakening" foregrounded in the previous chapter. Whether or not Woolf was consciously responding to *Ulysses,* it is clear that Joyce's text forms part of *Mrs. Dalloway*'s "textual unconscious." This is a process in which a prior generations of critics have also consistently participated by citing Woolf's novel as the "other" major masterpiece of high modernist technique and a "feminine" counterbalance to the "masculine" vision of *Ulysses.* Part of the technical audacity of both novels involves their parallel use of the temporal framework of a single day to unfold the entire inner history and psychology of their protagonists, all the while evoking the richly textured random flux of modern urban existence as it filters through the beholder's subjective vision. Although the external "facts" and realistic details of Bloom's wanderings in Dublin and Clarissa's preparation for her London party are carefully recorded, both novels foreground, through a variety of self-conscious, original narrative techniques, the erotics of mental activity— including random thoughts, memories, past regrets and doubts, unfulfilled yearnings, future hopes, subliminal fantasies, and incursions of repressed desire—that traverse the "inner" worlds of these protagonists and that simultaneously connect them to the "outer" world that exists on the other side of consciousness.

To demonstrate the enactment of sexuality in Joyce's mental theaters, the following section on *Ulysses* focuses on the two episodes, "Circe" and "Penelope," that most thoroughly reject traditional methods of realistic narration (and particularly the traditional "signposts" for indexing states of inwardness) in order to simulate mental and libidinal processes. In "Circe," this effect is achieved through a psychodramatic exteriorization of what are largely Leopold Bloom's subconscious fantasies and unconscious desires in the form of a hallucinatory dramatic "script." In "Penelope," it is achieved through an interiorization of Molly Bloom's reveries in a self-contained interior monologue that has become *the* example of modernist stream-of-consciousness in the popular imagination. By staging a textually mediated version of the Freudian return of the repressed in these episodes, Joyce uses his touted discursive and linguistic free play both to acknowledge and to celebrate the libidinal fluidity and desirous possibilities of the unboundaried subject. At the same time, as we shall see, what might be called *Ulysses's* textual unconscious complicates, indeed at times overwrites, this apparent *jouissance,* drowning out free play in acts of authorial derring-do and mastery.

Woolf resorts neither to psychodrama nor to uninterrupted interior monologue to represent the atemporal, random flux of consciousness that constitutes so much of *Mrs. Dalloway.* Rather, she makes use of fairly constant indirect free discourse filtered through a third-person voice, almost invisible slippages in narrative perspective, extended sentence structures, and even punctuation to create the sensation of a seamless narrative that weaves in and out of multiple characters' consciousnesses, and in and out of often disconnected scenes, in a process of ceaseless association and seemingly effortless flow. The tropes of diffusion, connection, and relationality suggested by the performance of this "seamless" textual erotics capture something fundamental about Clarissa's enactment of an identity that is never fixed but always in process, and I argue that this sense of the self's shifting boundaries also illuminates the syncretic eroticism that suffuses both her daily life and her less conscious desires. However, the narrative, psychological, and libidinal erotics of connection/diffusion promoted in *Mrs. Dalloway,* no less than *Ulysses's* valorization of polymorphous free play, depends on the repression of anxieties not only specific to but hidden within the text's unconscious—the return of which threatens to undermine the very ethos of connection that supports Woolf's vision of modern life and the modern novel. To prepare us to tackle the full implications of this paradox, this chapter will begin with an examination of the mechanisms of repression and return that inflect Joyce's staging of sexuality in the theater of the mind with its particularly modernist power and ambiguity.

JAMES JOYCE, *ULYSSES*
(RE)STAGING SEXUALITY IN "CIRCE", PERFORMING (AS) "PENELOPE"

For all these knotty points see the seventeenth book of my Fundamentals of Sexology or the Love Passion which Doctor L. B. says is the book sensation of the year.

—Virag in "Circe" (420)

if I could only remember half of the things [he says] and write a book out of
it the works of Master Poldy yes.
—Molly in "Penelope" (621)

I have already noted how Joyce explained his goals in writing *Ulysses* to
Djuna Barnes by declaring, "I have recorded, simultaneously, what a man
says, sees, thinks, and what such seeing, thinking, saying does, to what you
Freudians call the subconscious." Had he been more careful in his wording, however, Joyce might have more accurately stated his mission by *re-
versing* the latter half of his proposition, to state, "I have recorded, simultaneously, what a man says, sees, thinks, and *what you Freudians call the
subconscious does to such seeing, thinking, and saying*," since it is the impact
of the subliminal on the conscious plane that so clearly marks much of his
enterprise. Hence it is tellingly ironic that, having just identified "what you
Freudians call the subconscious" as one of his representational aims, Joyce
abruptly interrupts himself in order to dismiss psychoanalysis in no uncertain terms as "neither more nor less than blackmail"—a classic instance of
displacement that perfectly illustrates Jacques Lacan's observation, paraphrased by Patrick McGee, that "Joyce the symptom illustrates the psychoanalysis that Joyce the subject refuses." [17]

Indeed "Joyce the symptom" reveals a thoroughgoing investment
throughout *Ulysses* in the "tides" of consciousness, as well as the "subterranean" depths (to repeat his words to Arthur Power) of "what you Freudians
call the subconscious." By opening up a spatial dimension within narrative
that evokes the atemporal, nonchronological, associative processes of mental and libidinal activity, Joyce creates the fictive illusion of interiority, first,
by articulating the fundamentally split nature of identity—"those hidden
tides . . . run[ning] humanity counter to the apparent flood," as he put
it to Power—that has been psychoanalysis's most radical contribution to
modernity,[18] and second, by harnessing both the power and slipperiness of
language to express the dilemmas and theatricalize the impossible desires
of the radically divided self. This is a division, as we will see, that Joyce
plays upon in order to turn traditional understandings of interiority inside out.

Of particular relevance to this chapter is Joyce's prying open of novelistic form to make narrative space for the representation of what he called
those "ascending fumes of sex"—those incalculable psychosexual forces
that shape even as they subvert human identity. Hence my focus here on
the two episodes of *Ulysses* that most radically experiment with narrative
form in order to simulate the erotics of mental activity. Not coincidentally,
these episodes contain the novel's most graphic sexual content, manifested
in "Circe" in the libidinal perversities surfacing in Bloom's subconscious
as he journeys through Nighttown, Dublin's red-light district, and manifested in "Penelope" in Molly's uncensored erotic reveries, expressions of

marital and personal discontent, and thoughts of the affair she has initiated with Blazes Boylan earlier in the day, as she drifts to sleep by the side of her now-sleeping husband. Staging a return of the sexually repressed in both these scenarios in order to affirm eros in all its polymorphous variety, Joyce self-consciously participates in a poetics and politics of the perverse whose aim is to dismantle dominant culture's assumptions about sexuality, identity, and narrative as coherent wholes. However, while acknowledging this celebratory dimension of Joyce's fiction of sexuality, we need to account more precisely than has yet been done for the repressions manifested by *Ulysses*'s own unconscious. For these undercurrents—manifestations, as Lacan puts it, of "Joyce le symptôme"—complicate the authorial effort to open a textual space for the play of unrepressed, polymorphously perverse sexuality within the narrative. Rereading *Ulysses* from this perspective, I argue that "Circe" betrays an investment in those very mechanisms of narrative control that compromise the section's affirmation of sexual and textual plurality, while Molly's monologue in "Penelope" gives expression to a speaking subject who evades Joyce's authorial impositions, even as her enactments of subjectivity remain enmeshed in the theatricalization of self and sexuality that "Penelope"—no less than "Circe"—seeks to evoke and expose.

The Mental Theater of "Circe"

"Imagine the underside of a text," Hélène Cixous writes of "Circe," "where discourse becomes detached and fantasies imprint their anxiety." Cixous's description is right on target, since to read the "Circe" section of *Ulysses* for the first time is indeed to find oneself in a surreal, defamiliarizing realm of the "underside" where erotic desires, repressed guilts, subconscious fantasies, and symbols of the unconscious indiscriminately mingle, jockeying for position and displacing one another in turn. All this libidinal activity occurs on a textual plane composed of oddly familiar but estranging words, images, phrases—many of which the reader may vaguely recall having read earlier in the novel, but which, now pried loose from their meaning-bestowing contexts, have become open-ended, floating signifiers. And if "fantasies imprint their anxiety" on this "underside of the text," it is in no small part a function of the Nighttown setting, which triggers, as Cixous also so aptly puts it, "a feast day of the repressed" in Bloom and, we might add, in the text itself.[19]

Of course, Bloom's "repressed" has never been entirely absent from the narrative proper. The interior monologue technique that Joyce has intermittently used since "Calypso" to reveal the ongoing stream of thoughts coursing through Bloom's mind has indirectly revealed—through its approximation of the verbal slippages, condensations of meaning, metaphoric substitutions, tell-tale gaps, ellipses, and associative leaps that characterize the thought process—a great deal about Bloom's subliminal fears, guilts, and desires; the reader is encouraged to read his "quoted" thoughts as an analyst would read a patient's chain of associations as keys to what remains unsaid or suppressed. In contrast, as Karen Lawrence notes, the task of "Circe" is precisely to delve into "the ellipses of the stream-of-consciousness passages of the early chapters."[20]

To represent these subconscious processes, however, Joyce resorts to a narrative technique and point of view radically different than anything else that has appeared in the text to this point, for in "Circe" the narrative shifts from third-person narration—with its intermittent internal monologues—to the genre of dramatic script. The reader's eye is immediately assaulted by stage directions, scripted dialogue, scene shifts, changes in costuming, and multiple levels of role-playing—signs that we have entered a realm of mental theater, one in which the repressed is rendered visible in the form of scripted and enacted fantasy. Joyce's method of rendering psychic processes in this episode, then, is at once expressionistic and psychodramatic. The majority of the surreal "events" that subsequently unfold operate as literalized metaphors or externalized embodiments of unexpressed, indeed often inexpressible, desires and fears.[21] This expressionistic dissociation of the narrative from any mimetic reflection of Bloom's or any other character's sensibility plunges the reader headlong into a realm of opaque language that seems governed only by the unanchored drift of association. In this realm the words of "Circe" form, on the one hand, a depersonalizing, one-dimensional screen onto which repressed fantasies are projected and, on the other, a distorting filter through which any literal actions, such as Bloom's movements through Nighttown, are relayed to the reader. The resulting sensation is that of a hallucinating text either totally out of control or operating according to its own mysterious rules. This disorienting effect, as Joyceans since David Hayman have pointed out, has been anticipated throughout by the novel's gradual evolution toward a kind of narrative "autonomy" or arbitrariness: from at least "Aeolus" and certainly "Sirens" forward, each successive episode, more daringly experimental than its predecessor, has increasingly given the written word precedence over action, so that by "Circe" any sense of a controlling "narrator" (Hayman's formulation) or an "authoritative narrative voice" (Lawrence's) appears to have disappeared altogether.[22]

This seeming eclipse of a stable narrating center helps create an illusion of textual autonomy, and this illusion is, in turn, strategically abetted by "Circe"'s dramatic format: drama, after all, is the one genre that exists for its audience without direct authorial mediation, appearing to "happen" of its own volition. At the same time, because the written nature of *this* drama means that it is necessarily read as a script rather than witnessed as performance, the immediacy characteristic of theater is replaced by a sense of distance, an alienation effect which is enhanced by the hallucinatory, indeed *nonperformable,* nature of much of the scripted "action." Thus exploiting his dramatic medium, Joyce creates a textual universe in "Circe" that approximates the workings of the unconscious, appearing to run on its own libidinal energies (although like the libido it too is part of a larger organism) and to move forward via a dreamlike drift of association in which obsessive, repressed fantasies find expression by indiscriminately attaching themselves to whatever external stimuli are available.[23]

So radically unanchored a textual universe sets the stage for the explosion of the polymorphous perverse that accompanies Bloom's movement through Nighttown. All his sexual sins of the past, all his repressed erotic fantasies (to say nothing of his oedipal and marital nightmares), rise to the surface of "Circe" as comic actors—often with speaking roles—to accuse him of his deviation from a hypothetical sexual norm: even within Bloom's "private" psychic terrain, sexuality assumes a series of ever-shifting *public* masks, attesting to its essentially performative nature as one enormously Circean spectacle. On a thematic level, this revolt of the psyche, played out as a psychodrama of simultaneous guilt and desire, is largely precipitated by Bloom's internalization of a cultural ethos of manhood that exists at odds with a personal sense of well-being predicated on his often feminine identifications, passive preferences, and general empathy. Given the disastrous public and personal events of Bloom's day, the sources of this unwelcome insurgence of the repressed are not hard to fathom: made to doubt his adequacy as a man on multiple counts (by Molly's impending affair with Blazes, by his sensed difference from the hypermasculine and unfeeling world of his Dublin counterparts, by his failure to father a son), denigrated because of his Jewish otherness and his Christian idealism, torn in his allegiance to nation or empire ("Stage Irishman!" will be one of the accusations leveled against him in the judgment sequence [401]), the already marginalized Bloom undergoes a further process of social alienation on 16 June that results in the psychic state of self-division to which the expressionistic format of "Circe" gives articulation. Appropriately, then, Bloom's first appearance in the episode is literally marginalized: his walk-on occurs in a bracketed stage direction (a kind of textual margin) where it is reported that the "concave mirror" (a marginalizing mode of representation) in Gillen's hairdresser's window "presents to him lovelorn longlost lugubru Booloohoom" (354)—an image of alterity caught in the process of linguistic fragmentation.

It is psychologically appropriate that Bloom, unsure of himself as acting subject, almost immediately fantasizes about himself as passive object. Fearing that by the standards of Dublin's world of male camaraderie he isn't enough of a man, Bloom subconsciously punishes himself for his inadequacies by imagining himself transformed into his culture's icon of abject submission: the dominated, cowering, but delighted female. In the fantasy of sex-reversal that ensues in Bella Cohen's whorehouse, Bloom's internalization of his society's sexual values is at its greatest; summoning up the nightmarish fantasy of Bella-as-Bello, his subconscious exacts its revenge, masochistically whipping him for his supposed masculine failures: "What else are you good for, an impotent thing like you," Bella/o will torment Bloom, "Can you do a man's job?" (441).[24]

These manifestations of guilt and humiliation, however, are only one aspect of the repressed content to which "Circe" gives expression. Several of the personal revelations surfacing while Bloom subliminally imagines himself a woman and a sexual misfit attest to quite real, only barely suppressed, desires to explore avenues of sexual experience commonly denied men in his culture: passivity, homosexuality, autoeroticism, masochism, fetishism, coprophilia, anality, transvestism. Through the nonjudgmental representation of Bloom's subconscious fantasies, Joyce valorizes a kind of libidinal fluidity, a play of sexual variation and unending capacities of erotic stimulation, that complements Freud's hypothesis that the sexual instincts are multiple in direction, lacking a fixed or "correct" object or aim (*Three Essays,* 3–14, 37–38).[25] That Joyce finds this destabilizing *sexual* free play a matter for rejoicing rather than condemnation is evident in the much-touted *discursive* free play or linguistic promiscuity that characterizes "Circe" as text and *Ulysses* as a whole. Here the poetics and politics of the text's affirmation of the perverse most clearly complement each other, for not only Bloom's but the narrative's erotogenous zones are allusive, associative, amorphous, and objectless, as Caroline Cowie has astutely noted.[26]

In this convergence of psychic and narrative erotogeneity, Joyce's thematics of the return of the repressed resonate most profoundly on the textual level. For the linguistic texture of "Circe" can be likened to a mass of random associations and concentrated zones of erotic fantasy that, once stimulated into activity, trigger a series of multiplying intertextual references and allusions whose excitations (like those of the libido) ripple across the bodily surface of the text in multiple directions. Through this deployment of the polymorphous perverse on levels of content and technique at once, "Circe" challenges the liberal humanist assumption that sexuality, like narrativity, is a unified, singular entity. Even the most incidental details of "Circe" convey something of this multilayered challenge to humanist assumptions of self-coherence and sexual fixity. The humor of Bella/o's muddled injunction to the onlooking spectators, as he/she prepares to auction the "female" Bloom to the highest bidder—"examine shis points. Handle hrim" (440)—underlines the complicity of language, for instance, in the sex-gender stratifications that, in this fantasy, are being exposed as cultural fabrications. A more significant example involves the disintegration of the unitary "I" along both linguistic and gendered lines as Bloom defends himself to the "Gentlemen of the jury" in the judgment sequence: "Let me explain . . . I am a man misunderstood . . . I am a respectable married man . . . I live in Eccles Street. My wife, I am the daughter of . . . ." (373). Before the phallic "Law" that should uphold discrete masculine identity ("I am a man"), the juridical subject crumbles, cultural "misunderstanding" serving as the trigger for a far more profound psychosexual gender confusion. By so overloading his system of signifiers throughout "Circe," Joyce explodes, as Frances Restuccia has put it, the "phallologocentrism" that would have been inherent in "manfully . . . think[ing] up a signifier for every signified in Dublin."[27] The polymorphous play of signifiers that ensues becomes yet one more affirmation, rather than condemnation, of the unleashed perversities at play in Bloom's fantasy life.

Exhibitionist (Im)Postures

The achievement of such democratizing free play, however, is only part of the story of "Circe." In terms of plot, the episode's affirmation of Bloom's sexual fluidity is qualified by its valorization of the phallic arena that provides the overarching context for this release of the repressed. Because Nighttown's primary reason for existing is to foster and satisfy male fantasies, it in effect forms an extended men's club where men meet, compete, and bond in sundry ocdipal patterns.[28] This homosocial substratum of "Circe's" narrative helps explain Bloom's fantasized confrontations with his overbearingly misogynist grandfather Virag (who taunts Bloom for his lack of virility) and with the overbearingly virile Blazes Boylan (who displaces Bloom from his position as husband to that of unsatisfied voyeur). It also underlines the fact that the one thread of plot winding its way throughout "Circe's" otherwise plotless drift of associations is Bloom's quest for a son in Stephen Dedalus, whom Bloom has followed into Nighttown. Indeed, the Odyssean dimensions of Bloom's day-long wandering might best be summed up as the paternal quest for phallic succession, as Bloom's hallucination of the long-dead Rudi, "slim ivory cane" in hand (497) at the end of the Nighttown sequence poignantly (if also ironically) suggests. For all its fantastical content, relations between men shape the waking and dreaming worlds of "Circe."

The episode's libidinal fluidity or free play is further complicated by the fact that sex in Nighttown occurs almost exclusively as a linguistic-narratological experience. An evocative emblem of this continual displacement of the sexual onto the linguistic level is the stage direction where Bloom, walking in Nighttown, comes across some "obscene" graffiti: "*He gazes ahead, reading on the wall a scrawled chalk legend* Wet Dream *and a phallic design*" (369). Not only does sexual release here "occur" only in language, as a *scribbled* "wet dream"—where it is relegated, moreover, to the phantasmatic status of *dream*—but the phallus, instrument of men's wet dreams, also turns out to be pure text: a representational phantasm, a chalk outline or "design" without substance. Within the drama proper of

"Circe," one of the most extreme examples of this substitution of the linguistic for the sexual occurs when the disembodied "Voices" of Molly and Boylan make a stage appearance, mimicking the sounds of male and female orgasm (the former signified by its gutteral consonants, the latter by its throaty vowels):

> BOYLAN'S VOICE *(sweetly, hoarsely, in the pit of his stomach)*
> Ah! Godblazegrukbrukarchkhrasht!
> MARION'S VOICE *(hoarsely, sweetly, rising to her throat)*
> O! Weeshwashtkissinapooisthnapoohuck? (462)

Sex, here, is purely textual, nothing more. In addition to this element of linguistic displacement, both literal and fantasized planes of physical action are robbed of any climax, sexual or otherwise. Not only is there no orgasmic experience, as far as I can tell, for anyone in Bella's bordello, but Bloom's fantasies generally fade before they reach fulfillment. For instance, just as Bloom's "low, secretly, ever more rapidly" whispered words to Mrs. Breen incite her sevenfold "Yes, yes, yes, yes, yes, yes, yes" (foreshadowing Molly's orgasmic yeses at the end of the novel), the scenario teasingly fades, replaced by an image of coital impotence as "armless" loiterers "flop wrestling, growling, in maimed sodden playfight" (367) in the street. Similarly, just as Bloom's fantasy of being birched by Mrs. Talboys nears a climax, with our hero trembling in submissive anticipation of fulfillment, the scene abruptly shifts, rudely terminating Bloom's fantasized pleasure (382).[29]

There are, of course, various explanations that can be offered in justification of this process of endless deferral and displacement. On the thematic level these interruptions might be seen as an analogue of the frustrations Bloom has experienced throughout his long day; from a Lacanian perspective, they might be explained as the inevitable slippage along the chain of signifiers that constitutes desire in language; from a feminist point of view, they might be read as the workings of a feminine *jouissance* that disrupts male trajectories of desire. But despite such explanatory efforts, the disturbing fact remains that the Bloom-persona of "Circe" has become a mere pretext, a linguistic tool, for Joyce's narrative erotics in these instances. And this dehumanizing of the fictional subject points to a further complication in "Circe's" affirmation of sexual/textual free play: that, despite the illusion of textual autonomy or authorial erasure effected by the episode's dramatic format, Joyce's fascination with the mechanisms of narrative control inscribe within "Circe" a narrative erotics that often contradicts its proclamations of polymorphous fluidity.

Such textual authority is most overt in those frequent stage directions (the one dimension of a script in which the playwright's presence is palpable) where Joyce indulges in his signature punning and verbal bravado. This showmanship spills over into the sheer extravagance of many of the speeches assigned the dramatis personae, such as that in which the Papal

Nuncio unfolds a genealogy of "begats" stretching from the biblical Moses through twenty-nine generations to our own Bloom (404). Even more pointedly, the section's many self-reflexive moments call attention to the control inherent in the authorial function. Not only does the litany delivered by the suddenly appearing Daughters of Erin recapitulate the entire novel-to-date in encoded form, the following stage direction, announcing that *"A choir of sixhundred voices . . . sings the chorus from Handel's Messiah Alleluia for the Lord God Omnipotent reigneth . . ."* (407), typographically highlights the imprint of that other "Omnipotent" creator, Joyce himself, without whose reigning talents this *tour de force* would not be happening. Such textual moments, I suggest, function as sites for a kind of extreme authorial exhibitionism, a pyrotechnical flexing of literary muscle that becomes equivalent to an act of masturbatory display. Indeed, an apt metaphor for Joyce's authorial practice in these instances might be the fireworks that go off "with symbolical phallopyrotechnic designs" during the fulfillment fantasy (394). The irony, then, is that as much as Joyce decries the masculine ethos that oppresses Bloom with its emphasis on male prowess, the author is more than willing to put his own literary prowess on display for all takers.

Literary prowess or potency, I should add, is not in itself an automatically negative quality. In this regard, we need to be careful to distinguish the authorial derring-do weaving its way through the whole of *Ulysses* from the particular mode of authorial "exhibitionististicity" (417)—to borrow Virag's term for Bloom's voyeurism—at work in "Circe." Sandra Gilbert and Susan Gubar have taken Joyce to task for participating in a unilaterally patriarchal rhetoric of mastery—in their words, for "inaugurat[ing] a new patrilinguistic epoch"—through a show of linguistic "puissance" that "sentences" women to the material realm. In contrast, as Karen Lawrence has argued, and as a careful analysis of the narrative erotics inscribed in many of the novel's other "exhibitionistic" *tours de force* demonstrates, Joyce often uses style to deconstruct "the symbolic, encoded forms of his own representations," including those of women, and in the process he exposes the complicitous "workings of male desire" in producing such representations.[30]

What renders "Circe's" representation more problematic, in contrast, is the degree to which its mechanisms of narrative control work against its simultaneous proclamations of sexual fluidity. An example occurring near the end of the episode makes this process vividly clear. If, as I have argued, the narrative of "Circe" thwarts orgasmic release on both levels of action and fantasy, I would nonetheless venture that in the penultimate moments of "Circe" Joyce manages to have his *own* textual-narratological orgasm—and when Joyce comes, he indeed comes big. I have in mind the frenzied chase scene that follows Stephen's phallic shattering of Bella's chandelier with his ash-plant. In the episode's longest stage direction, which spills over two pages, the text virtually explodes as Bloom, chasing after Stephen, is in turn pursued by what turns out to be a cast of ninety-nine characters, culminating with "Mrs. Miriam Dandrade and all her lovers" (478–79). This gargantuan release of textual energy, collecting together the novel's component parts into one continuous ejaculation of words, in effect (re)assembles the entire text and even manages to foreshadow its ending.[31] It is hard to imagine a more audacious example of authorial fiat. If Clive Hart is correct—and I think he is—in suggesting that "Circe" charts Bloom's psychic acceptance of the fact that he doesn't *need* genitally oriented sexuality to be happy,[32] Joyce's maneuvers here suggest otherwise as regards the authorial function: the come-hither call of the prostitutes to their prospective clients that so intimidates Bloom—"Big comebig!" (387)—has become the invisible narrator's self-assumed badge of honor.

This exhibitionism, in turn, further complicates the playfulness, the polymorphous perversity, of "Circe" by subjecting the reader to a coercive dynamics of textual mastery and control. As the audience of such "phallopyrotechnical" displays, we become, like Bloom, quintessential voyeurs participating in an erotic enactment that depends on a relation of inequality rather than reciprocity, even if we have willingly consented to be mastered. This, as we will see, is a radically different position than the one that *Mrs. Dalloway* invites its reader to inhabit. In so flaunting his power as the ultimate authority of our pleasure, Joyce recapitulates on a narrative level the very dynamics of domination against which his representation of Bloom's libidinal outpourings is meant to work. Freeing the polymorphous perverse, in this Circean Nightworld, becomes another name for policing the other's desire.

Patrick McGee has argued that the sexual transformations of "Circe" illustrate "the ideology of the patriarch in a state of breakdown"[33]—a sentiment qualified, as we have just seen, by the degree to which Joyce's fascination with the mechanisms of textual mastery begins to overwrite the episode's poetics and politics of the perverse. This, however, doesn't mean that authorial fiat unequivocally has the last word, or that the polymorphous perverse is incapable of staging its own devious returns. For McGee's statement still holds true on the level at which patriarchal ideology unwittingly contains the source of its own deconstruction. A case in point is the chase scene, which not only proves that Joyce can "come big" when he wants to, but also exposes the anxieties of masculinity that instigate such phallic expenditures of sexual/textual energy. As just noted, the ejaculatory prose of this stage direction, summoning forth the entire novel in its breathless list of ninety-nine names, ends with the item "Mrs. Miriam Dandrade and all her lovers." Given the principles of association and substitution governing the dream-logic of "Circe," this reference clearly seems to anticipate the novel's finale, with the name "Miriam" standing in for "Marion"

(Molly's proper name), especially since Molly's erotic reveries about "all her lovers" indeed bring *Ulysses* to an end.

But is this mention of Mrs. Dandrade really, or only, a "mask" for Molly? It turns out that this obscure character is none other than the person at the Shelbourne Hotel, mentioned in "Lestrygonians," who has sold Bloom her black undergarments (132). These "short trunkleg naughties," it turns out, Bloom does not give to Molly but secretly dons himself, in order to practice "various poses of surrender" (437) in front of the mirror. "You were a nicelooking Miriam," Bella/o taunts Bloom in "Circe," "when you clipped off your backgate hairs and lay swooning in the thing across the bed as Mrs. Dandrade about to be violated by lieutenant Smythe-Smythe . . .," whereupon a list of eleven more names follows (437). In light of this transvestic revelation, we might well recast the phrase "Mrs. Miriam Dandrade and all her lovers" to read "Mr. 'Miriam' Bloom and all *his* violators": Mrs. Dandrade is at once a "cover" for Bloom's taboo desires *and* the vehicle of the cross-dressing masquerade ("swooning . . . *as* Mrs. Dandrade") in which he is privately engaging. Moreover, as one of the most overtly homosexual of "Circe's" fantasies—a man imagining himself anally penetrated by men—its climactic positioning in the chase sequence effects an unsettling displacement not only of the text's heterosexual climax in "Penelope" (husband and wife in bed), but also of the heterosexually charged masculine bravado characterizing the textual erotics of the passage itself.

Bloom costumed in drag thus becomes the agency whereby the text's polymorphous perverse makes a most playful return indeed, unsettling the "ideology of the patriarch" this time around in the role of the nonheterosexual, repressed other of the text's "phallopyrotechnic" designs. At the same time, Bloom's masquerade illuminates the crucial fact—already implicit in the dramatic format of "Circe"—that *all* sexual identification is a masquerade, a fluid exchange of roles and masks and words. Even in the most interiorized spaces of psychosexual fantasy, *the mind remains a theatre*, its sexual guilts and desires and polymorphous pleasures imbricated in a performative play of surfaces and exteriors whose status is never a given but always in the process of being constructed.

Engendering "Penelope"

To turn from the way in which Bloom's sexual playacting as "Mrs. Miriam Dandrade" ironically recasts the ending of *Ulysses* to the masquerade of "Penelope" that actually concludes the novel raises the question of Joyce's representational and formal goals in creating Molly's monologue. As in "Circe," the attempt to represent those "hidden tides" and "ascending fumes of sex" expressive of libidinal activity fuels Joyce's narrative experimentation here, where the "uncensored"—now of Molly's rather than Bloom's psyche—is spectacularly put on display. However, rather than repeating "Circe's" disorientingly surreal, pseudodramatic staging of desire, Joyce attempts to create, in what is perhaps the modernist example *par excellence* of uninterrupted stream-of-consciousness narration, a convincing mimesis of every thought and erotic reverie coursing though Molly's psyche as she drifts toward sleep. Not only is the gulf between "Circe's" technique of surreal expressionism and "Penelope's" autonomous interior monologue immense; because this *modal* difference is mapped over the axis of *sexual* difference, Joyce's narrative strategies also raise the question of how gender-marked his choices may be. In other words, what assumptions about differences in male and female modes of consciousness and repression are encoded in the very formulation and deployment of these two techniques?

Just as the psychodramatic expressionism of "Circe" throws up a screen of opaque language that automatically situates the reader at a remove from its record of psychic "events," so the waking Bloom exists at a certain *distance* from the feverish activity that "Circe" shows to be seething in his subconscious: repression seems to work more thoroughly, if destructively, to maintain the ego boundaries and psychological differentiation that, as the reading of Lawrence in chapter 2 illustrated, is constitutive of male identity in western culture. A sensation of *immediacy*, in contrast, is the inevitable effect of interior monologue; by simulating the associative drift of Molly's (literally unpunctuated) thoughts, the text of "Penelope" generates an illusion of transparency not only for the reader but for Molly herself, implying that she, as a woman, has more immediate access to her libido than, say, Bloom to his own. Not only do Molly's ego boundaries appear more permeable, more capable of admitting to consciousness the desires and dissatisfactions of the subconscious, in her monologue the term *consciousness* proves a very relative concept, describing a state that, however verbal in its presentation, exists in close proximity to and in communication with the less conscious aspects of mental and psychosexual life. At its most positive, such a representation could be taken to mean that women's access to the unconscious makes them less repressed individuals; at its most negative, it risks implying that women, lacking men's more highly developed egos or sophisticated strategies of repression, *are* their libidos, *are* the unconscious (hence, as noted in chapter 2, the persistent association of the plot of libidinal awakening with female rather than male sexuality).

If these modal distinctions highlight questions of the relation of sex to gender, so too does the manner in which these two chapters thematize the return of the repressed. In "Circe," what is repressed and seeks a return is definitionally psychological—Bloom's fears, doubts, anxieties, desires. In "Penelope," however, the repressed to which the narrative gives expression is frequently culture's—that is, all that has previously been repressed or censored in cultural and literary representations of women's sexuality. To put it another way: if "Circe" gives expression to the repressed *in* Bloom, "Penelope" gives expression to Molly *as* the repressed of culture. This subtle difference sheds light on the ambiguous sexual politics marking Joyce's narrative experimentation. For whereas "Circe" works to deconstruct the global category of "sexuality" in the name of a polymorphously perverse free play that is supposedly universal (but here made the province of the male subject), the more narrowly defined task of "Penelope" is to deconstruct the moral prohibitions accruing to the social category of "gender" in the name of "woman," freeing her sexuality from taboo (even if those prohibitions have "universal" implications for both sexes).

A corollary of these distinctions is that Joyce seems to accord his female protagonist a much more intuitive understanding of gender as a construction, a masquerade, that she must continually *enact* (which the ending of *The Virgin and the Gipsy* also suggests is the moral of Yvette's ascension to maturity). To the extent that Molly's implicitly dramatic monologue thematizes and foregrounds gender as a performance, however, an unexpected congruence emerges between "Penelope" and the explicitly dramatic, scripted format of "Circe." For, as Cheryl Herr has persuasively shown, both episodes have roots in the contemporary theater of Joyce's day. If "Circe" draws on the pantomime tradition of sexual impersonation to reveal sexuality and identity as an ensemble of constructed roles and discourses, "Penelope" emulates the music-hall tradition of saving the headline performer, the diva, for the star-turn or "topper" at the end of the bill.[34] Not only does the narrative positioning of "Penelope" as a kind of novelistic "topper" draw on theatrical precedent, the episode's method also has dramatic affinities. Precisely because Molly's interior monologue is uninterrupted and self-contained, it can quite literally be read as a *dramatic soliloquy*—a scripted address directed to a hypothetical audience that observes the dramatic unities of time, place, and action. We have already seen how the mental theater of "Circe" becomes a strategic mode of elaborating its psychosexual concerns; just how the theatrical components of performance subtend the representation of sexual subjectivity in "Penelope" will emerge as one line of inquiry in the following pages. To clarify the ramifications of this topos for modernist explorations of sexuality and narrative, however, we must look more closely at the sexual/textual dynamics of Molly's monologue and the controversies to which it has given rise.

The Double-Speak of Molly's Desirous Discourse

Not only is Molly a consummate actress, but her first-person monologue provides the vehicle for what many see as *Joyce's* show-stopping masquerade of femininity. And, indeed, it is the very intimacy of Joyce's simulation of a woman's voice that has spawned endless debate about the relative success or failure of his method for representing Molly's psychosexual complexities. Among feminist critics there is a widespread, although not unanimous, suspicion that Joyce "violates" Molly, first by penetrating her thoughts and then by appropriating her voice through his ventriloquism.[35] Whatever one's view of Joyce's characterization, the question also often becomes, as one of my students once wisely put it, whether we feminists have to apologize for liking Molly, and whether in reading Molly we are able to avoid collaborating in (what might well be) her author's reading of her.[36] I will shortly suggest two ways in which the phenomenon of Molly-as-fictional-creation gives us an "out," as her figural presence dodges some of the less desirable impositions of her maker, but first I would like to review some of those elements that seem problematic in Molly's articulation of her sexual identity and desires, bracketing for the moment the question of whether these thematized viewpoints attest more to Molly's limitations, Joyce's impositions, or some combination of the two.

Like Bloom, Molly harbors an often negative self-image ("I suppose Im nothing any more" [635]) that is directly related to the state of her marriage and her fears of sexual rejection. As her monologue obsessively reveals, the anxieties engendered by her cultural position as woman and wife mark her perception of sexuality and in particular of female pleasure in profoundly contradictory ways. For instance, of her capacity for erotic fulfillment, she fantasizes procuring sex with "some nicelooking boy . . . since I cant do it myself," only to reveal a few lines later that she indeed *can and must* "finish it off myself anyway," at least in the case of sex with Bloom, where there is "no satisfaction in it pretending to like it till he comes" (610). Heterosexual intercourse both is (with a nicelooking boy) and is not (with Bloom) the answer, just as autoerotic satisfaction both is ("finish it off myself") and isn't ("cant do it myself") an option to intercourse.

This double-speak of "both/neither" also characterizes Molly's contradictory relationship to her body. If she at times voices a classically Freudian definition of female anatomy as lack ("whats the idea making us like that with a big hole in the middle" [611]), she also evinces a pride in her breasts ("they excite myself sometimes" [638]) that hovers ambiguously among genuine appreciation, narcissistic self-love, and a male-identified view of women's bodies. Molly's references to oral sex provide another indication of her mixed sexual self-image. For whereas she imagines fellatio with Stephen's "lovely young cock there so simple . . . so clean and white" (638) as entirely pleasurable, she fantasizes that she will punish Bloom by making him practice cunnilingus on her ("Ill make him do it again if he doesnt mind himself and lock him down to sleep in the coalcellar with the blackbeetles" [636]). The metonymic process of association that links female genitalia to beetle-infested cellars is part of the same cultural anxiety that Molly internalizes in the upward displacement informing her valorization of "bubs" over "holes."

What these contradictions indicate is the simple fact that the objecti-
fying terms originating within male heterosexual discourse to describe
women's bodies provide Molly with the only *sanctioned* language she
knows for expressing her material sensuality. To appreciate her voluptuousness, much less another woman's, Molly automatically slips into a
male viewpoint. Hence her expression of pleasure in the smoothness of her
thighs immediately becomes the thought, "God I wouldnt mind being a
man and get up on a lovely woman" (633), and her admiration of her
breasts leads her to fantasize having a penis in order to conceive "the
amount of pleasure they [men] get off a womans body" (638). While some
readers have seen these statements as signs of latent lesbianism, and others
as evidence confirming Freud's theory of female penis envy, such thoughts
more crucially indicate Molly's entrapment in a sociolinguistic order that
simply does not provide her with a vocabulary capable of articulating her
specific bodily pleasures.

From conceiving of her body in terms of heterosexual male paradigms,
it is a small step to Molly's tendency to measure her self-worth in terms
of men's responsiveness to her sexuality. Thus whatever personal release
she finds in sex with Boylan is overshadowed by her preoccupation with
whether she has "satisfied" him (610), and she decides "the only way" to
solve her marital problems with Bloom is to "make him want me" (642).
Molly's personal metaphysics of being hence reduces to her sexual essence
as woman: "I suppose thats what a woman is supposed to be there for or
He wouldnt have made us the way He did so attractive to men" (642).
With her position as both cultural and narrative subject dictated from
above by her heavenly as well as earthly maker, Molly in her bed-ridden
immobility has struck many readers as the embodiment of the archetypal
Feminine, condemned to play the role of the willing and (im)passive female flesh that always says "yes" through a Joycean sleight of hand that
transforms her material substance into pure essence.

And yet, along with this narratively overdetermined acquiescence to
biological determinism, Molly's monologue simultaneously reveals much
more than she overtly says about her capacity for sexual self-pleasure. If
her standard complaint is that sexual enjoyment is a male privilege—"nice
invention they made for women for him to get all the pleasure" (611)—
Molly also subtly modifies this judgment when she inadvertently reveals
why men have "all the pleasure": "they want to do everything too quick
take all the pleasure out of it" (615). Pleasure, it turns out, is not exclusively male; the problem is that female pleasure is subjected to male demand within the framework of heterosexual coupling. Moreover, for all
Molly's psychological reliance on these sexist paradigms, her discourse positively reverberates with sensuality and the potential for self-enjoyment
as well as self-fulfillment: her monologue makes it clear that *she knows*
what it feels like "to let myself go," to "come again" and to "feel all fire

inside me" (621), and *she knows,* as the final pages of "Penelope" reveal, how to give herself satisfaction. However lackluster Molly's love life may be, however inadequate or limited her vocabulary for expressing her eroticism, she nonetheless, like Edna in *The Awakening,* exudes and acts upon a sensate eroticism that often proves sufficient unto itself, even if the overt thrust of the narrative might have us think otherwise. It is precisely this unconscious but nonetheless textually present knowledge-of-the-body, this autoerotic sufficiency, that forms one component of the textually repressed of "Penelope."

What Molly's monologue also makes clear is that she is perfectly comfortable with contradiction; any viewpoint she offers at one moment is likely to be reversed the next. However, to conclude that Molly's contradictions are evidence of her feminine illogic *or* of Joyce's stereotypical representation of female consciousness finally isn't sufficient. In fact, it is precisely this capacity to contain and withstand contradiction, along with what I have just called Molly's unacknowledged potential for autoerotic sufficiency, that brings into focus two routes by which her textually constituted subjectivity eludes—in an act of dodging the novelistic police reminiscent of Lucy Snowe—not only her maker but her readers.

The Diva Performs a Star-Turn

I take as my signposts to these escape routes two phrases Joyce used in writing Frank Budgen to explain the significance of "Penelope" to the rest of *Ulysses.* The first appears in a letter of 16 August 1921, where he calls "Penelope" the *clou* of the book.[37] In its literal meaning of "nail," "spike," or "stud," this French term would seem to summon forth a worst-case scenario of the authorial mastery involved in "pinning down" a woman's consciousness, precisely by affixing Molly to her bed. Taken in its aural sense as a "clue" to *Ulysses,* the term hardly serves Molly any better, ascribing to her monologue a superhuman explanatory power that makes woman's voice the existential truth or key underlying Everyman's quest—an only slightly less pernicious way of pinning Molly to a traditional literary function.

But *clou* can also mean the "star-turn" or "chief attraction" of a theatrical event, and to see Molly, as Cheryl Herr suggests, as the headline performer, the so-called topper, in *Ulysses'*s novelistic show provides an illuminating context within which to reinterpret the gendered implications of her star performance. Following Herr's cues, Kimberley Devlin has brilliantly argued that "Penelope" not only "foregrounds theatricality" but that "theatricality mediates Molly's visions of self and other." That is, cognizant of the role-playing element in all behavior, of the self-dramatizations underlying any "identity," Molly "dons multiple recognizable masks of womanliness" throughout her monologue, as her thoughts sift through the various props, costumes, gestures, appellations, and signifiers at her disposal in order to construct whatever "feminine" image she wishes to project in a given social or personal encounter. The past perfect tense of Molly's wistful claim—"I could have been a prima donna only I married him" (628)—is at least in part belied by the multiple performances she *continues* to enact, both in her everyday negotiations with others and in the roles she "does" or "pretends" in imagination and memory—for example (to list only a few of the illustrations culled by Devlin), "*Ill do* the indifferent [spouse]"; "*I could do* the criada"; "when I came *on the scene . . . I pretended* I had a coolness on with her over him"; "I pulled him off in my handkerchief *pretending* not to be excited" (642, 641, 612, 626; emphases added).[38]

In light of this ability to conjure up roles at a moment's notice, the contradictions in Molly's monologue that have stirred such debate among critics might more usefully be seen as a function of her half-conscious awareness that femaleness in her world is *always* an enactment, a series of sometimes mutually contradictory performances. Hence Devlin, returning to Joyce's description of "Penelope" as "the *clou* of the book," defines Molly's monologue as "a concatenation of roles, an elaborate series of 'star turns' that undermines the notion of womanliness as it displays it."[39] On the one hand, to the extent that Molly submits to cultural norms, she participates in the female masquerade in order to "become" woman through, in Mary Anne Doane's terms, a "hyperbolisation of the accoutrements of femininity"[40]—a phrase that well describes Molly's narcissistic flaunting of her figure, obsession with female dress, exaggerated reliance on male prowess, and the like. On the other hand, Molly's consciousness that she is always playing a role, a recognition heightened with every new act she performs, simultaneously turns female masquerade into a *parody* of the signifiers of gender, and this mimicry constitutes a very different mode of power: "Miming the feminine, playfully 'repeating' it," Carol-Anne Tyler writes, "produces knowledge about it."[41] Experiencing her subjectivity as an enactment, Molly not only performs "femininity" but plays on that very act of role-playing, thus becoming, in Devlin's engaging analogy, a modern-day "gender performance artist."[42]

An extension of seeing Molly as an actress, taken to its logical extreme, is to read "Penelope" as a *literal script,* a tack which leads Herr to argue that the speaking voice in "Penelope" has no mimetic value or fictive existence at all, that "Molly" is *only* a stage role to be filled by any competent actress—or, for that matter, actor.[43] If such an extreme reading risks stating the obvious about any fictional "character"—who is always a verbal artifact, nothing more or less—the conceit of "Penelope" as an(y) actor's script usefully points out the degree to which Molly's words (whether envisioned as spoken theatrical vehicle or internalized dramatic monologue) form a screen, a mask, behind which the character can hide and, in hiding, elude both reader's and author's impositions. Similarly, McGee argues that

"Molly's word . . . is a masquerade, a play of conventions. . . . But this does not mean that [her word] has no relation to something *like* a woman, to something *like* the feminine, to something that resists Molly's word and Joyce's writing. . . . To read Molly is to half-create her but never to possess her."[44]

Molly's theatrical self-presentation, moreover, resonates significantly with Judith Butler's theories of gender construction. As we saw at the beginning of this chapter, Butler argues that gender's "substantive effect," its appearance of a fixed essence or substance, is always "performatively produced," inscribing itself through various cultural codes *onto* the body rather than rising from *within* the subject. Indeed Molly's use of masquerade, her gender role-playing, is, to use Butler's terms, a "repeated stylization of the body" that reveals gender to be an *act* "that performatively constitutes the appearance of its own interior fixity."[45] This formulation sheds a crucial light on the theatricality that pervades Joyce's representation of the psychosexual complexities of Molly's "interior" life. For what promises to be a privileged glimpse into Molly's feminine "essence" or "core" turns out instead to reveal a series of masks, of performative *surfaces,* upon which are inscribed those gender prescriptions that culture produces, while it pretends they originate in some "interior fixity." Thus, however disparately weighted the deconstructive "tasks" undertaken in "Circe" (as regards sexuality) and "Penelope" (as regards gender), the representation of Molly's "inner" consciousness ultimately works to unsettle the assumed boundaries of interior versus exterior, surface versus depth, every bit as much as does "Circe's" flaunting of the unconscious as a theater of unending sexual masquerade.

Going Solo

If theatricality constitutes one path whereby Molly's representation evades authorial and readerly mastery, a second avenue of escape lies in the *formal* attributes of the literary technique Joyce employs in "Penelope." Critics have often noted the anomalous structural position that Molly's monologue occupies as *Ulysses's* final word or, as Joyce put it in a second letter to Frank Budgen, the text's "indispensable countersign."[46] In a narrative whose structure has been dictated by the criss-crossing trajectories of its male heroes—who finally meet in "Ithaca," the immediately preceding section—it may come as a surprise to find oneself lodged, at text's end, in a consciousness and a chapter that stands so completely apart from the interests of the rest of the narrative. In addition, this positioning of "Penelope" might, at first glance, seem to be Joyce's means of circumscribing Molly's power, adding to her objectification by stripping her consciousness bare and making its excavation the basis for a demonstration of his virtuoso pyrotechnics. Molly is kept in her bed, as it were, "framed" by the larger narrative of which she only forms a small part.

However, in its function as an "indispensable countersign" to the entire narrative, "Penelope" also establishes its separateness or autonomy by virtue of its formulation as, in Dorrit Cohn's words, "a self-generated, self-supported, and self-enclosed text." Seen from this perspective, the autonomous status of Molly's self-enclosed interior monologue becomes a vital sign of its formal independence rather than an effect of constriction. For technically speaking, this episode, beginning and ending within a single consciousness, forms, as Cohn wisely points out, "*the only moment of the novel where a figural voice totally obliterates the authorial voice throughout an entire chapter.*"[47] The point is crucial, because it implies that however much Joyce may (or may not) desire to impose his viewpoints on Molly, there is a sense in which her voice, *by virtue of its figural constitution as a self-sufficient "I,"* removes the author, and with him, his authority, from the picture: on a purely technical level, this "I" demands neither audience nor reply.[48]

The few times that Molly engages in the language of personal address, directing her thoughts to an imaginary audience, only serve to confirm the degree to which her position as speaking subject grants her a certain independence from the controlling powers in her life. It is no coincidence that each of the four interlocutors Molly imagines are *male* figures whose authority, tellingly, is successively desacralized by the contexts of her statements. Thus, to her divine creator she complains, "give us room even to let a fart God" (628); to her domestic lord she grumbles, "O move over your big carcass out of that for the love of Mike" (639); to her earthly creator she demands, "O Jamesy let me up out of this pooh" (633). Even what certainly is, on one level, the epitome of "Jamesy's" effort to assert control over Molly by making *her* articulate or voice her subjection to *his* whims ("O let me up") simultaneously ends up unmasking the anxieties that motor the desire for authorial mastery. For Joyce's name, his self-conscious signature, is left for all time stranded among references to menstrual blood (a countersign of Molly's creative fiat), thoughts about women's capacities to simulate virginity (and hence rob fatherhood of its certitude—the nightmare haunting Stephen's interpretation of Shakespeare in the library episode), and signs of incipient domestic rebellion ("whoever suggested that business for women what between clothes and cooking and children"). "Jamesy" is fairly outnumbered, Joyce's self-conscious authorial intrusion overwhelmed by those "countersigns" of insurgent female authority most calculated to whet his masculine anxieties. This series of mental addresses appropriately culminates in a prophetic statement of insurrection—putatively directed at Bloom but vague enough to include all men—that augurs a different, more empowering story for female characters such as Molly: "*Oh wait now sonny my turn is coming*" (642; emphasis added). And "coming" Molly indeed is, by text's end.

The way in which the term *sonny* potentially includes more men than Bloom alone also calls to mind the psychologically enabling use to which Molly puts the pronoun *he* throughout her reveries. One could select any number of instances where the reference of the third-person singular masculine pronoun is ambiguous; likewise, Molly's memories of the men in her life repeatedly collapse into one syncretic image: "what was his name Jack Joe Harry Mulvey was it . . . no he hadnt a moustache that was Gardner" (626–27). As this interchangeability suggests, Molly's thoughts attach no special privilege to any one man, not even Poldy; she receives continual pleasure, rather, from imagining, desiring, manipulating, an infinitude of men—or *he*-men, as Cohn jokingly but aptly calls them—ranging from those she has known intimately to those she has merely glimpsed on the street.[49] Early in her monologue, Molly mentions her fancy to have a "new fellow" every spring (625), and at least within the seasons of her imagination, she fulfills her desire.

Thus interchanging fantasies about men for private erotic gain, Molly becomes, in the realm of her imagination, an acting subject, not merely a passive object whose existence is entirely dependent on male approval. Amidst the referential instability of the pronouns *he* and *him,* her first-person *I* remains the one constant, the single fixity the reader can always depend on to be identical to itself—even if that self is divided, contradictory, and multiply positioned. Moreover, just as Molly's figural *I* strips Joyce of a direct authorial voice in her monologue, Moira Wallace suggests that what Molly means by her famous "yes" may not be identical to her author's infamous extratextual assertions to friends such as Louis Gillet, to whom Joyce confided that Molly's final word denoted "acquiescence, self-abandon, relaxation, the end of all resistance"—that is, feminine passivity in its most archetypal representation.[50] First, to the extent that Molly's "yes" intimates "self-abandon," *she only abandons herself to herself,* retreating to a private world of her own making as she fades to sleep during orgasm. Second, the very fact that she *is* bringing herself to orgasm, as the final series of lyrical "yeses" signals, makes it clear, as Wallace argues, that this sexual act of *auto*eroticism is one which, by its very nature, excludes us *even as* we voyeuristically look on. As such, Molly's "yes" also becomes an assertion of what *she* feels; its affirmation is her self-affirmation.[51] Simultaneously, Molly's "yes" is thus also a resistant "no," the refusal of an acting subject to subject her thoughts to others' desires and demands; it is another way of saying, as Molly already has, "I suppose he thinks Im finished and laid out on the shelf well Im not no" (630), or, "O wait now Sonny my turn is coming."[52]

Literally, of course, Molly, like any fictional character, cannot exist alone. It takes a Joyce to write a "Molly" into being, just as it takes the reader to give "her" textual life. Nonetheless, the very act of writing and reading Molly, *because of* her representation in a self-contained and self-generated interior monologue, also frees her figural presence—not of all male markings, which would be impossible, but at least of any absolute authorial attempt to "make" or "speak for" woman. For the *very grammar* of Joyce's representation of female consciousness ironically undoes his authority to make his language signify what he might want it to mean: *his* promiscuous "he's" become *her* access to erotic pleasure; *his* inscription of "female" contradiction through Molly's continual self-interrogation becomes *her* means of keeping the question open; *his* "yes" of feminine surrender becomes *her* affirmation of a private space and a public mask that, finally, resist appropriation. In so speaking of a fictional character's ability to slip through our policing grasps, I again think of Lucy Snowe; but whereas Brontë actively plots Lucy's escape from the disciplinary forces that attempt to contain female desire, Joyce unwittingly puts into Molly's hands, through his choice of format, the tools and discourse that allow her to resist even her maker's appropriation.

As Molly lies beside Bloom in bed, thinking back on her encounter with Boylan, another of these ambiguous third-person masculine pronouns crosses her mind: "I wonder is he awake thinking of me or dreaming am I in it" (610). Whether "he" refers to Bloom or Boylan, this pensive thought would, at first glance, seem yet another confirmation of Molly's incapacity to imagine herself apart from men: unless they "think" of or "dream" her, she feels she has no real identity or existence. But when Molly's words are applied to the authorial presence who has dreamed her into novelistic existence—Joyce himself—they take on a tantalizingly different valence. For, in fact, Joyce literally *did* dream about Molly, and his recounting of this dream on two separate occasions quite stunningly attests to what Karen Lawrence has called the authorial anxieties engendered by his intuition of the possible "presumptuousness" of his attempt "to lend voice to female desire."[53] Simultaneously, his dream attests to his uneasy intuition that Molly's "power" is precisely the power to "escape" his text's boundaries. In the dream, Molly comes calling on Joyce to reprimand him for meddling in *her* "business"—that is, for taking over her story—and in response to Joyce's passionate defense of his intentions in writing "Penelope," Molly flings a miniature *coffin* at him and announces, in words that recall Dora's leavetaking of Freud, "And I have done with you, too, Mr. Joyce."[54] In other words, refusing to be coerced by "Mr. Joyce's" insinuating explanations, she establishes her independence from his authorial control by finishing with him, symbolically diminishing and killing him off, instead of vice versa. Not coincidentally, Molly also appears *in masquerade* in the dream: she is wearing a black opera cloak "that looked like *La Duse*," the Italian actress who succeeded Rachel, the model of Brontë's Vashti, as the greatest female actress of the European stage. Having dismissed her creator, she is free to exist beyond his text in a realm to which his representational powers can only gesture. On some profound level that is not merely a critic's dream, Molly La Duse has indeed escaped the bedsteadfastness of *Ulysses*,[55] moving outside the constraints of her fictional context and making an extratextual appearance, a kind of curtain call, in the role of a consummate actress with the uncanny ability of returning without notice to haunt her creator's subconscious. What is interior and what exterior is hopelessly blurred as Joyce's attempt to represent Molly's "interiority" in "external" form becomes a manifestation of his own interior anxieties. In yet another ironic twist, *Ulysses*'s repressed has made a return, and this time the space of representation is not "Circe's" dream-text, but the theater of Joyce's own dreaming unconscious.

VIRGINIA WOOLF, MRS. DALLOWAY
REPRESENTING "THE UNSEEN PART OF US, WHICH SPREADS WIDE"

> And of course she enjoyed life immensely . . . (though goodness only knows, she had her reserves; it was a *mere sketch,* he often felt, that even he, after all these years, could make of Clarissa).
> —Peter Walsh in *Mrs. Dalloway* (118; emphasis added)

> But *to go deeper, beneath* what people said . . . *in her own mind now,* what did it mean to her, this thing she called life? Oh, it was very queer.
> —Clarissa in *Mrs. Dalloway* (184; emphasis added)

Neither Joyce's authorial ambition nor his technical bravado were lost on Virginia Woolf, whose diary reveals the depth of her engagement in reading *Ulysses* at the very time she was imagining the kernel of what was to become *Mrs. Dalloway*—her criticisms of the former are often immediately juxtaposed with remarks on her creative breakthroughs in imagining the latter. At this chapter's opening, I noted Woolf's praise of Joyce's courage in disregarding the "signposts" of traditional realist fiction in order to record "the flickerings of that innermost flame which flashes its messages through the brain" ("Modern Fiction," 107). But several of her impressions of Joyce and *Ulysses,* both published and private, are much less glowing. On the one hand, she freely admits that her ambivalence may be colored by her own authorial anxieties—as, for instance, when in 1920 she reflects that "what I am doing is probably being better done by Mr. Joyce," or when in 1922 she calls *Ulysses* a "mis-fire," only to confess a day later that "then again, I had my back up on purpose."[56] On the other hand, her critique of Joyce helps bring into relief some crucial distinctions between his "masterpiece" ("Modern Fiction," 107) and her own evolving aesthetic for exploring "the dark places of psychology."

Ever since the publication of Woolf's diary, critics have been fond of quoting her less-than-kind remarks about Joyce: for example, her acerbic comment that the writer is too "virile—a he-goat," or her feeling that *Ulysses* is ultimately an "illiterate, underbred book," the "self-conscious & egotistical" product of "some callow board school boy" (26 Sept., 16 Aug., and 6 Sept. 1922, respectively; 2: 202, 189, 199). While it is easy to criticize the class-bound elitism of such remarks, her criticisms—when stripped of their deprecatory overtones—pinpoint some of the contradictions that this chapter has already located in the tension between Joyce's celebration of polymorphous free play and his fascination with mechanisms of narrative control. For instance, Woolf's comment on his excessive "virility" or "goatishness" stems, one suspects, as much from Joyce's exhibitionistic display of his literary "prowess" as from any explicit sexual content; likewise, the pyrotechnical showmanship that increases with every episode no doubt feeds Woolf's judgment that "a first rate writer . . . respects writing too much to be tricky; startling; doing stunts" (6 Sept. 1922; 2: 199). Consequently, the element of Joyce's writing that seems most to disturb Woolf is what she perceives as its egotism (the word crops up repeatedly in the diary entries on *Ulysses*[57]); and the question of ego, tellingly, emerges as central in Woolf's hesitations about the ultimate efficacy of Joyce's stream-of-conscious technique. As she puts it in a notebook kept while reading the novel, "Perhaps this method gets less into other people *and too much into one.*"[58] She expresses the same reservation in "Modern Fiction." Having praised Joyce for discovering new ways to uncover "the quick of the mind," Woolf suggests that his "method" nonetheless imposes a certain "limitation" on the reader, who is left feeling "confined and shut in a bright yet narrow room, rather than enlarged and set free." This "narrow room," I take it, refers not only to the novel's focus on Bloom's consciousness but to the intensity of Joyce's authorial presence, for, as Woolf proceeds to ask, "Is it due to the [stream-of-consciousness] method that we feel . . . *centred in a self which . . . never embraces or creates what is outside itself and beyond?*" (107–8; emphases added).

Such comments pinpoint a salient difference in Woolf's evolving modernist poetics, one that has implications for the sexual-political values she attaches to her conception and depiction of subjectivity. For in her estimate, the novelist's goal of "look[ing] within," of imagining the "incessant shower" of "myriad impressions" as they "fall upon the mind" (2: 106), is not merely to draw a circle around or circumscribe the interiority of her fictional creations—the mind as conceived by Woolf is not a "narrow room" shut off from all external phenomena, even at its most egotistic or subjective. Rather, it constantly reaches out to and "embraces" those myriad impressions that come from "outside itself and beyond." Woolf's great achievement in *Mrs. Dalloway* is to create a narrative method and narrative form for charting this incessant fluctuation between those aspects of consciousness that lie "within" and those that lie "beyond," which taken together form what the novel calls "the unseen part of us, which spreads wide" (232). Hence, although an exploration of the internal world and subjective perceptions of Clarissa Dalloway is integral to the novel that bears her name, the narrative moves with equal ease in and out of multiple consciousnesses, often barely distinguishing among them; the mind's variable and random movements, furthermore, are mirrored in the arbitrary, haphazard flow of the actions and events that make up the novel itself. Although the phrase "stream of consciousness" is generally taken to apply to a character's immediate thought processes, in Woolf's case the phrase aptly conveys her vision of the fluidity of all life. As an early reviewer wrote of *Mrs. Dalloway*'s experimental form, "Here, Mrs. Woolf seems to say, is the stream of life, but reflected always in a mental vision."[59]

This emphasis on "mental vision" over clock time is also discernible in the spatial metaphors that Woolf employs in the most widely quoted paragraph of "Modern Fiction," where she advocates a complete break with the conventions of nineteenth-century realism. "Life is not a series of giglamps symmetrically arranged," Woolf passionately declares; "life is a luminous *halo,* a semi-transparent *envelope* surrounding us from the beginning of consciousness to the end." Intriguing here are the seemingly contrasting properties of the two metaphors—the halo, the envelope—that Woolf employs to evoke the mental "life." The image of the envelope connotes a container of sorts, a structural form provisionally enclosing and thereby demarcating the boundaries of individual identity, while the image of the luminous halo, its pulsations blurring the exact line separating self and other, represents consciousness in its diffusive, outwardly radiating, aspects. But if one effect of a halo is to make outlines indistinct, so too the envelope that Woolf figures as encapsulating consciousness is also "semi-transparent," its membrane permeable to the movement of light through and across its enclosing surfaces (106). In Woolf's vision of subjectivity the boundaries of identity are at once shifting and porous, for although consciousness may arise from within, it is not ultimately contained by the corporeal body.[60]

Significantly, Woolf's description of her evolving modernist project and compositional process in her diary evokes a similar pattern of expansion and enclosure. Announcing with great excitement on 26 January 1920 that she has just "arrived at some idea of a new form for a new novel"—the result of which is the experimental *Jacob's Room*—she proceeds to outline her goals:

> Suppose one thing should open out of another—as in An Unwritten Novel—only not for 10 pages but 200 or so . . . doesnt that get closer &

yet keep form & speed, & enclose everything, everything? . . . no scaffolding; scarcely a brick to be seen . . . everything as bright as fire in the mist. . . .
What the unity shall be I have yet to discover . . . [but] I think from the
ease with which I'm developing the unwritten novel there must be a path
for me there. (2: 13–14; emphases added)

Here the double pull of consciousness, simultaneously radiating outward
and inward, is raised to the level of narrative principle. For the "new form"
that Woolf envisions is composed of an *unfolding* process—"one thing . . .
open[ing] out of another"—that reciprocally "*enclose[s]*" that which it
opens up, in a continuous double motion that creates the illusion of a
seamless and unbroken whole: of text, perception, character, consciousness. The spatial image of the "fire in the mist" that follows (anticipating
the images of halo and semitransparent envelope of the essay) evokes the
desired effect of this narrative method; something central is captured or
netted by such writing-in-process, but it can only be apprehended indirectly, as if seen through a mist that diffuses its glow outward and dissolves
the solidity of its outline. To create a form capable of such fluidity and
indeterminacy, Woolf continues, the author must banish all traces of ego
from the writing process, even as she maintains enough narrative control
to "discover" the "unity" latent in the unfolding narrative. This delicate
balancing act underlies the authorial anxiety that causes Woolf to wonder
whether she is up to the formal challenge she has set for herself—
"Whether I'm sufficiently mistress of things—thats the doubt," she says a
few lines later—and, not coincidentally, this fear leads directly to a critique
of her peers: "I suppose the danger is the damned egotistical self; which
ruins Joyce & [Dorothy] Richardson to my mind: is one pliant & rich
enough to provide a wall for the book from oneself without its becoming,
as in Joyce & Richardson, narrowing and restricting?" (2: 14). The author,
like the text itself, must become "a permeating *and* permeable presence."[61]

Also noteworthy in this diary entry is the oxymoronic title that Woolf
gives the new fictional form she hopes will express her vision of life: "the
unwritten novel." Just what this phrase means is not immediately clear. At
first it appears to refer to "An Unwritten Novel" (1920), a recent short
story that Woolf cites, along with "The Mark on the Wall" and "Kew Gardens," as a prototype for the innovative novelistic form she envisions: "but
conceive mark on the wall, K. G., & unwritten novel taking hands and
dancing in unity. What that unity shall be I have yet to discover" (2: 14).
In "An Unwritten Novel" the representation of one extended act of perception forms the story's entire plot and becomes an analogue of the creative
process; the narrator of the story, sitting in a train, watches an unknown
woman seated opposite who absently gazes out the window and, in the
process of observing her unknowable companion, begins "almost automatically" to compose a novel in her mind. This novel is never written, however, for the woman disembarks and leaves the narrator with only her sub-

jective mental impressions. The narrator has, in the text's terms, "read" the woman, but she has not categorically defined or authored her.

So, too, Woolf implies with all fictional writing: *our subjects always escape,* leaving us only with the truth of our impressions, a partial "reading" for which the piling on of "realistic" details can never be an adequate substitute. This sentiment—which Brontë also demonstrates in Lucy's narrative refusal to pinned down, and which Joyce' s discursive construction of Molly less consciously effects—underlies Woolf's invention of the label "the unwritten novel": the perceiving imagination engages in a continuous process of internal "novel-writing" that at once never ends and forever undoes or "unwrites" itself. In Woolf's poetics of the textually perverse, the highest "truth" that fiction can aim to capture is this ever-unfolding, indeterminate process of perceiving and recording a reality that always eludes our summations. One important corollary, as Jennifer L. Kapuscik notes, is that the narrator of "An Unwritten Novel" comes to position herself *not* as the author but rather as a *reader*—and only one among many possible readers at that—of the "unwritten novel" that she observes.[62] This strategic reconceiving of author as reader, and of reader as perceiver, forms Woolf's response to the dangers of "egotism" and authority that she fears for her own craft and that she sees limiting Joyce's narrative experiments. Hence, in the place of authorial impositions *onto* character, Woolf through the device of the unwritten novel proposes to impose a web that is variable and flexible, open to and reflective of the flux inherent in human perception and human relations. By the end of the January 26 diary entry, the repetition of the phrase "unwritten novel" thus assumes a cumulative significance that goes well beyond its initial reference, for, as Kapuscik puts it, "it is clear that Woolf is no longer referring to her short story, but to something greater; certainly the novel she envisions, *Jacob's Room,* but also a new type of fiction, a new genre on which she would concentrate for the rest of her career."[63]

Even more than in *Jacob's Room,* Woolf's theory of a new novelistic form finds its realization in *Mrs. Dalloway,* a novel whose originality, Woolf realizes, lies in its implementation of a "design [that] is so queer & so masterful" (19 June 1923; 2: 249). From her early premonition that she is about to write something "rich, & deep, & fluent & [yet] hard as nails, while bright as diamonds" (6 Sept. 1922; 2: 199), to the latter stages of composition, Woolf's descriptions of the work in progress evoke an unfolding looseness and fluency that simultaneously embraces and contains everything: "It is reeling off my mind fast & free now," she writes on 26 May 1924; "I feel as if I had loosed the bonds pretty completely & could pour everything in" (2: 302). What Woolf "pours in," however, is also a result of what she has been digging out. "For my own part I am laboriously dredging my mind for Mrs. Dalloway & bringing up light buckets" (2: 189), she writes on 16 August 1922, and a year later she uses similar terms to describe her excitement over her "prime discovery so far" in creating the novel (now called *The Hours*): the "tunnelling process, by which I tell the past by instalments [*sic*]" (15 Oct. 1923, 2: 272).[64] This technique allows Woolf, in Elizabeth Abel's phrase, to "reshap[e] time as depth" and give the project's restricted temporal scheme—a single day in the life of Clarissa Dalloway—the psychological richness commensurate with her interest in unfolding consciousness, thereby escaping the "tyranny of sequence."[65] "I should say a good deal about The Hours, & my discovery," Woolf writes, "how I dig out beautiful caves behind my characters." These caves of memory—repositories of desire, loss, absence, repression—eventually "connect" and "each comes to daylight" in the present. "I think that gives exactly what I want; humanity, humour, depth" (30 Aug. 1923, 2: 263).

"Dig[ging]" "beautiful caves" behind her characters, "tunnelling" to retrieve the past, "dredging" the mind to bring up "light buckets": Woolf draws upon a repository of images for interiority that, as chapter 2 demonstrated, were also familiar to Freud, who frequently used archeological and topographical metaphors—buried ruins, underground channels, labyrinthine conduits—to invoke the psyche and the libido. This shared imagery serves as a reminder of the proximity of Woolf's fictional explorations of consciousness to the increased acceptance of psychoanalysis in the early 1920s. The simultaneity of these modernist projects has been expertly analyzed by Elizabeth Abel in *Virginia Woolf and the Fictions of Psychoanalysis* (1989). As Abel points out, in the same years that Woolf is digging caves behind her characters to give them psychological depth, Freud in his essay on "Female Sexuality" makes allusions to actual archeological digs to posit the significance of the preoedipal phase of female development.[66] More immediately, the Bloomsbury community was central in stimulating the interest of literary London in psychoanalysis throughout the 1920s. Virginia and Leonard Woolf's Hogarth Press was the first English publisher of Freud, providing "the turning point in the dissemination of psychoanalytic theory in England"; James Strachey, brother of Lytton, was Freud's primary translator; Virginia's brother Adrian Stephen became a psychoanalyst and his wife Karin a popularizer of Melanie Klein's matricentric revision of Freud's oedipal theory; Klein herself relocated to London in 1926.[67]

In the midst of this flurry of activity, however, Woolf remains curiously silent about her own opinions of Freud and the practice of psychoanalysis—a silence belied by her active production, throughout these same years, of a series of intensely psychological novels that not only incessantly probe the "borderland of various levels of consciousness between body and spirit," as one contemporary put it, but that might well be called revisions of the Freudian family romance.[68] A clue to this paradoxical silence in the face of such overly psychological subject matter lies in Edwin Muir's perceptive insight into Woolf's fictions of consciousness: "Although the psychology is subtle and exact, no trace remains of the psychoanalyst."[69] In vivid contrast, Freud as psychoanalyst (not unlike Joyce as novelist) leaves his traces everywhere, a trait that one suspects wasn't lost on his English publisher: his texts resoundingly attest to his investment in maintaining absolute control within the analytic encounter, in mastering the secrets of his patients, and in translating this will to power into textual authority, as indicated by the crises of authorial anxiety we have already noted in his composition of *Dora.* While deeply interested in the world of the mind opened by Freud's forays into the psyche, Woolf deliberately excises from her authorial practice any "trace . . . of the psychoanalyst," precisely because that role implies a degree of authorial omniscience antithetical to the tenets she assigns the "unwritten novel." The latter rubric, as we have seen, repositions the writer as a subjective "reader" of, rather than ultimate authority over, the text, while its larger reading audience ideally becomes the "partner" of the novelist "in this business of writing books." In refusing to speak from the position of the analyst, Woolf thus attempts to build that "wall for the book from oneself" that she saw as an essential instrument in keeping the "damned egotistical self" at bay when entering into (and identifying with) the psychology of one's fictional creation.

The result of these techniques in *Mrs. Dalloway* is a profoundly moving portrait of several hours in the life of a fifty-some-year-old woman preparing for an evening party. But in this portrait, the quotidian detail, the social fabric, of daily life that one might expect of a society-oriented novel is continually deemphasized, often cordoned off in parentheses, while Clarissa's expansive memories deluge the foreground and provide the novel with its primary tension and interest. These recollections not only give the reader intimate access to Clarissa's interior life but also provide links to the thoughts and feelings of those characters whose lives intersect with hers throughout the course of the day. In turn the strategic absence of an overtly omniscient authorial point of view, on the one hand, and an avoidance of the technique of intermittent first-person stream-of-consciousness narration that Joyce uses, on the other, create a text in which an apparently seamless movement between and among various characters' subjective points of view and private thoughts create a narrative erotics in which, to return to the 26 January 1920 diary entry, one thing opens out of another while simultaneously "enclos[ing] everything, everything." The following pages show how this interconnected web of textual relations becomes expressive of fundamental aspects of both Clarissa's sense of her identity and her latent eroticism. At the same time, this narrative erotics simultaneously effaces its origins in Clarissa's and the text's own repressions. To uncover the novel's hidden relays between connection and repression, I will first look more closely at the narrative operations that underlie its modernist form, then take up its representation of consciousness in flux, and penultimately analyze its staging of the libidinal currents flowing through the "beautiful caves" of Clarissa's memories.

Permeating and Permeable Narrative Webs

Thus far, my comments on Woolf's theory of the "unwritten novel" as a simultaneously radiating and contracting web have been primarily descriptive. Now I want to offer more precise evidence of the techniques that create *Mrs. Dalloway*'s sensation of seemingly unbroken flow. Mirroring Woolf's wish to create a novel without "scaffolding" and with "scarcely a break seen," the narrative of this novel glides in and out of the inner worlds of its characters, shifts from one viewpoint to another, leaps from past to present, and moves from one event to the next without a perceptible break. In part this seemingly effortless flow owes to Woolf's manipulation of syntax and grammar. On the level of the sentence, Woolf creates highly elliptical structures that can easily cover the space of a page or more, structures whose phrases and clauses, sutured by semicolons that allow an unbroken accretion or amplification of detail within the individual sentence, force the reader to keep reading forward. Similarly, the ubiquitous use of present-tense participial phrases generates forward motion; their litanic repetition creates the sensation of action about to be completed, of meaning about to emerge, if we just keep pushing ahead. Complementing the strategic use of commas, semicolons, and dashes to extend such clauses and phrases in what come to seem endless, unbroken lines, Woolf frequently uses parentheses to open up spaces within the sentence or paragraph whose content creates a simultaneity of action or laying of multiple viewpoints without breaking the grammatical unit.[70] Another syntactical strategy for creating the sensation of unbroken movement involves the insertion of pronouns with unclear antecedents to expedite unmarked transitions. Note, for example, the sequence where the crowd watches a mysterious motor car pass on its way to Buckingham Palace: in one sentence the pronoun "it" shifts from signifying the car to signifying an aeroplane overhead, which then becomes the narrative hook transporting the reader to another part of London (30). The subtlety of such shifts is further camouflaged by Woolf's reliance upon indirect free discourse within limited third-person narration to convey characters' thought processes, rather than first-person transcripts. The effect gives the text an overall homogeneity of tone and syntax, in which the third-person narrative and the variously represented consciousnesses seem to form one unbroken piece.[71]

These means of instilling constant movement, flow, and homogeneity into the text on the level of the sentence are complemented by Woolf's creation of thematic threads that effect seamless, virtually invisible transitions between scenes, characters, and perspectives. In several instances, as the preceding example of the motorcar and aeroplane illustrates, instruments of modern technology, often literally in motion themselves, become the narrative agents creating forward momentum and linking together otherwise random actions and geographically separated locations in one continuous trajectory. A classic example of this threading technique occurs at the beginning of the novel as Clarissa, hitherto the sole focal point of the narrative, enters a flower shop. When the backfiring of a car in the street brings her to the shop window to observe the passing vehicle, however, the narrative perspective shifts, reestablishing her as only one among many random observers. Dipping in and out of their viewpoints, the narrative follows the car all the way to Buckingham Palace, at which point the growing crowd of spectators is distracted by the sky-writing of the aeroplane overhead. With the nearly imperceptible shift of narrative focus from one mode of transportation to the other, this aeroplane now becomes the literal motor of narrative desire threading together the multiple perspectives of observers now scattered across the face of London. From the vantage point of the plane, moreover, the reader is privileged to a panoramic (and humanly impossible) view of the city, then of Greenwich, and then of the countryside unfolding on either side of London, where below, we are now told, in a patch of woods, "adventurous thrushes hopping boldly, glancing quickly, snatched the snail and tapped him on a stone, once, twice, thrice" (41). This abrupt vignette of nature "red in tooth and claw" thus becomes the narrative's destination, twenty-some pages after having abandoned Clarissa on Bond Street. In the space of a single sentence, readers find themselves transported along a mind-boggling chain of associations that reach from the thoughts of Mrs. Dempster, a working woman watching the plane in Regent's Park, to the aeroplane's overhead view of England, to the impalement of this insignificant snail on the bird's beak in the forest below.

These dizzying perspectival shifts from human spectator to aeroplane to snail also point to the invisible narrative presence of yet another mode of vehicular transport contributing to the illusion of seamlessness. As much a harbinger of modernity as the car and aeroplane, this vehicle is the mobile camera of early film technology.[72] For Woolf imaginatively simulates in prose of what is called in cinematic terminology the continuous take—the craning long shot moving in for a close up—which in turn allows Woolf to insert a mode of "impersonal" omniscience into the text without resorting to the antimodernist device of intrusive omniscient narration. Later in the narrative, this cameralike manipulation of viewpoint to create the impression of an unbroken thread is used to create a brilliant *tour de force* of modernist writing out of the simple event of the approach of the Warren Smiths to the Harley street residence of Sir William Bradshaw. Parked outside is a car that Rezia guesses belongs to the doctor. As the narrative subtly shifts from Rezia's observation of the car's exterior to her supposition of a human presence waiting within (is her ladyship in the car?), the narration focuses on Lady Bradshaw, whose hypothesized thoughts, conveyed in indirect free discourse, gradually extend to include those of her husband sitting in his office, within whose perceptions the narrative point of view now relocates itself. In the space of two pages the narrative focus established at the beginning of this sequence—the Warren Smiths nervously approaching the doctor's office, with Rezia's vision framing the scene—has been turned completely inside out, so that by the time they walk into Sir Bradshaw's office, they have become the depersonalized objects framed by his scrutinizing vision: "He could see the first moment they came into the room (the Warren Smiths they were called) . . . [that] it was a case . . . of complete breakdown" (144). Woolf effects this dramatic reversal of focus without breaking narrative continuity or using any of the traditional realist signposts that alert the reader to a change in perspective: hence the shock many readers experience upon realizing that Septimus and Rezia have somehow made it into the physician's office "sight unseen." The seamlessness of the transition evokes a moving camera's circumnavigation from outside to inside; modern technology replaces old-fashioned omniscience to remind us of the radical *permeability* of the borders separating realms of existence and perception.[73]

The sensation of interconnectedness that characterizes Woolf's narrative erotics is also facilitated by her tendency to subjectify the objective—that is, to animate or give the appearance of human life to insensate nature—and, in the process, to dissolve the boundaries distinguishing interior from exterior, the zone of the living from that of the inorganic. To cite only three examples, the "throb" of motor engines stalled in traffic come to sound "like a pulse irregularly drumming through an entire body," a breeze wafting down the Mall "lift[s] some flag flying in the British breast of Mr. Bowley," and the sound of the chimes of St. Margaret's "glides into the recesses of the heart and buries itself in ring after ring of sound, *like something alive* which wants to confide itself, to disperse itself" (20, 28, 74; emphasis added). Not only does the inanimate enter into and become a *living* part of the human organism in the latter example; in the simultaneous act of "confid[ing] itself" and "dispers[ing] itself" within the heart, it becomes a correlative for the double motion of contraction and expansion that Woolf assigns to consciousness and that, as I have been suggesting, Woolf makes a signature of her modernist poetics.

Enactments of Identity: Clarissa's Selves

The image of St. Margaret's chimes provides an appropriate transition from Woolf's formal techniques to her representation of Clarissa's psychology. For this figure of sound permeating the body's boundaries and filling the recesses of the heart turns out to be part of a passage of indirect free discourse originating in Peter Walsh's perspective as he walks past St. Margaret's, at which point the chimes remind him of what he takes to be the very essence of Clarissa's mysterious identity: "like something alive," the above passage continues, "which wants to confide itself, to disperse itself, to be, with a tremor of delight, at rest—like Clarissa herself" (74). From the novel's opening pages, where Clarissa's impression of the "particular hush, or solemnity; an indescribable pause; a suspense . . . before Big Ben strikes" (4–5) becomes an image of her own liminality (she is perched on a curb, pausing before plunging into the flow of traffic), to her appearance at her party at the end of the text, where she "ha[s] that gift still; *to be;* to exist; to sum it all up in the moment *as she passed*" (264; emphasis added), Clarissa's identity or being hinges on the paradox of a momentary suspension or "pause" in the midst of motion, the aura of seeming to "sum it all up" while "passing," that Woolf has also made a dictum of her "new form" (opening out yet enclosing all) and a tenet of consciousness (the envelope that surrounds, the halo that diffuses).

But to probe the psychological nuances of Clarissa's being, the deeper "recesses" of her "heart," is to encounter another paradox. For while Peter can locate imagistic equivalents of Clarissa's interiority in his surrounding environment, he also admits that after all these years he only can only make "a mere sketch" (118), a surface drawing, of the reserved Clarissa: "depth" escapes him even as he attempts to imagine and represent it. Indeed, all manifestations of identity in this novel at times appear no more than constructions—performances, representations, poses, costumes, set pieces— that defy even as they invite others' attempts to fathom their hidden recesses and underlying meanings. I will be suggesting that the tension between this performative aspect of Woolf's representation of subjectivity and the modernist impulse to depict life from within, in all its psychological depth, provides a key to understanding the multiple and shifting facets of Clarissa's permeating and permeable identity.

In fact, the entire world of this novel becomes a stage upon which gender, class, and other identities are continuously assumed and performed. A telling moment occurs as Clarissa, making her way up Bond Street, reflects that "often now this body she wore" seems "invisible; unseen; unknown," replaced by another costume: "this being Mrs. Dalloway; not even Clarissa any more; this being Mrs. Richard Dalloway" (14). Not coincidentally, the next paragraph makes it clear that what most fascinates Clarissa as she proceeds along Bond Street are its clothing stores. In a profound sense, a woman *is* what she wears, Clarissa realizes, as she pauses in front of a glove shop "where, before the War, you could buy almost perfect gloves. And her old Uncle William used to say a lady is known by her shoes and her gloves" (15). Performing identity is not, however, restricted to the upper-class lady. If Clarissa's role as "mistress" of a household preparing to entertain the Prime Minister later in the evening means that she must "assembl[e]" herself into "that diamond shape, that single person" (56) who commands the love (and labor) of her servants, her maid Lucy also intuits that aristocracy is a pose that can be copied. Not only does Lucy predict the "mincing tones" (56) the ladies and gentlemen assume later in the evening, but she can and does "imitate" those tones in her own mental fantasies of grandeur: "Behold! she said, speaking to her old friends in the baker's shop, where she had first seen service at Caterham. . . . She was Lady Angela, attending Princess Mary, when in came Mrs. Dalloway" (55–56). For Septimus, too, the world is a stage; the view in Regent's Park strikes him as "a length of green stuff with a ceiling cloth of blue and pink smoke high above"—that is, a painted theatrical backdrop—against which the play of children seems "music hall" acting (36–37).

Just as the world of London is presented as a vast theater where one either performs or watches performances, so too the inner worlds of Woolf's characters often take on the resonances of staged set pieces. When Peter Walsh unexpectedly shows up at Clarissa's door after an absence in India of several years, for example, the external dynamics of his and Clarissa's emotionally charged reunion assume the form of theater, while both internally perceive the reactions of the other as a kind of defensive role-playing, replete with props (he toying with his knife, she with her scissors and thread); such "play-acting" helps cover the unresolved feelings they harbor toward each other in an only partially successful state of repression. Imagining what life would have been like had she married Peter, Clarissa acts out the fantasy in her mind as a play: "and . . . it was as if the five acts of a play that had been very exciting and moving were now over and she had lived a lifetime in them and run away, had lived with Peter, and it was now over" (70–71). Woolf next shows how Clarissa breaks the spell of this fantasy by transforming herself from involved actor to distanced spectator of her own desires: "Now it was time to move, and, as a woman gathers her things together, her cloak, her gloves, her opera-glasses, and gets up to go out of the theatre into the street, she rose from the sofa" (71).

If present moments are insistently translated by the mind into ongoing performances that hide as they reveal their intensities, painful memories are also internalized as a kind of theater. Peter, for example, relives the decades-old breakup with Clarissa at Bourton as melodrama, its "final scene" (95) played out against the ubiquitous stage setting of the fountain in the garden. Such scene-making translates psychological trauma, the ultimate mark of inwardness, into theatricalized set pieces that are more manageable than the actual experience.[74] Precisely because they can now be represented (and hence ostensibly separated from the wounded ego), these "scenes" begin to take on a life of their own *within* the individual, and this alienation of the remembering self from the past through the agency of scene-making only deepens the rupture, the self-division, that already grounds subjectivity. Such a theatricalization of interiority not only resonates with Butler's theory of performative identity, but implies (as the analysis of *Ulysses* has also shown) that even within the realm of the interior, the mind remains a kind of representational theater, a performative play of surfaces and exteriors that makes any "full" apprehension of an originating inner "self" impossible, a fantasy of coherence belied by the novel's demonstration of the permeability of the boundaries separating inside and outside, self and other.

Primary among the multiple and sometimes contradictory enactments of identity that coalesce to make the "whole" of Clarissa Dalloway is the pose she assumes as the "perfect hostess" (93), an upper-class woman with a talent for creating social occasions where titled aristocrats, members of government, and the old guard mingle in a mutually sustained illusion of centrality, purpose, and power. It is this willingly assumed social identity that leads Peter Walsh to think Clarissa has lost her better self by opting for "rank and society and getting on in the world" in marrying Richard Dalloway (115). Indeed for Peter the "traged[y]" of Clarissa's married life is that "with twice [Richard's] wits, she had to see things through his eyes" and that "with a mind of her own, she must always be quoting Richard" (116). In effect she has assumed the *costume*—the perceptions and words—of an identity that Peter fears has now become her *essence*. At times Clarissa, too, internalizes the judgment of others that she is "frivolous; empty-minded; a mere silly chatterbox" (65) as the truth of her being, mistaking the *effects* of her participation in the world of society as a defining inwardness. But what Peter doesn't realize, and what Clarissa herself sometimes forgets, is how carefully constructed this pose of the "perfect hostess" (93) actually is.

A glimpse of Clarissa constructing this social identity—and the enabling function it serves—occurs when she returns home from her morning outing in Bond Street and retires to her bedroom. Woolf sets the stage (as it were) for a moment of psychological intensity, a descent into the depths of the self, from the moment Clarissa reenters her house, pausing on its "threshold" before mounting the stairs to her room as might "a diver before plunging while the sea darkens . . . beneath him" (44). As thoughts of her recent illness give rise to fears of death, Clarissa turns to her image in the dressing-table mirror to stop the onrush of time by "plung[ing] into the very heart of the moment, transfix[ing] it there." Looking at her reflection serves the analogous function of "fixing" not only the moment but *herself* as well, of creating an illusion of self-coherence and stability in the midst of flux. For in the act of "collecting the whole of her at one point," of "seeing the delicate pink face of the woman who was that very night to give a party; of Clarissa Dalloway; herself," Clarissa methodically wills into being the image of a self that is focused, unified, centered. The funneling process whereby Clarissa draws herself into "one point" is mirrored in the syntax of the ever-shorter series of modifying phrases used to describe the "pink face" in the mirror, which shifts from an anonymous party-giving "woman" to the bearer of a third-person name "Clarissa Dalloway," to the certainty of "herself" (54). Simultaneously, *Clarissa performs for herself the very identity she is in the process of creating* as she looks at her reflection and purses her lips "to give her face point," an act that lends to her face, her surface appearance, an effect of concentrated purpose essential to the successful performance of her social role as perfect hostess: "That was her self—pointed; dartlike; definite. That was her self when some effort, some call on her to be her self, drew the parts together." But Clarissa also knows this self is a radical construction, the product of an internalized fantasy of coherence rather than the outward reflection of an inward truth: "She alone knew how different, how incompatible and composed so for the world only into one centre, one diamond, one woman who sat in her drawing-room and made a meeting-point, a radiancy no doubt in some dull lives . . . never showing a sign of all the other sides of her" (55). Rather than participating in the cultural illusion that there is a hidden center to being, Clarissa strikes a pose that allows her—not totally unlike Molly Bloom in this regard—to enact an identity that is necessarily provisional, always shifting to accommodate both the pressures of the external world and the demands of inner need.

Clarissa's diamondlike "radiancy" is also composed of many "other sides," including facets "incompatible" with her "glittering and tinselly" social image.[75] In contrast to the legibility of this social self, Clarissa constructs for herself an inviolate privacy that no one can read, touch, or see. To those like Peter who feel frustrated by the "mere sketch" (118) that Clarissa's outward countenance presents, this self is the "impenetrabl[e]" (91) Clarissa, the cold and unyielding Clarissa whose walls of propriety and "reserve" (118) deflect the heat of others' seductive pleas for attention. But to Clarissa, this radically unknown and unknowable component of being is at once an embodiment of the existential condition of all humanity *and* a "solitude" that she in many instances, including her marriage to Richard, finds "priceless" (181). Like Brontë's Lucy Snowe, Clarissa discovers that remaining unknown to others—even at the price of psychic alienation—is sometimes preferable to the objectification that cultural norms of gender impose on all women, including those as unassuming in appearance as Lucy or as glittering as Clarissa. Elsewhere musing on those external forces that threaten to destroy this solitude, Clarissa tentatively gives to this protective, secretive self, "whatever it was," a name: "the privacy of the soul" (192). This mystification of the untouchable "soul" may seem to reinforce essentialist norms, confirming Kristeva's critique of the modernist focus on interiority as a covert means of recuperating a traditional western metaphysics of the self.[76] While I do not mean to suggest that there is no humanist residue in Woolf's thinking, her formulation of consciousness is much more complicated than Kristeva's reading of modernism assumes. For a phrase like "the privacy of the soul" does not so much reify a transcendental conception of the word *soul* as posit an alternative mode of subjectivity—again, like Lucy Snowe's—that only exists to the degree that it eludes categorical definition and escapes being pinned to one meaning. Moreover, if "identity" inevitably eludes representation, as Woolf implies, this doesn't make one's *experience* of identity, one's consciousness of self, any the less "real." To put it another way, Clarissa may pin down or "transfix" her *own* image, construct a provisional "center" to her identity, as she looks into the dressing table mirror, when it suits her needs, but she refuses to allow *others* to pin her to one meaning or narrow her multiple, "incompatible" facets to one "point."

In fact, the unified identity that Clarissa wills into being when called on by external pressures to be herself—which is to say, to enact *a* self—coexists with a vision, present from the opening pages of the novel, of all identity and being as radically decentered: "She would not say of any one in the world now that they were this or were that . . . [and] she would not say of herself, I am this, I am that" (11). In terms of the narrative's syntax, moreover, this refusal to categorize oneself or others strategically frames Clarissa's affirmation of the inviolate "privacy of the soul." For Clarissa comes to this epiphany as she watches the elderly woman who lives in the opposite building ascend her stairs, "gain her bedroom, part her curtains, and disappear again into the background. Somehow one respected that— that old woman looking out of the window, quite unconscious that she was being watched. There was something solemn in it . . . whatever it was, the privacy of the soul" (191–92). Ascending to her bedroom (as Clarissa has done earlier in the day), looking out the window (as Clarissa is now doing): this solitary woman is both Clarissa's *double,* a reflection glimpsed in a figurative mirror that prefigures Clarissa's future, and a *separate individual* whose life beyond the frame of the mirroring window Clarissa will never know. Hence, as the old woman recedes from view, Clarissa realizes that the "miracle" and "the supreme mystery" of existence "was simply this: here was one room; there another" (193). Just as she has earlier refused to say she is one thing or the other (11), both rooms exist "here" and "there," in a simultaneous relation of connection and separation that is reflected in the parallel syntax of the two sentences. Moreover the latter scenario, in its dual function as a mirror (Clarissa looking into a frame and seeing an image of self reflected there) and as a staged spectacle (Clarissa as audience watching the parting of the curtains onto the stage of the old woman's bedroom), replays and reverses the vignette of Clarissa looking into her dressing table glass earlier in the day. The masquerade of the definite self that Clarissa stages in that mirror is now replaced by the mirrored reflection of a radically decentered self, one that refuses the logic of either/or and that instead embraces a vision of symbiosis and difference.

For Clarissa, this decentering of stable or singular identity is closely linked to her unwavering belief that the boundaries of the physical body do not mark the absolute limits of the self or consciousness. "Why should our bodies end at the skin, or include at best other beings encapsulated by skin?" Donna Haraway has asked in her well-known "Manifesto for Cyborgs,"[77] and similarly Clarissa feels that her being, her consciousness, extends beyond her body and continues as a part of the fluidity of the world of interconnected objects. Neither absence nor death, therefore, spells out an absolute limit to being because subjectivity continues in the interconnections. "Somehow in the streets of London, on the ebb and flow of things, here, there, she survived, Peter survived, lived in each other," Clarissa muses, and she envisions death as "being laid out like a mist between the people she knew best, who lifted her on their branches as she had seen the trees lift the mist, but it spread ever so far, her life, herself" (12). Later in the day Peter ponders the logical conclusion to which she takes this metaphysics of connection: "So that to know her, or any one, one must seek out the people who completed them; even the places. . . . For she believed . . . [that] the unseen part of us, which spreads wide . . . might survive, be recovered somehow attached to this person or that, or even haunting certain places after death" (231–32).

Notably, Clarissa's articulation of "the unseen part of us" that spreads outward into the universe of animate and inanimate things not only evokes Woolf's description of human consciousness as a luminous halo, but also repeats, on a thematic level, the formal aesthetic articulated in the diary, whereby multiple narrative threads "open out" of one another in an unbroken "ebb and flow." This diffusion or "spreading" of the self beyond its visible boundaries also forms the exact counterpart to the dartlike, definite self that Clarissa composes in the mirror for the world to see. That Clarissa's sense of identity is pliant enough to embody both extremes illustrates a model of being that, as Patricia Yaeger has written in reference to Chodorow's theories of female psychological development, "permits both a saving maintenance of ego-boundaries and an exploration of the pleasures of intersubjectivity."[78] Earlier in this chapter, we saw how Joyce creates for Molly Bloom a subjectivity whose capacity to contain and withstand contradiction deconstructs rather than reinforces many of the oppositions and stereotypes that critics have traditionally attempted to foist onto her. The psychology that Woolf grants to Clarissa Dalloway also contains apparent contradictions without reducing them to simplistic oppositions: the glittering society matron who is all surface, the hostess who provides a unifying center, the existential solitary, the private soul unknown to others, the decentered self that is neither one thing nor its opposite, the intersubjective self that exists in others. All are equally valid facets and faces of a being who, like the chimes of St. Margaret's, is most fully her (whole)

self—possessed of the magical ability "to be; to exist; to sum it all up"—
in the moment of passing, change, and dispersion.

The Match Burning in the Crocus: Clarissa's Sexuality

If these multiple enactments of identity add up to the sum total of a self
that goes by the name of "Clarissa Dalloway," this multiplicity-in-oneness
is also closely related to the narrative's representation of the libidinal currents of Clarissa's inner life. However, Clarissa's conscious awareness of her
erotic and autoerotic potential is much more limited, reflecting the degree
to which she has internalized her culture's views of female sexuality. On
the sexual stage constructed by male perceptions of femaleness, Clarissa
judges her sexual performance to be lacking even the lack that according
to psychoanalytic theory is supposed to generate a woman's compensatory
heterosexual desire. This negative self-image is particularly pronounced in
the scene when she returns from her morning shopping adventure and,
learning that Richard will be lunching with Lady Bruton, suddenly experiences "an emptiness about the heart of life." Withdrawing nunlike to her
bedroom, Clarissa upbraids herself for the "virginity preserved through
childbirth which clung to her like a sheet" and the "contraction of this cold
spirit" that has led her to feel that she "ha[s] failed" Richard sexually. In
other words, she interprets her lack of sexual response as a sign of an essential frigidity that she assumes is tantamount to a basic lack of *any* sexuality:
"She could see what she lacked. It was not beauty; it was not mind. It
was something central which permeated; something warm which broke up
surfaces and rippled the cold contact of man and woman" (45–46).

However, as the immediately following stream of associations makes
abundantly clear, Clarissa *has* in the past felt, and indeed can *still* feel,
"something central which permeated." But Clarissa has only experienced
this erotic feeling in the presence of other women, as the phrase that completes the sentence quoted above reveals: "It was something central which
permeated, something warm which broke up surfaces and rippled the cold
contact of man and woman, or of women together. For *that* she could
dimly perceive" (46). An immense psychological and narrative weight
is brought to bear on Woolf's italicized word "that," recalling Nancy K.
Miller's argument for a feminist narratology where the "added emphasis"
reveals otherwise occluded narrative secrets.[79] For even as Clarissa proceeds
to disguise her passionate response to women by recasting it as a simulation
of men's feelings for women, Woolf's description of the sensations that
the "charm of a woman" (46) arouse in her protagonist's psyche exudes a
powerfully autoerotic current that gives the lie to her judgment of herself
as sexually frigid, lacking "something central," empty "at the heart of life":

> Only for a moment; but it was enough. It was a sudden revelation, a tinge
> like a blush which one tried to check and then, as it spread, one yielded to

its expansion, and rushed to the farthest verge and there quivered and felt the world come closer, swollen with some astonishing significance, some pressure of rapture, which split its thin skin and gushed and poured with an extraordinary alleviation over the cracks and sores! Then, for that moment, she had seen an illumination; a match burning in a crocus; an inner meaning almost expressed. But the close withdrew; the hard softened. It was over—the moment. (47)

Like Chopin's lyrical evocation of Edna Pontellier's sexuality, Woolf's language draws extensively on the physical senses in order to ground Clarissa's erotic "revelation" in the body's materiality.[80] Simultaneously, the evocation of Clarissa's libidinal rapture through indirect free discourse—in which the "expansion" to the "farthest verge" is met by a simultaneous contraction ("the world come closer")—creates a rhythm of dispersal/enclosure characteristic both of Woolf's theory of the unwritten novel and of consciousness. Writing, subjectivity, and eroticism thus share in an "ebb and flow" that replaces the linear trajectory associated with traditional narrative desire (rooted in male sexual expenditure) with one that evokes the currents of female orgasmic pleasure. That Woolf means to associate the orgasmic rhythms of Clarissa's moment of "illumination" with a female erotics is also suggested by implicit gendering of the floral image of the match burning in the crocus, one that anticipates the feminocentric artwork of Georgia O'Keefe and Judy Chicago.[81]

Crucially, this highly eroticized moment overwrites Clarissa's despondent feeling, expressed a few pages before, that she lacks "something central which permeated; something warm which broke up surfaces." To the contrary, the image of the "burning . . . crocus" allows the reader a glimpse of something "central," "permeating," and "warm" *that exists in the very place of that perceived lack.* But this figural attribution of interiority does not posit itself as an absolute origin of identity or function as the guarantee of self-presence; rather, the revelation of the "match burning in the crocus" only conveys "an inner meaning *almost* expressed." That is, its meaning can never be definitively pinned down to one and only one signified, because there is no single truth or stable center in Woolf's metaphysics of being. This indeterminacy is reinforced by the image of the crocus. Most notably, mirroring the properties of the figure of the "fire in the mist" that the 1920 diary entry uses to describe the "unwritten novel," the match burning in the crocus remains *unseen,* only apprehended through an intervening, translucent membrane that diffuses its outline and extends its borders indefinitely in a halo-like glow. Moreover, to the degree that the incandescent crocus or luminous mist becomes the vehicle of "illumination," traditional categories of surface and depth become inoperative: Who is to say that the light animating either flower or mist is located "inside" or "on" its container?[82]

The potent eroticism that the image of the match burning in the crocus reveals in Clarissa's psyche is confirmed by the memories that surge to her consciousness as her associations leap from the general ruminations on "this falling in love with women" that have triggered this lyrical outburst to thoughts of one woman—"her relation in the old days with Sally Seaton. Had not that, after all, been love?" (48). Elizabeth Abel has written persuasively that the youthful love relationship between Clarissa and Sally forms the "repressed" of the novel, its plot fragmented by the overt story of Clarissa's day and the inner reflections to which the return of her former suitor, Peter, gives rise. As opposed to her relationships with men—that with her husband Richard being advantageous but emotionally distant, and that with Peter being romantic but self-depleting—Clarissa's infatuation with Sally Seaton, a guest in her home at Bourton during the summer she makes her choice of Richard over Peter, is portrayed as idyllic and ecstatic, and thirty years later it still has the power to make Clarissa remember "going cold with excitement" (51) and, in the very act of remembering, to experience once again that rush of excitement in her body.

Woolf makes it clear that these intensely romantic feelings form a pinnacle in Clarissa's psychosexual life. Indeed, as memories of her devotion to Sally resurface in the closeted privacy of her bedroom,[83] Clarissa defines as "the most exquisite moment in her whole life" the night at Bourton that Sally stopped on the terrace by the stone urn, "picked a flower; kissed her on the lips" (52). And, significantly, this kiss is summed up in an image of inner radiance burning through that echoes the description of the match burning in the crocus, thus linking the homoeroticism of this moment to the preceding expression of sexual ecstasy. "And [Clarissa] felt that she had been given a present," Woolf writes of Sally's kiss, "wrapped up, and told just to keep it, not to look at it—a diamond, something infinitely precious, wrapped up, which as they walked (up and down, up and down) she uncovered, or the radiance burnt through, the revelation, the religious feeling!" (52–53). Three points are in order here. First, by ending these options with the unseen but felt quality of the diamondlike kiss, Woolf again creates a "meaning almost expressed" that, like the blaze illuminating the crocus from within, escapes direct representation. Second, the way in which the diamond's radiance burns through or permeates its wrapping, blurring the boundaries of inside and out, repeats the property of diffusion that Woolf sees as intrinsic both to eros and consciousness and makes a principle of her narrative art.[84] Third, by representing the gift of love from woman to woman as an infinitely precious diamond, Woolf tempers the less favorable connotations that accrue to the hard, faceted, centered, diamond self that Clarissa will shortly create in the mirror as an expression of her hostess pose. Whereas the latter image emphasizes the cold, geometrically exact surface that mirrors back what the world wants to see, the diamond kiss emphasizes a central warmth or radiance that has no absolute boundaries, that in emanating outward effaces the barrier between self and other.

This treasured kiss, however, like Clarissa's "dim perception" of her autoeroticism, only exists in the interstices of the narrative and her memory. Just as the "revelation" (47) of sexual ecstasy several pages earlier is ultimately curtailed by the heterosexual frame that allows Clarissa's thoughts to escape self-censorship (after all, she tells herself, she is only describing "what men felt [toward women]"), the "revelation" (53)—note the repeated wording—brought on by Sally's kiss is abruptly checked by the return of their male companions, whose abrasive intrusion into this moment of female intimacy is likened to "running one's face against a granite wall in the darkness!" (53). But, then again, Clarissa's infatuation for Sally has always been informed by and made psychologically possible by her foreknowledge that a wall will sooner or later descend to break off the union that she retrospectively acknowledges as precipitating "the most exquisite moment in her whole life"; she is haunted by the "presentiment of something that was bound to part them" that she proleptically associates with marriage, a "catastrophe" that both young women nonetheless consider inevitable (50).[85]

Once this wall descends, Clarissa's interpersonal life is cut off from the ecstasy that Sally has brought to it, and she reinscribes this loss as the lack of *any* sexuality—hence the blame she lays upon herself for being frigid, for sexually failing Richard through "some contraction of [her] cold spirit." Yet in the face of these claims, the narrative strategically works to reveal a powerful current of unacknowledged eroticism that suffuses Clarissa's present-day existence, a sensuousness that is often displaced from specific persons to generalized objects and that is manifested in her passion for "life" itself. From the very first page, the text illustrates Clarissa treating the daily experience of living as an amorous adventure, actively plunging into and encountering each moment ("What a lark! What a plunge!" [3]) with a "gaiety" and "ecstasy" that reestablishes on the noninterpersonal plane, yet in uncannily similar language, the passion once animating her relationship with Sally.[86] Further, Clarissa's diffusive eroticism is the source motivating her desire to create moments of connection for others to experience. As much a weaver of narrative relations as Woolf, Clarissa views her parties, where she becomes the diamondlike "centre" that forms "a meeting-point, a radiancy" for her guests, as an opportunity "to kindle and illuminate" (6)—the exact sensations formerly attributed to her sexuality (the match *illuminating* the crocus) and to Sally's kiss (the *burning* radiancy of the wrapped-up diamond). And if the diamond-wrapped kiss was once Sally's "present" to Clarissa, now Clarissa conceives her parties as her "offering" to the world (185). Clarissa's libidinally charged past thus continues to flow into the present, making itself felt in the charged autoeroticism with which her syncretic desires attach themselves in multiple relationships to a world of things that in turn simultaneously suffuse her consciousness and extend her being in a web of interconnections.

This modality of desire thus repeats on a libidinal plane what I have been calling the double motion that also dictates the flux of consciousness and manifests itself in the novel's formal attributes. Indeed, Woolf's most radical contribution to modernity's breakdown of logocentric conceptions of sexuality, identity, and narrative depends upon this continual slippage back and forth across the boundaries assumed to divide subject and object, self and other, interior and exterior, body and text. Challenging myths of the self's inner coherence by revealing its traversibility, plurality, and production within and as language, challenging the hegemony of sociolinguistic constructions of power by showing their infiltration by human desire, this dissolution of binaries in turn reinforces the ethos of diffusive connection and intersubjective fusion that bridges the modernist poetics and sexual politics of *Mrs. Dalloway*. This valorization of relation and connection also reminds us how closely Woolf's innovations in modernist form are tied to her difference of vision as a woman. In this regard, Luce Irigaray's lyrical evocation of the libidinal poetics and politics of women's language intriguingly echoes Woolf's own aesthetics: "One would have to listen with another ear, as if hearing *an 'other meaning' aways in the process of weaving itself, of embracing itself with words, but also of getting rid of words in order not to become fixed, congealed in them.* For if 'she' says something, it is . . . never identical with anything . . . rather, it is contiguous. *It touches (upon).*"[87] So, too, with Woolf's conceptualization of the unwritten novel, which "embrac[es] itself with words, but also [gets] rid of words in order not to become fixed." "Doesn't that give the looseness and lightness I want," Woolf asks in her diary, "doesn't that get closer and yet keep the form and the speed, and enclose everything, everything?" Like the "contiguous" writing that Irigaray posits as a characteristic of women's speech, the illusion of an unbroken weave of consciousness and narrative for which Woolf aims depends on an erotics of expanding relations, one that, in assuming the rhythms and pulsations of the living body, materially "touches (upon)" its readers and dissolves the boundaries separating written word and responsive reader.[88]

One effect of this slippage is radically to reposition the reader, as noted earlier, as a participant in the creation or writing of the unfolding text. This embrace of the reader, in turn, is related to Woolf's desire to efface her own narrative presence for the same reasons she criticizes Joycean egotism. As we have now seen in some depth, she largely effects this authorial self-erasure through her deployment of a uniformly removed third-person voice whose flux of indirect free discourse equally filters the musings of all the characters. If authorial effacement turns out ultimately only to be a *pose*—since the personal stamp of Woolf's style as well as the consummate artistry with which she creates the illusion of a seamlessly unfolding narrative are apparent everywhere in the text—it is a pose that nonetheless has an enabling effect, helping to create the illusion of a web of contiguous relations that underwrites Woolf's modernist poetics and inspires her vision of that "unseen part of us, which spreads wide," embracing everything, everything.

Rupture and the Return of the Repressed

Having demonstrated the deep enmeshment of *Mrs. Dalloway*'s artistic achievement in Woolf's vision of relation, I now want to examine the ways in which this vision is simultaneously built over and out of its antitheses: discontinuity, repression, loss, alienation, waste. Such terms are not unfamiliar to anyone who has thought about this novel's affinities with such bleak modernist manifestos as "The Wasteland" or who has charted its depiction of Septimus Warren Smith's harrowing progression from madness to suicide. But I want to point to another, perhaps less obvious, site of repression in this text, one that (like the Sally Seaton love plot) can only be read in the gaps in the narrative's interconnected web. Access to this level of the text's unconscious is provided by a muted thematics of rupture and loss emanating from the same idealization of female relations that, I have been arguing, inspire and sustain Woolf's libidinal and textual erotics.

A war veteran suffering from shell shock, a loss of ego boundaries, and the suspicion that "the world itself is without meaning" (133), Septimus Warren Smith functions as Clarissa's obvious double, a psychological and figural mirror of the fears she represses in the name of connection. But whereas Clarissa never knows Septimus, learning of him only when his suicide is mentioned at her party, the narrative contains another dark double of Clarissa, an other whom she not only knows but quite literally houses, in the form of Doris Kilman, her daughter Elizabeth's history teacher. A repressed and oppressive woman with a massive inferiority complex that underlies both her inflated egotism and masochistic self-abasement, Miss Kilman plays Bella/Bello to Clarissa's Leopold Bloom, her ominous presence teasing out a Circean underside to Clarissa's day-long journey into the psychological reaches of memory and desire. On the one hand, Kilman's costume, an unkempt green mackintosh, becomes to Clarissa the outward manifestation of all that she finds repulsive about the tutor's hungry "self love" (17); on the other, Clarissa's upper-crust pose of cool self-possession inspires Miss Kilman's brutal desire to "unmask" (189) and master Clarissa. I would suggest, however, that what each woman might find beneath the facade of the other is an unwelcome reflection of her own deepest anxieties and uncertainties. If Miss Kilman admits to herself that she cannot "get the thought of [Clarissa] *out of her mind*" the entire day (203; emphasis added), so too Clarissa senses, on her early morning walk to the florist's, that the very "idea" of Kilman has become part of her subconscious landscape, "one of those spectres with which one battles in the night" (16) and which vampirishly drain away "our life-blood" (17). In effect, Kilman has become a monster routing in the nightwood—to anticipate Djuna Barnes's metaphor—of Clarissa's unconscious: "It rasped [Clarissa], though, to have *stirring about in her* this brutal monster! to hear twigs cracking and feel hooves planted down *in the depths* of that leaf-encumbered forest, the soul; never to be content quite, or quite secure, for at any moment the brute would be stirring, this hatred" (17; emphasis added). As the monster/ghoul lodged within the soul who "stirs" up negative feelings that Clarissa would rather forget, Miss Kilman becomes an emblem of a hidden side of Clarissa's psyche, of repressed contents striving for expression that call into question the exaggerated love of life that animates her desire to serve as a meeting point, a site of connection, for others. Structurally Woolf emphasizes this antithesis by having Clarissa block these surfacing thoughts of the hateful Kilman with the rhapsodic paean to nature's beauty that fills her mind as she enters the florist's shop. In a telling act of repression, this celebration of natural connection creates within Clarissa a "wave" of fluidity that "she let[s] flow over her and surmount that hatred, that monster" (19).

But more precisely *what* is it that Miss Kilman represents that Clarissa so needs to hate, and, in so hating, repress? Why, more than two hundred pages later, does she still claim of this "enemy" that "she hated her: she loved her" (265–66)? To what degree are these ambivalently twinned feelings of "hatred" and "love" related to Miss Kilman's barely veiled lesbianism (suggested by the irony of her name), which manifests itself in the passionate relationship Miss Kilman and Clarissa's daughter Elizabeth have formed? Clarissa's melodramatic imagination indicts Doris Kilman as "Elizabeth's seducer" (266), and both Clarissa and her husband are aware that their seventeen-year-old daughter has what they prefer to think of as a "school-girl crush" on Miss Kilman. "But it might only be a phase, as Richard said, such as all girls go through," Clarissa thinks, only immediately to qualify herself by adding, "It might be falling in love. . . . Anyhow they were inseparable" (15–16). In turn, the language of Miss Kilman's yearning to possess Elizabeth—"if she could grasp her, if she could clasp her, if she could make her hers absolutely and forever and then die" (199–200)—clearly expresses a passionate obsession that Kilman only barely manages to control through ascetic denial of the flesh. Given the intensity of this bond, its subliminal effect on Clarissa, I want to argue, is to remind her of the *absence* in her present life of any similar, sustaining affiliation with a woman: what *no longer* unites Clarissa and Sally now links Miss Kilman and Elizabeth. Only on a figurative plane does Clarissa possess the qualities of relationality and identification that Woolf's text associates with the world of women.

However much Clarissa might consciously deny that the loss of her own bond with Sally contributes to her ambivalent feelings about Miss Kilman, such a link finds expression throughout the text's and Clarissa's unconscious. For example, the language used to express Miss Kilman's unrequited love for Elizabeth (see 199–200 above) directly echoes the ecstatic language used in the "match burning in the crocus" sequence to express the intensity of Clarissa's love for Sally. Clarissa's actions also repeatedly and symptomatically betray the textually repressed connection between these two lesbian moments. Particularly vivid is the occasion (recalled by Elizabeth) when Clarissa, with an overacted show of goodwill, forces upon Miss Kilman a hamper of flowers that has just arrived from Bourton, creating an unflattering juxtaposition between Kilman and the physical site and primary emblem of Clarissa's "pure" love for Sally (whose "way with flowers" was legendary at Bourton [49])—small wonder Kilman's agitated, awkward response is to "squas[h] all the flowers in a bunch" (198)! Clarissa's subconscious speaks quite clearly through her action; she wants to embarrass Miss Kilman in front of Elizabeth, and she counts on the fact that her ladylike graciousness will only make Miss Kilman look all the more unfemininely disagreeable.

As this latter scenario implies, not only does Miss Kilman's relationship with Elizabeth subliminally remind Clarissa of her forfeited bond with Sally; more immediately Clarissa fears that she has been replaced in her daughter's affections by another woman. And to the degree that the newfound inseparability of Elizabeth and Kilman displaces the original dyad of mother and daughter, it also deprives Clarissa of the one remaining arena of female intimacy in her life. "This woman had taken her daughter from her!" (190), Clarissa inwardly rails, experiencing "a violent anguish" (191) at the sight of the two women leaving the house together without her. This disruption of the maternal tie, moreover, hints at another level of psychological and textual repression at work in the novel, one tied to the plentitude associated with the preoedipal phase of female development and the premarital world of "female pastoral" that Abel convincingly associates with the Bourton episodes. For what Clarissa's unfolding memories and Woolf's enveloping narrative cooperate in repressing is perhaps the most formative event in Clarissa's psychic development: *the traumatic, repeated experience of violent loss and rupture characterizing all her early intimate bonds with women.* The most striking of these losses involves the death of Clarissa's older sister, Sylvia, about whom the reader only learns, tellingly, through Peter's, not Clarissa's, recollections. "To see your own sister killed by a falling tree (all Justin Parry's fault—all his carelessness) before your very eyes, a girl too on the verge of life, the most gifted of them, Clarissa always said, was enough to turn one bitter" (117–18). Abel notes that the offhanded manner in which the fate of Sylvia is "written both into and out of the text" suggests "a story intentionally withheld, forcibly deprived of its legitimate proportions."[89] And just as this story gestures toward but ultimately suppresses the effects of this forfeiture of sororal intimacy on Clarissa, so too Clarissa represses the psychic rupture that such loss inevitably entails.

Behind the loss of the sister Sylvia, moreover, looms another virtually unrepresented story of early female symbiosis and subsequent loss: the unremarked-upon death of Clarissa's mother. In fact, Clarissa entertains no recorded thought whatsoever of her mother until, in the briefest of asides during the party sequence that ends the text, an old guest, Miss Hilberry, comments that Clarissa "looked to-night . . . so like her mother as she first saw her walking in a garden in a grey hat" (267). Woolf juxtaposes this observation with the off-color conversation of a nearby group of men who, as Clarissa archly notes to Miss Hilberry, "won't tell us their stories"—another seemingly incidental aside that reminds us of the cultural imperatives that permit certain stories while censoring others, especially female-related ones. Hence Clarissa's reaction to Miss Hilberry's primordial memory (her eyes fill with tears that she immediately represses) reveals *both* her participation in such censorship *and* the tremendous inner division that such willed excision masks: "Her mother walking in a garden! But alas, she must go" (267). A repeated, shattering experience in Clarissa's psychological development, then, this loss of female symbiosis, both revealed by and hidden within the larger narrative, occurs yet again as the "granite wall" of male need interposes to separate Clarissa and Sally on the terrace, and it appears about to repeat itself with the loss of Elizabeth to Miss Kilman. Clarissa's identity is grounded in a schism, a rupture that she represses and that the narrative cooperates in keeping under cover.

In a profound sense, the seamless, almost effortless, unfolding of consciousness that composes the fabric of this novel is the *product* of this repression. For in a pivotal effort of sublimation, Clarissa's psyche replaces the feelings of rupture, fragmentation, and hurt that accompany the loss of the female world of relation with a private metaphysics based on an affirmation of the values of interconnection, symbiosis, and identification. What Clarissa no longer possesses in actuality—meaningful bonds with living women—is thus reconstituted on psychological and narrative levels, where it becomes the foundation of the very erotics driving this text and generating its trove of images and metaphors: permeability, nondifferentiation, fusion. These imagistic displacements—analogous to the mechanism by which psychic repression works—recur throughout the text. We have already noted one such example in the instance in which Clarissa's mind immediately covers over her disturbing thoughts about Miss Kilman with images of natural beauty as she goes into raptures over the flowers (whose many-hued beauty she likens, no less, to a coterie of "girls in muslin frocks" [17–18]). A second example of displacement involves Sylvia's death. On two occasions Peter's thoughts link Clarissa's witnessing of this senseless tragedy and the evolution of her "aetheist's religion of doing good for the sake of goodness" (118). In effect, the experience creates in Clarissa a "horror of death" that she attempts to ameliorate with the philosophy that "the unseen part of us, which spreads wide," exists "everywhere," in myriad relations to the people and places that "complete" us (231–32).

But an even more striking example of the return of the textually repressed occurs, as Carla Mazzio has brilliantly noted, upon the very first mention of Sylvia's name, which appears in the text well before she is identified as Clarissa's deceased sister.[90] Just a few lines after Sylvia's name crops up in a list of various people whom Clarissa associates with Bourton, Clarissa gives expression to her philosophy of life extending beyond death. What is curious, given the gruesome nature of Sylvia's death (crushed by a felled tree), is the imagery that springs to Clarissa's mind and the narrator's pen to express this pantheistic creed of ongoing life: "on the ebb and flow of things, here, there, she survived, . . . she being part, she was positive, *of the trees at home;* of the house there, . . . part of people she had never met; being laid out like a mist between the people she knew best, who lifted her *on their branches as she had seen the trees lift the mist,* but it spread ever so far, her life" (12). As my italics make clear, the "trees at home" that are the cause of Sylvia's meaningless death have been transformed, with no apparent sense of irony, into the metaphoric vehicle of Clarissa's inspirational vision of continuing life. At the same time, the Latinate root of Sylvia's name reiterates, as if in code, the link between "trees" and the "sylvan" source of her death that Clarissa represses. Likewise, the symptomatic fact that Sylvia's unattributed name has *just* crossed Clarissa's mind in the same flurry of associations that imaginatively recasts trees as a positive emblem betrays Clarissa's subconscious *knowledge* of the very loss that gives rise to her creed and at the same moment reveals the psychological and linguistic operations whereby horrific reality is transformed into a seemingly benign metaphor of continuing relation and connection.

Just as these instances supplement the loss of female plentitude with the fantasy of connection, so too Clarissa's parties become a stay against the death and division that has marked her psychological development. In an important passage that most clearly aligns the thematics of *Mrs. Dalloway* with those of other classic modernist texts, Woolf depicts Clarissa sinking "deeper . . . in her own mind now" to ponder "this thing she called life" as she rests prior to the party. Musing on the disconnected lives that exist everywhere, she feels "what a waste," "what a pity," and "if only they could be brought together; so she did it," giving her parties in order to "combine" and "create" in the face of meaninglessness and fragmentation. "Anyhow, it was her gift," Clarissa thinks of her parties, her metaphor recalling Sally's gift—the diamond kiss—decades before: as such Clarissa's "gift" to the world both replaces and represses the loss of the "most exquisite moment" of her life. Following this implicit reference to the lost bond with Sally, the deepest origin of Clarissa's urge to create an unbroken web of relations surfaces a few sentences later with the spontaneous thought: "It was enough. After that, how unbelievable death was!—that it must end" (184–55).

Yet simultaneous with this soothing thought—indeed interrupting it—is the ominous presence, on the opposite side of the drawing room door where Clarissa rests, of none other than Miss Kilman with Elizabeth in tow: a return of the repressed that serves as a reminder that "enough" is never enough when it comes to the death of female intimacy that impels Clarissa's effort "to combine; to create; but"—as she tellingly puts it—as an offering "to whom?" (185).

The Curtain Rises

If Clarissa's parties thus become a way to fight death and division—which is also to fight Kilman, the dark emblem of all that she has lost—the question arises whether such open-ended "offerings," such ultimately compensatory gestures, can ever make up for the actual lack in Clarissa's life of those intimate female bonds so closely knit to her personal metaphysics of connection. To see how Woolf attempts to plot a way out of this quandary we need to turn to the final party scene, or rather, to its most intensely psychodramatic moment, as "death" itself enters the party. Upon overhearing Dr. Bradshaw's story of Septimus's suicidal plunge, Clarissa instantly removes herself to "the little room" abutting the drawing room where the party is in full swing. In this private space—an architectural equivalent of the psyche—Clarissa simultaneously withdraws into herself and, in working through the implications of Septimus's death, recovers a key to her own psychic survival that hinges, tellingly enough, on a kind of theatrical set piece involving two women. First empathetically entering into and imagining the stages of Septimus's leap as if she too is experiencing it, then paying tribute to his choice to die as a valid "attempt to communicate" in the face of "the impossibility of reaching the centre" (280–81), Clarissa walks to the window and, instead of taking the plunge that Septimus has chosen, sees once again the old lady who lives opposite, who is this time "star[ing] straight at her!" (283).

The moment is intensely (psycho)dramatic: the mini-theater that Clarissa watches in the opposite window mirrors Clarissa back to herself by giving exterior expression to a truth of being that is both created and validated in this very moment of literal and psychological reflection: the truth that the "miracle" of existence, as Clarissa has put it upon seeing the old woman earlier in the day, depends on the simultaneous embrace of difference and sameness. These, as we saw earlier, are the principles that at once fortify one's ego-saving boundaries yet allow the self's enriching diffusion into otherness without its becoming, as in Septimus's case, an all-encompassing immersion into a world with no boundaries at all. Engaging in this momentary theater of self-reflection, Clarissa not only redeems her philosophy of living but recreates a spiritual bond, however tenuously, with another woman whose direct gaze (a confirmation of identification/connection) and whose drawing of her curtain (a confirmation of separation/difference) gives Clarissa the courage to return to the party in the drawing room: "But she must go back. *She must assemble.* . . . And she came in from the little room" (284; emphasis added).

In the context of the miniature drama that has just unfolded, Clarissa's choice to "assemble" upon leaving the little room becomes all the more pregnant with meaning. We have noted the potentially restrictive implications of her previous act of "assembling"—composing a face in the mirror for the world to see—since the persona of "perfect hostess" is also a pre-scribed female role that causes others to judge Clarissa in gender-biased terms as feminine, "tinselly," or "superficial." But if one root meaning of the verb "assemble" is to *masquerade* or *seem,* another is to *mirror*—and it is precisely Clarissa's ability to mirror herself in others, to identify both with Septimus and with the old woman opposite in order to get a measure of her own difference, that proves lifesaving, enabling her to "assemble" and thence perform a self at once resilient and expansive. Performing identity is not simply to wear an external disguise, masking some inviolate, unchanging core of being, but, Woolf implies, *the only way* "to be" in a world of perpetual flux and change: identity, the marker of self or psychic "depth," exists only in process of creating and recreating itself.

The mini-drama that is staged in "the little room" and reflected across the way can of course simply be read as a repetition of the pattern, traced in the prior section, by which Clarissa continues to repress the painful knowledge of personal loss and the horror of death by replacing these grim realities with fictions of endless relation. But something else happens, I think, when Clarissa confronts Septimus's suicide. For she simultaneously confronts the possibility that death, rather than being horrific, might in fact be an "embrace," an attempt to connect in face of the reality of loss that has become the pattern of her own, not just Septimus's, life. In this moment of simultaneous empathy and projection, Clarissa experiences, I suggest, a deeper truth than her conscious mind is capable of articulating—a truth to which the textual unconscious of *Mrs. Dalloway* provides access by making Clarissa's poetic evocation of death's embrace a verbal echo of her previous expression of the passionate ecstasy she shares with women.[91] In deciding to "go back" to rejoin the world of the living, then, Clarissa transforms the repression or denial of loss that has motivated her celebration of life into a *sublimation* of that loss, a process which begins by acknowledging, however fleetingly, the enormity of the divisions that have left her "alone" and devoid of "rapture": "And once she had walked on the terrace at Bourton" (282). This process of transformation and recognition has been ongoing throughout the day but, at this moment of heightened psychodramatic intensity, under the stimulus of Septimus's death, it finally achieves articulation.

Having commented at such length on the operations of the repressed in this text, I should also point out that repression is not always a bad thing; it can also work, productively, to create those epiphenomena that Freud calls love and affection. In this light, it is important that when Clarissa decides that "she must go back" and "assemble," she exits the inner room with a very specific object to go back to in her mind: "She must find Sally and Peter" (284); for the two principal players in the memories of Bourton that have dominated Clarissa's day have both turned up as unexpected guests at her party. As *material* manifestations of love and affection that—however changed, transmuted, or displaced over time—have allowed Clarissa to go on living in the face of rupture and division, the presence of Peter and Sally at the party provides her with the chance to forge a meaningful connection between the past and the present. As Woolf says in her diary of the tunneling process for representing consciousness, the caves of memory that give the novel its psychological depth ultimately "connect" and "com[e] to daylight at the present moment." With Clarissa's exit from the little room and her resolution to find Sally and Peter, that moment has arrived. It is also the moment that will bring the narrative to a close.

For the hope, however tentative, with which the novel concludes—the hope that there may still remain for Clarissa some viable link between her past, with its riches of relationship, and the possibility of shaping meaningful human connections in the present—becomes the driving principle behind the remarkable technical feat that brings the text to an end. With the lines, "But she must *go back*. She must assemble. She must find Sally and Peter," the third-person voice uses the device of indirect free discourse to paraphrase Clarissa's thinking process *for the very last time,* though we are not yet aware that we have "exited" Clarissa's consciousness as surely as she has exited the small room. The immediately following sentence—"And she *came in* from the little room" (emphasis added)—sets into motion one of Woolf's nearly invisible transitions in viewpoint, as the narrative perspective reestablishes itself *outside* of the room, with Clarissa walking into its field of vision as the object of its cameralike gaze. But only as a temporary object—for at this point Clarissa vanishes from sight, not to reappear until the final sentence of the novel, twelve pages later. With the interjection of the question, "But where is Clarissa?" by Peter Walsh as he keeps Sally (now Lady Rosseter) company, the narrative seamlessly shifts its perspective to this pair as they sit ruminating about their old friendship with Clarissa, each wondering whether she will live up to her promise earlier in the evening to return to them. The reader, meanwhile, is put into an analogous position of suspense, keenly aware that the novel is in danger of drawing to a close without her return. Then, in the final line, as if in answer to the sudden thrill of "ecstasy" and "excitement" that Peter feels, Clarissa walks back into the narrative field of vision, her entrance simultaneous with the last words of the novel: "For there she was" (296).

What Woolf has masterfully crafted in these twelve pages (an agonizingly long wait at the end of a relatively short novel) is an erotics of suspension that depends on the narrative thread that runs, unbroken, from Clarissa's *exit* from the little room to her *entry* into Peter and Sally's angle of vision: nothing less than her arrival can satisfy the desire for connection, as opposed to further loss or rupture, creating a suspense that now exists on the level of both plot and structure. This narrative erotics of suspension/connection, completing the narrative frame begun twelve pages before, ultimately restores to the waiting reader a character who, tantalizingly, has been represented throughout the text as *the very embodiment of suspension*—akin to the "hush, or solemnity; [the] indescribable pause; [the] suspense . . . before Big Ben strikes" (4–5). And what this final stroke, narratively speaking, delivers is a representation of self that Clarissa has "assembled" out of her confrontation with repression and loss, a self who strikes a pose that not only seems to sum up her ability to be ("For there she *was*"), but a pose that also signifies closure, a fulfillment of narrative desire (as in summing up a story). And yet, of course, at the very instant that this pose seems "to sum it all up," to attest to Clarissa's ability "to be" (264) in face of the onslaught of time, the unreported story of the encounter between Clarissa and Peter, between Clarissa and Sally, begins to unfold in a future beyond the threshold signified by the text's final image and words.[92] As such, the last line—"For there she was"—serves both as a summation *and* a springboard into the unknown, simultaneously enclosing *and* opening outward in the double motion intrinsic to Woolf's vision of consciousness, eroticism, and narrative itself. It is one more thread, a lifeline cast in the direction of some unknown recipient in the unknown future—perhaps the reader who becomes the cocreator of this "unwritten novel"—and as such it embodies the hope for a connection between past and present, self and other, that will transform Clarissa's metaphysics of relation into more than just a displaced metaphor for, a repressed ghost of, all that she has loved and lost and, perhaps, will love again.

The sheer talent, originality, and insight with which Woolf and Joyce shape their experiments in modernist form to reflect the flux of consciousness lie behind their current reputations as the two most important novelists writing in English in the first half of the twentieth century. Even as concepts of canonicity have been fiercely debated in the past decade, and as the value of "modernism" as a movement and as a category of analysis has come under harsh scrutiny, resulting in the dethroning of certain authors (farewell Hemingway) and rise of hitherto neglected ones (welcome Hurston), both Joyce and Woolf have retained a position of preeminence that I, for one, am happy to grant them. But their now canonical status has also come at a certain expense, particularly insofar as their individual achievements have been subsumed into a set of aesthetic practices and beliefs that more properly describe the institutionalization of "high modernism" begun by Eliot and Pound and reaching an apogee in American new criticism in the 1950s.[93] Classifying Woolf and Joyce solely within these terms serves to efface the more radical poetics and politics that, as this chapter has attempted to show, motivates, drives, and ultimately complicates their representational aims. This erasure is especially evident when we consider the libidinal politics of *Ulysses* and *Mrs. Dalloway*, where the exploration of psychosexual states—manifested in the play of polymorphous desire in Joyce, the diffusive narrative erotics of Woolf, and the return of the repressed in both—opens onto narrative and existential possibilities that cannot be contained by acts of authorial fiat.

In composing *Mrs. Dalloway* Woolf records in her diary—as we have already seen—her great excitement in realizing a "design [that] is so queer and so masterful." The oxymoronic coupling of these two adjectives applies equally well to the balancing act that both *Ulysses* and *Mrs. Dalloway* execute, combining the deviant, wandering, elusive qualities of their narrative designs with the patterns, the overall unity, the technical mastery, that each text exemplifies, even when (as in Woolf's case) mastery itself is overtly disavowed. In the following chapter, we will see what happens when the "queerness" of such narrative designs becomes an overtly thematized component of the text, as I argue happens in a submerged modernist tradition originating among gay and bisexual writers who locate their fictions in the modern metropolises of the United States and Europe. It is a critical commonplace that the rise of modernism was integrally tied to the evolution of the twentieth-century city (to wit the importance of London in *Mrs. Dalloway* and Dublin in *Ulysses*), whose myriad stimuli and paradoxical congregates of isolated individuals living in proximity to millions of other unknown selves suggest many of the concerns of the modernist novel.[94] The next chapter, however, will trace the even greater significance that the urban setting assumes for those experimental fictions issuing from the largely homosexual enclaves hidden in the topography of the modern city, enclaves that turn to their distinct advantage the autonomy and anonymity more often seen as the bane of urban life. Transforming the mysteriously labyrinthine, technologically complex spaces of the urban setting into libidinal stages upon which their literally and figuratively perverse fictions of sexuality unfold, these writers pioneer a spe-cifically queer modality of modernism, one in which the depiction of consciousness not only comes to resemble theatricalized spectacle, as in Woolf's and Joyce's representations of the mind's sexual theaters, but one in which the masquerade of sexuality becomes, for the queer inhabitants of the modern urban geography, the final "truth" of subjectivity itself.

CHAPTER FOUR

Theaters of the Mind II

Bruce Nugent, "Smoke, Lilies, and Jade"
· · · · ·

Djuna Barnes, Nightwood
· · · · ·

Charles Henri Ford and Parker Tyler, The Young and Evil
· · · · ·

Blair Niles, Strange Brother
· · · · ·

> So I lie, who find no peace
> Night or day no slight release
> From the unremittant beat
> Made by cruel padded feet
> Walking through my body's street
> —Countee Cullen, "Heritage"[1]

> In Bohemia everything and anything is in season.
> —Charles Warren Stoddard, *For the Pleasure of His
> Company: A Tale of the Misty City*[2]

In contrast to the institutionalization of high modernism that the names
Joyce and Woolf have come to signify over the course of the twentieth
century, this chapter investigates a much less institutionalized, indeed deviating and deviant, modernist practice emanating from the gay urban spaces
of Harlem, the Left Bank, and Greenwich Village in the 1920s and 1930s.
I want to argue that this neglected alternative modernist enterprise created
linguistically complex, highly experimental fictions as well as popular texts
of mass culture and modernity that are not only worth examining in their
own right but whose circulations of sexual and textual desire foreshadow
the rise of what is now being called "queer" in current gay studies, arts,
and politics.

205

The writers surveyed in this chapter—Bruce Nugent, Djuna Barnes, Charles Henri Ford, Parker Tyler, and Blair Niles—do share many concerns with Joyce and Woolf: the attempt to reorganize fictional narrative along spatial, nonlinear coordinates as a way of breaking out of a narrowly defined code of mimetic realism; the exploration of human subjects divided by repression and driven by unconscious impulses; the mining of language's signifying properties and disjunctiveness to provide a self-reflexive commentary on the slipperiness of all desire. Likewise, these writers share with Joyce and Woolf a profound interest in the psychosexual and libidinal forces associated with the world of the interior, those mysterious psychological undercurrents whose representation has been the concern of the previous three chapters. But despite this shared interest in "the dark places of psychology" that Woolf touts as the modern writer's special province, the writers I am bringing together under the affiliation of "queer modernists" do not, by and large, follow Woolf's charge to "look within" and simulate the flux of consciousness in prose narrative. Nor do they categorically discard those external signposts associated with traditional realism and viewed by many high modernists as barriers to a higher truth of being. Rather the surface of quotidian reality itself often becomes a siting for those libidinally charged forces that Woolf and Joyce locate within the consciousness of their fictional subjects. Indeed, the tentative play of surface-as-depth at work in Joyce's and Woolf's representation of consciousness as a mental theater—a phenomenon the previous chapter linked to Judith Butler's explanation of identity and sexuality as performative rather than constitutive of an originary core of being—is pressed to an even greater extreme by these writers, for whom the unceasing, always provisional enactment of identity, desire, and gender often becomes the primary textual marker of the interiority of their fictional characters. But if these texts choose to represent the externalities of "reality," they do so with a vengeance that borders at times on the surreal, exposing the visible plane of the everyday as a disguise and (dis)simulation itself. In such fictions, the inverted Circean nightworld momentarily depicted in *Ulysses*—in which "inner" guilts, "hidden" desires, and subconscious impulses are exteriorized as performed actions—threatens to become the entire fictional world, a carnival of shifting constructions, chameleon roles, and enigmatic codes that compose a totalizing universe of pure difference.

Such a slant of vision is not unrelated to the nonmainstream sexual subcultures that these texts represent—those sexual dissidents and outcasts tentatively allied under the sign of the "homosexual." Nor is their perverse reading of the performative as the real unrelated to the modernist practices both appropriated by and originating within these marginalized gay literary communities. And, as the term *community* indicates, all these characteristics cannot be separated from the quintessentially modern *urban* experience that provides the specific geographical and textual siting for the rise of this queer modernist enterprise. But before linking these characteristics further, I need to justify the applicability of the adjective *queer*—once a term of homophobic disapprobation—to this historically specific context. I will do this, first, by turning to recent theoretical appropriations and redefinitions of the term and, second, by intimating its relevance to the revisionary modernist project this chapter investigates.

In what has been an amazingly short span of time, the proliferation of the word *queer* in lesbian and gay politics, arts, and culture, in the academy, and on the street indicates a term whose radical usefulness is quickly superseding its sometimes contradictory meanings.[3] Part of its appeal has to do with the hope that "queerness" is not simply a passing trend but the marker of an epoch-making shift in modes of conceiving sexuality that portends the breakdown of the hetero/homo binary characterizing twentieth-century western epistemology.[4] By shifting the debate on sexuality from a straight/gay opposition (in which one's sexuality is defined by the biological sex of one's partners) to that of normative/non-normative behaviors (which recognizes the fluidity of *all* sexuality), queer thinking strategically attempts to free homosexual desire from its dependence on and secondariness to heterosexuality as the privileged term within dominant sexual codes. Governed instead by a logic and a politics that is at once radically anti-assimilationist (I refuse to be like you) and radically antiseparatist (we are not a single minority defined by one agenda), this embrace of "a common identity on the fringes," as Jeff Escoffier and Allan Bérubé put it, positions same-sex desire as part of a more general celebration of difference.[5] As a means of reconceptualizing sexual categories, spaces, and boundaries, the queering of identity and academic theory alike is a strikingly contemporary phenomenon, rooted in a postmodern aesthetics of performance and pastiche that, in the words of Ann Powers, "has turned closet inside out, making the projection of a queer attitude enough to claim a place in homosexual culture."[6]

Without denying the relevance of the social and psychological transformations signaled by the concept *queer* to the contemporary moment, this chapter suggests that in another liminal epoch—the 1920s and 1930s—something very like what Powers calls "the projection of a queer attitude" was at work in the making of urban gay spaces in the early-twentieth-century modern city, as well as in the representation of these urban spaces in a variety of fictional texts. As my chapter title indicates, I want to focus in particular on the gay bohemian enclaves of Greenwich Village and Harlem in New York City and of the Left Bank in Paris, all of whose complexly intertwined literary communities became the locus in this period of various modes of noncanonical modernist writing. The following pages argue that the conjunction of sexual subculture, urban geographies, modernist practice, and queer theory provides an intriguing blueprint for rereading the subversive energies of several hitherto marginalized modernist texts, four of which I examine in this chapter: Bruce Nugent's "Smoke, Lilies, and Jade" (1926), Blair Niles's *Strange Brother* (1931), Charles Henri Ford and Parker Tyler's *The Young and Evil* (1933), and Djuna Barnes's *Nightwood* (1936).[7]

A few caveats, however, are in order before I proceed. First, in speaking of a queer modernism of the 1920s and 1930s, I do not mean to suggest that the meanings we now associate with the term *queer* were available, or even latent, in its usage then. On the contrary, rather than signaling an unruly fluidity in excess of the homo/hetero binary, the term *queer* emerged in the interwar period among homosexuals to signal an innate orientation toward persons of the same sex. Those of "us who are born 'queer,'" as Mark Thornton, the gay protagonist of *Strange Brother*, explains, exist "at the opposite pole from the entirely normal man," and, unlike those "border-line cases" that the psychoanalyst hopes to influence, can never be "push[ed] . . . over into the safe region of normality—into the happy pasture of the herd": hence, for Mark and his "tribe," queerness is a birthright, not a choice (154–55). Second, I am not interested in making a cause-and-effect argument that purports to have uncovered the "origins" of contemporary queer theory in an earlier period—in this case, the modernist era—thereby vitiating the impact of the present moment by revealing queerness to have been around all along. Rather, my interest is in the ways in which many of the most challenging implications of contemporary queer identifications, attitudes, and "theory" retrospectively shed light on various questions about same-sex desire and its representations circulating in the early decades of this century and intimately linked to the rise of the twentieth-century metropolis. In other words, while the project of this chapter may indeed be historiographical, intent on rendering intelligible certain aspects of the past, it does not aim to provide a teleology that traces an unbroken history of influence from "then" to "now."

Crucial to the siting of queer desire in these modernist texts is the specifically modern experience of urban space as uncontrollably vast, internationally diverse, and spectacularly unknowable. Georg Simmel has argued that the explosion in the size and complexity of the modern metropolis at the beginning of this century fundamentally reshaped the *mental* life of the city dweller, whose psyche responded to the city's myriad stimuli with increased feelings both of anonymity and of unprecedented freedom.[8] This dual response is confirmed by Raymond Williams's observations in an essay suggestively titled "Metropolitan Perceptions and the Emergence of Modernism," which links the new psychology created by this increase in anonymity/autonomy to the development of modernism: if the sense of isolation, of being lost in the crowd, created for many individuals those extreme states of distorting, alienated consciousness that have since become hallmarks of modernist art, so too the "liberating diversity and mobility of the [modern] city," in Williams's words, awakened in others a sense of openness, of new horizons, and of the "exceptional liberties of expression" that served as a crucial spur to modernist experimentations. For, as Williams also notes, within the great, international, metropolitan centers emerging after the turn of the century, "small groups in any form of divergence or dissent could find some kind of foothold, in ways that would not have been possible if the artists and thinkers composing them had been scattered in more traditional, closed societies."[9]

Hence, along with the anonymity and autonomy that Simmel cites as intrinsic to the experience of modern city life, the possibility of establishing such "footholds" served to attract increasing numbers of homosexually disposed men and women to the metropolis. The protagonist of *Strange Brother* provides a paradigmatic example of this migration: taking to heart the advice of an older gay mentor to leave Iowa for "a place big enough for a man to be different safely" (74), Mark Thornton moves to New York City, where the relative tolerance of Harlem's community provides him the space to be more open about his sexuality. Likewise, the action proper of *The Young and Evil* begins with the disembarking of a homosexual youth named Julian, flushed with "lush expectancy," from a ship that has carried him from the repressive South to the docks of New York City: here he is met by the mascara-eyed Karel, a hitherto unseen pen pal whose body, undulating "like a tall curved building," seems a personification of knowing urbanity.[10] The possibility that *any* person moving through the diverse urban landscape might experience hitherto unimagined possibilities of sexual gratification—as well as the likelihood that the daily physical movements of lesbian and gay individuals exponentially increased their chances of crossing paths with others sharing the same desires—gradually helped to carve out enclaves within the urban grid where, as George Chauncey's impressive study of New York City has documented, increasingly visible gay subcultures took root and flourished into active, self-sustaining communities from the turn of the century forward.[11] The geography of gay identity, it is clear, becomes synonymous with the occupation of urban space in this century.

It is essential to note, however, that none of the urban sites and texts that I am considering are exclusively homosexual. Rather, these communities exist in a fluid and contingent relation to other disenfranchised populations: the bohemian artist community, political extremists, sexual profligates, the entertainment demimonde, the criminal underground. Similarly, these sites are characterized by a polymorphously labile sexuality whose expressions may run in any of several directions.[12] Such characteristics anticipate some of the more salient features of queer theory, three of which are particularly relevant to the fictions of modernity investigated in this chapter. First, these texts presage the contemporary understanding of queer subjectivity as the assumption of a defiantly *non-normative identity* that defines itself primarily in terms of its opposition to the status quo rather than in terms of an opposition between heterosexual and homosexual categories. Hence, in addition to accommodating lesbians and gay men of various races, classes, and ethnicities, the urban spaces represented in these texts embrace drag queens, straight-identified male hustlers, "fag hags," impoverished artists, bisexuals, panhandlers, anarchists, and straight women exploring their own oppression. Second, this strand of renegade modernism shares with current queer theory a sense of queerness as a *communal affiliation* shared by sexual dissidents and otherwise marginalized members of society who find in the proclamation and celebration of their common difference the basis on which to begin to build alternative worlds. Hence, the creation of affiliations and identifications that cross and recross hitherto segregated sexual/social categories of oppression becomes the pivotal defining feature of these marginal communities. At the same time— and this is a crucial point—the self-proclaimed outcasts who populate these texts also typically find a common rallying point, whatever their sexual orientations, under the sign of the "Homosexual," the modern identity category based on same-sex desire. In their embrace of homosexuality as a governing trope, these fictions anticipate Eve Kosofsky Sedgwick's argument in *Tendencies* that any politically viable use of the term *queer* today must acknowledge the centrality of same-sex expression to its present definition. "Given the historical and contemporary force of the prohibitions against *every* same-sex sexual expression," Sedgwick writes, "for anyone to disavow those meanings [of queer], or to displace them from the term's definitional center, would be to dematerialize any possibility of queerness itself." [13]

Third, these "fringe" modernist texts share with current theory a sense of queerness as an effect of representation and hence of style, whether played out in fantasy, on the body, or in writing. Modernist writing, of course, is nothing if not a self-conscious performance of style, of textual inscriptions that—like the coded gay body—simultaneously flaunt and conceal "meaning" in a masquerade of allusion and self-referentiality. [14] On the textual plane, the appeal of modernist style, language play, and experimental formats to gay writers seeking both to convey and to disguise taboo subject matter is obvious. In the interplay of gay argot and linguistic experimentation in Ford and Tyler's *The Young and Evil*, for example, the novel's verbal difficulty—a typical trait of modernist prose—directly relates to the reader's knowledge or ignorance of the camp slang it employs to describe the homosexual subculture it gleefully depicts. If the specific language of such texts lends itself to queer readings, so too do their larger narrative formats often enact modes of narrative desire that defy heterosexualizing or oedipalized definitions of textual movement. Creating structural patterns based on principles of intersection, linkage, breakdown, and coupling, these fictions map out a deliberately perverse textual circuitry within whose spaces something akin to queer desire is produced and circulated. In the process the concept of narrative space itself is reconfigured. To the degree that a major project of the modernist aesthetic was to reconceive the spatial-temporal coordinates of written and visual art, the queering of narrative movement in the modernist text provides a particularly salient instance of the degree to which the more general modernist revolution in conceiving space and time was accompanied by a specific if largely unacknowledged subcultural politics of sexuality. At the very least the experimental forms of these texts unsettle the primacy of heterosexuality as the novel genre's governing trope; at the most they espouse a protoqueer narrative politics by positing their objects of desire as representative of the queerness that constitutes *all* desire.

Such literary mappings of queer desire raise the related question of the topographical mapping of queer sites in the early twentieth-century city. In the following paragraphs, I hope to show how an application of theories of social space, particularly those of urban geography, may expand our understanding not only of the historical formation of such enclaves but also of the conceptual and imaginative projections that such spaces may engender. I would like to outline five general directions that theorizing urban gay space might take, with an eye to how these directions may enhance our understanding of the "queer sites in modernism" taken up in the rest of this chapter. First, however, I suggest that in order to realize the subversive potential of such conceptions of queer space, queer theorists need to reconsider some of the Foucauldian paradigms that have come to be taken for granted in thinking about social space, particularly as regards the relation of social space to the sexualized body. For Foucault, space most often functions, in David Harvey's paraphrase, as a metaphor "for a site or container of power [that] constrains,"[15] and the spatial organization of the post-Enlightenment city is no exception: within its newly organized, disciplinary spaces of social control, the body is subjected to a regime of faceless, technocratic surveillance and figurative when not literal incarceration. Foucault does acknowledge the possibility, however circumscribed, that the body may occupy particular "points, knots, or focuses of resistance," temporary "heterotopias" from an otherwise all-encompassing disciplinary world.[16] "Resistance," however, may not provide us with a sufficient theoretical handle for imagining, much less articulating, *alternative systems* of experiencing, living in, manipulating, and creating social space—systems of being-in-the-world that the conjunction of the desiring queer body and urban space in all its liberating anonymity, mobility, and diversity holds out as a radical, differently configured, possibility. Keeping this caveat about Foucault in view, the following paragraphs outline five general approaches to theorizing gay urban space, particularly as it comes into being in the 1920s and 1930s and enters modern(ist) textual representation.

APPROACH #1: POCKETS AND GRIDS

First, we might consider how the imposition of the ubiquitous city models of *the urban grid and/or the axial radius* contributes to the formation of specific pockets where cultural difference is not only encouraged but, in its containment, becomes advantageous to those located both outside *and* inside its parameters. As Rosalind Krauss notes in her famous monograph on modern art, the grid pattern is *the* quintessential emblem of modernity—"like that other symptom of modernity, the large city." In spatial terms, the grid—whether imposed over the space of the canvas or the topography of the city—creates an "antinatural, antimimetic, antireal" flatness that not only replaces "the dimensions of the real . . . with the lateral spread [across] a single surface," but also upholds the absolute autonomy of the artifact itself. "The grid is a way of abrogating the claims of natural objects to have an order particular to themselves," Krauss writes.[17] This description of the modernist repudiation of the terms of "natural" "order" is particularly evocative when juxtaposed with the simultaneous emergence, in the modern urban landscape, of communities of homosexually identified men and women whose objective was the similarly "modernist" one of dissociating sexual desire and object choice from the tyranny of the "natural" and the "order" of heterosexuality.

These aesthetic/spatial considerations have important correlatives in the social history of urban design. As the product of urban planning, the grid is most often seen as an American innovation, an utopic attempt to reconceive the hierarchized space of the European city by using right angles to create equal or democratic relations among its sectors and hence its citizens (the nearly uniform grid of Franklin's "city of brotherly love," Philadelphia, stands as a quintessential example of this democratizing impulse). As a relatively recent historical phenomenon, then, the grid pattern forms a contrast to the most traditional feature of urban organization in European cities: the radial axis, which, from medieval Italian hill-towns to Haussmann's restructuring of Paris to Mussolini's Rome, monumentalizes the city center as the source from which power flows.[18] Hence, in contrast to the putative democracy of the grid, the radiating axis is often equated with an authoritarian impulse to police human social relations through a hierarchical division of space (although, one hastens to add, the monotony of the grid can prove as tyrannical as the subordinations created by the axial radius). In reality, most cities—even the newly styled American ones—consist of some overlay of the two patterns, of which Washington, D.C., provides a fascinating example, as anyone driving in the city for the first time learns: an axial grid of streets, radiating from the White House, is laid over a square grid, planting a firm "center" of power in the midst of this political experiment in establishing democratic relations between parts and the whole.[19]

Indeed, such overlays often create the interstices or pockets within the urban grid where "forgotten" or "invisible" subcultures first take root and flourish. This is particularly true of the two quintessential cities of modernity that become such evocative sites of queer social and textual innovation, Paris and New York. It is worth thinking about how, in both cities, the actual physical layout or mapping of street patterns within particular sectors has worked to make these sites more amenable to emerging gay lifestyles.[20] Note, for instance, the historical positioning within Manhattan of Greenwich Village as an old-world, virtually unreconstructed "village" whose tangle of small streets, influenced by the curve of the Hudson, defeats the larger grid pattern and creates an insular neighborhood in which it is much easier (1) to lose oneself (in all senses of the word); (2) to maintain a sense of privacy and therefore safety from interlopers; and (3) to execute the "cruise," creating spontaneous intersections of covert glances and direct looks as often as one crosses and recrosses the maze of streets. Likewise, the medieval Latin Quarter of the Left Bank functions both physically and symbolically to create a hidden pocket within Paris. (A French *quartier*, as Aldo Rossi comments, denotes a residential area that has evolved *within* a sector of the city rather than one that has been superimposed *upon* it.[21]) By and large escaping the nineteenth-century city planning of Haussmann, whose scheme of grand boulevards imposed over old Paris was ostensibly designed to open up city perspectives but actually created routes by which the militia could more easily defeat popular unrest, the Latin Quarter's labyrinth of ancient, narrow alleys and *cul-de-sacs,* peppered with cafes, bars, and seedy hotels, has maintained an atmospheric insularity, mystery, and autonomy conducive to artistic and so-called alternative lifestyles.[22] Even Harlem's more recent development and positioning in the grid of New York, while lacking the small "old-world-village" feel of Greenwich Village or the Left Bank, maintains a physical insularity and symbolic resonance—given its location on the "other" side of the "wilderness" of Central Park—as the repressed other of establishment Manhattan.[23] The hierarchizing implications of this spatial distinction are evocatively captured by the title of Carl Van Vechten's controversial Harlem novel *Nigger Heaven* (1926). For the phrase "nigger heaven" refers to the balcony to which theater-going blacks were relegated, a position of spatial subordination from which, however, in terms meant to suggest Harlem's uptown relation to midtown and lower Manhattan, those "on top" look down on and potentially threaten their unaware oppressors.[24] Likewise, even though Harlem occupies a symbolically invisible position in relation to mainstream white New York, James Weldon Johnson reminds us in *Black Manhattan* (1930) that this pocket nonetheless exists "in the heart of Manhattan": it may be overlooked, but it is still, on one level, "central" to the whole city. Johnson contrasts this black metropolis to the black sectors of other cities, which form "a nest or several nests situated somewhere on the borders; it is a section one must 'go out to.' In New York it is entirely different. Negro Harlem is situated in the heart of Manhattan. . . . It is not a fringe, it is not a slum, nor is it a 'quarter' consisting of dilapidated tenements. . . . Three main highways lead into and out from upper Manhattan, and two of them run straight through Harlem. So Harlem is not a section one 'goes out to,' but a section that one goes through."[25]

APPROACH #2: MOVING, WALKING, CRUISING

In addition to the topographical spaces carved out by such pockets, we might consider the effect of the ceaseless mobility of metropolitan modernity on the evolution of dissident sexual identities and communities. Of obvious importance in this regard is the evolution of various modern technologies of transportation—such as the subway system—that not only enhanced the relative ease with which one could move among the city's districts, making an appearance and then disappearing at will, but also created a complex layering and simultaneity of movement that radically reordered the early-twentieth-century city dweller's spatial experience of urban life. (Think, for instance, of the strata of movements created by the simultaneous existence of underground trains, pedestrian movement on the sidewalks, automotive transportation—cars, buses, taxis—on the streets, and overhead "elevated" trains.)

Of equal relevance to any discussion of the interimplications of urban mobility and sexual identity is the "creative" role played by individual pedestrian movements in demarcating and thereby constructing social space. Theorizing the impact of the urban pedestrian on the cityscape in *The Practice of Everyday Life,* Michel de Certeau argues that the very activity of walking through the city defines "spaces of enunciation," resulting in a proliferation of "pedestrian rhetorics" that, taken together, resist the oppressive, totalizing attributes of social space diagnosed by Foucault. For what appears to be a swarming mass in motion is also, for de Certeau, "an innumerable collection of singularities," individual human agents whose different, multiple, yet intersecting paths throughout the city inscribe "an allusive and fragmentary story whose gaps" make space for the evolution of nonhegemonic vernaculars and popular street cultures that can in turn give rise to viable social practices.[26] The multiplication of these pedestrian rhetorics liberates (rather than localizes) social space and social practice, de Certeau asserts, *and thus daily creates the city anew.*[27] Such an explosion of movement, moreover, renders all urban mobility, to use gay parlance, a form of cruising. Indeed, cruising may be said to become the "pedestrian rhetoric" *par excellence* in the modern era, taking the place of the role Walter Benjamin attributes to the *flâneur* of the nineteenth-century city.[28]

APPROACH #3: DISSEMINATING NODES

We also might usefully theorize these gay urban enclaves as a series of traversable sites, nodal points (1) across which the enclave's "native" inhabitants move in a continual flow of desirous possibility that constantly redraws the community's shifting parameters of tolerance and relative safety and (2) though which other segments of society are also always moving, taking away with them impressions that thus travel elsewhere. As a node of transit and point of intersection, the queer enclave participates in the dissemination of contraband sexual knowledge to unfamiliar terrains outside its immediate borders, and it encourages the cross-identifications that constitute the queerness of its community. "Gayness" thus permeates beyond the geographical boundaries of its specific locales, in the form of information from which no city-dweller is absolutely immune.

APPROACH #4: METONYMIC MIGRATIONS

Conversely, it is also fruitful to conceptualize these urban gay sites as simultaneously mobile, shifting entities. As Ernest Hemingway nostalgically recalled years after his prolonged residence on the Left Bank of Paris, "If you are lucky enough to have lived in Paris as a young [adult], then wherever you go for the rest of your life, it stays with you, for Paris is a *moveable feast*."[29] Greenwich Village, the Left Bank, and Harlem, that is, are *imaginary* as well as actual sites, their meanings floating and attaching to other locations: thus we find manifestations of "Harlem" in the midst of a midtown jazz and supper club, venerable institutions of Greenwich Village bar life rebuilt twenty blocks to the north, and the expatriate queer world of Paris turning up in Vienna and Berlin. The latter shift, whereby Berlin metonymically "becomes" an imaginary Paris and vice versa, also underlines the fluid and interchangeable *internationalism* of these urban sites, as metropolises whose cosmopolitanism exceeds the patriotic, often parochial boundaries of nationhood. In a profound sense, such "world-class" cities, along with the queer denizens they shelter, share a system of values, an aura of sophistication, an appreciation of high culture, and, as Raymond Williams argues, an awareness of "a wide variety of subordinate cultures" due to patterns of immigration and the heritage of imperialism,[30] that makes them *more like one another* than like the national populations whose spatial boundaries contain them.

In this regard, it is also fascinating to note that the urban spaces under investigation here—Harlem, Paris, Greenwich Village—are often rendered analogous to one another in the literature by and about them. During the 1920s and 1930s, "downtown" gay New York (or the "fanciful aggregation of Greenwich Village uranians," as Wallace Thurman caustically put it in his novel *Infants of the Spring*[31]) increasingly came "uptown" to Harlem, particularly to participate in its rent parties and drag balls. And Harlem in this period is often represented as the "Paris of New York": "Overcrowded, vulgar, and wicked, Harlem was Afro-America's Paris," writes Lewis.[32] Conversely, jazz-age Paris is seen as a version of Harlem, a perception fostered by the presence of the black colony at Montmartre, the sensational debut of Josephine Baker on the Paris stage, and the numbers of expatriate Harlem Renaissance writers—including Langston Hughes, Claude McKay, Nella Larsen, and Jessie Fauset[33]—taking up temporary residence in Paris's more racially and sexually tolerant environment.

APPROACH #5: PRIVATIZING PUBLIC SPACE

In addition, theories regarding the spatial transformation of the everyday can suggest how the appropriation of public social space—the park, the café, the store window, the subway, the bathhouse—often radically reorganizes what is considered public and private space, and in ways that become especially constitutive of modern gay male identity.[34] The letters of Parker Tyler describing Village life, for instance, underline the way in which he and his gay friends act out "private dramas" in the public eye, which, even when staged as campy public spectacles, nonetheless occlude the (in)sight of the uninitiated. Similarly, Chauncey reports how the plate-glass windows of the Life Cafeteria, a well-known gay hangout in the Village, provided a sort of stage where gays would perform a "show" for the voyeuristic weekend tourists who came to the Village to watch the faggot parade; at the same time, this public venue is being appropriated by these same faggots as a domestic space in which to carry on their "private" lives.[35] Walter Benjamin, writing about the Arcades Project and its transformation of Paris's public spaces, comments that the creation of these glass-enclosed shopping thoroughfares transformed the city's streets into one vast interior.[36] Conversely, we may hypothesize that, in much gay life, interiorized space becomes *one vast street,* a thoroughfare accommodating social, intimate, and anonymous interchanges impossible in the realm of the bourgeois home and its rarefied interior space. Numerous examples abound: the tradition of the Harlem rent party and the buffet flat; the artistic and literary salon (including Gertrude Stein's and Alice B. Toklas's Saturday evening gatherings and Natalie Barney's lesbian revelries at 35, rue Jacob); the democratizing brotherhood of the YMCA (in which the hallway onto which all the rooms open becomes the public thoroughfare); and the public bathhouse.[37]

Theorizing urban sexual subcultures through the filters offered by these five approaches may also help us rethink certain tropes that have become commonplaces in lesbian-gay criticism, particularly Sedgwick's theory of the closet.[38] For instance, if we think of gay urban enclaves as *physical* sites of intersection through which people of all dispositions travel, and as *conceptual* sites with the power to migrate elsewhere, the idea that there is a distinct "inside" or "outside" to "gay life" (an idea that has served to police the hetero/homo divide) begins to lose its descriptive force. Likewise, who is to say that Greenwich Village, for example, is a margin, a "closet," or even a "*sub*culture" when the very conditions of its making and dissemination, like those of postmodern queer world-making, call into question the normalizing and hierarchizing assumptions upon which a term like "*sub*culture" is founded?

The bulk of this chapter details the various paths whereby the desires that circulate and proliferate on the streets, in the clubs and speakeasies, and in the private residences that compose these queer sites become models for the spatial and temporal formal experiments characterizing the defiantly perverse fictional narratives surveyed in the following pages. In representing the nonhegemonic sexual identities that such queer spaces at once fostered and made possible, these narratives constitute an overlooked modernist practice whose study promises to revise and enlarge our understanding of literary modernism. Before turning to the specific examples of Nugent, Barnes, Ford and Tyler, and Niles, I would like to suggest some of the more general tactics by which these queerly experimental fictions succeeded in translating the various ideas about the modern city, urban space, and gay experience sketched above into quite specific literary equivalents.

The first of these potentialities can be seen as a formal correlative of Chauncey's claim that in the first three decades of this century the urban gay enclave constituted a much more self-sufficient and autonomous entity than has been hitherto suspected. For these queer examples of modernism tend to transform the "footholds" of dissent that they depict into self-contained, self-regulating, and entire textual worlds. Generally speaking, that is, these texts do not merely offer the reader voyeuristic glimpses of the gay community from some safe vantage point; rather they make this world the encompassing focus of their representational efforts. In novels like *The Young and Evil* and *Nightwood,* we *only* see a queer world, from which the status quo is entirely banished; in "Smoke, Lilies, and Jade" and *Strange Brother,* the privileging of the point of view of their gay protagonists subsumes all other nongay perspectives, facilitating a crossing of multiple categories of identity that results in a queer world-vision if not in an entirely queer world. Consequently, readers must wholly immerse themselves in the text's self-contained and self-referential realm of significations for its entirety, imaginatively entering a space of otherness from which the only exit is the closing of the book itself.[39]

Second, to the degree that these alternative, totalizing visions of urban queerness set themselves against traditional novelistic representations of quotidian reality, it is not surprising that their authors repeatedly turn to the world of the night—and, more specifically, to the social activities summed up by the word *nightlife*—as a primary locus of their narratives. The one constant in all these texts is the number of seemingly insomniac characters who wander the city by night, finding under its cover a realm of uninhibited, polymorphous, fluid desires. This realm of desire often borders on the extravagantly carnivalesque, as the elaborate set pieces and backdrops to the narrative action illustrate: exotic stage shows, drag balls, circus acts, all-night speakeasies, private parties, sidewalk cafés, and illuminated street festivals come to mind. Traditionally the world of carnival has served as a ritualized space for the inversion of social order, allowing a temporary suspension of its rules and values.[40] In making the shadow world of night a totalizing realm of feverish activity, these texts also invert the outsider's (and by proxy certain readers') conceptions of what is natural or not. Thus in *Strange Brother* the female protagonist feels, upon her liminal entrance into the homosexual subculture to which Mark's revelations have given her access, turned "mentally upside-down" (158), for "what still seemed to her as inverted as skyscrapers pointed earthward, Mark regarded as perfectly natural" (194). As the figure of the skyscraper intimates, this inverted order is intrinsically connected to the modes of life made possible by the very form of the modern city. And to the degree that the text's space contains an entire world, it represents a world of multiplying difference in which "inversion" has become the new norm, that which Mark regards as "perfectly natural."

Third, these fictions evince manifestations of the two psychological characteristics, anonymity and autonomy, that Simmel associates with modern urban experience. The sense of anonymity produced by the daily encounter with sheer numbers of unknown beings is reflected in the anonymity or elusiveness that often marks the characterization of the protagonists in these texts. Rendered primarily through their poses of worldliness, sophistication, or disaffection, such characters deny the reader easy access to their "inner depths" and demand to be read in terms of the surfaces they have constructed as signifiers of their difference. This resistance to interiorization is one reason why the characters of novels like *Nightwood* and *The Young and Evil* appear so utterly amoral or morally blank: they refuse the logic of a core identity within which prevailing moral values can or should be located. Closely related to this elusiveness is the autonomy that these characters exhibit as independent agents, most pronounced in the ease with which they shed not only dominant values but dominant conceptions of fidelity, relationship, and even friendship. Their random physical movements, mirroring their tendency to drift in and out of each others' lives, attest to a willed freedom from commitment—including any commitment to the reader—that at once renders them all the more unknowable and protects the autonomy they have achieved from assimilation into a disciplinary order.

Fourth, in many of these fictions the denaturalization of committed relationships finds a textual correspondence in a kind of denaturalization of linguistic relations, a severing of the assumed organic link between signifier and signified that the performance and/or masking of "homosexual" affiliation as a costume, as pure surface, has also already set into motion. Likewise, as earlier noted, the language play and stylistic indirection that characterize several of these texts contribute to this denaturalization of language by encoding and disclosing discourses specific to the queer enclaves taking root in the interstitial spaces of the modern city. The evolution of specialized argots or localized vernaculars that emerge as the signature of and password to these self-contained sexual cultures is a particularly *urban* phenomenon in that vernacular language is always dependent on the geographical and spatial proximity of its in-group practitioners.[41] Such urban-specific vernaculars, in "queering" expected meanings, also help produce queer desires, queer subjects, and, not least, queer readers by initiating those unfamiliar with its ideolect into a new linguistic/sexual order. The connotative force of such gay argot, disseminating its content beyond the represented world of the text and into the world of the reader, thus performs a function similar to the third approach above: for the entire text, like the gay ghetto, becomes both a point of intersection and a traversable site, a space of transmission that fosters the spread of "gay" knowledge beyond its immediate boundaries.

Fifth, if the mobility of the autonomous gay urban subject as he or she navigates the geography of the metropolis shapes modes of characterization, it also marks the modernist formulations of narrative movement in these texts. The multiple yet intersecting paths or "stories" traced out by the individual human agents whose footsteps daily redefine urban spaces constitute, as we have already seen, what de Certeau calls a pedestrian rhetoric. De Certeau's description, tellingly, bears striking resemblance to standard descriptions of the modernist text: splintered, disjunctive, paratactic, yet creating a multilayered "wholeness" from the intersections it renders among simultaneously unfolding scenes, actions, and thoughts. In fact, the reformulations of traditional narrative movement that often typify these queer examples of modernist practice spring from the same spatial redefinitions of temporality that the proliferation of these pedestrian rhetorics on the streets creates within the city dweller and the urban commentator. The textual desire that drives these texts does not simply flow, but moves, like the urban subject, in fits and starts, seeking points of intersection and/or crossing that serve as switch points from one outpouring of energy to the next, tracing out a circuitry of restlessly mobile desire that derails linearity in favor of a dispersed temporality through a space that is multiple, simultaneous, and constantly changing. This description of narrative movement calls to mind Deleuze and Guattari's definition of nonoedipal desire as a flow created by a proliferating series of attachments and detachments among partial objects: such a series of temporary couplings and blockages perfectly evokes the erratic, nonlinear trajectories that characterize both metropolitan space and the modernist text, as well as the spaces of enunciation that both enclose. Hence the trajectories in several of these deviant modernist texts not only serve a de-oedipalizing function by defying the contours of the Freudian masterplot (Oedipus's discovery that his end lies in his beginning) but also work against heterosexual presumptions in their rejection of the structural dictates of the marriage plot (where the cessation of the need to narrate is equated with the perfect union of two— male and female—into one).[42]

As a sixth and final point in pursuing these theoretical connections between urban gay space and experimental writing, we need to consider how these reconfigurations of narrative desire help reconceptualize narrative space in order to make room for the representation of homoerotic content. These experiments with narrative's spatial possibilities take any number of forms: Nugent's extreme use of ellipses, which break the horizontal flow of language with wordless gaps that, repeating from line to line, visually create vertical "paths," literal openings, on the page that evoke the protagonist's aimless footsteps as he cruises the city; the desultory or dilated temporality that ensues from Ford and Tyler's near hallucinatory, surreal stylization of the continually shifting sexual alliances of their characters; Barnes's refraction of key actions through Cubist-inspired verbal repetitions that create a sense of suspended motion; Barnes's and Niles's use of nonstop monologues that bring the forward momentum of their narratives to a near standstill, a technique that strategically clears space for the emergence of Doctor O'Connor's and Mark's counterhegemonic visions of the "Night" and the "shadow world," respectively. In all these examples, there is a deliberate perversion of narrative temporality that is at once a general characteristic of modernist writing and, I would argue, a strategy specific to "queer" writing, transforming its narrative form into a material embodiment of the sexually dissident, queer communities that these texts struggle to usher into the field of representation. To these struggles we now turn.

BRUCE NUGENT, "SMOKE, LILIES, AND JADE"
HARLEM AS A HOMO STATE OF MIND

> Avenues of dreams
> Boulevards of pain
> Moving black streams
> Shimmering like rain.
> —Lewis Alexander, "Streets"[43]

Published in 1926 in the first and only issue of the Harlem Renaissance literary magazine, *Fire!!: A Quarterly Devoted to Younger Negro Artists,* Richard Bruce Nugent's experimental short story "Smoke, Lilies, and Jade" forms a paradigmatic example of the modernist appropriation of urban and textual conceptions of space for protoqueer ends. The journal's claim to speak for "younger Negro artists" is particularly apt in Nugent's case. Only 21 years old when this remarkably sophisticated story appeared in print, Nugent arrived in New York City a few years earlier as part of the vast influx of African-Americans to Harlem throughout the first decades of the twentieth century.[44] This great migration, as it has been called, inalterably transformed the urban landscape of metropolitan Manhattan, creating a world north of Central Park in which, as a character puts it in Niles's *Strange Brother,* "We have our own place. For Harlem's complete in itself. It's got everything. . . . A colored man can be happy if he stays in Harlem. He can almost forget that all the world's not Harlem" (29–30). The product of a series of complex factors, Harlem rose to national prominence within the space of a decade to become not only the largest black city in the United States but also, as Chauncey puts it, "the symbolic . . . center of a vast cultural experiment."[45] For in the 1920s and 1930s the existence of Harlem as "our own place" fostered among African-Americans the movement now known as the Harlem Renaissance—a movement whose participants became, for a short period of time, the focus of national attention and praise.

From the very beginning of Harlem's ascendance as an urban and a cultural phenomenon, a series of evocative spatial metaphors—refuge, mecca, paradise, home—were deployed to describe its promise and appeal. These metaphors are especially compelling in light of this chapter's focus on imaginative transformations of urban space. One such designation, "the city of refuge," taken from the title of a story by Rudolph Fisher, was quickly adopted by Harlemites to evoke the safety experienced within the boundaries of this geographically and symbolically complete world.[46] To the population that found a refuge here, this "city within a city," as James Weldon Johnson called it, also beckoned like the promised land, a notion echoed in the title of the special issue of the March 1925 *Survey Graphic,* "Harlem: The Mecca of the New Negro," that is often credited with inaugurating the Harlem Renaissance proper: here the word *mecca* specifies a designation that renders Harlem the spatially realized spiritual goal of a temporal progression or pilgrimage. Similarly the artist Arna Bontemps likened Harlem to "a foretaste of paradise" for new arrivals who, like himself, found it miraculous to discover a location in the United States where it was "fun to be a Negro."[47] The Jamaican-born Claude McKay gives fictional representation to the affirmative sense of identity that this urban space conferred on its inhabitants in *Home to Harlem* (1928), a novel in which Harlem is truly "home," a site of ecstatic liberation and an "Afro-

New World landscap[e]," in James de Jongh's words, to which the roaming protagonist Jake always returns to "be himself."[48] The euphoric tenor of all these images supports Aldo Rossi's contention that the city whose many parts "are complete in themselves" is the city that "truly permits freedom of choice." While one might want to qualify Rossi's optimism, since such freedoms also often prove fleeting, the "Harlem" perceived by its residents as an entity "complete in [itself]" becomes more than a physical site—most important, it becomes, in the black novelist Wallace Thurman's words, "a state of mind."[49]

As attested by the number of gay and bisexual characters in the fiction of the Harlem Renaissance and by the homosexual proclivities of several prominent Harlem personalities and supporters, including Wallace Thurman, Claude McKay, Alain Locke, Countee Cullen, Carl Van Vechten, Richard Barthe, Bessie Smith, Ethel Waters, and (more ambiguously) Langston Hughes, part of this touted "freedom of choice" was a "live and let live" attitude that led to the emergence of a distinctively gay African-American subculture in Harlem.[50] Even when officially discouraged, the presence of this urban, gay subculture on any number of levels (from clubs and private parties to sex orgies at buffet flats and drag balls attended by thousands) constituted a visible presence in Harlem that, as Eric Garber has shown, rivaled the simultaneously emerging gay reputation of the Village. Nor did this presence go unnoted in the popular black press, where, for instance, Baltimore's *Afro-American* reported with mild but witty disapproval the "erotics, neuretics [*sic*], perverts, inverts and other types of abnormalities, cavorting with wild and Wilde abandon" in Harlem's public spaces.[51]

Given this atmosphere, Richard Bruce Nugent, an aspiring young artist with no doubts about his sexual attraction to men, arrived in New York City at a propitious moment in his own and Harlem's development—a time, as Nugent quipped years later, when "gender was becoming more and more conjectural."[52] Upon meeting Langston Hughes in 1925, Nugent was swept up into the crowd of young intellectuals and artistic rebels—including Hughes, Thurman, and Zora Neale Hurston—who conceived the journal *Fire!!* to challenge the assimilationist, middle-class politics of their elders by celebrating within its pages a more complete range of black life, including the folk traditions and sexual freedoms of its underclass.[53] This context sheds light on the homoeroticism of Nugent's story, which was designed not only to be shocking but also to startle its audience into an awareness of the full implications of the "freedom of choice" conferred by Harlem's position as a "city of refuge" and as a shelter from oppressive social values. Indeed, it is the ultimate realization that "one *can*" choose—and, more specifically, that one can honor multiple racial and sexual choices—that forms the climax of "Smoke, Lilies, and Jade."[54] Drawing on the urban phenomenon of Harlem that ensured these freedoms as well as on the New Negro literary movement (many of whose notables appear in the story), "Smoke, Lilies, and Jade" is also the most recognizably modernist of the texts examined in this chapter, written in a mode of stream-of-consciousness narration that owes to Joyce (Nugent's protagonist is also a would-be artist in the mold of Stephen Dedalus). This experimental style, as is true of the fictions surveyed in chapters 2 and 3, is expressive of a deeply psychological interest in plumbing the less conscious, more taboo reaches of the mind—a device that, in Nugent's text, works to disclose the stages by which the protagonist Alex gradually "comes out" to himself as a man who loves another man.

Not least among Nugent's achievements in this story is the representation of an African-American character under the sway of libidinal desire that avoids the pervasive racist equation of the Negro with instinctual, "animalistic" sexuality.[55] The persistence of this stereotype, coupled on the one hand with the Freudian elevation of the libido and on the other with the modernist embrace of the primitive, often put the black writer in a no-win position, forced to choose between avoiding the representation of certain psychological truths (the realm of the instinct that underlies consciousness) and confirming a stereotype of blackness (in which the Negro is rendered synonymous with sex and instinct, lacking the more highly developed capacities of reason). It was precisely the danger of confirming the latter stereotype that led W. E. B. DuBois to urge Harlem's writers to avoid scandalous topics or low-life depictions, and instead inculcate a vision of a thoroughly respectable black middle-class. This, however, was precisely the mandate against which Nugent's circle was rebelling in making "younger Negro artists" the focus of their new journal. "We younger Negro artists who create now intend to express our individual dark-skinned selves without fear or shame. If white people are pleased we are glad. If they are not, it doesn't matter. . . . If black people are pleased we are glad. If they are not, it doesn't matter," Langston Hughes wrote.[56] Indeed, stirring up trouble was an explicit goal of *Fire!!* As Nugent reminisced, "Wally [Thurman] and I thought the magazine would get bigger sales if it was banned in Boston. So we flipped a coin to see who [got to write] the bannable material. The only two things we could think of that [were] bannable were a story about prostitution or about homosexuality."[57] Evidently both men thought they won the flip, Thurman producing "Cordelia the Crude," the story of a female prostitute, and Nugent contributing "Smoke, Lilies, and Jade," the first piece of literature by an African-American to engage the subject of homosexuality by dramatizing the internal process by which a black person comes to acknowledge, give name to, and act upon his homosexual desires.

Yet if the result is a variant of the coming-out paradigm of much gay fiction, this coming-out narrative is produced through a series of identifications that cross and recross multiple categories—in particular, those of sexuality (hetero/homo/bisexuality), biological sex (male/female), race (black/white/Latin), and aesthetics (Wildean decadence/high modernism/Harlem Renaissance). While these cross-identifications are ones that the urban phenomenon of Harlem makes uniquely available to Nugent's protoganist, they also enact a slippage between categories that, as in contemporary queer theory, cannot be stabilized and that consequently produces a "queer" desire for which the label most often applied to this unsung modernist text—a "gay" fiction—now seems inadequate.

Cruising the Modernist Text

Characteristics of metropolitan modernity, literary modernism, and marginalized identity intersect in the formal structure of "Smoke, Lilies, and Jade," whose technique is spelled out in Alex's paraphrased musings in the first lines of text: "It was so comfortable just to lay there on the bed . . . his shoes off . . . and think . . . think of everything . . . short disconnected thoughts—to wonder . . . to remember" (98; all ellipses are Nugent's). The entire story is constructed of precisely such "short disconnected thoughts," generally reported in indirect free discourse. As such, the text of Alex's mental world resembles a vast thoroughfare, a space crossed by myriad, conflicting impressions, sensations, and desires. And to the extent that Alex's mental world forms a crossroads, it evokes both the story's primary setting (the streets) and its primary action (walking). For the associative flow of language that Nugent uses to indicate Alex's random thoughts is mirrored in the equally random footsteps of this young artist's movements as he wanders the streets of New York City night after night. Moreover, if Alex's aimless thoughts are echoed in his (apparently) aimless steps, so too, the narrative technique forces the reader to submit blindly to the flow of Alex's thoughts and movements, experiencing the drift of unconscious desire as Alex experiences it. Simultaneously, this technique puts the reader in the ambiguously eroticized position of cruising Alex's mind, sifting through his recorded thoughts for telltale signs to confirm the suspicion that the restlessness pervading his actions and the "difference" he ascribes to himself are signs of an unvoiced crisis of sexual identity.

Nugent's experimental form abets this intuition that there is more to Alex's musings than meets the eye, for the "short, disconnected" phrases that make up the written text are in fact connected by an equally preponderant series of ellipses. On one level these ellipses represent bridges or lulls in the process of free association as the mind shifts from one topic to the next. But, on another level, these wordless gaps, regularly puncturing the narrative, also signal the possibility that some things are best left unsaid, both in the text and in Alex's psyche.[58] The Freudian resonances of this self-censorship (and the use of modernist technique to represent this repression) point to one of the affinities between Nugent's text and the "dark places of psychology" that Woolf designated as a primary concern of the modern novelist; not coincidentally, one of Alex's favorite authors is Freud, and Alex's dreams become (as we shall see) a crucial determinant in decoding the unspoken desires that drive this narrative.

In addition to signaling the unsaid or repressed, these ellipses also contribute to the text's spatial experimentations, breaking the horizontal flow of language with wordless gaps whose repetition from line to line create visual "pathways" that spiral from bottom to top of each page. For some readers, these breaks evoke the ascending spiral of smoke of the title and, for others, Alex's desultory footsteps as he meanders throughout the city: the space of the text thus becomes a map of the city itself, imprinting a labyrinthine system of movement and flow that is constitutive of Alex's identity as a black man with gay desires. In conjunction with the "short disconnected" thoughts they bridge, these ellipses participate in a strategic queering of narrative that transforms modernist techniques for registering the flux of consciousness into a palimpsest of gay urban subjectivity in the making.

Crossing Categories of Difference

For Nugent, then, modernist technique becomes a crucial tool in representing the psychology of his protagonist, whose conflicted identity and suspect desires are integrally tied to his self-reflexive questioning of his "differen[ce] from other people" (100). The ambiguity of the desires that lead Alex to ponder this difference provides the opening note of the narrative, which begins, "He wanted to do something . . . to write or draw . . . or something . . .," a sentiment echoed a few lines later as he "wish[es] he were writing. . . or drawing . . or something . . ." (99). This is a quintessential expression of unfulfilled desire—although the repetition of the indefinite phrase, "or something," only makes it clear that Alex himself is prodigiously unclear about precisely *what* it is he "wants," and his supine position as he lounges in bed imbues this opening tableau with a voluptuousness that exceeds the stated desire to "write or draw." The ambiguity of this opening note is compounded by the seemingly incongruous memory that next floods Alex's consciousness, as he recalls the night six years ago when "his mother awaken[s] him" to tell him his father has died. While Alex's recollection might on first glance seem the prelude to a Freudian oedipal plot in which the son realizes the fantasy of replacing the father in the mother's affections, on the narrative plane I would argue that this symbolic and psychological killing off of the father has quite the opposite effect, freeing both Alex's psyche *and* the narrative to proceed along nonoedipal erotic trajectories. For this memory triggers Alex's feelings not of sadness ("yet it hadn't been tragic . . . or weird . . . not at all as one should feel when one's father died") but of almost smug self-satisfaction: tellingly, this recollection· is immediately followed by Alex's "puff[ing] contentedly on his cigarette," feeling "comfortable" and "nice" as he lies in bed, which in turn leads him to observe that he is "so different from other people" (99–101).

Alex's contentment in his difference, it is clear, is linked to this break from paternal interdiction. At the time of the father's death, his mother has articulated the normative oedipal narrative of sons and fathers: "But you mustn't cry Alex . . . remember you have to be a little man now." Alex, however, refuses to be a "little man" in the mold of his father; and when he overhears people at the funeral saying, "Alex is just like his father," he knows differently: "And the tears had run fast . . . because he *wasn't* like his father." Instead of identifying with the father, he seems to *desire* him. For what Alex's associations now unearth, as he lies in bed remembering the past, is his fascination with his father's "beauty." This desire for, rather than identification with, the same-sex parent, reverses the usual terms of oedipal maturation (whereby the boy's identification with the father's desire for the mother is the guarantor of adult heterosexuality). No wonder, then, that memories of his father's "beauty" lead to the double-handed observation, "maybe it was wrong to think thoughts like these . . . but they were nice and pleasant and comfortable" (100–101).

The proclamation of difference from the norm foregrounded by placing this memory of severance from paternal origins at the narrative's beginning continues in the associations that immediately follow. Alex's thoughts leap from his father's death to his mother's incomprehension of his artistic ambitions, summed up in her disparaging remark, "Really you're a mystery to me . . . and who you take after . . . I'm sure I don't know" (101). Psychologically this denial of family resemblance completes Alex's separation from his birth family and the bourgeois world it represents—a separation that in fact he (like Stephen Dedalus) seems fervently to desire. He wants, that is, to be repudiated by the claims of blood in order to realize a fantasy of exile, for relocating in Harlem allows him, first of all, to construct a metropolitan persona whose "difference" is no longer estranging and, second, to be admitted to a substitutive kinship structure composed of the Harlem artists who, in contrast to his mother, "accepted and liked him . . . no matter how he dressed" (101). In figurative terms, Alex undergoes an act of self-orphaning that becomes an act of self-authorization.

This reference to Alex's dress refers to the flamboyant style and mannerisms that he affects in his new urban life as an aesthete with decadent leanings and artistic pretensions. Pondering why he is "different from other people," Alex overtly ascribes this otherness to the fact that he is a struggling bohemian artist—an identity category for which a certain deviation from the norm is accepted. As such, the label of "artist" also becomes a mask behind which Alex hides, from himself and others, his unacknowledged homoerotic feelings. In Alex's mind, to be a struggling artist justifies both his pennilessness and his pride; a "great artist" is inevitably, Alex rationalizes, "misunderstood" (103), a member of an elite in-group the larger world spurns. This proves a minoritizing identity that, unlike his homosexuality, he can publicly embrace: "In truth he was tragic . . . that was a lovely appellation . . . The Tragic Genius . . . think . . . to go through life known as The Tragic Genius" (102). Alex draws on two artistic models to authorize his membership in this elite. One is provided by the world of Harlem, where the artistic community that Alex adopts as his new family is composed of some of the most prominent names among Harlem's advocates of the New Negro—(Jean) Toomer, Langston (Hughes), Wallie (Thurman), Zora (Neale Hurston), (Countee) Cullen, Harold (Jackson), and Paul Robeson are just a few of the artists with whom Alex proudly (and narcissistically) claims friendship. Indeed, his compulsive tendency to list such names in his reveries, inserting himself among their ranks as an equal, forms a psychological strategy for defending himself against the anxieties of authority that come with the identity he has constructed for himself as a Dedalean artist-in-exile.

The second model that Alex uses to justify his self-conception as aspiring artist derives from the English tradition of the aesthete-dandy, to which his mannerisms, affectations, pose of world-weary sophistication, and favorite writers are indebted. Chief among the latter is Oscar Wilde, a "Tragic Genius" if ever there was one, and the one artist, above all others, whom Alex explicitly takes as a role model. Not only is the text interlaced with implicit and explicit references to Wilde, but on two occasions Alex substitutes Wilde's words for his own, in effect inhabiting the voice of his master.[59] Such hero worship is not uncommon among young, struggling artists, but the fact that it is specifically Wilde whom Alex has makes the model of his artistic persona begins to suggest, ironically, the very deviation that the pose of artist is, on at least a subliminal level, meant to conceal. Indeed, in artistic circles of the 1920s and 1930s, mention of the name Wilde often served as a code word to signal homosexual propensity. Thurman's *Infants of the Spring* provides a humorous example of this phenomenon, in a scene in which its flamboyant aesthete Paul Arbian—a thinly veiled portrait of Nugent—announces, "I think Oscar Wilde is the greatest man that ever lived" to a handsome young man that he hopes "is one of us," then archly adds, "Unless you're dumber than I think, I've told you all you need to know" (24).[60] The same coding also accrues to Alex's Wildean modes of dress that so upset his mother, since such sartorial extravagance can either connote bohemian eccentricity or homosexual effeminacy, depending on the context and the interpreter. In Alex's assumption of the identity, persona, and style of The Artist, then, Nugent underscores the complex ways in which one minoritizing category of identity may mask or, just as important, *make possible* another. "A homosexual, if he was artistic and intellectual, was just another bohemian," Parker Tyler quipped of life in New York in the interwar years.[61]

Simultaneously, both Alex's self-construction as a dandy-aesthete and his incipient gayness work to keep race—his most visible mark of difference—in the background of the narrative. In an overt sense, "Smoke, Lilies, and Jade" is the least race-conscious text in *Fire!!* Nowhere in the story is Harlem—or for that matter, the ethnicity of the characters—explicitly named as such: the reader infers race and setting indirectly, through markers such as the mention of 136th Street, references to members of the Harlem literati, and the story's appearance in a Harlem-based quarterly. This raises the question of whether Nugent has subordinated a thematics of race to that of sexual and artistic identity, relegating issues of racial oppression to the closet of Alex's psyche. I would argue, however, that "race" permeates the text, but in a manner that takes as a given the interiorized perspective of its black protagonist. In keeping with the narrative's stream-of-consciousness format, Alex's awareness of his blackness is simply presented as part of his life, rather than as a fact that needs to be spelled out for uncomprehending readers. Simultaneously, through Alex's painterly gaze, Nugent *does* indeed write race into the narrative, but in a manner that deconstructs the traditional perception of race in America as an absolute opposition between blackness and whiteness; for those distinctions in skin color that the dominant culture reads as racial designations exist for Alex primarily as *aesthetic* elements. Thus, when Alex looks at the skin tones of his friends, his eye discerns a myriad of colors—features "tinted proud purple," "lids colored mysteriously green," "skin a blue" (103). Concomitantly, it remains unclear what ethnic category is signified by the "olive-ivory" used to describe Melva's skin or, for that matter, the "whiteness" used to describe the body of Alex's male lover Beauty (especially given the fact that Beauty's first spoken words in the text are in Spanish). This ambiguity, I take it, is one of the strengths of the story: we are forced to read "color" only *as* color, as a hue in a palette rather than a categorical designation of racial difference. Both physically and conceptually, Alex inhabits a world where his identity need not be read exclusively *against* "whiteness" but rather *as part of* the immense spectrum to which Harlem had become home in the 1920s.

Cruising the City Streets

Alex's ability to cross among all these signifiers of difference—racial, sexual, artistic—that constitute his identity, using one when necessary to mask or front the other, is crucially related to the urban space in which Nugent situates Alex's coming-of-age story. As already noted, by the 1920s Harlem had achieved the status of a near-autonomous "city within a city," sheltering a wide range of talented young African-American artists and promoting a vibrant culture that helped to foster an unusual degree of toleration among racial, gay, and other socially disenfranchised groups. As in the other texts discussed in this chapter, the fluid commingling of these various subcultures is most apparent under the democratizing cover of night. Like Paris, Harlem became famous for its exciting nightlife. "A blue haze descended at night and with it strings of fairy lights on the broad avenues," Arna Bontemps wrote of Harlem's magical allure. Likewise Langston Hughes's poetry evokes the rhythms that transformed the jazz parlors of Lenox Avenue into what James de Jongh calls a "dreamscape of the blues." [62] The "blue" terrain of night is also Alex's special realm; like a true decadent, Alex spends his days lounging in bed, only leaving his room when darkness falls. "To wander in the night was wonderful," he effuses as he strolls out into "the dusky blue" (102), becoming one of the manifold, anonymous pedestrians whose individual pathways, in de Certeau's terms, intersect to produce those "gaps" in the "allusive and fragmentary story" of the city that at once elude the forces of discipline and create those clandestine sites where nonhegemonic social practices—including homosexuality—come into being and eventually succeed in occupying social space. In fact, venturing out into this nightworld to meet up with his artist friends provides Alex the perfect subterfuge with which to disguise his "blue thoughts" (105) as he cruises the "narrow blue" (104) of the city's streets after hours in search of, as he tells himself, artistic inspiration. [63] Once again, "art" provides the excuse for and avenue to the as yet unnamed. And if art provides the excuse, then Harlem provides the site. For Alex's night-long wanderings finally hit pay dirt when he happens upon living "poetry" at four o'clock in the morning, in the "perfect" form of a man whom he meets and poetically renames Beauty (105).

The initial meeting of the two men as they walk the streets of New York by night forms a crucial turning point, both in Alex's emerging acknowledgment of his homosexual desires and in the narrative's disclosure of his hitherto ambiguous sexuality. Because, however, he is unable consciously to admit the goal toward which his steps are leading him until he has irrevocably crossed its threshold, the scene unfolds with a minimum of talk, leaving the reader merely to intuit that the men are cruising each other. In place of words, Alex responds first to the musical echo of Beauty's footsteps behind him, which he instinctively knows are a man's, then as their steps fall into the same rhythm, he begins to wish this stranger "would speak . . . but strangers don't speak at four o'clock in the morning . . . at least if they did he couldn't imagine what would be said" (105). The "at least" clause is telling; it implies that men who *do* speak at this hour say the unimaginable, that is, make explicit their illicit desires. In contrast, Alex's ability to avoid words is what enables him to follow the drift of erotic attraction and attain the union for which he subconsciously yearns; to name his desire would break the spell by forcing him to acknowledge a homosexual act for what it is, as well as subject it to the disciplinary forces that ban it from legitimated social space. Nonetheless, the only words exchanged between the men are a classic of gay cruising in their very innocuousness: Beauty asks Alex for a match, by the glow of which light Alex is overcome by the beauty of this stranger's face; in response to a smile from Beauty, Alex's heart "sing[s]" and the two continue to walk "in silence," their union anticipated by "the castanets of their heels clicking r[h]ythmically." This dance of desire reaches a climax when they reach Alex's room, "[undress] by the blue dawn," and proceed—with "no need for words" but with an extended ellipsis to signify more than the usual hiatus between thoughts—to make love.

Even as this encounter propels Alex across the liminal threshold separating hetero from homo, he simultaneously transgresses another culturally constituted binary in entering this relationship, for the two men form an interracial couple.[64] In turn, this sexual identification across racial categories leads to another cross-identification, one that is the narrative's most heavily guarded secret. For if Alex has a skeleton in the closet with the power to shock, it is not his unadmitted love of men (which all the clues have led us to suspect) but rather the presence of an actual girlfriend (which nothing in Alex's consciousness has led us to infer). Structurally, this disclosure reverses the usual trajectory of gay coming-out stories, where a hetero relationship often *precedes* and serves as a feint for the more controversial homosexual love story that follows. In Nugent's strategic reversal, however, the opposite proves true: just when we think we have reached the "gay" climax of the narrative—Alex's sexual initiation—the plot opens onto the more ambiguous and indeed queerer terrain of bisexuality that dominates the rest of the story.

It is fascinating that the reader only arrives at the knowledge of Alex's bisexuality through his mental struggle to articulate the depth of his attraction to Beauty. Echoing the term he has previously used to evoke his own sense of otherness, he thinks, "[This feeling] was *different*" (105; emphasis added), adding that he has not felt this way about anyone else except— and here the narrative revelation appears—Melva: "But then he was in love with Melva . . . and that explained that" (106). The circularity of the latter phrase, however, explains little except that Alex cannot voice romantic love for Beauty until he has first named his socially legitimized love for Melva. In typically male homosocial fashion, the intrusion of Melva's presence into his consciousness becomes the mediating agency that allows him to articulate his feelings for Beauty and thus transgress the mental division he has previously constructed between sex (which men can do without words) and love (espousals of which belong to the province of heterosexual romance): "They [Melva and Beauty] were both so perfect . . . such compl[e]ments . . . yes he would like Beauty to know Melva *because he loved them both . . .* there . . . he had thought it . . . *actually dared to think it . . .* but Beauty must never know . . ." (106; emphasis added).

This tortured desire to think, to give voice to the implications of "love" between men, coupled with Alex's need to reconcile his love of Beauty with his "equal" love of Melva, finds expression in the two-tiered dream sequence that follows as Alex drifts to sleep with Beauty at his side. In the first segment Alex is on his hands and knees in a field of black poppies and red calla lilies searching for a mysteriously lost object, when he happens upon the legs, then the thighs, buttocks, torso, of a standing nude man: *fort/da* indeed. This turns out to be Beauty, who says, "I'll wait," which causes Alex to grow confused. In the second segment, he continues his search, this time happening upon the legs, hips, waist, breasts, of a nude woman, Melva, who also says, "I'll wait"—but in this instance, Alex's confusion is followed by an action: "and [he] kissed her" (106). This single phrase, the only difference between the two segments, reveals the one taboo that Alex has not yet been able to transgress in his new relationship with Beauty. It is no coincidence then that upon awakening, Alex immediately looks at Beauty's lips and quotes lines from Wilde's *Salome* to himself in order to express his hitherto repressed desire to kiss Beauty: *the dreaming unconscious has forced its wish onto the plane of reality.* Ironically, though, Alex is not ready to act on his wish, and in this variant on the Sleeping Beauty motif, Alex pretends to be asleep as Beauty now awakens and proceeds, in an extended lyrical passage, to awaken Alex with the kiss that Alex has desired to give. When, a few nights later they both kiss with their eyes open, neither pretending to be asleep, an ultimate barrier to self-realization has been crossed.

Given the libidinal intensity with which these scenes are imbued, one might well deduce that this story is, after all, a fable of gay self-discovery, and that Alex's proclamations of equal love for Melva are simply a psychological feint allowing him to pursue his "true" desire for Beauty. Certainly the homoerotic aspects of the plot carry the greatest libidinal charge. But to dismiss Melva as an example of the expendability of women within the homosocial paradigm ignores her continuing presence and importance in Alex's psyche as well as the unpredictable fluidity of desire that Nugent is attempting to represent. For the rest of the story charts the oscillation in Alex's consciousness as he attempts to come to terms not only with his love for Beauty, but also with the fact that he loves two people—who happen to be a man and a woman—at the same time. For example, in a scene at a local church where Langston's spiritual, "Fire!"[65] is being performed, Alex is inundated by thoughts of both Melva ("and he had kissed her") and Beauty ("[his] lips had pressed hard"; [108]); on another evening Alex takes Beauty to Forno's, in a kind of public coming-out, when Melva enters the restaurant and meets Beauty; the story ends with a scene at Coney

Island, to which Alex has taken Melva, where his emotions wildly vacillate from the euphoria of Melva's kissing him ("and the sea sang for them") to depression at Beauty's absence ("the sea *dinned*"). Leaving Melva at her door and walking home to Beauty, Alex's thoughts alternate repeatedly between the names of his two lovers ("Beauty . . . Melva . . . Beauty . . . Melva"), building to the climactic epiphany that begins the last paragraph, "one *can* love two at the same time" (Nugent's emphasis). Thoughts of Melva's farewell kiss and then of Beauty's beauty follow, each memory ending with the declarative refrain "one *can*," both of which are then followed by the expanded phrase that forms the final line of the story, "one *can* love" (109–10). This ending note, I think, is deliberately ambiguous (in place of the typical "finis" to signal the story's end, Nugent inserts the phrase "to be continued"), keeping open the question of whether one can successfully love two at once, as well as whether (since his final thoughts fix upon his desire for Beauty) Alex is being totally honest with himself in maintaining that he loves both equally. Or, to put it differently, one might say that Nugent's intent is to represent a "portrait of the artist as a young man" who is still in the process of discovering himself, and as such his bisexuality remains an open-ended possibility as well as a question that cannot (and should not) be glibly answered.

To the extent, then, that this story is an exploration of consciousness that traces in modernist form the process whereby Alex comes out to himself, admitting his love for another man, it also becomes, importantly, the story of homosexual realization that cannot exist outside a complex network of cross-identifications—identifications across sex, race, gender, and status to which the newly formed metropolitan space and identity of Harlem were uniquely conducive in the early twentieth century. Tracing his steps across the face of the city, Alex creates an intricate network of intersecting, overlapping possibilities, a pedestrian rhetoric that not only comes to define his subjectivity but becomes a blueprint for the representation of the mobile workings of his consciousness, through whose textual mappings the reader-as-pedestrian moves as well. Disclosing a continual slippage between categories of difference—artistic decadence/sexual decadence, homo/bi/heterosexuality, black/brown/white, male/female—that cannot be stabilized, Nugent appropriates modernist technique for something that might well be called queer ends, creating the fiction of a textual and social space where queer desires may take root and begin, like Alex, to flourish.

DJUNA BARNES, *NIGHTWOOD*
WORLDS OF NIGHT IN THE CITY OF LIGHT

In fact my great virtue is that I never use the derogatory in the usual sense.
—Doctor Matthew O'Connor, in Djuna Barnes, *Nightwood*[66]

For many black artists the dazzle of Harlem's cultural burgeoning was not enough to overcome its circumscription within racist America, and, for longer and shorter periods of time, a number of talented African-Americans sought relief from racial typecasting across the Atlantic, in the more enlightened cultural milieu of Paris. David Levering Lewis has commented how in a parallel movement a number of white artists and writers were "drawn to Harlem on the way to Paris."[67] That many of these expatriates were also homosexual or bisexual is a well-known fact, for the relative freedom from discrimination that many African-Americans experienced in Paris extended to other oppressed groups, including gay men and lesbians. By 1900, as Sheri Benstock writes in *Women of the Left Bank,* Paris had already established "an international reputation as the capital of same sex love among women and was designated 'Paris-Lesbos.'" Hence the emphatic declaration of one of the city's most famously open lesbian expatriates, Natalie Barney, whose Left Bank salon formed the center of the city's lesbian demimonde: "Paris has always seemed to me the only city in which one can live and express oneself as one pleases."[68]

These freedoms of expression, encompassing both the personal and the artistic, played a significant role in the experience of another American woman and writer, Djuna Barnes, whose participation in "Paris-Lesbos" is wittily immortalized in her *Ladies Almanack,* a fictional parody of Barney's coterie. Leaving Greenwich Village, where she had begun her writing career as a journalist, Barnes joined the wave of expatriates who flooded Paris in the interwar years to participate in the artistic and literary movement that was making an international name for itself on the Left Bank. Remaining in Paris until 1931, Barnes became a well-known if enigmatic fixture in the city's often overlapping literary and lesbian cultures: emerging, for example, as the one woman writer whom male arbiters of modernism such as Eliot and Joyce treated as a peer; involving herself in a devastatingly unhappy love affair with the American sculptor Thelma Wood; and writing the book that would guarantee her lasting reputation as, in her own words, "the most famous unknown of the century."[69] So too has that work, *Nightwood* (1936), remained one of the "most famous unknown[s]" of this century, despite the increasing critical attention it has garnered as a modernist classic.

Attempting to categorize *Nightwood* as either "classic" or "modernist," however, is a tricky affair. Even though the novel's first American edition carried the imprimatur of Eliot's preface, it is a text that resists categorizations of all sorts, "slapp[ing] down," as Marilyn Reizbaum aptly puts it, the reader's attempts to naturalize or "know" it.[70] Moreover, despite its modernist affinities—which include its experimental narrative style, intricacy of literary allusion, thematics of alienation, and representation of the power of unconscious desire—the novel can only with the greatest difficulty be assimilated into the canon of high modernist practice. Indeed, if

Nightwood maintains a relationship to mainstream modernist literary efforts, it only does so by making, in Jane Marcus's memorable and often-quoted phrase, "a modernism of marginality."[71] The same difficulty of classification inheres in numerous attempts, however well intended, to interpret the novel as the expression of a single social or sexual agenda—for instance, to categorize it as a "woman's text," a "feminist fiction," or a "lesbian narrative."[72] Unlike the former two positions, which are relatively recent, the mythic claim that *Nightwood* is a lesbian novel has been in circulation since its first reviewers zeroed in on its "homosexual" elements. From Philip Rahv's jibe that Barnes has "exploited" the theme of sexual "perversion" in order to dramatize "psychic disorder" and thereby display "a certain modernist attitude," to the opinion of the anonymous reviewer (possibly Rebecca West) in the *Newstatesman and Nation* that Barnes's account of modern-day "Lesbos" is not only welcome but long overdue, the consensus seems to have been that a novel in which "the central character is a homosexual, and the three chief characters are dominantly sapphic," is by definition a gay text.[73]

This is not to imply that the world of expatriate lesbianism is incidental to the novel—far from it, as we shall see—but to suggest that reifying same-sex love as *the* lens through which to read its narrative proves an oddly unsatisfying enterprise. On one level such an effort is problematic simply because it is difficult to apply an identity politics (particularly one that primarily understands "character" in a mimetic relation to plot) to a text that is often resolutely antimimetic and whose characters, such as they are, more often than not serve as symbols of the unconscious or as psychodramatic projections of states of desire. On a related level, it makes sense that a text that refuses literary labels (such as "high modernism") would also avoid identity labels of all sorts.[74] In light of this resistance to categorization, I suggest that the term *queer* in its current usage comes closer to providing an appropriate theoretical medium for making sense of the realm of polymorphous desire that circulates among *Nightwood*'s wandering community of outsiders, outcasts, and orphans.[75]

Articulations of queer theory shed light on at least three aspects of the ranks of the disenfranchised that make up the "nightworld" of this "nightwood." First, in choosing to represent "the mad strip of the inappropriate that runs through creation" (105), Barnes creates a universe that transcends the limits of the hetero/homo divide in order to include a dizzying cross-section of the sexually and socially dispossessed: circus performers and trapeze artists, transvestites, mock aristocrats, bohemian artists, a quack doctor, racial others and wandering jews, and alcoholics join ranks with "my Sodomites" (93) to form Barnes's demimonde of the "inappropriate." These outcasts revel in their outlaw and pariah status, embracing their supposed "damnation" and parading their abjection as a sign of divine election. Even those who hopelessly yearn to be counted among the dominant culture's "insiders" nonetheless find themselves irresistibly drawn to its fringes, surreptitiously "com[ing]," as does Felix Volkbein, "upon the odd" in order to "dazzle [their] own estrangement" (10–11).[76]

By thus privileging "the people of the underworld" (31) who make up the entire universe of the novel, Barnes transposes those who generally exist on the margins (of society, of texts) to center stage. As in contemporary queer theory, this tactic undoes the imprisoning cultural binaries of inside/outside, dominant/marginal, upon which the hetero/homo divide depends. For in imagining a world of otherness that is both all-encompassing and central, Barnes creates a *conceptual space* in which the normative becomes, for once in history, the excluded, the taboo, and the unmentionable. As Reizbaum has pointed out, the effect is as if the nightworld that Joyce creates in "Circe" has overrun and become the entire text of this "nightwood."[77] There is no "mainstream" in this novel—or, rather, its social misfits and undesirables have *become* the mainstream. This inversion of the social order is carried out on any number of textual and thematic levels: the world of day has become the realm of night (which, as in Nugent's story, is ubiquitous); the litanic repetition of words such as "derangement," "depravity," and "damnation" become indices of an inversed morality that displaces the regulatory Enlightenment concepts of "order," "sanity," and "salvation." The result is a world of carnival and circus in which the deliberate suspension of the rules of social order and class becomes a cause for celebration and revelry, as well as for anarchy and estrangement.[78]

These inversions point toward a third affinity between the universe Barnes creates and contemporary idioms of queer world-making. For while I have suggested that reading *Nightwood* primarily through a lesbian lens fails to capture the range of queerness that the text embraces, nonetheless I would simultaneously argue that the novel's representation of its underworld of aliens and outcasts organizes itself under the sign of same-sex love. "What is this love we have for the invert, boy or girl?" (136), O'Connor asks in one of his monologues, taking the ubiquity of such love as a given.[79] And in a world of deliberately "inverted" values and terms, the Sexual Invert—as homosexuals, following Havelock Ellis, often called themselves in this time period—becomes an especially evocative figure for the despised and rejected of society. As we have seen, Sedgwick warns in *Tendencies* that any politically viable use of the term *queer* today must begin by acknowledging the centrality of homosexuality to its definition, especially given the viciousness with which homosexuality has been demonized as the ultimate "perversion" of natural order throughout history. *Nightwood*'s deliberately perverse depiction of an entire universe of outcasts banded in solidarity under the sign of inversion, I suggest, exists as an early formulation of the same principle.

Parisian (In)Versions

In the urban settings that form the primary backdrop of this novel, this queer contingent enjoys a heightened relationship to city space, particularly as experienced under the cover of night. "Was it at night that Sodom became Gomorrah?" Matthew asks Nora in one of his telling conversational detours. "It was at night, I swear. A city given over to the shades, and that's why it has never been countenanced or understood to this day" (86). In this formulation, the concept "city" has become a metonym for the inverted population that haunts it by night, a population whose desires have "never been countenanced or understood to this day." "Those who love a city," so the third-person narrator begins the narrative of Nora and Robin's lesbian affair, "become the shame of that city, the *détraqués*, the paupers" (52). This relation between the city and its queer fringe also dictates the simile that Nora uses to explain to Matthew her suffering when Robin leaves her for another woman. In this passage the city's abjects and outcasts become a symbol of the repressed element that the city proper—like the psyche of the dominant culture—needs to expel: "All that we have loved becomes the 'forbidden' when we have not understood it all," Nora says, "as the pauper is the rudiment of a city, knowing something of the city, which the city, for its own destiny, wants to forget" (156). This forgotten city, of course, is the city that exists by night, the city of disconsolate lovers, the city recreated every evening by the wandering steps of its insomniacs: all that the nightworld of Paris's Left Bank comes to signify in *Nightwood*.

The queer subjects of Paris inhabit a space well suited to their formation and promulgation. Following the political and technological revolutions of the eighteenth and nineteenth centuries, Paris had emerged in the international popular imagination as *the* symbol of metropolitan modernity: the city of new boulevards, the metro, and electric illumination; home of the cultural and intellectual avant-garde; capitol of fashion; vendor of outrageous pleasure and vice. "Paris was where the twentieth century was," Gertrude Stein categorically asserts in *Paris France* (1940).[80] But like Stein's residence on rue de Fleuris, just off the Luxembourg Gardens, the Paris of the twentieth century for most avant-garde artists and thinkers was more specifically located on the Seine's Left Bank, where bohemian, expatriate, homosexual, and politically radical subcultures had long been at home. The Left Bank's Latin quarter in particular held a special appeal to the various fringe elements of society drawn to its antique charm, crumbling buildings, and medieval tangle of streets and alleys; indeed, the philosophy espoused by the novel's resident philosopher, Matthew O'Connor (himself a habitue of Place St. Sulpice, a hub in the midst of the quarter), might well be taken as a description not only of Barnes's labyrinthine style but of the Latin quarter itself: "There is no direct way. The feotus of symmetry nourishes itself on cross-purposes" (97). The cramped physical spaces and circuitous pedestrian byways of the sector, which had long been associated in the popular imagination with moral degeneration and political radical-ism (the Communards made especially effective use of its narrow streets to erect barricades and halt the government troops during the 1871 uprising), represented to progressive city planners the nightmarish inverse of the sym-metries that Haussmann's scheme of boulevards imposed on the Right Bank. "It is impossible to traverse the narrow streets which go from the Quai de Conti to the old abbey of Saint Germain des Pres," a contributor to the journal *Urbanisme* complained,

> without seeing again the horrible days of the revolution of which they were the theatre, where the walls themselves have retained the cries of the victims of September. . . . Where the disorders were [once] unchained, prostitution and disease has [now] erected its domicile. History and a concern for human dignity . . . order us, imperiously, to abolish, together with this past, the present-day misery.[81]

In Barnes's transformation of this "theatre" of social "disorder" into the textual site of literary experimentation, the Left Bank's nightworld also comes to represent a universal condition. As O'Connor warns Nora Flood when she seeks him out in the middle of the night to explain its mysteries, "neither are the nights of one city the nights of another. Let us take Paris for instance. . . . French nights are those which all nations seek the world over" (82). That is, the desires of the body associated with "French nights"—and embodied in the nightlife of Paris, with its sidewalk cafés, pedestrian flow, and sexual electricity—provide a more easily traveled "roadway" (84) into the psychosexual reaches of the "night" of the human condition. Simultaneously, "Left Bank" comes to designate more than a geographical space: it is a state of mind, one that exists the world over in the anonymous corners of every twentieth-century metropolis where queer cultures gather. "Every city has its left bank," notes Ford Madox Ford, "I should like to call attention to . . . the many Left Banks of the world. For something mournful—and certainly hard up!—attaches to almost all uses of the word *left*." Ford then moves from the metaphysical to the geographi-cally specific, as he continues, "every great city has its left bank. London has, round Bloomsbury, New York has, round Greenwich Village, so has Vienna."[82] Likewise, representatives of *Nightwood*'s Left Bank world turn up in Berlin, Vienna, and America. But even as the queer significations that attach to this specific urban conceit prove mobile and shifting, the Left Bank of Paris remains Barnes's *primary* site for such significations, just as homosexuality remains the privileged "perversion" representing the queerness of the quarter at large. Ned Rorem, the gay composer, has poi-gnantly written of the square where Barnes locates Matthew's favorite bar and the hotel where Nora and Robin make their first home, "I can never stroll through the Place Saint Sulpice . . . without being invaded by a sense of the past so intense that the *quartier* seems to have been invented by Djuna rather than the reverse."[83] The city that has inspired and indeed promulgated queer desires and subjects has become, in Rorem's imagining, the space of queer invention itself.

Estranging and Orphaned Words

It is the representation of the marginal, the queer, and the "inappropriate," moreover, that gives rise to Barnes's distinctive brand of literary experimentation, resulting in a text that is at once modernist, avant-garde, surreal, and expressionist. As a springboard to my discussion of *Nightwood*'s form, I would like to turn to a cluster of metaphors—birth, the infant, the child, the orphan—running throughout the text whose thematics provide a corollary of its formal effects. The state of estrangement and permanent wandering, of ostracism and dispossession, that envelops the narrative's all-inclusive society of outsiders is a condition that begins with birth: entering the world is figured as a *thrusting away*, a violent act of orphaning, that is simultaneously a *descent into* human consciousness and decay. This process is epitomized in the account of Felix's birth, with which the novel begins, as his mother, Hedvig, "named him Felix, thrust him from her, and died" (1). The idea of birth as an estrangement and a descent is echoed by Doctor O'Connor, who claims to be the gynecologist who has "delivered" Nora Flood: "I . . . wail for all the little beasts in their mothers, who . . . have to step down" (105). This radical estrangement (the condition of becoming human as opposed to remaining "beast") is exacerbated by the alienation pervading modernity in particular: "The modern child has nothing left to hold to . . . —we go up—but we come down" (40). Hence the abandonment experienced by every citizen of *Nightwood*'s inverted universe comes to define the entire human condition, which is to say that the novel transforms queerness into a universal principle. In Barnes's heretical metaphysics, we are *all* queers, orphans wandering in search of a never-to-be-attained home or resting place.[84]

So too with Barnes's formal aesthetics, for her use of estranging language redoubles this condition of radical dispossession by holding the reader at a calculated distance from the text. Just as the narrative's queer subjects exist in states of permanent alienation, their outcast state is mirrored in the tendency of signifiers in the novel to divorce themselves from their signifieds and become "linguistic orphans" thrust out into a sea of uncertainty where other equally homeless, "lost" words drift in search of an anchoring meaning. This dissociation of words from meaning gives rise to the frequent sensation, in reading *Nightwood*, that one sign refers to another in an endless chain without, in the words of Jacques Maritain, "the intermediary of any concept. . . . Two things are not compared, but rather one thing is made known through the image of another." The disorienting effect of this strategy is most palpable in what Jane Marcus calls the "oxymoronic frenzy" of *Nightwood*'s overwrought, bizarre, and labyrinthine imagery. Noting that the novel at once works by means of its heavily imagistic language and baffles its readers on the same account, Kannenstine draws on Felix's insight that an image is nothing more than "the stop the mind makes between uncertainties" (111) to argue that Barnes's images function as momentary suspensions—"essentially a verbal equivalent of the photographic image"—in an ongoing flux. Operating on the sheerly textual plane, on the level of surface, sound, and combination with other word-images, rather than serving as an index of rational meaning, Barnes's imagistic prose, Kannenstine perceptively notes, "snatch[es] the *sensation* of a thought out of the conscious thought process that would normally erase it," thus capturing a dimension of reality that reaches beyond language and outlasts—as nonverbal aftereffect—"the commonplace temporal."[85]

Such imagistic dissociation resembles the surrealists' juxtaposition of dissimilar elements in order to stimulate the unconscious into creative activity. Barnes, too, employs the surrealist technique of wrenching objects from their familiar contexts, but unlike the surrealists (whose antipathy to homosexuality was notably more pronounced than in other avant-garde artistic movements of the period[86]), she does so not only to overturn ordinary perceptions of normal reality but also to chip away at sexual categories of the norm(al) that militate against recognition of the "mad strip of the inappropriate that runs throughout creation." Related to this imagistic rebellion against the norm is Barnes's cultivated inorganicity of style, which in its baroque play of surfaces privileges the artificial, the ornamental. Erin Carlston convincingly demonstrates that this denial of an inherently organic function to language is indebted to the decadent aesthetic that privileges artifice over nature. In support of her argument, Carlston cites Arthur Symons's definition of decadence as "that learned corruption of language by which style ceases to be organic and becomes . . . deliberately abnormal." To the degree that Barnes's valorization of stylistic artifice echoes this decadent precept, however, this "learned" *linguistic* "corruption" certainly also suggests another, more *bodily* "corruption"—since homosexuality, according to early-twentieth-century popular sexual discourse, was also assumed to be "learned," nonorganic, abnormal, and characterized by excessive artifice.[87]

The fascination with text-as-surface that results from the coupling of aestheticizing impulse and representations of the homosexual outcast has several implications for Barnes's narrative: first, these verbal surfaces act as screens upon which, as in Joyce's "Circe," repressed desires can project themselves; second, this surface play means that the "action" of the narrative comes to exist primarily in the movement of the words and images themselves; third, the fixation on the "baroque intricacies" of the surface becomes, as Joan Retallack argues, a way of avoiding the linearity and futurity associated with mimetic narrative and hence the inevitable decay and death that such realism (as well as marriage, when viewed as a way of perpetuating a lineage that outlasts the self) implies.[88] Deliberately frustrating, artificial, ornamental, inorganic as opposed to natural, hybrid, and impure in its eclectic mix of discourses and genres, Barnes's prose style is "queer" in multiple senses but particularly in its refusal of any easy coupling of the label and the labeled, dominant culture's most effective tool for categorizing and quarantining its misfits and thereby eliminating difference.

This strategic queering of words, imagery, and style occurs in tandem with Barnes's deliberate perversion of narrative temporality through various experimental techniques: dilating or disrupting linear sequence, creating verbal equivalents of suspended motion, and, most significantly, foregrounding the spatial dimensions of the text itself. "In time everything is possible, and in space everything forgivable" (126–27), Matthew O'Connor says, and the emphasis on the spatial over the temporal in *Nightwood* tends to open up pockets within the text where its outcast subjects may flourish in full "forgiveness" for their non-normative behaviors. In addition, the opening up of such textual spaces makes room for the representation of the atemporal, nonchronological forces shaping the inner lives of these protagonists. Thus Sharon Spencer comments on the way in which the "narrative time" of the fourth section or chapter begins "to slow down and to stand still," until "waking time" ceases altogether as the narrative descends into the timeless "nightwood" of subconscious and preconscious motivation in the next section. From this point onward, Nora and Matthew, then Felix and Matthew, then Nora and Matthew again, engage in static monologues where the movement of their words ultimately becomes the *only* significant action in the narrative. "Plot" has been brought to a virtual standstill.[89]

This breakdown of narrative temporality and breaking open of narrative space is facilitated by the structural use of repetition. In Barnes's case, this involves the refraction of the same event (Robin's betrayal of Nora) through various narrative perspectives, so that the climaxes of the third, fourth, and fifth sections keep returning to the same moment, as if all time for Nora has stopped at this one cataclysmic instant. Occupying the still heart at the very center of the novel's polycentric form, this replaying of the catastrophic severance of Nora and Robin from differing points of view creates a sense of spatial simultaneity *across* rather than progression *through* time. Such temporal retardation or blockage also occurs on the microlevel of the narrative, in surreal images that effect a suspension of forward motion: note, for instance, Hedvig "moving toward [Guido] in recoil" (3), or Nora's "body eternally moving downward but in one place" (51), or the analogy likening Robin to a ship's figurehead in a museum, which "though . . . static" seemed "yet to be going against the wind," turning its face "toward itself in time, as an image and its reflection in a lake seem parted only by the hesitation in the hour" (38). Such spatial/temporal displacements also characterize more extended descriptive moments in which the repetition of phrases and words transforms key events into verbal equivalents of Cubist painting, as time itself seems to fracture into many pieces. Some of these instances are among the novel's most famous passages, such as the moment at the end of the "Night Watch" chapter when Nora slowly drops to her knees as she looks out her window and in horror sees the statue in the garden below her window dissolving into the image of Robin embracing Jenny (64), and Matthew's description to Nora of the fatal carriage ride to the Bois, during which Jenny viciously strikes Robin, who repeatedly "goes forward" and "sinks down," like "something seen in retarded action," for an entire page (76).

The overall shape of *Nightwood* participates in this spatialization of narrative, forming a trajectory that—disavowing the dynamics of narrative succession—is radically nongenerative and, by implication, productively queer. On both thematic and formal levels, Barnes's narrative frustrates the generative and generational premises governing oedipal understandings of traditional fictional plot. According to Peter Brooks, the Freudian masterplot is driven by the desire for an ending that returns us to and explains our origins, thereby repeating the agonized oedipal relation of child to parent; in contrast, as Donna Gerstenberger has noted, *Nightwood* emphatically frustrates the reader's desire for a narrative progression that leads to a "serviceable end."[90] The same point holds true for the novel's beginning, an "origin myth" that is in fact a story of failed and fraudulent origins (turning on the instant rejection of Felix at birth, as Hedvig thrusts him from her, and the counterfeit ancestral portraits that are Felix's paternal legacy). It also holds true for the failed dream of dynastic succession that governs Felix's obsessive pursuit of ancestral origins and miscalculated marriage to Robin Vote so that "she might bear him sons who would recognize and honor the past" (45). This desperate genealogical ambition is wrecked by the fact that the only son Robin bears Felix is a weakling imbecile who will not live to inherit his patrimony (and who, like Felix before him, is violently rejected by his mother).[91]

Complementing this wholesale repudiation of children are all the nonreproductive adults who populate the text, underlining Barnes's rejection of the dynastic plot of succession as an underlying structure for the novel. Likewise, the absolute devaluation of the monogamous (and heterosexual) couple as the desired "end" of love (or, for that matter, the ending of a novel), which is most forcefully thematized in Robin's random promiscuity, contributes to the novel's deviating and deviant movements; the way in which Robin is "moved out of death's way by the successive arms of women" (64) becomes a model for the queer circulations of narrative desire that constitute the novel's trajectory—a trajectory that, working in concert with Barnes's experimentations in estranging language, surreal imagery, and nonorganic style, thwarts any "sense of an ending" that would impose final meaning on the queer desires of the sexually disenfranchised that this text so defiantly champions.[92]

Descent into Night

If Barnes's modernist practices, as I have been arguing, buttress her representation of the marginal or queer, her experiments in technique also support her vision of the underside of consciousness, of the psychosexual and libidinal currents that traverse the thin wall separating dreaming and waking states of being. Kannenstine has observed that in this novel "the concrete Paris of the twenties fades into an interior landscape and becomes part of an anatomy of night." In turn, the narrative's "preoccupation with the nocturnal, with sleep and dreaming," points the way to the psychic regions signified by such key metaphors as the "night" (the subject of Matthew's monologues), the "nightwood" of the title (an oblique reference to the "dark wood" that inaugurates Dante's *Inferno*), and "the underworld" (that, in Barnes's inversion of dominant and marginal, has become this novel's entire world).[93]

While her interest in exploring the darker reaches of the psyche aligns Barnes's modernist practice with that of the other writers in this book, finding a way of representing these interior forces proves a very different matter for Barnes than for writers who attempt to capture the immediacy and activity of the "inner" life by simulating the associative flow of thought. Alfred Kazin pinpoints this difference in a 1937 review of *Nightwood*. Citing the passage from "Modern Fiction" in which Woolf enjoins novelists to record the rain of atoms upon consciousness, he notes that "Miss Barnes has gone beyond Mrs. Woolf's practice of her own theory. For Miss Barnes is not . . . concerned with the immediate in time that fascinated the stream-of-conscious novelists . . . [but with] the blood stream of the universal organism." Kannenstine glosses this difference, too, when he notes that Barnes's exploration of the psyche does not aim to provide an "index of thought"—that is, to get inside a character's mind to relay what that character is thinking or feeling—but hinges on "a pattern of cross-reference of image and symbol" that leads to the "gradual breakdown of rational and sequential perception," at which point "the daylight narrative is effectively submerged and an interior reality rises to the surface of the work." What Kannenstine's wording implies is that Barnes's technique for representing this "interior reality" is an *expressionistic* one that depends on psychodramatic exteriorization. As in "Circe," the psychological is projected onto the work's surface, charging words, images, and tableaux with the fleeting sensation, rather than articulation, of thought or desire. Without directly indexing psychic interiority, the novel remains profoundly invested in the "psychological," as might be expected of a text that opens in Freud's Vienna of 1880, parodies the psychoanalytic encounter in Nora's visits to "Doctor" O'Connor, and prominently features dream material.[94]

Rather than conveying a character's *conscious* thoughts, then, the representational goal of Barnes's technique is to explore the *unconscious* and, beyond it, the *preconscious* that lies outside history, in the primitive "night" of the mind before we become "human." This is the state to which "the universal organism" (in Kazin's phrase) is always returning—whether in sleep, in waking dreams, or in the throes of irrational desire. In Matthew's monologues, the omnipresent night—the obverse of the rationality of daylight—becomes the emblem for this vast, archetypal universe inhabited by sleepers, lovers, the possessed and the dispossessed. Variously referred to as the "secret land" (7), the "lost land" (45), the "foreign land" (57), and the "unknown land" (87), the night of unconscious desire is the world to which all Barnes's wandering, lost orphans gravitate. In the Gospel according to Matthew, there is only one path into the night, and that is utter submission—hence the litanic expressions of "going down," "going back," "coming down," "stepping down," and, most important, "bowing down" (Barnes's original title). Similarly, the text's frequent references to animals and beasts, as well as to "blood" and "racial memory," become indices of the primitive or vestigial origins of being, the collective unconscious of the human race, that exist within each individual and that silently shape conscious life.[95]

Of all the sleepwalkers in *Nightwood*, Robin Vote is its purest emblem of those aspects of the unconscious that human subjects paradoxically attempt both to repress and recapture. "Utterly unknown" even to herself, thinking "unpeopled thoughts," turning a "timeless" gaze onto the waking world, Robin becomes a source of attraction to others because her presence stirs in their memories and longings the "image of a forgotten experience" (138, 46, 37). "She carried the quality of the 'way back,' as animals do" (40), the narrator reports, to "some place that we have forgotten and would give our life to recall" (118). Robin thus figures both the "way back" (that is, the avenue of escape from history and time) and the wishful goal of that escape: the bliss of nonbeing experienced only in earliest infancy and in the womb, the "home" that everyone has lost in becoming human. The text's initial presentation of Robin brilliantly condenses many of these associations, and the effect renders her less a "realistic" character than a densely charged archetype of unconscious desire. In this scene, reported in the chapter titled "La Somnambule," Robin has fallen in a deep faint from which she cannot be awakened. When Doctor O'Connor (with Felix in tow) appears on the scene to attend to her, she is lying sprawled on a bed surrounded by a riot of "potted plants, exotic palms, and cut flowers, faintly over-sung by the notes of unseen birds," that makes the room appear "a jungle trapped in a drawing room," as in a painting by Rousseau (34–35). Robin's deep sleep is thus associated with the primeval, and her struggle to awaken becomes an emblem of "a woman who is beast turning human" (37). In marked contrast to the downward movement (unearthing the hidden libido) traced by the awakening plots of chapter 2, awakening here forcibly drags Robin "upward" into "threatened consciousness" (34). Later in the novel, Nora likewise comes to realize that the greatest sin she has committed against Robin has been to "str[ike] her awake" when "she was asleep," waking her to human corruption and a fall from the mythic plenitude of being that Robin "ha[s] managed in that sleep to keep whole" (145).

If sleep symbolizes Robin's intimate connection to the nightworld of the unconscious, then sleepwalking becomes an emblem of the barely human condition in which Robin negotiates waking reality. Characterized as a "born somnambule, who lives in two worlds—meet of child and desperado" (35), Robin moves through the demimonde of the Left Bank in a dreamlike haze reminiscent of the drifting movements of Lawrence's and Chopin's protagonists as they give themselves over to the inner rhythms of libidinal desire. Sleepwalking between "two worlds"—day and night, consciousness and unconsciousness, human and animal—Robin inhabits a psychic borderland reminiscent of the liminal urban sites occupied by the queer outcast, its marginal space simultaneously home to the outlaw (the "desperado") and the orphan (the "child"). Even in her incarnation as an adult woman, Robin straddles two worlds on multiple levels—as a bisexual whose erotic practices admit both men and women, as a gender outlaw who dresses in the men's clothes, as an American living in Paris.

This liminality helps explain Robin's physical movements as she takes to the streets of Paris with "the ample gait of the night-watch" (41), moving "from table to table, drink to drink, person to person" in a "slowly increasing rhythm," all the while "directing her steps toward that night life" that acts as a dividing line between those who wish to claim her and the world of anonymity in which she can, literally, lose herself by shedding the vestiges of knowable identity in stages of stupor and collapse (59). Barnes's evocation of Robin's forays into the "turbulent night" (59) underlines the thematic importance of the urban topography that gives her solitary wanderings a specific context. Indeed, one might push this observation further and argue that the aspects of Robin's characterization that make her so effective a symbol of the unconscious can be directly linked both to Simmel's analysis of urban anonymity and autonomy, and to de Certeau's theory of the resisting rhetorics paced out by the city walker. Tellingly, Robin's wandering is triggered by the discovery that she is pregnant. This bodily transformation awakens Robin to a "lost land within herself" that is both the child she is carrying and the quiescence she has lost in becoming a thinking subject, and it precipitates her impossible quest to recapture this lost state through a descent, by way of the night, into the primordial realm of polymorphous desire. At this point the narrative becomes a kind of road map charting Robin's increasing movements across the face of the city: "She took to going out" (45); "she strayed into the *rue Picpus*" (46); "[she] took to wandering again" (48). As she maneuvers the streets of Paris (and eventually beyond) with the dazed semiconsciousness of a sleepwalker, her mobility—like that of Alex in "Smoke, Lilies, and Jade"—mirrors her mental activity. "Her thoughts were in themselves a form of locomotion," Barnes tells us as Robin strides the quarter in "a formless meditation" (59–60). And to the degree that her mobility is also a mode of cruising, it anticipates the lesbian destination to which this mental "locomotion" leads. For as Robin increasingly leaves Felix to "wander" in the streets, the narrative reports that her mind also "wander[s]"—"to thoughts of women that she had come to connect with women" (47). These thoughts become reality when, after a four-month absence, Robin returns to the quarter in the company of a female lover, Nora Flood. But, as Nora will also learn, no single person is capable of holding Robin in place, for the desires motivating Robin's straying movements are, in the most radical sense, promiscuous.

Both Robin's promiscuity and her love of women point to the deeper psychosexual currents at work in the novel's inverted nightworld of the unconscious. Underlying Robin's progression through a series of female lovers are two conflicting impulses intrinsic to individuation: the desire to be recognized by (and hence connected to) others, yet the desire to be a fully autonomous self (hence separate from others).[96] The novel identifies these "two spirits" at work in Robin as "love and anonymity. Yet they were so 'haunted' of each other that separation was impossible" (55). That is to say, Robin wants to be loved, to be claimed by others in order to avoid utter alienation and meaninglessness, while her promiscuous straying simultaneously enacts the existential desire not to belong, to achieve the freedom of complete separation, a desire that, if taken to its extreme, leads to the radical anonymity that obliterates the "self" altogether. This conflict between love and anonymity, between yearning and loss, thus explains Robin's "tragic longing to be kept, knowing herself astray" (58). Yet, as we have seen, this "wish for a home, as if she were afraid she would be lost again" (55), is counterbalanced by the opposing impulse to escape the very haven she craves in order to preserve her autonomy: hence her infidelities and broken relationships. O'Connor attempts to instruct Nora, who is devastated by Robin's desertion, that these leave-takings are thus less personal slights than the ritual enactment of an overpowering need to be reassured of her separateness and, ultimately, her anonymity: "Every bed she leaves, without caring, fills her heart with peace and happiness. She has made her 'escape' again" (146). In escaping into anonymity, Robin realizes a fantasy of nonpossession that, paradoxically, at once confirms her autonomy and annihilates this autonomous self by severing all the ties that would affirm its reality.

The compulsion to repeat that underlies this pattern of erotic bonding and disengagement leads one to suspect that Robin is replaying an original trauma of separation from which she is unable to free herself—or, perhaps, it might be more accurate to say, *the* original trauma of separation, specifically the loss of union with the mother. In turn, this originating libidinal scenario finds "adult" expression in the text's lesbian relationships, which provide the arena in which Robin plays out the most important of these escapes. On the one hand, in seeking out female lovers, Robin recaptures something of this lost unity (Nora quite explicitly plays the role of mother to Robin's child); on the other, in choosing "anonymity" over committed "love," Robin strives to achieve a state of undifferentiated being that approximates the condition of original symbiosis with the mother. In Barnes's psychodrama of the pain involved in becoming an individuated human subject, the universality of this desire to recapture the unmediated space of the womb is hauntingly summed up in O'Connor's howl of despair, "It's my mother without argument I want!" (149). Along these lines, Erin Carlston demonstrates how the text's manifold and otherwise ambiguous images of oral sadism and partial objects serve as expressions of the "primitive rage and desire provoked by [a] separation" from the idealized mother, a separation that Carlston suggests is "figured in and recuperated by lesbianism."[97]

This primitive rage, in turn, underlies and helps explain the psychic violence pervading the erotic bonds established in this nightworld. According to Jessica Benjamin, the failure to achieve successful differentiation lies at the origins of all relations of erotic domination; hence the sadism with which Robin enacts her repeated "escapes" from commitment is counterposed by the extreme abjectness of her equally strong desire to submit utterly to the domination of others. "There are some people," Felix says of Robin, "who must get permission to live" (117), precisely because, like the incompletely individuated Robin, they have never developed a sense of self or ego strong enough to confirm their being. As Benjamin puts it, they masochistically seek out domination by "an other who [alone] is powerful enough to bestow this recognition."[98] This slave mentality surfaces in Robin's "tragic longing to be kept," which leads her passively to yield to whomever most forcefully attempts to possess her. For instance, she considers that "she belong[s] to Nora" as long as Nora makes their relationship "permanent by her own strength" (55). But all that Jenny—a far inferior person—has to do to win Robin from Nora is to exercise, through psychic and physical violence, a greater degree of domination. Jenny's victory is cinched by the horrific scene during the evening carriage ride to the Bois where she repeatedly strikes Robin's face, drawing blood as Robin passively sinks to the floor: "It was not long after this that Nora and Robin separated; a little later Jenny and Robin sailed for America" (77).

On the level of unconscious fantasy, then, erotic violence not only serves to reenact the traumatic loss of a primal unity but also represents an attempt, however doomed, to break through what Benjamin calls "numbing encasement" in individual solitude (the estranging condition of becoming a human subject) in order to achieve a transcendence of ego that recaptures the semiotic register of the maternal/infant bond. When that infant is a girl, Benjamin argues, issues of separation are further complicated by the fact of sexual sameness, which mitigates the infant's repudiation of the mother and establishment of rigid ego-boundaries.[99] The difficulty if not impossibility of complete separation seems to underlie Barnes's representation of the psychosexual dynamics that dictate Robin's infantile relation to the female lovers who become Madonnas and mothers to her. As Nora puts it, "A man is another person—a woman is yourself, caught as you turn in panic; on her mouth you kiss your own" (143), and she retrospectively admits that Robin has been both "my lover and my child. For Robin is incest, too; that is one of her powers" (156). And like a child, Robin's narcissistic self-involvement affords her the "power" to wound by forgetting the presence of the other, which forms the inverse side of her masochistic desire to be dominated. It's reductive of course to assume that adult lesbian erotics simply mirror the mother-infant bond; for Barnes, however, love between women crystallizes the ambivalences of separation and fusion that psychoanalysts since Freud have seen as the libidinal "truth" driving all erotic desire.

The conflicts and fantasies that underlie the dilemma of becoming human also help explain the psychosexual dimensions of the inner dramas of the novel's other queer habitués. Most notably, Nora's obsessive desire to possess the beloved totally forms the antithesis of Robin's compulsion to break away from others. This desire changes, upon Robin's departure, into a masochistic fixation on loss and pain to which Nora perversely clings, as if to compensate for Robin's absence.[100] A related dynamic governs Felix's compulsive, utterly abject desire to "bow down" to others, which is the result of his negative internalization of his Jewishness. This same abjection dooms him to wander the globe, like Robin and the other orphans of the nightworld, in search of that primary recognition and original home whose attainment is impossible, because such goals only exist "out of time," in the deepest reaches of the unconscious. So, too, Matthew O'Connor's lamentations express his frustration at his limited condition as a human, exemplified in his impossible desire to escape his biological maleness and become the mother to whose womb he also wishes to return, a desire that he can satisfy only in transvestite fantasy.

In depicting with compassion the states of abjection suffered by these outcasts and orphans of the dominant culture, *Nightwood* stages a descent into the night that reveals that the "abnormality" reigning on the "other" side of consciousness is a universal condition. Thus the cry with which Matthew exits the text—"can't you let me loose now, let me go?" (165)—transposes the protests of a persecuted sexual and social minority, concretized in this text's representation of the nightworld of the Left Bank, into a vision of the frailty of human identity that is, in the end, metaphysically queer.

Carnival of Surfaces

One of the most seductive aspects of queer theory for contemporary theorists and activists has been its emphasis on an aesthetics of performance, pastiche, and surface. Grounded in a refusal of the essentialist logic of a core identity that presumes a natural sexuality, queer theory strategically positions sexuality as an effect of representation and style, played out in fantasy and on the body, rather than as an overdetermining cause. This emphasis on sexuality as an enactment is not only a postmodern phenomenon, however, but a vital component in the history of gay and lesbian culture, which has always used the props of performance—including dress, pose, affect, and language—to mark its difference from the mainstream. The demand to be read in terms of the surfaces that one constructs to signify one's subcultural affiliation has served multiple purposes: first and most simply, it affirms the possibility of self-creation and hence suggests that identity is a construction rather than a given; second, it serves as a visual code to signal sexual desires to other initiates; third, it provides a mask that protects the hard-earned autonomy of the gay subject from assimilation into the disciplinary order (in this regard, Lucy Snowe's depolicing narrative is not only protomodernist but presciently queer).

In Barnes's writing practice, this emphasis on the surface translates into a resistance to interiorization. For, while *Nightwood*'s "descent" into the psychology of the unconscious is as total as that of any text examined in this study, Barnes does not represent the individual thought-processes or inner worlds of her characters. Rather, the intensely psychodramatic material of *Nightwood* is projected outward onto the narrative plane, rendering interiority a textual theater where sexuality and identity are self-consciously staged and performed.[101] Even those narrative moments that the reader may think provide glimpses into the inner depths of these characters ultimately reveal that what lies "behind the surface" is pure theater, a facade of surface upon surface that underscores the secondariness and estrangement inherent in all representation. Two examples are instructive. I have already made reference to one of the novel's great psychodramatic set pieces, the scene in which O'Connor has been summoned to Robin's hotel to rouse her from a faint. The positioning of the narrative viewpoint with Felix behind the greenery, as he voyeuristically gazes at Robin, then at the doctor gazing at Robin, abets the sensation that this is a portrait of Robin in her primordial "essence," when her guard is down. But in fact both Felix and the Doctor are spectators viewing a *staging* of the primitive, one whose artifice is underlined by the junglelike room's resemblance to Rousseau's paintings of "framed nature." The theatricality of this tableau is also underscored by the fact that when Robin finally awakens she speaks in "the low drawling 'aside' voice of the actor who, in the soft usury of his speech, withholds a vocabulary until the profitable moment when he shall be facing his audience" (38). One cannot help but wonder what else is being withheld, particularly from the readers who also form part of Robin's captive "audience." The illusion of a character's inner "truth" being psycho-dramatically revealed also characterizes the scene in which Nora arrives unannounced at O'Connor's apartment at three in the morning to learn "everything you know about the night." Finding him waiting in bed for someone else, dressed in golden wig, make-up, and nightgown, Nora real-izes this is "the hour when he had evacuated custom and gone back into his dress" (79–80). Again, while the image of "going back" to some state exists before "custom" implies that Nora is witnessing a private expression of Matthew's innermost nature, this natural essence is itself dressed in full regalia: behind one covering ("custom") lies another ("dress"). As in the sexual/mental theaters of *Ulysses* and *Mrs. Dalloway,* the blurring distinc-tions between interior and exterior denaturalize the fantasy of the self as the repository of an organizing coherence, and of gender and sexuality as the expression of an inner fixity. Rather, Barnes's distanced mode of pre-senting character, like her estranging use of language, drives the point home that the performative play of surfaces is *all* we ever get.

Connections between these exterior masks, questions of psychosexual representation, and the Left Bank's queer habitués weave throughout *Nightwood.* Foremost, these issues intersect in the text's frequent imagery of the circus and carnival. Despite T. S. Eliot's well-intended warning that readers not dismiss the novel as a "horrid sideshow of freaks" (xvi), it is difficult *not* to notice Matthew O'Connor's designation of himself as the "bearded lady" (100) or Felix's identification with the "splendid and reek-ing falsification . . . [and] pageantry of the circus and the theatre" (11). Such references support Jane Marcus's claim that the novel is a comic "cir-cus epic," rooted in a bawdy Rabelaisian celebration of the body and "the good dirt" (84).[102] Early on, *Nightwood*'s narrator comments that the "emotional spiral of the circus"—its magnetic pull—paradoxically takes flight from its "immense disqualification [in the eyes] of the public" (12), and this sense of disqualification from the norm is what draws both the homosexual Matthew and the Jewish Felix into the spiraling orbit and the fringe world of the circus as a space where they have "to be neither capable nor alien" (11). Moreover, the plot of the novel, such as it is, often finds its inspiration in or around sites associated with the circus or theater. In the first chapter, the narrative proper begins with the bringing together of Felix, Matthew, and Nora at a party attended by performers from the Cirque de Paris; Nora and Robin's love affair starts at the Denckman Circus; the fantastical home the two women create on the Left Bank is decorated with circus, carnival, and theatrical memorabilia; Robin's seduction by Jenny (who is associated with the commedia dell'arte) commences at the Paris Opera. The novel fairly abounds in highly theatricalized sites of "splendid and reeking falsification."

Second, if the carnivalesque atmosphere of the circus highlights the pleasures of theatrical self-creation, the text's emphasis on dress and costume similarly underlines the performative dimension of all constructions of identity. Matthew's midnight female attire and Robin's boyish clothes function as signs that not only express, but *create* their "inverted" desires, while Jenny's ridiculously inappropriate historical get-ups call attention to her second-hand, borrowed emotions. The same principle applies to names as costumes of the self; these include the circus people's gleeful assumption of fabricated aristocratic titles, Felix's questionable assumption of the title of "Baron," and Matthew's equally suspect self-designation as "Doctor." Third, and linked to these sham titles, the queering of identity and desire implicit in the unending costuming of the self surfaces in the discourse of imitations, forgeries, and falsehoods running throughout the novel. Felix's inherited ancestral portraits, for instance—the only evidence backing up his claim to aristocratic heritage—turn out not only to be fakes purchased by Felix's father but *reproductions* that, to make matters worse, represent two *actors* dressed in improbably extravagant stage-costumes. Not only do these portraits thus debunk any true "origin" to the Volkbein dynasty, they also, like all the instances of forgery in the narrative, destabilize the binaries of original/copy and pure/impure, since it is no longer clear that there *are* any originals behind the copies. Such a destabilization takes on added importance in a culture in which homosexuality has traditionally been seen as a pale imitation or inferior copy of an "authentic" heterosexuality. Instead, the text implies, all life is a secondary condition, a stepping down, and heterosexuality, no less than homosexuality, is a construction, a "lie" that the ego constructs to contain the anarchic libido. "I am my own charlatan" (96), Matthew thus proudly proclaims, upholding the lie and the inauthentic as virtues in the inverted nightworld of which he serves as self-proclaimed prophet.

And in the end, even night—emblem of the unconscious and the preconscious—proves to be yet another covering or costume: "The night is a skin pulled over the head of day so that the day may be in a torment" (85). But this "skin" is a costume that, once again, strategically inverts normative assumptions of interior and exterior, of the rational and the irrational.

Night, not day, is ultimately the one common raiment that all human subjects wear; it is neither something deep within nor something on the far horizon but the constitutive surface on which identity is inscribed and read. In such a universe, the abject can begin to stand upright, the marginal move to center stage, and the underdogs of society join together to attest to the queer communion that exists on the other side of day's "torment." For in this series of inversions, the fabled City of Light, Paris, has become all cities of the night "given over to the shades," those "Sodom and Gomorrah[s]" that O'Connor defiantly pronounces have "never been countenanced or understood to this day" (86). In the linguistic realm of the normatively unintelligible—the world in which the norm, that is, becomes the unintelligible—the nightworld that is *Nightwood* becomes a home if not a final resting place for Barnes's estranged and orphaned children.

CHARLES HENRI FORD AND PARKER TYLER, *THE YOUNG AND EVIL*
A WALK ON THE WILD SIDE

> . . . words can
> always afford to be tolerant of that which we
> misunderstand . . .
> — *The Young and Evil,* p. 159

A brilliant version of Barnes's nightworld, preceding the publication of *Nightwood* by three years, exists in Charles Henri Ford and Parker Tyler's *The Young and Evil* (1933), a novel that remained out of print for three decades. The brain-child of two young men "anxious to rebel in every arena from sex to punctuation,"[103] this coauthored fiction depicts the gay culture of New York City's bohemian enclave, Greenwich Village, in the late 1920s in a dizzying combination of nonstop stream-of-consciousness narration, free-associative techniques, surrealist image and action, and in-the-know gay argot that adds a camp twist to the carnivalesque atmosphere pervading Barnes's queer universe.

If *The Young and Evil* and *Nightwood* share similarities, these affinities have a basis in historical fact, for in the late spring of 1931, the Left Bank world of expatriate artists welcomed a new compatriot, Ford, just arrived in Paris to find a publisher for his and Tyler's manuscript *Love and Jump Back* (the working title of the novel), since its explicit sexual content guaranteed no American press would take it up.[104] The twenty-one-year-old Ford had met Barnes a few months earlier in Greenwich Village (to which Barnes had temporarily returned), and—in an example of the migratory patterns linking these urban spaces—they had gone dancing at Harlem's

Cotton Club before Ford set sail for Europe. Soon after, Barnes returned to Paris, and within months Ford was sharing her Left Bank apartment. By February 1932 (as Ford was putting final touches on the manuscript) mutual friends were speculating that the two were on the brink of an engagement—a very queer prospect indeed, given both authors' equal if not primary interest in members of their own sex. No engagement ensued, but Barnes and Ford clearly shared artistic tastes and visions. And one mark of this affinity is the role played by both in forging a renegade brand of modernism whose innovativeness is tied to its queer vision of urban life.[105]

Like *Nightwood, The Young and Evil* uses the city setting to give fictional representation to an autonomous, insular universe in which homosexuality is the norm rather than the exception. Its characters may quip that "ninety-five percent of the world is just naturally queer" (159) without fear of creating a scandal, in part because such a statement encoded a psychological truth for the inhabitants of the Village in the 1920s, who, in an unprecedented manner, were constructing lives in which the majority of their intimates may well have been "naturally queer." While a no-holds-barred celebration of homosexuality serves as the novel's primary organizing principle, *The Young and Evil* delineates a world that, as in *Nightwood,* is also queer in the contemporary sense. Numbering among the ranks of the "young and evil" in this text are fairies (effeminate gay men), queers (men who consider themselves innately or "naturally" homosexual), bisexuals, male trade (men who sleep with men but espouse their heterosexuality), straight women who fall in love with gay men, political dissidents (anarchists, communists, and socialists), policemen who patronize gay bars, con artists and thugs, representatives of various oppressed races, wealthy benefactors in search of low-life kicks, and countless impoverished *artistes*. Indeed, the one constant activity linking nearly all the novel's episodes is that of writing or talking about writing: characters greet each other by asking what the other is composing, recite their poems in speakeasies for cash, contemplate their unwritten masterpieces, and generally take advantage of any spare moment to scribble bits of verse.

As is true of Alex in "Smoke, Lilies, and Jade," artistic identity becomes for these Village scribblers a sign of membership in an elite cadre of like-minded individuals. Being "artists" at once justifies their eccentric behavior and dress, explains their penury (the impact of the Depression is just beginning to be felt), and, for the majority of these Villagers, becomes a coded expression of their sexual "exception from the rule."[106] The terms that Eve Kosofsky Sedgwick uses in *Epistemology of the Closet* to distinguish among twentieth-century models of homosexuality prove very illuminating here. For in upholding the superiority of the misunderstood artist— and, by extension, of the persecuted homosexual—to the plebian masses, Ford and Tyler's gay bohemians assume a minoritizing model of identity ("we are the elect"). Yet in the actual degree of variation that characterizes their sexual practices, something closer to a universalizing model (homosexuality as one aspect of the wide spectrum of sexual possibilities inherent in everyone) emerges. These two models converge in the arch comment, cited above, that "ninety-five percent of the world is just naturally queer," since this percentage pivots, the speaker adds, on "the degree of resistance" involved: "I don't say I *do* and I don't say I *don't* but if the fur coat had fit me he would have had a DIFferent answer" (159). Fur coats aside, declarations (or denials) of sexual orientation in this novel shift according to context: if homosexuality provides the dominant "perversion," the desires that run rampant throughout these pages are notoriously fluid, precisely because, as Chauncey's study of gay New York evinces, it is only in this period that the opposition between heterosexuality and homosexuality as mutually exclusive poles begins to take shape.[107] Hence our present-day understanding of *queer* quite vividly captures the range of polymorphous sexualities given free reign in Ford and Tyler's high-spirited paean to same-sex desire. In light of these slippages, I find particularly intriguing the phrase "turning queer" as it is used by Karel, an unabashedly gay character, to describe the sexually ambiguous Louis: "But Karel was thinking of Louis turning queer so beautifully gradually and beautifully like a chameleon like a chameleon beautifully and gradually turning" (124). In Karel's articulation, same-sex desire has become more than an innate or inborn state (e.g., the "naturally queer" ninety-five percent of the population); rather, it is figured as a process of becoming or "turning" from which a man like Louis—who sleeps with men, who seems to have romantic feelings for men, but who nonetheless protests his straightness—is no longer immune. One is not simply born on one side or the other of this newly emerging, regulatory divide; one chooses—or, worse, is seen by others as belonging to—one side or the other, and what one does in bed suddenly portends, at least for the heterosexual man who occasionally sleeps with other men, a definitional crisis of tremendous consequence.

That the sexual misfits and social outcasts of this novel share with contemporary theorists a sense of queerness as the assumption of a defiantly non-normative identity that supersedes sexual binaries is further confirmed by the number of alliances across multiple categories of difference and oppression represented in the novel. These cross-alliances underscore the point that Ford and Tyler's goal is *not* simply that of replacing the traditional boy-meets-girl formula with an equally reductive boy-meets-boy plot. While the most important relationship in the novel is that of two overtly gay men, Julian and Karel, they are involved in an intense friendship that is (against conventional expectation) *non*sexual. Their lives are intertwined with those of the con artists Gabriel and Louis, whose relationship remains erotically suspect (are they *only* friends?), while they both position themselves as "normal" men while carrying on affairs with "homos."[108] The intricacies of the bond between a gay man and straight woman are delineated in the friendship of Julian and Theodosia, who have known each other since childhood and who temporarily live together as lovers. Other sexual allegiances appear to shift with ease: the bisexual Mexican dancer Santiago first appears as the artist Osbert Allen's male escort, then as the wealthy arts patron Mrs. Dodge's boy-toy,[109] and he ends up confessing that Julian is the only "sissy boy" he's ever "loved" (106); the "straight" bantamweight boxer who comes to Julian's housewarming party to meet girls seems quite happy to dance with mascara-eyed boys; and some relationships, such as that of Harold (very effeminate) and So-So Flower (woman, man, transvestite?), simply defy categorization.

While these identifications across categories of difference are often fleeting and not necessarily admirable (I will return to the amorality that runs throughout the text), they nonetheless underscore an important resemblance between the reign of polymorphous sexuality within the Village milieu as gay identity was gaining visibility in the 1920s and articulations of queerness in the 1990s as a communal affiliation shared among oppressed groups. The wonder and power of such "community" is the implicit message, I take it, of the extended stream-of-consciousness passage that concludes chapter 3. By evoking Julian's thoughts as he recalls Theodosia's discovery of his homosexuality, the narrative produces a phenomenology of queerness *as the linguistic and material sign of a difference that is also a point of contact and alliance.* A lyrical and experimental *tour de force,* the passage is worth quoting at length:

> Theodosia walking in sunlight, walking in morning, walking in sun paths, walking, walking and walking . . . drinking in the morning, drinking the noon, Theo in moonlight, in darkness, walking, walking and saying he is queer. I wonder. Theo bearing wonder. Theodosia finding queer, saying I love you. In strange smoke-thick yellowed air of speakeasies, over wine, over liqueurs, over smoke, over dreamings, Theodosia chanting words like broken musics: I love you . . . Theo finding *queer:* walking slowly in sunlight and saying slowly: I almost believe, except there is a difference and if you are? then there IS a difference. Theodosia walking in sunlight of morning . . . and saying queer, I love you. (35–36)

I find enormously provocative the rhetorical shift from the initial expression of Theodosia's discovery and reaction, "finding queer, saying I love you" to the single speech act in which she pronounces "queer, I love you." The performative force of the latter statement creates a bridge across categories (gay man/straight woman) that creates a conceptual space for imagining a truly queer bond of love to exist. At this textual juncture, the novel's poetics and politics of the perverse interpenetrate, anticipating contemporary theories of queer performativity.[110]

In Writing: Divine Slang

As a variation upon modernist poetics, *The Young and Evil* deliberately carves out an alternative niche for itself within the modernist tradition. On one level, as Ford later reminisced, the novel owed its inception to the fact that "at this time many of us had been introduced to *The Sun Also Rises* and everyone wanted to write a novel about their life like that novel." Actually, the experimental text that he and Tyler produced is not only stylistically but thematically worlds removed from Hemingway, for its "lost generation" is composed of the queer fringe that Hemingway's novel continually attempts to excise (it is instructive to consider how Jake's sexual dysfunction and Brett's "faghag" propensities would fit right into the world of Ford and Tyler's novel, instead of wreaking the havoc they do in Hemingway's text). Tyler reminisces that *The Young and Evil* was written rapidly and un-self-consciously enough "to escape being officialized modernism."[111] What is clear in hindsight, however, is that this "escape" from canonical modernism is also indebted to the self-conscious affiliations that the text everywhere espouses, from its dust jacket (carrying publicity blurbs from Stein and Barnes) to the discussions of modern art that fill its pages. Its ruthlessly irreverent young artists dismiss Eliot and Pound, and they blithely—if erroneously—report Joyce's death (a "mistake" the text lets slip by!—Joyce died in 1941), gestures that tend to de-oedipalize the patriarchal founders of "officialized" modernism. Meanwhile they privilege Barnes as the one modern writer with whom they would most enjoy discussing poetry: "Julian said I think I like Djuna Barnes which is a good way to think. . . . Yes and if Miss Barnes were to come past my gate [Karel replies] I'd say come into my yard Miss Barnes and sit upon my porch and I will serve you tea and if you will recite one of your poems I will be glad to learn it backwards" (18): "inverted" poetry, indeed!

This is also a novel in which the difficulty and obfuscation associated with modernism serve strategically queer ends. The lack of punctuation and quotation marks creates a confusion among subjects and objects that contributes to the sense of desire's polymorphous fluidity (as in, for example, the exchange, "You'll have to sleep on the couch Gabriel said Karel. . . . Jesus Karel Louis said" [148]). Passages that appear to be unreadable modernist prose are often composed of "men-bewildered words" (17) designed to hide their gay content from outsiders while revealing themselves to those readers who share what is in fact a highly developed use of gay argot. At one point, Julian rhetorically asks, "What is divine besides slang[?]" (134). The implication, of course, is that *nothing* is more "divine" than such camped-up rhetoric, and this precept governs the two most experimental chapters in the novel, both of which bend modernist technique to queer purposes with a vengeance.

The first of these, chapter 1's "Well Said the Wolf," creates a hallucinatory impression of New York City's gay bar culture in the late 1920s through a combination of free-associative style, fairytale allusions, and homosexual slang. The chapter begins by plunging the reader without warning into a surreal realm of make-believe and "fairy" tale:

> Well said the wolf to Little Red Riding Hood no sooner was Karel seated in the Round Table than the impossible happened. There before him stood a fairy prince and one of those mythological creatures known as Lesbians. Won't you join our table, they said in a sweet chorus.
>
> When he went over with them he saw the most delightful little tea-pot and a lot of smiling happy faces. (11)

Only the reference to the "Lesbians"—who have mistaken Karel for "a Lesbian in drag"—clues the reader in to the fact that the elfin creatures who populate this wonderland on the other side of the looking glass may be fairies in more than one sense. This realization, in turn, casts suspicion on *all* the fairytale references that punctuate the chapter, beginning with its framing device. If the relation of text to reader, as the opening sentence implies, is analogous to that of leering wolf to Little Red Riding Hood, one cannot help but recall that the wolf is making an elaborate attempt at seduction that hinges on his disguise in grandmotherly drag: into what, then, is the reader being seduced, and by whose dissimulating enchantments? The innuendos do not stop here: as Chauncey informs us, the term *wolf* in gay culture of the 1920s served as a code word for a masculine man who exhibited "a decided preference for male sexual partners" but was still not considered homosexual.[112] Reading between the lines, we also find that the "nice fat old bullfrogs," "horrid ogres," "satyrs," and cooing "naiads" who surround Karel at the tea table are either leering older men or part of their gay entourages; second, that the "tea" which everyone is drinking (shades of *Alice in Wonderland*) is contraband liquor; and, third, that the Arthurian-sounding "Round Table" is in fact a gay speakeasy, as is the childish-sounding "Doll's House" to which this crew of "little boys and girls" dispatches itself in a "lovely little speedboat"—a taxicab—midway through the scene. That "tea" is the beverage of choice, moreover, makes these establishments, figuratively, "tea-rooms"—a phrase which in 1920s gay argot signified men's public restrooms where sex occurs—thus signaling to the knowing reader yet another level of subversive connotation at work.

An even more dramatic example of modernist style encoding explicit gay content occurs in the account of the immense Harlem drag ball of chapter 12, "I Don't Want to Be a Doll."[113] As Julian swirls across the dance floor, his consciousness overlaps with fragments of overheard conversation to form a surreal collage of thought detached from character, phrases detached from context, and fantasy material. This takes the form of a ten-page prose-poem composed of unpunctuated, irregularly indented lines. The most difficult as well as the most experimental writing in the entire text, this passage contains the narrative's densest concentration of gay slang (characters dish each other as "old auntie," "Miss Bitch," "Miss Suckoffski," "Miss 69") and camp innuendo, as in the following excerpt:

> . . . Byzantine
> baggage grand cocksucker
> fascinated by the fairies of the Better
> Class chronic
> liar fairy
> herself sexual
> estimate crooning
>   I'M A CAMPfire girl
>   gratuitous sexually meaning
>   (163–64)

On the one hand, the content of this imagistic collage could hardly be more graphic; on the other, its fragmented status ensures a certain degree of difficulty, luring the reader who cares to make sense of its prose into a game of linguistic hide-and-seek. For instance, a seemingly blatant reference to anal intercourse—"feature it / adores me to stick it in his and flew into a temper last night when after the regular party my poor thing wouldn't get a hard on enough to go in and STAY in" (162)—is nonetheless missing its key term (stick it in his *what?*), which shows up out of context on the facing page, in the aside, "*never say anus* you mUst have been stunned" (163; emphasis added). What must never be said—anus—is of course being said in this instant, thereby filling in the missing word in the previous bit of dialogue. The frenzied anarchy of such language play becomes an apt correlative for the sexual and psychic anarchy unleashed by the free-for-all of the drag ball, an event in which sexes, races, and sexual proclivities all indiscriminately mingle and confound each other. Throughout *The Young and Evil,* then, experimental style becomes the agent creating "gratuitous[ly] sexua[l] meaning[s]" that proliferate in patterns as gleefully promiscuous as the postures assumed by its sexual actors.

In Transit: Bodies in Motion

More overtly than any of the other examples examined in this chapter, *The Young and Evil* links configurations of urban space to the marginalized sexual identities and the practices that such sites engender. I have already noted how, throughout the first decades of this century, the public perception of Greenwich Village shifted from that of artistic haven to "mecca" for "degenerates" and "perverts of all kinds."[114] As Chauncey's *Gay New York* shows, various historical and demographic factors—the prevalence of single-room residences, cheap eateries, and newly constructed subway stops—coalesced to make the Village an enticing mecca for young, single, and increasingly gay men and women. Ford and Tyler's text, a veritable catalogue of the names of the streets, bars, restaurants, and other haunts that composed the social matrix of gay Village life in the late 1920s, corroborates Chauncey's thesis, illustrating the manifold ways in which this interstice within the larger urban grid lent itself to the needs of an increasingly visible queer population in both its public and private domains.

But it is the novel's representation of the life of the streets, above all else, that marks the Village as a gay arena, its criss-crossing roads charged with the constant flow of sexual energy. Whether strolling down Fourteenth Street, which "at five o'clock is . . . invariably alive with the sex-starved" (29), being chased down Fourth Street by fag-bashers at dawn (46), cruising "the plate-glass windows of one after another cafeteria" off Union Square (133), or being "picked up on Eighth Street" after being mistaken "for trade [o]n Christopher" (157), the characters of *The Young and Evil* are inveterate city walkers whose steps map the city's erotic routes and zones. Charting the flow of movement outlined in any of several episodes reveals the range of queer-friendly spaces that this urban enclave incorporates. Chapter 10, for example, opens inside Julian's West Third Street apartment, into which Theodosia has temporarily moved; they decide to go dancing at the Dragon Tavern, and while getting ready, Julian recalls a recent party in which the apartment has provided a forum for communists, poets, and queers to argue about sex and politics; on the way out the door, the two decide to stop into Frankie's basement bar on Macdougal for a drink, where, after avoiding a chance encounter with Gabriel (who is crossing the same street), they run into more poets and ex-lovers; next they move on to the racially, sexually, and nationally mixed crowd at the nearby Dragon Tavern. Here, Santiago is doing his infamous whip dance; two Russian aristocrats attempt to pick up Julian and Theo; Theo leaves with a woman named K-Y; Santiago's male lover Osbert storms out in a snit over the dancer's flirtation with the bejeweled society maven, Mrs. Dodge; and in the wee hours of the morning, Julian, Santiago, and Mrs. Dodge end up naked in the same bed back at the Third Street apartment. Within the Village's closed circuit, *everything* is in transit: bodies, identities, desires.

The libidinal streams unleashed by this ceaseless physical movement work in tandem with the sexual mobility that also characterizes the lives of these characters. For not only does the Village become a haven to any number of figurative orphans who, like Nugent's Alex or Barnes's Robin, appear completely detached from familial roots, the neighborhood's insularity within the larger urban grid encourages a constant freeflow of desire in which characters attach, detach, and reattach to each other in temporary alignments that are mirrored in their constantly shifting living arrangements.[115] Sheltered by the anonymity of modern urban life, these characters have shed the constraints of bourgeois morality, including its ethos of committed relationship. Instead, they live by an alternative standard in which multiple sexual partners, simultaneous lovers, and inevitable "betrayals" are the norm. The ease with which these characters discard relationships shares affinities with Robin's promiscuity in *Nightwood,* for in both novels the denaturalizing of monogamous relationships becomes the sexual outcasts' means of defying the normalizing pressures of the dominant order. One result of this spurning of conventional moral codes is the perceived *amorality,* or acceptance of a morally blank universe, that runs throughout this world. The promotional blurb that Djuna Barnes supplied for the novel's dust jacket highlighted precisely this quality, relating the novel's title to its refusal of conventional standards of morality. After saluting the authors' "genius" in evoking the modern "homosexual," Barnes somewhat caustically notes that "[the characters'] utter lack of emotional values—so entire that it is frightening; their loss of all Victorian victories: manners, custom, remorse, taste, dignity; their unresolved acceptance of any happening, is both evil and 'pure' in the sense that it is unconscious." Years later, Tyler would say much the same thing, noting that "the world calls 'evil' . . . whoever rejects label and methods and systems."[116] As in *Nightwood,* queerness thus emerges from the deliberate severing of signified from signifier.

Significantly, this promiscuous play of desires, bodies, and words "in transit" becomes a model for the novel's elliptical trajectory. One of its most pronounced experimental features is its narrative structure, which breaks completely with organic models of plot development. Events do not link together to form one continuous trajectory or a sequential organization that proceeds logically from beginning to ending. To the contrary, most of the chapters could be rearranged without substantially affecting the reader's understanding of event (there is no inevitable chronology) or of character (characters in this novel do not "develop" but "are"). Rather than constituting an unbroken flow, the textual desire that drives *The Young and Evil* and threads through its disparate parts takes its cue from the intricate circuitry of the city grid: like the urban subject, the narrative moves in bursts of energy, halts at temporary junctures, abruptly changes directions, leaps across intersections, and merges with competing flows in a multidimensional textual space.[117]

One effect of this derailing of linear sequence in favor of a dispersive temporality is the extreme dilation of narrative time, in which the heightened attention to the present moment, stripped of past or future, calls attention to the spatial components of textuality. Joseph Litvak suggests that such narrative dilation, in which time is "wasted" or "lost" in the self-indulgent and leisurely proliferation of narrative that has no pressing goal beyond its own being, demonstrates a deliberately sophisticated naïveté (that is, a knowing regression to the self-absorption of childhood), and that this knowing innocence is a constitutive feature of gay narrativity. Litvak's theory fits this novel on two fronts. First, it meshes with the psychological profile of Ford and Tyler's bohemian artists as dilettantes with all the time in the world to kill; Julian and Karel assume the pose of both the world-weary sophisticate and the perpetual adolescent or pampered narcissist who refuses to "settle down," as Litvak puts it, to the adult responsibilities of "a maturely genital heterosexuality." Second, it makes sense of the deliberately wayward, perverse pace of *The Young and Evil*, in which the narrative propensity to "waste" meaningful time in pursuit of immediate pleasures becomes a (queer) textual end in itself.[118]

Such promiscuous narrative pleasures also return us to the promiscuously shifting relationships that the novel's sexually marginalized Villagers map out in their desirous connections to and departures from each other. If there is one narrative thread that links events in this otherwise nonlinear fiction, it is the chain of couplings and uncouplings that the main characters compose: Julian moves to New York, Julian and Karel attempt to sleep together but fail, Julian and Karel meet Louis and Gabriel, Karel moves uptown with Louis, Gabriel attempts to seduce Julian and then Theodosia, Theodosia moves in with Julian, and so on. However, rather than forming a simple daisy chain, these shifting alignments are often facilitated by some version of a *ménage à trois* that serves as a switch-point that makes way for the formation of a new coupling or new narrative direction.[119] The narrative repetition of such sexual threesomes holds a symbolic importance that is greater than any of the individuals involved: first, on the thematic level, these repeated scenarios participate in the devaluation of the unit of the monogamous couple against which these sexual renegades position themselves; second, on the formal level, these triads create nodal points or intersections in the narrative where textual energy may accumulate before expending itself in any number of possible new directions. At first glance, the conceit of "threesomes" might seem to suggest various theories of triangulated desire, but in fact nothing could be further from the case. These polymorphous encounters conform neither to the Girardian paradigm of mimetic desire (the "lover" desiring the "beloved" through the presence of a "third," which for Girard composes the underlying structure of realist fiction) nor to the Freudian paradigm of triangulated, oedipal, incestuous desire. In these often spontaneous, anonymous, and ultimately meaningless liaisons, no one assumes or is assigned one and only one position, because all the participants are simply sexualized bodies in transit. In frustrating heterosexualizing as well as oedipalized paradigms of fictional structure, then, the trajectory of *The Young and Evil* provides a provocative template for theorizing the production and proliferation of queer narrative desire.

In Style: Gay Incognitos

For all the play it gives to libidinal energies, *The Young and Evil,* like *Nightwood,* avoids representing states of interiority. "Wearisome and tediousness is this business of mirroring the mind" (94), Julian says of his own writing, and Ford and Tyler seem to agree, offering characterizations singularly devoid of psychological depth. If this resistance to narrative interiorization appears to be an implicit rebuke to the modernist aesthetic advocated by Woolf and Joyce, nonetheless, this resistance should not be confused with a denial of the psyche or of the power of the psychosexual to shape subjectivity. In the place of depth, the novel's authors celebrate a Wildean (anti)aesthetic of surface, appearance, and artifice, promoting in particular the art of illusion that, in elevating the seen or visible over substance, disrupts the presumed organic relation between "form" and some preexisting "content." Historically, such an inversion of traditional aesthetic norms, as the discussion of Nugent and Barnes has begun to suggest, played an important role in the formation of modern gay identities and gay urban cultures. Not only does the articulation of identity-as-surface, rather than identity-as-depth, become a powerful tool for combating homophobia (which depends on reading homosexual "signifiers" as exact indices of homosexual "signifieds"), but it also allows for the affirming fantasy of self-creation by stressing the performative dimension of identity. By manipulating the outward signifiers of one's chosen identity, the homosexual subject asserts control, to some degree, over the way his or her sexual difference will be read in the larger sphere of the visible.

A corollary of this emphasis on the surface as the site of difference is the implicit understanding of Ford and Tyler's characters that all manifestations of sexuality are enmeshed in representation. One effect of this awareness is the excessive attention they pay to their physical appearances, practicing in front of the mirror the poses with which they intend to slay the world: Karel has been known to set an "endurance record in front of the mirror" (32), and Julian, preparing to go out, examines his reflection "from multiple angles" before he decides that "he would do" (26)—exaggerated extremes of Clarissa Dalloway's self-confrontation in the looking glass. For Julian this intensely narcissistic self-absorption is a factor of the desire to make himself legible as a sexual being, taking advantage of his youthful beauty while it lasts to position himself as the object of other men's gazes and thereby assert publicly his availability. Karel's concern with appearance is more complicated, for it involves constructing a hyperbolic persona as The Poet, one whose fame exists less in his immortal writings than in his theatrical self-presentation; he *is* his ultimate work of art.[120] The decadent flamboyance Karel exhibits as part of this image simultaneously allows him (like Alex in Nugent's story) to flaunt his sexual difference and "get away" with it. It appears Karel has learned much from his and Julian's gay supermodels, Wilde and Stein, geniuses at commodifying larger-than-life images of themselves for general public consumption; in both cases, Wilde's and Stein's personae as celebrity artists with odd mannerisms and even odder wardrobes encode the sexual difference they disguise as "eccentricity." Julian's and Karel's manipulation of appearance in addition participates in a selective violation of gender norms that is calculated to place themselves outside the bounds of normative masculinity—Julian's, by orchestrating his sexual objectification (a traditionally feminine position), and Karel's, by using the artifice of makeup (a cultural practice deemed essential to the masquerade of femininity but antithetical to masculinity).[121]

Karel's and Julian's obsession with wardrobe carries over to their circle of gay Village friends, for whom the theatricality of appearance also becomes a salient indicator of self-assumed (and equally discardable) identity. The most extreme manifestation of the power of self-theatricalization to create a social space for queer identity is the Harlem drag ball that forms the centerpiece of chapter 13 ("I Don't Want to be a Doll"). The liberating, euphoric possibilities of performing and wearing identity, of valorizing surfaces as a way of authorizing one's difference, however, are balanced by their opposite, since such theatricality simultaneously reinforces cultural stereotypes of male homosexuality as narcissistic fixation and secondary copy (of an original heterosexuality). The anxieties engendered by such readings of gayness beset Julian once he leaves the ball and is overcome by the fear that, in the key term of the chapter's title, he is *nothing but* a fairy doll—that is, he fears that nothing lies beneath the beautiful facade, rendering his homosexuality *only* superficial, void of genuine life: "A doll does not believe itself he thought it only believes in its dollness." In turn these self-doubts generate Julian's authorial anxiety that his poetry may also simply be a way of dolling up—without which, he deduces, "I would be practically nothing . . . unless a DOLL"—which leads him to the despairing conclusion that "my homosexuality is just a habit to which I'm bound which is little more than a habit in that it's not love or romance but a dim hard fetich [*sic*]" (170).[122]

As a simulacrum whose exterior masks the lack of any core, Julian's icon of the mass-produced doll resembles the detached or floating linguistic signifier of poststructuralist theory. And it is in this signifying function that the doll becomes such a potent symbol to Julian of his internalized fears about homosexuality, for, as Lee Edelman has persuasively argued, male homosexuality has been relentlessly constructed as "inherently textual" in the modern era—indeed, the homosexual attentiveness to surfaces traced above is in part a response to heterosexuality's persistent textualizing of the gay body as a composite of legible signs in the attempt to make that body available to visual recognition. In *Homographesis,* Edelman shows how the cultural need to "see" or "read" homosexuality as a distinctive type, a body that can be discerned through its categorical difference from heterosexuality, serves as a mechanism for controlling a difference that is *actually invisible* and that thus potentially renders all sexual meaning indeterminate. As Edelman writes, "A vast cultural project of bringing the homosexual into the realm of representation, and especially into the realm of visually recognizable representation, [has been] mounted strategically in order to circumscribe the dangerously indeterminate borders of 'homosexual difference.'" But to focus so obsessively on the search for homosexual signs is to betray the fear that signifiers and signifieds never match, that every sexual signifier is open to infiltration by "alien" signification.[123] In a sense, then, Julian's anxiety about his authority to script his sexual identity is the mirror inverse of heterosexual culture's fear, first, that such alternative scripts *do* in fact exist and are being enacted every day, and, second, that these urban scripts escape the policing mechanisms of straight legibility precisely by mining the queer disjunctions of meaning inherent in the self-subverting practice of signification itself.

This tension between the heterosexual imperative to read homosexuality when and where it needs to see it and the queer counterattempt to write homosexuality into being on its own terms becomes the subject of the novel's self-reflexive commentary. In one such instance, (gay) Karel asks (supposedly straight) Gabriel "how would it feel . . . to consider meaning instead of being meant?" Gabriel's reply is unexpected: he proceeds to tell of narrowly escaping assault by a group of fag-bashers the week before, and adds, "They were probably drunk or I don't see how they mistook *me*." Gabriel, a putatively "straight" character, has just experienced what it means to "be meant" ("They saw me and called out hey faggot!") instead of controlling the "meaning" (45–46). This question of who controls sexual meaning also lies behind the exchange that occurs when Gabriel's buddy-in-petty-crime-and-hustling, Louis, says that he is "waiting for the day . . . when I can destroy all definitions," and Karel counters, "But until then . . . they are the most that matters" (112). If Louis's sexual ambiguity thrives in the absence of definitions, the oppression that Karel has suffered as an openly gay man makes him all too aware of both the freedom *and* the perils that lie in categories of meaning. Given Louis and Gabriel's personal history of unacknowledged sexual relationships with men, their resistance to being "meant"—which in Louis's derisive lingo is to be labeled a "homo" or "queer" (143, 144)—furnishes an especially vivid example of a turning point in the history of sexual discourse as the pressure to identify one's sexual stance on one side or the other of the homo/hetero binary begins to overshadow and constrain the Village's reputation for sexual fluidity.

This struggle among competing sexual discourses, as queerness gradually yields to the hetero/homo imperative, is vividly concretized in chapter 14 ("Cruise") when Karel and a friend, Frederick, are picked up by the police on Riverside Drive for having solicited a sailor who violently turns on them. Karel's primary concern is to wipe off his mascara before the police see it, since this "sign" would "type" him as a fairy and de facto guilty. Equally telltale is the fact that the sailor who has assaulted him "had his fly open the white showing" and can only "weakly" reply, "I don't know" when Frederick demands, "What did you do it for?" (183, 189). This exchange suggests that the ambiguity of the sailor's desires (why has he been loitering on Riverside Drive in the middle of the night anyway?) has resulted in a moment of homosexual panic or terror at "being meant," which he then seeks to alleviate in the act of bashing queers (making *them*, not himself, bear the brunt of "meaning"). The imperative to impose labels is underscored by the parodic description of Karel and Frederick sitting "as straight as this: ii" (189) as they wait to appear in court. Using *typeface* to reinforce the power inherent in sexual *typing*, Ford and Tyler underscore the performative element of all sexual identity, which renders even straightness ("ii") a pose, stripped of its natural or self-evident status.[124]

Thus the modernist self-reflexivity of *The Young and Evil* provides a presciently Foucauldian glimpse into the way in which the modern homosexual subject is both produced by and produces sexual discourses. To the degree that gay men like Karel and Julian successfully participate in this discursive production by harnessing the slippery power of signification to serve their own agendas, the urban setting of Greenwich Village proves an indispensable backdrop to their efforts. As a relatively circumscribed urban space where marginal identities flourish, where sexual definitions remain fluid, and where experimentation is the norm, the Village serves as a kind of cultural laboratory for testing alternative identities in the crucial decades of the 1920s and 1930s. These characteristics of radical experimentation and "the slippery power of signification" are everywhere evident in the queer *textual* body of *The Young and Evil*, whose subversively avant-garde style and form, as well as its sexually explicit content, place it at the margins of official modernist practice, in a position comparable to that of the outcast queer fringe it brazenly represents.

As avant-garde as this novel is, however, it also contains seeds of contradiction that help explain why, historically, the ferment of protoqueer attitudes in such urban enclaves as the Village eventually gave way to a stricter reinforcement of the heterosexual imperative and the even greater demonizing (and closeting) of homosexuality. These contradictions can be located, in particular, in chapter 11 ("Love and Jump Back"), in which Karel addresses the subject of the artist and political liberty at a forum at The Round Table. After acknowledging the appeal of political movements such as socialism and communism that seek "political freedom for the mass" (119), Karel nonetheless concludes his long-winded speech by declaring that the ultimate expression of political liberty lies in the supreme "spirituality" of the individual artist rather than the material needs of the democratic masses. While the rhetoric of the artist as the member of a privileged elite, superior to the common masses, provided for many homosexuals a particularly appealing analogy for self-legitimation (by making one's minority status a source of pride rather than shame), this same rhetoric also recapitulates a standard trope of canonical modernism: the transcendent vision of the individual artist who brings order out of chaos. Karel's championing of this often reactionary expression of modernist aesthetics is ironic on at least two levels. First, this artistic credo does not in fact reflect with any accuracy the avant-garde vision of *The Young and Evil.* Second, by downplaying the "liberty" of the common "mass," Karel's words militate against the text's representation of queerness as a communal affiliation that cuts across and unites multiple categories of oppression.

This confusion over politics, or the place of "queer art" in relation to politics, gets to the heart of the failure of the sexually fluid alliances arising in interwar New York City to combat successfully the binaristic opposition of "hetero" to "homo" that would shortly become definitive of twentieth-century sexuality—the very binary that 1990s queer activism self-consciously attempts to challenge and break down. For, exciting and revolutionary as it was, the ferment of queer attitudes and behaviors in the 1920s and 1930s lacked any organized or conscious *sexual* politics beyond the politics of pleasure or the politics of art. Yet it is also too easy to use hindsight to judge this potentially revolutionary urban eruption as a failure or a falling off from its original potential. It might be wiser to take a cue from Kristin Ross's comments on another urban revolution that failed to materialize (specifically, the workers' takeover of Paris's streets in the 1871 rebellion): for those who lived such moments of rupture and transformation, Ross writes, "the fulfillment was *already there.*"[125] The same might be said of the protoqueer lives that, however temporarily, began to transform urban space in the 1920s and 1930s; for them, the fulfillment was also "*already there,*" in the present-tense, lived experience of daily world-making. From this perspective, *The Young and Evil* deserves to be recognized for the truly daring social and formal experiment that it was then and is now.

BLAIR NILES, *STRANGE BROTHER*
STRANGE PASSAGES

> I dream'd in a dream I saw a city invincible to the
>   attacks of the whole rest of the earth,
> I dream'd that was the new city of Friends,
> Nothing was greater there than the quality of
>   robust love . . .

It was seen every hour in the actions of the men
    of that city,
And in all their looks and words.
        —Walt Whitman, "I Dream'd in a Dream"[126]

The nightworld of homoerotic desire that pervades the cityscapes of "Smoke, Lilies, and Jade," *Nightwood,* and *The Young and Evil* lives on as "the shadow world" (154) of Blair Niles's *Strange Brother* (1931). Repeatedly used by the character Mark Thornton to describe the vast but unacknowledged gay population that, like himself, inhabits New York City, the phrase "shadow world" connotes not only a liminal space but a condition of secondariness, obscurity, and nonmateriality, associations which eventually extend to include the equally "shadowy" position accorded both race and female sexuality in the world of this text.[127] Because of its representation of the homosexual demimonde, *Strange Brother* is usually found in the gay section of bookstores; because of the novel's racial sympathies, literary studies tend to group it with productions of the Harlem Renaissance. In point of fact, Blair Niles was neither gay nor black but a white female novelist, journalist, and travel writer whose interest in and empathy for "foreign" cultures marks all her writings.[128] These complexities suggest, once again, that Niles's novel might be better served by our current understanding of the term *queer,* not the least because of the multiple identifications across categories of race, sex, and gender that make up its plot. In *Strange Brother,* Harlem becomes a space of passage and transit (rather than, as in Nugent's story, the primary setting): its world of *black* nightclubs and speakeasies provides the locus bringing together two *white* visitors, Mark Thornton and June Westbrook, whose crossing paths interlock to form the "queer" union—of gay man and straight woman—that emerges as Niles's focal point. Mark, an aspiring artist, has sought out Harlem because its tolerant atmosphere offers him, in the words of his literary idol Whitman cited above, a place of refuge from "the attacks of the whole rest of the earth." For June, a journalist, the freedom of bodily expression that she finds in Harlem triggers an awakening to sexual desires that she has hitherto repressed. The racial otherness of Harlem thus provides a liminal space that allows both characters to come to terms with their oppression and find mirror-selves in the other that become the basis for their "strange siblingship" across differences of gender and sexuality. A sustained look at this queer siblingship, I will be arguing, does not simply rehearse, in Kobena Mercer's phrase, the "all too familiar . . . mantra of 'race, class, gender' (and all the other intervening variables)," but rather attests to "the complexity of what actually happens 'between' the contingent spaces where each variable intersects with the others."[129]

If the phrase "the shadow world" suggests some continuities between

Strange Brother and the queer fictions we have already examined, it also suggests some important differences. Foremost, in this novel "the shadow world" never becomes an autonomous universe. Rather, the gay subculture depicted in *Strange Brother* remains, as the word *shadow* implies, a *closeted* realm, one that exists on the margins, under cover, yet always susceptible to surveillance and persecution. Such a representation exists in stark contrast to the openness of *The Young and Evil*, which takes as a given the possibility of creating and living in an almost entirely gay world. A measure of this difference can be seen in an action repeated in both texts. When Karel and Julian preen in front of mirrors, they are practicing self-consciously "gay looks" with which to broadcast their difference to the world. On the contrary, when Mark Thornton anxiously inspects his reflection, he is looking for any telltale signs that might betray the secret of his homosexuality to others. In large part Karel and Julian's candor is an effect of their life in the Village. Likewise, Mark's very different experience of urban life dictates his fears of disclosure. His original purpose in moving to Manhattan has been to find "a place big enough for a man to be different safely" (74), and while he finds respite in Harlem, he does not make this sanctuary his home, nor does he find the "new city of Friends" that his reading of Whitman has led him to expect elsewhere in New York.[130] Rather his job as art instructor at a Settlement House in the tenement district of the upper East Side forces him to inhabit a ghetto in which survival depends on passing and in which disclosure portends tragedy. Instead of discovering Whitman's visionary city where "robust love" would be "seen every hour in the actions of the men . . . and in all their looks and words," Mark occupies an alienating landscape in which homosexuality only becomes visible as a derisive spectacle, a "circus" show of "freaks," as June's cousin Phil callously puts it:

> "Oh, come on now . . ." Phil interrupted. "Get back to science. Freaks don't interest me. I'm a naturalist. I'm not in the circus business. Sex is for the purpose of reproduction. Anything else is a farce. . . . As for abnormalities . . . I'd turn them over to the psychoanalyst." (178)

In *Nightwood*, the circus world signifies an inversion of the norm and a consequent centering of the margin, but within the somber realism of Niles's novel the same metaphor is transformed into a chilling reminder of the regulatory forces—of science, psychology, popular opinion—that conspire to keep "the shadow world" in the shadows, at the very edge of social legibility. The only counterweight that the novel proposes to this conspiracy of silence lies in the creation of those queer alliances—such as the friendship arising from Mark and June's "freak" encounter in Harlem—that span segregated worlds and collapse psychological and physical distance. The by-product of twentieth-century cosmopolitan life, such chance collisions and spatial reorganizations attest to the ever-evolving possibilities that the narrative associates with New York City as the embodiment of modernity.

As what I've just termed Niles's somber realism attests, the novel's vision of metropolitan modernity is not, by any stretch of the imagination, "modernist" in the formal sense. Nor does it aspire to the status of "high art," such as Karel preaches in *The Young and Evil* when he asserts the superiority of the artist to the masses. To the contrary, *Strange Brother* is geared to mass consumption, nearly every page bearing the impress of high, popular, or mass cultural interests, and its straightforward realism complements its desire to reach a broad rather than select audience.[131] Nonetheless, I suggest, the novel remains a quintessential expression of modernity, forging a distinctive vernacular for addressing many of the same concerns motivating modernist writing and inspiring postmodern inquiry. And it is the role of the city, above all else, that marks an emphatic place for this novel in the discourses of modernity and modernism: for the novel is nothing less than an ecstatic celebration of urban life as *the* ultimate expression of "the modern," the desire (to borrow from Ezra Pound) to "make it new." These affiliations can be glimpsed on several fronts. Whereas *The Young and Evil* advertises its modernist affiliations (and differences) by announcing Joyce's death within its pages, Niles's *Strange Brother* situates itself within the realm of modernity by incorporating into its plot the completion of the Chrysler Building, a feat of contemporary engineering that becomes the novel's primary symbol of "the beauty and the magic of this New York" (280). Likewise, Niles self-consciously translates the aesthetic principles voiced by Woolf in "Modern Fiction"—in particular the commission to record the "myriad impressions" that score the "ordinary mind" in "an incessant shower of innumerable atoms" (106)—into the concrete, everyday experience of her city-dwelling characters. Consider, for instance, Mark's thoughts as he sits by his tenement window and is bombarded by the raucous sounds of street life. "How . . . were *men's minds*," he asks himself in perfectly Woolfian cadences, "to survive the bewilderment, the noise and the turmoil of the *myriad impressions incessantly* forced upon them?" Consider, as well, June's acknowledgment of the randomness inherent in the immensity of the city: "Anything may happen in New York. . . . I'm just one *atom* in New York, but I'm part of it and I love it" (300, 111; emphases added). At such moments June's and Mark's perceptions become vernacular extensions of Woolf's highbrow aesthetic proclamations.[132] Niles's representation of the modern metropolis also reflects the modernist practice of bricolage in the anthropological and ethnographic impulse that fuels her depiction of New York as a "living museum" (231), one that extends horizontally from borough to borough and vertically from its sublime heights to its underground depths. As such, the temporal-spatial disjunctions and fragmentation associated with high modernist technique are rescripted on the level of theme and plot, particularly via June's role as an urban investigator intent on uncovering the various spaces and populations of the labyrinthine, multilayered city. "Why should I go on a journey to study people when they're all around me—here?" (52) June asks in a statement that makes explicit the anthropological desire that motivates her exploration of urban enclaves such as Harlem, and of urban subcultures such as Mark's "shadow world."[133]

As the "living museum" that forms the site of June's study, New York City is represented by Niles as a microcosm of the entire world. "All the world is here in your great New York" (85), marvels one immigrant, and Mark echoes the sentiment, "What an extraordinary place New York is! The world is here!" (231).[134] The multidimensionality of New York, like that of the modernist text and that of the museum collection, radically reorders time and space: all three entities are composed of disparate parts that are yoked into self-regulating wholes through laws of contiguity, adjacency, and juxtaposition rather than through principles of organicism. This temporal-spatial simultaneity is brought home to the reader of *Strange Brother* when June looks up at the soaring spire of the Chrysler Building, then down at the hordes of people disappearing into a nearby subway that will shunt them, within minutes, to the "other worlds within the New York which had just shown her its splendor." Just as quickly, June's process of association carries her from thoughts of these "other worlds" within New York to a contemplation of Mark's "furtive world, unrecognized by the forces which raised the skyscrapers of New York" (324), but which has nonetheless carved out a space for itself within the anonymity and bedlam of the city. In a related observation, Mark reflects that "only in the bigness of New York lay any security; only in its hardness and its loneliness, and in the fact that nobody cared anything about you" (124). Here, in a nutshell, is the paradox outlined by Simmel, whereby the psychological alienation fostered by the enormity of metropolitan life simultaneously becomes the guarantee of personal autonomy, including the freedom—however precarious—to enter the shadow world of queerness. For Mark, this tug between the freedom to desire and the anonymity of the city is played out in his endless "midnight prowlings" (292) in this city of "ceaseless movement" (322). Like Nugent's Alex, he "walk[s] the streets hour after hour" (319), filled with an "everlasting restless urge" that is less about sex than the desire to forge community, or as he puts it, "[the] chance to talk to someone suffering like myself" (256). It is this unfulfilled desire—both fanned and frustrated by the excitations of urban life—that has led Mark and, as we will see, June to Harlem in search of a reprieve from the loneliness fostered by being outsiders in mainstream culture.

Rites of Passage in Harlem

The setting for the opening segment of *Strange Brother*—taking up nearly a fifth of its entire length and occurring over the course of one evening— is the fabled Harlem of the Harlem Renaissance. Historically, this is the same Harlem we have already glimpsed in "Smoke, Lilies, and Jade": Nugent's plot unfolds in 1925, Niles's in 1927. Like Nugent, Niles represents a vibrant world that has recently come into its own and that boasts a self-sufficiency unparalleled among black communities in the United States. Mark's black friend Caleb, a journalist with the *Harlem Star,* speaks with pride of what it means to have "our own place": "It's got everything . . . complete. Shops and hotels, theaters and restaurants, doctors and lawyers, churches and dance-halls, rich and poor. Everything" (29). This "black city . . . contained within vast complex New York" is also a world that, as June's investigative eye reveals to the uninitiated reader, is "in its turn complex, divided and subdivided into cliques and classes" (207). But it is also a world, as June's presence in Harlem attests, increasingly invaded by white tourists drawn to the glittering spectacle of its nightlife. Yet the less conscious reason that "downtown comes up to Harlem," June argues, is to find "the very joy" (52) that sophisticated white people of the 1920s felt missing in their own lives and projected onto what they perceived to be the more natural, less complicated, and hence, in Nancy Cunard's words, more "real" Negro: "Notice how many of the whites are unreal in America: they are *dim.* But the Negro is very real; he is there. And the ofays know it. That's why they come to Harlem—out of curiosity and jealousy and don't-know-why."[135] The geographical position of Harlem within New York, moreover, an apparently entire world bracketed away on the far side of Central Park, played into the tendency to fetishize it as a symbolic site of otherness for the white thrill-seeker: to travel to Harlem was to cross a social and psychological threshold into the unknown. At such a distance Harlem became a safe space where the dominant culture could indulge its fantasies and fears of the forbidden, marginalized, and repressed.[136]

Of course, as the opening set piece at the Magnolia Club illustrates, most visitors experienced Harlem's allure under the cover of night, in the regulation nightclubs whose extravagant, exotic revues only confirmed, to the voyeuristic gaze of most white patrons, the association of the African-American with the erotic and the libidinal.[137] In contrast to these calculated spectacles of otherness, Niles posits a more authentic Harlem, embodied in a small basement dive called the Lobster Pot to which the narrative shifts in the second chapter. Moving from one location to the other, June marvels, "The Magnolia Club is staged. It's the white man's Harlem. . . . This is natural. Here everything just happens" (49). While this equation of the "other Harlem" (34) with nature and spontaneity also verges on a racist stereotype, I want to suggest that something much more radical is being effected by Niles's transformation of this site of *natural* impulse into a meeting point for all those whom the dominant culture dismisses as *unnatural:* for the Lobster Pot, as microcosm of the "real" Harlem, becomes the locus where gays and straights, blacks and whites, rich and poor, commingle without self-consciousness or judgment. This queer ambience is brilliantly epitomized in the commanding presence of the bar's pianist and singer, Sybil. This huge black woman is rendered at once as the epitome of the natural life force in all its "fecundity," possessed of a voice that transports her audience back "to the source of life, sweet, wild, elemental" (43), *and* as an unapologetic butch lesbian who jokes about her femme lover Amy between musical sets.[138] Before the evening is over, the community of listeners created by this black lesbian fount of natural fecundity not only includes June, but Mark in the company of his black friends Ira and Caleb, a threesome of cross-dressed white lesbians (47), five effeminate white men in makeup (49), a few prostitutes, and a group of young Negro dandies joined by a black man in pearl earrings named Pansy (58), all served by a waitress with "the hair and high cheekbones of a North-American Indian, the nose and mouth of an Ethiopian, and the skin of a mulatto" (40–41). The "other Harlem" that June has expressed such a passionate desire to see, it appears, is the home of the queer and the outcast, its space anchoring a diverse community that cuts across categories of sexual orientation, race, gender, and class.

Principal among the cross-identifications that interests Niles is the relationship struck up between June and Mark on this pivotal night, which begins when June notices Mark at the Magnolia Club and continues into the early hours of the morning when Mark directs June to the Lobster Pot. As a white woman drawn toward black culture in a racist society, and as a straight woman who comes to identify with a gay man in a homophobic society, June provides an intriguing example of the complex affiliations and contradictions that, in her case, produce the phenomenon of the "straight queer."[139] Described as "simultaneously aristocratic and Bohemian . . . entirely unconventional in spirit and thought and manner" (18), June exemplifies the would-be emancipated woman of the jazz age: she has defied tradition by divorcing her wealthy husband, and she revels in the "independent, free and easy world" (20) to which her career as a professional journalist has given her access. This partial freedom, however, only accentuates the repressions and oppressions she experiences as a heterosexual woman, filling her— much like Edna Pontellier—with a vague "troubled longing for something which she did not have" (15). What she "does not have" might more accurately be rephrased as what others deny her. For her male companions, she realizes, are interested only in her "surface life," remaining blind to "the seething inner June" (36). This dissatisfaction is precisely what subconsciously draws June to Harlem, for its nightlife provides an environment that allows her denied interiority and eroticism to begin to emerge.

This awakening occurs through a fascinating process of doubling, identification, and projection as she watches Glory and Sybil, the black female
performers at the Magnolia Club and Lobster Pot. Whereas her male companions only see a "dressed-up" version of the primitive in the singer
Glory's performance, June sees—in an intriguing echo of Molly Bloom's
final words—a woman who "knows how to say 'yes' to life." This sensed
affirmation leads June to "project herself *into* Glory's body," and the act of
visualizing herself "inhabiting [Glory's] lithe brown body," in turn, triggers
June's awakening to the "deep fires burning within her, waiting to leap
into flame" (10–11; emphasis added).[140] If June's empathetic spectatorship
revives her latent eroticism, it is also telling that during these scenes her
gaze is split equally between the stage on which Glory performs and the
corner of the audience where Mark sits with his black friends: for the narrative's extended opening sequence in Harlem, it turns out, not only provides
the liminal site of June's erotic awakening, but also forms the figurative
and literal threshold through which June passes—and, along with her, the
reader—into the strange, unknown shadow world signifying Mark's sexuality.

Mark's familiarity with the Harlem scene that June is seeing for the first
time raises the question of the desires and identifications that have drawn
him to this liminal urban space. Ever since discovering his homosexuality
at the age of 16, Mark has felt himself bereft of "family . . . or home" (149),
and when this figurative act of self-orphaning is literalized by the death
of his remaining parent, he moves to New York City in search of a new
constellation of "family," thus echoing the migrations of Nugent's Alex and
Ford and Tyler's Julian to the city. Although Mark doesn't find the city of
brotherly love that his reading of Whitman has led him to hope exists,
he does discover another sort of "strange brotherhood" in Harlem.[141] The
achievements that this community has made "under such heavy odds,"
Mark reveals to June, forged "a bond. I started going to Harlem" (151).
That bond lies in his recognition of shared, though different, experiences
of discrimination and marginality. As he says to Ira and Caleb of Harlem's
regulation nightclubs for white patrons, "As for your being 'segregated' . . .
I know how that makes you feel. Nobody does any better than I do" (28),
and Mark's eyes fill with tears as he reads June lines from Countee Cullen's
"Heritage," for "he always identified himself with the outcasts of the earth.
The negro had suffered, and that bound Mark to him" (234). If a bond
forged in oppression draws Mark to Harlem, what he finds in this urban
enclave is an unprecedented degree of sexual tolerance, confirming
Chauncey's and Garber's theses regarding the relative acceptance of gay life
in Harlem in the interwar era. "In Harlem I found courage and joy and
tolerance. I can *be myself* there," he confides to June, "They know all about
me and I don't have to live a lie" (152). This freedom to exist outside the
closet, however temporarily, is critical to Mark's psychic well-being. For

the fact that "with them I can be honest" brings him a temporary peace of mind, even though he confesses that "I'm still lonely . . . I'm still a stranger there, too. But it calms me" (155). In drawing an equation between racial and homosexual oppression, as well as in gesturing toward their differences, Niles maps out an alliance of outcasts and dissidents that contemporary queer politics strives to realize.

Such a mapping, however, is not unproblematic. For this identification across categories of race and homosexuality is borne out in a series of spatial and territorial metaphors whose implications call into question the narrative politics of Niles's decision to make Harlem the point of entry to her study of gay and female oppression. June's perception becomes the vehicle of these imagistic connections. "We are in a strange land," June says of Harlem when she appeals to Mark, still a stranger to her, to help her "explore" the "other Harlem" (34), whose imagistic association with "darkness" is repeatedly emphasized (41). When Mark reveals his homosexuality to June the following day, June feels herself carried on a tide "into a strange, dark country" and transported into a "place of strange, dark desire" (131, 168). Not only is June's entrance into this "dark place" (157) of homosexual desire quite clearly represented as a psychological rite of passage—"the veil which separated the normal from the shadow world had been lifted, to let her pass in" (158)—but this threshold event now takes precedence over Harlem's function as the liminal space, the threshold, through which the reader enters the text. Simply put, one "dark" and "strange" realm of otherness makes way for another. In the process, issues of race become secondary as Mark and June's developing relationship resumes outside its original framing in Harlem.

Despite this retreat from race as the primary narrative focus, the unlikely relationship that unites this straight woman and gay man retains its basis in the very identifications that have drawn each to Harlem in the first place—a sense of shared oppression, the quest for lives of vibrance and joy, the unfulfilled yearnings for romantic love that lead both to identify instantly with the passionate emotions expressed in Glory's song. From the very moment Mark tells his sexual secret to June, she finds herself "identif[ying]" with Mark "so suddenly that she had no time to understand the bond which surprisingly existed between them" but which she intuitively understands to be "something more" than a simple response to his pain (162). One is reminded of the relationship of straight Theodosia and gay Julian in *The Young and Evil* ("finding queer, saying I love you"), for this "something more" that June senses resides in the literal and figurative queerness of their bond as woman and man who are "friends without any complication of sex. It was a different relationship than any that June had ever known before. . . . Mark's friendship had brought into her life something entirely new" (193). Ultimately, June comes to realize that Mark means more to her and that his love is more satisfying than anything her suitor, Seth, can ever offer—and this displacement of heterosexual romance as the plot's emotional climax is, indeed, one of the narrative's queerest turns of all.

Sexual Suspects

A related effect of this text's queerness involves the role that homosexuality assumes as Niles's privileged subject and rallying trope for all the modes of oppression explored in the novel. We have just observed how, on the level of narrative structure, the spatial locus of Harlem problematically operates as a kind of feint, providing the potentially squeamish reader a gradual entry into the even more controversial topic of homosexuality. As the metaphoric "darkness" of Harlem's nightlife gives way to the darkness of Mark's "shadow world," the reader, like June, is transported without quite being aware of it into uncharted terrain from which there is no turning back. Predictably, June's anthropological impulse finds a fresh outlet in Mark's revelations. On the one hand, her curiosity becomes Niles's vehicle for imparting crucial information about the gay underground to the uninformed reader, as Mark enumerates for June's knowledge the various gay spaces, from subway tea-rooms to restaurants and parks, that compose this invisible city-within-the-city, and June's empathy becomes Niles's strategy for propagandizing on behalf of this minority population. On the other hand, despite the immensity of this subculture, Mark's confessional narrative—indeed, the very fact that it is couched as a confession—makes painfully apparent the ever-present threat of discovery—and, worse, blackmail and incarceration—that renders the closet *the* modus operandi of his life. Even though Mark has migrated to the city to find a place to be "different safely" (74), his metropolitan experience teaches him, all too quickly, that *no* place, not even Harlem, is "really safe" (124).

This lesson is driven home in the opening segment, when he and June witness the arrest of Nelly, an effeminate gay man, outside the Lobster Pot. At this very instant, Mark's dream of Whitman's "new city of Friends" is replaced, in his psyche, by something "furtive" and "sordid" (79). Attending Nelly's trial the following morning, Mark is awakened to the sobering reality that "every one who is different is liable to the penitentiary" (130); then he proceeds to internalize the law in a classically Foucauldian example of the mechanisms of self-surveillance, hurrying away from the Court House "as though infallible eyes watched him" (102), and stopping to scrutinize his reflection in a store window in order to assure himself that his "manly" appearance hasn't, as in Nelly's case, "testif[ied] against him" (97). Simultaneous with this intensified fear of discovery is the equally heightened desire to "throw off the masks" of "deceit" (105) and escape the closet whose power he is in the process of demonstrating. In a very real sense, Nelly's arrest triggers in Mark an epiphany that serves as his ultimate self-awakening: not to sexual desire, as in the awakening plots enumerated in chapter 2, but rather to the necessary repression of sexual desire that eventually leads him to despair and suicide.

The self-policing that Mark undergoes duplicates the attempts of a number of competing historical sexual discourses attempting to define homosexuality in the 1920s and 1930s; this categorizing impulse, as David M. Halperin among others has shown, originated in the late-nineteenth-century construction of homosexuality as a universal identity category rather than a range of discrete acts.[142] Indeed, one of the markers of this narrative's contiguity with the forces of modernity and popular culture is its representation of culture's obsessive attempt to make legible this newly constructed homosexual "personage," the better to regulate its being.[143] In *Strange Brother*, we not only hear of these competing discourses but see them *put to work*, entering the text through its vocabulary, through the spoken words and inner thoughts of its characters, and through Niles's interpolation, via citation and quotation, of actual texts and authorities. At least seven such discourses—legal, scientific, psychoanalytic, moral, ethnographical, poetic, and political—can be singled out.

First, the most striking instance of a proscriptive legal discourse that becomes a part of the novel occurs when Mark goes to the public library after the sentencing of Nelly and looks up the definition of homosexuality in the "Crimes Against Nature" section of the Criminal Code, which Niles reproduces verbatim. As Mark experiences the awful "power of words" to "alter the whole aspect of facts" (124), his subjectivity is radically transformed, and this discourse of criminality *now becomes part of his way of thinking about himself*. Second, a biological/medical explanation of homosexuality as a genetically determined characteristic enters the text through the enlightened views of the Jewish character Irwin Hesse, on his way to attend the International Sexual Reform Congress in Vienna (164).[144] Third, the text also provides a forum for a variety of popularized versions of psychoanalytic theory. These range from Mark's citation of Ellis's rhetoric of "inversion" to explain his feeling of being a "half-man" (153–55) to Phil's designation of homosexuality as a type of "degeneration" or "retarded mental development" best handled by psychoanalysts (55). Fourth, the shaming discourses of popular morality that view homosexuality as an aberration of nature are illustrated in Phil's disgusted dismissal of gays as "freaks" in a circus sideshow, as well as the opinion of Mark's mother that she would rather see her son dead than gay (138). Fifth, to combat this prejudicial discourse, Niles draws on ethnographic discourse to proselytize for the diversity of homosexual behavior by creating a typology that reaches from the Hellenic masculine ideal embodied by Mark to the lower-class fairy culture constituted by effeminate men such as Pansy and Nelly, and from the closeted upper-class world of June's gay ex-husband to the cross-dressing milieu of the Harlem drag ball. Finally, a more positive image of male love is created by the text's inclusion of, first, a series of literary allusions, often taking the form of actual quotations and including Plato, Shakespeare, Whitman, and Cullen, and, second, the politically charged rhetoric of notable sexual reformers who provide Mark with moments of inspiration (Carpenter, Ellis, Hirschfield, Symonds, and Forel).

As these various languages seep into and shape Mark's consciousness, he in turn begins to create his own counterdiscourse in the form of the anthology "Manly Love" that June has encouraged him to edit. A bricolage of quotations from literary sources and homosexual thinkers, this projected text serves two strategic purposes: first, through the citation of names and epochs, it creates an empowering history of homosexual desire (not only for Mark's projected audience, but for the gay readers who have stumbled onto Niles's text); second, it creates a forum where a diversity of homosexual voices articulate an identity that is plural, flexible, and heterogeneous. Not only do we see, in the narrative's representation of Mark's work on the anthology, a Foucauldian reverse discourse on homosexuality becoming a tangible part of Niles's text, thereby offsetting the negative power of naming epitomized in Mark's reading of the Criminal Code, but the elements of pastiche and juxtaposition that go into Mark's arrangement of its many parts suggest that it may technically be far more "modernist" than Niles's novel itself. The tragedy that *Strange Brother* leaves unanswered at its conclusion is the fate of the "Manly Love" manuscript after Mark's suicide. All the narrative reveals is that his belongings have been shipped off to his homophobic relatives. From our contemporary vantage point, we can read into the disappearance, and likely destruction, of this text an allegory of the erasure—as Chauncey has documented in *Gay New York*—of a particularly vital chapter in queer history before the Second World War.

In inverse proportion to these discursive efforts to stabilize and contain homosexuality within definitional boundaries, the plot of *Strange Brother* vividly illustrates the way in which imputations of homosexuality tend to spread, casting a "shadow" over nearly every straight male character in a process of connotation that, as D. A. Miller argues, both reinforces homophobia and exposes the constructedness, the fragility, of the lines drawn up to separate normative from non-normative behaviors.[145] To the degree that this wildfire multiplication of homosexual possibility begins to destabilize heterosexual assumptions, it becomes another of the novel's protoqueer attributes: "You make it seem everywhere," June wonderingly says to Mark. June has good reason to be concerned, given that the primary character implicated in this process of connotation is her reluctant suitor Seth Vaughan. All talk and no action when it comes to lovemaking, Seth remains an "enigma" (44) and their unconsummated relationship "inexplicable" (168) to June. "Labeled" a man who is "perfectly safe . . . for women's clubs" (21), withdrawing into "strange silences" (the adjective "strange," as already noted, connotes various sorts of queerness in this text), absenting himself for long periods of time without an explanation (44–46), and mysteriously confessing to an inner "weakness" that his pride will not allow him to admit and that he cannot undo (119), everything about Seth is so shrouded in the language of the closet that even his unambiguous dismissal of homosexuality—"It's never interested me. I've always been perfectly normal, thank God" (205)—only becomes a further source of ambiguity: might he not protest too much? The process of connotation at work here is reinforced by the narrative's calculated juxtaposition of straight Seth and gay Mark. Immediately after Seth has spoken of his mysterious "weakness" to June, Mark arrives at her apartment, and, as if Seth's double, sits in the chair Seth has just vacated as he proceeds to confess his queerness to June. During his revelation, June's thoughts are drawn back to the memory of Seth's "trying to tell her something, which for all her swift intuitiveness, had escaped her. What was it that Seth had been trying to say?" (127). The sequence of associations makes it appear as if, in her subconscious mind, Mark's present confession analeptically provides the answer. Seth's heterosexuality is indirectly called into question, furthermore, by June's discovery of her ex-husband Palmer's secret gay life (the clues to which have been available to the astute reader all along), which invites us to wonder whether June is repeating a pattern of falling in love with a closeted man.

Niles also represents a category of violently homophobic men whose over-eagerness to persecute the gay men they pride themselves in being able to spot implicates them in the cruising activities at which they appear, ironically, all too adept. The situation recalls Edelman's dissection of how the cultural mandate to read homosexuality as a set of visible signs, in order to designate it as other, simultaneously raises the suspicion of *knowing too much* (hence the adage, "It takes one to know one").[146] A classic example of such a case is the plainclothes officer who has arrested Nelly. "Oh, I can spot 'em! Can tell 'em as far as I can see 'em," he boasts in the courtroom, "I know 'em all right" (96–97). Similarly suspicious is the homophobia of Mark's boss, Mr. Rotheby, who gives Mark a set of photographic prints of nude Greek and Roman statuary (73) yet has a local barber's assistant fired because of the rumor that he is a "boy-lover" (291). Likewise, when Rico, the neighborhood boy Mark has befriended, viciously attempts to blackmail him ("I've found you out! . . . It'll cost you!"), the boy's denunciation reveals a depth of unacknowledged yet frankly homoerotic desire. "Liked you? There wasn't anyone else in the world for me," Rico lambasts his victim, "But you didn't see me. I wasn't on the map for you. And I thought it was *because you weren't* that kind, *even though* I'd always had a suspicion *that you were*" (315; emphasis added). The dissonance between Rico's "because . . . you weren't" and his "even though . . . you were" reveals the incoherence that lies at the heart of a definition of heterosexual masculinity that must disavow as totally distinct ("you weren't") the homosexuality ("you were") upon which straight definition depends. Once the process of guilt-by-association has been set into motion, no man is immune. Hence even the novel's most sympathetic heterosexual male, Evan Rysdale (who in current jargon might be called a "straight queer" for his unequivocal support of gays), falls under the shadow of homosexual suspicion simply because he knows too much; in the imagination of a homophobically constructed society, which depends on maintaining an unbridgeable gulf between hetero and homo categories, his repeated admission to June, "Yes, I have known many" (266), raises the question of precisely "how many" and, even more damningly, *why*.

Songs of the Year

The tension traced above between the desire to quarantine the homosexual as a separate, always identifiable, species of being and a process of connotation that finds homosexuality everywhere is mirrored in *Strange Brother*'s alternating views on whether sexual identity is essential or constructed. Homosexuality, for example, is simultaneously positioned as both natural and a state of artifice, even within single scenes (Sybil's dance of fecundity versus Nelly's making up his face at the Lobster Pot). Similarly, the text's valorization of June's "inner" life (which others don't see) as the *essential* June exists in tension with the external stimulants that the text also represents as constructing her desires. Niles does not take sides in this debate; indeed, she may not always be aware of the ideological confusions to which her plot sometimes gives voice. Nonetheless, in repeatedly asking us to consider the relation of identity to modes of discourse and the exercise of social power, *Strange Brother* raises questions about the constitution of modern subjectivity and queer identity that traverse, in popular idioms, the same intellectual terrain as the experimental fiction of Nugent, Barnes, and Ford and Tyler.

Foremost among the novel's explorations of the determinants of identity is its representation of the tremendous impact of popular culture—of which hit music becomes Niles's privileged trope—in creating as well as expressing the desires of its characters. As June says to Seth in defense of her love of popular songs, "No matter how cheap you may think them, we do live and love and dance to them, don't we? They are somehow the heartbeat of the year. . . . My point is that we live to the beat and the words of our dance tunes" (17–18). The text, indeed, is cut through and through with songs of the year, as June calls them, each of which takes on a special significance to those characters who "find" themselves and their desires in the lyrics that their minds continually recycle.[147] In one instant Sybil is singing, "Why do I cry? . . . You never hear me," and in the next the narrative reports June's internalization of the lyric *as her own emotion:* "No, it was useless to cry, June thought. Seth never heard her" (43).[148] This is only one example of the many times Niles represents the artifacts of popular culture infiltrating the consciousness of her characters, both predicting and articulating the very desires that these artifacts are simultaneously constructing.[149] The urban subject, Niles insists, *is* the product of his or her modern context. As she puts it in a moment of Whitmanesque expansiveness, the popular lyrics June hums in her head are culture's living bloodstream: "the words of current songs, the songs of the music halls and the movie-houses, of the phonographs and the radios and the dance orchestras, songs that for a season are heard everywhere," all these form "the accompaniment of living" (120). Not coincidentally, at this very moment June is humming a song lyric to herself: "What is the good of me by myself" (120); ironically, it is only through the "impersonal" intervention of modern technology—here in the form of the phonograph, the movie hall, the radio—that June finds relief from the sense of isolation she is expressing. Not only do the words and rhythms of popular music implant within the modern subject the fiction of an entirely subjective world of private emotion, this soulful "accompaniment of living," insofar as it is broadcast across the city and the globe, unites a circuit of otherwise unconnected listeners in the shared project of "living."

This impress of external phenomena on inner life is part of the novel's interrogation of the interplay between traditional discourses that posit an origin or essence to the self and representations that suggest that all identity is a performative effect, the inscription of the exterior world. And to the degree that identity is performative, sexuality is also revealed to be an enactment. This fact is driven home in Niles's depiction of the masks Seth and Mark wear. Seth, in attempting to explain to June his mysterious weakness, asserts that "character" is something that a man "builds," like civilization; and although we fool ourselves into believing that we can always return to "what I *essentially* am," that *essence* has in fact been replaced by what we have *constructed* in its place: "The thing you've built so carefully, so painfully throughout the years, that thing comes to own you in the end. . . . And so Seth Vaughan must be what I've *made* him" (119–20; emphases added). In this articulation, the "made" man *becomes* Seth's essence; there is no natural self, no origin, that underlies and dictates the edifice of "character" that Seth has deliberately "built." In contrast to Seth's self-constructions—erected to hide something that remains ambiguous but that nonetheless seems suggestive of the closet—Mark undergoes an inverse process, yearning increasingly to strip away the mask that hides what he on several occasions identifies as his real "nature" or inborn essence. Yet time and again the narrative demonstrates the degree to which a "naming" that comes from outside the self precedes and thus determines Mark's sexual identity. For instance, Mark's adolescent awakening to his homosexuality occurs when his friend Tom Burden "break[s] the truth" to him—a "truth" that Tom has already read in Mark, in advance of Mark's self-knowledge, and into which Mark then steps as the preexisting "truth" of his being (134–35). And, yet, as Mark recollects the impact of this revelation, his wording clothes this truth-claim in the language of performance: "And, suddenly, it was just as if we were in a theater," he says to June of the mirror that Tom holds up to him, "and the curtain had gone up, and I saw my life . . . acted out. And I knew it to be true . . . everything Tom had said" (141; Niles's ellipses). When the curtain goes up to reveal the so-called truth that lies hidden behind the veil, Mark sees, in its place, "*my life . . . acted out*"—a representation, a performance that accords perfectly with the script that, however "true" to Mark's preexisting sense of difference, has nonetheless been hand-delivered by Tom and whose truth can only be retrospectively determined by rereading his entire history in its light.

These performances of identity, these stagings of sexuality, run throughout the text, eventually enveloping all the marginalized cross-identifications—gender, homosexuality, and race—that lend to the the novel its distinctively queer ambience. These enactments are most overt in the large, theatrical set pieces (such as the opening nightclub sequence and the drag ball scene in Harlem) where otherness is quite literally transformed into the site of spectacle. The regime of the gaze that seems to dominate in such scenes, however, turns out to be very unstable: what is a regulatory or voyeuristic gaze from one point of view (Mark and June's participation in the white spectatorship of black Harlem[150]) may turn out to be an identificatory or desirous gaze from another; the object of the gaze in one context (June as object in her ex-husband's collection of valuables) becomes an active agent elsewhere by exercising the right to look (June watching Glory and Mark in the Magnolia Club). The binaries of seer/seen, visible/invisible, are radically destabilized,[151] in large part because of the way the text's queer cross-identifications complicate, if never fully dismantle, the system of surveillance upon which the mechanism of the closet depends.

The Return of the Repressed

Despite these slippages, it is nonetheless apparent that racial otherness—specifically, African-American blackness—and not homosexuality becomes the most "invisible" of the text's marginalized subjects. This differentiation is in large part an effect of Niles's sexual politics, which makes the "outing" of gayness the novel's central narrative project; even within a communal world of queer alliances, some positions stand to gain more than others, just as some oppressions remain more repressed than others. Ironically, the fact that the two most "spectacular" scenes of theatrical display are set in Harlem (the nightclub acts at the Magnolia Club and the drag ball of chapter 11) only drives this point home. I have already noted how, in structural terms, the opening setting in Harlem serves as a kind of masking strategy to introduce the even more explosive and taboo topic of homosexuality. After the immense amount of narrative energy expended in creating this initial focus, the reader expects, reasonably enough, that Harlem will continue to play a major textual role. Yet after chapter 2, Harlem drops from sight, only to reappear very briefly in the circumscribed form of chapter 11, as Ira and Caleb give June a whirlwind tour of Harlem society and culture. At this point Harlem has become merely an interstice, a digression, in the narrative. While the educational goal of chapter 11 is admirable (to expose white readers to the diversity and richness of African-American life), it nonetheless renders Harlem the contained object of an ethnographic survey that conveys information rather than contributes to the forwarding of the plot. And when the chapter culminates in June's attendance at the annual Harlem drag ball, *black* Harlem is transformed into a *gay* space, whose narrative function, moreover, is to facilitate a minor climax in one of the gay subplots—namely, June's discovery of her ex-husband's homosexuality.

In a curious way, though, the novel ends where it begins despite itself. For the disappearance of Harlem once it has served its primary function as a liminal site of discovery for June and Mark is counterbalanced by its sudden reappearance, in condensed symbolic form, on the very last pages of the novel as the text's ultimate locus of knowledge and wisdom.[152] In a striking demonstration of the return of the textually repressed, the plotting of *Strange Brother*'s final chapter turns on the pivotal role that two black characters, June's Trinidadian maid Beulah and Mark's African-American friend Caleb, play as speaking subjects whose words reconcile June to the recent deaths of the two most important men in her life: Mark, who has committed suicide, and her erstwhile lover Seth, who has been killed in an airplane crash. First, it is Beulah who provides a solution to the mystery of Seth's strange behavior by explaining to June that he was impotent and ashamed to admit it ("At last she understood it all. . . . Yes, Beulah was right. 'An old man, mom, can't give what he wants to give'" [330, 339]). However implausible the reader may find this revelation, Beulah's proverbial wisdom brings June the consolation she needs. Second, it is Caleb who brings the news of Mark's suicide to June. This triggers, however, one of the queerest moments of all in the novel as Caleb launches into a three-page reverie about bucolic life back on the "old plantation" in Virginia where he grew up (and to which he is returning for a visit). The ostensible function of this digression, which temporarily halts the novel's momentum toward closure, is that Caleb is giving June time to absorb the news of Mark's death as he rambles on. Further, his story turns out to be something of a moral fable designed to inspire June to recommence the business of living, for when she asks how he'll able to leave the rural "peace" of the plantation, he replies that New York "brings you back to itself. Maybe it's because it's alive" (338).

One cannot help but wonder, however, whether the textual unconscious of *Strange Brother*—whose repressed contents I have already associated with its elision of race—is relaying a more complex and contradictory message. For in fact Caleb's narrative of "the old days" centers on the memory of toting his master's gun and fetching the fallen quarry when the "white folks went hunting," an activity that he cheerfully looks forward to resuming, though presumably without the company of white masters, on his return visit to the Deep South. This reminiscence would not be extraordinary except for two facts: first, that Mark, after likening himself to a wounded animal, has just blown his brains out *with a gun*—in fact, with his grandfather's pistol, his one patrilineal inheritance and a reminder of his own rural upbringing; and, second, that Caleb likens the flight of the quarry before it drops to earth to that of *airplanes,* in one of which June's suitor Seth has recently crashed to his death. This narrative "coincidence"—in which two images associated with violent death reappear in a context of ostensible uplift—makes Caleb's extreme thoughtfulness (in calming June) seem, on second sight, to conceal a certain thoughtlessness, one that not only speaks to Caleb's own repressions (in only remembering a happy South), but also inserts a just-audible undercurrent of hitherto suppressed black anger and murderous violence into the novel's climax. Such a return of the repressed functions similarly to the moment in *Mrs. Dalloway* when Woolf, without any apparent self-consciousness, transforms those very tree branches that have led to the senseless death of Clarissa's sister into a metaphor of everlasting life.

The moment of Mark's suicide, moreover, is marked by an even more circuitous return of race as the text's repressed, again through the agency of Caleb's southern heritage. Just before he kills himself, Mark's thoughts return to a childhood memory—the sick cow that the herd turns on and gores to death—that the narrative has previously established as an allegory of Mark's internalization of society's view of homosexuality as a sickness and of his subsequent alienation. Given the violence of this image, it is perhaps no coincidence that the one time that Mark is depicted recalling his friend Caleb's tales of the South occurs the very night of Nelly's arrest, as Mark, upset, walks home and sees the word *chitterlings* in the window of a Harlem grocery store. This, Mark remembers, is one of the first words Caleb learned in his childhood: "Hog-killing time was a great event, Caleb said. And at hog-killing time you ate chitterlings. The word, Mark remembered, meant entrails" (68). Butchery, death, violence, the herd instinct—these less pleasant manifestations of "pastoral" nature not only foreshadow Mark's fate but, fascinatingly, circle back not once but twice to Caleb's narratives of a seemingly benign South in which acts of bird-hunting and

hog-killing mask a level of black anger that goes unspoken and racist violence that surfaces instead in displaced allegories of homophobic violence
(Nelly as butchered meat) or as a subtle narrative violence (the way Caleb's
story to June almost derails the movement to narrative closure).[153]

If issues of race thus make a somewhat shadowy return in the text, issues
of gender are more graphically underscored in the final pages. For the fact
that the recipient of Beulah's and Caleb's parting wisdom is June underscores her ambiguous position in the queer trajectories of desire that the
novel has been tracing. On the one hand, in a twist whose pathos is both
fitting and ironic, June comes to a final awareness of her interiority, of the
psychological depth that the *straight* men in her life have consistently denied her as a woman, by the death of her oppressed gay friend. "Through
Mark," June realizes, "she had learned to see life, not in one dimension,
but with a depth of focus which penetrated to the hidden places of the
heart" (340). Given the queer terrain of male/female friendship that June
and Mark's relationship has staked out, it may seem appropriate that the
final stage in June's quest for a fuller life has been facilitated by her encounter with the shadow world of male homosexuality. However, this affirmation is mitigated by the more troubling way in which the narrative unconsciously transforms June—the straight woman who empathizes with both
gay men and black people—into the bearer of *all* male sexual dysfunction,
gay and straight alike. In the process, June internalizes their "failure" as her
own: the instant Caleb breaks the news of Mark's suicide, she thinks, "I
failed [him]" (333); when her thoughts turn to Seth's unwillingness to confide the secret of his impotence to her, she asks herself "whether she too
had not failed" him (340). The guilt June assumes for the deaths of both
men vividly attests to the contradictory position occupied by the emancipated woman of the late 1920s, at once a "free woman" and a prisoner of
the anxieties of assuming her own authority.

Guilt, however, is not all that June internalizes. In the last moments of
the text, she also incorporates within her psyche what she deems the best
of both men: Mark's courage and Seth's valor. Not only do these attributes
give June the courage to live; in the text's queerest touch of all, the images
of Mark and Seth are "strange[ly] fused" (341) within June's spirit in a
"marriage," as it were, of two men, one gay and one straight. Of all the
utopian cross-identifications that the text forges, this is one that can *only*
exist between men who are dead, or in the imaginative space of a woman's
consciousness. While this may seem like the ultimate cliché—only women
understand; men would rather be dead than be intimate—it is one that is
ratified by the operative mechanism of heterosexual masculinity in patriarchal society, which at once depends, as the novel goes to such lengths to
show, on the subordination of women and the scapegoating of homosexuality. And, as a cliché that speaks a disturbing cultural truth, this is a mes-

sage that *Strange Brother,* as a popular fiction that necessarily speaks in the language of simplified truisms, makes uniquely available, in all its banality, for serious critical interrogation.

"We do seem odd in a wonderful city like this" (282), muses Lillie-Marie, a forlorn homosexual whom Mark Thornton befriends toward the end of *Strange Brother,* as the two walk through the majestic heart of central Manhattan. Their steps eventually lead them to the Italian tenements of the upper East Side where Mark lives. Entering his neighborhood, they must pass through a religious street-festival where a surreal collage of "wax counterparts of the human body," miniature and life size, moist and sticky in the heat of the summer night, are displayed in the surrounding stalls and carts for the diseased to buy and then "wait for [their] cure" (285–86). The two vignettes, occurring side by side, serve as apt companion pieces with which to conclude this chapter's inquiry into the hopeful and hellish dimensions of the queer inhabitant's experience of the modern metropolis. In the first instance, the "oddity" that Lillie-Marie assigns himself and Mark in order to underline their sexual difference in fact is shown to be as much a part of the "wonder" of the cityscape as its inspirational and dwarfing skyscrapers, for the heterogeneity of the new urban geography makes room for all things, great and small. But when viewed as part of the larger body politic of American society, the homosexual subject becomes the abject, the "odd" or literally queer appendage that fragments the whole body into diseased parts, in need of an amputation if not a cure. Yet, for "his sort," Mark reflects as he and Lillie-Marie walk through the nightmarish street festival (this text's closest approximation to a Circean descent into the underworld), there is no single "body part" that will purchase their "cure." The implication is that homosexuality is an essential state of being, a defining identity that suffuses one's totality, inside and out. As this chapter has shown, the emergence of this modern conception of homosexual identity is very closely related to the rise of the modern metropolis; without the anonymity and autonomy afforded by urban life or the establishment of viable gay enclaves within its interstices, the concept of "homosexual" as we know it would not exist.

To bring this chapter to a close, I'd like to turn to some pairings to which the queer modernist fictions I've discussed in the previous pages lend themselves, since these pairings sum up several of the potentials and paradoxes involved in the representation of gay urban space. The setting in Harlem, for example, makes it logical to read Nugent's and Niles's thematics of race in conjunction with each other. Despite the use of the same urban site, however, these two texts highlight the most sharply diverging formal approaches covered in this chapter: Nugent's deployment of a Joycean stream of consciousness to relay his gay subject matter is the most recognizably modernist (and hence, ironically, "mainstream"), while Niles's realist investigation of urban geography is the least overtly experimental (and hence "low-brow") of the four examples of queer modernist practice examined here. And while both Nugent and Niles share a profound interest in creating identifications across categories of racial/sexual difference—hence their contemporary "queerness"—the more fluid depiction of consciousness in Nugent's story yields the more radical destablization of categories, whereas Niles's articulation of cross-identifications tends to expose the slippages that reinstate hierarchies of difference (for example, the way in which racial and female otherness is subordinated to gay otherness on levels of plot and structure). The latter effect also calls to mind one of the major criticisms launched at queer politics and theory today: which others does the term privilege, and which others does its ethos simultaneously render invisible? Nugent's and Niles's contrasting visions are not unrelated to the way in which each narrative treats Harlem as a narrative locus. In "Smoke, Lilies, and Jade" the black city-within-a-city forms the larger frame within which the story's shifting desires and identities unfold, whereas in *Strange Brother* Harlem becomes a space of transit, a passageway that is left behind once it has served its inaugural function. Alex embraces the wholeness of his geographical siting; Mark remains a visitor on its fringes. In this regard, it is telling that the former text represents the *fulfillment* of sexual desire between men, whereas all we get in Niles's novel are Mark's frustrated longings—as a visitor to Harlem and disdainful of the Village, Mark figuratively has no "home" or equivalent psychic space where such desires might reach fruition.

If the Harlem setting creates a thematic link between Nugent's and Niles's texts, so *Nightwood* and *The Young and Evil* share many connections beyond the fact that Barnes and Ford were friends who read and critiqued each other's manuscripts. For these two novels most explicitly link the queer subjectivities they depict to the dispossessed urban sectors of the cities where their characters roam, and in the process their texts become narrative equivalents of these self-contained city spaces where sexual nonconformity is the norm rather than the exception. Significantly, these texts also transform this conjunction of non-normative sexual identity and spatial topography into the basis for the most linguistically experimental and most stylistically avant-garde of the fictions investigated here: in both *Nightwood* and *The Young and Evil* narrative desire is rerouted into what might be called deviant narrative circuits, reconceptualizing textual space and temporality to accommodate the geographical and psychic domains that their protagonists inhabit.

At the same time, however, the radical modernism of these two novels also betrays certain repressions in the form of oversights that anticipate certain aspects of queer theory that have come under attack by some gay and lesbian critics. In *Nightwood,* for instance, the queerness of Barnes's inverted world of the night becomes an entire metaphysics, a universal malady. However empowering it is on one hand to see queerness every-where, on the other hand the *social* implications of being sexually dispos-sessed or oppressed sometimes fade from Barnes's consideration, despite the efforts of sympathetic critics (including myself) to keep them fore-grounded. And Ford and Tyler's sexually and linguistically promiscuous celebration of the random, democratizing flow of queer desire paradoxi-cally leads to a celebration of an elitist (and essentialist) notion of the artist and "high" art that opposes the constructedness of desire so forcefully promulgated on its thematic and structural levels. In both novels, as well, the valorization of the polymorphously perverse that is effected by divorc-ing the reign of eros from conventional morality sets into motion degrees of psychosexual use and abuse that these fictions represent without a full awareness, I suspect, of the negative implications that such power dynam-ics involve. For the reinstitution of psychically wounding hierarchies of domination and oppression is, ironically, one result of the hedonistic valo-rization of sexual and libidinal anarchy. These sadomasochistic tendencies manifest themselves in the heartlessness with which Robin sheds her lovers, as well as in the passive-aggressive behavior that attends her desire to be-long to and yet sever herself from others who care for her; and this coercive dimension of erotic power underlies the amorality that typifies all Ford and Tyler's characters, and that is especially evident in the absolute cal-lowness with which Louis and Gabriel walk over others. We also see the negative repercussions of inhabiting a world where "anything goes" in the abjection of Nora's suffering—creating the illusion that her (specifi-cally) lesbian desire and her (universal) degradation are part of an inescap-able lesbian narrative of damnation—and in the utter masochism with which Karel allows the bullying Louis to denigrate him in ways that seem to script Karel as the stereotypically tragic queen fixated on the heterosex-ual masculinity he cannot possess.

These, however, are also obviously historical as well as literary problems, and they do not detract from the *legitimacy* of the alternate worlds that all these texts—even Niles's depressing account—imagine into being. Like-wise, in so far as it helps make possible the articulation, creation, and insti-tutionalization of queer identities and communities, the anarchy or occa-sional cruelty engendered by such libidinal free play is infinitely preferable to the ideologies of totalitarian control and the eradication of sexual and racial difference looming on the horizon of public consciousness as the euphoria of the jazz age yielded to new historical constraints. These con-straints included, most notably, the economic depression of the 1930s, which lessened the expatriate fervor that made internationalism so vital a part of the queer urban experience I have been describing, and the rise of fascist and totalitarian regimes that increasingly portended global war and holocaust.

I take as an emblem of the intersection of this new era of uncertainty with the queer visions that I have argued constitute a neglected aspect of modernist history the melancholic reflection of one of the characters of Wallace Thurman's gay-inflected Harlem novel *Infants of the Spring:* "I'm one of Gertrude Stein's lost generation . . . or rather post-lost generation. I'm too busy trying to find borderlines in this new universe of ours ever to strike out on my own. I'm afraid of the dark, I suppose." [154] The following chapter turns to one source of the "darkness" halting the bold sexual and textual experimentation that had flourished among the "post-lost generation" of queer modernist writers and artists up to the mid-1930s: the long shadow cast by the rise of European fascism, whose rhetoric of nationalism, racial purity, and heterosexual universality marks a fearful return of the father-figure of patriarchy so emphatically exiled from these queer sites in modernism. In turn, as I will now argue, the resurgence of and transformations in oedipal formulations of narrative in this decade illuminate the psychological, cultural, and novelistic ramifications of the historical rise in paternal authoritarianism and its impact on the modernist attempt to formulate a viable poetics and politics of the perverse.

CHAPTER FIVE

Under the Shadow of Fascism

OEDIPUS, SEXUAL ANXIETY, AND THE DEAUTHORIZING DESIGNS OF PATERNAL NARRATIVE

William Faulkner, Absalom, Absalom!
• • • • •

Christina Stead, The Man Who Loved Children
• • • • •

> Society it seems was a father.
> —Virginia Woolf, *Three Guineas*[1]

> There is too much fathering going on just now and
> there is no doubt about it fathers are depressing.
> —Gertrude Stein, *Everybody's Autobiography*[2]

The specter of paternal fiat has cast a long shadow over the history of western literature, and at least since Freud's adaptation of the Oedipus myth to explain the psychological and gendered development of human subjects, the image of the monolithic, monumental father has also loomed large in the theories of several critics who have attempted to locate the motor of narrative desire, the origins of plot, in the story of Oedipus. "Death of the Father would deprive literature of many of its pleasures," Roland Barthes writes in *The Pleasure of the Text*. "If there is no longer a Father, why tell stories? Doesn't every narrative lead back to Oedipus?" Barthes's supposition that every story is a "staging of the (absent, hidden, hypostatized) father" calculated to whet our appetite "to know, to learn [like Oedipus] the origin and end," has been shared by some of the most important and influential accounts of narrativity to have emerged in the past decade or so. One thinks, for example, of Peter Brooks's brilliant re-appropriation of psychoanalysis for novelistic studies in his theorization of the narrative desires that drive the Freudian masterplot—most typically figured in the genealogical story of failed fathers and rebellious sons—and of Teresa de Lauretis's equally compelling feminist argument that stories inevitably construct their acting subjects as masculine, that is, as mirrors of Oedipus questing for answers to riddles through a text-space inexorably gendered feminine.[3]

In the following pages, however, I would like to suggest not only that we probe a bit further this assumed universality of the oedipal scenario as the basis of all narrative, but also that we pause to ask whether *any* paradigm based on origins can sum up the myriad desires that novelistic fictions engender. Simultaneously, we might ask whether there are specific historical moments—such as the decade preceding the outbreak of the Second World War—in which fictional claims to paternal ubiquity are given greater emphasis than others, and whether such emphases may therefore express cultural as well as fictional anxieties of authority that expose the father's plot as something less than absolute. In other words, might it not be, as Susan Stanford Friedman has suggested, that "the concept of all narrative as necessarily oedipal is a plot *against* narrative," perhaps a plot of the father himself? Following this logic, various feminist theorists over the past decade have begun to propose alternatives to paternally grounded fictional narrative by turning to lyric modes of structuration, Chodorovian theories of preoedipal bonding between mother and daughter, and models of female sexuality, both gay and straight, to describe a female-based textual erotics within the canon of women's fiction.[4] But what would happen were we to scrutinize father-centered fictions with the same diligence, scratching the surface of Oedipus to see what lies beneath? Might there be ways in which even paternal masterplots deauthorize their proclaimed originary power? What is the relationship between this masterplot and modernist fiction, and between the anxieties of authority that each manifests? And how absolute—to continue a line of inquiry begun with the discussion of *Villette* in chapter 1—is de Lauretis's assertion that the female position in such plots can never serve as their motive desire or shaping force, but only as a marker of their limits?

These are some of the questions this chapter explores by examining the political and aesthetic ramifications of the psychosexual and textual perversities set into motion by William Faulkner's *Absalom, Absalom!* (1936) and Christina Stead's *The Man Who Loved Children* (1940), two modernist novels published within a few years of each other that foreground, in overwhelming and often nightmarish detail, the father's brutal exercise of his power—as lawgiver, as namer, as literal and figurative author of being. If Faulkner and Stead reveal an obsession with the relation of authoritarian fatherhood to narrativity, so too the fathers in these textual variants of Southern "modernist gothic" are obsessed with imposing their dominion over the "family texts" they have created; in the process the story of the father's seemingly absolute, shaping power becomes a mirror of larger textual operations that, on a first reading, might appear to confirm Barthes's hypothesis about the origins of all narrative in oedipally engendered struggle. To gain some measure of the sheer intensity with which these two experimentally daring texts foreground and investigate paternity's claim to omnipotence, it might be helpful to think about the quite different representations of fatherhood encountered in the preceding chapters. In *Villette* Lucy Snowe's paternal origin is never named, befitting a text whose "heretical" shape knows no definite origins or ends, whose most powerful characters are women, and whose trajectory inscribes a distinctively female autoerotics. In the turn-of-the-century narratives of sexual awakening examined in chapter 2, the once all-powerful paterfamilias of the Victorian family is exposed as a fraud (just think of the shoulder-padded Colonel of *The Awakening* or the cowardly Rector of *The Virgin and the Gipsy*); these fathers are obsolescent reminders of a past order, their blundering attempts at influence and control never touching the deeper psychosexual currents of their daughters. Even Dora's father, a powerful influence in her formative years, becomes an object of scorn and ineffectuality, doomed to give way to Freud's surrogate authority. The fathers that make an appearance in the modernist texts examined in chapters 3 and 4 are also often figures of failed manhood, or worse, impotence: ever since the death of his son Rudi, *Ulysses*'s Bloom is no longer capable of procreative intercourse, and in *Nightwood* Felix's wish for lineage is ironically countermanded by the birth of a weakling son who, like Rudi Bloom, is doomed to die before his father.[5] In addition, several of the noncanonical queer fictions examined in chapter 4—in which ejection from or rejection of one's birth family is the norm—construct fatherless (and often motherless) narratives. The opening passage of "Smoke, Lilies, and Jade," for example, deliberately stages the death of the father, not to posit him as a narrative origin but to dismiss him altogether from the following account, and *The Young and Evil* cleverly replaces the paradigm of triangulated oedipal desire with a chain of shifting sexual threesomes, creating a circulation of perverse narrative desire that defies the vectors of the Freudian masterplot.

The downplaying of the role of the father in this sampling of fiction is not meant to suggest that the institution of fatherhood or the patriarchal structures supporting it had necessarily fallen out of power, either in the domestic realm of the nuclear family or in the cultural imagination at large, in the first decades of the twentieth century. Indeed, the continual retooling of the middle-class family unit to fit the exigencies of modern technological culture—a process in which Freud's articulation of the oedipal family participated—worked largely to reconsolidate the symbolic, when not literal, dominance of the father in the social hierarchy. And yet the relative inattention to fatherhood in these texts contrasts glaringly with the reappearance of the figure of the seemingly omnipotent, patriarchal father as a subject of heightened social and literary concern in the mid-1930s. This reengagement, reflected in the nearly contemporaneous comments of Woolf and Stein selected as epigraphs to this chapter, was directly related to the emergence, on the international political scene, of an ideology of totalitarian fatherhood within the German and Italian fascist movements. Woolf's reactions provide an illuminating example. For, as Elizabeth Abel has argued, the disturbing sequence of political events in Europe in the late 1930s compelled Woolf, attempting to come to terms with the resurgence of patriarchal dominance that she saw so clearly inscribed in fascist ideology, to reexamine the father-centered aspects of Freudian theory that she had earlier set aside in favor of the mother-centered psychological theories of Melanie Klein.[6] The result of this shift is laid out in *Three Guineas* (1938), which, written as a response to the question of "how to prevent war," creates an explicit link between patriarchal fatherhood and fascist totalitarianism. Audaciously declaring that the "Dictator, as we call him when he is Italian or German, . . . is here among us . . . in the heart of England" (53), Woolf identifies "the black night that now covers Europe" as one with the cry of the father across history, the infantilizing father who in his desire for omnipotence seeks "to keep his daughter in his own power" (141, 132). Hence, Woolf argues, women fight the same enemy in "the tyranny of patriarchal state that you [men] are fighting [in] the tyranny of the Fascist state" (102). Woolf's somber conclusion—that "society it seemed was a father," only more oppressively so than ever—echoes Gertrude Stein's lament one year earlier, in *Everybody's Autobiography* (1937), that "there is too much fathering going on just now and there is no doubt about it fathers are depressing." Like Woolf, Stein links this "depressing" fact to the political scene by representing all world leaders as oppressive patriarchs: "father Mussolini and father Hitler and father Roosevelt and father Stalin and father Lewis and father Blum and father Franco." For Stein, too, the enemy not only resided in Italy or Germany but "at home"—ergo "father Roosevelt."[7]

Despite its willful isolationism during the 1930s, America was not immune to the shadow cast by the rhetoric of the Fatherland; both the wish to distance itself from the monolithic, "bad" Father of fascist politics and the desire to find within the democratic model of nationhood a positive image of domestic paternity fueled an intense national preoccupation with fatherhood on intellectual and popular levels alike; as Stein observed, "there is too much fathering going on just now." Moreover, U.S. culture was not as resistant to the seductions of fascist ideology as many of its citizens liked to believe. As Kathryne V. Lindberg has shown, the very fact of the six-month serialization of Mussolini's pseudo-autobiography in the 1928 *The Saturday Evening Post,* the most influential organ of popular culture in America, attests to the degree that (as Woolf sardonically wrote of England) the "Dictator . . . is . . . here among us"—in this case, the story of his ascent decked out in startlingly all-American images of "Teddy Roosevelt-like manhood," Whitmanesque individual expansiveness, and the Yankee ingenuity of Franklin.[8] The threat—or fantasy—of the literal invasion of America by fascism in the form of a Hitler-like dictator who might, chameleonlike, assume all-American coloration is given expression in Faulkner's *Go Down, Moses* (1940), when a character sardonically says of the nation, "After Hitler gets through with it? Or Smith or Jones or Roosevelt or Wilkie or whatever he will call himself in this country?"[9] Such a scenario becomes, in fact, the plot of Sinclair Lewis's *It Can't Happen Here* (1935), in which a fascist dictator's mesmerizing personality leads to his rise to power in the United States.

Even more to the point, as Laura Doyle's impressive study of the interplay of American eugenics, race politics, and modernist literature reminds us, U.S. culture had long been receptive to what was to become one of the chief tenets of German fascism, the practice of "negative" eugenics. The series of sterilization laws passed in various states between 1907 and 1931—whose overt goal of inhibiting the reproduction of the "unfit" was implicitly designed to secure the racial "purity" of the ruling white elite—became the model that Nazi Germany explicitly imitated and only surpassed in its own 1933 compulsory sterilization law, a move that "[led] one American scientist," as Doyle notes, "to lament that 'the Germans are beating us at our own game.'"[10] Moreover, the simultaneous promulgation in American culture of an ethos of "positive" eugenics, emphasizing the procreative and marital duty of the "pure" race-mother, not only foreshadowed the Nazi propagandistic idealization of submissive Aryan motherhood as the guarantor of nationhood, but also worked to uphold an ideology of patriarchal fatherhood. "Race and woman must not be left to their own devices," wrote one such proponent of eugenics, "Women of Aryan stock must be protected by heroic Aryan males."[11] In the attempt to distance itself from the eventual atrocities committed by Führer in the name of the Fatherland, the American psyche, one might hypothesize, both recognized and disavowed something uncomfortably close to its own collective belief in, and desire for, the primacy of heroic "founding fathers." And it is this unconscious desire for a paternal origin—an origin that is also patriarchal—that both Stead and Faulkner's novels, written under the shadow of fascism and the approach of war, make the subject of their modernist experiments in form.

In *The Man Who Loved Children*, set in Tidewater Virginia in 1936, the link between "benevolent" fatherhood, American race patriarchy, and the rise of European fascism becomes explicit in the title character Sam Pollit's advocacy of a system of state-controlled eugenics to his young children. To amuse his captive audience, he describes his personal vision of utopic society (named, tellingly, *Monoman* or *Manunity*), which he argues will be made perfect by "weed[ing] out the misfits and degenerates"[12]—in other words, by eradicating all those signifiers of difference that call into question the homogeneous "unity" of "man" (*Man/unity*). The fascistic underpinnings of Sam's vision of eugenic control, and its relation to this all-

American father's engulfing paternal egotism—his "*Monoman*-ia," as we shall see—emerge in his bald admiration of totalitarian regimes. He brags to his daughter Louie's school friend Clare that "if I had my way—if I were a Stalin or Hitler, Clarigold—I would abolish school altogether for children like you and Looloo, and would form them into communities with a leader, something like I am myself, a natural leader" (352). Sam also tells his children that if he were "autocrat of all nations," he would kill off nine-tenths of the population "to make room for the fit," a task that Stead uncannily and presciently has him say he would achieve "by gas attacks on people living ignorant of their fate in selected areas, a type of eugenic concentration-camp" (372).

Published in 1936, the year in which Stead's novel is set, *Absalom, Absalom!* unfolds the tale of another father's equally monomaniacal urge for absolute dominion in a parallel period of national crisis and racial division—in this case, the decades encompassing the American war between the states that the character Rosa Coldfield repeatedly refers to as a "holocaust."[13] Even though various leftist critics of the 1930s and early 1940s, as Robert H. Brinkmeyer Jr., has noted, charged that "Faulkner's imagination flirts with fascism,"[14] Faulkner's text has, curiously enough, never been read as an allegory of or even implicit commentary on the rise of European fascism. In part this may be because the novel's mythicizing and universalizing tendencies—apparent in its presentation of history as cyclical repetition—seem to eclipse "real" history altogether, even the historical specificity of the Civil War that sets Sutpen's downfall into motion (thus its battlefield scenes, in which Sutpen confronts his son Henry, are most often compared to Greek tragedy). And yet, ironically, this collapsing of historical epochs to evoke a cyclic or static conception of time (such that the biblical paradigm of King David and his sons becomes the story of Sutpen and his children, which in turn becomes the story of the Compson family in the narrative frame) is not unlike the fascist interpretation of history, which hinges on a belief in the transhistoricity of the Aryan nation—hence its immutable destiny. Such a cyclic or mythic view of history is also intrinsic to the nostalgic mythicizing of the agrarian South and its *Volk,* as well as to the cyclical blurring of past and present by its multiple storytellers, that Faulkner's narrative at once recreates *and* counters by recording the patriarch Thomas Sutpen's failed dream of creating a great dynasty of sameness, a lineage of "pure" little Sutpens. And if the grand design, the already predetermined blueprint, that Sutpen ruthlessly attempts bto impose on others has suggestive affinities with Hitler's monomaniacal plot to implement a "final solution" that would ensure the racial purity of the German family-state, so too the very monumentality of Sutpen's superhuman effort to transform his dream into a lasting edifice, a work of art, echoes in intriguing ways the aestheticization of politics by which Walter Benjamin claims fascist ideology gained its popular base of support.[15] Also in common with fascistic ideology, Sutpen practices his own version of racial and sexual eugenics as a means of securing his vision of a pure dynasty, casting off his supposedly black son Charles Bon and proposing to breed with Rosa Coldfield before marrying her to make sure she can produce the legitimate son his scheme demands.[16]

Despite the suggestiveness of these analogues, it is not my intention in this chapter to read either of these novels as parables of fascism per se, but to suggest that their grappling with "universal" issues of fatherhood and patriarchy cannot be separated from their grounding in a politicized moment in history that subtly inflects the sexual/textual politics of Faulkner and Stead. Likewise, theoretical claims to the ubiquity or universality of the "plot of the father" as a determinant of narrative cannot ignore, entirely, the degree to which such literary plots and theories themselves have historical determinants. To return to the era of the 1930s, one might suggest that the "shadow" cast by the burgeoning rhetoric of fascism, Führer, and Fatherland—and here I intend the word *shadow* to indicate the ineffable and subconscious as well as conscious effects of such a discourse—is precisely what created among some modernist writers an active, if anxious, reengagement with father-centered fictional plots—a reengagement that, in bringing the mythic oedipal paradigm to the fore as a possible explanatory model of narrative desire, also places that paradigm under its greatest stress and challenge.

For the next few pages, I would like to look more closely at the related psychological mechanisms underlying Thomas Sutpen's and Sam Pollit's claims to textual/sexual authority and creative/procreative fiat, in order to see what Faulkner's and Stead's representations of fatherhood reveal about the intertwined dictates of sexuality, narrative, and psychology motivating their modernist reworkings—or, more evocatively, perversions—of the patriarchal plot of fatherhood. To examine these psychological mechanisms will go some way, I hope, in attempting to posit an implicit answer to the question that Klaus Theweleit's study of fascism and masculinity asks: namely, how did a "specifically masculine organization of life—in short, 'patriarchy' . . . —use fascism to ensure its own survival?" (89). Despite the different time periods in which the two novels are set, both make painfully immediate, through narrative techniques that we will examine shortly, the will-to-power of two fathers who share a nearly identical obsession that fuels all their mental fantasies and material schemes: that of generation, of *producing* generations, as an exercise of their patriarchal privilege as namebearers and at the expense—or neglect—of the women who actually bear their namesakes. There are, to be sure, some differences. Sutpen's goal, like his presence, is more abstract—to create a male dynasty that will immortalize his name forever—and Sam's more tangible—to envelop himself in the daily materiality of his children, sons and daughters alike. But for both fathers the *psychological* impetus is the same: to use their progeny as a means of imposing their ego—"the citadel of the central I-Am's private own," as one of Faulkner's characters puts it (139), or the "Great I-Am" as Henny Pollit calls Sam (165)—on a recalcitrant external world, recreating its threatening otherness, its difference, in their own image. Both men thus practice what Luce Irigaray has identified as a specular logic of the same, striving to confirm their autonomy, power, and superiority as men and fathers by producing offspring who will seamlessly mirror their desires back to them: sameness begetting the same.[17]

By envisioning themselves as the autonomous creators of their own dynasties, moreover, both Sutpen and Sam effectively *treat their families as texts,* subject to their authorial whims and control: as such, both men might be said not only to exist *within* but be producers *of* oedipal narrative. And yet, fascinatingly, these family texts, these paternal designs, prove inherently self-subverting; they not only unravel themselves, but they do so in ways that exceed the generational rebelliousness of child against parent that critics like Barthes and Brooks have taught us to expect in examples of oedipally plotted fictional narrative. In fact, the frayed designs of the fathers in *Absalom, Absalom!* and *The Man Who Loved Children* should begin to make us suspicious of the way in which western cultural institutions have forced a duplicitous link between the materials of male procreativity and critical metaphors of narrativity, a link as duplicitous in its way as the rhetorical bridge that fascist politics created between fatherhood as a biological state and the State as the Fatherland. For the fictions of interiority that Faulkner and Stead finally narrate, once we read through and into the various lacunae punctuating them, end up being less a demonstration of the ubiquity of the father's power than of the concrete and ever-present threats to paternal ubiquity that strip the father's story of its status as origin and end of meaningful narrative. The self-proclaimed authority of both Sutpen and Sam reveals itself to be not an abstract universal but a highly ambiguous construction, one founded on a profound anxiety about the meaning of authoritarian patriarchal masculinity, and this anxiety suffuses their all-too-tangible identity as men, as sexual beings, and as fathers for whom the status of paternity must always be ambivalent rather than assured—for fatherhood, as Stephen Dedalus puts it in *Ulysses,* remains a "legal fiction" founded upon "incertitude" (170).

And these are anxious narratives, indeed, if the sheer frustration that their modernist styles and modes of narration provoke in many readers is any reliable indication. However much one may praise Faulkner's achievement, for instance, one can hardly deny the extreme perversity, the downright irritability at times, of his modernist self-reflexivity and indeterminacy: readers inevitably find themselves trapped in a labyrinth of repeating stories, proliferating viewpoints, and multiple interpretations that remain frustratingly incomplete, irresolvable, and partial. Similarly, the overbearing verbosity of Sam Pollit in *The Man Who Loved Children,* burdening the narrative with a solipsistic discourse that is as exasperating as it is exhausting, threatens to keep some readers from finishing the book. Admittedly, all stories by definition provoke some degree of anxiety, temporarily frustrating us with detours and digressions in order to heighten our anticipation of their resolutions; and modernist writing elevates this waywardness into a narrative principle of deliberate complication (as in Joyce's and Woolf's associative patterns of logic) and frustration (as in Stein's use of repetition). The monologic verbosity that threatens the readability of *Absalom, Absalom!* and *The Man Who Loved Children*, however, plays out this tendency to an extreme that points to the anxieties and frustrations embedded in their historically specific representations of paternal authority. For in both novels this anxiety-producing verbosity takes on a coloration, as it were, that can be distinguished from general modernist stylistics. In *Absalom, Absalom!* the sonorous cadence of Southern storytelling that we generally associate with Faulknerian narration is blended with—deliberately, I suggest—another tonality common to Southern political oratory: that of the demagogue, whose rabid pontifications of racial superiority and regionalist insularity, of blood and soil, are geared, not unlike the unstoppable staccato of the words that fill *Mein Kampf,* to appeal to and give expression to the visceral emotions of wounded pride, hatred, and inferiority of the defeated American Southern agrarian community or *Volk.*[18] In Faulkner's novel, traces of this alternately mesmerizing and badgering voice pervade the rhythms of the third-person voice as well as the spoken dialogue and quoted thoughts of each speaker, including Sutpen; in Stead's novel, this demagogic vocality is more specifically located in Sam Pollit's ranting speeches and sermons to his captive audience, his children. The fact that Sam's great aspiration is to have his own radio show—where he can become, in the persona of "Uncle Sam," the invisible voice of America—eerily echoes the mastery of sound waves for propagandistic uses that Hitler himself was perfecting in the same era to exhort and drill his "national progeny" into compliance and submission, via the enhanced technology of the loudspeaker and the radio broadcast.[19] Analyzing the "compulsion" of the type of the fascist leader "to speak incessantly," Theodor Adorno has discerningly noted, in terms that certainly apply to Sam's voice and the voice of Southern demagoguery in general, that "language itself, devoid of its rational significance, functions in a magical way and furthers those archaic regressions which reduce individuals to members of crowds."[20] And if the main tactic of fascist rhetoric is to appeal to the desire of the masses to close ranks in solidarity against the incursions of those "on the outside," as Adorno puts it, the primary source of the anxiety that underlies Sutpen's and Sam's verbal tirades and acts of domination also involves precisely the socially and politically repressed elements of their plots, all those unwonted reminders and hidden signifiers of otherness or nonmaleness—female sexuality, racial difference, latent homosexuality, daughter-texts—that their dynastic schemes have been constructed to subdue or contain. But despite such efforts at containment, these subversive elements *do* escape the father's fascistic plotting, and, in the form of the return of the textually repressed, threaten to wreck his transcendent designs and call into question the invisible, hypostatized authority upon which his identity as the superior sex and superior race rests.

For the reader attentive to the psycho-political dynamics of gender, race, and sexuality in this century's fictional and cultural narratives of modernity, as well as for the literary theorist in search of Oedipus, the result of such textual maneuvers is profoundly important. For these "escaped" strands of narrative reconstitute, reorder, our perception of where we've been and what we (might mistakenly think we) have been reading: that which confronts us is no longer "simply" an oedipal retelling, for the paternal design has been deauthorized, shown to be illusory even in its supposed origin. Out of such rereadings, a much more tangible, pathological, and even vulnerable father, stripped of his guises and abstractions, his powerful absences and preordained plots, may emerge—a father whose material presence immediately problematizes, indeed politicizes, the cultural ethos that constructs fatherhood as a heroic if doomed narrative, and a father whose story is always other than the specularity of his self-representation would have us believe.

WILLIAM FAULKNER, *ABSALOM, ABSALOM!*
CREATION BY THE FATHER'S FIAT

I didn't realize until Hitler got into the newspapers that I had created a Nazi before he did.
—William Faulkner to Malcolm Crowley [21]

. . . all boy flesh that walked and breathed stemming from that one ambiguous eluded dark fatherhead and so brothered perennial and ubiquitous everywhere under the sun—
—William Faulkner, *Absalom, Absalom!* (299)

Given Faulkner's resentment at having been labeled a "Gothic fascist" by critics of the literary left in the 1930s, his boast to his editor that he created Nazism before Hitler—"I invented him in 1931," he says in reference to a character in *Light in August*—is more than a little ambiguous: who, after all, would want to be claimed as the father of fascism? Prominent among those accusing Faulkner of promulgating a literary version of fascist ideology was Maxwell Geismar, the author of the influential tome *Writers in Crisis* (1942), where he argued that blacks and women had become Faulkner's scapegoats for all the vitriol and hatred he felt toward the forces of history and social conscience slowly eroding the ethos of the Old South.

Despite the modernism of Faulkner's form, Geismar argued, the writer was part of the antimodern revolt "from which fascism [also] stems," working within "the larger tradition of reversionary, neo-pagan, and neurotic discontent" driving European fascism.[22]

Judgments such as Geismar's, however, need to be read in the context of the period and the circumstances that produced them; throughout the 1930s and early 1940s, as Robert H. Brinkmeyer Jr., has amply demonstrated, national patriotism in the United States tended to associate Southern regionalism with a mode of "antidemocratic parochialism" that was viewed as tantamount to the "fanatical nationalism embraced by fascist countries."[23] W. J. Cash's classic *The Mind of the South* (1940), for instance, makes an explicit equation between outbreaks of mob violence in the South and those rampant in "Fascist Italy, in Nazi Germany, and in Soviet Russia," and Katherine DuPre Lumpkin in *The South in Progress* (1940) equates the racist rhetoric used by the Ku Klux Klan with that of National Socialist anti-Semitic propaganda. Even one of the defenders of the South, Richard M. Weaver, claiming it to be the bastion of the democratic tradition, nonetheless concedes in "The South and the Revolution of Nihilism" (1944) that "one of the obvious features" of an agrarian culture irrationally attached to its "belief in the influence of blood and soil" and the "glorification of the martial spirit" (the ironic legacy of the region's defeat in the civil war) is the degree to which "Southern whites considered themselves *Herrenvolk* in relation to the Negro."[24] Ironically, simply because of his Southern roots, settings, and subject matter, Faulkner was regularly classified as a merely "regional" writer by literary critics throughout the 1930s, a designation that gave critics like Geismar an excuse to collapse their general political critiques of Southern regionalism into their interpretations of an author who happened to represent this region; indeed, as Lawrence H. Schwartz has argued, it was only *after* Faulkner was "reinterpreted" as a writer of "universal" rather than "local" themes in the latter 1940s that his critical reputation soared.[25] In fact, not only may Faulkner's fiction be read as a devastating critique of the very parochialism, authoritarianism, and ethos of blood purity that his critics associated with fascist politics, but in 1938 the author donated his typescript of *Absalom, Absalom!* to a relief fund for Spanish loyalists, and he went on public record with the League of American Writers in expressing his opposition to the rising tide of fascist oppression throughout Europe.[26]

If the typescript of *Absalom, Absalom!* thus materially entered the explicit realm of the international politics of the late 1930s, the motivating spirit behind those written words may be said, albeit less consciously and more circuitously, to have already ventured into the same arena; Faulkner's boast that he had in effect "created" Hitler in advance of the man himself (in the character of Percy Grimes) might be even more appropriately applied to Thomas Sutpen, the mythically powerful, charismatic, yet dreaded protagonist of *Absalom, Absalom!* (1936). The fact that the novel charts the failure of Sutpen's overweening ambitions and dictatorial paternalism, does not, of course, in itself provide an answer to Faulkner's political sympathies or the lingering traces of textual authoritarianism that some readers have sensed in his fiction. But they do help us refocus the issue, realizing that the question of whether Faulkner entertained a "flirtation with fascism"— as Geismar claimed—is less important than recognizing the degree to which the shadow of fascism had already entered the American cultural psyche and its literary manifestations in the decade which saw Hitler's and Mussolini's rise to power. And the vehicle of that entry, as I will now trace in more detail, was the revived interest among writers such as Faulkner in stories of the father, of his mythic powers over his progeny, and of his creative fiat—stories that reach back to Oedipus and forward to Freud's diagnosis of modern civilization's discontents and his analysis of the psychology of mass movements in *Group Psychology and the Analysis of the Ego* (1922).

Set in the strife-torn American South in the decades surrounding the Civil War, *Absalom, Absalom!* slowly and elliptically unfolds the legend of the larger-than-life Thomas Sutpen—a man without a past who arrives godlike in Yoknapatawpha County, Mississippi in 1833 out of nowhere, takes up land, builds a magnificent house, and sets about creating a dynasty. The history of this mythic progenitor is unfolded through a quintessentially modernist sequence of multiple, overlapping, interweaving, often nonsynchronous narrative voices whose verbose flow of words keeps the ghost of Sutpen alive in 1909, the present time of the narration. These narrators include old Rosa Coldfield, who summons young Quentin Compson to her house to tell him her embittered version of the Sutpen legend; Quentin's father, who reveals to his son parts of the story passed down to him from his father and parts as he himself poetically imagines them to have occurred; and Quentin and his college roommate Shreve, who create "out of the rag-tag and bob-ends of old tales and talking" (303) their own fiction of what might have happened. Adding to the novel's notorious difficulty is the fact that some of this information is conveyed to the reader in dialogue, some in (often italicized) interior monologues, some in thought patterns conveyed in indirect free discourse, and some in breathless, run-on passages of third-person narration that take on the characteristics usually associated with interiorized stream-of-consciousness narrative. Hence, although the ghost of Sutpen is everywhere in the text as a linguistic trace, the actual sequence, to say nothing of the "truth," of his life story and motivations remains maddeningly difficult to grasp. Like these narrators, we are forced as readers actively to construct our own version of Sutpen—and in this participatory effort, the shadow that Sutpen's "ambiguous eluded dark fatherhead" casts over his progeny also threatens to make us accomplices in perpetuating his name and fiat, as well as the transmitters of the dangerously reactionary poetics and politics embedded in his paternal plots.

Masochistic Narrators and Godly Masterplots

Those readers of *Absalom, Absalom!* left frustrated by Faulkner's elliptical narration may take comfort in the fact that the novel's narrators find themselves left in equal states of frustration, fated to repeat a story that refuses to die. "That was all. Or rather, not all," Rosa Coldfield says of her version of the Sutpen myth, "since there is no all, no finish" (150). This open-endedness makes for a particularly masochistic narrative erotics, both in regard to its tellers and to the psychosexual complexities that underlie the subject of their protracted telling. But what, exactly, are the investments of Rosa, Mr. Compson, and Quentin and Shreve in retelling this already-told legend, and what can their proliferating interpretations of Sutpen's life tell us, in turn, about the self-subverting plot of the father enacted in this novel? Quite a bit, I suggest, once we look at their urge to narrate in light of Freud's conjectures about the human compulsion to repeat repressed or traumatic psychic materials as a means of exorcising the tyranny of the past. To Rosa, Mr. Compson, and Quentin, at least, the myth of Sutpen is not simply a fascinating source of endless speculation but a specific threat to be expunged. Each of their retellings hence becomes, in a real sense, a fight to master a story that threatens to master them. For Sutpen represents to these narrators, as he does within his own plot, an authority figure whose interdiction, like that of all fathers, appears irrevocable, "perennial and ubiquitous everywhere under the sun" (299), when in fact his powers of persuasion have always been backed by a strong arm. In the psychodrama of narrative transference that ensues, therefore, Rosa, Mr. Compson, and Quentin weave their tales to ward off what they intuitively sense to be the castrating power of this demonic, now absent, but still ever-powerful father—the "dreaded primal father" of the primal horde, "towards whom only a passive-masochistic attitude is possible, to whom one's will has to be surrendered." [27]

Simultaneously, however, their narrations reveal a paradoxical investment in *not* mastering this story, in letting it continue without end. At least subconsciously, all three tellers repeat (and listen to and then repeat again) Sutpen's story as a way of putting their own lives on hold, of postponing a confrontation with present-day reality. Examining their compulsion to repeat from this perspective begins to shed light on how intimately their roles as narrators are linked to the sexual anxieties that drive Faulkner's entire enterprise. The example of Rosa is the most complex, a point to which I will return, but in terms of the narrative's initial representation of her "lonely thwarted old female flesh embattled for forty-three years in the old insult" (14) of virginity, her narration is presented as the garrulous outpouring of a spinster's "impotent yet indomitable frustration." Talk has become her only way of wreaking vengeance upon the "long-dead object" (7) of her hatred, Sutpen, for having jilted her those forty-three years before. Rosa's constant recapitulation of Sutpen's affront and insult simultaneously becomes an eroticized substitute for the life that she claims has ended in that past moment and an eerie reflection of her continued sexual frustration, which, caught up in a past-without-end, can never resolve itself. The world-weary Mr. Compson, in contrast, uses the saga of Sutpen's dynasty as a pretext for indulging in decadent fantasies of desire whose dilatory narration allows him to avoid the reality of his present dynasty's decline and his impotence to do anything to halt it. For Quentin, too, the sexual and textual are inextricably, masochistically, linked: by relaying to Shreve the incestuous triangle formed by Sutpen's progeny, Quentin allows himself to participate verbally in the incestuous desires that he too harbors (for his sister Caddy) yet fears to initiate.[28] Internalizing his inaction as a failure of manhood, Quentin turns to the erotics of narrating, as do Rosa and his father, as a substitute for the erotic fulfillment that is missing in his life.

If these methods of postponement, of infinitely delayed climax, shed light on the *whence* of Faulkner's formal experiments with repeating, layered perspectives, the psychosexual anxieties that underlie the narrators' deferrals of completed story simultaneously point to the existential—and quintessentially modern—landscape in which such doomed efforts at repetition unfold. The defeated and divided state of the South becomes a microcosm for the post–World War I Eliotic wasteland itself. For Faulkner's narrators occupy an emptied-out world, a world characterized by belatedness and haunted by the impossibility of bridging the gap between truth and its record, meaning and its expression, signified and signifier. This condition, *the* condition of modernity, is evoked in an image of Quentin's self-division and consequent alienation that occurs at the novel's beginning; finding himself divided into "two separate Quentins" (9) as he listens to Rosa's tale, Quentin senses that "his very body was an empty hall echoing with sonorous defeated names; he was [no longer] a being, an entity . . . [but] a barracks filled with stubborn back-looking ghosts" (12). So, too, with *Absalom, Absalom!*'s narrative structure, another kind of echo-chamber haunted by "garrulous outraged baffled ghosts" (9), its seemingly endless repetitions attesting to the fact that neither words, nor language, nor story can ever retrieve anything from the past but those ghostly absences that are already its only present reality; in the wake of this void, all that remains is repetition, secondariness, perpetual speculation. The result for the narrators, caught and *caught up* in the empty, echoing halls of their labyrinthine attempts to explain the mystery of Sutpen's dominion, is a sense of unrelieved frustration that mirrors, on the thematic level, the text's continual deferral of meaning on its formal and linguistic levels. In what could be a gloss on Faulkner's representation of the obdurate open-endedness of modern experience and modernist narrative, Rosa concludes her rumination on the fact that there is no end, "*no all, no finish*" to Sutpen's story with the thought, "*It is not the blow we suffer from but the tedious repercussive anticlimax of it*" (150).

The "tedious repercussive anticlimax" of lives doomed to "no finish," to an irreparable separation between the word and the thing, helps explain the masochism that links the textual and sexual erotics of the narratives of Rosa, Mr. Compson, and Quentin. But this explanation does not yet answer a related question: What are the anxieties hidden within Sutpen's story that so powerfully summon forth the doomed narrative desires of these story-tellers? To begin to answer this question, we need to look more closely at Sutpen's desire to be the omniscient, omnipotent author of his personal history, for he often treats his life as if it were a plot-in-progress, a narrative "design" that already exists as a Platonic whole in his mind. "You see, I had a design in my mind" (263), he will repeatedly explain to General Compson, his one confidant and Quentin's grandfather. To be sure, whatever expressions of desire or intention that this text presents as Sutpen's own are filtered through three generations of narrators and hence liable to profound distortion and mythologization. Significantly, however, the repeated trope of Sutpen as a maker of "designs" originates in the two episodes in chapter 7 in which Sutpen tells his story in his own words to General Compson (who passes it on to Mr. Compson and thence on to Quentin); both occasions are presented as the text's most nearly unmediated moments of access to Sutpen's thoughts. And as far as this would-be creator is concerned, the "plan" or blueprint that already exists as a "whole" (274) in his mind only awaits physical realization or consummation. The operative words here are "physical" and "consummation," since Sutpen's design more precisely depends on creating a dynasty of sons who will immortalize, monumentalize, his name. Sutpen wishes to become the author, that is, of nothing less than a paternal plot—or, in Peter Brooks's terminology, an explanatory myth of origins and endings that will at once give his identity retrospective significance and proleptic authority. "You see, I had a design," his confession to General Compson continues, "To accomplish it I should require money, a house, slaves, a family, . . . [and] incidentally, of course, a wife" (263).

Likewise, the Sutpen legend inherited and embellished by Jefferson's community of tellers also attests to the powerful stakes involved in Sutpen's self-assumed status as founding father of his own nation-kingdom and author of his familial design. In Rosa's estimation, Sutpen is a consummate if demonic master artist who orchestrates his godlike arrival in Jefferson as high mythic drama, willing the plantation called Sutpen's Hundred out of swampland, marrying into respectability, begetting his family. The biblical allusions that Rosa's narrative uses to describe Sutpen's imperialist enterprise only accentuate his self-appointed pose as archetypal, disembodied Father-Creator who exists outside or at the origins of human time. Not only does he seem to summon a world into being "out of the soundless Nothing . . . like the oldentime *Be Light*" (9), but he remains, like the unspeakable, indivisible divinity of Jehovah, "not articulated in this world" (171). This tendency of others to see Sutpen as the actor in his own time-less creation-myth allows Sutpen, ironically, to create the aura of existing outside the historical and political moment that in fact offers him the means to his dominance, an illusion that in turn—as in the fascist mythi-cization of German destiny—proleptically guarantees the community's assent to his totalizing design as not only inevitable but immutable. Com-plementing the role of divinity Sutpen assumes as creator, his human incar-nation conjures forth the first man in his unfallen state, the original patri-arch Adam who is the sole "namer" of his progeny and possessions: "He named them all himself: all his own get and all the get of his wild niggers . . . naming with his own mouth his own ironic fecundity" (61–62). Nam-ing others, he metaphorically as well as literally controls their very exis-tence, subduing their independent differences by making them reflections of his all-imposing omnipotence as their begetter.

Underlying the authorial control that Sutpen attempts to exert over his design, then, is the transcendent desire "to make his position impregnable" (15). And yet, as Faulkner's wording ironically betrays, the only means to this abstract ideal of impregnability is by the very *real* sexual act of impreg-nation. Hence the narrative's accounts of Sutpen's creative enterprise—even before his marriage to Ellen Coldfield—are constantly imbued with phallic imagery. Hyperbolically described as a "thunderclap" orgiastically "abrupt[ing]" upon the scene (8), he claims his "virgin" land (40) in an act of archetypally masculine aggression, "overrun[ning] the astonished earth" in a sexualized conquest that is a violent act of usurpation (8). Analogously, the Sutpen of communal legend penetrates the Coldfield sanctum to claim his virgin bride "with the abruptness of a tornado" that wreaks "irrevocable and incalculable damage" (47) and is gone. Always appearing to others to "project himself ahead," as if "in some fierce dynamic rigidity of impa-tience" (159) to consummate his design—a rigidity evocative of Thewe-leit's account of the soldier male—Sutpen effectively masquerades as the phallus; even the terms of his decline and death remain unapologetically and mythically phallic. Repudiated by his one legitimate son, Henry, he sets out to father an illegitimate one, his attitude likened to "an old worn-out cannon which realizes that it can deliver just one more fierce shot" (181), and that "next time there might not be enough powder for . . . a full-sized load" (279).

The male act of sexual impregnation, as all this exaggerated, disturb-ingly violent phallic imagery would seem to indicate, is fraught with more anxiety and uncertainty than Sutpen or the inheritors of his myth might care to acknowledge; until the symbolic father proves he also has a body, that the abstract word can indeed be made flesh, his dream of an "impregnable" position is left open to constant challenge (tellingly, Sutpen confides to General Compson that he has remained a virgin till his first marriage as a "part of the design which I had in my mind" [248]). Thus, when his final plot to sire a male heir by Milly Jones misfires, as it were, it is appropriate that Sutpen meets his death in an act of symbolic castration, felled by the scythe that Milly's incensed grandfather raises against him: one thwarted Bearer of the Phallus topples another in an act of now-meaningless conquest.

Plainly, it is neither old-fashioned lust nor romance that prompts Sutpen's phallic aggressiveness. A much more abstract, narcissistic desire motivates his monomaniacal urge to procreate, for Sutpen essentially conceives of his "family plot" as an extension of his own ego, a blueprint for imposing and imprinting his identity on all his surroundings. Paternity, like the godly power of naming, becomes a way of subsuming one's anxieties about authority by rendering one's possessions miniature, hence inferior and less threatening, versions of oneself. As Adorno says, "The libidinal pattern of fascism and the entire technique of fascist demagogues are authoritarian."[29] Given such an overwhelming and solipsistic imperative, the authority of fatherhood inevitably becomes sadistic, for Sutpen's entire sense of himself rests on the psychic, when not physical, violation and penetration of the identities of all his dependents—whether his wife, children, slaves, or, on a textual level, the narrators and readers who inherit his story.

Sutpen's anxious desire for complete mastery over his story, his paternal text, however, turns on a very ambiguous relation to the Southern caste system he purports to uphold. Only at the novel's midpoint do we learn, via his retrospective explanation to General Compson, that Sutpen's entire design springs from humiliations undergone as an adolescent, turned away from the front door of *his* master's plantation as poor white trash by a "monkey-dressed nigger butler" (231). In effect, the rest of Sutpen's life is spent—and here sexual, social, and psychological meanings of the word *spend* interpenetrate—in a series of violent entries to make up for this one barred threshold; class, race, and gender come together in a devastating illumination of the very specific anxieties underpinning this father's desire for an identity based on *disembodied* authority rather than the *all-too-embodied* inferiority he has felt as a youth. In Brinkmeyer's terms, Sutpen ironically occupies both the position of thematic fascist (in his driving ambition to succeed by ruthless means) and the structural Jew (the pariah never fully accepted into the Southern society to which he pays court).[30] Designed to cover over the vulnerability briefly exposed in this childhood experience of shaming, Sutpen's paternal plot thus turns out to be a compensatory narrative, one that tries not merely to explain his origins, but to explain *away* the ignominy of his beginnings by means of his more successful ends. The vicissitudes of temporality and location are more involved in Sutpen's transhistorical scheme than he wishes to admit.[31]

All this may have begun to sound like the stuff of a classically oedipal narrative—the father who was once an ashamed son begets sons who in turn rebel against him—a narrative, moreover, with specifically American analogues, given the Republic's "oedipal" revolution against its parent country. When, however, we look more closely at the narratological implications of Sutpen's attempt to give shape to the plot his own life, something rather different begins to emerge. For as an artist, Sutpen is so fixated on the final product—establishing a genealogy that will immortalize his single-handed rise to an "impregnable" position of authority—that he forgets the necessary "middle" that constitutes the very substance of narrative plot, the living "middle" that is always and necessarily transgressive, a deviation from the straight line that in linking the beginning and end would obviate the need for "story." In narrative terms, that is, Sutpen neglects metonymy, the flow of events that is the means to an end, in favor of metaphor, the illumination conferred by the end itself. And this oversight critically dooms Sutpen's aesthetic design, precisely because, like all plots of the father, life is *not*, in the final measure, a written text, however much patriarchy or totalitarian regimes may treat it as such; Sutpen's story will have no final illumination until it is *over*, leaving him quite literally unable to ratify its "meaning."[32]

Hence, by definition lacking the retrospective vision of a completed whole, Sutpen is actually too involved in the making of his history to be either the removed, omniscient author that he impersonates or the all-powerful abstraction whose disembodied law he would have his subjects obey without question. Nor is Sutpen's premature determination of his "ends" his only oversight. He also fails to see that the very goal, the fixed metaphor, toward which he drives is itself contrary to the stasis he desires. For the achievement of a genealogy of Sutpens-in-perpetuity, far from being final, must necessarily remain metonymic, depending on a continuing line of generations which must occur *in* time, not out of time. Sutpen's desire to summon into creative being the "fixed goal in his mind" (53), whose meaning Sutpen has already determined, will always escape his impositions since he, a living man, cannot freeze history into a final shape while it is still in the process of unfolding.[33]

Unruly Children, or Sons in Love

Most obvious among the transgressive elements disturbing the synchronic reading of the "end" that Sutpen attempts to impose on the narrative "middle" of his paternal plot are, of course, his children. Male and female, black and white—the straight and pure line of patronymic descent that Sutpen means to create deviates rather wildly from his Platonic intentions.

The case of his two sons is particularly telling. Sutpen's entire masterplot, after all, depends on male progeny, yet neither son fits comfortably into his plan, and each, in falling victim to the paternal design, becomes a catalyst precipitating its ultimate destruction. Sutpen's legitimate heir Henry quite simply repudiates his birthright, choosing fraternity with his illegitimate half-brother Charles Bon over fealty to his father. Forcing a break in Sutpen's design by depriving him of his heir, Henry effectively abandons the family text, and he returns only to die and bring the House of Sutpen to an apocalyptic close more final than any of Sutpen's projected ends. However, as the very fact of Henry's return home at the end of his life suggests, his revolt against Sutpen's command has never really ceased, nor have his acts of defiance ever entirely escaped the Law of the Father. Eventually murdering Charles, the beloved brother for whom he has repudiated his inheritance, Henry in fact executes "the office of the outraged father's pistol-hand" (179), perversely fulfilling Sutpen's desire while thwarting his own. In the vicious circle of patriarchal logic in which Henry finds himself trapped (doomed to rebel against, yet serve his father), we seem to have the most unadulterated evidence of a strand of oedipal narrative at work in Faulkner's text: according to classic Freudian theory, sons wish to replace the father but do so by acceding to the father's law, learning to wield the same phallic power. Yet the fact is that Henry does not *simply* become Sutpen or, for that matter, a representative of phallic authority. Self-exiled to an unknown plot, a figurative no-man's land outside the text where he exists under an alias as a non-Sutpen,[34] he becomes an emblem of an element of (in)difference that Sutpen's design cannot control; simultaneously refusing the rules of male procreativity (as far as we know, he sires no heirs) *and* creativity (by becoming a creative absence), Henry in his small way reveals the "outraged father's pistol-hand" to be no more than an "outrage": a victimizing authority whose only law is violent coercion of others.

If the son Henry comes to repudiate his father, in a chiasmic reversal, the father Sutpen has already rejected his firstborn son, Charles Bon, for not being "adjunctive or incremental to the design which [he] had in mind" (240)—the consequence of Sutpen's belated discovery that Eulalia Bon, his first wife, is partially black. As the taint which Sutpen's plot attempts to discharge, Bon represents a return of that plot's textually repressed contents when he appears at the door of Sutpen's Hundred as Henry's best friend. But the repressed in Sutpen's design, the already written that cannot be erased, is not only this son's blackness. It is also Sutpen's own unconscious, governed, as we have already seen, by a pathology of lack and need that reaches back to that fateful day when he was denied access to his master's plantation and made so painfully aware of his own inferiority in a white man's world of power. Thus, it is ironically appropriate that the specter of the "boy-symbol . . . on the outside of a white door" (261) that was once Sutpen himself makes its return in the *very body* of Sutpen's disenfranchised son, knocking (as Sutpen once did) at the entrance to a plantation that is now Sutpen's; and this incursion of the past into the present introduces an element of repetition into the father's fiction of progress that subverts its desired linearity. The successful transcendence of origins for which Sutpen has plotted so long and hard cannot, after all, cover over its narrative beginnings in a boy's anxiety-striken crisis of identity.

The self-defeating nature of authority derived from such ambiguous origins is exposed by Sutpen's reaction to this unwanted reminder of the past. In refusing to acknowledge his kinship to Bon, the mirror-image of his youth, Sutpen denies, in a literal as well as figurative sense, his own flesh and blood. As such, Bon's return catastrophically threatens to disrupt Sutpen's plot. But at the same time, Sutpen's overshadowing presence deprives this son's life of any retrospective ordering perspective, hence of any narrative shape, other than that of inaction; for as long as Sutpen withholds from Bon "that flash, that instant of indisputable recognition" that would allow the son "[to] know for sure and forever" their kinship (319), Bon's identity lacks the origin, the starting point, that would allow the rest of his life to assume an intentional or meaningful pattern (Shreve's reconstruction of events, in particular, focuses on Bon's desperate need for that very acknowledgment of beginnings that his father's plot attempts to suppress).

Sutpen thus exerts a stultifying, castrating effect on both his sons. He has in a sense "unmanned" Henry by condemning him to serve as his unwilling "pistol-hand," and he condemns Charles Bon to a life of hopelessly masochistic waiting, textually underscored by the feminizing imagery evoked to describe Bon.[35] But in so victimizing his sons, Sutpen also dooms his own plot, which, as we have seen, depends on male heirs, and thereby provides a clue to the self-subverting nature of sexual and paternal authority. For, ultimately, the stymied desires of Henry for autonomy and of Bon for recognition—identified by Jessica Benjamin as the twin components of the successfully individuated self[36]—stand less as proof of Sutpen's incontrovertible power than as signifiers of the profound anxieties underlying his phallic identity—anxieties that are given narrative figuration as the plot excrescences, "castrations" (in Henry's case), or "feminizations" (in Bon's) of the parent plot, formed by sons whose sin is to reflect imperfectly the father's image.

While the conflict of sons and fathers in our culture will always to some degree be oedipal, nonetheless the deviant narrative energies generated by this conflict—just described as plot excrescences—begin to deauthorize the story of the father at its putative origin. If we turn from a consideration of Henry and Bon as sons to their role as siblings, linked with their sister Judith in an incestuous triangle, the text reveals an even more powerfully transgressive permutation of antipaternal narrative. Early on, the intense affinity of Henry and Judith establishes incest as a brother-sister attraction;

described as a "single personality with two bodies" (91–92), Ellen Cold-field and Sutpen's two children grow up sharing "a relation closer than the traditional loyalty of brother and sister even" (79). But it is the introduction of Bon (not yet known to be their half-brother) into the Henry-Judith dyad that makes possible the the "pure and perfect incest" (96) that Mr. Compson's decadent imagination attributes to Henry in one of the novel's most famous passages. For by plotting the engagement of his best friend Bon to his sister, Henry makes possible a doubly satisfying displace-ment of his own incestuous desire. Not only does this matchmaking scheme or plot allow Henry to possess his sister "in the person of the brother-in-law, the man whom he would be if he could become, metamor-phose into, the lover, the husband"; it also allows him the homoerotic satis-faction, via Judith's mediation, of uniting with the object of his worshipful infatuation, Bon, "by whom he would be despoiled, choose for despoiler, if he could become, metamorphose into the sister, the mistress, the bride" (96). Or, as Shreve imagines Henry schooling Bon, "*Hers and my lives are to exist within and upon yours*" (325). The incestuous implications of this configuration are not confined to Henry and Judith, once it is revealed that Bon is Sutpen's son: the subsequent engagement of Bon and Judith and the attraction between the half-brothers also become literally incestu-ous possibilities.

Which is to say that the incestuous, as nearly all of Faulkner's critics have acknowledged, forms an extremely powerful undertow in Sutpen's paternal plot. To what degree the structure of incest supports an oedipal reading of this novel is another question. John Irwin has most prominently linked the two patterns as refractions of the same wish, a move facilitated by his reading of Freud, in which the boy's incestuous desire for his sister forms a displacement of an original desire for the mother.[37] But in the world of *Absalom, Absalom!*, Ellen Coldfield, Henry's mother, is strikingly absent as an object of desire for Henry or anyone else, and Charles's mother, Eulalia Bon, only has textual life insofar as she is a projection of the narrators' fantasies of her existence. What Henry and Bon seek in in-cestuous union with Judith has very little to do with a return to the mater-nal womb and much more to do with their ambivalent relations to their father and to each other.

In fact, all three of the incestuous variations formed by these siblings covertly work to pervert, in the strongest sense of the word, Sutpen's de-sign. For example, if we look at the violation of the incest taboo incipient in Henry and Judith's closeness from an anthropological perspective, it be-comes clear that their endogamous exclusivity undermines Sutpen's need for those external family alliances (such as he has sought by marrying into Coldfield respectability) that will strengthen his dynasty and better its chances for survival. The incestuous union of Bon and Judith, on the other hand, threatens to adulterate the racial purity of the central family line with the impermissible taint of Negro blood (Sutpen, of course, is not bothered by issues of racial purity when he beds his slaves, such as Clytie's mother, because these aren't eugenically "fit" mothers, only sexual conveniences for the master's pleasure). And, third, the pairing of Henry and Bon would strike the biggest blow of all to Sutpen's design, since their nonproductive union would ensure no line of descent.[38]

As a thematic element of this text, then, the sexual perversion of sibling incest stands in direct opposition to the desire of the father, threatening to wrench his plot beyond recognition. Translated into structural terms, one of the threats of incest is that it augurs a continual return of the same, hence a break in temporal and genealogical progression. Thus, what I have been calling the narrative perversity of the novel—manifest in its nonchronological ordering, doublings of character and narrative layers, and continual loopings back in time—might be seen as a structural analogue of this thematically represented incestuous impulse, working equally to frustrate the straightforward progress upon which Sutpen's dynastic narrative model depends.[39] What, then, does the fact that Sutpen's design depends on progeny whose desires subvert that plan reveal about his exercise of paternal fiat? Most simply put, all of these children become tangible emblems of the patriarch's worst fears about otherness: whether in the form of femaleness (as in Judith's case), blackness (as in Bon's), or latent homosexuality (as in Henry's), these siblings in their myriad incestuous alignments bring to the palpable surface of Sutpen's text precisely those repressions upon which its constructions of masculine privilege, racial superiority, and heterosexual procreativity have depended.

The anxieties that gender, race, and sexuality create for Sutpen's phallic identity become all the more apparent once the extent to which the world of this novel is structured by a complex network of male bonding is acknowledged. Designed to confirm men's power through their exchange of women, the male homosocial bond, as Eve Kosofsky Sedgwick has shown, simultaneously generates men's deepest anxieties about their manhood precisely at that point where culturally fostered comraderie between men becomes barely distinguishable from sexual intimacy.[40] Male identity within patriarchal society—no less Southern patriarchy—depends, that is, on a very fine, often ambiguous line separating the acceptable from the unacceptable, the "real" man from the sexual suspect. And this is the very boundary on which Henry and Bon's relationship dangerously hovers. There are the obvious explanations, of course, including blood affinity, for their bonding—Henry sees in Bon the sophisticated and worldly mentor figure he would like to become; Bon sees in Henry the confirmation of his paternal origins ("*[He has] my brow my skull my jaw my hands*" [314]). But "love" is the quality that Faulkner's narrators constantly invoke to describe the youths' mutual attraction; and, as we have seen above, one of the functions, perhaps *the* primary function, of the sibling incest triangle is to bond

Henry and Bon over the body of Judith in a homoerotic union whose psychosexual structure is also irreducibly homosocial: "It was not Judith who was the object of Bon's love or of Henry's solicitude. She was just the blank shape, the empty vessel in which each of them strove to preserve . . . what each conceived the other to believe him to be—the man and the youth, seducer and seduced, who had known one another, seduced and been seduced, victims in turn each by the other" (119–20).

Given the novel's title, critics have understandably made much of Faulkner's use of the Absalom-Tamar-Amnon biblical analogue to elucidate its incest triangles.[41] But if we dig behind this analogue to the preceding generation of Absalom's father, David, we will uncover another, equally applicable biblical archetype—that of "the love that passeth understanding" shared by the youthful David and Jonathan. And this archetype, presenting homoerotic male comradeship in its most idealized and disembodied form, can be seen at work in the way the various narrators (especially the men) invoke Henry's love for Bon, poeticizing the tragic division that comes between the two youths while relegating Judith, the metaphorically blank page on which the story of their division is written, to the background.

The tragedy, however, is not simply that Henry and Bon fall out in the end. It is that from the very beginning of their friendship they are only able conceive of their mutual desires within the homosocial and consequently heterosexual terms provided by the Father's law, in which "the similarity of gender" looms as an "insurmountable barrier" (95), a final and hopeless intervention, to realized love (the scenario recalls, in its way, Clarissa Dalloway's tacit acceptance of the wall of compulsory heterosexuality whose inevitable descent will separate her and Sally Seton). Given this cultural repression of the homoerotic, along with the paternal anxieties about masculinity that it inevitably reproduces, it is ironically fitting that the act of murder serves as the brothers' final, and only, consummation. The gunshot that Henry fires at Bon, "heard only by its echo" (153), becomes a devastatingly apt metaphor for a sexual climax that never occurs, itself only "heard" in the narrative via its reverberating absence. With this image, we return, circuitously, to the militaristic metaphor—the nearly exhausted "cannon" with its one good last load—used to describe Sutpen's procreative, protofascistic imperialism. But whereas the father's rusty weapon invoked the act of sexual intercourse as unfeeling violence, the firing of Henry the son's pistol connotes an act of anguished violence deprived even of the frisson of sex: all that is left is an empty, unanswered, erotic charge. Seen in this light, the thwarted homoerotic plot of this modern-day David and Jonathan, "heard only by its echo," becomes the symbolic equivalent of the alienated modern condition summed up in the characterization of Quentin Compson as "an empty hall, echoing with sonorous defeated names . . . [and] stubborn, back-looking ghosts" (12). In the emptied-out world of the decimated South that Faulkner makes a symbol of the modern wasteland and of language itself, such ghostly absences and echoes become the sum total of being, as well as emblems of modernist fiction emptied of discernible meaning.

The homosocial structure that turns love into murder also suffuses and disturbs the historical, psychosexual, and narrative levels of Sutpen's dynastic plot. Historically speaking, if Henry and Bon can be seen as fraternal soul mates at war, so too the Civil War from its inception was viewed in familial terms as the struggle of brother against brother—a struggle, moreover, fought over the figurative body of the mother-country herself. Second, in psychosexual terms, *Absalom, Absalom!* includes a terrifyingly visceral primal scene in which the act of heterosexual parental copulation to which the young child is exposed is *replaced* by an emblem of the homosocial, exclusively male, network of power that governs Sutpen's world. For the set piece serving as the climax of the very first chapter, the wrestling spectacle that Ellen discovers her children furtively watching from the barn-loft, forms this text's most authentic equivalent of the Freudian two-backed beast—only this vision is not of heterosexual copulation but of two naked men locked in an embrace, a public display, that is actually a deadly struggle for "supremacy, domination" (29). Nor are the wrestlers "the two black beasts [Ellen] had expected to see but instead a white one and a black one . . . her husband and the father of her children standing there naked and panting and bloody and the negro just fallen evidently" (29).

Here, finally, is the father's uncovered, carnal body. And, here, too, is the David and Jonathan archetype stripped of its ideality, caught in a violent embrace that not only embodies the underlying structure and fate of men's relationships in patriarchy, but that also encodes, quite visibly, the ugly truth of hierarchical relations in the American South: white rising triumphant over black. That the father *forces* Henry to watch this overtly public display of aggressive male virility, and that the mother's entrance into the tableau virtually makes no difference ("I don't expect you to understand it," Sutpen rebuffs Ellen, "because you are a woman" [30]), powerfully suggest that exposure to the homosocial paradigm—not simply heterosexual coitus—*has become the affective experience in the formation of male identity in the world of this novel,* as well as in the creation of its oedipal plots.[42] The same might also be said of the Oedipus myth itself, once we look at the story of the father that precedes, in narrative time, the drama of discovery that Sophocles records. For the fact is that the curse leading King Laius to abandon his son Oedipus in the first place originates in an international crime that is at once homosocial *and* homosexual in nature: it is none other than Laius's violation of his brotherly bond with a neighboring king (Pelops) by raping that ruler's son (Chrysinus) that precipitates the curse on the House of Laius, a curse carried out by *his* son's unwitting enactment of the "oedipal drama" of incest and patricide. Faulkner's text may thus be said unconsciously to supplement Freud's paradigmatic scenario of male identity development by restoring to the oedipal myth its hidden pre-text, its suppressed origin, in homoerotic desire transmuted into homosocial violence.

The complicities of male bonding infiltrate *Absalom, Absalom!* on a third level, that of its narrative retelling. For Quentin and his roommate Shreve, the novel's final narrators, participate in a creative intercourse of words that intimately bonds them, via Sutpen's story, in a quasi-erotic "marriage of speaking and hearing . . . in order to overpass to love" (316). This act of imaginative union, nonetheless, also becomes a shouting match, as we shall see, a battle for mastery not only over this story but over each other, a frustrated dialogue that ends in an ejaculation of love-hate ("*I dont hate it,* [Quentin] thought, panting in the cold air . . . *I dont. I dont!*" [378]) as abrupt as the gunshot at the gate of Sutpen's Hundred beyond which Henry and Bon, unable to "pass" (133), stop forever.[43]

Maternal, Racial, and Daughterly Others

As these instances of male bonding suggest, the place allotted to women in Sutpen's construction of his family text, even more than that of wayward or unclaimed sons, is extremely peripheral. "So it was no tale about women," Mr. Compson says of the life story Sutpen confesses to his father the General, "and certainly not about love" (248). As noted in chapter 2, Claude Lévi-Strauss has argued that in patriarchally structured societies women primarily serve as items of exchange that make possible transactions of power between men, and this reality is dramatically reflected in the secondary, mediating position women occupy in Sutpen's family plot: Eulalia Bon, Ellen Coldfield, and Milly Jones are the price their fathers or guardians pay for Sutpen's services or company. Sutpen accepts Eulalia from her father in exchange for saving his Haitian plantation during the slave uprising; Ellen is the reward of Sutpen's demonic dealings with Mr. Coldfield ("whose daughters he might even have won at cards," Rosa says [20]); Milly is the understood price that her grandfather Wash Jones pays for the privilege of drinking scuppernong wine with the master. Predictably, then, passionate eros has no place in Sutpen's work-in-progress, and, since he views women as no more or less than the reproductive bodies required by his eugenical scheme of a fit and pure dynasty, he feels free to discard Eulalia, marry Ellen, propose to wed Rosa if she proves fertile, and cast off the fifteen-year-old Milly when her child turns out to be a useless daughter.

Yet the very inconsequentiality of the roles accorded women in Sutpen's plan, like its other suppressed elements, becomes a potent sign and symptom of the anxieties that fuel the plot of this father as well as his white cohorts in Southern patriarchy. For beneath the flowery encomiums embellishing antebellum rhetoric about women, its representations of the

Southern belle reveal a profound misogyny and fear of female sexuality. A case in point is the fundamentally contradictory attitude underlying the eroticized images that Mr. Compson, for one, uses to describe women—on the one hand as empty "vessels" (108, 119–20) waiting to be filled, and on the other as parasitic "vampires" (67, 86) actively draining life from others: he who bases his power on the phallus as an instrument of penetration stands, in his worst nightmares, to be penetrated, to be sucked dry.[44] And if men like Mr. Compson and Sutpen—and perhaps Faulkner himself—see women as endangering their potency, it is precisely because female sexuality harbors the one element—the bodily ability to reproduce—that men's ostensible power and designs can never completely control. Women's sexuality has an authority, a creative fiat, to which all the father's fictions of authority in the world can only presume, can only possess by way of metaphor.

The most striking textual manifestation of the male anxieties engendered by female sexual procreativity in *Absalom, Absalom!* involves the striking absence of mothers throughout the entire novel. Both in Sutpen's plot and in the text at large, motherhood by and large forms an invisible state. Those mothers who are represented in any depth are literally disembodied male projections (such as Shreve's fiction of Eulalia Bon, Charles Bon's vengeance-mad mother, or Mr. Compson's evocation of Ellen in "the absolute halcyon of her butterfly's summer" [74]). Other mothers—Sutpen's, Clytie's, Ellen and Rosa's, Milly Jones's, even Quentin's—are simply striken from the text, often without explanation. Sutpen's mother, for example, is granted textual life and death in the space of one sentence, where she is described as "a fine wearying woman" who died in Sutpen's youth (223). Clytie's mother is presumably one of the two nameless slave women Sutpen has brought with him from Haiti, and Milly's mother is even further marginalized, cited only in the chronology that ends the novel. But there are two especially striking cases worth examining, for in both these instances of repressed motherhood the absence of information is so extreme that it creates unexplained gaps and inconsistencies in Faulkner's otherwise scrupulously woven narrative design.

The first occurs early in the novel, as Mr. Compson in chapter 2 recounts the events leading up to Sutpen's and Ellen Coldfield's wedding in 1838. Mrs. Coldfield, oddly, is not mentioned once, the maternal role in supervising a daughter's wedding plans entirely given over to "that grim virago fury of female affront" (54), the parodic figure of the aunt who "cajole[s] Mr. Coldfield into the big wedding" (51) that forms the chapter's seriocomic climax. We might well begin to doubt whether there *is* a living Mrs. Coldfield except for the one brief appearance that she makes *in a parenthesis* at the beginning of the very next chapter, where Mr. Compson notes that she has died giving birth to Ellen's sister Rosa—an event that occurs, however, in 1845, a full seven years *after* Ellen's wedding. In effect, by substituting an exaggerated female stereotype, that of the sexually re-pressed "virago," for the mother, the text sacrifices probability (after all, where *was* Mrs. Coldfield during her firstborn's wedding?) for easy laughs.

A similarly revealing lacuna occurs in the postwar narration, when the light-skinned Charles Etienne (son of Charles Bon and his octoroon mis-tress) defiantly counters Judith's and Clytie's attempts to save him from his racial heritage by marrying a "coal black and ape-like woman" from some distant "two dimensional backwater" (205). To emphasize Charles Etienne's tragic self-destructiveness, the narrative voice goes out of its way to ridicule the atavistic and "automaton-like state" (205) in which his mate, who is not even accorded the dignity of a name, exists—*despite* the fact that she single-handedly and heroically conveys her husband, too "se-verely beaten and mauled" (205) to assist her, from wherever they have met to Jefferson, a place she has never been. Once she has served her pri-mary function in the plot by giving birth to a son, Jim Bond, the chapter makes no further mention of her; "the old woman" with whom this son is now said to share the cabin turns out to be Clytie (210, 215–16), not his mother. Another mother has disappeared from the text without a trace. Her description as a "black gargoyle" (209) thus becomes prophetic of her narrative function; like the gargoyle she supposedly resembles, she be-comes one of those extraneous plot figurations, one of those unwanted, gothic excrescences, that the paternal plot relegates to ghostly invisibility.

As the example of Charles Etienne's wife also indicates, the lack of mothers in this text is complemented by the quite visible, disruptive rise of black sons. For, ironically, the one realized dynasty in the novel, the only fruit of Sutpen's efforts to create and control a racially pure empire of miniature Sutpens, is the genealogy that stretches from his repudiated son, Charles Bon, through Charles Etienne, to his great-grandson Jim Bond, a genealogy that is at once male (the fulfillment of Sutpen's dream) *and* characterized by an exponential increase in degrees of blackness (the night-marish inversion of his dream). Once again, an aspect of the otherness—here, the taint of racial otherness—that Sutpen has attempted to exclude from his design redounds upon his authorial control, and, once again, the outcome points to the unresolved anxieties of identity that have under-mined this father's authority and his plot from its inception. For Sutpen's greatest fear has always been an adulteration of the family plot by those extraneous narratives—the stories of mothers and daughters, half-caste sons, "unmanly" men—that potentially stand outside, hence threaten the hegemony, of his desired identity as all-powerful patriarch, the great white father. It is fitting, then, that a "foreign" woman—Eulalia Bon—is made the culprit responsible for (supposedly) introducing the strain of "unfit" Negro blood that upsets Sutpen's projected ends by "defiling" the family line; in the novel's complex symbology—as in early twentieth-century eu-genics discourse—femaleness, and particularly wayward female sexuality, is often equated with an equatorial darkness personified by the black races.[45]

Indeed, the specific challenge that the pairing of fecundity and racial otherness poses to authoritarian white male identity, and hence to the racially defined borders of Sutpen's plot, is the message of the novel's spellbinding closing statement, as Shreve taunts Quentin about the horror that the very idea of miscegenation holds for the Southern imagination:

> I think that in time the Jim Bonds are going to conquer the western hemisphere. Of course it wont be quite in our time and of course as they spread toward the poles they will *bleach out again* like the rabbits and the birds do, so they wont show up so sharp against the snow. But it will still be Bond; and so in a few thousand years, I who regard you will also have sprung from the loins of African kings. (378; emphasis added)

Shreve's vision is not simply that the black race (like narrative metonymy run wild) will conquer the world, but more precisely that Aryan whiteness will cease to be a marker of difference, the absolute metaphor of achieved ends, once the various races eventually mix *under the guise of whiteness.* For the Southern establishment, then, the great fear is the threat of nondifferentiation, of the collapse of the boundaries and polarities that allow for the repression and subjugation of otherness that, as we saw in chapter 2, Klaus Theweleit has shown to be historically constitutive of white male identity in western culture and that he persuasively links to the rise of fascism in the era of modernity. That this threat is particularly threatening to the male psyche can be glimpsed in Shreve's final words. Despite all his sardonic distance as a non-American (he is Canadian), Shreve tellingly refers to the Jim Bonds of the future springing from the "loins of African *kings,*" whereas technically speaking it will be the African "queens"—Eulalia's descendants—whose "loins" will give birth to, create, this final debacle of Southern white patriarchy.

If Sutpen's paternal masterplot cannot successfully do away with his black descendants, neither can it totally neutralize the covertly transgressive perversities that characterize his daughters, Judith and Clytie.[46] Unlike their white and black counterparts in Henry and Bon, these half-sisters seem doomed to haunt the background of Sutpen's family text, ever-present but useless in furthering Sutpen's patronymic designs (both remain childless), except as the keepers of his house. Their joint *impassivity,* however, should not be mistaken for traditional feminine passivity; they may keep Sutpen's house, but they do not necessarily keep to his plot. It is worth noting that Judith and Clytie, along with their cousin Rosa, form an all-female triumvirate whose combined strength keeps Sutpen's plantation running throughout the last months of the war—a break in the usual order of male domination that illuminates for the reader the paradoxical position these daughters occupy in his paternal plot. On the one hand, this period of absolute female rule works because it is temporary, because all three women still perceive their existence as dependent on the return of the now-absent father—"he was all we had, all that gave us any reason for continuing to exist," Rosa tells Quentin (154). On the other hand, Sutpen's very absence disproves his necessity to their autonomous survival. "No," Rosa continues,

> it did not even require the first day of the life we were to lead together to show us we did not need him, had not the need for any man so long as Wash Jones lived or stayed there—I who had kept my father's house and he alive for almost four years, Judith who had done the same out here, and Clytie who could cut a cord of wood or run a furrow better (or at least quicker) than Jones himself. (154)

With the one man on the plantation, Wash, relegated to the position of functionary, the three women weave a narrative shaped to their own desires, creating what could be called a Story *without* Designs in contradistinction to Brooks's description of the Freudian masterplot, which Rosa aptly identifies in her description of the "furious . . . desire" and "mad intention" (154) that fuels Sutpen's monomaniacal impulse to climax and completion, and that inspires his increasingly frantic because futile effort to restore the plantation to its former glory upon his return from the war. "Not even that. Neither Judith nor I wanted that. Perhaps it was because we did not believe it could be done, but I think it was more than that: *that we now existed in an apathy which was almost peace,* like that of the blind insentient earth itself which dreams after no flower's stalk nor bud, envies not the airy musical solitude of the springing leaves it nourishes" (154–55; emphasis added).

That this female counterplot exists *within* Sutpen's design points to the ambiguous relationship his daughters maintain to their father's supposedly incontrovertible law. At first glance Judith appears totally identified with her father, silently yielding to his fiat when Henry is exiled and when Bon's death leaves her one of the war's "still unbrided widows" (123). Indeed, as a young girl Judith has manifested a strong, even phallic, identification with her father.[47] Yet of all the Sutpens, it is also Judith who most actively concerns herself with preserving a written record that will allow for the handing down, even to strangers, of the suppressed stories underlying the official history of the family's rise and fall. Thus, "to make that scratch, that undying mark on the blank face of the oblivion" (129) that is also her own silenced story, Judith passes Bon's crucial letter to her on to General Compson's wife, in an act of female-to-female transmission that makes possible Mr. Compson's retelling of these events to his son Quentin forty-five years later: the transmission of father-to-son, the ostensible basis for this (and all oedipal) narrative, here depends on a prior transaction that is an exchange between women.

This is not to ignore the importance of the "man-to-man" transmissions between Sutpen and General Compson (the subject of which, appropriately, is a father-son narrative), passed on to Mr. Compson and thence to Quentin. My point, rather, is that this male chain of narrative transactions often depends on unrecognized female exchanges, ones that not only make possible the father-son story that the men want to tell, but that keep certain counteroedipal strands of subversive narrative in play. The daughter's effort to make a mark, a protesting counterstatement, does not stop with Judith's passing on of this letter, either. For as Deirdre d'Albertis has brilliantly shown, Judith constructs her own textual equivalent of Sutpen's family plot, and even hides it out in the open, in her arrangement of the family graveplot upon the successive deaths of Ellen, Sutpen, Bon, and Charles Etienne. Within this demarcated plot of land, Judith places the various tombstones—each itself a text, a "block of stone with scratches on it" (127)—so that Sutpen is surrounded by the denied, disruptive elements of *his* plot; to complete *her* counterplot, she orders her own headstone from her deathbed, which is tellingly placed "at the opposite side of the enclosure, as far from the other four as the enclosure could permit" (210).[48] On the one hand symbolically fulfilling the role of her biblical namesake, the Judith who beheads, castrates, the patriarchal oppressor, by so encompassing Sutpen's grave, Judith on the other hand also leaves behind a lasting statement of eloquent protest, in the form of a silent testimonial to the marginal position that, as an expendable daughter, she has always occupied in his plot.

Like Judith, Clytie also proves a covertly destabilizing force in Sutpen's design. "Free, yet incapable of freedom," she is the embodiment of the "perverse inscrutable . . . paradox" (156) of slavery: she is at once too proud to think of herself as chattel, yet she never questions the fact that Sutpen is her absolute master. On a conscious level, Clytie functions as the everfaithful retainer, working to promote Sutpen's cause and protect his kindred as if they were her own family—which, ironically, they are. Yet this unacknowledged daughter is also "the presiding augur of [Sutpen's] disaster" (62), her face a mute text, like the marble gravestones, that attests to the "debacle" (156) of miscegenation lying behind Sutpen's fall.[49] And it is she, significantly, who with the murderous fury of her classical namesake Clytemnestra brings destruction down on the House of her father, setting fire to Sutpen's Hundred rather than cede to Rosa her guardianship of the dying Henry. As in Judith's passing on to Mrs. Compson of Bon's letter, it is once again an act of transmission between women—Rosa's telepathic decoding of the secret Clytie has kept hidden at Sutpen's Hundred—that has kept this story going all the while. Authorial fiat, it would seem, does not lie entirely in the hands of the father.

Rosa's Unwriting of the Masterplot

Thus I return, at long last, to Rosa Coldfield and the role she plays in the making and unmaking of the father's story. The symbolic recipient of Clytie's secret and youngest in the female triumvirate that temporarily reigns at Sutpen's Hundred, Rosa is not, of course, literally one of Sutpen's daughters, but she is none the less the figurative offspring of his paternal text, as her aggrieved narrative voice overwhelmingly demonstrates. I have already observed how Rosa's "outraged recapitulation" (8) of the Sutpen legend may be read as a spinster's "impotent" act of revenge, the perverted child, as it were, of her years of sexual frustration and (in conventional eyes) unreproductive and emotional sterility. But there is another, much more actively subversive side to Rosa's role as narrator that we should consider—one that is productive, indeed potent, rather than powerless or self-defeating. Established at the very beginning of chapter 1 as Yoknapatawpha County's "poetess laureate," Rosa is the only *published* writer, however open to question the quality of her writings may be, among the novel's narrators, "issuing . . . poems, ode, eulogy, and epitaph, out of some . . . implacable reserve of undefeat" (11). One might also take note of the fact that she only begins writing when her neurotic, Yankee-sympathizing father nails himself in the attic of their house during the war, becoming—as will Henry Sutpen, hidden in his own attic half a century later—a *male* version of the "madwoman in the attic," Gilbert and Gubar's evocative figure for the woman writer's angry double. Even more important, Rosa's authorial status is reflected in the fact that she is the narrator who initiates this text by summoning Quentin to her house, first to listen to her tale and then to serve as her witness on the revelatory night trip to Sutpen's Hundred where Henry is discovered: without Rosa, there would be, to put it bluntly, no novel for us to read.[50]

Nor is Rosa's garrulous narrative style, elongated by seemingly endless and frustrating repetitions, simply an emblem of the speaker's lack of erotic fulfillment or her passive entrapment in a long-dead past, however much both may be contributing factors. Rather, the technique of deferral and postponement that marks her retelling may also be read as a sign of her subversive if partial power *over* Sutpen's text and its desired climaxes. At the beginning of this discussion, I suggested that Sutpen's story itself refuses to die, exacting its revenge on its auditors by dooming them to perpetual frustration. But in Rosa's case, we can also reverse this proposition to state that it is *she* who refuses to let Sutpen's story die. In effect, by using her role as narrator to keep the unruly plot-in-process, the transgressive narrative "middle" that Sutpen would rather ignore, alive and anxiously disruptive, Rosa rebels against what I have already characterized as his compulsive desire for metaphor, for the completed goal or monumental design. If oedipal narrative is an explanatory myth of beginnings and endings, the search for the "proper" narrative death that will bestow retrospective meaning on the irregularities and deviations of the individual's life career, then Rosa's refusal to lay the myth of Sutpen to rest *de-oedipalizes,* in a real sense, its power. Rewriting Sutpen's deeds as undying and communal legend, she "unstrings"—to repeat Susan Winnett's memorable metaphor, cited in chapter 1—the oedipal logic of the Brooksian "masterplot that wants to have told us in advance where it is that we should take our pleasures and what must inevitably come of them."[51] Like Lucy Snowe's heretic narrative in *Villette,* like the queer deviations of *Nightwood* and *The Young and Evil,* Rosa's monologues create whole texts that emphatically take their pleasures elsewhere, as we can see in the metonymic play of the middle to which her "outraged recapitulation" of "undefeat" gives vent. And in inserting this "elsewhere" into the overarching plot of the father in *Absalom, Absalom!,* Rosa's narrative retelling clears space for our illuminated rereading of the self-subverting forces, the plot excrescences, generated by Sutpen's textual enterprise. Following Walter Benjamin's critique of the fascist aestheticization of politics, we might hypothesize that this *de*oedipalization of Sutpen's authority in effect *re*politicizes the narrative, stripping away the aesthetic design to expose the unruly contents it attempts to hide.

Moreover, given the fact that hidden origins and proleptic endings are the essential cornerstones of Sutpen's masterplot, it is fascinating to note how Rosa usurps control over both the beginning and end of the novel. Not only does she determine the text's opening—without her summons to Quentin, as we have seen, there would be no occasion for the telling that becomes this novel—but by making Quentin her companion, her witness, on the revelatory night trip to Sutpen's Hundred, where the dying Henry is discovered hidden in the attic, she also summons into being the climactic event of the Sutpen family plot—the fire, set by Clytie, that burns down the house, destroys its last white descendant, and sends Rosa "to bed because it was all finished now, there was nothing left. . . . And so she died" (376). These are simultaneously the last events narrated by Shreve and Quentin in their college dorm months later, and within a page of their mention of her death, the novel ends. It is as if the literal "story" must cease when Rosa is no longer alive to keep it going. Thus, even in death, Rosa continues to usurp Sutpen's desire for metaphoric finality, preempting his "proper" end by breaking off the account of *his* story where and when *she* desires (one is reminded of Dora's breaking off of her analysis and thereby thwarting Freud's desire for a complete narrative). In the war between Sutpen's formidable will to power and her own authorial stratagems, Rosa finally succeeds in turning the castrating power of the father against the "eluded dark fatherhead" (299) itself: the psychic wounds he has inflicted on his progeny redound posthumously to rend his own suddenly vulnerable narrative.

The primary recipient of the narrative transmission that Rosa initiates and symbolically brings to a close is the young Quentin Compson. "Maybe someday you will remember this," she tells him, "and write about it" (10). The fictional improvisation that he and Shreve weave from the "rag-tag and bob-ends of old tales and talking" (303), forming the reader's most immediate link to the novel's record of events, becomes another retelling that, like Rosa's, will not let Sutpen's story die easily. Yet if Rosa's habits of deferral amount to a covert counterplot against the father, the boys' obsessive reliving of his history indicates that what cannot die for each of them involves the unresolved anxieties of masculine and racial identity that have *also* driven Sutpen to his doom. For Quentin especially, the anxieties of sexual and creative generation that have beset Sutpen's design have become his own personal nightmare: "*Yes, we are both Father. Or maybe Father and I are both Shreve, maybe it took Father and me both to make Shreve or Shreve and me both to make Father or maybe Thomas Sutpen to make all of us*" (261–62). In other words, because both Quentin and Shreve *are* the white sons, the Harvard-bred male inheritors of the dominant culture (and not dispossessed daughters like Rosa, Judith, or Clytie), they cannot escape the crises of authority and conflicts of identity embedded in the story of ambiguous fatherhood that they retell.

One can see this truth, first of all, in the way their creative dialogue begins to repeat the pattern—and contradictions—of homosocial bonding characterizing the world of Sutpen and his progeny, as their "marriage" of words is transformed into a struggle for mastery ("Wait, I tell you! . . . I am telling [it]" [277]); their very intimacy has become the grounds for an increasingly anxious contest of one-upmanship. Second, at least for Quentin, storytelling only enmeshes his fragile sense of self and even frailer sense of masculinity more disastrously in the self-subverting struggle of fathers and sons; the attempt to make himself the primary narrator of the events that his father has told him, indeed to become his father's superior in knowledge by telling the story better than his progenitor, dooms him to repetition and psychic impotence.[52] Third, even the lacunae in Quentin and Shreve's fiction refer us back to tremendous anxieties of racial and sexual identity motivating Sutpen's desire to establish a dynasty in his own image. For the questions that remain unanswered in *Absalom, Absalom!*—Is miscegenation really the key to Sutpen's repudiation of Bon? How does Bon learn (if ever) that he has black blood? What does Henry actually reveal to Quentin in the climactic attic encounter?—all turn on questions of racialized masculine identity, of which the narrative's only explanations are those *created* by the boys, which are hence "fictions" in the most fundamental sense of the word. The essential uncertainty of the status of such fictionalized explanations—upon which not only the novel's "mystery" but Sutpen's otherwise inexplicable repudiation of his sons rests—thus self-reflexively echoes the uncertainties lying at the core of phallic identity, and hence of racial patriarchy the "eluded dark fatherhead" itself (299).

An emblem for the sexual and textual anxieties produced by such uncertainties exists in the climactic moments of the novel. When Quentin finally confronts the dying Henry, hidden away in the attic of Sutpen's Hundred, a much-discussed gap in narration occurs, as the two engage in a surreal, italicized dialogue consisting of a short series of repetitive phrases that eventually move full circle without confirming anything; this elliptical conversation, as Peter Brooks has noted, "seems to constitute a kind of hollow structure, a concave mirror or black hole at the center of the narrative."[53] And the fear of empty centers, of dark "holes" and gaps into which all meanings tumble and out of which nothing certain emerges—imagery powerfully evocative of female sexuality and racial difference in modern western culture—is very much, and on very many levels, what the modernist and masculine anxieties haunting *Absalom, Absalom!* (and often its critics) are all about.

For years critics have pointed out how Faulkner's foregrounding of issues of intelligibility have made this text a quintessential fictional example of modernist self-reflexivity. The fundamental uninterpretability of this anxiety-producing text, I am also suggesting, has everything to do with its interrogation of the grounds on which all plots of the father erect their dubious beginnings. For underneath those masterful designs, *Absalom, Absalom!* reveals a story not of the power of the father, but of how one man's sexual anxieties, occurring in one epoch of historical crisis and retold in another portentous moment, dismantle the very notion of his transcendent, abstract authority. Oedipus, however empowered by our society or its myth-making processes, is finally and nonetheless a vulnerable man caught in the middle of a story that he has indeed helped create but cannot control—caught, as it were, with his pants down, his fallacies exposed, his repressive efforts showing for the ineffectual cover-up they are. Moreover, as Shreve's prophecies on the last page warn of Sutpen's dynastic dreams, there is always the "nigger" who gets away: all those fractious, marginal excrescences of plot, all those perverse emblems of "non-maleness," of otherness, that refuse to mirror the dictatorial father or confine their desires to his authoritarian masterplot. Thus Shreve says of any and all attempts to give a balanced, tidy explanation of Sutpen's failure: "Which is all right, it's fine; it clears the whole ledger, you can tear all the pages out and burn them, except for one thing. And do you know what that is? . . . You've got one nigger left" (378). Escaping the shapers of dynastic and narrative designs by their exclusion or their cunning, these transgressive elements remain, then, to unravel the ends whereby the father would explain his origins and to return the reader to the obsessions that remain in play, despite the paternal effort to repress difference, in the midst of a story doomed by its very premises never to end.

CHRISTINA STEAD, *THE MAN WHO LOVED CHILDREN*
AT THE CROSSROADS OF MYTH AND PSYCHOANALYSIS

> You do not do, you do not do
> Any more, black shoe . . . //
> I have always been scared of *you*,
> With your Luftwaffe, your
> gobbledygoo,
> And your neat mustache
> And your Aryan eye, bright blue.
> Panzer-man, panzer-man, O You . . . //
> Daddy, daddy, you bastard, I'm through
> —Sylvia Plath, "Daddy"[54]

> There was an old woman who lived in a shoe
> She had so many children she didn't know what to do.
> —Mother Goose Rhyme

How much of a conclusion can we extrapolate from one text's demonstration of the self-subverting law of the father? Does the example of *Absalom, Absalom!* allow us to assume that all of our culture's paternal plots so systematically deauthorize their proclaimed powers? What do such narratives and their cultural contexts imply about father-centered theories of narrative? I want to continue this discussion by putting Faulkner's text in dialogue with Christina Stead's *The Man Who Loved Children* (1940), a tale of fatherhood that vies with the story of Sutpen in its relentless depiction of paternal authority and its textual poetics of the perverse. Billed by Marilou B. McLaughlin as one of the most "famous nearly-famous novels of the century,"[55] *The Man Who Loved Children* was published four years after *Absalom, Absalom!* and, despite its apparent realism, is as daringly experimental as Faulkner's more renowned modernist classic. Despite her Australian birthright, Stead—who lived an expatriate life in several countries—situates her portrait of the patriarch, as Faulkner does his dynastic saga, in the American South, where allegiances to the family are as fierce and potentially conflictual as regional loyalties: the war-torn milieu of Mississippi from which Sutpen's legend springs has become, in Stead's novel, the foreboding atmosphere of Washington, DC and Tidewater Virginia in the years immediately preceding World War II. And, as we have also seen, if certain of Sutpen's monomaniacal and genocidal impulses seem protofascistic, Stead's Sam Pollit, in the face of his patriotic and humanitarian professions, fancies himself a "natural leader" (352) in the mode of Hitler who, were he "autocrat of all nations," would employ eugenical methods disconcertingly similar to those used by the Nazis to make "room for the fit" (372). There is, however, one crucial distinction between these two novels that illuminates the gendered coordinates of the father's plot. And that difference lies in Stead's focus on a daughter as the primary opponent to her father Sam Pollit's text of paternal authority and family bliss; the Judiths and Clyties of Faulkner's world have moved to center stage in the person of Louisa Pollit, an action relegating the sons (and there are several "little Sams" in Stead's novel) to the wings. Such a shift in emphasis creates a permutation in oedipal logic that both speaks to the anxieties of authority that disable the imperialist claims of paternal narrative and calls into question the assumptions governing those critical analyses that have made special claims for Oedipus as the origin of all story.

Not surprisingly, Sam's aggrandizing impositions of ego, calculated to uphold the integrity of his paternal plot, become all the more fraught with anxiety given the femaleness of his oldest child Louisa: his *narcissistic* desire for self-perpetuation through offspring is forced to reveal its other face as an *incestuous* desire to control Louie's sexuality through the mechanisms of erotic domination. The eroticized struggle of father and daughter that ensues also illuminates the textual implications of Stead's narrative enterprise; their struggle becomes a life-and-death battle—such as that recounted by Sylvia Plath in her famous poem, "Daddy" cited above, and as analyzed in Dora in chapter 2—for the mastery of a story whose ownership is suddenly up for grabs. What is at stake, crucially, is the question of female desire and its relation to narrative authority. For beyond the morass of pathological paternity that comprises Sam Pollit's family text glimmers the possibility of one daughter's mythic power to create a plot in which she is the subject not only of her own but the *narrative's* quest for meaning—a quest that replaces Oedipus's anxieties, the motor of male narrativity, with the pleasures of female narratability.

I began this chapter by citing Peter Brooks and Teresa de Lauretis as two of the most prominent theorists who have argued for the (omni)presence of father-related models of narrative fictions. As my references to Brooks's reading of *Absalom, Absalom!* have indicated, there are many points where I feel he admirably captures the narrative dynamics of Faulkner's novel. Yet, at the same time, one of my implicit goals in examining *Absalom, Absalom!* has been to offer a critique of the gender-related blindspots in Brooks's reading. These blindspots, indeed, are symptomatic of a bias that underlies his entire genealogical model of narrative transmission, with its nearly exclusive reliance on fathers and sons and its male-oriented interpretation of the sexualized energy of novelistic beginnings and endings. What I would like to initiate in the following pages is an inverse move, reading *The Man Who Loved Children* with an eye to de Lauretis's (rather than Brooks's) theory of oedipal narrative. Unlike Brooks, de Lauretis aims to expose the operation of sexual difference informing the deep structures of all narrative. And yet, although one may applaud her welcome attention to gender, her methodology leaves itself open to question; for in the process of assigning masculine and feminine designations to subject and object positions in the oedipal quest for self-knowledge, de Lauretis authorizes a set of assumptions about the relation of gender to narrative that are as delimiting, in their way, as Brooks's elision of all but masculine trajectories of narrative desire from his schema.

In assessing the theories of Brooks and de Lauretis in light of these two novels, moreover, I want to point out the chiasmic structure governing the intersections I have created among these two novels and two critics. To the extent that Brooks relies on an oedipal paradigm to elucidate the production of narrative, his primary interest may be said to be *psychoanalytic:* the Oedipus complex theorized by Freud underwrites the dynamics of succession highlighted in the classic, male-authored texts from which Brooks draws his theory. De Lauretis's argument, in contrast, begins with the *mythological* rather than psychoanalytic dimensions of this paradigm: she is interested in Oedipus's story as a quest through the gendered coordinates of time and space. But the fact is that Faulkner's text is most overtly invested in the *mythos* of paternity, whereas Stead's focus on "the man who loved children" is more immediately *psychological.* Thus, to the extent that my reading of Faulkner has attempted to uncover the psychosexual contours sometimes obscured by the text's mythologizing of Sutpen's fatherhood, my task in the following section will be to uncover the myth-making power (in this case, of the questing daughter) that emerges from Stead's "case-study" of Sam's pathological paternity.

The House That Sam Built

Sam Pollit's obsessive desire to create a paternal plot that will reflect his own glory takes place against his unhappy second marriage to Henny Collier, the upper-class daughter of a Southern aristocrat whose pampered upbringing has given way to a grotesquely embittered vision of the world. Literally hurling competing "texts" of invective against each other (35), husband and wife wage a war of words that pits Sam's self-aggrandizing pieties and humanitarian orations against Henny's sardonic ironies and black moods. If marriage has yoked the two in everlasting enmity, that hatred has produced, ironically, five children (a sixth is born in the course of the narrative) in six years. And these progeny, happily oblivious to the rancor that seethes around them, form with their older half sister Louisa— Sam's child by his first marriage—the basis of this father's plot: a charmed circle into which Sam, the "loving" father of the novel's title, insinuates himself, shielding himself from the failure of his marriage by claiming this world of children as his own private paradise. Nor is *paradise* too strong a word to describe the fantasy world that Sam builds within the bounds of Tohoga Place, the Pollits' Eden-like Georgetown estate. However, in counterpoint to Sam's fiction of perpetual paradise, Stead traces the family's "fall" from this private sanctuary, as Sam's loss of his state department job forces his clan to leave Tohoga Place for Spa House, an "ugly old castle comedown" in a deteriorating section of Eastport, Maryland. With this geographical move, the dramatic focus also shifts. In this unfamiliar environment, Henny's role as Sam's principal antagonist wanes, and her stepdaughter, the adolescent Louisa, increasingly assumes the role of primary blocking figure. As the escalating conflict between father and daughter overwhelms the second half of the text, the volatile tensions of this "war at home" increasingly expose the rents in the fabric of Sam's fictions of domestic paradise and strip bare the dangerously dictatorial nature of his all-engulfing paternal love.

So summarized, Stead's harrowing portrait of domestic life might sound like it would best be served by an exacting mimeticism. But while the surface of *The Man Who Loved Children,* narrated from a seemingly omniscient, third-person point of view, often *seems* realistic, its mode of depicting family turmoil more accurately embodies what R. D. Laing calls a psychological representation of the "internalized family," in which the largely unconscious configuration of familial relations as they exist within the individual's psyche have been projected, in exaggerated form, outward onto a screen of familiar events. In other words, as Joan Lidoff has put it, Stead's highly charged descriptive and expressive language attempts to "[explore] subterranean, emotional fields of force rather than imitating the way people *really* talk and act."[56] Structurally, this method of representing "the subterranean reaches of the unconscious" through external event has points in common with Chopin's and Lawrence's method of using resonant image and metaphor to charge seemingly straightforward action with unconscious and subconscious motivation. Stylistically, it shares with Barnes and the Joyce of "Circe" a surrealist manipulation of language and event, juxtaposing incongruous objects in order to stimulate within the reader that dissociation of consciousness that activates the irrational.

The subtle warping of narrative realism that ensues from these methods produces an erotics of narration every bit as perverse, and perversely frustrating, as that of *Absalom, Absalom!* If the paramount source of the frustration experienced by Faulkner's readers is the novel's entrapping layers of narration, in which the same story is told again and again without resolution, the primary cause of frustration in *The Man Who Loved Children* is Sam Pollit himself, whose incessant stream of badgering, coaxing, engulfing words overwhelms the text with a monologic intensity that merits Henny's derisive characterization of her husband as "the Great Mouthpiece" (172). Just as Sam threatens to engulf and consume his children's identities, so his verbosity threatens our status as autonomous readers, forcing our submission to his words and will. As in *Absalom, Absalom!* Stead's story of paternal fiat thus engenders a particularly masochistic erotics of reading. Such textual perversity is intensified—again as in Faulkner's text—by the gaps that the father's story creates; the reader's frustration increases in proportion to his or her gradual intuition of all the viewpoints and stories that have been repressed or glossed over by virtue of Sam's verbal prolixity.

The frustrations generated by this mode of narration, moreover, are very much related to the anxieties fueling the plot of paternal authority that is Stead's subject matter. No less than Thomas Sutpen, Sam Pollit views himself as the author of his family, and consequently he quite literally treats his progeny as a "text" that he alone has the power to shape and control. The degree to which Sam sees his *procreative* function as an act of *creative* fiat—and consequently his progeny as elements in a plot of his sole making—is illustrated throughout the novel. Simultaneously assuming the godly role of prime creator and the human role of first man and original patriarch, Sam ensconces himself in a veritable "Garden of Eden" (47) within the walls his many-acred Georgetown estate, populating it with pet animals, birds, and reptiles that, God-like and Adam-like, he proceeds to name, exulting all the while "what it must be . . . to taste supreme power!" (17). It is thus no wonder that Henny repeatedly calls him "the Great I-Am" (165, 268, 371, 411), a denigrating appellation that Sam no doubt secretly takes as a complimentary testament to his "supreme power."[57] He also asserts his fiat by renaming his children in terms that consolidate his godly dominion ("Louisa" thus becomes the nonsensical "Looloodirl" and "Loolabulloo," Evie his "Little Womey," his sister Bonnie "Bonniferous"). If Sam names others, Stead in turn bestows on him a name that slyly reveals his pretensions to authorial fiat and control. His middle name, "Clemens," aligns him with Samuel Clemens, one of America's most beloved fiction writers (and a notorious teller of stretched truths), and his first name, Samuel, becomes a sign of his egotistical vision of himself as a genial "founding father," revealed in his dream of hosting a patriotic radio show under the appellation of "Uncle Sam."

In assuming the mythic role of prime mover of this children's paradise, Sam attempts to perpetuate a very specific myth: that of the ever-happy, ever-growing, all-American family. "By Gee . . . but we're a cheerful bunch" (18), he effuses, and boasts that he "c[an] never have . . . enough" of "the pleasure of being a father" (215). Therefore he periodically invites the whole neighborhood to play at Tohoga: "Sam himself did all he could to attract the very small boys and girls of all ages to Tohoga House. . . . He beamed, he bloated with joy, to see how they feared and loved his great house" (46–47). The grotesque image that results from Stead's substitution of the word "bloated" for the expected *glowed,* however, is one indication that there is something disturbingly out of balance in the psychic joys Sam reaps from fatherhood. Moreover, his "dewy-eyed" sentimentality blinds him, conveniently, to the selfish egotism underlying his utopian claim that his only purpose in procreating has been to turn out "a little nucleus of splendid men and women to work for the future" (131). Rather, Sam's aim in immersing himself so totally in the lives of his children is to achieve a kind of eternal present: it is for himself—not for his children or the "future"—that he attempts to freeze time and achieve a changeless realm of infantile pleasure.

Unlike Thomas Sutpen, then, Sam-as-Father desires less the metaphoric finality of achieved ends than the metonymic continuity guaranteed by a perpetual chain of "little-me's." That is, rather than committing Sutpen's sin of overlooking the "middle" that constitutes the substance of narrative, Sam wishes to plunge into and fix that very middle and make his children's worshipful love an end in itself. But despite this difference in method, each father has the same goal: to impose a kind of stasis on the family text—whether in its middle or in its culmination—that will ensure his immortality as its supreme shaper and his unchallengeable authority as "keycarrier, childnamer, and riothaver" (36). Ironically, though, in Sam's case it is precisely his *over*involvement in his children's daily existence that proves how far from transcendent or omnipotent such a conception of authoritarian fatherhood really is: the myth of immutable paternal fiat is for Stead *only* myth, daily contravened by Sam's materiality as a man and father. In contrast to the power of the Symbolic Father of Lacanian theory, Sam's power is not simply located in a vortex of "absence" but in an overbearing plentitude of presence that, Stead demonstrates, simultaneously makes his authority vulnerable to challenge.

To understand both the extent and precariousness of Sam's paternal rule, we need to consider in more detail the narcissism underlying his need to become "one" with his children. As in Sutpen's case, the act of fathering children and then claiming their independent existences as his own becomes a way of denying their (and the world's) threatening otherness by recreating it as sameness. "You are myself," Sam coaxes Louie (136), and in face of her resistance, prophesies that, if not now, in the near future "you will be like me" (354). The very terms of Sam's pathological demand, however, begin to deconstruct his claim to paternal superiority. For example, in traditional psychoanalytic terms the father serves as the voice of prohibition that makes possible the child's successful individuation and healthy participation in culture, precisely by enforcing a separation from the dangerous engulfment of the mother. But in *The Man Who Loved Children* the absolutely devouring narcissism of Sam's claim on Louie ("you are me") serves as a forceful reminder that fathers as well as mothers can be experienced as engulfing threats. In the case of Louie and her siblings, it is explicitly the father who fills the role of the narcissistically threatening mother, while it is Henny who inspires their desire to separate.[58] Sam's claim to self-sufficient authority is also belied by the *extremity* of his need to see his children as extensions of his ego; the fact is that without their devotion Sam would possess no self at all—his identity has come to depend on their presence every bit as much as theirs on his. Hence, in the narcissistic attempt to make his children mirrors of himself, Sam becomes what he sees: an overgrown child, caught in a juvenile competition of one-upmanship with his progeny. Again, the *reality* of paternal narcissism begins to counter the *myth* of paternal authority.

To the degree that Sam's psyche is so absolutely invested in fatherhood, his "love" also becomes a sadistic expression of power and control, the politics of which dovetail, in uncanny ways, with the fascist ideology of fatherhood being espoused in Germany and Italy. In his explanation of the psychology of fascism, Theodor Adorno argues that the successful dictator, like Sam himself, "has to appear himself as absolutely narcissistic," one who "does not love" but commands the love of his followers in the form of irrational discipleship and the masochistic surrender of their ego boundaries to the leader's more omnivorous ego.[59] The same narcissistic libidinal investment dictates Sam's ultimately sadistic relationship to his children; to possess his offspring totally, he violently transgresses the psychic, emotional, and even physical boundaries of their independent existences. Hence the discomfiting scene in which Sam first makes a "loving" show of joining his lips to those of his youngest son, Tommy, to funnel chewed sandwich into the infant's mouth; "mottled with contained laughter," he then attempts the same with Louie, "trying to force . . . banana into her mouth with his tongue," until she breaks away in fright and disgust (57–58).[60] Part of the horror of such moments is the way in which Sam couches his seductive appeals in a "honeyed, teasing voice" that leaves the children powerless to resist his triumph of will (47). However, the power that resides in Sam's manipulative charm just as easily manifests itself as sadistic cruelty. During the Sunday as "Funday" set piece that occupies the first hundred pages of the novel, Sam encourages a fight between Ernie and Saul (calling their locked fists an expression of love), and when Saul breaks away in "tears of rage and humiliation," Sam leads the whole pack howling after him with cruel taunts. Ultimately Sam turns the event (which he, after all, has instigated) into a pious object lesson: a "man-to-man fight" cleans out the bad blood and makes for the happy family—"Hey, presto! we're wholesome and clean again, good citizens and good brothers" (84–86). The political implications of the sadistic streak underlying Sam's notion of good "citizenry" and brotherhood become clear, as noted earlier, in the vision of a better society that Sam unfolds to his impressionable audience this same day. This utopic world, which Sam proposes to name *Monoman* or *Manunity*, will attain perfection through the practice of eugenic control, "weed[ing] out the misfits or degenerates" (50) in the name of the "unity" of "man" (*Man/unity*). Such a state, as Louie wisely interjects, might more aptly be called "monomania," and, indeed, its monomaniacal insistence on sameness mirrors Sam's ruling principle of totalitarian fatherhood. Paternal authoritarianism, Stead implies, is part of a larger global totalitarianism that creates dictators who not only preach (as does Sam) theories of racial superiority but who also put them into deadly practice.

Consequently, Sam's domestic territorialism demands that he wipe out, in the name of the father, all traces of maternal authority. Stead uses the occasion of his very first appearance in the novel to underline this equivocal relation to the maternal. Approaching Tohoga Place in the evening, he witnesses Henny half-strangling Louie through a lit window, only to turn his back on this scene of domestic violence and deliver a strangely inappropriate encomium of love to "Mother Earth" (20–21). Ironically, what disturbs Sam here is less Henny's violence toward Louie than its demonstration of her unwomanly *power* that betrays the ideal of universalized Mother Nature that he shares in common with the fascist leaders he admires; within the Führer's ideology women are fecund earth mothers whose fulfillment of biological destiny is a social duty serving the national good. Nonuniversalized, all-too-human mothers, in contrast, pose a tangible threat to Sam's fantasized self-image as autonomous creator of his family plot. Sam's reaction is literally to attempt to appropriate Henny's procreative labors for himself, as the occasion of the birth of their son Charles-Franklin (reported in the "Morning Rise" chapter) horrifically illustrates. Forcing all the bewildered children awake "to hear the new baby come" (287)—itself a dubious parental decision—Sam begins to chant low before their eyes and then, in a virtual simulation of Henny's delivery, turns "red with delight and success" (289) when the baby's cries join its mother's off-stage screams.[61] Henny remains invisible throughout the whole chapter; Sam's antics have entirely monopolized the narrative's focus, just as he has usurped Henny's act of creation in order to restage it as *his* "success," the "morning rise" of *his* sun/son.

Sam's attitude towards female procreativity reflects his ambivalence towards sexuality in general. For Sam, sex is double-edged: he is driven by sexual needs that his puritanical self-image tells him are repulsive, and hence he represses those desires, only to have them resurface in inappropriate, childish ways (his puerile flirtation with the "child-woman" Gillian Roebuck, his erotic domination of his children). These contradictions carry over into Sam's attitude towards his own body. On one hand, unlike Thomas Sutpen, this is a father who prides himself on his corporeality, parading half-naked in front of his children while preaching (like the Hitler Youth leagues) physical fitness and the benefits of naturism: "The morning was hot, and Sam had nothing on beneath his painting overalls. When he waved his golden-white muscular hairless arms, large damp tufts of yellow-red hair appeared. He kept on talking. . . . He was not ashamed of his effluvia, thought it a gift that he sweated so freely" (49–50). On the other hand, when it comes to Louie's body, Sam is repulsed by thoughts of the maturation she is undergoing:

He feared, with the shrinking of the holily clean, the turpitudes of adolescence, and although boys might go through it, he heartily wished that bright
pure womanhood could leap straight from Little-Womey's innocence to the
gentle sobriety of Gillian Roebuck's nineteen or twenty years. The swelling
thighs and broad hips and stout breasts and fat cheeks of Louisa's years . . .
were repugnant to Sam: he wanted a slim, recessive girl whose sex was
ashamed. (329)

Underlying Sam's fastidiousness is the fear of a sexuality whose productive
fecundity (Louie's broad hips versus Gillian's recessive sex) stands to challenge his identity as the autonomous male creator of his family text.
Within the parameters of Sam's paternal plot, sexual desire must yield to
functionality: one has sex not because one desires the other or enjoys the
act but because heterosexual coitus is the only way to produce the progeny
that will bolster one's position of supremacy.

In this regard, it is noteworthy that Sam has intercourse with Henny
only twice during the course of the novel, and each occurrence is calculated
to ensure the success of his paternal plot. The first incident occurs the
night of the long Sunday/Funday sequence. Having just announced his
upcoming departure for Malaya on a work assignment, Sam proceeds to
seduce Henny, impregnating her in order to guarantee her compliance during his nine-month absence. As she angrily declares on his return, "Didn't
he fix me up, pin me down, make sure no man would look at me while he
was gallivanting with his fine ladies?" (269). Even more revealing is the
second sexual encounter between Henny and Sam, elliptically reported toward the end of the novel. Sam has received an anonymous hate letter
intimating that he is not the father of the baby Charles-Franklin, which
unearths all his anxieties about paternity's uncertain status and hence about
his own masculinity. The result is a domestic battle that rages into all hours
of the night. Louie, waking to the sounds of scuffling, fears her parents are
murdering each other, then hears Henny's "fretful hysterical laugh"—"Oh
leave me alone, you make me sick"—after which there is more "violent
struggle," and then Louie hears "Sam groan" (435). What Louie imagines
to be Sam's cry of distress from a death wound inflicted *by* Henny turns
out to be the orgasmic climax of Sam's forcing himself *on* Henny, in order
to prove, in advance of the fact, that he is the father of any future child
Henny might bear. In a profound sense, Sam's rape of Henny literalizes
Sutpen's ravishment of his land in *Absalom, Absalom!* Both acts are aggrandizing impositions of ego calculated to secure the interest of the father's
estate in the face of the incertitude underlying his claim to authority.

The "Great Mouthpiece" Gets Off

The conceit of Sam authorizing a "family plot" becomes much less abstract
when we turn to the role played by his use of rhetoric in constructing this

text. Language, above all, is Sam's special tool for enforcing his rule. "The Word was sacred to him" (265), Stead summarizes Sam's boast to his children, who from their earliest years have intuited that "their father was the tables of law" (34). As such Sam becomes the symbolic author and keeper of the linguistic realm into which they have been born: "The children listened to every word he said, having been trained to him from the cradle" (328). As "the Great Mouthpiece" (172), however, Sam's linguistic power is not simply that of the abstracted Lacanian father and lawgiver; rather, it is an ever-present, oppressive reality, both in the world of his family and in the experience of Stead's readers. Badgering and whining and charming his listeners into compliance with a tongue of "quicksilver" (36) that easily shifts among scraps of baby talk, "perennial humanitarian orations" (36), sing-song rhymes, pious moral pronouncements, and "little speculations and homilies" (340), Sam demonstrates a linguistic prowess worthy of Joyce's exhibitionistic verbal flexing in "Circe"; as Lidoff notes, Sam creates "entire worlds" with his rhetoric alone.[62] Captivated by his verbal magic, the children literally become Sam's captives. Hence Louie muses, in Stead's paraphrase toward the end of the novel, that "she [had] no longer thought of Sam as . . . anything but a mouthy jailer for months" (503). For Sam's command of words also perniciously extends itself into the lives of the children by becoming a command over *their* language: he demands their written allegiance by placing them under orders to write him individual letters while he is in Malaya; he assigns Louie her reading material and requires her to give recitations every morning. Despite the apparent heteroglossia of his many voices, then, the ultimate narrative effect of Sam's manipulation of his words and the words of his dependents is to create an overwhelmingly monological discourse. In truth, Sam resists any openly dialogic encounter with alterity, responding only to echoes of his own words (or their mirrored reflections in his children), and this defiant monologism not only flattens the surface of the narrative into virtually a one-dimensional plane—that of Sam's self-glorifying paternal text—but also produces a discourse unusually successful in drowning out alternative linguistic realms, including those occupied by Henny and the children, along with the stories these dependents might wish to invoke.[63]

The intensity of Sam's dominance over the narrative has two crucial, interrelated formal consequences for the text that is *The Man Who Loved Children*. One of Stead's brilliant narrative strategies is to make it appear as if Sam's language has inundated all the usual narrative functions—including authorial viewpoint, realistic presentation, imagery—so that the third-person text often seems scripted by its internal creator figure, Sam.[64] But at the same time, Sam's self-involved monologism fosters, on the level of story, his (oedipal) blindness to the operations of everyday family life, and this blindness sets up the situation for a text that at times strikes the reader—and this is Stead's second masterstroke—*as being dizzyingly, gro-*

tesquely, out of control. Once again, this lack of control, in the face of its ostensible operation, can be measured on the level of technique, and as such, it is part of Stead's overall narrative strategy: the unreliability of omniscient focus during crucial episodes, disorienting shifts in the use of indirect free discourse, distortions of viewpoint, and abrupt cessation or repression of significant plot threads, all become symptomatic of a text whose authority is in imminent danger of collapse.

I have already commented on the quality of "warped realism" engendered by Stead's narrative erotics. This warping effect, I suggest, is largely the product of the way Stead "allows" the narrative to present its portrait of reality as it occurs to Sam, as if filtered through his viewpoint. This is not to say that Stead entirely erases her authorial presence from the text's third-person narration, but that what "omniscience" there is in the text exists in a very volatile relation to the subjects of its narration. More often than not, as McLaughlin has observed, the "omniscient voice denies us overt help in finding a focus,"[65] and throughout the reader is brought up short against seemingly objective passages of narration that turn out, in retrospect, to be subjective and partial. This is particularly true of Stead's deceptive use of indirect free discourse, the novelist's traditional tool for approximating a character's thought-processes within third-person narration. Not only does Stead set into motion disconcerting shifts in perspective from indirect free discourse to authorial commentary, but she also utilizes a narrative voice that often *pretends* to enter into the field of a given character's perspective, when in fact it remains at a distance, thereby only creating the illusion of indirect free discourse and a privileged "inside" view of character.[66] Whenever we think we are getting an unbiased representation of the Pollit world, the subtle instability infusing Stead's narrative reminds us that we are not.

Accompanying this mimetic distortion, especially in the first half of the novel, is the text's ongoing omission of crucial, unpleasant truths that would undermine Sam's wishfully benign vision. Some critics have faulted Stead for withholding facts or inserting them "in the wrong place" (for example, nearly forty pages pass before we discover that the parents are not talking to each other!).[67] Conversely, I would argue that these elisions deliberately and perversely mimic Sam's textual enterprise, omitting those facts which cast doubt on his paternal authority while painting the most negative portrait possible of Henny as the source of the family's economic ruin and the embodiment of chaos. It is no coincidence that our most poignant glimpses of Henny's trials and of the unconditional love that the children bear her occur only when Sam is offstage, figuratively absent from the text he is attempting to control.

Numerous secondary textual "distortions" follow from these excesses and gaps in representation. There is, for example, Stead's use of elaborate, exaggerated imagery throughout, as when the third-person narrator begins one chapter, "On Sunday morning the sun bolted up brash and chipper from the salad beds of the Atlantic and with a red complexion came loping towards them over the big fishing hole of the Chesapeake" (24), and when we read, at the end of the same day, that "the sun went down in yellow pulp, and Sam's New Jerusalem was dissolved in a milk soup" (130). Here images from the familiar domestic world (salad beds, yellow pulp, milk soup) combine with the grotesque to evoke a grotesquely surreal landscape.[68] Another manifestation of this process of textual distortion can be located in the exaggerated intensity of Stead's chapter titles—"The meridian of murder," "Beautiful and childlike was he," "What will you shut up?"—which prepare the reader for the heightened representations of "reality" they contain. The frame of the familiar is further warped by Stead's disproportioning of temporal sequence, creating an offsetting rhythm of dilation and contraction that disrupts a sense of smooth succession between events. A single day takes up nearly one-third of the novel, whereas months rush by in the following chapter; other scenes unexpectedly evolve into major set pieces that seem to overrun the surrounding narrative space.

Stead also disrupts the traditional continuity of plot by inserting, seemingly at random, several quite surreal events that have no directly discernible or interpretable relation to the developing action. One example is the macabre incident in which Louie (having momentarily wandered away from Sam's games) is invited into the Kydds' house to drown their pet cat. Others include Louie's one-time encounter with the evil-spirited schoolgirl Olive (which leads nowhere), and her bizarre grilling by her grandmother's maid Nellie, who maliciously tells Louie that she is both a bastard and a "norphan" and who seems clairvoyantly informed about the petty "crimes" of Louie's youth (174–75). Simply present in all their oddity, these "non-narrative" moments form seemingly unnecessary encumbrances—or, to recall my terminology in discussing Faulkner's text, grotesque excrescences—to the paternal plot.

Such a poetics of the perverse gives rise to the question of its underlying politics. Not insignificantly, all these examples depict Louie interacting with others *outside* the family nexus, suggesting rents in the fabric of Sam's paternal narrative through which other plots, however secondary or fragmentary, may temporarily be glimpsed. Given the fact that Sam's most important paternal tie is to Louie and that the oedipal dimensions of his family plot are chiefly conveyed through their father-daughter relationship, these deviations from the parent plot become all the more important. For in Stead's vision of the unwittingly deauthorizing designs of the father, it is precisely Sam's repressed desires for Louie—rather than, as in Freudian theory, her incestuous cathexis to him—that reveal those anxieties hidden within paternity that render its authority not only destructive but, as we shall now see, *self*-destructing.

Sins of the Snakeman, or Sam's Sham

The implications of this incestuous undercurrent in *The Man Who Loved Children* are present in the oedipal battles that "the man who loved children" wages with all his progeny, not just Louie. He sadistically reduces his namesake, Little-Sam, to an appalling state of "savage mutism" (393) in the hellish marlin boil episode, unmanning the boy in front of his siblings to ensure that he remain *little* Sam, a castrated version of the father; his blithe denial of the family's financial crisis leads his oldest son, Ernie, to hang himself in effigy during the novel's climax; he promises the aptly named Evie, the prototype of the dutiful daughter, that she can take Henny's place ("Why, Little-Womey, soon you got to be my wife, I speck" [385]).[69] But it is Louie who most fully awakens Sam's incestuous desires, precisely because she is most nearly his intellectual equal and because she most obstinately resists his manipulative charm. Hence, the more that the rapidly maturing Louie begins to differentiate her adolescent self from Sam, the more her father forcibly attempts to impose his identity onto hers through the process that Irigaray identifies as a masculine specularity: the act of consuming her individuality, making it identical to his, becomes Sam's psychological means of countering his fear of losing his own self, his male autonomy, through her individuation. In the process, what we have seen to be Sam's narcissistic wish, "You will be like me" (354), becomes the eroticized command, "You and I must cleave together" (479), and Sam's reaction to all that he cannot know or possess in Louie is the violent desire to destroy. "Was this tall, powerful girl with stern, hangdog face really Louie, the child of love? . . . Sam wanted to strike her across the face to obliterate that . . . mask" (276). What Sam desires to obliterate, of course, is the threat that Louie's otherness poses.

Because this threat of difference is most apparent in the bodily processes that are rapidly transforming Louie into a woman, the combat between father and daughter takes on an increasingly sexualized tenor, with Sam attempting to control Louie's sexuality through the mechanisms of erotic domination. That there is something dangerously prurient in these attempts to police Louie's eroticism is also conveyed in Sam's earlier violations of her privacy, as he surreptitiously "poke[s]" and "prie[s]" into her bedroom, "investigating her linen, shivering with shame when suggestive words c[o]me into her mouth" (329). This "mental lip-licking" (330) escalates when he discovers that Louie keeps a coded diary and forces her to translate it to him. The connotations of this textual violation as displaced sexual violence become even more glaring when Sam, "looking for fresh worlds to conquer" (423), discovers the Aiden sonnet cycle that Louie has been writing and mockingly declaims it in front of the other children, accusing her of "trying to practice poickry without a poick's license" (427).

Shift the *o* in "poick" to *r,* and Sam's unconscious subtext becomes quite clear; he is staking his phallic supremacy as the "lawful" manipulator of words on the traditionally Freudian myth of female sexuality as a lack.

Such eroticized combat—as in the case of the "unspeakable depravities" the Rector thinks about Yvette in *The Virgin and the Gipsy*—raises the specter of father-daughter incest, nowhere more evidently than in Sam's suspect methods of initiating Louie into the mysteries of sex. Telling her that "it is the father who should be the key to the adult world, for his daughters," this keybearer decides to "take the bull by the horns" and correct Louie's "'unscientific' view of procreation" by giving her, along with Shelley's *Poems* (including *The Cenci*) and Frazer's *Golden Bough,* James Bryce's account of the Belgian atrocities, whose graphic accounts of violent rape haunt Louie's "daydreams and night thoughts" (378–79).[70] As if in confirmation of these incestuous overtones, the episode in which Sam provides Louie with her "sex education" materials is immediately followed by the report of a local scandal, in which a pregnant "girl child" accuses her father of incest.[71] Sam immediately identifies with the father, whom he self-righteously claims *must* be innocent, excoriating those who would dare "attack a father in his own home" (379–80). While Ernie simply stares at Sam with the challenge of disbelief, Louie, having felt a shock of recognition in the reported story, boils "with a murderous revenge" (381). Her desire for vengeance takes the form, ironically, of a gift to her father, a one-scene verse-drama titled *Tragos: Herpes Rom,* or *The Tragedy of The Snake-Man, or Father,* that she writes in an invented language for her siblings to perform on Sam's birthday. Inspired by her reading of *The Cenci,* Louie's play centers on a father whose incestuous embrace kills his daughter (the plot anticipates Djuna Barnes's verse drama *Antiphon* [1958], which is set during World War II and directly links the threat of father-daughter incest to authoritarian fascism). With this single gesture, Louie begins to challenge the authoritative status of Sam's paternal fiction by inserting her own subversive countertext within its framework. Just as significantly, all Sam can do is "feebly" complain that it isn't in English and, when presented with its translation, mutter "I don't understand: is it a silly joke?" (401, 404). In a sudden turnabout, it is no longer clear just who has the upper hand in this "battle for control" between father and daughter—a sexual battle that, as Joan Lidoff states, is necessarily "fought in and over language."[72] More than one author, it would appear, is competing for control of Sam's precious family text.

The degree to which Louie's "silly joke" begins to destabilize the grounds upon which Sam has erected his fatherly designs, leaving him suddenly "enfeebled," calls attention to the many other self-subverting, half-hidden elements that his paternal text has just managed to cover over to this point. For every so often, a fissure in Sam's plot appears, disclosing a perspective that undermines his own. Most of these gaps center, tellingly, on Sam's failure to measure up to the traditional paternal role of wage earner. If there is one fact that Sam's narrative perspective persistently conceals, it is the *extremity* of the impoverishment his family undergoes once Sam is fired from his state position during the height of the Depression and the family is forced to leave Tohoga Place. In fact, we don't really have a clue to the degree of this extremity until, a full three-quarters of the way through the novel, Louie's English teacher, Miss Aiden, visits for dinner, providing the reader's first outside view of the family. Her horror-stricken realization that "the Pollits lived in a poverty that to her was actually incredible" (418) thus shocks us as much as Miss Aiden, for we have hitherto been shielded from such harsh realities by Sam's narrative control over the text's vision of the family. In Henny's response to one of Miss Aiden's questions, we also learn, for the first time, that her doctor has warned her to have only two children—but, as Louie innocently laughs, "they came" regardless (419). As more rents appear in Sam's text, it also becomes clear that Henny, not Sam, is the family's *actual* breadwinner; between her "promises, lies, and tricks" to borrow on credit and her dividends from her father's estate, the family barely manages to survive, while Sam, still out of work, pretends "to ignore where the household money [comes] from. . . . About their money, as about everything, he was vague and sentimental" (369–70).

With this gradual rewriting of the myth of paternal fiat, the increasing bedlam generated by Sam's assumption of authority becomes more and more visible. Chaos is not, as Sam's version of the family text preaches, the exclusive property of Henny's chthonic realm. This fact is graphically illustrated at the novel's end when, in Henny's absence, the family descends into hellish anarchy, slop pails standing unemptied, the baby Charles-Franklin eating his excrement, and Sam, ever the disinterested scientist, proclaiming it "natural" (458). This is indeed "gothic" horror, disguised by Sam as naturism but conveyed by Stead as surrealist psychodrama.

The stark reality and pathos of Sam's failure to live up to the myth of fatherhood when it comes to the level of immediate, material need is mirrored in the failure of the male-ordained structures of patriarchy to support and sustain Sam in his hour of need. In *Absalom, Absalom!* we saw how these structures of male homosocial bonding—perpetuating the sexual commerce in women upon which patriarchy rests—also generated the very anxieties of masculinity that helped deauthorize that plot of the father. At the same time, we noted that such bonds exert an undeniably powerful *imaginative* control over Faulkner's text—they are central to the whole mythos it is attempting to recreate. Stead's paternal plot, in contrast, gradually exposes the male homosocial network as a fabrication hardly worth its name. Even though, in a classic instance of the homosocial barter in women, Henny's father has handpicked Sam Pollit to be his son-in-law, advancing him in government service as a business investment, this male bond is totally undercut when Mr. Collier dies, leaving his son-in-law with nothing but his debts (which strip the family of Tohoga Place); even more significantly, the end of his father-in-law's patronage leads to Sam's loss of his government job.[73]

Incapable of measuring up in a world of men that either bullies him or lets him down, Sam increasingly turns to his children because they are indeed *all* he has got; thus in their dilapidated new home in Maryland he creates for them a fantastical, self-enclosed, and wishfully static world because here—and only here—can he exercise the absolute command denied him in the "real" world of men. But the more he exists in this world of illusion, the more that world becomes susceptible to the fissures and breaks that call his version of the family myth into question. And one of the possibilities that glimmers through these cracks is the simple fact that there may be a covert *female* homosocial network, not a male one, that ultimately holds sway, determines identity development, and initiates narrative progression in Stead's vision of Pollitry.

Outlawed Languages and "the Natural Outlawry of Womankind"

The idea of a secret alliance of women working to undermine Sam's paternal plot returns us to a phenomenon observed in *Absalom, Absalom!*—namely, the subversive role played by mothers and daughters in deauthorizing the oedipal designs of which they are an ineluctable part. Initially, Henny appears to be the most avid deconstructor of the myth of authoritarian fatherhood that Sam is attempting to construct. "Sam was household czar by divine right, but Henny was the czar's everlasting adversary, household anarchist by divine right" (34), the narrator comments in politically charged metaphors that abut the novel's undercurrent of antifascist allegory. In Stead's version of paternal narrative, as opposed to Faulkner's, the mother's presence simply cannot be expunged, and the oppressed Henny's protesting voice, however garbled and splintered by Sam's engulfing textual presence, is never completely silenced. Although Sam attempts to contain Henny's disruptive power by writing it into his text as the personification of archetypal, chthonic anarchy, Stead's terms make it clear that Henny's resistance as "household anarchist," is an intuitively political act, a response to enforced oppression and marginalization by what Woolf calls in *Three Guineas* the "Dictator . . . at home" (53).[74]

In addition, the text's many images of Henny as an "old witch," whose "black fits" are legion and whose famous "black look" is feared by all, dimly reflect the subversive if ambivalent power that is still hers (here, again, Stead and Faulkner share in a mode of Southern modernist "gothic"). Evidence of this power resides in the way all the children respect Henny and accord her "natural rights" that they never grant their father. For to them she is not, as Sam would have it, a personification of diabolic monstrosity but rather "a charming, slatternly witch, their household witch; everything that she did was right, right, her right: she claimed this right to do what she wished because of all her sufferings, and the children believed in her rights" (368). In all her otherness, in her exemption from Sam's law, Henny thus holds open to the children an alternative world and language, epitomized in her room (into which Sam is never allowed) with its treasure-troves of mysterious cabinets and drawers (32), "her wonderful yarn[s]" (8) of a world populated with freaks and outcasts narrated in a vivid language of her own creation, and the riddles and "rigmaroles" that she, Sphinx-like, tells the spellbound children only "when Daddy [is] out" (5). Even when Daddy isn't out, Henny has a voice: another one, to be sure, embattled, shrill, and half-maddened, pouring out in nonstop, virtuoso, nonsensical, page-long paragraphs that temporarily interrupt the flow of Sam's pontifications and dredge up those embarrassing facts that his text would prefer to ignore.

But despite her occasional ability to disrupt Sam's text, Henny nonetheless remains, like Chopin's Edna Pontellier, psychologically embedded in the chain of male exchange that has defined her existence, dictated her traditional expectations—of money, adoration, leisure—and, furthermore, distorted her self-image as a woman and sexual being.[75] It remains for Louie—who eventually refuses to participate in this chain—to subvert her father's text by learning to write her own story. In fighting for control of the words with which to express her creation of a self born phoenixlike out of the struggle for separation and individuation, Louie rewrites in an even more dramatic sense than Faulkner's Rosa Coldfield the oedipal logic of narrative. To break out of this life-denying logic, Louie must first break free of Sam's verbal power—a power which, as we have already seen, allows him to impose upon his family a stifling homogeneity that flattens dissent and outlaws difference. In antithesis to Sam's use of language as a tool of domination, the story of Louie's growth as the figurative author of her own life and literal author of actual texts demonstrates the life-affirming ability of Stead's characters to "speak . . . their world[s] into existence"[76] by renewing language's outlawed multivocality.

An initial stage in Louie's rebellion against Sam's discursive fiat is simply silence, a refusal to enter dialogue on the "great mouthpiece's" terms. A related tactic is that of covertly disrupting the master discourse. Hence the episode in which Louie, instead of taking notes during one of Sam's self-interested "perennial humanitarian orations" (as he supposes her to be doing), produces a countertext inimical to his fatherly instruction: "*Shut up, shut up, shut up, shut up, shut up, I can't stand your gassing, oh, what a windbag, what will shut you up, shut up, shut up*" (363). Powerful as this statement of protest is, it is nonetheless conceived in reaction to, and thus to some degree is contained by, the paternal exercise of linguistic authority against which it directs itself. Much more self-empowering, in contrast, is

Louie's development of her own artistic voice in the series of texts, both verbal and written, that she produces. While Sam is absent in Malaya, Louie uses her inventive talents as a storyteller to soothe her siblings with the bedtime tale of "Sam-the-Bold" and the weretigers; her harrowing fable of "Hawkins, the North Wind," narrated the night that Sam rapes Henny, serves a similar purpose by distracting the children from their parents "going it hammer and tongs" downstairs (428).[77]

Simultaneously, Louie begins to conceive of her imaginative capacities as forms of art. Her gift to Sam upon his return from Malaya consists of three spontaneously composed and recited lyrics in the style of Confucius (275–76); upon entering high school at Annapolis, she begins to write, first in jest as she combines themes of social marginality and linguistic perversion in her pun-filled, Djuna Barnes-like story of the circus wedding (337), then in solemn earnest as she falls in love with her English teacher and begins the monumental Aiden Cycle, "which would consist of a poem in every conceivable form and also every conceivable meter in the English language, each and every one, of course, in honor of Miss Aiden" (340). In terms of Louie's search for modes of expression free of Sam's influence, it is telling that the Aiden Cycle's proliferating love sonnets—which Louie daily circulates among her equally infatuated schoolgirl friends—rewrite the Petrarchan tradition from which they spring by inscribing a circuit of female-female passion. Proclaiming Miss Aiden their "Onlie Begetter" (340), these sonnets implicitly challenge Sam's status as prime mover or "only begetter" of Louie's life—hence the otherwise inexplicable affront he feels upon discovering and reading them.

In direct relation to Louie's growing awareness of her renegade female status, she also finds empowerment, however temporary, in the prototypically subaltern exercise of "writing from the margin." Her coded diary is a classic example of the outlawed woman writer's attempt to find a private space for self-expression. Likewise, Louie's immediate reaction upon writing the *Herpes Rom* drama is to translate it into "a secret language" created on the spot: "So that she could write what she wished, she would invent an extensive language to express every shade of her ideas. 'Everyone has a different sphere to express, and it goes without saying that language as it stands can never contain every private thought'" (385). Given *Herpes Rom*'s debt to *The Cenci,* one might argue (setting aside Shelley's own feminism) that Louie still remains under the shadow of a male literary tradition, or that coded writing at best only subverts the status quo from within its structures. But it is crucial to note that Stead makes a point of stating that on this occasion Louie, for the first time in her adolescent writing career, primarily "wrote for herself," not for her brothers and sisters or even Miss Aiden (385): Sam's approval or disapproval is ultimately less important than the statement her text makes. In this regard, the play's final line, "Mother, Father is strangling me. Murderer!" (404), which rewrites the scene at the beginning of the novel where Sam spies on Henny throttling Louie, resonates with several possible layers of meaning. Although doomed to die like Beatrice Cenci, the daughter in this drama gives voice to the possibility of parental incest evaded in Freud's account of the girl's oedipal dilemma, in which the burden of incestuous desire is shifted to the child. For in Louie's rewriting, the *fantasy* of seduction by the father postulated by Freud is given a murderous *reality,* and his conclusion that the preoedipal "powerful attachment of the girl to her mother . . . is destined to make room for an attachment to her father" ("Femininity," 106–7) is countermanded by the daughter's last words, which attempt to reestablish a dialogue with the absent mother rather than conciliate or "make room for" the father. Although Louie's play concludes with the silencing of the daughter, Louie herself remains alive and her message clearly if covertly expressed; as such, Sheridan has commented, Louie becomes "the prototype of the woman writer, as Julia Kristeva and others would now see her, struggling to speak against the Name-of-the-Father, discovering the feminine repressed by the discourses of a patriarchal symbolic order, breaking into the pre-symbolic, semiotic space below."[78]

Contrary to the Kristevan prototype, however, Louie's artistic and linguistic growth does not remain restricted to "the pre-symbolic, semiotic space below." This fact can be measured in Sam's growing uneasiness when faced with the reality of Louie's rapidly developing verbal capabilities and her pleasure at participating in and even controlling the "symbolic order" of language he thinks his special domain. It is precisely this sense of competitive territorialism that leads Sam to humiliate Louie (under the guise of good-natured humor) in front of her best friend Clare by belittling her intellectual skills: "Looloo [thinks] of nothin' but eating all the dickshunairies she [can] find and [goes] around chock-full of big words aspewin' em out and destroyin' the peas of mind of the famerlee" (351). It might be going too far suggest that the phallic reference that Sam's baby talk "inserts" into the word dick-tionary is deliberate, an intentional effort to reclaim language under the sign of the phallus, the "Name-of-the-Father" to which Sheridan refers. But it does seem clear that Sam subconsciously imagines Louie's "eating" of language as resulting in a kind of self-impregnation ("chock-full of big words"), and it is her capacity, both as woman and as author, to give birth ("aspewin' em out") to meaning that Sam sees as threatening his own status as primary progenitor of the "famerlee" text. This crisis of authority helps explain the extremity of Sam's negative reactions to Louie's literary creations (whereas, earlier, he has encouraged her intellectual development as long as he deemed it a reflection of his Apollonian wisdom): hence his violent desire to slap her when she recites her Confucian poems, his public humiliation of her Aiden sonnets as "sickening tommyrot" (426), and his reaction to her play as "stupid and silly" (404).

The very nature of this battle over words goes to show that the so-called law of the father does not, in fact, extend unconditionally over the realm of language. The discursive order is not, as Lacanian and French feminist theory of the 1980s argued, a uniformly patriarchal realm, nor is language inevitably the medium of women's oppression. For Louie, rather, the materiality of words serves an empowering and potentially emancipatory function. This is not meant to imply that women have not often found language exclusionary and alienating, but to suggest, as Patricia Yaeger forcefully argues, that the multivoicedness of language has *also* made historically available to women a realm of linguistic inventiveness, orality, and play. The destabilizing properties inherent in all language, that is, free potential artists like Louie to "seize words and use them for [their] own purposes," turning language against the assumptions of a "prior, masculine authority" with which others, like Sam, may have hitherto invested it.[79]

A fascinating example of the process by which Louie's reappropriation of language assumes an emancipatory power capable of withstanding her father's claims to linguistic priority occurs in the wonderfully named chapter, "Sam Suspended," as Sam lasciviously pokes and pries into the privacy of Louie's room. To measure the impact of this moment, we need to review the stages leading to it. A few chapters earlier, shortly after the occasion of Charles-Franklin's birth, Louie combats Sam's claims to omnipotence by quoting Nietzsche at him:

> "I know something. . . . I know there are people not like us, not muddle-headed like us, better than us. . . . I know something else: if it is chaos, it will not be chaos forever: 'out of chaos ye shall give birth to a dancing star.' Nietzsche said that."
>
> Sam blushed, and he said gently, "You mean, out of confusion we will bring order."
>
> "No," cried Louie, "no, no; you understand nothing." (302)

Sam's ineffectual attempt to replace Louie's understanding—that chaos may be productive, leading to the birth of the dancing star that is herself—with his more conservative reading of chaos as the negative precondition of "order" comes back to haunt him when, prying into Louie's room, uneasily sniffing out signs of her sexuality, the inspiring words that she has learned from Nietzsche *unconsciously infiltrate and subsume his thoughts*: "His nice Louisa, . . . he could see (much as he closed his eyes), was a burning star, new-torn from the smoking flesh of a mother sun, a creature of passion" (329).

This is an absolutely pivotal moment in Sam's and Louie's war of words, for, as Stead's use of indirect free discourse reveals, in this moment Sam articulates his thoughts *within a set of terms whose meanings have now been set by Louie, rather than vice versa:* the daughter's language has begun to (re)shape her father's view of reality by putting it into dialogue with her own. In sum, what Louie's inventive, joyous use of words, both in her speech and in her writing, does to Sam is to render his discourse only "one among many modes of speech,"[80] and the effect is to destabilize Sam's claim to paternal fiat and transcendent meaning (hence his fears of a "creature of passion" born of the "*flesh* of a *mother* sun"). The linguistic freedom to which Louie aspires in her art is, of course, exactly what Stead's dazzling use of language-play has been demonstrating throughout the novel.

One consequence of Louie's mining of language's emancipatory potential is her construction of an individuated self, a triumphant and expansive "I am" (part Whitman, part Sappho, part Hélène Cixous *avant la lettre*), whose realm of being is literally and figuratively worlds removed from her familial role as domestic servant, substitute mother, and ugly duckling. As she ebulliently writes to her friend Clare,

> Everyone thinks I am sullen, surly, sulky, grim; but I am the two hemispheres of Ptolemaic marvels, I am lost Atlantis risen from the sea, the Western Isles of infinite promise, the apples of the Hesperides and daily make the voyage to Cytherea, island of snaky trees and abundant shade with leaves large and dripping juice, the fruit that is my heart, but I have a thousand hearts hung on every trees [*sic*], yes, my heart drips along every fence paling. I am mad with my heart which beats too much in the world and falls in love at every instant with every reflection that glimmers in it. (436)

This is the expression of a self that is "other" in every way to Sam's reality, a self freed from the mirror of his narcissism and capable of capturing, as the final image conveys, its own reflections of alterity. And if the cadences and images of Louie's intoxicated prose anticipate the language of Cixous's now classic essay, "The Laugh of the Medusa," one of Louie's main defenses against Sam's authoritarian commands turns out to be the Medusa-like laughter that Cixous celebrates, laughter which cuts through the cant of Sam's pontifications and silences his platitudes.

Another crucial ingredient in Louie's emerging authority is her increased identification with Henny ("the mother sun") rather than Sam. Drawn together in "a strange affection" based on what Stead calls "the natural outlawry of womankind" (258), the problematical bond between this stepmother and stepdaughter again suggests the presence of a subterranean, *female* version of Sedgwick's homosocial network at work in the novel, informing its final actions as well as its narrative trajectory in subtle, surprising ways. We have encountered versions of this female homosocial world in the female-dominated enclosures of *Villette* and on Grand Isle in *The Awakening,* speculated about its existence in *Dora,* and measured the psychic impact of its loss in *Mrs. Dalloway.* Even in the latter example, however, vestiges of a subterranean system of female communication exist, connecting women as disparate as Clarissa and Lady Bruton, whose "How's Clarissa?" to Richard Dalloway over lunch "infallibly" signifies to other women, Woolf writes, "a signal from a well-wisher, from an almost silent companion, whose utterances (half a dozen perhaps in the course of a lifetime) signified recognition of some feminine comradeship which went beneath masculine lunch parties and united Lady Bruton and Mrs. Dalloway who seldom met, and appeared when they did meet indifferent and even hostile, in a singular bond" (160–61).

From the novel's beginning Louie has suspected "that perhaps there was something to say on Henny's side" of the Sam/Henny divide, precisely because she, like Henny, is also always "guilty, rebellious, and . . . chastised" (35). In turn Henny is identified as "one of those women who secretly sympathize with all women against all men" (36), and her murderous rages against Louie simply underline the identification that exists between them—"I beat her until *I* can't stand," Henny cries in a revealing slippage of pronouns (94; emphasis added).[81] Furthermore, the centrality of female bonding in Louie's quest for self-recognition and autonomy is made manifest in the same-sex relations she begins to form outside the family circle. Some of her encounters, as her run-ins with Mrs. Kydd, Nellie, and Olive indicate, are inevitably ambiguous or negative. But there are also the self-affirming female models: Clare, the "blue-eyed female Caliban" (339) with whom Louie shares her dreams of freedom and fame, and the great "love" of her adolescent life, Miss Aiden, whose encouragement inspires her creative efforts. That these two relationships pose a real danger to Sam's paternal designs is revealed by his defensive reaction: he quite brazenly undertakes to woo and win over both Clare and Miss Aiden, using all the heterosexual charm he can muster in an attempt to displace Louie in their affections and thereby break up a female homosocial economy that excludes his participation. But the maneuver fails, for, as Louie declares to Sam in their final confrontation, "I'm my own mother" (524). With this affirmation of her partisanship in the "natural outlawry of womankind," Louie signals, at least on the level of language, her intention to break from the plot of the father by becoming her own parent and her own authority.

Renegotiating Oedipus: The Daughter as Quester

Yet there would seem to be an overwhelming paradox involved in Louie's declaration of emancipation: after all, she becomes her "own mother" by murdering, quite literally, her stepmother, Henny. Is this not merely a female version of the Oedipus story? To answer this question, we need to look at the grotesque events that form the simultaneously surreal and gothic climax of Stead's plot, which originates in Louie's desperate decision, as the parental war grows more hellish by the day, that the only way to "save the children" (502) is to poison both Sam and Henny. The scheme backfires, however, when Henny intuits Louie's plan and defiantly gulps the arsenic-filled tea before Louie has had time to prepare a second cup for

Sam.[82] The tragedy of Henny's death raises the question, then, of whether Louie's revolt against the plot of the father has been worth the effort; after all, she has only succeeded in killing the parent for whom she feels the most sympathy and in the process consolidated her father's dominance. In fact, to the accompaniment of an unbelievably rapid series of turns in good fortune, Sam's totalitarian powers reassert themselves with a vengeance, his narrative presence once again engulfing the novel and his paternal authority emerging triumphant: he is vindicated by the community, gains an instant replacement for Henny in the form of his hapless sister Bonnie, and is on the verge of a new profession, as radio host of "The Uncle Sam Hour." Just as he has become, again, sole mouthpiece of his family, this fascist-sympathizing domestic tyrant now intends to become the voice of American democracy on the eve of war. In the face of this rebirth of Sam's hitherto collapsing paternal power, the only solution left to Louie is to run away from home, and this action is narrated as the novel's final event. With her departure, the version of the family text over which Sam claims authorship (which he would no doubt also title *The Man Who Loved Children*) has expelled its two most disruptive elements—his wife and eldest daughter—leaving his authority over the remaining children, along with his titular status, unchallenged.

Stead qualifies this ostensible story of patriarchal success, however, by simultaneously allowing the reader to view Sam's rehabilitated family plot from its margins, and from this vantage point the plot of the father begins to look less like a clear-cut or total success. The image that Stead uses to describe Louie's matured view of Sam's equivocal paradise poignantly suggests this "other side" to Sam's story: "She was on the other side of a fence; there was a garden through the chinks [in the fence] that she had once been in, but could never be in again. Yet she did not care" (517). Given Louie's pressing need for differentiation from this incestuously engulfing father, her expulsion from this garden is truly a *felix culpa;* it allows her to see that Sam's circumscribed realm no longer occupies, indeed has never occupied, the center of the larger world, but rather is relegated to the sidelines, visible only through the "chinks" in the dividing line between innocence and experience. The implications of this shift in perspective for the status of Sam's text become manifest in the final encounter of father and daughter. As Sam begs her to "stick to him and be happy," Louie rejects his plea by finally naming it for what it is: "'The same old story,' Louie muttered at last" (521).

And with this refusal of the same old story, the possibility of creating a new textual space outside the plot of the father—anticipated throughout the narrative by Louie's emerging status as an author in her own right—becomes reality. This textual hope receives symbolic expression in the novel's last scene as Louie runs away from Spa House in the early hours of the morning. Pausing on the Eastport bridge, a liminal boundary between past and future, Louie experiences a magical liberation of vision as the blinders imposed by Sam's "old story" drop away: "How different everything looked, like the morning of the world, that hour before all other hours. . . . 'Why didn't I run away before?' she wondered. . . . Things certainly looked different: *they were no longer part of herself but objects that she could freely consider without prejudice*" (525; emphasis added). Readers have sometimes questioned whether Louie has really freed herself from Sam's influence, whether her euphoria in escaping has merely blurred her vision. The implication that Louie has traded blindness for sight in leaving home begins to suggest a more hopeful answer. So too, I think, do the narrative terms of Stead's ending, whereby Louie's escape from the paternal text and the final lines of the novel are presented as one and the same event, with any hint of turning back soundly negated: "As for going back towards Spa House, she never even thought of it. Spa House was on the other side of the bridge" (527).[83] In psychological terms, the division of self and object ("they were no longer part of herself but objects") that Louie becomes aware of while crossing Eastport bridge—a separation that Sam's myopic vision consistently lacks and that his incestuous mode of bonding with his children has disavowed—gives her the aesthetic distance necessary to begin the authorial task of recasting, on this Thoreauvian "morning of mornings," her life as a continuing, open-ended story.

The sequence of events that brings Louie to this threshold, moreover, contains an ingenious revision of the psychosexual dynamics assumed to be constitutive of paternal narrative. For in making the latter third of the novel the story of Louie's growth to maturity, Stead brilliantly models the progress of Louie's individuation *on a step-by-step inversion* of the constitutive elements of the Oedipus story, creating too neat a reversal, as David Wingrove has proposed, to be unintentional.[84] In Sophocles' version of the myth, Oedipus's patricide leads to union with the mother, a violation of the incest taboo for which he is punished with blindness. The questing Louie's *matricide,* in contrast, leads to her *severance* from the *father,* an escape *from* incest for which she is rewarded with quite literal *sight* ("How different everything looked"). As matricide is substituted for patricide in the daughter's story, so severance from the father replaces union with the mother, escape replaces violation, and sight replaces blindness. Moreover, if Oedipus's blinding brings about his insight into the truth that his end lies in his origin—the pattern that narrativists like Barthes and Brooks have made the foundation of their theories—the difference in *outer* perspective granted to Louie by her new vision is precisely the marker of her removal from Sam's narratological economy of predetermined origins and endings—and, we might add, from the economy of oedipal theories of narrative.

Stead's story of the daughter's struggle for separation from the parent also challenges the role and aim assigned the oedipal conflict in traditional psychoanalytic theories of female development. Ironically, Freud's account of the daughter's desire for the father anticipates the narrative that the father in Stead's text desires to impose on his daughter. Hence Sam paints Louie's stepmother Henny as the "bad mother" to be rejected, sets himself up as the true object of her desire, attempts to force her secondary identification with an "ideal"—that is, powerless—mother (the dead Rachel), and fantasizes that Louie will grow up to be a nice, feminine woman who will make a man like himself (if not him) happy. Louie, as we have seen, ultimately turns a deaf ear to all these appeals. As Sheridan notes, she refuses the usual psychoanalytic "resolution of the feminine oedipus complex" by refusing to submit to "the passive aim of father-attachment," which would entail "becom[ing] (like) the mother."[85] This rejection of paternal cathexis *and* negative maternal identification is implicit in Louie's plan to murder *both* parents: on the one hand, she realizes that she has ceased to "[think] of Sam as her father . . . for months," while on the other she conceives of Henny's death as a kind of mercy killing ("as for Henny she did not see how her fate would be better if she went on living" [503]). Through this double rejection, Louie escapes the shadow of paternal law that demands her subjection and instead becomes an *acting* subject, one whose "walk around the world" (527) has just begun.

As such, Louie has become a quester par excellence, replacing Oedipus's anxieties—the male origin of narrativity—with the pleasures of female narratability. To portray Louie as an able and acting subject, creating her own story as she searches it out, also returns us to the discussion of *Villette* in chapter 1, and to my suggestion there that Lucy Snowe's heretic narrative raises serious questions about Teresa de Lauretis's argument that the very definition of narrative negates the possibility of representing female desire as its moving force. Stead's representation of Louie raises similar questions about the ubiquity of de Lauretis's claim that the oedipal story of the questing hero's movement into unknown space is "in fact paradigmatic of all narrative." As the active transgressor of boundaries and spaces that must be conquered en route to self-knowledge, the heroic mythical subject, de Lauretis continues, is inevitably constructed as a human being *and* a male, just as those inert markers of passage on his quest are inevitably gendered inhuman (or monstrous) and female: "Female is what is not susceptible to transformation . . . she (it) is an element of plot-space, a topos, a resistance, matrix and matter." This inscription of sexual difference into the mythic structuration of narrative leads to de Lauretis' resigned acceptance of "*the inherent maleness of all narrative movement*" and the impossibility of ever representing woman's desire as the moving force, the subject, of narrative: "her story, *like any other story,* is a question of *his* desire."[86]

While such a statement might ultimately describe Henny's fate in *The Man Who Loved Children,* how true is it of Louie's story and her desires? It strikes me that Stead, like Brontë before her, has created in Louie a female character who in the most profound sense *does* become an acting subject, the subject of not only her own but also the narrative's quest for meaning. It is Louie, after all, who in place of the mythical male subject becomes the agency of transformation dictating the text's final trajectory of desire. The result is that, in the final analysis, Louie's story is hardly a question of "his" desire—that is, of man's narrative-making capacities—as de Lauretis puts it; more accurately, *Sam's story has become a question of her desire*. For in Stead's boldest imaginative stroke, not only does Louie come to occupy the position of the questing hero who generates narrative movement, but, inversely, Sam, prime "mover" of the paternal plot, becomes the symbolic, static "text-space" through which she moves to maturity, and as such the mythical landscape confronting the questing (female) subject has here been *refigured as the father himself*. Fixed into place by the boundaries of the paternal fiction he has created in his own image, Sam ironically comes to embody the enclosing, devouring stasis that de Lauretis sees as "morphologically female and indeed, simply, the womb";[87] he becomes that liminal marker of positions whose stationary boundaries help define the progress of the hero but cease to authorize it.

Nor is the female quest of Louie just an interruption, a moment of resistance, in what de Lauretis (erroneously, I think) defines as the larger "masculine" structures of narrative movement. It is Sam, after all, not Louie, who at the end is left behind, trapped within a world that the reader knows is chaos and misery, whatever the appearance of success he manages to establish in the public sphere, just as he is trapped, figuratively speaking, between the material covers of the book that, ironically, bears his name. In narratological terms, one might say that the very anxieties of masculine authority that have inspired the domestic imperialism of this father, impelling him to subsume all difference under his name and law, have thus circuitously returned, in the disguise of "feminine" morphology, to transform him into his sexual/textual other: the abject, "monstrous" mother. What this slippage forcefully suggests is the textually, rather than biologically, constituted nature of the sexual distinctions upon which Sam has grounded his authority all along. The hypothesis that "the primary distinction" established by narrative "rests, first and foremost, on what we call biology," turns out to be the father's fantasy.[88] At the cross-roads of myth and psychoanalysis, then, one finds a very different story than the one extrapolated from the Oedipus legend by theorists from Freud to Brooks and de Lauretis.

With Louie's developing authority to act upon her own desires, to leave the paternal plot without looking back at the world "on the other side of the bridge," not only is Sam's authority, even over his fantasies, thrown into question, but what de Lauretis defines as "the work of narrativity itself"—"the production of Oedipus"—is radically redefined.[89] In Stead's brilliant revision of oedipal narrative, the deauthorizing designs of the father make way for an alternative myth, that of the female/daughter quester for whom the Oedipus story is a pre-text, neither the first nor final word, neither the beginning nor culmination, of her infinite desires.

If the plots of the father represented in *The Man Who Loved Children* and *Absalom, Absalom!* demonstrate that the "work of narrativity" might be more complicated than various theories of narrative based on the search for paternal origins suggest, it is in large part because the domestic imperialism of Sam and the regional imperialism of Sutpen—as the word *imperialism* betrays—exceeds the psychoanalytically defined boundaries of the oedipal scenario of fathers and sons (or daughters) and spills into the political and indeed global sphere of material human relations. In these novels, that is, the desire that drives the plot does not conform to one universal paradigm of narrative so much as it responds to, and thereby exposes, those historically specific ideologies of fatherhood, race, and nation whose claim to universalizing power depends on promulgating the myth that there *is* a definitive beginning and ending, an explanatory narrative that will counter the chaos and lack of meaning associated with twentieth-century modernity. The plot of the father, the story of Oedipus, does not exist in isolation but responds to its historical contexts in ways that subtly inflect the desire of and for narrative. In the era of the 1930s, this political context was provided, as this chapter has shown, by the specter of fascist engulfment that culminated in World War II.

Given the international repercussions of the conflict that looms on the horizon of these fictions, it makes sense to ask what world lies for Louie Pollit on the "other side of the bridge" once she makes her escape from Sam's claustrophobic realm at the end of *The Man Who Loved Children*. The global order I imagine her entering is the world of the war-exile and postwar diaspora, the world of crumbling colonial empires and the beginning of the Cold War, the world in which the "Third World" assumes unprecedented importance. This political and psychic landscape also becomes the backdrop for the late modernist experiments in novelistic form to which I turn in the next chapter—novels at once fictions of psychosexual intensity and attempts to create, like Joyce's *Ulysses* before them, an epic vision of the contemporary world. Written during the Cold War era of the 1950s, Lawrence Durrell's *Alexandria Quartet* is set in Egypt—a former British possession—just before and during the World War, and Doris Lessing's *The Golden Notebook* begins on the African continent during the war and traces its aftermath in England of the 1950s. In these texts, the issues of race and fascism that underlie Faulkner's and Stead's paternal narratives resurface as issues of race and colonialism, while the political threat of fascism is transmuted into that of totalitarianism (figured in the anti-Communist fears that surround Lessing's protagonist, a former Party member, as well as in the fear of an united Arab front that underlies the political intrigues of the *Quartet*). In representing the fragmentation of consciousness of their protagonists, Durell and Lessing turn to the psychological theories of Jung, Reich, and others, in addition to Freud; one consequence is that the oedipal conflicts and family romances foregrounded in chapter 5 yield to the heightened depiction of the battle between the sexes. In this war, the latent strands of homoeroticism present in Faulkner's and Stead's family dramas emerge as real and present dangers to the normative definitions of masculine and feminine behavior undergirding postwar sexual ideology.

In leaving the world of Pollitry "on the other side of the bridge," then, Louie may effectively escape Sam's paternal plot, and she may enter a new world where she becomes the questing agent who authors her own desirous plots. But such desires are complicated by an external world in the process of "crack-up" and inner worlds increasingly subject to social and sexual pressures that transform the struggle for subjectivity into a psychosexual battlefield and threaten mental stability. Just how the multiple anxieties created by these contradictory pressures affect the authorial enterprise lies at the heart of Durrell's and Lessing's sprawling, experimental, self-reflexive novels—novels in which the attempt to embody and confront the specter of "fifties writing gone mad" creates a permutation in modernist narrative as it crosses the threshold into the era of postmodernity.

CHAPTER SIX

Fragmented Selves, Mythic Descents, and Third World Geographies

FIFTIES' WRITING GONE MAD

Lawrence Durrell, Alexandria Quartet
· · · · ·

Doris Lessing, The Golden Notebook
· · · · ·

> What a culture designates as alien, utterly
> other and different, is never so.
> —Jonathan Dollimore[1]

> In the objectification of the scopic drive there is always the threatened return of
> the look; in the identification of the Imaginary relation there is always the alien-
> ating other (or mirror) which crucially returns its image to the subject.
> —Homi K. Bhabha[2]

Lawrence Durrell's multivolumed *Alexandria Quartet* and Doris Lessing's *The Golden Notebook* stand at the end of a half-century of modernist experiments in representing interiority. While both share in common with the novels taken up in the previous chapters the attempt to represent the vicissitudes of psychic life, their gargantuan narratives go further than most of their predecessors in also attempting to propound an epic, indeed global, vision of life in this century that spans the philosophical and political as well as psychological foundations of human subjectivity. It is now perhaps difficult to imagine the intense excitement and international attention that greeted the publication of these works in the five years spanning 1957 to 1962: both were widely touted as worthy if controversial successors to the modernist tradition associated with Joycean experimentation. Not only did the *Alexandria Quartet* win glowing praise from reviewers as well as the popular reading audience, who awaited the publication of each of its four volumes from 1957 to 1960 with the sense of participating in the making of a late modernist masterpiece, but it triumphed in academic circles, spawning literally hundreds of scholarly articles and turning up on Ivy League syllabi in the following decade. The appearance of Lessing's novel in 1962 had a similarly catalytic effect. Praised by many establishment critics as the achievement of the decade for its moral and political vision, the novel was further catapulted into visibility when its representation of the relation of the sexes from a woman's point of view became a rallying point for the first phase of the contemporary women's liberation movement—the novel had been so swept into the feminist temper of the times as an indispensable "weapon" in the war against patriarchy, Lessing complained in 1971, that it had ceased to be read on its own merits.[3] Lessing's objections not withstanding, the novel was embraced, as Molly Hite writes, by an entire generation of intelligent, dissatisfied women "because of its subject matter," and it became a mainstay of women's studies courses throughout the next two decades. By 1985, no less than 59 dissertations, 300 articles, and 17 books had appeared on Lessing, the majority focusing on *The Golden Notebook.*[4]

Yet, ironically, neither Durrell's nor Lessing's reputation has fared so well over time. Durrell's stock couldn't be lower than it is today; his blend of lush romanticism and existential soul-searching stands at a far remove from current postmodern critical sensibilities, belying the fact that critics once seriously debated the status of the *Alexandria Quartet* as *the* masterpiece of the century. In contrast, Lessing's novel, while sometimes considered a bit heavy-handed in the wake of the postmodern fictional experiments that followed it, has attained a certain canonical status over the years, but it too is neither written about nor read with the fervor it once aroused. In 1989 Claire Sprague commented on how few of her students "in the past two or three years had heard of, [much less] read Lessing";[5] and in the 1990s, serious criticism on *The Golden Notebook* has dropped to a minimum as Lessing's increased involvement in science fiction has moved her further from the novelistic mainstream.

I am going to be arguing that the issues of erotic perception, gendered subjectivity, and narrative authority presented in both these works, if submitted to the insights that have marked recent modes of cultural criticism—particularly postcolonial and queer theory—make them well worth our attention today. From such perspectives, these novels become valuable not merely as the last gasps of a modernist aesthetics but because they reveal many of the normalizing pressures of post–World War II sexual ideology that continue to riddle western culture at the end of the century. Before making this argument, however, I want to draw our attention to a school of psychology that reached the height of its popularity in the same years that saw the appearance of the *Alexandria Quartet* and *The Golden Notebook,* but that, like those novels, has since fallen from critical favor—namely, Jungian theory as a mode of understanding the relation of the individual psyche to the collective. Two prominent markers of the spread of Jungian, myth-based ideas to literary and cultural fields of study were Northrop Frye's *Anatomy of Criticism,* published in 1957, the year that the first volume of the *Alexandria Quartet* appeared, and Joseph Campbell's

The Mask of the Gods, the first three of its four volumes appearing between 1959 and 1962. I will not be applying either Frye or Campbell directly to the materials examined in this chapter, but I find it illuminating to consider the similar concerns, approaches, and energies driving all these mid-century works, fiction and nonfiction alike. The resemblance lies not only in the obsessive tendency of these authors to churn out multiple volumes or multiple refractions of the same schema (Durrell's and Campbell's four-volume works, Lessing's five notebooks, Frye's four archetypal modes), but also in the descent into the realm of the irrational that both Durrell and Lessing make a necessary stage in their protagonists' process of individuation. The ideal goal of such quests is the emergence of an integrated self that can withstand the pressures of personal and global chaos. This process of descent into the underworld of the interior and the integration of the darker sides of the individual and collective unconscious resembles the universal paradigm that Campbell ascribes to the mythic quest in *Hero with a Thousand Faces* and that Jung evokes with his concepts of the shadow self and the anima/animus. The important exception is that Durrell and Lessing give their questing figures a much more specific sociopolitical and historical grounding. If the existential journeys that their multilayered narratives trace bear the marks of this timeless pattern of descent, psychic fragmentation, and return, in both novels the "universality" of this mythic paradigm is simultaneously reshaped by the contexts of modernity, particularly that of colonialism, within which it occurs.[6]

This tension between the mythic and modern, the timeless and the political, becomes apparent in a thematic (and ultimately formal) contradiction that I will be investigating. For the exploration of the libidinal energies and repressed desires triggered by the descent into the irrational is in both novels paradoxically checked by an ultimate reaffirmation of quite traditional gendered subjectivity that hence fulfills a fantasy of normalization quite specific to the national politics and dominant sexual ideology emerging in the Cold War period of the fifties and early sixties. The mechanism that causes this withdrawal from the more radical implications of the dissolution of ego experienced in the descent into libidinal anarchy is predicated, I will suggest, on the threat that male homosexuality represents in both texts, a threat that is intricately if incoherently connected to the colonial landscapes—Egypt in the *Alexandria Quartet,* Southern Rhodesia in *The Golden Notebook*—that provide the foreground and background, respectively, of these two narratives.

It is also informative to consider the many other similarities that make these shared dramas of release and repression so emblematic of their time, including the authorial anxieties besetting the writer hovering on the threshold between modernism and postmodernism. In this regard, both novels' protagonists are writers who are experiencing severe cases of writers' block, the fruit of which, ironically, is a *proliferation* of writing, in which

Durrell's volumes and Lessing's notebooks retrace the same events from multiple points of view. This technique of proliferating and often conflicting narratives—from which the reader must slowly extract a composite text that is never really "complete"—at once reflects the chaos of an external reality whose ordering principles have broken down and speaks to the perceived loss of meaning that makes the production of art, specifically fictional art, seem all the more pointless to the *Alexandria Quartet*'s Darley and *The Golden Notebook*'s Anna. In each novel, furthermore, the crisis in narrative authority that confronts these blocked writers fosters an emotional numbness, an inability to feel or act, that manifests itself as a crisis in sexual authority. These sexual inadequacies are most overtly played out in the protagonists' self-destructive love affairs with members of the opposite sex who represent impossible, hence "foreign," objects of desire: Darley's with Alexandria's mythic femme fatale Justine Hosnani, and Anna's with the blacklisted Jewish-American scriptwriter Saul Green. The ultimately sadomasochistic, as well as delusional, currents set into motion by both these love affairs unlock a degree of psychosexual activity in the narrating protagonists that each text represents through largely psychodramatic techniques. As the "interior" dramas signified by these "exterior" relationships deluge the realistic plane of the narrative, these novels stage increasingly dreamlike descents into the underworld of the unconscious, the libidinal, and the irrational.[7] In the *Alexandria Quartet,* this "underworld" (explicitly referred to as such by Durrell) is figured as the mutating, fluid realm of polymorphous perversity and of anarchic desire, ruled by the "dark tides of Eros";[8] in *The Golden Notebook,* the breakdown of ego boundaries that Anna's descent into the world of the interior occasions marks her entrance into the equally mutating, fluid, polymorphous realm of madness and schizophrenia.

In line with this descent pattern, the crises in sexual and textual authority that occupy Durrell's and Lessing's protagonists provide the occasion for the intensely psychodramatic encounters with externalized embodiments of their repressed desires and fears. These projections assume multiple forms of otherness, including *gendered otherness,* most apparent in Darley's and Anna's problematic relationships with members of the "opposite" sex; *racialized or colonialized otherness,* most apparent in the Third World settings of each novel; and, *homosexual otherness,* most apparent in the way such desires destabilize both protagonists' assumptions about normative masculinity and femininity. The following paragraphs examine each of these three manifestations of otherness in turn, and after indicating some of the intersections between the psychological projections and displacements that they enact, I turn to the sexual ideology of the Cold War 1950s and early 1960s that makes the anxieties of authority represented in Lessing and Durrell so illuminating an index of their late-modernist endeavors to plumb the world of the interior and to find a novelistic form capable of addressing a global order in the process of rapid breakdown, temporary reconsolidation, and radical transformation.

GENDERED OTHERNESS

On a very basic level, Darley's and Anna's tempestuous love affairs trigger archetypally figured encounters with the opposite sex that come to represent the other of gender that exists within the psyche. In Jungian parlance, this amounts to a confrontation for Darley with his female anima and for Anna with her male animus, those archetypes of gender that supposedly dwell within the deepest reaches of the collective unconscious and are shared by all men and women. As in the myth of Tiresias, the blind seer who dwells in Hades and possesses the coveted knowledge of both "sides" (he has lived seven years as a female),[9] Jung and his followers argue that the incorporation of the anima/animus is a necessary stage in becoming a healthily adjusted male or female, and this psychic process has often been read into the quests of Lessing's and Durrell's protagonists for wholeness.[10] However, as feminists have long pointed out, Jung's conception of psychic androgyny as an ideal incorporation of male and female attributes—the "outward persona" and "inward face" of the anima/animus—nonetheless depends on a problematic understanding of "masculine" and "feminine" components of the psyche as *universal* principles, rather than as internalized social constructions of gender. Note, for example, Jung's description of the anima: "Every man carries within him the eternal image of the woman, not the image of this or that particular woman, but a definite feminine image. This image is fundamentally unconscious . . . an imprint or archetype . . . a deposit, as it were, of all the impressions ever made by woman." The whole person who successfully emerges from the underworld of libidinal desire remains a distinctly male or female self, richer for the largely subconscious integration of his or her gendered, but hierarchically secondary, complement. Because the "masculine" remains associated with valor, strength, and powers of mind, and the "feminine" with intuition, passivity, and lack of decision, such a theory implicitly maintains the hierarchical superiority of male over female in terms of the values culture assigns to these characteristics. It also assumes the normativity of heterosexual desire, yoking together male and female within the psyche as well as in the socius as the model of successful harmony or wholeness. As Jung continues, "Since this image [of the man's anima] is unconscious, it is always unconsciously projected upon the person of the beloved, and is one of the chief reasons for passionate attraction."[11]

Several of these attitudes, widely and popularly disseminated in the 1950s and 1960s, can be seen carrying over into the anxious concern with norms of masculinity and femininity that contributes to the psychodramatic frenzy underlying the epic scope of both these novels. For instance, Durrell's boast of producing a "man-size piece of work" that "goes straight up among those books . . . which men have built out of their own guts"[12] is reflected in his protagonist Darley's obsession with the status of manhood in a rapidly changing sexual and social order that threatens, at every turn, to "unman" his phallic superiority, to leave him impotent to act, either as a man or writer. *The Golden Notebook,* too, revolves around the anxieties of sexual and textual authority that beset the "modern" or "free" woman in a transitional period of sexual and global strife. As single woman, mother, writer, and lover, Anna must not only strive *for* agency as a female subject but strive *against* the seductive masochism that the cultural legacy equating femininity with Freudian lack has instilled in her subconscious. Yet even as Lessing works to free representations of women from patriarchal definitions of femininity that keep woman "in her place," her protagonist seeks to find a proper masculine complement, a "real" man whose presence in her life will confirm her own heterosexual desirability as a feminine woman. "I'd forgotten what making love to a real man is like" (561), Anna approvingly writes of Saul—who, if his sadistic behavior exemplifies "real" manhood, offers a depressing portrait of the future prospects facing women in heterosexual relationships.

FOREIGN OTHERNESS

On a second level, the specters of otherness that Darley and Anna confront in their interior quests intersect with the phantasm of the "exotic other" created by British imperialism. For the mythic descents of both protagonists take place against the backdrop of colonized Third World landscapes, which, as Edward Said argues in *Orientalism,* have come to represent "one of [the West's] deepest and most recurring images of the Other." Within the orientalizing imagination, these images of the other have almost inevitably been tinged with suggestions of the erotic, Said notes, transforming the mythic East into "a place where one could look for sexual experience unattainable in Europe."[13] Thus, in Durrell's *Alexandria Quartet,* the colonial setting in British-occupied Egypt on the eve of World War II becomes a screen onto which Darley projects his fantasy of illicit desires forbidden in England (that "home of the eccentric and the sexually dispossessed," as Durrell whimsically puts it in *Mountolive* [71]). In transforming the nonwestern world into a fantasized image of sexual promise and excess, the orientalist project has most often relied, as Said demonstrates, on a set of metaphors equating the Anglo-European colonizer with phallic conquest and the colonized other with stereotypes of feminine receptivity, fecundity, and availability, a discursive move that psychologically functions to justify the penetration and appropriation of the mysterious riches of the latter by the "superior" rationality of the western mind. This tendency to feminize the East—and conversely, to transform sexual relationships into imperial conquests—can be seen in the ruminations of the young British diplomat Mountolive in the third volume of the *Alexandria Quartet,* who repeats the name "Egypt" to himself "as one might repeat the name of a woman" (*M* 2) and who feels he is now "really penetrating a foreign country" (12) when he falls in love with an older, sexually wise Egyptian woman. In Lessing's novel the colonial backdrop is presented in Anna's very first notebook entry, in which she recalls the war years that she, like Darley, spent abroad, in her case in the British Crown Colony of race-segregated Southern Rhodesia. This formative event has provided the inspiration for Anna's best-selling novel, *Frontiers of War*, an interracial love story that dramatizes the sexualized relation of white colonist and colonized other. But even more subtly, Anna's traumatizing experience of the color bar in Southern Rhodesia is responsible for creating the internalized template for understanding oppression that Anna takes back to England, in the form of "sexual apartheid." To the degree that the Third World symbolically occupies a feminized, degraded position as "one of [the West's] deepest and most recurring images of the Other," Anna's conflation of racial and sexual apartheid, which comes to a head in her descent into madness when she falls in love with the sadistic Saul Green, thus makes profound psychological sense.

HOMOSEXUAL OTHERNESS

In both these novels the discourse of foreign otherness is projected onto the ambivalently represented trope of homosexuality, which, despite the overridingly heterosexual focus of these fictions, plays a pivotal role in their plots. Whether literally embodied in specific characters or presented as a recurring motif, the shadowy presence of homosexual desire becomes a site of threatening otherness that gives external expression to another face of the "alien other" existing in Darley's and Anna's subconscious depths. As such, homosexuality also serves both as the trigger of and target for the anxieties of heterosexual masculinity and femininity that beset these protagonists. In the *Alexandria Quartet*, the specter of homosexuality is explicitly related to that of the colonialized other. "The sexual provender that lies at hand is staggering in its variety and profusion," Darley notes as he uneasily surveys the seemingly pansexual universe of Alexandria. As the repressed contents of Darley's feverish imagination gradually reveal, the European voyeur who gazes too long, or too longingly, at the profusion of Egypt's sexual provender is apt to find himself implicated in its variety of perverse permutations. Homi Bhabha puts it well: "In the objectification of the scopic drive there is always the threatened return of the look; in the identification of the Imaginary relation there is always the alienating other (or mirror) which crucially returns its image to the subject."[14] In Lessing's *The Golden Notebook,* the link between homosexuality and Africa is no less telling, attested to by the bisexuality of the RAF pilots who are Anna's best friends and political allies in Rhodesia and by the intersection of homophobia and apartheid that, as we will see, precipitates the climactic events of the segment of the novel set in Africa. What both novels make fascinat-

ingly clear, moreover, is the degree to which the unprecedented sexual freedom experienced by *both* men and women in the postwar period—including the frankness in speaking about sexual variation spawned by Kinsey's
revelation of the homosexual "10 percent"—proceeded hand-in-hand
with a retrenchment of traditional gender ideals. Ironically, this conservative reaction can be seen as the outcome of the destabilization of accepted
social assumptions about "masculine" and "feminine" behavior occasioned
by a new era of sexual permissiveness, which I take up below. In the process, homosexuality increasingly became the scapegoat for an array of sexual, gender, and textual anxieties, its status as the "other" face of heterosexuality never far beneath the surface of the dominant fifties' discourse of
sexuality in England and America.

Two examples, both involving issues of authorial fiat, illuminate this
process of scapegoating, whereby fears stemming from primarily heterosexual anxieties are displaced onto homosexuality. The first is biographical,
involving the events that inspired Durrell to create the *Alexandria Quartet.*
Writing to Henry Miller from Alexandria in 1942, Durrell describes Eve
Cohen, his future wife and original model for the *Alexandria Quartet's*
archetypal Woman, Justine, in language that echoes the orientalizing trope
of the eastern woman as fecund, supine, passive, and (sexually) available.
For Eve becomes, quite literally, Durrell's means of access to an "inside" of
eastern sexuality that he penetrates not only as a lover but as voyeur and,
ultimately, British writer of colonialist narrative. "She sits for hours on the
bed and tells me all about the sex life of Arabs," Durrell writes to Miller,
and he then lists what sounds like a précis of the various exotica forming
the orientalizing backdrop of the *Alexandria Quartet:* "perversions, circumcision, hashish, sweetmeats, removal of the clitoris, cruelty, murder . . . she
has seen the *inside* of Egypt to the last rotten dung-blown flap of obscenity."[15] What Durrell's female informant tells him about the "sex lives of
the Arabs," however, raises the phantom of those ambiguously unspecified
"perversions" that include the association of Arab sensuality not only with
the delights of the harem but with serviceable boys. For in a second letter
to Miller, Durrell sardonically comments that "Love, hashish, and boys
[are] the obvious solution to anyone struck here [in Alexandria] for more
than a few years," and a few months later he adds, "One could not continue to live here without practising a sort of death—hashish or boys or
food."[16] The latter equation of the sensual enjoyment of "hashish or boys
or food" with death of the self is followed by Durrell's mention to Miller
of the "wonderful novel on Alexandria" he has just conceived, which he
cavalierly describes as "a sort of spiritual butcher's shop *with girls on the
slab.*"[17] The narrative sequencing of these epistolary comments rather
strikingly suggests that underlying the inspiration of the *Alexandria Quartet* as a heterosexist fantasy of girls as meat-to-be-devoured is the fearful
image of pederasty (enjoying "boys") as an ultimate indulgence in passive

pleasures (like drugs, like food) that spell a "sort of death" to a western definition of masculine agency. The process of repression enacted by the letter's overwriting of "boys" by "girls" as consumable objects (food, meat) of male appetite foreshadows the process whereby the repressed returns in the *Alexandria Quartet* in the form of a series of talismanic figures of homoerotic desire that very nearly derail Darley's heterosexual love-interests and his quest for writerly manhood.

The Golden Notebook dramatizes a similar authorial displacement in its account of the origin of Anna's novel *Frontiers of War*. As in the *Alexandria Quartet,* the context is again explicitly colonial. Not only is the dashing heterosexual hero of Anna's story of love across the color bar, as she reveals in her Black notebook entries, modeled on a *bisexual* British trooper, Paul Blackenship, whose sole claim to heterosexual manhood depends on the single night he has sex with Anna, but also the crisis at the Mashopi hotel that precipitates Anna and Paul's lovemaking, as we will see, hinges on an allegation of same-sex desire between a black man and white man. None of these originating causes make it into Anna's novel. Instead, onto these events Anna has grafted a highly romantic fiction of heterosexual love across the color line. This slippage between heterosexual anxieties and ho-mosexual subtexts is restaged throughout the non-Rhodesian section of the novel, as homosexual characters back in England increasingly become the target of the negative energies generated by feelings of heterosexual inade-quacy. The trajectories of both Lessing's and Durrell's texts thus move to-ward a climactic excision of perceived homoerotic threat and a subsequent rechanneling of perverse or wayward libidinal energies in order to facilitate their protagonists' regained confidence as woman and man, respectively, and as freshly inspired rather than impotent writers.

In both the *Alexandria Quartet* and *The Golden Notebook,* then, homosexu-ality becomes the wellspring for a degree of sexual and textual anxieties and scapegoating that has wide-ranging implications for the depiction of the sexes that forms the psychodramatic core of these late-modernist nov-els. These anxieties, as I have implied, are intimately related to a crisis of authority in masculine and feminine self-fashioning in the postwar period. In England, America, and indeed western Europe, the sexual ideology emerging from the Cold War era of the 1950s and early 1960s is a particu-larly riven one, split by contradictions that a newly articulated notion of gender performance only barely managed to cover.[18] On the one hand, the postwar pre-Vietnam era was the beginning of the "sexual revolution"; for coexisting with the era's heightened ideal of the suburban home and the planned, nuclear family—ideals held out, in a profound sense, as the "re-wards" of peacetime—was the heightened eroticization of both middle-class men and women as sexual agents and sexualized bodies, increasingly engaging in premarital sex and affairs outside of marriage. Writing in 1966 about the "current acceleration of sexual freedom," British feminist critic Juliet Mitchell noted in *Women: The Longest Revolution* that "the major structure which at present is in rapid evolution is sexuality," manifested in the (liberating) failure of "marriage in its classical form" to regulate "spontaneous behavior" or hold in abeyance "the liberalization of relationship."[19] And a touchstone for making Americans aware of the "widespread deviation from accepted sexual standards" in everyday middle-class life was the research of Alfred Kinsey, whose groundbreaking volumes, *Sexual Behavior in the Human Male* (1948) and *Sexual Behavior in the Human Female* (1953), had a more tangible influence on "modern sexual consciousness," as Paul Robinson puts it, than any research published before Foucault's *The History of Sexuality*.[20]

Women's roles were especially complicated by these changing sexual mores. Even as the end of the war forced many middle-and working-class women out of civilian jobs and back into domestic lives serving their men, the "career woman" and "city girl" also became more familiar and accepted types (the metropolitan locus of this "type" reaches back, interestingly, to Lucy's migration to Villette and resonates with the queer urban spaces analyzed in chapter 4). Indicative of a new class of educated, professional women for whom marriage was less an immediate necessity, the city girl also helped make possible a less virginal conception of femininity that no longer depended exclusively on her sexual purity or innocence. Yet in such a formulation, it is less the notion of women's sexual independence than a cultural belief in an essential femininity that is actually being recuperated, an emphasis that underscores the straitjacket of gender typing that indeed *intensified,* throughout the fifties, as a certain image of essentialized *hyper-femininity*—performed on the accessorized female body, with push-up bras, wasp-waisted dresses, nylons, high heels—was mass-produced with a vengeance, as the period photography in *Life* and *Look* magazines vividly attest.[21] It is no coincidence that the book often credited with triggering the modern feminist movement was titled *The Feminine Mystique,* or that it was published in 1962, the year that Lessing's novel appeared, for the production of the "mystique" that Betty Friedan critiques in this volume was not simply the product of centuries of oppression (although it was also that) but a very specific creation of the postwar years.

If definitions of femininity were increasingly complicated in the postwar years, so too was the Anglo-American understanding of masculinity for soldiers returning from the front and male youths attaining maturity under the shadow of the war, all of whom had to find new ways of demonstrating their manhood now that the battlefield was a thing of the past. One product of this shift, as Leo Braudy has suggested, was the emergence of a new prototype of vulnerable, bodily present, and countercultural masculinity, epitomized in film by James Dean, Montgomery Clift, and Laurence Harvey, and in writing by Jack Kerouac and John Osborne. Yet, as in the case of the newly sexualized woman, the unconventional vulnerability demonstrated by these male icons worked to confirm their essential masculinity, and it did so by proffering a revitalized definition of virility that could coexist with a capacity for feelings, for confusion, and even for existential despair.[22] Braudy's thesis that the dual impulse of the general public toward outsidership and convention throughout the fifties is mirrored in the unresolved tensions of its characteristic art forms—method acting, the plastic arts, and Beat literature, all with an emphasis on the body in motion—is surely applicable to the contradictory constructions of masculinity proliferating in the period and performed with a heightened intensity as both men and women jockeyed for position in a world striving to return, as Linda Kauffman puts it, to "normality" after the devastations of World War II and its enforced separation of the sexes.[23]

This uneasy jockeying for position between men and women in a transforming sexual, social, and global order recalls Lessing's introductory disclaimer that *The Golden Notebook* was being wrongly read as "being about the sex war, or . . . claimed by women as a useful weapon in the sex war" (this introduction was added in 1971). While Lessing goes on to uphold the cause of "Women's Liberation," she does so in order to "get the subject . . . over with" (viii) and pronounce her presumably ignored authorial concerns: first, to present the theme of division, crack-up, and breakdown as a way to a new unity; second, to "give the ideological 'feel' of our mid-century"; third, to represent an artist with a "block"; fourth, to find a viable way to address issues of subjectivity from a Marxist perspective without being reviled for abandoning the collective or the political; fifth, to create a self-reflexive novel whose innovative structure comments on the status of the novel as a conventional literary form (xi). Intriguingly, all five of these declared themes are also evident in Durrell's *Alexandria Quartet;* it, too, makes fragmentation (of identity, sexuality, narrative) part of its thematic and formal structures; gives an ideological feel to global politics at mid-century by representing the waning of the British empire in the Near and Middle East; presents an artist whose writing block is symptomatic of personal and public worlds in increasing chaos; engages the problem of subjectivity by revealing the relativity of individual perception; and, finally, creates a thoroughly self-reflexive fiction that problematizes its status as fiction on nearly every page. Beyond these five shared topics, however, I would propose that Lessing's text most emphatically shares with Durrell's the one theme that Lessing irritatedly brushes aside. For the "sex war"— that is, the oppositional relation of the sexes, the masks of gender that the men and women in these texts feel obliged to wear, and the desires that such norms of sexuality and gender are supposed to foment—seems to me not only to lie at the heart of the manifold "ideological" issues that Lessing's novel so bravely attempts to address but also to tie her text, as if to its mirror inverse, to Durrell's exploration of western masculine anxiety in an ideologically displaced global setting. As Lessing notes in an aside about the cowardice that has often characterized women's writing, "Most women will still run like little dogs with stones thrown at them when a man says: You are unfeminine, aggressive, you are unmanning me" (ix). Anna Wulf, as we will see, has done her share of running to escape the imputation of being a "woman-hater," and one of her greatest fears in maintaining the life of a "free woman" is that she may actually have become less "womanly" and hence less desirable. And Durrell's Darley epitomizes the male fear of being "unmanned," rendered ineffectual and impotent, that accompanies men's sense, however imaginary, of women in charge—or, in the case of Justine and Darley, of women "on top."

The way in which these particular anxieties about a postwar norm of masculinity and femininity, itself in flux, intersect with the late-modernist challenge to narrative authority in a literally and figuratively decentered world order leads us directly, as the following pages suggest, to the two most intriguingly absent themes in criticism of either novel—themes that are, paradoxically, quite precise indicators of what is at stake in the "war of the sexes": the exploration of heterosexual desire against the backdrop of colonialism, and the specter of homosexuality that first makes itself visible on foreign terrain and then migrates "home," where it works to deconstruct those verities of sexual and national identity that such a conception of home was founded, ironically, to support.

LAWRENCE DURRELL, *ALEXANDRIA QUARTET*
HOMOEROTIC NEGOTIATIONS IN COLONIAL NARRATIVE

> What follows would be a drama freed from the burden of form. *I would set my own book free to dream.*
> —Arnauti on his *Moeurs,* in Lawrence Durrell, *Justine* (61)

> Lying with one's own kind . . . sex has left the body and entered the imagination now.
> —Balthazar to Darley in *Justine* (82)

Durrell lacked no confidence in positioning himself as the heir apparent to Proust, Lawrence, and Joyce, among other famous male modernists, touting the *Alexandria Quartet*'s attempt to synthesize Einstein's theories of relativity and the modern novel as the latest advance in experimental fiction. In the prefatory note to the second volume, *Balthazar,* where he explains the narrative design of the *Alexandria Quartet,* Durrell also announces his "central topic" to be "an investigation of modern love" (n.p.). Given these thematic and formal concerns, it is appropriate that the principal subject whose "relative" viewpoint dominates three of the four volumes is a writer who is in love. The only problem is that this protagonist is not yet very good at either writing or making love: up to the final pages of the last volume, Darley remains a pitiably blocked writer, a deluded lover, and, as a consequence of both, a confused sexual subject for whom issues of erotic perception, masculine subjectivity, and narrative authority are fatally linked. The result is a knot of sexual and textual anxieties that it takes, with no exaggeration, four volumes and nearly one thousand pages of writing to allay.

Both the radical relativity of viewpoint that underlies Durrell's multi-layered format and the "investigation of modern love" that is his declared subject pivot, moreover, on his protagonist's precarious negotiation of the mazes of Near Eastern sexuality, of which the city of Alexandria, the fabled meeting point of "East" and "West," becomes a larger-than-life symbol. Born and raised in India in a family whose Anglo-Indian roots go back three generations, stationed in Alexandria as a press officer during World War II, living in a self-imposed exile from England most of his adult life, Durrell disdained the notion of empire—"I don't give a damn about British empire," he announced in an interview—in the same breath that he allowed himself to be labeled a "colonialist."[24] These complex, sometimes contradictory attitudes toward empire and colonialism inform the process by which Egypt becomes much more than an exotic backdrop to the *Alexandria Quartet*'s modernist pyrotechnics. For in Durrell's modern epic, Egypt's geopolitical realities become a screen onto which characters like Darley project their most forbidden erotic desires. Engaging with libidinal fantasy through this mechanism of displacement, not coincidentally, frees Darley to emerge as mature novelist and successful lover at the end of the fourth volume.

But Darley's response to the lure of foreign otherness is double-edged: such figurations of sexuality, for all their attraction, are also terrifying, not the least because they give vent to possibilities unthinkable within western constructions of masculinity. Within the psychodramatic landscape of the *Alexandria Quartet,* that unthinkability is time and again coded as the danger of homosexual metamorphosis. The possibility—the fear *and* the desire—of being "unmanned" by homoerotic impulses gives the *Alexandria Quartet* its deconstructive frisson. In effect, its four novels map out an unstable geography of male eros in which Darley's psychological quest depends on a descent into a surreal dreamscape that repeatedly confronts him with the one taboo, male homosexuality, that throws his primary goals—heterosexual fulfillment and a written text—into jeopardy. If the Near East first seems to hold the promise of literary inspiration and sexual freedom for the western traveler, these discursive manifestations of same-sex desire suggest another side to his story, one that points to the highly explosive crossing of sexual and authorial anxiety triggered by the very enterprise of colonial narrative.

Epistolary Ejaculations

An intriguing place to begin to decipher the sexually ambiguous desires that haunt the *Alexandria Quartet,* pervading its representations of both Egyptian sensuality and western male psychology, is Durrell's correspondence with Henry Miller, his literary mentor and closest male friend. This correspondence began in 1935 when the yet unknown Durrell wrote a gushing fan letter to the current *bête noir* of literary letters, proclaiming the infamously graphic *Tropic of Cancer* to be "the only really man-size piece of work which this century can . . . boast of." Miller, his "man-size" ego no doubt flattered by such praise, quickly wrote back, touting Durrell's views as a mirror of his own: "It's the kind of letter I would have written myself." Thus began a series of narcissistically enabling epistolary exchanges that would bond the two writers, man-to-man, in a life-long correspondence.[25] The terms of Durrell's adulation also reveal the young writer's desire to produce his own "man-size piece of work," a goal which in terms of sheer bulk he accomplished twenty-odd years later with the publication of the enormously successful *Alexandria Quartet.* It is not surprising, then, to find an echo of this early ambition espoused by the *Alexandria Quartet*'s successful writer-figure, the larger-than-life Pursewarden, who announces that he wants to write a novel "characterised by a *total lack of codpiece!*" (*C* 130). But precisely how, under Miller's tutelage, did Durrell learn to divest himself of *his* "codpiece," to let it all hang out, as it were, in order to display a "piece of work" that, as he says of *Tropic,* "goes straight up among those books . . . which men have built out of their own guts"?[26] It is but a slight leap from this blatant phallicism to another of the young Durrell's epistolary homages to his literary master. "In telling anyone about myself these days," he boasts, "I always say I'm the first writer to be fertilized by H. M."[27] If, as one critic puts it, "Miller's seed obviously fell on fallow soil,"[28] we may reasonably wonder what it meant for Durrell to find himself in a position so diametrically opposed to his "man-size" ambitions, playing bottom to Miller's top. "Creative" intercourse this may only be, but Durrell's choice of metaphors nonetheless places him in a biologically female relation to his mentor, one in which the fledgling novelist's task is that of serving as "fallow soil" to Miller's "seed." Language, one is tempted to deduce, subtly contaminates the platonic terms of this manly friendship.

Even more fascinating, in the light of language's destabilizing potential, is the literary metaphor that Durrell uses to describe Eve Cohen, his future wife and the model for Justine, the *Alexandria Quartet*'s archetypal femme fatale, when he writes Miller from Alexandria seven years later. Attempting to convey the sex appeal of this "strange, smashing, dark-eyed woman," Durrell declares that she "is *Tropic* . . . walking."[29] Miller's "man-size" ouevre seems to have grown altogether feminine legs in Durrell's imagination. And with this figurative metamorphosis of one text (Miller's) into a woman (Eve) who will become the basis for another text (Durrell's), the younger partner in this literary collaboration adroitly reverses the sexual dynamic inscribed in the earlier letter. It is now Durrell who assumes the male authorial role and Miller's text, via its leggy incarnation in Eve, that is metaphorically penetrated. For Eve becomes, as noted earlier, Durrell's means of access to an "*inside* of Egypt" whose "sex life" she reveals to her new lover as part of their bed-play.[30]

Durrell fertilized by H. M., Miller's *Tropic* penetrated by Durrell: such thorny intersections should inspire us to take another look at the sexual negotiations that underlie the lush romanticism of the *Alexandria Quartet*. On one level, the Durrell-Miller relation that I have been sketching resembles the homosocial pattern of male bonding we have seen rehearsed in *Absalom, Absalom!* and elsewhere. Such homosocial behavior, as Eve Kosofsky Sedgwick has pointed out, is not antithetical either to patriarchal formations or to male heterosexual (and often homophobic) norms.[31] On another level, however, the premise of homosocial bonding, pervasive as it is in the world of the *Alexandria Quartet,* may not be the most telling method for understanding the elliptical negotiations of "other" sexualities that not only keep rearing their heads in the Miller-Durrell correspondence, but that also determine the paths whereby the whole problematic of masculine sexual identification and its attendant uncertainties are continually brought to bear on the act of writing in the *Alexandria Quartet*. Durrell-as-writer obviously holds to an at least partially phallocentric creed—as his desire to emulate Miller's man-size work attests—but the fact is that the very tools of his formal experimentation in the *Alexandria Quartet*—language, structure, point-of-view—evoke a flux of libidinous desire that, once freed *into* his text, threatens to overwhelm the coherence of its representations of masculine heterosexual competence. What ensues, as we shall now see, is a profound case of authorial anxiety in which the imaginary geography of Durrell's eroticized Egyptian landscape throws the modernist and masculinist tenets of his text into disarray.

Relativity, Modernism, and Orientalism

Not unlike the interweaving narrative voices and time periods that make up *Absalom, Absalom!* the four interlocking volumes of the *Alexandria Quartet* are shot through with multiple, shifting, unstable points of view that emphasize the subjective, the interior, and ultimately the spatial aspects of consciousness. This modernist affinity for attending to the unspoken nuances of inner life carries over into the novel's representation of sexuality, where issues of erotic perception and writing are never far apart. "Loving is only a sort of skin language, sex a terminology merely," Darley writes (*J* 177), and the novelist Pursewarden dreams of a novel that will "have the curvature of an embrace, the wordlessness of a lover's code" (*B*

235). Thus *Justine*, the first volume of the *Alexandria Quartet*, begins with Darley's retrospective, highly subjective attempt to come to grips with his essentially narcissistic love affair with the Egyptian-Jewish beauty Justine Hosnani by recording events not in chronological sequence but associatively, "in the order in which they first became significant for me" (100). The blinders imposed by his romantic solipsism become painfully clear in *Balthazar*, where Darley is forced to relive the "truth" of the sensations he has recorded in *Justine* from a completely different vantage point, that of the Alexandrian doctor Balthazar, whose corrected version of the *Justine* manuscript reveals that Justine has possibly engineered the whole affair with Darley to conceal her more important liaison with the novelist and diplomat Pursewarden. As if to underline further the relativity of sexual and narrative perception, *Mountolive* relegates Darley to the background of its action; the now omnisciently narrated action reveals *all* the love plots of the first and second volumes to be covers for a much more wide-reaching political plot (involving the attempt of Justine and her husband Nessim to return the Coptic Christian minority in Egypt to a position of influence by supporting the Zionist overthrow of Palestine).[32] Only in the final volume, *Clea*, does time move forward, as Darley's first-person narration resumes, recording his return to Alexandria and successful wooing of Clea, another expatriate European artist.

In employing multiple points of view to dramatize the relativity of known reality and the provisionality of narrative truth, Durrell gestures toward the legacy of literary modernism, whose tenets, he intimates, his formal experiments in the *Alexandria Quartet* have revivified for a post-Freudian, post-Einsteinian, nuclear age. This impress of modernist aesthetics is most directly felt in Durrell's first major novel, *The Black Book* (1938), where the character Lawrence Lucifer, a writer-figure in self-imposed exile like the *Alexandria Quartet*'s Darley, proclaims, "I am such a vatful of broken, chaotic material that it will be a miracle if anything can ever reassemble this crude magma, detritus . . . into a single organic whole—even a book."[33] Lucifer's elation or despair—it is hard to tell which—expresses a foundational principle in Durrell's theory of the modern novel, as evinced in the series of lectures on modern art he delivered in Argentina on behalf of the British Council in 1948. These lectures, later published as *A Key to Modern British Poetry* (1952), make explicit the connections Durrell sees between the notion of stable reality exploded by Freud's decentering of human personality, Einstein's theory of relativity, and the consequent challenge facing the contemporary novelist to "reproduc[e] something like [Einstein's] space-time continuum" in a narrative form that contains "all time in every moment of time."[34] This innovative if grandiose agenda becomes the motivating aesthetic idea behind the *Alexandria Quartet*, as the prefatory note to *Balthazar* makes explicit: "I have turned to science and am trying to complete a four-decker novel whose form is based on the relativity proposition. . . . The first three parts . . . are to be deployed spatially . . . and are not linked in a serial form. They interlap, interweave, in a purely spatial relation. Time is stayed. The fourth part alone will represent time and be a true sequel."

In case we have missed the point, Durrell inserts several self-reflexive statements on his craft into the text. In the first volume, Darley recalls Justine's exclamation as she studies her reflection at her dressmaker's: "Look! five different pictures of the same subject. Now if I wrote I would try for a multi-dimensional effect in character, a sort of prism-sightedness" (*J* 16). Later, Balthazar says of the interlinear commentary he has scribbled into the margins of Darley's *Justine* manuscript, "Unwittingly I may have supplied you with a form, something out of the way! Not unlike Pursewarden's idea of a series of novels with 'sliding panels' as he called them. Or else, perhaps, like some medieval palimpsest where different sorts of truth are thrown down one upon the other, the one obliterating or perhaps supplementing another" (*B* 177). Pursewarden also makes free with his advice, suggesting that Darley attempt "a four-card trick in the form of a novel; passing a common axis through four stories, say. . . . A continuum, forsooth, embodying not a *temps retrouvé* but a *temps délivré* [note the pun on *livre*, "book"]. The curvature of space itself would give you a stereoscopic narrative, while human personality seen across a continuum would perhaps become prismatic? . . . I can imagine a form which, if satisfied, might raise in human terms the problems of causality or indeterminacy" (*C* 126). Everyone, writers and nonwriters alike, seems willing to serve as muse to the novel that Darley is too blocked to write.[35] Meanwhile, all these descriptions remind the reader of the technical feats that Durrell— as opposed to Darley—is in the process of achieving by writing a novel that "stays time" through its overlapping volumes and that dramatizes the relativity of truth through its interplay of multiple texts and often conflicting texts-within-texts, all of which work to destabilize the realist premise of traditional fiction.[36]

As the concept of the prismatic "human personality" also indicates, Durrell shares with his modernist forebears the desire to find a way of representing the spatiality of consciousness in narrative form, of capturing the flux of interiority and the drift of subconscious desire. "*I would set my own book free to dream*" (*J* 61), another of the *Alexandria Quartet*'s writer-figures says, and Durrell comes closest his goal of setting his novel "free to dream" in those sections that transform Alexandria's sensual nightworld into the stage for a series of intensely psychodramatic set pieces that function as externalized representations of extreme mental states. If the technique sounds familiar, it is because we have seen Joyce and Barnes do much the same thing with Dublin's Nighttown and the Left Bank of Paris respectively. Durrell's mining of psychodramatic technique is particularly pronounced in two sequences, both of which occur in *Balthazar*, the most densely psychological and psychosexual of all the volumes. In the first, Narouz, who as we will later see functions on a literary level as one of Darley's many alter egos, wanders through Alexandria's prostitute district on the night of the Moslem festival of Sitna Mariam, watching scene upon scene of spirituality and sex blurring in the crush of delirious celebrants. Durrell's quite evocative representation of the color and cacophony of the night's riotous festivities—a surreal blur of whirling dervishes, acrobats, musicians, prostitutes, children, snake-charmers, freaks, and muscledancers—becomes an externalization of the archaic images and polymorphous desires abiding in humanity's collective unconscious. "The night accommodated them all" (149), Durrell says of the riot of elements that compose this carnival-like spectacle. In this orgasmic atmosphere where "reality [runs] down like an overwound spring" (148), Narouz launches on a descent into his ancestral unconscious, "burrowing deeply into the silence of his own mind . . . where the archetypes of . . . marvellous images waited for him," triggering "desires engendered in the forest of the mind, belonging not to themselves but to remote ancestors" (158, 157). The second set piece worthy of note is the city's annual celebration of Carnival, which occurs towards the end of *Balthazar*. This masked celebration also becomes an occasion when the libido, "delivered from the thrall of personality," is given free reign: "The dark tides of Eros . . . burst out during carnival like something long dammed up and raise the forms of strange primeval creatures—the perversions" (184). As these costumed revelers enact their illicit desires under the cover of darkness and anonymity, "plunging . . . ever deeper into the loneliness of their own irrecoverable identities, [and] setting free the polymorphous desires of the city" (196), Carnival, like the festival of Sitna Mariam, becomes an externalized representation of the limitless realm of anarchic desires that the daylight fiction of the coherent self has been evolved to hide.

In such depictions, Durrell's modernist technique and psychological intentions seem to work in tandem. On the one hand, his multidimensional, dispersive, polyphonic text approximates the fragmented, anarchic, psychic terrain of the component instincts sketched out by Freud, and on the other, his evocation of the archetypal images buried in the "forests of the mind" complements Jung's notion of the collective unconscious that can only be reached through a descent into the underworld of the psyche. But this equation of the formal and psychological brings us to a less overt but nonetheless troubling aspect of Durrell's representation: namely, that these "dark tides of Eros" (*B* 185) have been projected onto the foreign geography of a literally dark-skinned, Third World nation. As such *The Alexandria Quartet* unwittingly participates in the enterprise of colonial narrative, its modernist poetics and its sexual politics inextricably bound to its representation of Egypt as an alluring but dangerously foreign other.

This orientalizing tendency calls to mind Durrell's report to Miller of his *tête-à-têtes* with Eve Cohen, whose rudimentary checklist of the "the sex life of the Arabs" conjures up the West's stereotypical association of the East with sexual license and sexual aberration. The *Alexandria Quartet* takes this sampling, and adds to it yet more sexual variations that transform Alexandria into a living symbol of the polymorphous perverse sprung loose from the restraints associated with cooler, calmer western minds. Perhaps the one "perversion" that becomes the text's most sensational emblem of Egypt's sexual depravity and difference is child prostitution, which the narrative declares to be the fate of all orphaned children in Egypt; not only has Justine been raped as a child, but she fears her missing daughter has been sold into prostitution, and the narrative circles back to the haunting scene of Justine searching through child-prostitute dens filled with "horrifying beauty" (*J* 33) and, even more chillingly, of the diplomat Mountolive mistakenly stumbling into another of these dens, where he is set upon by sexually ravenous prepubescent girls. Beginning with pedophilia as the ultimate signifier of the sexual degeneracy of the Arab world, the *Alexandria Quartet* includes a spectrum of variant sexual practices and behaviors that include rape, incest, nymphomania, pederasty, sadomasochism, bestiality, pornographic rings, lesbianism, female circumcision, transvestism, and male castration. All the component instincts, all the perversions, are given free reign in Durrell's phantasmagoria of Egyptian eroticism.

I have already noted how the threatening excess of this illicit otherness is part of the "almost uniform association between the Orient and sex" that underpins Edward Said's theory of the West's fascination with the East. "Since the time of the Prophet fabulous Araby has reeked of aphrodisiac excitement," one such example of orientalist writing declares; and, of the many regions of so-called Araby, Egypt perhaps has the longest history of being, in Sir Richard Burton's phrase, "that classical region of all abominations."[37] Gustave Flaubert's travel diaries recounting his 1849–50 journey to Egypt—upon which Said draws extensively—have come to be seen as paradigmatic of the European writer-traveler's tendency invest the Near East with excessive libidinal content to serve his psychic needs. This move is epitomized in Flaubert's transformation of the "luxuriant and seemingly unbounded sexuality" of the female courtesan with whom he has a torrid affair into the poetic inspiration for his writings. Such textual appropriation of the foreign other, Said argues, is a typically orientalizing move: eastern exoticism is deliberately experienced at a remove as a titillating spectacle, as a "living tableau of queerness," which the tourist can voyeuristically enjoy but nonetheless stand apart from, thus theoretically remaining untouched by its difference.[38]

Yet what Said forgets to mention in analyzing the West's sexualized response to the Orient is precisely what his wording—"living tableau of queerness"—nonetheless betrays. For many western observers' eyes (including Flaubert's), it is not only female flesh that rivets their attention. A return to Durrell's text underlines this truth. For Narouz's dreamlike journey through the festival grounds of the mulid of Sitna Mariam in *Balthazar* is literally interrupted by one such "living tableau of queerness," when he comes to a standstill, first, before "the great canvas theatre outside which the muscle-dancers stood, naked except for loin-cloths to advertise their skill, and motionless, save for the incredible rippling of their bodies—the flickering and toiling of pectoral, abdominal and dorsal muscles" (149), and, then, half a page later, as he stands mesmerized before the riveting spectacle of a "magnificent-looking male prostitute, whose oiled curls hung down his back and whose eyes and lips were heavily painted," as his breast is being tattooed (150). It hardly needs to be added that what is erotically alluring in such representations of unleashed sensuality is not only female, however "feminized" these objects may at times appear. This intuition is also confirmed by Flaubert's travel experiences. "Speaking of bardashes," he writes in a letter home to Louis Bouilhet, his best friend, "here it is quite accepted. One admits one's sodomy, and it is spoken of at table in the hotel. Sometimes you do a bit of denying, and then everybody teases you and you end up confessing," whereupon he proceeds to tell of his adventures in attempting "to indulge in this form of ejaculation" with a "quite nice young [boy]" at the baths.[39]

The erotic possibility that Flaubert discovers in Egypt is echoed, one hundred years later, in the expression of delight that the self-confessed "peddyrast" Scobie expresses in the *Alexandria Quartet* upon his arrival in Egypt: "Looking from east to west over this fertile Delta, what do I see? . . . Mile upon mile of angelic little black bottoms" (*J* 108). Beneath the sexual allure of the colonized Orient's "fertile delta"—an archetypal symbol of female fecundity—there lurks a not-too-hidden penchant for the equally colonizable "black bottoms" of boys. Male homosexuality, whether in the form of pederasty or adult liaisons, is clearly an important if covert component in the mythos of Egyptian sexual license and perversity. Accounts of the prevalence of male-male eroticism in Egyptian history reach back to Josephus and Herodotus, and they take on added propagandistic value with Napoleon's invasion of Egypt, the event credited with launching modern orientalist scholarship. Typical is the near hysteria that enters a French naval officer's travel memoirs when lamenting "the passion contrary to nature" that forms "the delight" and "infamy of the Egyptians," which, he claims, is "generally diffused all over Egypt: the rich and poor are equally infected with it."[40]

This fluid movement across sexual (and social) boundaries turns out to be equally terrifying to the *Alexandria Quartet*'s questing Darley, for personal reasons we will investigate; but nonetheless the *possibility* of such effortless transgression remains very real for him, a situation heightened by the continually blurring boundaries of Alexandria, a polyglot universe comprising, Darley writes at the beginning of the *Alexandria Quartet*, mul-

tiple races, languages, creeds, and "more than five sexes, [with] only de-
motic Greek . . . to distinguish among them" (*J* 4). But this heterogeneity
is also precisely what attracts Durrell, and others before him, to Egypt as a
symbolically feminized terrain onto which one can project western male
fantasies of the sexual otherness and unbridled eroticism considered less
available in the more puritanical moral climate of Europe. And although
Durrell adds that "for the artist in [one]self some confusions of sensibility
[are] valuable" (*B* 46), the defamiliarizing experience of Alexandria's sexual
"variety and profusion" (*J* 4) is as contradictory for Darley as it is instructive. For the fact is that his quest for sexual identity cannot escape a continual negotiation of the homoerotic in the guise of foreign otherness, and
these negotiations threaten the status of the personal and public texts he
wishes to produce. But to make sense of the "confusions of sensibility" that
ensue from the novel's homosexual subtexts, we need first to consider the
overt *hetero*sexuality of its love plots, which pivot on Darley's textual affair
with Alexandria the city and his sexual affair with Justine the woman.

"Her Infinite Variety": City and Woman

The mysteriously strange, always protean world of Alexandria holds a tantalizing allure for Darley, a seductive appeal that he attempts to fend off by
assuming the role of curious but detached artist-spectator. This pose of
uninvolvement, however, swiftly breaks down when he meets and falls
"blindly and passionately in love" with Justine—or rather, with "one of
the many selves she possessed and inhabited" (*B* 121), for Justine is the
ultimate embodiment of Alexandria's legendary variety. To Darley's orientalizing imagination, this protean quality makes Justine the eternal feminine, ever evading capture yet hopelessly yearning to be possessed by the
right man. Simultaneously, this quality renders her a variant of the archetypal eastern woman, a "voluptuar[y] . . . of pain" (*J* 35) in whom a vast
array of apparent contraries meet: sensuality and asceticism, mystery and
knowledge, fecundity and sterility, pain and pleasure.[41] So too, Alexandria,
"the capital of Memory" (*J* 169), is a combination of discordant elements,
its divided origins reflected in a mythic history intersected by Alexander's
library, Cleopatra's court, and Plotinus's philosophy. A city lacking one
unified national or racial origin, Alexandria thus becomes a mirror not
only of Justine but of the *Alexandria Quartet* itself, whose shifting points
of view also reveal that there is no single interpretation or representation
that will capture its multiple realities.[42]

Neither one thing nor the other, Alexandria, like Justine, lends itself to
gender stereotyping. Figured by Darley as a "whore among cities" (*B* 13),
the city functions as a passage, a threshold between different cultures and
ways of being. Similarly, within Darley's imagination, Justine becomes a
sexualized site on his route to manhood—or, in Pursewarden's characteris-

tically misogynistic rhetoric, "a tiresome old sexual turnstile through which presumably we [men] must all pass" (*B* 105). The degree to which Justine serves as a stationary marker in Darley's mobile quest for self-knowledge also raises the specter of the Sphinx, whose presence confronts the questing Oedipus with the archetypal riddle of Woman.[43] Both enigma and riddle, Justine becomes the text's overdetermined symbol for the instability of truth and language in an existential world—that belated and bitter knowledge awaiting all the *Alexandria Quartet*'s male seekers.[44] Darley's description of Justine's appeal to men betrays what is at stake for him in the act of transforming her archetypal femininity into a sign of modernist uncertainty: "There was no question of true or false. Nymph? Goddess? Vampire? Yes, she was all of these and none of them. She was, like every woman, everything that the mind of man (let us define 'man' as a poet . . .) wished to imagine. . . . I began to realize with awe the enormous reflexive power of woman" (*C* 47–48).

Significantly, this conceptualizing of woman as man's mirroring other points to an even more suspect feature of Darley's desires, namely, the degree to which his projections onto Justine are narcissistic, reflecting, as Irigaray says, the masculine back upon itself ("everything that the mind of man . . . wished to imagine") in an example of the male specular logic of the same that chapter 5 illustrated at work in the paternal plots of Faulkner and Stead. Such male worship of the same also begins to suggest the possibility of a homoerotic underside to Darley's passion for Justine, and, indeed, to Durrell's plotting of male heterosexual desire. Hence Alexandria—elsewhere feminized as "princess and whore" (*C* 54)—is equally figured as "a city of incest" in which the "lover mirrors himself [as] Narcissus," and in which love itself is "something subtly androgynous, inverted upon itself" (*J* 82, 4). Not only does Darley meet and fall in love with Justine through her reflection in a mirror, but mirrors become Durrell's self-reflexive metaphor for the text's destabilizing, multidimensional refractions of points of view. Thus when Darley speaks of those lovers who emerge from Alexandria's "great wine-press of love . . . deeply wounded in their sex" (4), he subconsciously confirms the degree to which Alexandria's mirroring inversions have undermined the security of his authority as removed, all-seeing observer. The spectacle of Egyptian sensuality has become a reflecting glass, "inverted upon itself," for in a world of fluid boundaries, he who gazes ultimately finds himself penetrated in turn by his reflection in the mirror of the other.

Moreover, as the unsuccessful outcome of Darley's affair with Justine indicates, he has reason to feel "wounded in [his] sex," unsure of his "masculine" status, and by extension, his heterosexual competence. A curious impotence has dogged this would-be writer and dazed voyeur ever since his arrival in Alexandria, leading him to experience a failure in all domains of feeling: "to write; even to make love" (*J* 11). His first Egyptian lover, the nightclub dancer Melissa, will confess that "he never excited me like other men did" (*C* 214). And when Justine sweeps Darley across the borderline of voyeuristic detachment into the libidinal anarchy of her interior world, Darley assigns to himself the grammatical position of passive object of her desire: "She had achieved me" (*J* 21). Hence, it comes as no surprise that this "timid and scholarly lover with chalk on his sleeve" (*B* 121), having left Alexandria for an island retreat where he can lick his wounds in solitude, acquiesces with hardly a word of protest to Balthazar's revelation (in the latter's heavily annotated and edited draft of the *Justine* manuscript) that the most important love of his life has been a total sham. Balthazar's argument that Justine has used Darley as a "decoy" (12) to conceal her affair with Pursewarden—already Darley's rival as successful novelist—only underlines Darley's authorial and psychic impasse. His entire framework of reality radically transformed by this wounding knowledge, he must begin the work of "learn[ing] to see it all with new eyes," accustoming himself "to the truths which Balthazar has added" (12), among which he seems to accept as a given the revelation of his "unmanning" at Justine's hands.

Hence, as Darley begins this process of reevaluation, a series of memories and events repressed from *Justine* spontaneously rise to the surface of his recording consciousness, making up the reader's text of *Balthazar*. And, tellingly, what these hitherto repressed incidents obsessively reveal are less instances of Justine's infidelity (which we might expect from a deceived lover), than instances of Darley's profound uncertainty about his status as a man and about male sexuality in general, giving rise to anxieties that cannot be unknotted from the pulsations of homoerotic desire generated by the colonial encounter with otherness.

The Repressed Returns: Talismans of Gay Desire

It is no coincidence that *Balthazar* is named after the character whose text—nicknamed the Interlinear—undermines the sexual and narrative authority that Darley has attempted to establish over his passion by writing *Justine*. Unexpectedly appearing on Darley's island "like some goat-like apparition from the Underworld," sporting "dark Assyrian ringlets and the beard of Pan" (*B* 8), Balthazar, a doctor who also dabbles in the Cabal, is the perfect archetypal guide to initiate the next stage of this jilted lover's quest: descent into the mythic "Underworld" of polymorphous desire that Alexandria evokes. Not insignificantly, Balthazar is also a lover of his own sex, as Darley well knows, since he is "often" prone, he casually notes, to walking in unannounced on Balthazar in bed with various sailors (*J* 78). If Balthazar is the first in a series of homosexual figures to flood the psychodramatically charged landscape of *Balthazar*, he is also the one man whose "inversion" Darley claims to admire, since, to Darley's view, it doesn't compromise "his innate masculinity of mind" (*J* 77, 78). Darley's phrasing is worth note; the pronoun "his" obviously refers to Balthazar, but like so much else that is objectified as a third-person observation in this volume, the following description could apply equally to its speaker—"innate masculinity of mind" is precisely what Darley wishes to claim for himself, as well as what Balthazar's text has thrown into question. "And so, slowly, reluctantly," Darley writes at the end of the first chapter of *Balthazar,* "I have been driven back to my starting-point. . . . I must set it all down, in cold black and white. . . . The key I am trying to turn is in myself" (13).

Darley's words prove more prophetic than he knows, for the seemingly objective "facts" that he proceeds to record in this volume are indeed often none other than hidden "keys" to himself. Nothing could make this fact more clear, as David Wingrove has deftly elucidated, than the series of four triggering events whereby the psychologically and textually repressed resurfaces to rewrite the story of *Justine:* a recollected photograph, the memory of a kiss, the religious festival of Sitna Mariam, and Alexandria's celebration of Carnival.[45] I will take up these triggering events in the order in which Darley remembers them. As soon as Balthazar leaves, Darley turns to a photograph taken outside Mnemjian's barbershop, the hub of the *Alexandria Quartet*'s male homosocial world whose owner serves as the "archives of the city" (*J* 25). Examining this visual text for clues that he has hitherto failed to see, Darley fixes on two figures, Toto de Brunel and the unfortunately named John Keats—characters who have both gone unmentioned in *Justine.* First, Darley takes up the case of Toto, an aged and effeminate homosexual whose marginal position in the photograph is, tellingly, *the inverse of Darley's own:* "And in one corner there I am, in my shabby raincoat—the perfected image of a schoolteacher. In the other corner sits poor little Toto de Brunel . . . the darling of old society women too proud to pay for gigolos" (*B* 15). As we might suspect from Darley's condescending tone—which markedly contrasts with his professed tolerance for Balthazar's sexual practices—Toto has become a projection of the speaker's own inadequacies and uncertain self-image. For in serving as the "lapdog" of rich society women, Toto's position subconsciously reminds Darley of the passive role he himself has assumed as Justine's decoy. The fear of having been emasculated by Justine's use of him helps to explain the intensity of his virulent put-down of Toto's effeminacy: "There was . . . nothing to be done with him for he was a woman" (15).

Having trashed "poor little Toto," Darley's associations bring him to consider "poor John Keats," the newspaper correspondent who has snapped this photograph. As the recording eye behind the camera lens, Keats symbolically occupies the position of invisible but all-knowing author—that is, until Darley makes sure we know better: "Once he had wanted to be a writer but took the wrong turning" (16). Yet the more Darley ridicules Keats's counterproductive "mania to perpetuate, to record, to photograph everything!" (16), the more these traits sound suspiciously like Darley's own. Darley, after all, is the blocked writer whose failure to produce a novel is tied to the disabling belief that he can contain everything within one frame of reference—which Balthazar's Interlinear, in literally spilling over into the boundaries of the *Justine* manuscript, has emphatically disproved.

As the inaugural event in Darley's imaginative recovery of a repressed past, then, it is no accident that his memory exhumes two figures who illustrate, respectively, the impasses of sexual and narrative authority that have precipitated his own identity crisis. Both Toto and Keats, furthermore, illustrate the inextricability of the sexual and literary. Toto's sexual perversion is reflected in his comic perversion of language, for he speaks in "a Toto-tongue of his own," composed of three languages, whose destabilizing logic subverts the status quo by undermining the assumed relation between signifier and signified: "Whenever at a loss for a word he would put in one whose meaning he did not know and the grotesque substitution was often delightful. . . . In it, he almost reached poetry" (15–16). A more orthodox yoking of sexual potency and the word recurs in Keats's case. In the last volume of the *Alexandria Quartet,* this nondescript writer undergoes a radical transformation, returning from the war front not only a true writer but the epitome of sexy masculinity, as Darley learns when he finds his double taking a shower in the bathroom of his former apartment and is stunned by the sight of the now bronzed, athletic physique of a "Greek god!" standing under the water (*C* 170). Yet as Darley's telltale exclamation point suggests, even this now-positive projection of his dual goals of writerly and masculine authority is not without a homoerotic undertone that ever so slightly destabilizes its apparent signification, a slippage that falls in line with the other anxieties of masculinity that surface throughout *Balthazar* to haunt Darley.

The last figure Darley notes in Keats's photograph, Scobie, brings to the plane of consciousness even more blatant thoughts of sexual and linguistic perversion. "No mythology of the city would be complete without its Scobie," Darley has earlier written of this colorful ex–merchant marine and befuddled employee of the Egyptian Vice Squad and Secret Police. "Origins he has none—his past proliferates through a dozen continents like a true subject of myth" (*J* 105–6). At the same time, Scobie is depicted as an authentic British colonial, sporting "the comprehensibility of a diagram—plain as a national anthem" (*B* 19). Yet, curiously, Darley's train of associations as he observes Scobie's photographed image reveals that this old friend's signifying capacities are not so apparent after all: he instantly flashes on the day Scobie confesses to him that he has pederastic "Tendencies" (23) for which he is not "fully Answerable" (33). Exiled from a homeland which has not appreciated his zeal as a scoutmaster, Scobie has found a paradise for his proclivities in the colonized Orient. Nor are Scobie's transgressive tastes limited to brown (or in British parlance "black") boys, for the old man also confesses to Darley, as a popular jazz melody, "Old Tiresias," plays in the background, that he doesn't mind "slip[ping into] female duds . . . when the Fleet's in" (32–33; readers of *Nightwood* may have already guessed at Scobie's cross-dressing propensities from his recitation of "Watchman, What of the Night?" [*J* 106], Durrell's sly reference to Barnes's equally garrulous transvestite expatriate, Matthew O'Connor). The frighteningly swift and altogether convincing transformation of Scobie into "a veritable Tuppenny Upright" (*B* 32) as he puts on his "female duds" exposes Darley to another slippage in signification (from "male" to "female") that, by analogy, raises the haunting possibility of his own metaphoric unmanning. Moreover, as in Toto's case, this destabilization in sexual meaning is marked by a subversion of linguistic content; Scobie speaks in so arcane a dialect that his verbal perversions necessitate a glossary at the end of the volume.

The fear that being unmanned may vitiate one's artistic powers becomes the even more explicit subject of the next chapter, as Balthazar's reconstructed text causes Darley to travel back in memory to the inception of Justine's lesbian affair with the artist Clea. This is another event that Darley has known about all along but that he largely suppresses from *Justine,* since it runs counter to his romanticizing vision of the consuming heterosexual passion he assumes Justine feels for him. "Distasteful" as Darley now claims to find the subject of female homosexuality, he dwells on the affair at length. First, because the women's lovemaking literally interrupts Clea's artistry, her kisses "[falling] where the painter's wet brush should have fallen" (*B* 41), the tableau that Darley mentally constructs serves as a cautionary fable for one whose own creative productivity has been blocked by his love for Justine. Second, Clea's break with Justine provides Darley with a model for avoiding inappropriate desires—the homosexuality that he here denigrates as "the consuming shape of a sterile love" (42)—and Clea is a particularly relevant model, considering she becomes Darley's ideal love object at the end of the *Alexandria Quartet.* Hence Darley subconsciously depicts Clea's experience as the complementary inverse of his own: her naive encounter with lesbianism proves "that relationships like these did not answer the needs of her nature," that "she was a woman at last and belonged to men" (46). This investment in maintaining Clea's "innocence" (42) attests to the strength of Darley's pressing need to establish his own innocence, his untainted masculine integrity, in the midst of the sexual perversions that increasingly surround him and threaten (following the logic of the Freudian switch-word) the presumed "needs of *his* nature" as much as *hers.*

Given the welling-up of forbidden desires signified by Balthazar, Toto, Scobie, and company, it is fascinating to turn to the next textually repressed event reported for the first time in *Balthazar.* This involves chapter

7's long account of the orgiastic mulid of Sitna Mariam, whose dreamlike, Circean atmosphere I have already briefly noted. It only takes a few jotted words by Balthazar in the Interlinear—"So Narouz decided to *act*"—to "detonate" in Darley's "imagination" (143) the latter's entirely *fictional recreation* of Narouz's movements throughout the evening, the account of which is disguised as objective, omnisciently narrated text. What this narrative sleight of hand fails to conceal, however, is the fact that the sensations Darley attributes to Narouz, the "desires engendered in the forests of the mind" (157), are not Narouz's, but in fact projections of *his own* imagining and hence of his own psychic needs. Darley's account of the mulid, thus, becomes an act of creative fiat, a weaving of the fiction he needs to hear, that vies in intensity with Quentin and Shreve's collaborative "marriage" of minds and words when they conjure out of the rag-tag and bob-ends of old stories Sutpen's confrontation with his son Henry, and Henry's with his half brother Bon.

But why does Darley choose Narouz to stand in as actor in his own imaginative fantasy? Because, it turns out, Narouz in many ways embodies Darley's ideal of archetypal masculinity. Clad in loose peasant clothes that "expos[e] arms and hands of great power covered by curly dark hair," possessed of a powerful body from which emanates "a sensation of overwhelming strength" (58–59), Narouz epitomizes untamed sensual virility. This is a man who can easily, not to say sadistically, dismember animals with one crack of his whip, and who, like Lawrence's Gerald Crich, experiences delirious orgasm when taming a wild horse. Narouz's unrequited love for Clea reinforces his function as Darley's heterosexual role model, outlining the proper route for the timid schoolteacher's wayward drives. From Darley's narrating perspective, then, Narouz looms, in perhaps too many senses of the word, as a man's man—so much so that an ambiguously homoerotic element begins to infiltrate the narrator's appreciative descriptions of the person who, after all, is established as his guide to heterosexual fulfillment. Not only might Darley's lingering evocation of Narouz's orgasm on horseback sound slightly suspect, but the muted feminization that infiltrates his description of Narouz's "splendid" eyes, "of a blueness and innocence that made them almost like Clea's," along with the "deep and thrilling . . . magic of a woman's contralto" (59) that he reads into Narouz's voice, points to an erotic intensity barely contained by the appeal to sexual difference. Within Durrell's symbolic geography of desire, masculine heterosexuality is once again complicated by its proximity to the homoerotic.

That there is more going on here than first meets the eye is confirmed in Darley's evocation of Narouz's night-odyssey through the mulid's festival grounds. Narouz's movements lead him, finally, to an aged, fat prostitute with whom he engages in feverish intercourse, because (so Darley conjectures) Narouz imagines that he hears in her voice Clea's presence: "A voice spoke out of the shadows at his side—a voice whose sweetness and depth could belong to one person only: Clea. . . . The voice was the voice of the woman he loved but it came from a hideous form, seated in half-shadow—the grease-folded body of a Moslem woman. . . . Blind now to everything but the cadences of the voice he followed her like an addict" (158–59). Having entered a mutable and sightless realm where sexuality takes any and all forms, Narouz in effect creates his desired love object out of this amorphous and anonymous body, imbuing the prostitute with his desires for Clea. When we remember that Narouz's perceptions are being hypothesized by the narrating Darley, moreover, this moment becomes pivotal in exposing the stakes involved in this text's constitution of male sexual identity. For what this encounter reveals about the nature of sexual attraction is the fact that *all desire is unfixed,* or, to put it in Freud's terms in the *Three Essays,* that there is no necessary link between sexual instinct and object-choice: the only "natural" objects of our desires are those that our fantasies construct, just as Narouz has done with the decrepit prostitute.[46] In practical terms, Narouz's example teaches Darley the manifold options that are also his: Darley, too, can put his love for Justine aside and redirect his desire to a more "appropriate" object-choice. What Balthazar has said in praise of homosexual relations—"Sex has left the body and entered the imagination now" (*J* 82)—thus turns out to be true of all negotiations of desire. The Circean world of libidinal fluidity, of polymorphous free play, that Joyce celebrates in the Nighttown episode of *Ulysses* lives on in Durrell's exploration of the nature of desire.

And Darley—even more than, say, Leopold Bloom—should know something about the constructed nature of sexual fantasy, because, in a riveting return of the repressed, it turns out that he has not only been a participant in this festival, he has *witnessed* Narouz's copulation with the prostitute first-hand: "*My memory revives something which it had forgotten;* memories of a dirty booth with a man and woman lying together in a bed and myself looking down at them, half-drunk, *waiting my turn . . .*" (160; emphasis added). Waiting his turn, that is, to do the same as Narouz, and spend the image of his lost love for Justine on this nameless body; which, literally, also means waiting his turn to *take* Narouz's place, to *become* his eroticized masculine ideal, a "real" man. Unless Darley subconsciously means to take the place of the prostitute, *to be with* rather than become his ideal—a possibility that accentuates the sexual ambiguities continuing to plague Darley's quest for manhood.[47] Given Darley's spectatorial role in this "forgotten" but now recovered "memory," it is noteworthy that his voyeuristic tendencies are especially pronounced when it comes to potentially homoerotic displays of naked male flesh: visiting Balthazar in bed with his boyfriends; walking in on Keats's newly godlike body under the shower; and, now, interrupting Narouz's orgasm. Given these recurrences, it no longer suffices to explain away Darley's obsessive thoughts of homosexual taint solely as an internalized reaction to his failure as Justine's lover; it becomes more and more possible that he also subliminally searches out that which he fears because it speaks to his unarticulated desires.

Thus it is ironically but psychologically appropriate that the welter of polymorphous desires unleashed by Darley's vivid recreation of the mulid of Sitna Mariam in chapter 7 is immediately set against an account of Scobie's murder (which is recorded out of chronological order) at the beginning of chapter 8. Once again the narrative sequencing takes its cue from the associative drift of Darley's mind, rendering the novel's form a simulation of psychic processes, as Darley recalls how the genial old "Peddyrast" is gruesomely kicked to death while cruising the docks in his female clothes. In so manipulating the sequential ordering of events, Darley unconsciously uses his textual authority to serve warning on his analogous potential for perversity: not only do Scobie's "Tendencies" catch up with the roguish old sailor, but the latent homoeroticism just given expression in Darley's account of Narouz has also been, if not literally punished, at least *overwritten*.

This report of homophobic violence, moreover, prefigures the psychodramatic climax of *Balthazar*—the Carnival ball during which the effeminate Toto de Brunel is also discovered brutally murdered, his head run through with a hatpin—yet another psychodramatically charged event suppressed from the earlier text. "Why have I never [before] mentioned this [incident]?" Darley muses in terms that repeat almost exactly, as we will see, Anna Wulf's admission of her suppression of homosexual material in *The Golden Notebook*. "I was even there at the time," Darley continues, "yet somehow the whole incident though it belonged to the atmosphere of the moment escaped me in the press of other matters. . . . Nevertheless, it is strange that I should not have mentioned it, even in passing" (182). Even more so than the mad jumble of color, sounds, and human grotesques at the festival of Sitna Mariam, Alexandria's celebration of Carnival assumes the contours of a dream-text that taps into the collective unconscious of the human race. "The dark tides of Eros . . . burst out . . . like something long dammed up and raise the forms of strange primeval creatures—the perversions," Darley says of this three-day-long debauch, noting that its "ruling spirit" is the "utter anonymity" that comes when "we are delivered from the thrall of personality, from the bondage of ourselves" (182, 185). Hence the ubiquitous black costumes and dominos donned by the participants become "the outward symbols of our own secret minds," "shroud-[ing] identity and sex," blurring the borders "between man and woman, wife and lover, friend and enemy" (196, 182). In this world of dissolving boundaries, of unmoored sexuality and uncertain identity, Darley finds an exhilarating freedom implicitly linked to the homoeroticism that has haunted him throughout *Balthazar*:

One feels free in this disguise to do whatever one likes without prohibition. . . . You cannot tell whether you are dancing with a man or a woman. . . . Yes, who can help but love carnival when . . . all crimes [are] expiated or committed, all illicit desires sated . . . without the penalties which conscience or society exact? (185)

To do "whatever one likes," for Darley, seems intimately connected to the "criminal" pleasure of just perhaps finding oneself dancing with a member of the same sex. But if Carnival, through its exteriorization of desire, seems to make such "illicit" crimes possible by temporarily escaping the socially repressive laws of "prohibition," "penalties," and "conscience," the festival is simultaneously the siting for the much more ambiguous reinforcement of repression. One is reminded of the surveillance of the gaze that goes hand-in-hand with the liberation of spirit that Lucy Snowe feels in her quest into the midnight fête in the park in *Villette*. For Darley's reference to criminal acts "expiated and committed" takes on a more ominous meaning once we learn that the costumed Toto, Darley's negative alter ego, meets his doom against this ambisexual backdrop. The satiation of "illicit desires" exacts a high payment.

Significantly, Toto is mistaken for Justine when he is killed; on the way to the Cervoni ball, Justine has given him her well-known intaglio ring to wear, so that she can slip away from the ball unobserved, granting him in the meantime "a miracle long desired . . . to be turned from a man into a woman" (195). The unintended result of this substitution assumes significance on several levels. First, it enacts the death of the feminized man that Darley fears he has become through his "unmanning" by Justine; second, it marks the death of a scapegoat for Justine herself, the negative love object who has engendered his self-doubts. But, third, the death of Toto also symbolizes the scapegoating of Darley's homosexual impulses. For just as significant as the fact that Toto dies mistaken for Justine is the fact that she has marked his black sleeve with white chalk so that she may later identify him among the costumed revelers. Crucially, this signifying mark echoes an image that Darley has already used to describe himself as "this timid and scholarly lover with chalk on his sleeve" (121); imagistically he and Toto become interchangeable.[48] Hence Toto functions not only as Darley's negative foil, not only as a scapegoat for Justine, but as a double or mirror—in this world of incestuously multiplying mirrors—of Darley himself.

And who is it that kills Toto? None other than Narouz, the masculine heterosexual principle incarnate. For, as David Wingrove astutely deduces, in the act of narrating Toto's death Darley allows his hypermasculine double (Narouz) to assert itself by carrying out the psychic slaying of his feminine self-image (Toto) and with it his guilty homoerotic desires.[49] This purgation allows Darley to reposition himself as a sexual being and a productive artist, which becomes the project of the rest of the *Alexandria*

Quartet. The primary male task, Durrell implies, is to create a love object appropriate to one's desired self-image. But for Darley such a goal involves several paradoxes. For that which Darley is exorcising is any expression of the polymorphous play, the slippages in signification, that Carnival (like the preceding mulid) has revealed to be the underlying "truth" of all sexual desire. Without his psychic descent into the anarchy and anonymity of Carnival's dreamscape, moreover, this knowledge would never have occurred to Darley, nor would this symbolic exorcism have been possible. In "hunting from room to room . . . for an identifiable object to direct our love" (196), as Darley says of the Carnival revelers, we find that there are no destined objects *except* those we construct . . . or those we need to kill.

Pygmalion and the Reinstatement of Phallocentric Discourse

The quintessential Carnival story of unmasked true love, interestingly enough, turns out to be all about the (quite literal) construction of one's desired sexual object, and as such it sheds light on Durrell's resolution of Darley's anxieties at the end of the *Alexandria Quartet.* It is at Carnival that the doctor Amaril falls "madly in love" (*M* 133) with a masked lady who disappears without leaving her name. The next year, Amaril meets her again, and after a frenzied pursuit, strips her of her mask, only to learn her nose has been eaten away by disease. Undeterred by this revelation, Amaril uses his surgical skills to reconstruct a nose for his beloved—in effect, to replace her lack with his phallic projection. As Clea, who relates this fable, notes, "You see, he [was] after all building a woman of his own fancy . . . only Pygmalion had such a chance before!" (*M* 137). Once Amaril has successfully "author[ed]" this "lovely nose" (*C* 80), he bestows on his bride a very special wedding present: a doll's surgery, where she can repair children's wounded dolls, inert Galateas like herself, the rest of her life. "'It is the only way,' says Amaril, 'to hold a really stupid woman you adore. Give her something of her own to do'" (81).

It is ironically fitting that Clea narrates this story: not only has she helped Amaril engineer Semira's transformation by sketching models for the new nose, but Semira's fate becomes Clea's own. As already noted, the fourth volume details Darley's return to Alexandria and the self-confidence that he gains as he lays to rest Justine's dangerously oriental allure by redirecting his sexual energies toward the serenely virginal, blonde beauty of Clea. To become a part of this text's economy of male desire, however, Clea must first be remade by man in his image, no matter how perfect she may appear to be, and this symbolic act of rebirth forms the symbolically charged climax of the entire *Alexandria Quartet.* Darley and Clea have been deep-sea diving when Clea's hand is accidentally harpooned to a submerged wreck. Unable to free the harpoon, Darley is forced to hack Clea's arm off with a knife, and then, on shore, pump her nearly drowned body back to life (she gasps for air like "a newly born child") in a grotesque "simulacrum of the sexual act—life saving, life-giving" (244–45). Not surprisingly, even Durrell's most ardent supporters have had problems justifying the heavy-handed (pun intended) construction of this scene. Rather than attempt to justify this flurry of melodrama, I suggest its *inevitability*, given the *Alexandria Quartet*'s unfolding themes. That is, the strain that the text places on credulity at this point has everything to do with the difficulty (and desperation) involved in the attempt of Darley to construct an appropriately heterosexual object of desire.

Durrell's symbolism, indeed, is painfully obvious. Not only is Clea pinioned by one phallic object and castrated by another, not only does a simulated sex act by a man bring her back to life, but it is her painter's arm—her means of independent creative productivity—that she loses: the "necessary sacrifice of a useless member," according to one critic.[50] In turn, Darley's role in reanimating Clea transforms him into a Pygmalion-like "life-giver" (244) whose powers of creation thereby subsume the threat that women's reproductive powers—like Egypt's emblematic fecundity—have traditionally posed to the questing male (the same threat, as we've seen, underlies Sutpen's and Sam Pollit's efforts to appropriate maternal procreativity).[51] The parallels to the Pygmalion-Galatea myth are clinched by the fact that it is none other than Amaril who treats the wounded Clea, replacing her missing hand with a mechanical one that paints even better than her original: her artistry is thus rendered a product of male instrumentality. Simultaneously, Clea reveals that Amaril was the unnamed lover to whom she has earlier lost her virginity, "turn[ing]" her "into a woman" (249) ready for Darley's advances. "I suppose I was even a bit eager to be wounded," she says of her sexual initiation (101), and wounded she indeed becomes in this final bit of psychodrama.[52] Durrell's narrative has forcibly fashioned a feminine love object that answers to his protagonist's desired self-image as a heterosexually competent man: via the agency of Greek myth, a perfect (and perfectly Hellenic) mate is born from Darley's descent into the dangerously torrid zone of middle eastern sexuality.

In order to construct his female counterpart, however, Darley must first refashion his own image, a project that recalls the sexual ambiguities besetting his negotiations of masculine subjectivity throughout the *Alexandria Quartet*. Just as Darley's doubts have been expressed through externalized self-projections, so now one of his many doubles becomes the measure of his potential for self-fashioning: in this case, the journalist Johnny Keats, recently returned to Alexandria from the front (World War II has commenced) newly metamorphosed: "And . . . you know what? The most unaccountable and baffling thing. [War] has made a man of me, as the saying goes. More, a writer! . . . I have begun it at last, that bloody joyful book of mine" (173). If Keats can undergo such a sea change, there might be hope for Darley yet. Keats's doubling function also explains his pronouncement that he now considers himself a worthy competitor for Clea: manhood, writing, and wooing Clea all appear part of the same agenda in Durrell's textual universe.

But the actual moment of reencounter between Darley and his masculine double unleashes an extraneous erotic energy that belies the assumed coherency of this formula. This scene, noted earlier, occurs when Darley returns to his old apartment to find Keats in the shower: "Under the shower stood a Greek god! I was so surprised at the transformation that I sat down abruptly on the lavatory and studied this . . . apparition. Keats was burnt almost black, and his hair had bleached white. Though slimmer, he looked in first-class physical condition" (170). While Keats dries himself, the two men make conversation:

> "God this water is a treat. I've been revelling."
> "You look in tremendous shape."
> "I am. I am." He smacked himself exuberantly on the buttocks. . . . "You look in quite good shape, too," he said, and his blue eyes twinkled with a new mischievous light. (170)

Taken out of context, this exchange might seem more the prelude to sex in gay porn fiction than the encounter of straight hero and his straight role-model. For under Darley's intense gaze, Keats's body becomes as much an object of consumption, a living spectacle, as the glistening, "magnificent-looking male prostitute" who mesmerizes Narouz during the festival of Sitna Mariam. But there is a significant difference between these two eroticized objects: this new-born Adonis is as unmistakably English as the Pygmalion-like artist whose vision metaphorically (re)creates him. Just as Justine's dark exoticism has been replaced with Clea's rational clarity, the swarthy foreignness of Darley's former male ideal Narouz—murdered at the climax of the third volume—is overwritten by a newly fantasized masculine self-image whose Aryan good looks perfectly complement Clea's own and whose name associates him with canonical English literature. Yet even the retreat from oriental sexuality implicit in this pair of substitutions does not completely eradicate the homoerotic possibility—or threat—that Egypt has already unlocked in Darley's psyche and the text's unconscious, as the exchange of "mischievous" glances in the shower attests. It is thus inevitable that Keats dies in battle almost immediately after this encounter. Not only does his death free Darley to become the new Keats, as it were, it also ensures that those lingering glances go no further. In death, Keats thus joins those other silenced signifiers of homoerotic taboo, Toto, Scobie, and Narouz. Within the libidinally charged world that Durrell has created, the price of masculine subjectivity is repressing the very desires that make its construction such a pressing necessity.

The impact that this restructuring imperative has on the psychological level is repeated on the formal level, as the concluding pages of *Clea* illustrate. In Darley's last walk about town (it is the eve of his final departure from Alexandria), he comes across a religious procession that echoes the Sitna Mariam festival and Carnival scenes of *Balthazar*. But the erotic, ecstatic, and perverse energies of those events have been subtly homogenized, routed into one linear trajectory, in this reprise: "And to all this queer discontinuous and yet somehow congruent mass of humanity the music lent a sort of homogeneity; it bound it and confined it. . . . Circling, proceeding, halting, the long dancing lines moved on towards the tomb, bursting through the great portals . . . like a tide at full" (262). This rechanneling of the multiple tributaries of desire into one massive "tide at full" not only uncannily recalls Lawrence's flood and Freud's description of the way sexual instincts are brought into the service of a single drive, but also inscribes the physiological process of male orgasm. And with this climactic ejaculation, the dispersive energies of this multilayered text are "bound and confined" within a specifically phallocentric model of narrative that has little to do with the polymorphous free play that Durrell's formal experimentations and embrace of the relativity principle have encouraged. Ironically, the goal of the processional is Scobie's former lodging: this lecherous old Tiresias has been resurrected by the Moslem population of his quarter as El Scob, a fertility god to whom barren women pray. With this rewriting of the very type of male sexual ambiguity into an emblem of heterosexual productivity, the narrative's homogenizing of its deviant impulses seems finally to have cleared the way for Darley to produce, at long last, his "mansize" masterpiece.

So how does the reinvigorated manly artist feel, proverbial pen in hand and facing the blank page? Well, we can only take Darley at his word: "like some timid girl, scared of the birth of her first child" (275). Perhaps this return of the feminine whereby Darley identifies himself as a *her* is only a joke, or a slip of the pen, or an assertion of mastery over former anxieties. Nonetheless, this age-old conflation of masculine artistic productivity and female reproductivity betrays the shadow of a fear that lingers to disturb Darley's newborn confidence. Perhaps he should join the barren wives who pray to El Scob for succor.

Writing Couples Redux

This mass of contradictions circles us back to Durrell's problematic relation to phallocentric discourse, in the case of the *Alexandria Quartet* exacerbated and illuminated by the sexual and representational politics of colonial narrative. For Durrell, we have seen, is attracted to Alexandria as the locus of his narrative precisely because its exotic foreign otherness allows him to indulge in fantasies of, as Said puts it, "a different type of sexuality"—certainly one more open to experimentation. Likewise, the polyphonic execution of his late-modernist endeavor evokes a geography of the instincts freed from constrictions of time and space and, to the writing western consciousness, from sexual-moral orthodoxy. But such representations of foreign sensuality and free play, for all their appeal, simultaneously prove unnerving, precisely because they expose the contradictions embedded in western culture's traditional plots of masculine maturation and articulation. Hence Darley's compulsion to code the "possible" as "homosexual," the absolute antithesis of Eurocentric manhood, and hence his impulse to *colonize* these fantasies by equating them with the "feminine," thereby categorizing their difference within familiar hierarchical terms that grant him the fiction of control over their subversive attraction.

But this desire to control, to pin down as one thing and not the other, is also what the *Alexandria Quartet,* with its paean to the relativity of all truths and its repeated illustration of the slipperiness of all signification, works to counter. For if the multiple, overlapping perspectives engendered by the *Alexandria Quartet's* refracting linguistic and formal structures suggest the subjectivity of all viewpoints, so too its evocations of the sensual Alexandrian nightworld suggest that the only "truth" of sexuality or sexual identification is its similarly fluid and individually constructed nature. The irony, then, is that Darley's discovery of the arbitrariness of sexual choice, of the role that imagination plays in creating any object of desire, makes all the more urgent his formulation of a choice towards sexual fixity, towards an absolutism of heterosexual identification and "straightforward" artistic productivity. Thus *Clea* ends with an exchange of letters between Darley and Clea, letters tremulous with the anticipation of a not-too-distant reunion on safe European soil, followed, on the last page, with the narrator's declaration that he has just penned the first words of his long-deferred novel: "Once upon a time . . ." (275). At this moment, with Clea practically in his arms, Darley has become the apotheosis of the western writer, and the Near East a successfully colonized other whose perversities he can survey from the authorizing distance of myth and fairy tale.

The catch, though, is that Clea really *isn't* in Darley's arms. Despite the fact Darley has begun to write, his romantic desires remain in a state of suspension; the concluding exchange of letters gives an illusion of romantic closure where none exists. And with this image of Clea writing from Paris and Darley writing from his island retreat, I inevitably think of that other writing couple mentioned at the beginning of this discussion—Miller in Paris, Durrell on a Mediterranean island—for whom correspondence also whets rather than consummates desire. In turn this correspondence reminds me of the letter Flaubert excitedly writes from Egypt to his best friend, Louis Bouilhet, back home in Paris. Having just gone into exacting detail about the sodomitical proclivities of his fellow Egyptians, he concludes:

Dear fellow how I'd love to hug you—I'll be glad to see your face again. . . .
At night when you are in your room and the lines don't come, and you're
thinking of me, and bored, with your elbows on the table, take a sheet of
paper and write me everything—I devoured your letter and have reread it
more than once. At this moment I have a vision of you in your shirt before
the fire, feeling too warm, and contemplating your prick. (86–87)

Whatever one may want to argue about Flaubert's tone or his overwhelmingly heterosexual orientation, this letter inscribes the body of a homosexual rather than merely homosocial desire. Nonetheless, the framework
within which Flaubert encases this masturbatory scenario presupposes a
relation of writing to sexuality as potentially disabling as that which generates Darley's crisis of masculinity in the *Alexandria Quartet*. For Flaubert
must first represent the homoerotic revery as that which takes place when
"the lines don't come," when Bouilhet is "bored" with his poetry and abdi-
cates pen for prick; so too, the homoerotics of the *Alexandria Quartet* figuratively take place between the lines, precisely because the exotic otherness
of sexual perversion is figured as the threat of erasure, the negation of artistic vitality or "sap." Thus in his journal Flaubert will use nonreproductive
sexual play as a metaphor to express his despair at not having yet achieved
his writing goals: "Where is the heart, the verve, the sap? . . . We're good
at sucking, we play a lot of tongue-games, we pet for hours: but—the real
thing! To ejaculate, beget the child!" (199). Against this phallocentric
model of narrative creation, in which the pen is the penis only if the desire is heterosexually productive, the substance of the narrative that Flaubert relays to Bouilhet simultaneously inscribes another story. For the
erotic tableau he unfolds is, first of all, *of* writing—"take a sheet of paper
and write," he enjoins Bouilhet—and, second, on Flaubert's part, it has
taken the *form of* writing: "At this moment," he *writes,* "I have a vision
of you . . ."

Hence, that which takes place between the lines, as in Durrell's case,
or when the lines don't come, as in Flaubert's, writes itself into the text
nonetheless, engendering a homoerotic discourse of foreign otherness that
is already inscribed its denial. In the case of the *Alexandria Quartet,* the
sheer effort of Darley's attempt to construct a nonperverse, productive
model of sexuality and narrativity—underlining the extremity of the masculine and textual anxieties that at once drive and undercut his story—
ends up only clearing space for the play of the desires that it ultimately
attempts to write out of its narratives. Meanwhile Darley corresponds ex-
pectantly with Clea in Paris, and Clea replies in kind, serenely awaiting a
consummation that never comes; and in the gap between these two lovers,
one the constructed mirror-projection of the other, exists an other
"other"—the phantasm raised by the conjunction of colonialism and homoerotic possibility—that will not disappear from this mid-century text's
mappings of the problematic terrain of male desire.

DORIS LESSING, *THE GOLDEN NOTEBOOK*
SEX-RACE WARS ON THE FRONTIER

> I have no time for people who haven't experimented with themselves, deliberately tried the frontiers.
> —Anna in Doris Lessing, *The Golden Notebook* (542)

An acute awareness of modernity, to paraphrase Linda Kauffman, runs throughout Doris Lessing's *The Golden Notebook* (1962),[53] a novel that attempts to impart a sweepingly global vision of what Lessing calls "the ideological 'feel' of our mid-century" and of the "great debates of our time" (xi). Confronting what she sees as the cataclysmic breakdown of existing systems of Enlightenment order, Lessing tackles a number of "major" issues and debates, most of which have been amply dissected by the Lessing industry: (1) the status of Marxism, socialism, and collectivity as political ideals; (2) theories of individual psychology ranging from Freud and Jung to Laing and Rank; (3) the loss of the writer's authority in a relative universe; (4) use of experimental, fragmented form to capture the sense of reality in a state of breakdown and to gesture toward a less unitary mode of envisioning order; (5) the rise of the women's movement in response to the destructive warfare of the sexes; and (6) issues of Empire and colonial oppression. However, one seemingly "minor" issue illustrating Lessing's "awareness of modernity" that has gone unmarked in criticism on *The Golden Notebook* is, as I have already indicated, the curious role played by that "modern" creation, the homosexual "personage,"[54] in the trajectory of the novel, linking together its much more visible debates. In fact the novel is bracketed by two seemingly offhanded references to "queers," made to Anna Wulf by her best friend Molly in the first and last sections of "Free Women," the narrative that encases Anna's notebook entries. Occurring as they do at the novel's beginning and end, these references suggest that what has been said offhandedly is perhaps of some consequence after all. What are the sexual anxieties being bracketed by these throwaway references, and what do either these references or the anxieties that they index have to do with the psychosexual and libidinal trajectories of this politically charged novel?

The first reference occurs when Molly, who is an actress, talks about what it is like to return to England after having spent time on the Continent. Currently, she is rehearsing a play in which, she jokes to Anna, "Every man in the cast is a queer but one, and he's sixteen. So what am I doing here?" In this case, the "queer" reference forms a segue to Molly's real point: the inadequacies of *heterosexual* English men, who know neither how to make women feel "like women," nor how to put women at ease sexually: "As soon as you set foot here, you have to tighten your belt, and remember, Now be careful, these men are Englishmen. . . . And you get all self-conscious and sex-conscious. How can a country full of screwed up people be any good?" (47). The problematic heterosexual politics of nation and manhood thus seems to be the logical outcome of the stream of associations set into motion by Molly's throwaway reference to the sexual orientation of her fellow cast members but one. The second reference occurs within a page of the end of the text, when Anna asks Molly how her ex-husband's second wife (Marion) is faring now that she too has left Richard. Throughout, the pathetically weak-willed, alcoholic, and helpless Marion has provided a foil to the "free women" that Anna and Molly aspire to be, and in response to Anna's inquiry Molly reveals that Marion has abandoned her latest fashionable cause—African racial politics—for another kind of chic: setting up a dress shop in Knightsbury. Molly delivers a final twist to her putdown of Marion when she sardonically adds, "She's already surrounded herself by a gaggle of little queers who exploit her, and she adores them and she giggles a lot and drinks just a *little* too much, and thinks they are ever such fun" (665). A truly "free" or independent woman, it is clear by inference, does not surround herself with imitation men who, like Toto in Durrell's *Alexandria Quartet,* serve as rich women's companions in the absence of the real thing. This portrait of Marion not only diminishes Marion's break from Richard by infantilizing her behavior but also denigrates male homosexuals (note the repetition of the word *little,* linking these men and Marion) by implying that they exploit women whom they cannot sexually satisfy, perhaps *because* they cannot satisfy them.

The common denominator in both of these instances, it seems, is less the condescending attitude that Molly and Anna display toward "queers" than the paucity of heterosexual men willing to engage women such as themselves on a level of parity. The following pages take up, in more detail, the complex and often devious routes by which the "male problem" for free women like Anna and Molly—precisely because such men have cast themselves as the enemies when not the victims of liberated women—is deflected onto, as it were, other "others"—a category that includes the victims of racial oppression with whom Anna identifies in Africa as well as the homosexual men in her present-day London life, with whom she and Molly strenuously try *not* to identify. The failure of heterosexual men and women to establish nonantagonistic relationships in the mid-twentieth century, Lessing implies, is emblematic of the larger breakdown in communication, as well as in language itself, that is constitutive of contemporary civilization, whose increasing meaninglessness, division, and disorder are responsible for the impasse that informs Anna's inability to write or to relate as a "whole" person to others. The thematic and ultimately formal tension between Lessing's sense of the "the split, divided, unsatisfactory way we all live," and the "need for [the] wholeness" (161) that will heal such fragmentation, underlines the novel's status as one of the last great modernist attempts to impose artistic coherence on a vision of a world in the very moment of its passing.

Cracking Apart, Cracking Open

The Golden Notebook begins on a note of division and fragmentation, as revealed in the first words that Anna Wulf speaks on the novel's opening page: "The point is, that as far as I can see, everything's cracking up" (3) On the one hand, "the point" of the novel could not be made more explicit, for the topos of things falling apart extends in all directions—Anna's disillusion with the political ideals she has espoused in the British Communist Party; the failure of relationships (foregrounded in this section by the imminent arrival at Molly's flat of her ex-husband Richard, to complain about Marion); the psychic divisions signaled by the states of depression, nervous breakdown, and insanity that beset various characters in the novel; and the dissolution of traditionally unifying concepts such as nation and Empire. Nor is modern art, as Anna realizes, immune to such fragmentation. As she writes in the Black notebook, "The novel has become a function of the fragmented society, the fragmented consciousness," that is, of the divisions both inside and outside us: "Human beings are so divided, are becoming more and more divided, *and more subdivided in themselves, reflecting the world*" (61).

On the other hand, Anna's "point" about "everything cracking up" is true only insofar as it expresses her subjective and hence limited viewpoint: "as far as I can see," Anna says. In face of this relativity of perception (which Lessing's layered narrative structure shares with Durrell's), Anna dreams of writing "a book powered with an intellectual or moral passion strong enough to create order, to create a new way of looking at life" (61). So saying, she aligns herself squarely within the modernist tradition that flourished before World War II, expressing, in terms identical to Woolf's in *To the Lighthouse*, the desire to impose coherence on the "awful black whirling chaos . . . just outside [us]" (367), and by doing so to inspire "a new way" of envisioning the future. At the same time, Anna despairs that she is no longer able to write such a novel, that the moment for such modernist belief may have been rendered obsolete by the prospect of "general annihilation" (243) that the political crises marking the Cold War world seem to augur: the Korean war, the Suez crisis, the McCarthy hearings in America, Communist atrocities in eastern Europe, A-bomb and H-bomb testings, rumors of germ warfare.[55]

Nonetheless, as an artist and intellectual, Lessing like her characters works out of an explicitly modernist legacy. In an interview published the same year as *The Golden Notebook*, Lessing places her self-reflexive fiction in a lineage that includes Joyce, Lawrence, Mann, and Proust.[56] Likewise, in the novel, Anna's friend Molly is the daughter of parents who participated in the 1920s in the "intellectual and bohemian circles that spun around the great central lights of Huxley, Lawrence, Joyce" (7). In theme and content, moreover, *The Golden Notebook* frequently alludes to its modernist forebears. Lessing deliberately attempts to do Joyce one better when she has Anna record a minute-by-minute description of an entire day in one of her diaries (a day in which Anna, like Molly in "Penelope," begins her period, which causes Anna to contrast Joyce's freedom of expression and that of women writers [340–41]); the tug of sexual attraction and repulsion and the critique of "sex-consciousness" in Anna's incomplete novel, *The Shadow of the Third* vividly evokes D. H. Lawrence;[57] and Anna's dream of dried up springs, spurring a quest through the desert and mountains in search of water (407–8), self-reflexively refers to Eliot's "The Wasteland."

Furthermore, *The Golden Notebook* evinces its affiliations with modernist experiments in form by embodying its concern with fragmentation and "crack-up" in its convoluted narrative structure. The text is composed of excerpts from four colored notebooks into which Anna attempts to segregate or "subdivide" the components of her life: Black for her African years and first novel, Red for her political involvement, Yellow for the draft of her unfinished novel, and Blue for her diary (the fifth or Golden notebook represents Anna's late attempt to synthesize these components into one document). These entries are interspersed with the contemporary narrative, "Free Women," which appears to be a realistic, omnisciently narrated account of Anna's life but which turns out to be a novella that Anna has written, thus comprising, in addition to *Frontiers of War* and *The Shadow of the Third*, yet another fictionalized version of her life. The continual alternation between the notebooks and the "Free Women" novella creates a series of spatial and temporal overlaps and disjunctions that are reminiscent not only of Durrell's volumes but also of Faulkner's multiple narrative voices in *Absalom, Absalom!*[58] Such layerings achieve several purposes. First, the divided, fragmented narrative form reflects Anna's—and Lessing's—perception of a radically alienated world. In the notebooks, "everything's divided off and split up" (274), mirroring "the split, divided way we all live" (161). Second, by offering the reader multifaceted, often contradictory portraits of Anna through the various personae she creates, the dispersive narrative structure reflects a modernist sense of the relativity of perception. Like a palimpsest, each narrative layer reveals a dimension of experience or fantasy obscured, omitted, repressed, in the other narratives. The intended effect is to destabilize the hierarchy maintaining truth's superiority to fiction, and, indeed, at times certain "facts" of Anna's life are more accurately conveyed in her fiction than in the supposedly more objective narrative passages. Reading the summary of the novel *Frontiers of War* against Anna's recollections of Rhodesia in the Black notebook, or the incomplete novel *The Shadow of the Third* in the Yellow notebook against

Anna's largely unrecorded relationship with a past lover named Michael, or "Free Women" against the entries in the Blue and Golden notebooks documenting Anna's descent into madness with "Saul," who may or may not be an actual person, sets into play a series of mirroring refractions that refuse a single truth and create a quintessentially self-conscious novel that is as much about the process—or (im)possibility—of writing modern fiction as it is about the events it "represents."[59] Only through the paratactic juxtaposition of all these multiple pieces within the covers of one book does the text arrive at a provisional wholeness, one whose imaginative order exists, like the fragments that Eliot's Fisher King has "shor'd against my ruin," in the unresolvable play of its many parts.

This destabilization of narrative truth carries over into Lessing's representations of the psychological divisions that exist within consciousness as well as in the contemporary political world.[60] Increasingly propelled by recent events to the edge of a breakdown, Anna finds herself wondering, "What then am I, Anna. . . . So try again: Who am I, Anna?" (389), and she enters a state of self-division that she begins to realize *is* her "identity": "What is happening is a breakdown of me, Anna" (476). The depiction of Anna's descent into madness and schizophrenic dissociation—occupying much of the "Free Women" text and the Blue and Golden notebooks—becomes Lessing's vehicle for exploring those subliminal psychological states whose depiction, as we have seen, has inspired many of the experimental narratives associated with modernist fiction. Importantly, however, Lessing not only associates the loss of the boundaries imposed by the ego—"the breakdown of me, Anna"—with self-destructive impulses but also sees such breakdowns of the ego as a means of access to levels of psychic reality denied by the normative world. In a book on Lessing appropriately subtitled *Breaking the Forms of Consciousness,* Roberta Rubenstein observes that the experience of madness and psychic disintegration propels Anna into a necessary encounter with and recognition of the "underside of her own personality."[61] This "underside" parallels the realm of anarchic impulse that Barnes explores in *Nightwood* and that Leopold Bloom enters in Nighttown—as Claire Sprague notes, "in [Anna's] long night of the soul, *The Golden Notebook* [becomes the] equivalent of the Circe episode in *Ulysses.*"[62] While such descriptions are suggestive of a Jungian night journey into the dark or denied side of the personality, this "underworld" also evokes Freud's description of the realm of the libido, whose dispersive, nonunitary component parts, flowing without check or boundaries, find an analogue in the dispersive, nonunitary narrative structure that Lessing uses to reveal "the rifts and splits that permeate Anna's psychic reality."[63]

The theme of "crack-up" announced on the first page of the novel, then, reverberates on social, formal, and psychological levels, and all of these attest to the modernist legacy of Lessing's enterprise. Lessing's privileging of states of interiority that exceed conscious ones, moreover, raises the question of the repressions that underlie the artistic and emotional paralysis that drives Anna into psychoanalysis. On the one hand, she asserts to her Jungian therapist, Mrs. Marks, that she is "not here become I'm suffering from a writer's block" (232); rather, she makes the case that "because the world is so chaotic art [has become] irrelevant" (42), thus voicing an even more extreme version of the anxiety of authority confronting her modernist predecessors. On the other hand, because she actually never stops writing (as the notebooks attest), she also admits that "my changing everything into fiction is simply a means of *concealing something from myself*" (229; emphasis added).

I have already indicated that one return of the repressed confronting Anna in the present time of the novel takes the form of her disdainful attitude toward male homosexuality. But the text's most overt example of narrative repression and return occurs in the initial entry in Anna's Black notebook. Under a column headed by the word "Source," Anna unearths her wartime memories of Southern Rhodesia, especially the weekends she spent in the country with her leftist friends at the Mashopi hotel—gatherings that inspired her best-selling novel, *Frontiers of War*. But the actual events that Anna now remembers and records in the Black notebook reveal the degree to which her novel has covered over and romanticized its "Source" material. Just as this notebook's account becomes a conscious revision of the repressed aspects of this past—a past which forms the silent backdrop against which Anna's current emotional and writerly impasse occurs—I want to suggest that her African experience also functions as the "Source" underlying the textual repressions upon which the entire novel rests. That is, the entire text of *The Golden Notebook* may form a reworking and displacement of the catastrophic events—in which race and homophobia collide—revealed in this chronologically displaced narration of Anna's sojourn in Africa during World War II.

Practices of Apartheid, at Home and Abroad

The colonial experience of racial division that shadows Anna's past sets the terms for the uneasy relation of the personal and the political that stymies her subsequent efforts as a writer and whole human being. Gradually settled by British entrepreneurs in the late 1880s, Southern Rhodesia—referred to as "the Colony" in *The Golden Notebook*—was formally annexed by Britain in 1923 and granted the status of a British Crown Colony with the right to self-governance. Only as the grip of the British empire began to wane in the aftermath of World War II—paralleling the case of Egypt—did the country gradually move toward a very fragile independence in the 1950s and 1960s.[64] In the novel, as in Lessing's personal experience, the war introduced into the racially divided colony a number of "alien influences," including not only restless, independent women like Anna (arriving in the country on the eve of the war in 1939), but Cambridge-educated young RAF men filled, as Michael Thorpe puts it, with "the fresh Marxist idealism of the 'thirties,"[65] and various political and intellectual refugees from Hitler's Europe. To the novel's exiles, the color bar in colonial Rhodesia forms an obvious political cause, and it galvanizes their formation of the Communist discussion group so pivotal to Anna's developing political consciousness. I will show, shortly, how Anna's fictionalization in *Frontiers of War* of her past experience of apartheid significantly alters these facts, as the Black notebook makes clear. What I want to emphasize at the moment is the way in which Anna "imports" this knowledge of minority discrimination "home" to England, to which she returns at the end of the war, in the displaced form of *sexual* apartheid, the systematic oppression of women that depends on the division between and opposition of the sexes. That is, Anna's awakening to her second-class status as a woman is profoundly if largely subconsciously shaped by her prior experience of racial discrimination and oppression in Africa.

The substitutive logic that underlies this slippage from racial to sexual discrimination can be glimpsed in Lessing's offhanded comment, in a 1966 interview with Florence Howe, that "the relationship between the sexes everywhere, not just in Western society, is so much a melting pot, that *it's like the color bar,* all kinds of emotions that don't belong get sucked in."[66] Even more to the point, we can see this and other related displacements at work in Anna's subconscious when, at the height of the "sex war" that precipitates her and Saul's ultimate descent into madness, she dreams of being at the Mashopi hotel, where she must fight to "re-enter" and reclaim her body from colonization by others. In the immediately following dream sequence, she envisions herself inhabiting "dark" skin and her "pen" transformed into a "gun" as she confronts an unknown "enemy" on a distant battlefield. At this point she realizes that she is an Algerian rebel fighting for independence against the French colonizers (600). The axis of colonized/colonizer that makes possible the substitution at the end of this dream of Algeria/France for Rhodesia/Britain prefigures, as well, the conflict of man (colonizer) against woman (colonized)—and, more specifically, Saul against Anna—that frames the entire dream sequence. Anna has gone to sleep with the sex war being waged between her and Saul on her mind, and she awakens as Saul returns to her bed fresh from the arms of another woman, "smiling, a man conscious of his power with women." His challenge to Anna, "Why don't you fight me? Why don't you fight?" thus recapitulates the content of her dream on a sexual rather than racial level (603).

Another example of the psychic process whereby Anna's subconscious uses race to signify sexual conflict occurs a few pages earlier, as Anna, lying in bed with Saul, hallucinates that she has become the mad Charlie Themba, a black nationalist leader "hated by the white men and disowned by his comrades" (593). Shortly afterwards, she feels herself metamorphosing into Charlie's antithesis, the noble South African populist Tom Mathlong: "I tried to imagine myself, a black man in white-occupied territory, humiliated in his human dignity" (597). In both cases, the stated terms of racial difference could as easily gloss Anna's perception of her minority status as a woman; for in her experience, her sex too is "hated by white men," and she too feels herself an interloper in "white, male-occupied territory." Such metaphors, in turn, make explicit the connection between Anna's experience in Rhodesia and the sex wars that she experiences back "home" in England, experiences that transform her "native" land into a menacing frontier, a constant battleground, and the ever-present site of her own colonization.

And what of these sex wars themselves? Fascinatingly, Lessing's most trenchant commentary on Anna's insights into the deeply destructive antagonism of men and women is conveyed not in Anna's own voice but in the displaced form of the new novel, *The Shadow of the Third,* that Anna is secretly writing in the Yellow notebook. The depiction of the dance of attraction and repulsion binding the characters Ella and Paul (thinly veiled portraits of Anna and her ex-lover Michael[67]) in an unceasingly antagonistic relationship becomes a trenchant critique of the operations of power and gender hierarchy that render the cliché equating "sex" with "war" all too descriptive of the present state of male-female relationships. "Men. The enemy. They" (452), the character Ella in Anna's novel uncompromisingly declares. This language anticipates the imagery of war and revolution in the dream, mentioned above, in which Anna imagines herself as the dark-skinned North African soldier fighting colonial oppression by firing at an "enemy" implicitly identified with Saul. And as Ella's lover Paul says with defensive sarcasm, "My dear Ella, don't you know what the great revolution of our time is? The Russian revolution, the Chinese revolution—they're nothing at all. The real revolution is, women against men." The occasion for this diatribe, significantly, is the acceptance of Ella's first novel for publication. "Well, we men might just as well resign from life," Paul comments upon reading it, his sense of male authority challenged by this sign of his mistress's textual authority (213). The transformation of the sexual stakes of this war into textual ones is driven home in Anna's love affair with the out-of-work Hollywood writer Saul Green, whose aggressively self-defensive words strike Anna like bullets: "I, I, I, I—I began to feel as if the word I was being shot at me like bullets from a machine gun. For a moment I fancied that his mouth . . . was a gun of some kind" (556). As the metaphor of deadly combat indicates, this so-called war of the sexes is not an isolated problem but intrinsic to the larger schisms and hatreds hastening the disintegration and fragmentation of modern life. "And I knew that the cruelty and the spite and the I, I, I, I of Saul and of Anna were part of the logic of war," Anna realizes near the end of the novel; "and

I knew how strong these emotions were, in a way that would never leave me, would become part of how I saw the world" (589). The enemy is not only "out there," on a distant battlefield or the invisible "front" of some "cold" war, but also here, at home, in the most personal of human interactions.

The responsibility for this deeply ingrained antagonism, Lessing takes pains to illustrate, lies in the attitude and behavior of men who take the entitlements of masculinity for granted. For the 1950s London that Anna inhabits is a world in which male chauvinism has been honed into a fine art, enacted and displayed with the ease of class privilege. All the men in the novel operate according to a socially sanctioned sexual double standard that works to confirm their sense of power over women by allowing them to cheat on their wives or lovers as often as possible, all the while condemning those women who attempt to exercise a similar freedom. The chauvinism of Anna's father, who defends his adultery with the comment, "What did you expect?" (462), serves as a template for virtually every man with whom Anna has a sexual relationship. Either they are married, relegating her to the position of the "third" (hence the title of the unfinished novel, *The Shadow of the Third*), or they flaunt their sexual conquest with other women in front of Anna to let her know that she cannot expect an exclusive relationship or commitment from them. This ethic of sexual promiscuity, of course, is not extended to Anna: her lovers Michael and Saul are consumed with jealousy at the thought of her sleeping with other men. Closely related to this proprietary sense of exclusive ownership of "one's woman" is the degree of sadism that underlies nearly every heterosexual relationship in the novel. Typical is the extreme "hostility and aggression" with which a casual lover, De Silva, forces Anna to listen to his accounts of abusing other women. Even though Anna realizes he embodies her archetypal dream of the incarnate "principle of joy-in-giving-pain," she nonetheless passively accedes to his verbal humiliation with a deadened passivity and "listless terror" that frightens her (503, 501).

De Silva's behavior, as well as the helpless response it calls forth in Anna, anticipates the harrowing depths of the sadomasochistic relationship into which Anna and Saul ultimately plunge. For Saul's "totally self-pitying, cold, calculating, emotionless" behavior (571) is simply an extreme version of the masculine front displayed by all the male lovers Anna has known. Likewise, his split personality, which alternates between abstract empathy with the position of women in the modern world and frighteningly abusive sadism, writes large the inner division between reason and emotion that characterizes every man in the novel, each of whom is psychologically sundered by the demands of the masculine role he has internalized. What men's sadistic behavior toward women simultaneously reveals and attempts to hide, Lessing dramatizes, is a desperate desire for mastery that coexists with the fear that any show of emotion will betray the fictitiousness of their power. The talismanic sign of this always-suspect male authority, of which these men are all too aware, is the constant threat of being exposed as sexually incompetent, or worse, impotent. Molly's gleefully roguish ex-husband Richard—one of the Captains of English industry—reveals he cannot get it up with his wife Marion; Anna and her Rhodesian lover, the German exile Willi, have a sexless relationship; Comrade Nelson, whom Anna knows from her Party connections, is a "sexual cripple" who hysterically browbeats himself for evincing "a mortal terror of sex" (484); Milt (who appears in the final interlude of the "Free Woman" novella as a more benign double of the notebooks' Saul) confesses he cannot sleep with women he *likes*. In turn, this sexual incompetence is almost inevitably projected by the men back onto the women, either for being sexually unresponsive or for being "castrating" bitches (451), that is, sexually active agents whose independence challenges men on their own turf.

Understandably, such attitudes affect the self-conceptions that women such as Anna and Molly carry with them. As Anna laconically notes, being a "free" woman in this society ironically doesn't mean being an autonomous self, but rather being viewed as "free" sexual goods that any man thinks he has a right to fuck. This situation creates a contradictory psychological bind for women like Anna: on the one hand, it increases her hatred of the male sex as an utterly alien species, while on the other it creates the crisis of hyperfemininity typical of the 1950s—the desire to be perceived by men as a "real woman" rather than a castrator, a woman whose soft femininity will one day attract a "real man" rather than an abusive or infantile lover. The burden created by this psychosexual impasse, Lessing shows, is a sense of emotional numbness that enforces a posture of terrorized passivity before, and masochistic submission to, these unrelenting male assaults: this is truly the "cold war" brought home to the heterosexual bedroom of the 1950s with a vengeance. "The sex was cold, an act of hatred, hateful," Anna says of an encounter in which Saul virtually rapes her, turned on by her "No," even as she finds herself "obediently" bowing to this violation: "I could not have refused" (585).

Perhaps the most damning commentary the text offers of the psychological consequences of this enmity on the thinking modern woman is the image Anna creates of her fictional double, Ella, masturbating to the "accompaniment of fantasies of hatred about men," feeling absolutely "humiliated" by her sexual dependence on men "for 'being satisfied,'" even as she "uses this kind of savage phrase to humiliate herself" as she reaches orgasm alone, fantasizing her hatred of the very men she thinks she needs (455). Such an image provides a chilling culmination to the scenarios or images of female orgasmic pleasure that have been noted throughout this study— Edna's response to Mlle. Reisz's piano-playing, the ecstasy that the memory of Sally's kiss brings Clarissa Dalloway, even Molly's series of orgasmic yeses (indeed Ella's masturbatory fantasy as she falls asleep rewrites with bitter realism the affirmative lyricism with which Joyce sends Molly to sleep, alone but not alone, at the end of *Ulysses*). Given Anna's similar experience of solitude in sex, the degree of internalized rage she feels—free but not free, having affairs but unfulfilled—is inevitable. "Sleeping with the enemy," Lessing makes clear, is an age-old female dilemma that in this supposedly more enlightened sexual era also proves neither the path to individual peace of mind nor one to a vision of social harmony.

Colonial Lessons in Homophobia

What happens to this rage, however, is curious. Unable, or unwilling, to admit the utter insufficiency of heterosexual men to fulfill a modern woman's needs, Anna projects her rage onto another "species" of men, namely those nonheterosexual men who become scapegoats for what remains unspeakable about their straight counterparts. This is an effect not only of Anna's subconscious displacements but of Lessing's own blindspots in the sex wars she otherwise so incisively lays bare. A key to understanding the complicated dynamics at work in this process of projection and displacement lies in the Black notebook's record of the events that occur at the Mashopi hotel during the war. For Anna's attempt in this notebook to recover the significance of her African past without the blinders of nostalgia opens the door through which the previously repressed subject of homosexuality dramatically enters both her consciousness and the text.

Crucial to this past is the group of unlikely friends—including Anna, her lover Willi, the three Oxford-educated RAF pilots, and Maryrose, a colonialist born and raised in Rhodesia—who have bonded over their shared leftist political ideals. When they discover the Mashopi Hotel, an unbelievably "British" establishment "in the middle of the bush, all surrounded by kopjes and savages and general exotica" (84), they take to patronizing it in a spirit of camp colonial parody, filling their weekend holidays there with drink and political discussion. Beginning her recollections by describing the pilots, Anna mentions, as if passing, the fact that "at Oxford these three had been homosexuals." She then confesses, "When I write the word down and look at it, I realise its power to disturb . . . the word *homosexual,* written—well, I have to combat dislike and disquiet" (74). While Anna on one level seems aware of her homophobia, noting the way she has immediately qualified the term by adding that eighteen months later the men are joking about "'our homosexual phase'" (75), she nonetheless collaborates in the men's rhetoric of deniability (homosexuality as only a passing phase) in her selective descriptions of their sexualities. For instance, when Paul, the charismatic object of everyone's desires (and the model for the dashing hero of Anna's best-selling *Frontiers*), writes off his sexual past with a quip—"I'm reluctantly coming to the conclusion that not only I am not a homosexual, but that I never was" (123)—Anna conveys his verdict as truth, despite the fact, as she well knows, that he has at this point never put his putative heterosexuality to the test. Only when he loses his (heterosexual) virginity do we learn that this has been a "first"; and, not coincidentally, his partner in this encounter is none other than Anna, who has always been infatuated with Paul and who thus has her own reasons for upholding his "real" heterosexuality.[68] Of the pilot Jimmy, who is hopelessly in love with Paul, Anna claims that he, "unlike the others," is "truly homosexual, though he wished he wasn't," and paints a pathetic picture of his groveling abjection before Paul and the later closeted life he leads (79). And Anna transforms the third pilot Ted's statement that he "sometimes said he preferred being homosexual" into a meaning that is more convenient to her narrative: "This meant he had a string of protégés" (80), young working-class men for whom he serves as mentor. Likewise, Anna rather strenuously avoids reading anything unusual into her lover Willi's total lack of interest in having sex with her, though she does mention the fact that he experienced "a little conventional homosexuality at the age of thirteen" in the "decadent" (73) atmosphere of 1930s Berlin where he grew up. All Anna's closest male companions in the Colony appear to have had sex with other men, yet only one is a bona fide "homosexual," that word which gives rise in Anna to those feelings of distaste and discomfort that even in the narrative present she must force herself to "combat" (a telling word choice, since it usually appears in the context of heterosexual and racial conflict).

Seen in one light, Anna's reluctance to label her friends' sexual preferences bespeaks a sexual fluidity that, as in the *Alexandria Quartet,* is heightened by the group's sojourn in an exotically foreign Third World locale. Even though the African setting itself doesn't present, as in Durrell's novel, a smorgasbord of "perverse" sexual activity, Lessing's Colony does provide a liminal space, a hiatus from the "real" world where freedom from old forms and customs, coupled with a devil-may-care pursuit of immediate pleasure fostered by the imminence of posting to battle for the RAF pilots, fosters an atypical lack of restraint and expression of nonconventional sexual behaviors. Africa thus provides an extension of the "time-out" from responsibility that university life previously offered the Englishmen, where they partook of a "loose group of about twenty, all vaguely left-wing, vaguely literary, all having affairs with each other in every kind of sexual combination" (75). Even if the men, other than Jimmy, now joke about their collegiate flirtations with homosexuality, they are freed to laugh about their experiences without fear of judgment and indeed with a sense of gaining stature for having dabbled, Bloomsbury-style, in "every kind of sexual combination." As with sex, so too with politics: Africa provides a safe space to experiment with radical ideas, as illustrated by the Communist reading group to which they belong. What Anna says of the young men at Oxford—"it was clear in retrospect that they were deliberately creating a mood of irresponsibility as a sort of social protest and sex was part of it" (75)—applies equally to the political and sexual community they form in exile in Rhodesia, a community whose boundaries remain fluid and open to a variety of otherwise marginalized experiences: "We were all, at various times, in love with each other" (77).

The crisis that brings the idyllic weekends spent at the Mashopi Hotel to an end overtly occurs over the issue of the color bar, when the hotel's proprietor, Mrs. Boothby, fires Jackson, her black cook of fifteen years, whom she accuses of not keeping in his place when Anna's comrades attempt to befriend him. Evicted from the hotel's premises, Jackson's family wanders off on foot to one of the black townships, doomed to an uncertain future and virtual separation. But the trigger that allows Mrs. Boothby's racism to find permissible expression and precludes criticism of her actions, tellingly, is homophobia. Even more interesting, this homophobia serves as the linchpin in the sequence of events that break up the Mashopi group of friends. Not only has its occurrence been omitted from the sanitized fictional account of these events in *Frontiers of War*, but Anna herself has completely repressed the event from her memory until the associative process of writing the Black notebook forces it into consciousness. "*It seems I've forgotten the most important thing of all*—Jimmy's having upset Mrs. Boothby," Anna writes, then proceeds to explain that the weekend *before* Jackson's firing, Jimmy has drunkenly put his arms around Paul and kissed him in the presence of Mrs. Boothby. As Anna explains, Mrs. Boothby's sudden realization that Jimmy's unmanly behavior has a name incites her shock and disgust: "But the word 'homosexual' put him outside her pale. 'I suppose he's what they call a homosexual,'" she says, "using the word as if it, too, were poisoned" (145; emphasis added).

The events of the following weekend make clear the degree to which the racial contradictions of colonial power are played out through the agency of such homophobia. Anna and her friends, who have been drinking and dancing all night, realize that Jimmy has disappeared and begin searching the hotel for him, at which point Jackson, the cook, finds the youth curled up in drunken sleep in the hotel kitchen. As Jackson, trying to be helpful, stoops to raise him to his feet, Jimmy wakes and puts his arms around Jackson's neck, murmuring in a haze, "You love me Jackson, don't you . . . none of the others love me" (147). Black and white men in a misinterpreted, taboo embrace—the moment eerily recalls the "primal scene" witnessed by the Sutpen children in *Absalom, Absalom!* It is at this unfortunate moment that Mrs. Boothby, already upset by the liberal behavior of her guests and frustrated by her own unacknowledged infatuation with Paul, chooses to walk into the kitchen and, in a blaze of righteous glory at this spectacle of disgust, orders Jackson's immediate departure. The next day she apologizes to Jimmy—after all he is a paying customer—but of Jackson and his family she can only say "Gone and good riddance" (152).

This sequence of events, moreover, is followed by another "climax" that helps to explain the mechanisms of repression that have contributed to Anna's "forgetting" of the homophobic virulence of Mrs. Boothby's outburst. For it turns out that the one fortuitous consequence of the evening's harrowing events is that Anna has a fight with Willi (whose strict Marxist ideology prohibits him from feeling sympathy for Jackson's plight—it is the black masses, not the victimized individual, who matter), and then runs off into the veld with Paul, which leads to the sexual encounter that proves to be Paul's first (and only, seeing that he dies a few days later) intercourse with a woman. The emotions Anna remembers are tantamount to Clarissa Dalloway's recollection of Sally Seton's kiss as the most exquisite moment of her entire life: "I have never, in all my life, been as desperately and wildly and painfully happy as I was then. . . . I remember saying to myself, This is it, this is being happy" (150). Just how these multiple events are transformed into the seemingly anomalous *interracial* love story of *Frontiers of War* hinges on an ingenious series of displacements indicative of the repressive forces at work in Anna's unconscious. For another Marxist comrade who joins the visitors at the Mashopi hotel, George Hounslow, is having an affair with the cook's wife, by whom he has fathered a half-caste son whom the guilt-ridden George fantasizes (like Sutpen in *Absalom, Absalom!*) will one day show up at his father's door to claim his denied patrimony. In Anna's novel, however, the miscegenation is much more romanticized, occurring between Paul's fictional prototype and the young, beautiful, neglected wife of the hotel's cook, one of the local African agitators (neither is Jackson an agitator nor his wife neglected), ending in tragedy when the hotel's "Mistress Boothby" surprises them in a romantic rendezvous. Instead of the illicit embrace of black man and white man that unlocks the real Mrs. Boothby's race-hatred, then, the novel substitutes the more acceptably erotic interracial embrace of black woman and white man. But even this pairing, signifying the romance that should have been but that tragically is nipped in the bud, is *also* a displacement, for it rewrites into a full-blown love affair the *single* evening of passion between Paul and Anna, who, like Mrs. Boothby, has always been attracted to Paul and hence never convinced of his bisexuality, despite evidence to the contrary.[69]

This doubling of Anna and Mrs. Boothby raises the disturbing but nonetheless pertinent question of whether the Anna who returns to England has subconsciously imbibed from Mrs. Boothby a lesson in how to displace the rage she feels at others onto homosexuality: for if the latter bigoted woman uses the "false" issue of same-sex desire to give voice to her racial prejudices in the firing of Jackson, so too, as we will now see, does Anna latch onto the figure of the male homosexual, in the narrative present of "Free Women," as a convenient scapegoat for the ill feelings that she bears the bigoted heterosexual men who repeatedly have disappointed her. And, again, eviction from the premises—Mrs. Boothby's solution—becomes Anna's only recourse against what she sees as a threat to her "home" (again, paralleling Mrs. Boothby's defense of the honor of her hotel), to her femininity, and, ultimately, to her sanity.

Getting Rid of Ronnie; or, Homosexual Housecleaning

The event to which I am referring—Anna's working up the courage to evict from her flat two gay boarders—occupies an inordinate amount of the dramatic action of the third and fourth sections of "Free Women" (thus falling right in the center of *The Golden Notebook*). Not coincidentally, it occurs in tandem with an acceleration in Anna's fear that she is "cracking up" (389). Although Ivor has been living in the extra bedroom in Anna's flat for some time without having warranted more than passing mention in the narrative, it is only in the third segment of "Free Women," as Anna's hysteria grows, that he suddenly commands a degree of attention disproportionate to the issues that have occupied the first two chapters of "Free Women." "Ivor had moved *into their lives*" (391; emphasis added), the text announces midway into the third installment of "Free Women" ("their" refers to Anna and her young daughter, Janet). Not just into "their home," but into "their lives": the phrasing signals the psychodramatic intensity of the coming conflict, first as Ivor befriends and increasingly caretakes Janet, who adores him (exacerbating Anna's uneasy sense of having been displaced in her maternal function), then as Ivor's boyfriend Ronnie also moves in, which Anna considers the price she is expected to pay for Ivor's caretaking of Janet. At this point Anna begins to suffer the increasingly paranoid sensation of being trapped in her own home, unable to "move freely because of those two." This causes her initial "dislike" of Ronnie to blossom in the space of a page to outright "contempt" for *both* boarders because they are not "real men" (391–92). As Anna's anxieties increase, warping her sense of reality, she admits to feeling "off balance" in the same breath that she attributes her mental instability to the men's presence in the flat: "I feel as if the spirit of this flat were being poisoned, as if a spirit of perverse and ugly spite were everywhere" (394). This reaction echoes, eerily, Mrs. Boothby's reaction when she is forced to use the word *homosexual* to categorize Jimmy's proclivities, "using the word as if it, too, were poisoned" (145). Anna freely admits her reaction is irrational, but irrationality is precisely the name of the game, now, and Anna's uncontrollable disgust and almost obsessive desire to evict the two men leads to the climax of this section of "Free Women," as she orders Ronnie out of the flat.

When the fourth section picks up after a break of one hundred pages, however, this homosexual subplot is immediately resumed; for it appears that Ronnie has moved back into Ivor's room, at which point Anna decides "she was very likely mad" (507). In the psychodrama that is now clearly being depicted, the incident signals another return of the sexually and textually repressed: neither Anna nor the text can so easily shake off the demon that Ronnie and Ivor have come to represent. The section ends with a second scene of expulsion, as Ronnie again leaves and Ivor attempts to conciliate Anna with a bunch of flowers. Anna's reaction quite chillingly brackets the psychological intensities set into motion by this inserted sub-plot: "trembling with anger," she viciously strikes Ivor (who unlike Ronnie is a well-meaning character) across the face with the flowers and repeats the words of Mrs. Boothby to that British matron's despised other, Jackson: "'Get out,' said Anna. *She had never in her life been angry like this*" (523; emphasis added). In this uncanny conjunction between disparate narrative moments, the intensity of the rage that fuels the expulsion of two different minorities takes on exactly the same emotional valence, raising the question of just what scapegoating is being effected in the name of cleaning the house of these "poisonous" and "perverse" influences.

In Anna's case, at least, the source of her displaced rage is not hard to pinpoint, once the Ivor-Ronnie incident is located within the larger narra-tive structure. The psychological displacements enacted in Anna's homo-phobia, in fact, follow closely upon a series of actual displacements that have recently occurred in the flat. Only when Anna's lover Michael leaves her (to work in Africa, no less) does she decide to rent out her vacant room to fill the psychological and physical void left by his absence. In contrast, the leavetaking of Ronnie and Ivor makes way for the arrival of a new tenant, Saul Green, who becomes Anna's new lover. Within this larger schema, then, the gay Ronnie and Ivor are not only insufficient replace-ments for straight Michael, but are destined to be replaced themselves be-cause they are not, in Anna's lexicon, "real men." This context suggests that Anna's anger toward Ronnie and Ivor is not only homophobic disgust but also an expression of the anger she feels toward the absent heterosexual lover(s) for whom Ivor and Ronnie can only be inadequate stand-ins (even as their own coupledom serves as a bitter reminder to Anna of what is missing in her own life).

The fact that these two gay men have become scapegoats for the multi-tude of heterosexual men who have abused Anna over the years is also confirmed by the narrative sequencing of the specific day on which Anna's "contempt" for her gay boarders erupts. For, ironically, this strong emotion is the culmination of a series of incidents of male aggression that have plagued Anna since the morning. This sequence begins with Richard's summons of Anna to his office, where he verbally assaults her and implic-itly comes on to her, and it culminates with the lewd man on the train who attempts to rub up against her, then follows her off the tube, "grinning in triumph" at having "humiliated [her] and triumphed" over her (390). Filled with a sense of panic that feeds the mounting hysteria and sense of "crack-up" that she is already experiencing, Anna leaves this psychopath on the sidewalk outside her door, only to enter the apartment and project all her contempt for such menacing men on her homosexual boarders.

What makes these gay men so apt a vehicle for Anna's rage, however, is not simply the fact of their being, so to speak, in the wrong place (Anna's flat) at the wrong time (just after she's been harassed). It has more to do with her own conflicted feelings about gender—or, more specifically, how her assumptions about what constitutes a real man ultimately affect her understanding of her own femaleness. The first complaint Anna articulates against the gay men, for instance, betrays her internalization of Freudian norms of female development. For the primary concern that Anna consciously articulates about Ivor is that her fatherless daughter Janet is growing too close to the young man and that Ivor's gayness therefore constitutes a deprivation in Janet's oedipal development: "Janet needs a man in her life, she misses a father. Ivor is very kind to her. And yet because he's not a man . . . with a 'real man' there would be a whole area of tension, of wry understanding that there can't be with Ivor" (391). As insensitive to children as Michael was, as much a misogynist as Richard is, Anna asserts that "there is no doubt I feel that their quality, their liking women rather than men, would be better for Janet than what Ivor has" (392). And when Anna decides to evict, first of all, Ivor's lover Ronnie, she justifies it, ironically, in the name of Janet's future (hetero)sexual development: "By God . . . I'm going to see she grows up to recognise a real man when she meets one. Ronnie's going to have to leave" (404). Although Lessing has Anna self-reflexively ponder her distinction of heterosexual males as "real men" by initially putting the phrase in quotation marks, by the latter passage the quotes have been dropped, in part, I submit, because Anna's views on this issue are very close to Lessing's own. For whereas Lessing is remarkably, and often brilliantly, sensitive to the oppressed status of women in modern patriarchal society—as her early feminist following indicated—her views of femaleness become conflicted precisely when she accepts as a given the heterosexual *dependence* of women's eroticism on male agency. As Mark Spilka intelligently argues, it is Anna's "asserted heterosexuality" in her relationships that brings out the more conservative, indeed in many ways Laurentian, side of an author whose sexual politics are otherwise diametrically opposed to those of the Lawrence we surveyed in chapter 2.[70] This confusion is ironically apparent in Anna's wry acknowledgment that only "so long as she [is] loved by a man" is she "immune to the ugliness of perverse sex, violent sex" (407)—a circumlocution that conflates Ivor and Ronnie's "perverse" sexuality and the "violent" sexuality of the man on the subway who has just assaulted her. She is thinking specifically of the "new, frightened, vulnerable" Anna that has emerged when Michael abandoned her. But in fact the security that she fantasized with Michael was nonexistent—so the sadism of Michael's hot-cold reactions to Anna's love, always coming and leaving, has amply demonstrated. The "immunity" that Anna fantasizes, rather, is the desire to *pass as normal,* to be validated as a woman who *can* be loved by a man: indeed, the only "proof" of being a "woman" at all, in the Freudian framework that Anna and many women of her generation have inherited, is to be made one by the right man—or, in Anna's terms, a "real" man. This is, as we have seen, the lesson Durrell also drives home in the *Clea* volume of the *Alexandria Quartet,* only from the male perspective: for Darley to become a "real" man, he must first mold Clea into the feminine (castrated) woman who then complements his own masculinity.

Anna's dependence on men for self-validation—even when she, like the reader, suspects that these very men are unworthy of the task—carries over into one of the text's more controversial assertions: its extended commentary on the superiority of vaginal over clitoral orgasm. The mere fact that such a discussion occurs in the novel is an indirect testament to the sexual frankness and self-questioning, despite the overwhelming conservative political climate of the 1950s and 1960s, ushered into being by "respectable" sexual investigators like Kinsey and Masters and Johnson. At issue in the debate over the "site" of women's orgasm, as Freud's assertions in the "Femininity" essay confirm, is an ideological contestation between female erotic self-sufficiency (symbolically associated with clitoral stimulation) and the heterosexual imperative (symbolically associated with vaginal penetration), and these same associations, however fictitious, also color Lessing's commentary.[71] A clitoral orgasm may offer a "thousand [more] thrills, sensations, etc.," Anna writes in the voice of her fictional double, Ella, and a so-called vaginal orgasm may only be "emotion and nothing else," but *nonetheless* Anna categorically upholds the superiority of the latter as the "one real female orgasm," namely because "[it] is created by a man's need for a woman. . . . Everything else is a substitute and a fake, and the most inexperienced woman feels this instinctively" (215–16). The use of the adjective "real" to distinguish among "types" of orgasms echoes Anna's use of the same word to distinguish among types of men. "A woman's sexuality is, so to speak, contained by a man, if he is a real man" (455), Ella muses, and Anna comments after her first sexual encounter with Saul Green, "I'd forgotten what making love to a real man is like" (561).

The flaw in such logic that Anna overlooks, however, is that it measures a man's realness solely in terms of his sexual capacity, ignoring the fact that in her experience "real men" almost inevitably turn out to be both sexist and misogynistic. If such *real* men are seen as the sole source of women's *real* orgasms—especially if a clitoral orgasm is admittedly more powerful—then it becomes clear that Anna's defense of the vaginal orgasm hinges on her desperate desire to be viewed, in the only terms society has provided her, as a "real woman." And, as a self-declared free woman, single mother, and professional writer of some renown, Anna subconsciously fears that she may have already passed beyond the pale, into the ranks of the "unfeminine" and hence the undesirable, in most men's eyes. The fear of non-normativity, when it comes to her own gender status, infiltrates and subconsciously molds Anna's very definition of erotic pleasure.

In turn, the desire to remain womanly-desirable—that is, in culture's terms, "feminine"—in order to attract the elusive real man helps to explain the particularly strong antipathy Anna expresses toward effeminately acting gay men. And this quality Ronnie, Ivor's boyfriend, represents with a vengeance. The first thought Anna expresses about Ronnie is that she "dislikes" him, but she attempts to keep her dislike in check since she realizes that her dislike is directed toward "the type rather than the person" (391). The "type" Anna has in mind is that of the limp-wristed, narcissistically self-involved, effeminate homosexual, which the text's hyperbolic descriptions of Ronnie take pains to emphasize: his "charming coiffured head" is likened to that of "a boyish young girl" (393); he speaks with "winning charm" that reminds Anna of "a well brought up young girl, almost lispingly correct" (394); he gestures "with a little writhing movement of the hips that was quite unconscious" (405); he "trip[s]" rather than walks up the stairs (406); and, foremost, Anna senses he is filled with jealousy and malice toward women, his "competitors" in the sexual market. Such a representation, in a text published in 1962, inevitably tilts the reader's sympathies against Ronnie, thereby paving the way for Anna's confession that she doesn't merely "dislike" Ronnie, but rather that she is shamefully "disgusted" by him. This expression of what amounts to *physical revulsion* surfaces when Anna comes upon Ronnie toying with her cosmetics in the bathroom, in a feeble effort to appeal to her as "one girl to another" (405).

This scene, it seems to me, is key to understanding the psychic origins of Anna's extreme homophobia. Not only are gay men such as Ronnie and Ivor scapegoats onto whom she can displace the rage she feels toward "real" heterosexual men; given her stereotypical equation of gay men with effeminacy, it is also quite possible that Anna is displacing onto Ronnie the anger and anxiety she feels at the image of her own enacted femininity that the effeminate gay man mirrors back to herself. For seeing Ronnie making up *his* face in *her* mirror, with *her* cosmetics, uneasily reminds Anna that her own "femininity" is not a natural birthright but a masquerade that she creates out of her desire to be desired by straight men whose "masculinity" she has accepted as the indispensable complement to her sexual satisfaction and self-esteem. If women are doomed to represent otherness in phallocentric culture, Lessing adds a twist to this formulation by figuring male homosexuality as the straight woman's other. For the feminine gay man's very imitation of female characteristics calls into question the "real" femininity that Anna needs to exude if she is to succeed in the game of heterosexual mating. Read in light of this displacement onto Ronnie of her own anxieties about "realness," the wording of Anna's climactic explosion of rage in the bathroom takes on an added resonance: "Good Lord! she thought, to be born a Ronnie! to be born like that—I complain about the difficulties of being my kind of woman, but good Lord!—I might have been born a Ronnie" (405–6). As the psychodramatic pitch of the scene reveals, the disgust that culminates in Anna's decision to evict Ronnie (and, later, even Ivor) forms an instance of the extreme heterosexist panic that is the inevitable consequence of the contradictory position Anna assumes in attempting to be "my kind of woman" in the heterosexual and misogynistic culture of 1950s England. The sex wars are indeed enough to drive one "mad."

The role that male homosexuality assumes in the London section of *The Golden Notebook* as a site of displaced anxieties about heterosexual norms of masculinity and femininity is also subtly linked to the valences that have attached, via the issue of the color line, to homosexuality in Anna's memories of Africa. First, it turns out that Ronnie and Ivor are not the only boarders that Anna, in her single state, has desired to evict from the flat because they are "disturbing her peace of mind." In fact, as Anna remembers in a brief aside, her sentiment that "Ronnie must go" is the exact feeling that she had about Jemmie, a previous student boarder from Ceylon whom she also disliked but whom she "couldn't bring herself to give . . . notice [to] because he was coloured" (404). One is reminded, uneasily, of Jackson's expulsion from the Mashopi hotel. If Anna's experience of African colonialism has given her an intuitive understanding of the analogies binding women and blacks in parallel systems of apartheid, she resists the similar (if also partial) identification that exists between herself and gay men, because acknowledging it would delve too deeply not merely into her oppressed status as a woman but into the masquerade of femininity that her identification as a heterosexual woman forces her to assume.

Second, the narrative of Anna's eviction of Ronnie is immediately juxtaposed with another return of the textually repressed: an excerpt from the Black notebook in which the subterranean network of associations linking homosexuality and the African landscape again rise to the surface of Anna's consciousness in the form of a forgotten incident. Significantly, this is the only African memory that is related out of chronological order, long after the other recollections. Anna opens this entry with the account of an accident she has witnessed on the London streets in which a man inadvertently kicks a pigeon to death, which she then proceeds to dream about. "It reminded me of something, I don't know what," Anna says about the dream, at which point she suddenly remembers the "something" she hasn't "thought of in years . . . an incident from the Mashopi Hotel week-ends" (413). This incident is a hunting trip on which Anna and her friends accompany Paul in order to shoot pigeons, so that Mrs. Boothby can cook that quintessentially British dish, a pigeon pie.[72] This invasion of the bush to satisfy colonial appetites quickly becomes an allegory of sex and death, of so-called natural fecundity and unnatural carnage, played out against the primordial African landscape. Most obviously, Lessing uses this symbolically charged tableau, as Anna sickens at the senseless killing of the pigeons, to underline the novel's critique of the British colonial presence, which has wreaked a parallel destruction on Rhodesia's indigenous populations. But, less obviously, the scene of cruelty and slaughter also provides the tableau for an underlying homosexual drama, in which Paul sadistically torments the doggedly lovelorn Jimmy by ordering him to retrieve the fallen birds, despite Jimmy's nausea, then demeans Jimmy for abjectly obeying him ("'We don't need a dog, after all,' remarked Paul" [423]. Publicly baiting Jimmy like this becomes Paul's psychic mechanism for disavowing his own homosexual inclinations—a ploy that simultaneously attests to Paul's unresolved desires by exposing his subconscious pleasure in prolonging the ritual of erotic domination that bonds the men together.

This hitherto repressed incident, in which colonial allegory and homosexual psychodrama exist side by side, occurs, moreover, against the backdrop of the African veld, which Anna represents as a fount of boundless, mindless, fecundity. On their way to the glade where the pigeons roost, the group has come across the mind-boggling sight of millions of grasshoppers copulating in the grass: "In every direction, all around us, were the insects, coupling . . . in thousands, crude green and crude red, with the black blank eyes staring—they were absurd, obscene, and above all, the very emblem of stupidity" (415). On the one hand, the narrative here momentarily falls into the orientalist stereotype equating the Third World with unthinking, untamed, "stupid" nature and procreative excess, not unlike Durrell's eroticized vision of Egypt's "infinite variety." On the other hand, this demonstration of natural fecundity turns out to be an exposé of the concept of "natural" behavior itself. First of all, Anna and her group spot among the mating insects two grotesquely mismatched pairs. In one an over-large grasshopper is being mounted by a "tiny ineffectual mate," and in the other the reverse is happening. Paul and Jimmy (themselves one such ineffectual coupling) attempt to separate the insects to create "two well-matched couples" (416–7), but the grasshoppers immediately revert to their previous alignments, rendering copulation an ever-desired, but always impossible achievement. Second, as Jimmy sardonically notes, there is nothing at all in this orgy of "what we refer to as nature" to guarantee that these couplings are formed by male mounting female, as the group has assumed: "For all we know, this is a riot of debauchery, males with males, females with females" (417). The snag in the "natural" scheme presented by the mismatched grasshoppers is next likened to the human scheme, as the beautiful Maryrose and handsome Paul stroll ahead of the rest of the group, to all appearances the "perfectly matched couple" (433)—a verbal echo deliberately linking these human players to the futilely mating grasshoppers a few pages before. Appearances to the contrary, however,

Paul and Maryrose are as likely to make a perfect, heterosexual fit as the mismatched grasshoppers—what with the solely incestuous nature of her desires (fixated on a dead brother) and his homosexual leanings.[73] As Egypt functions in Durrell's colonial narrative, so too the backdrop of the African wild in this scene facilitates a denaturalizing of "nature" that returns the very concept to its polymorphously perverse potential and that disrupts the tendency to equate nature with normativity. This critique of the cultural meanings embedded in terms like *nature, sexuality,* and *couple* helps to explain why Anna has hitherto repressed this powerfully experienced incident, which returns only through the associations set into motion by a chance sighting (the London pigeon) and an elusive dream.

The event that follows this Black notebook entry repeats these elliptical links, tying together Anna's heterosexual anxieties, the topos of (male) homosexuality, and Africa as mythic setting, for a few pages later Anna relates with glee the deception she and a writer friend have played on two male editors by writing fake literary diaries that these editors take seriously as high art. In one such attempt, they pitch a journal they claim to have been written by a "lady writer of early middle-age, who has spent some years in an African colony" and who is writing a play with a tragic, interracial love plot (white man, black woman) to illustrate "the superior spiritual status of the white man trapped by history, dragged down into the animal mud of Africa" (437, 439). This concept, which is Anna's clever parody of her best-selling *Frontiers of War,* is designed to deceive an editor named, of all stereotypical names, Rupert, who—surprise—is gay, described by Anna as "wet, limp, hysterical, homosexual, intelligent" (437). If this description betrays a note of unconcealed contempt, its vitriol is made all the more intriguing by the fact that its language of denigration turns up in a description, two hundred pages later, of Anna's self-loathing of her own female body.

The latter passage occurs in the midst of Anna's psychic disintegration as she and Saul Green descend into mutual, claustrophobic madness, reported at the beginning of the Golden notebook that Anna begins when the previous four notebooks reach dead ends. Sitting in bed and looking at her naked body, while Saul sleeps beside her, Anna comments, "I looked at my thin white legs and my thin white arms, and at my breasts. My wet sticky center seemed disgusting. . . . I was experiencing, imaginatively, for the first time, the emotions of a homosexual. For the first time the homosexual literature of disgust made sense to me" (612). What this very odd displacement of Anna's bodily self-disgust onto homosexuality manages to do is avert any self-recognition that her dislike of her sexual body, her "wet sticky center," is itself the product of heterosexual *male* ambivalence toward women (expressed as castration anxiety) that she has in turn internalized.[74] Again, the profound ambivalences emanating from the ongoing "war" between "mismatched" men and women turn out to be the trigger for the text's overt expressions of homophobia. The conclusion, for Anna, of this alienation from her body is further disintegration and descent into madness: "I knew I was moving down into a new dimension, further away from sanity than I had ever been" (613).

Anna's allusion to the "homosexual literature of disgust," moreover, begs the question of what works she might have in mind. The most prominent candidate in British fiction would be Radclyffe Hall's *The Well of Loneliness*, and, intriguingly, Anna's discomfort with her body is tied closely to her ambivalent feelings about those women, like Hall's protagonist Stephen Gordon, who unambiguously love women's bodies: lesbians. In comparison with Lessing's use of male homosexuality as theme, subplot, and index of psychological disintegration, the novel's references to lesbianism are few and far between. Nonetheless, these few allusions shed light on the normalizing pressures imposed on Anna by her culture's systematic reinforcement of compulsory heterosexuality, which causes Anna to shy away from those bonds with women that might otherwise provide a source of self-affirmation and community outside the sex wars that pit men and women against each other. The question of the relationship between "lesbianism" and "female bonding" is especially interesting in light of the frame narrative, "Free Women," which highlights Anna's close friendship with Molly Jacobs. While some critics have positively interpreted this relationship as a mirroring bond between women through which Anna finds her female identity (functioning as do Edna Pontellier's female friendships in *The Awakening*), I am struck by the growing distance, gaps in communication, and even distrust that come to characterize this relationship. In fact, one could make the case that Anna's comments on lesbianism are part of a subconscious strategy to remove any possible homosexual imputations from this friendship, deeroticizing its contours in order to render unthreatening the act with which the "Free Women" section (and *The Golden Notebook* as a whole) ends: "The two women kissed and separated" (666).[75] As the final sentence of the novel, after all, this line forms, in textual terms at least, the "goal" toward which Anna's psychological descent into and return from the Circean underworld of libidinal perversity, irrationality, and chaos has been leading all along.

The text's first allusions to lesbianism are filtered through the fictional alter-egos of Ella (Anna) and Julia (Molly) in Anna's unfinished novel in the Yellow notebook, *The Shadow of the Third*. Ella's lover jealously sees the two women's closeness as a "pact" working to exclude him, and thus he derides it by making defensive "professional jokes"—he is a psychiatrist—"about the Lesbian aspects of this friendship" (208–9). We later see Ella beginning to internalize this opinion when she decides not to continue confiding her romantic travails to Julia, because she fears that "two women, friends on the basis of criticism of men, are Lesbian psychologically if not physically" (455). Similarly, Anna writes in the Blue notebook that the problem for "women of our time" is that their self-consciousness about the failure of men will "turn them bitter, or Lesbian, or solitary" (480). In all these instances, "Lesbianism" is stereotypically defined as a reaction to a failed heterosexual ideal, rather than a desire that exists independently of men. Likewise, Anna's single recorded fantasy of making love to a woman depends solely on Saul's proximity. These thoughts occur in tandem with Anna's and Saul's descent into madness, as Anna grows obsessively jealous of the other women with whom he is sleeping. She remembers that her former psychologist, Mrs. Marks, has argued that obsessive jealousy is always partially homosexual—and now she begins to wonder whether she secretly wishes "to make love with that woman [Saul] was with now." Not because she really desires the woman, however. Rather, she has become so much a part of Saul that she wants what he wants, while, simultaneously, she desires to become Saul's object of desire by possessing that object. If this jealousy amounts to "homosexual desire," as Mrs. Mark declares, it is entirely theoretical (sex in the head, as Lawrence would say), produced and performed entirely, as Anna admits, "for Saul's sake," not out of her own inclinations (587–88).

Anna's inability to conceptualize lesbian desire outside of a heterosexual frame is not unlike the difficulty she has in thinking positively of her sexuality unless it is "contained by a man . . . a real man." "When she loved a man again," Anna attempts to assure herself, "she would *return to normal:* a woman, that is, whose sexuality would ebb and flow in response to his" (455; emphasis added). As the word "normal," in comparison to the capitalized category "Lesbian," implies, the novel's discourse on homosexuality assumes the superiority and desirability of hetero-normativity to other sexual expressions. Without a real man's love—which is to say, without the concrete evidence of being *desired by* a man—Anna feels denied her complementary "realness" as a woman. For all its feminist protest against the social and psychological oppression of women, the narrative at such moments comes dangerously close to echoing Lawrence's construction in *The Virgin and the Gipsy* of Yvette's sexuality as dependent on the natural man's superior, because phallic, knowledge.

In these regards, the psychological contradictions that underlie Anna's social position as a single woman illustrate the extreme hold that mid-twentieth-century gender ideology maintained on even its most enlightened, politically aware women: women for whom, ultimately, the act of being looked upon by men *as* women—however duplicitous or hate-filled those men—becomes the only convincing validation that they are "women" and hence worthy of feeling desire. To the degree that this acculturated understanding of sexual difference echoes Freud's scheme of female oedipal development, the analogy that Deleuze and Guattari make between Freud and colonialism becomes especially appropriate in light of Anna's conjoined experience of racial and sexual apartheid: "Oedipus is always colonization pursued by other means, it is the interior colony . . . even here at home, where we Europeans are concerned, it is our intimate colonial education."[76]

Mad Love

In these multiple allusions to same-sex desire, then, Lessing represents homosexuality in gay men as what might be called the "other face" of femininity (its negative mirror), and homosexuality in lesbians as what might be called the "defacement" of femininity (its erasure).[77] Crucially, Anna's unsettling encounters with the specter of homosexuality mark her gradual disintegration and entry into the realm of the irrational. In terms of narrative structure, as the extended middle sequence in "Free Women" illustrates, the presence of Ronnie and Ivor precipitates Anna's feeling that she is cracking up, going mad, and their eviction only clears the way for the advent of Saul Green, whose tortured relationship with Anna pushes her across the threshold of sanity into madness and self-destructive masochism. To be sure, within Lessing's cosmology, the loss of stable identity represents a necessary stage in human growth toward psychic wholeness; the descent into the darker side of the psyche is valuable because it reveals deeper truths of being and realities denied by custom, habit, and reason.[78] This affirmative view of a descent into the self echoes those Jungian archetypal patterns that posit the questing hero's journey into the underworld (mythic prototypes include Orpheus in Hades, Odysseus on Circe's island, and Persephone's abduction), where the hero undergoes an incorporation of the "dark other" within, after which he or she ascends to rejoin the daylight world of reason as a more complete person. Hence, many critics have interpreted Anna and Saul's descent into madness through the lens of Jungian archetype, positing Saul as a projection of those destructive aspects within Anna herself that she must acknowledge before she can regain the equilibrium needed to pick up the pieces of her life and begin writing again.[79]

Such a reading, it seems to me, lets Saul off the hook too easily; it is too facile to reduce Saul's sadistic aggression toward women only to self-destructive components already latent within Anna, when the text so clearly associates his actions with a larger cultural crisis in masculine authority that precipitates the sexual anxieties and feelings of inadequacy that, in fact, engender Anna's conflicted and self-destructive responses as a woman. Nor is the effort to "excuse" Saul's violence by pigeonholing him as Anna's animus, her unintegrated "masculine" component, finally commensurate with the parallels Lessing draws between the deadly sexual warfare that binds the two and the "logic of war" that is threatening to destroy the entire globe. Saul may or not be a "real" character, depending on one's interpretation of Lessing's psychodramatic narrative techniques, but the specific violence he represents is, as the text makes graphically clear, not only internal to Anna. It is part of the external reality of the male oppression that is an *active* force in the Cold War world that forms the backdrop of the novel. A climactic moment of confrontation between Anna and Saul, recorded in a harrowing passage at the end of the Golden notebook as Saul dangerously lapses in and out of his schizophrenia, illustrates the deep division on which masculine heterosexuality is founded; in this formation of subjectivity, sexual desire cannot be divorced from hatred and the will to dominate:

> His face was white, blood-drained, his eyes grey and strained and full of horror because I was lying there screwed up with pain. He said, in his own voice: 'Anna, for God's sake, don't look like that,' but with a hesitation, and back came the madman, *for now it was not only I I I I, but I against women.* Women the jailors, the consciences, the voice of society, and he was directing *a pure stream of hatred against me, for being a woman.* . . . As I wept *I saw his prick stand up* under his jeans . . . and I thought, derisive, oh so *now he's going to love me.* (630; emphases added)

By highlighting the historical specificity of the sex wars that Lessing analyzes, I do not mean to deny her simultaneous use of (as well as critique and parody of) Jungian archetypes—the novel, particularly in its accounts of Anna's dreams, is strewn with them.[80] But I do suggest that a contradiction arises in attempts to see the novel entirely in terms of a Jungian framework of universal archetypes, because they leave no room for the immediacy of the historical/political siting that Lessing simultaneously gives to Anna's psychological descent into madness. "It's all due to the times we live in" (574), is the response of the doctor whom Anna consults about Saul's terrifying memory lapses as he fragments into multiple personalities: a pat answer that holds more than a grain of truth.

And, in a profound sense, it is the haunting image of Africa, however distorted, as it persists in Anna's subconscious while she lives "inside" madness (582) that provides the grounds for her intuitive knowledge of oppression as an external, active force in history, one intensified by various complexly interrelated psychological and ideological incitements to achieve domination over others. Likewise, the recollections of the struggle for political autonomy on the African continent that filter through Anna's madness—via memories, dreams, and hallucinations—become the basis for her hope that the act of mental breakdown or "cracking apart" may in fact be the prelude to a larger "cracking open" of those metaphoric dams representing the old order. Through these gaps, Anna dreams, "the future might pour in [in] a different shape—terrible perhaps, or marvellous, but something new" (473). In particular, Anna's attempt to imagine herself as the heroic anti-apartheid black leader, Tom Mathlong, provides her with a model both for surviving as an oppressed minority in "white-occupied territory" and for creating a new mode of being adequate to the new world order. For Anna realizes that the self-possession Mathlong maintains in the face of overwhelming colonial opposition (unlike the black leader Charlie Thembla, who goes mad) is the result of his ability to detach himself by "perform[ing] actions, play[ing] roles, that he believed to be necessary for the good of others, even while he preserved an ironic doubt about the results of his action. It seemed to me that this particular type of detachment was something we needed very badly in this time" (597). To *perform* political action is not to disbelieve in its efficacy or necessity but to find an alternative means of catalyzing its possibilities.

This conflation of racial mimicry, politics, and survival calls to mind the work of an intellectual whose analysis of colonialism in Africa began appearing in the same time period that Lessing and Durrell were writing their novelistic accounts of the Third World—Frantz Fanon, whose *Black Skin, White Masks* appeared in 1951 and *The Wretched of the Earth* in 1961. Whether or not Lessing knew the work of Fanon, his inquiry into the psychodynamics of racial identity under colonial rule provides yet another theoretical context within which to understand the imaginary identification that Lessing stages between Anna Wulf and Tom Mathlong, between First World woman and Third World black. In many ways, Mathlong's performative mimicry of colonial stereotypes and anti-stereotypes, which works both to protect him and to advance his agenda, exemplifies Fanon's double-hinged argument about the instability of racial identity. For while racial identity depends on masquerade and projection, it is also the product of the colonized subject's internalization—or what Fanon calls "epidermalization"—of the gaze of the white colonizer on the African's bodily surface or skin. Considered from this perspective, the ironic detachment that Anna admires in Mathlong and that she imitatively incorporates as her own modus operandi is also, less positively, a product of self-division within one's consciousness and alienation from one's body. To the "man of color," Fanon writes, "consciousness of the body is solely a negating activity. It is a third-person consciousness." To put it slightly differently, as Gwen Bergner explains in an analysis of Fanon, "The white man's gaze produces a psychic splitting that shatters the black man's experience of bodily integrity."[81]

While acknowledging the dangers of indiscriminately collapsing the different histories of racial and female oppression, I find it productive to bring Fanon to bear on Lessing's novel because his analysis of the split subjectivity of the colonial subject also rings true of the psychic divisions that accompany Anna's psychic shattering and her doubled sense of her body as an occupied land overrun by enemy forces and as a territory that remains foreign to her, an interior frontier. One of Fanon's key terms, *masking*, also illuminates the lesson in potentially successful resistance that Anna learns from Mathlong's mimicry of the colonial stereotype. For the collage of notebooks, journals, newspaper clippings, and fictional "out-takes" that make up *The Golden Notebook* are nothing less than a series of shifting masks—masks taking the form of the "third-person conscious-ness" of which Fanon writes, usually parading in fictional first-person voices—worn by the narrating Anna in order to perform the multiple roles that may, or may not, insure her survival when history "cracks open."

To this degree, then, Anna's experience of colonialism and the color line in Southern Rhodesia becomes the internal anchor that gives substance to her struggles and a context to her historical positioning as a modern woman in the Cold War western world who is attempting to be "free" and a "woman." But if this historically specific politics of gender, informed by race, forms a counterweight to the universalizing tendencies of the Jungian-inspired dimensions of Anna's descent into the realm of the id, nonetheless *The Golden Notebook* finally enacts, not unlike the last volume of the *Alexandria Quartet,* a purgation of the most threatening (and hence politically revolutionary) aspects of the polymorphous perversities un-leashed by Anna's quest. The novel achieves this effect by rechanneling its dispersive, libidinal energies into a final narrative trajectory that upholds the normativity of heterosexual desire and the complementarity of gender roles, in the face of the novel's otherwise feminist call to emancipation. This rechanneling process begins in Anna's last notebook, the so-called Golden notebook, whose purpose is to supersede the prior effort at com-partmentalizing the contradictory facets of her life by gathering them into a single, unified narrative account; the fact that the overall novel takes its title from this notebook intimates that even Lessing privileges this effort at consolidation over the various "component parts" that precede it, as if it holds some final, or at least more conclusive, answer to the novel's exis-tential questions. The Golden notebook thus operates, on the structural level, as a kind of reining-in of libidinal energies that makes possible Anna's break from the self-destructiveness of her psychologically overdetermined relationship with Saul, her return to the world of everyday sanity, and, ultimately, her overcoming her writing block by composing a new autobio-graphical novel (as the last sentences of the Golden notebook reveal the "Free Women" text to be).

Likewise, the final section of "Free Women," which follows the Golden notebook and ends the novel, operates as a further streamlining of the nar-rative desires that have been in play since the opening pages. First of all, this "fiction" recasts Anna's psychological descent into "mad love" in a much tamer form, replacing the notebooks' account of her tormented rela-tionship with Saul with her brief, and relatively sane, affair with an Ameri-can writer in exile named Milt, thus corralling the perverse and dangerous energies into which the former relationship has tapped. Second, the resolu-tion of the "free women" theme in this final segment represents a retreat from the more utopian social and artistic ideals of the novel overall: Anna cynically decides she is going to work at a marriage welfare center (rather than recommencing her novelistic career), and Molly decides to marry a nice bourgeois man with a house in Hampstead. "So we're both going to be integrated with British life at its roots," Molly quips (666), and whatever Lessing's note of irony, the novella leaves us with the two women in retreat from the greater aspirations of their professions, politics, and freedom, opting, instead, for something closer to the status quo.

Furthermore, as already mentioned, the final sentence only underlines the lengths to which the text seems willing to go at this ultimate moment of closure to exorcise its demons—including, by implication, the specter of homosexuality—as Lessing represents the two women chastely kissing and separating. No shadow of the lesbian here; no shadow, for that matter, of the feminist ideal of sisterhood as a refuge from the heterosexual warfare that has ruptured every male-female bond in the text. I am reminded of the ending of the final volume of the *Alexandria Quartet,* where the religious festival honoring Scobie after his death marks this cross-dressing homosexual's ironic transformation into a deity of heterosexual fertility; this conversion, as we have seen, has its analogue in the contrast between the outburst of the polymorphous perverse in the festival scenes of the earlier novels and the procession that, in honoring Scobie as fertility god, pours down a single street in one unified flow, toward one goal. If such movement metaphorically encapsulates the linearity that overtakes the *Alexandria Quartet*'s otherwise dispersive narrative trajectory and that eclipses its queer fringes, so too the ending of Lessing's novel—whatever its ironic intentions as yet one more "fictional" refraction of Anna's consciousness—has the same effect, folding the text's manifold narrative energies into a single narrative line that stays all action: the women's kiss and separation has the same effect of closure, if only in reverse, as does Darley's anticipation of his reunion with Clea. There is, of course, a difference, one to which I have just alluded: whereas Durrell's ending can only be read as pointing to a future time outside of the text, the fact that "Free Women" is now unmasked as Anna's latest fictional effort, not the "final word" on her present life, means that there is no basis for positing any certain truths to her life, present or future.

For in a sense, we know no more of the narrating Anna's present circumstances outside the time-frame covered by the text than we do of Lucy Snowe's in *Villette;* both writer-protagonists elude us in the very act of writing. But what Lucy writes as the ending to her story, I would posit, is more radically open than the material with which Lessing's Anna leaves us. Anna the writer may not have capitulated to convention; but "Anna," the protagonist of "Free Women," may well have. And, beyond a doubt, this "Anna," as well as the narrating Anna, indeed as well as Lessing herself, remains trapped in those aspects of the gender ideology of the late 1950s that dictate a norm for heterosexual femininity that *needs,* as its scapegoat for the failures of heterosexual men, the homosexual other whose presence it must also deny. Anna's projections onto racial "others," via her experience of colonialism and apartheid rule, have given her access to a politicized knowledge of her position in western patriarchy as a woman who by definition is seen as man's mirror and secondary refraction, but this understanding comes at the expense of those simultaneous projections onto male homosexuality as femininity's "other face," or, to a lesser degree, onto lesbianism as the "defacement" of heterosexual femininity altogether—projections that also work as displacements, ultimately shielding Anna from the compromises involved in her performance of a woman's "natural," which is to say heterosexual, desire. As such, colonialism and homosexuality, first brought into conjunction in Anna's resurfacing memories of Southern Rhodesia, become evocative figures for the sexual and textual anxieties involved in attempting to become in the mid–twentieth century a free woman who possesses the authority to write a story that will express not only the cracking apart of a now defunct old order, but the cracking open of a radically new frontier of future being where, it is to be hoped, the recuperation of the self's repressed desires no longer depends on racial or homosexual others.

In this book, I have undertaken to investigate the libidinal politics that have very often contributed to the shaping of modernist narrative. E. M. Forster noted years ago in *Aspects of the Novel* that the reader doesn't really pick up a novel to seek action—we can get enough of that elsewhere in our lives. Instead we read novels, Forster claims, in order to experience "[the] secret life which each of us lives privately."[1] This interest in the privately lived "secret life"—what Woolf calls "the privacy of the soul" (*Mrs. Dalloway*, 192)—is of course a hallmark of the modernist turn to modes of interior representation; it has also been the subject of this study, which has focused on those novelistic experiments that have attempted to evoke the flux of consciousness and the erotics of mental activity in new or altered narrative forms. One result of the revolution in representation entailed by this inward turn is the emergence of what I have characterized in these pages as a poetics of the sexually and textually perverse. This "poetics" in turn invites our reexamination of the sexual, cultural, and aesthetic "politics" of the phenomenon of modernism itself, both as it has traditionally been defined and as it is actively being redefined in contemporary critical discussions.

In exploring the errant narrative desires summoned forth by putting the dispersive energies of the libido into writing, this book aims to contribute to three related arenas of critical debate: modernist studies, narrative theory, and theories of sexuality. The vexed question of just how (and whether) to read politics into the texts of modernism has been the impetus of much recent scholarship, and, in terms of issues of canonicity, it has also raised the question of what qualifies as modernist writing, to whom, and for what reasons. This book has attempted to participate in this discussion, first, by arguing that standard definitions of canonical modernism (and the assumptions of aesthetic autonomy associated with such definitions) have never quite adequately described the deviant desires inspiring much experimental modern fiction and, second, by using its chapter divisions to emphasize the historically shifting contexts giving rise to multiple variations of modernist writing. By giving historical specificity to novelistic attempts to represent the libidinal currents of psychic life—registering, for instance, the difference between the turn-of-the-century sexual discourse of hydraulics bearing on Lawrence's innovations and the impress of colonial and Cold War ideology on Lessing's themes—we enable ourselves to see more clearly both the varying shapes that modernist narrative has assumed and the causations, temporal and contextual, underlying these variations. Interpreting the complexity of modernist modes of representation as the product of an ongoing process not only counters the tendency to mythicize modernist aesthetics as a monolithic entity but also allows us to link more accurately fictional to cultural anxieties of authority, localizing *both* the poetics and the politics that have accompanied these shifts in representation. Finally, my expanded definition is also meant to counter the tendency to impose a barrier between modernist practice and poststructuralist theory, as if postmodern art is the only repository of a "truly" poststructuralist understanding of decentered identity, language, and reality. Rather, the indeterminacy (and breakdown of unitary modes of perceiving sexuality, identity, and narrative) that I find operating *within* the dynamics of much modernist fiction—and not just within its authors' visions of twentieth-century angst and fragmentation—attests to an ongoing process of redefinition that has anticipated what we now think of as poststructuralist thought.

If one project of this book, then, has been to demystify the cultural politics of modernism by looking at its libidinal politics, a related goal has been to engage the ideological assumptions of narrative theory, particularly in their ramifications for studies of the novel as genre. Like most students of the novel, I have always been drawn to theories—from Northrop Frye's "anatomy" of generic modes to Peter Brooks's search for the "design and intention in narrative" inciting us to "read for the plot"—that take broad, panoramic views of the genre in an attempt to lay bare its constitutive elements and paradigmatic desires. While I don't mean to refute claims that narrative may consist of paradigmatic elements, I do think that the desire to uncover such originary narratives and then claim their universality can blind us both to the ideological functions that those patterns may serve and to the ideological purposes that the very search for such origins may mask. Hence my unease, documented in chapter 5, with the assumed transhistoricity of the masterplot that Brooks locates in the Oedipus narrative. Clearly the genealogical imperative, the desire to uncover the beginnings that explain one's ends, is vital to many classic Anglo-European novels. But seeing its ubiquity everywhere, as *the* determinant of *all* plot, tends to obscure (for instance) the cultural reasons that this desire has found such a happy home in western culture and to deflect attention from the political reasons that such paternal plots surface with more energy in certain historical epochs as opposed to others. In contrast to the efforts of some critics to read one masterplot *into* the shape of fiction, other critics of the novel as genre have erred in an opposite direction, imposing one critical paradigm *onto* the heterogeneous, often conflicting levels of discourse and the myriad, "heretic" desires that this study attempts to reclaim for novelistic fiction. For example, as chapter 1 argues, the tendency among critics inspired by Foucault's work to see the novel *only* as an extension of social discourses of power, as the policing arm of a disciplinary society in which any and all appeals to a world "outside" power illustrate another covert inscription of power's omnipresence, flattens the dialogical quality that, according to Bakhtin, makes the novel unique among genres—its intrinsic multivocality as a contemporary form imbued in "living," open-ended language, which creates both in the narrative and in the experience of the reader a space for indeterminacy and imaginative free play that cannot be simply, or fully, folded into the regime of an all-encompassing power.

If certain aspects of the novel as a genre facilitate radically indeterminate forms of expression in my view (which is not the same as denying the novel's role as an enforcer of social ideology, nor does it disavow the myth of individual autonomy the bourgeois novel often promulgates), so too the thematic that has provided the primary constant of these chapters—sexuality in all its changing avatars—remains the most radically indeterminate, ambiguous, slippery aspect of human subjectivity. The third arena to which this book therefore attempts to make a contribution is that of contemporary studies of sexuality. As I noted in my introduction, the tenets underlying Freud's and Foucault's groundbreaking work on sexuality have too often been set against each other in an either/or binary—a move for which Foucault, of course, is in part responsible, since he presents his theory of sexuality's implantation and inscription in explicit contrast to Freud's language of internalization. However, given the complex and mobile ways in which culture and psyche inform each other's operations, it seems to me that there should be ample room to conceive a theory of sexuality that admits both to the constructedness of desire as it discursively presents itself in our social lives and the inextricability of those libidinal and psychic energies that give rise to subjectivity; the polymorphous perversities postulated by Freud are no less "real" than the polymorphous proliferation of sexual discourses whose operation Foucault brings to light. In all its variability and indeterminacy, sex forms *the* meeting point between individual subjectivity and social formations, dissolving the boundaries traditionally distinguishing inner and outer selves. The body of sexuality and the sexuality of the body are necessarily interimplicated in each other.

My attempt to mediate—if not reconcile—psychoanalytic and materialist-discursive imperatives finds its reflection in another thematic that has run throughout my readings of modernist practice and sexual fiction, a thematic best articulated in Jessica Benjamin's injunction that critics begin to conceive a "transitional space in theory" where "competing ideas [may be] entertained simultaneously" without necessarily canceling each other out.[2] Addressed primarily to psychologists, but relevant to all critics of gender, representation, subjectivity, and sexuality, Benjamin's concept owes to the renewed emphasis in psychology on concepts of intersubjectivity, in which the dynamics of relationship are conceived not only within the hierarchical paradigm of self and other or subject and object, but also of self and self, subject and subject. While envisioning intersubjective spaces certainly does not do away with relations of power, I would argue, in the spirit of Benjamin, that the act of holding open the *possibility* of a space in which one subject encounters other subjects who cease to be "other" in the imaginary intercourse that ensues may help us redefine our positions, not only as human and sexual subjects continually negotiating self/object relationships, but also as readers of texts and as critics engaging other critics. For the act of imagining a surrender to otherness that is a desirous yielding rather than an act of submission or coercion—the concept with which I began this book—is not only an ideal to be sought in interpersonal relationships; it is a precondition, as well, of the kind of empathetic reading that Faulkner immemorializes in his representation of the "overpass to love" created by Quentin and Shreve in recreating Sutpen's story in *Absalom, Absalom!*:

> That was why it did not matter to either of them which one did the talking, since it was not the talking alone which did it, performed and accomplished the overpassing, but some happy marriage of speaking and hearing wherein each before the demand, the requirement, forgave, condoned and forgot the faulting of the other—faultings both in the creating of this shade whom they discussed (rather, existed in) and in the hearing and sifting and discarding the false and conserving what seemed true, or fit the preconceived—in order to overpass to love, where there might be paradox and inconsistency but nothing fault nor false. (316)

Like the similar phenomenological concept of intercorporeal space (note how the boys "exist in" the very "shade" they create),[3] theories of intersubjectivity speak to the numinous dimension of individual experience that—as lovers, readers, critics—we already *know* in our bodies and in our knowledge of each other and the world, even if it escapes direct representation: the "overpass to love" where there is "nothing fault nor false."

So what of that intuitive understanding of sexuality and narrative that exists on the borderlines of consciousness, mediating the psyche, the body, and the social spaces we daily inhabit, inspiring and resisting our efforts at and participation in fictional representation? A telling image has recently surfaced from my past which, while hardly answering this question, speaks to these issues, and since I began this book with personal reflections on its composition, it seems fitting to return to the autobiographical as I bring this inquiry into the intertwined dictates of sexuality, psychology, and narrative to a close. Since I also began my analysis proper in chapter 1 with *Villette,* it also seems fitting to return to Lucy Snowe—whom I transformed into this text's privileged figure for the libidinal currents and "heretic" narrative energies that compose modernity's fictions of sexuality—in order to begin these personal reflections. I am thinking of the scene in chapter 20 where Lucy, having entered the grand concert hall in the company of Dr. John and his mother, catches a reflection of their party in a mirror and momentarily doesn't recognize herself *as she is.* Of this moment she muses, "Thus, for the first, and perhaps only time in my life, I enjoyed the 'giftie' of seeing myself as others see me" (286). Something like this unsolicited revelation was also my experience recently when a former playmate of my younger brothers, whom I barely knew—he was perhaps ten years my junior—wrote me a letter, revealing his memory of me as an adolescent. While he and my brothers romped on long summer days in the backyard dressed up as their favorite, gun-wielding comic book superheroes, there I always sat, he wrote, in a chair in the den, "reading, reading, reading": an emblem to him of perfect contentment in my choice not to play at boys' games in the backyard, enveloping myself without apology in a world of imaginative pleasure that he wished he could have claimed as his own. Reading his letter, I had the uncanny sensation, like Lucy, of suddenly catching a hitherto hidden glimpse of myself as seen from the outside, at least as my image has lived in a virtual stranger's imagination for decades; more uncanny still is the fact that the fourteen-year-old boy so immersed in his reading (no doubt a nineteenth-century novel) that he hardly registers the world around him is very much the person whom I have become as an adult: the professor who reads in order to write about reading. As I contemplated the unexpected "giftie" of this image as it reformed itself as a static tableau in my mind's eye—struck by the seeming contentment and containment of this younger version of self—I found myself returning to the very issues occupying me as I completed this manuscript. Thinking of Jessica Benjamin's theory of the twin components, separation and connection, necessary to successful individuation, I had the sensation that I was witnessing something very similar, the emergence of an autonomous (and adult) subject. On one level, the image bespoke a fully differentiated self whose successful separation from the world of otherness was manifest in his contented retreat into a "secret life" (to repeat Forster's formula) of imaginative pleasure as he sat turning page after page in that chair; yet on another level the same image revealed the paradox of psychic individuation, a subject who in the very act of reading was enacting the search for recognition and connection equally necessary to autonomous identity, looking for confirmation of his existence in the mirror of the other provided by the open pages of the book.

Thus, superimposing Benjamin's understanding of identity formation onto this image, I experienced a second shock of recognition, another of those externally bestowed gifts when "theory" suddenly "comes to life," registered in the body's responsive tremor to a truth conveyed: namely, that in my adolescent surrender to the world of fiction, I was repeating and hence rehearsing a subliminal awareness of the *expense* at which individuation is achieved, since, as Freud well knew, loss underwrites the desire for connection, the desire for an imagined merging with some other. Indeed, that boy sitting reading—myself in the mirror of my correspondent's eye—was engaging in his version of *fort* and *da,* the infant's game of mastery explicated by Freud in *Beyond the Pleasure Principle.* Freud argues that the infant's activity—throwing the toy out of the crib and then pulling on the attached string to retrieve it, activities accompanied by the exclamations *fort* and *da* respectively—forms a quintessential example of the need to master the primary loss to which all humans must submit: the disappearance of the mother into the external world of otherness. This loss of primal symbiosis, of course, is the source of the libidinal desires that resurface, in displaced form, as the craving for sexual and spiritual love, in order to know and be known in romantic bonds that substitute for this original and unspeakable deprivation.[4] If the infantile game of *fort* and *da*—acting out the trauma of the unspeakable—becomes a blueprint for the currents of erotic desire that shape the adult quest for love and relationship, this game also forms a blueprint, as Peter Brooks reminds us, for the mechanisms that motivate narrative desire: putting the unspeakable into words, the child creates the skeletal components of narrative to make sense of loss—something has disappeared (the inciting of desire for explanatory story), then it is found (the closure that effects a return to quiescence, the cessation of story).

So, there I sit in what is now a recovered but also a shared memory, reading no doubt a love story—perhaps, at not too far a stretch of the imagination, reading *Villette,* since my first copy of the novel is dated to the same year as this memory; reading in place of relating to the outside world, yet at the same time reading as a psychic exercise in bridging the gap between self and other, in learning the terms (and penalties) of desire by giving myself over to an imaginary world of narrative pleasures in which the exercise of empathetic identification and interaction with purely fictional beings creates the desire, continually deferred but nonetheless real, someday to "overpass to love" in a perfect union of subject and subject. What does this nexus of desires and investments, personal and professional, mean, in the end? Simply that the libidinal currents that underlie and shape the dynamic energies of sexuality and narrative alike have always been inherent in the (human) subject who, sitting quietly at the center of this memory, is also the subject (matter) inspiring the writing of this book.

NOTES

INTRODUCTION

1. Jürgen Habermas, "Modernity versus Postmodernity," *New German Critique* 22 (Winter 1981): 5; emphasis added.

2. Michel de Certeau, "History: Ethics, Science, and Fiction," in *Social Science as Moral Inquiry,* ed. Norma Hahn, Robert N. Bellah, Paul Rabinow, and William M. Sullivan (New York: Columbia Univ. Press, 1983), p. 128; emphasis added.

3. Muriel Dimen, "Seven Notes for the Reconstruction of Sexuality," *Social Text* 2, no. 3 (Fall 1982), p. 27; emphasis added.

4. See Michel Foucault, *The History of Sexuality,* vol. 1, *An Introduction,* trans. Robert Hurley (1976; rpt., New York: Vintage, 1980), and D. A. Miller, *The Novel and the Police* (Berkeley: Univ. of California Press, 1988). As Foucault states, "these discourses on sex did not multiply apart from or against power, but in the very space and as the means of its exercise" (32); in Miller's words, the novel's covert "enterprise" is to habituate subjects to the "totalizing power [that] circulates" in the social order (xii–xiii), for "the novelistic Panopticon exists to remind us that we too inhabit it" (32).

5. Emmanuel Ghent, "Masochism, Submission, Surrender: Masochism as a Perversion of Surrender," *Contemporary Psychoanalysis* 26, no. 1 (1990): 108–36.

6. The project of shifting the emphasis from subject/object relations to that of subject/subject within psychoanalysis marks an important new movement among psychotherapists, one exemplified by the work of Jessica Benjamin in *Like Subjects, Love Objects: Essays on Recognition and Sexual Difference* (New Haven, CT: Yale Univ. Press, 1995), where she eloquently argues for the recognition within psychoanalysis, both as a practice and as a theory, of relations as comprised of "two subjectivities, each with its own set of internal relations": "When we recognize the outside other as a separate and equivalent center of subjectivity, she is a 'like subject,'" Benjamin explains in reference to her title; "when on the other hand, we identify with the other as an inner representation, taking the other as the ideal of who we might wish to become, we also set up a relation of 'like subjects'" (3, 7). See also Ghent, "Masochism."

7. As a heuristic exercise, I begin a seminar I frequently teach titled "Modernity's Fictions of Sexuality" by passing out notecards and asking students to define the word *sex.* Their confusion at being asked to produce a simple definition provides an ironic confirmation of Foucault's observation in *The History of Sexuality* (see note 4 above) that in inces-

santly speaking, thinking, and obsessing about sex, we "speak verbosely of [our] own silence" (8). The terms *sex/sexuality* encompass what is more commonly meant by "sexuality" (e.g., the realm and range of sexual instincts and drives), a designation of one's biological sex (as in "What is the baby's sex?"), the physical act of coitus (which, in itself, begs further definition—what bodily parts, in what conjunctions, does it take to "make sex"?), sexual orientation ("What's your sexuality?"), sexual attraction or appeal (as in "What a sexy guy!"), base lust ("The pig just wants sex!"), and the prelude to or payoff of romantic desire ("sexual ecstasy").

8. Sigmund Freud, *Three Essays on the Theory of Sexuality,* trans. James Strachey (1905; rpt., New York: Basic Books, 1962), p. 15. All further references to this work are cited in the text.

9. Ann Snitow, Christine Stansell, and Sharon Thompson, eds., "Editors' Introduction," *Powers of Desire: The Politics of Sexuality* (New York: Monthly Review Press, 1983), pp. 42–43. The passage continues, "[Sex] is an area for play . . . to test out what the possibilities might be for an erotic life and a social world that would answer our desires." While the word "play" might at first seem inappropriate for a description of the cataclysmic change in late-twentieth-century ways of thinking about and perceiving sexuality occasioned by the onset of AIDS, this health crisis, which was just emerging into public consciousness at the time of the collection's publication in 1983, provides a singular illustration of the editors' point, for the dangers involved in contracting the HIV virus, as history has now come to demonstrate, have not simply provided disciplinary powers with a propagandistic tool to extend their regulation of our private lives; the shifts in sexual practice necessitated by AIDS have also reopened the question of what sexuality *is,* and what it is *to be,* reinvigorating its "possibilities" as "a comparatively open subject" whose future is not yet determined. See also Steven Marcus's observation, in his introduction to Freud's *Three Essays,* that sexuality represents that part of our psychic make-up most recalcitrant to civilized constraints (xxiv).

10. While I disagree with some of its implications, Miller's challenge in *The Novel and the Police* to the long-standing belief that the novel is "the most free" and "lawless" of genres (Miller is quoting Gide here), a successful truant, and a transgressor of boundaries (1–2) serves as a valuable reminder of the dangers of over-romanticization addressed above. Where Miller errs, I feel, is in collapsing a now outdated mode of reading fiction, derived from New Criticism's celebration of autonomy (both of the text and the individual), and more recent poststructuralist and Bakhtinian-inspired accounts of novelistic "free" play and emancipatory possibilities. Ironically, if one were forced to name the most widespread belief or axiom prevalent in novel criticism today, it would be a view much closer to that of Miller, one emphasizing, in the wake of new historicist criticism, the novel as a function of social discourses of power, rather than as a Trillingesque affirmation of the independent "human spirit." I return to these issues and their pertinence to this book later in this introduction and in chapter 1.

11. M. M. Bakhtin, *The Dialogic Imagination: Four Essays,* trans. Caryl Emerson and Michael Holquist (Austin: Univ. of Texas Press, 1981), pp. 7–11; and Freud, *Three Essays,* pp. 14, 33–34, 37–38. The quotation is from Jeffrey Weeks in *Sex, Politics, and Society: The Regulation of Sexuality since 1800* (London and New York: Longman, 1981), p. 153.

12. For representative attempts to categorize the use of stream of consciousness as a method, see Robert Humphrey, *Stream of Consciousness in the Modern Novel* (Berkeley: Univ. of California Press, 1954) and Melvin Friedman, *Stream of Consciousness: A Study in Literary Method* (New Haven, CT: Yale Univ. Press, 1955), works whose sometimes limited

applications need to be set against Dorrit Cohn's more rigorously sophisticated and typological distinction between levels of fictional discourse involved in representing states of interiority in *Transparent Minds: Narrative Modes for Presenting Consciousness in Fiction* (Princeton, NJ: Princeton Univ. Press, 1978) and Judith Ryan's probing into literary representations of the sensations of consciousness stemming from American empiricist psychology in *The Vanishing Subject: Early Psychology and Literary Modernism* (Chicago: Univ. of Chicago Press, 1991). For an overview of the evolving history of the concept of modernism, see Andreas Huyssen, *After the Great Divide: Modernism, Mass Culture, Postmodernism* (Bloomington: Indiana Univ. Press, 1986) and Astradur Eysteinsson, *The Concept of Modernism* (Ithaca, NY: Cornell Univ. Press, 1990). For recent attempts to expand the definitional boundaries of the field by introducing perspectives of gender, race, and empire often missing from traditional accounts, see Sandra Gilbert and Susan Gubar, *No Man's Land: The Place of the Woman Writer in the Twentieth Century,* vol. 1, *The War of the Words* (New Haven, CT: Yale Univ. Press, 1988), vol. 2, *Sexchanges* (New Haven, CT: Yale Univ. Press, 1989), and vol. 3, *Letters from the Front* (New Haven, CT: Yale Univ. Press, 1994); Marianne DeKoven, *Rich and Strange: Gender, History, Modernism* (Princeton, NJ: Princeton Univ. Press, 1991); Michael North, *The Dialect of Modernism: Race, Language, and Twentieth-Century Literature* (Oxford: Oxford Univ. Press, 1996); Laura Doyle, *Bordering on the Body: The Racial Matrix of Modern Fiction and Culture* (Oxford: Oxford Univ. Press, 1994); Houston Baker, *Modernism and the Harlem Renaissance* (Chicago: Univ. of Chicago Press, 1987); Vincent J. Cheng, *Joyce, Race, and Empire* (Cambridge: Cambridge Univ. Press, 1995); Bonnie Kime Scott, ed., *The Gender of Modernism: A Critical Anthology* (Bloomington: Indiana Univ. Press, 1990); Margot Norris, "Modernist Eruptions," *The Columbia History of the American Novel,* ed. Emory Elliot (New York: Columbia Univ. Press, 1991), pp. 311–30; Lisa Rado, ed., *Modernism, Gender, and Culture: A Cultural Studies Approach* (New York: Garland, 1996); Lisa Rado, ed., *Rereading Modernism: New Directions in Feminist Criticism* (New York: Garland, 1994); Ellen G. Friedman and Miriam Fuchs, eds., *Breaking the Sequence: Women's Experimental Fiction* (Princeton, NJ: Princeton Univ. Press, 1989); Gillian Hanscombe and Virginia Smyers, *Writing for Their Lives: The Modernist Women, 1910–1940* (Boston: Northeastern Univ. Press, 1987).

13. Virginia Woolf, "Modern Fiction" (1925), in *Collected Essays,* 4 vols. (New York: Harcourt, Brace & World, 1967), 2: 108. All further references to this work are cited in the text. Thanks to Brenda Silver for alerting me to an earlier version of this essay that appeared in the *Times Literary Supplement,* 10 April 1919: 189–90.

14. Useful here is Susan Stanford Friedman's comment, in her tentatively titled work-in-progress, *History's Return: The Politics of Rupture and Repression in Modernism,* that "I assume permeable boundaries between modernist and non-modernist modern writers. The less writers of modernity disrupt literary conventions the more they exist in a fluid borderland where their texts can be read as modernist in one sense and realist (for example) in another" (11). I am very grateful to Friedman for allowing me to quote from this impressive forthcoming work.

15. Malcolm Bradbury and James McFarlane, eds., *Modernism, 1980–1930* (Harmondsworth, England: Penguin, 1976), p. 27.

16. See Elizabeth Hirsh, "Utopia Here and Now: Women's Experimental Fiction," *Contemporary Literature* 30, no. 4 (Winter 1989): 578, and Alice Jardine, *Gynesis: Configurations of Woman and Modernity* (Ithaca, NY: Cornell Univ. Press, 1985), p. 69.

17. Roland Barthes, "The Death of the Author," *Image-Music-Text,* trans. Stephen Heath (New York: Hill, 1977), p. 146. My lists of formal and thematic traits are loosely

drawn from Friedman, *History's Return*, p. 11, and David Harvey, *The Condition of Post-modernity: An Inquiry into the Origins of Cultural Change* (London: Blackwell, 1989), p. 23.

18. David Bennett, "Periodical Fragments and Organic Culture: Modernism, the Avant-garde, and the Little Magazine," *Contemporary Literature* 30, no. 4 (Winter 1989): 484–85.

19. Harvey, *Condition of Postmodernity*, p. 11.

20. Snitow et al., eds., *Powers of Desire*, p. 9; Jonathan Dollimore, "The Cultural Politics of Perversion: Augustine, Shakespeare, Freud, Foucault," *Textual Practice* 4, no. 2 (Summer 1990): 188.

21. Sigmund Freud, *Dora: An Analysis of a Case of Hysteria,* ed. Phillip Reiff (written 1899, published 1905; rpt., New York: Collier Books, 1963), p. 96. All further references to this work are cited in the text.

22. See Foucault, *History of Sexuality,* pp. 10–13, 44, 47–49. A further look at the passage just cited from *Dora* bolsters the Foucauldian critique of internalization; for the "task of making conscious the most hidden recesses of the mind," as Freud puts it here, falls to the psychoanalyst/writer whose primary tool is the disciplinary one of surveillance, reading the patient's unconscious body language (the surface) for "signs" of what is presumed to lie within (96). I return to these complexities in chapter 2's analysis of *Dora*.

23. Judith Butler, *Gender Trouble: Feminism and the Subversion of Identity* (New York: Routledge, 1990); Butler's argument is addressed in more detail in chapter 3.

24. Foucault deliberately plays on the Freudian concept of the polymorphous perverse in order to reverse its meaning when he counters the repressive hypothesis with the concept of the "polymorphous techniques of power" (*History of Sexuality,* p. 11), a phrase that he puts in quotation marks.

25. Analogously, Benjamin in *Like Subjects* notes how the intersubjective model she has derived from object-relations theory has stimulated her attempt to "to formulate psychoanalytic theory in ways that allow competing ideas to be entertained simultaneously" (4). This endeavor, she suggests, necessitates entertaining "a transitional space in theory" that "can encompass the paradoxes that arise when we are aware that two or more competing and convincing perspectives apply to the same phenomenon. At times, it is important to put aside how a particular point of view is exclusive of another, to defer the contradiction in order to entertain more than one idea" (7). Isobel Armstrong makes a similar point in "Textual Harassment: The Ideology of Close Reading, or How Close Is Close?" *Textual Practice* 9, no. 3 (Winter 1995): 401–20, in which she builds a model of reading, based on affect, that is not caught up in the desire for mastery over the text underlying the dialectical relationship of subject/object, master/slave, traditionally found in theories of reading and interpretation.

26. Benjamin, *Like Subjects,* pp. 7, 4. See the preceding note.

27. Armstrong, "Textual Harassment," p. 417.

28. Dollimore, "Cultural Politics of Perversion," p. 192.

29. Thus Freud writes of the return of the perversions in adult life, "If such perversions admit of analysis, that is, if they can be taken to pieces, then they must be of a composite nature. This gives us a hint that perhaps the sexual instinct itself may be no simple thing, but put together from components which have come apart again in the perversions" (*Three Essays,* p. 28).

30. Teresa de Lauretis, *The Practice of Love: Lesbian Sexuality and Perverse Desire* (Bloomington: Indiana Univ. Press, 1994), xii. Dollimore says much the same thing: "So

one does not become a pervert but remains one; it is sexual perversion, not sexual 'normality,' which is the given in human nature" ("Cultural Politics of Perversion," p. 179).

31. See de Lauretis's argument, very close to the one proposed here, for the practice of an adult sexuality "of the component instincts, which, unlike infantile polymorphous perversion, is inclusive of phallic and genital drives but, unlike 'normal' sexuality, is not bound to a necessary phallic, genital, and heterosexual primacy" (*The Practice of Love,* p. xix).

32. Dollimore, "Cultural Politics of Perversion," pp. 182, 179 (emphasis added). See also Dollimore's book, *Sexual Dissidence: Augustine to Wilde, Freud to Foucault* (Oxford: Clarendon Press, 1991). Another critic who works in a similar vein as de Lauretis but uses "deviance" rather than "perversity" as his analytical touchstone for theorizing gay male subjectivity is Earl Jackson Jr., *Strategies of Deviance: Studies in Gay Male Representation* (Bloomington: Indiana Univ. Press, 1995).

33. De Lauretis, *The Practice of Love,* p. xv; Freud, "The Instincts and Their Vicissitudes," in *The Standard Edition of the Complete Psychological Works of Sigmund Freud,* 24 vols., trans. and ed. James Strachey (London: Hogarth Press, 1953–74), 14: 122. De Lauretis cites this passage as she introduces her concept of fantasy, rather than biology, as that which "is at the origin of sexuality as a social, as well as subjective, construction."

34. A brilliantly detailed analysis of this "necessary" interimplication can be found in Lee Edelman, *Homographesis* (New York and London: Routledge, 1994).

35. In Felman's argument, literary debates enact a process of transference as critics end up repeating the text's own contradictions—contradictions in fact never resolved but repressed in the text—in their critical disagreements; Jameson's theory of the political unconscious forges a method for reading modernist texts symptomatically to uncover the historical and political content their linguistic forms attempt to conceal. See Shoshana Felman, "Turning the Screw of Interpretation," in *Literature and Psychoanalysis: The Question of Reading: Otherwise,* ed. Shoshana Felman (Baltimore, MD: The Johns Hopkins Univ. Press, 1980), and Fredric Jameson, *The Political Unconscious: Narrative as a Socially Symbolic Act* (Ithaca, NY: Cornell Univ. Press, 1981).

36. See Friedman, *History's Return,* especially chapter 2: "Reading the Political *within* Modernism," and "Editor's Introduction," in *Joyce: The Return of the Repressed* (Ithaca, NY: Cornell Univ. Press, 1993), pp. 5–8. This division of modernist writers into warring camps on the basis of gender is the premise of Sandra Gilbert and Susan Gubar's monumental three-volume *No Man's Land,* whose often rich materials and analytical insights are ultimately constrained, in my reading, by the overarching emphasis on the categorical war of the sexes within the literary domain.

37. Eve Kosofsky Sedgwick, *Epistemology of the Closet* (Berkeley and Los Angeles: Univ. of California Press, 1990), pp. 31–32; Gayle Rubin, "Thinking Sex: Notes for a Radical Theory of the Politics of Sexuality," in *Pleasure and Danger: Exploring Female Sexuality,* ed. Carol S. Vance (Boston: Routledge and Kegan Paul, 1984), pp. 307–8, quoted in Sedgwick, p. 30. Sedgwick's proposition is echoed by Andrew Parker, who quotes Simon Watney as saying that gender "may not be the correct starting point for the study of sex at all," in "New Age Guys," *Lesbian and Gay Studies Newsletter* (March 1993): 32–33. Even where I disagree with some of the conclusions he draws, I credit Parker's thoughtful review of my own work for making me ponder the issues addressed in this "working proposition" all the more thoroughly.

38. Sedgwick, *Epistemology of the Closet,* p. 32.

39. Some of this bad rap, as is now widely recognized, is the legacy of mainstream feminism's early dismissal of certain aspects of sexuality—power, fantasy, aggression, danger—as "simply" patriarchal. These issues are addressed explicitly in the essay collections *Powers of Desire,* ed. Snitow et al., and *Pleasure and Danger,* ed. Vance, both direct products of this debate, especially as it crystallized in the Barnard Conference on Sexuality of 1982, where sexuality emerged as the "repressed" of straight, white, 1970s feminism. It should be noted that Sedgwick readily admits to the unknown consequences, the provisionality, of her axiom's call for a separation of the axes of sexuality and gender.

40. Ken Corbett, "Homosexual Boyhood: Notes on Girlyboys," *Gender and Psychoanalysis* 1, no. 4 (1996): 429–61; quotations are from pp. 432 and 437. See Judith Butler's use of the term in *Bodies That Matter: On the Discursive Limits of 'Sex'* (New York: Routledge, 1993), p. 239.

41. *Oxford English Dictionary,* 2d ed. (Oxford: Clarendon Press, 1989), pp. 887–88.

42. The subtitle was also designed to mimic the subtitle of my first book, *Love and the Form of Fiction,* to which this study is in many ways a sequel. The earlier book's focus on "love" is thus replaced with "sexuality," while the analysis of the narrative "form" of Victorian fiction is succeeded by an interest in the "shaping" of modernist fiction.

43. To those who might complain that the term *modernism* is ambiguous, I can only reply that *modernity,* however intuitively appealing, is even more so: for Habermas, modernity signifies the Enlightenment project that comes into being in the eighteenth century; for Foucault, the era of modernity begins in early- to mid-nineteenth-century Europe during the Industrial Revolution and is accompanied by the rise of a disciplinary order in which a social system of regulation based on spectacle is replaced by one based on surveillance and internalization of the law; for Alice Jardine, modernity denotes the twentieth-century breakdown of the master narratives (of progress, of faith in humanity, of human emancipation) that Habermas, in contrast, sees as definitive of modernity.

44. Virginia Woolf, *Three Guineas* (1938; rpt., San Diego, CA: Harvest/HBJ, 1966), p. 63.

45. Tillie Olsen, "Tell Me a Riddle," in *Tell Me a Riddle* (New York: Delta, 1956), p. 87.

46. Susan Stanford Friedman has analyzed this phenomenon in depth in "Creativity and the Childbirth Metaphor: Gender Difference in Literary Discourse," in *Speaking of Gender,* ed. Elaine Showalter (New York and London: Routledge, 1989), pp. 73–100.

47. Charlotte Brontë, "Farewell to Angria," in *Legends of Angria,* ed. Fanny Ratchford with William Clyde DeVane (New Haven, CT: Yale Univ. Press, 1933), pp. 315–16.

48. I quote from Joseph Litvak's abstract to *For a Narrative Criticism,* which advocates both the study of the novel as an overarching narrative structure and the use of narrative as a powerful critical tool in its own right. Various of these opinions on cultural and narrative criticism are also found in his book, *Strange Gourmets: Sophistication, Theory, and the Novel* (forthcoming Duke Univ. Press, 1997), and in the essay, "Proustian Anachronisms: Sophistication, Naïveté, and Gay Narrativity," presented at the 1994 MLA meeting in San Diego. I am grateful to Litvak for permitting me to quote from these sources.

49. Eve Kosofsky Sedgwick, *Tendencies* (Durham, NC: Duke Univ. Press, 1993), pp. 3–4.

50. This is Theodor Adorno's position, which Andreas Huyssen demystifies at length in *After the Great Divide.*

51. Edelman, *Homographesis,* xvi–xvii

52. James Clifford, "Introduction: Partial Truths," in *Writing Culture: The Poetics and*

Politics of Ethnography, ed. James Clifford and George E. Marcus (Berkeley: Univ. of California Press, 1986), pp. 12, 15.

53. Armstrong, "Textual Harassment," pp. 410, 403, 418.

54. Roland Barthes, *The Pleasure of the Text,* trans. Richard Miller (New York: Hill and Wang, 1975), p. 47.

CHAPTER ONE

1. Kate Millett, *Sexual Politics* (New York: Avon, 1969), p. 146.

2. Charlotte Brontë, *Villette* (1853, Harmondsworth: Penguin, 1979), p. 349. All further references to this work are cited in the text.

3. Dorrit Cohn, *Transparent Minds: Narrative Modes for Presenting Consciousness in Fiction* (Princeton, NJ: Princeton Univ. Press, 1978), pp. 7–9.

4. Michel Foucault, *Discipline and Punish: The Birth of the Prison,* trans. Alan Sheridan (1975; rpt., New York: Vintage, 1979), pp. 201–3; the quotation is from p. 200. All further references to this work are cited in the text.

5. D. A. Miller, *The Novel and the Police* (Berkeley: Univ. of California Press, 1987), p. viii. All further references to this work are cited in the text.

6. For a useful mapping of the benefits that might come from a combination of feminist and Foucauldian methodology, see Irene Diamond's and Lee Quinby's introduction to *Feminism and Foucault: Reflections on Resistance,* ed. Diamond and Quinby (Boston: Northeastern Univ. Press, 1988), pp. ix–xx. On the pockets of resistance to discipline, sometimes submerged in Foucault's writings, that a feminist perspective is suited to tease out, see Frances Bartkowski, "Epistemic Drift in Foucault," in the same volume, pp. 43–58. *Villette* has attracted the attention of several superb feminist critics over the years; I have particularly profited by the analyses of Sandra Gilbert and Susan Gubar, Karen Lawrence, Nina Auerbach, Nancy Miller, Patricia Yaeger, Brenda Silver (all cited below), and Mary Jacobus, *Reading Woman: Essays in Feminist Criticism* (New York: Columbia Univ. Press, 1986), chapter 2: "The Buried Letter: *Villette,*" pp. 41–61.

7. See Foucault's description of Napoleon as "the individual who looms over everything with a single gaze which no detail, however minute, can escape" (217); in the nineteenth-century imagination, Napoleon represented, Foucault argues, the modern exercise of discipline married to the power of the sovereign, from which conjunction the modern state was born. Indeed, M. Paul's uncanny ability "to wear eyes before, behind, and on each side of him" (310) aptly echoes Foucault's evocation of the century's new model of the police as "thousands of eyes posted everywhere" (214).

8. Foucault comments on the confessional as a productive, rather than repressive, site of nineteenth-century discourses of sexuality in *The History of Sexuality,* vol. 1, *An Introduction,* trans. Robert Hurley (1976; rpt., New York: Vintage, 1980), pp. 58–70. Brontë's imagistic equation between "magic" and "mystic" lattices is also noted in Sally Shuttleworth's "'The Surveillance of a Sleepless Eye': The Constitution of Neurosis in *Villette,*" in *One Culture: Essays in Science and Literature,* ed. George Levine and Alan Rauch (Madison: Univ. of Wisconsin Press, 1987), p. 320. Tracing the contemporary medical discourses informing Brontë's representation of female psychological illness, Shuttleworth's insightful essay tallies the many levels of Foucauldian supervisory discipline at work in the novel. Shuttleworth also notes (314–15) that Dr. John, a physician with an unflappable belief in his ability to penetrate to the innermost truths of all his patients, including Lucy, is another of the text's emblematic agents of disciplinary supervision, embodying the new power of

the nineteenth-century medical institution analyzed by Foucault in *The Birth of the Clinic: An Archaeology of Medical Perception*, trans. A. M. Sheridan Smith (1963; rpt., New York: Pantheon, 1973) and anticipating Freud's psychoanalytic methods in his ability to uncover the heart of his patients' hidden secrets.

9. One page later Brontë makes the analogy between the two women explicit, when the visit of Dr. John to the pensionnat leaves Lucy searching for a "key" to the "riddle" of his demeanor "almost as sedulously as madame had sought a guide to useful knowledge in my toilet drawers" (187). When Lucy receives her first letter from Dr. John, it is appropriate that she is figured as "gliding" through the schoolrooms and "mounting noiseless" (323) to the dormitories as she searches for a private space in which to read it, her ghostlike movements parodying those of her sister in surveillance, Mme. Beck. For two influential perspectives on the doubling functions of these women, see Sandra M. Gilbert and Susan Gubar, *The Madwoman in the Attic: The Woman Writer and the Nineteenth-Century Literary Imagination* (New Haven, CT: Yale Univ. Press, 1979), pp. 408–9, and Nina Auerbach, *Communities of Women: An Idea in Fiction* (Cambridge, MA: Harvard Univ. Press, 1978), pp. 103, 110–13.

10. Feminist inquiries into the male gaze and its impact on female representation begin with Laura Mulvey, "Visual Pleasure and Narrative Cinema," *Screen* 16, no. 3 (1975), and Mary Anne Doane, "Woman's Stake: Filming the Female Body," *October* 17 (1981). For a range of work on the possibility of a female gaze, not only in film but other genres, see also E. Ann Kaplan, "Is the Gaze Male?" in *Powers of Desire: The Politics of Sexuality*, ed. Ann Snitow, Christine Stansell, and Sharon Thompson (New York: Monthly Review Press, 1983), pp. 309–27; Jacqueline Rose, *Sexuality in the Field of Vision* (London: Verso, 1986); the various essays in *The Female Gaze: Women as Viewers of Popular Culture*, ed. Lorraine Gamman and Margaret Marshment (Seattle: The Real Comet Press, 1989); and Beth Newman, "'The Situation of the Looker-On': Gender, Narration, and the Gaze in *Wuthering Heights*," *PMLA* 105 (1990): 1029–41.

11. For an excellent analysis of Brontë's motifs of the stage, theatricality, and spectacle, along with their destabilizing propensities, see Joseph Litvak, "Charlotte Brontë and the Scene of Instruction: Authority and Subversion in *Villette*," *Nineteenth-Century Literature* 42 (Winter 1988): 467–89, a longer version of which appears in his *Caught in the Act: Theatricality and the Nineteenth-Century English Novel* (Los Angeles and Berkeley: Univ. of California Press, 1992). The world of *Villette* abounds in grand spectacles and dramatic set pieces, including, in addition to the concert chapter, the school play in which Lucy performs on Mme. Beck's birthday fête, the performance of the legendary Vashti to which Dr. John takes Lucy, Lucy's trip to the museum where the Cleopatra is on display, and the various impromptu theatricals, as it were, enacted on the estrade or before the school examiners in the classrooms of Mme. Beck's academy. As Litvak demonstrates, the school play in which Lucy (half) cross-dresses as a man is a particularly vivid example of the dissolution of the normative boundaries separating actor and audience, those who see and who are seen (478–81); for as Lucy discovers the "private" drama that is unfolding in the audience, and its parallel to the triangular "public" drama being enacted on stage, she modulates her role until she (like her costume) is playing on both sides of the boundary at once.

12. In addition to these instances, figurative and literal, of incarceration, one might also note the images of constriction that characterize Lucy's various living abodes, from the "two hot, close rooms" she occupies near the beginning of the novel to the "walled-in and guarded" recesses of Mme. Beck's pensionnat (97, 348), within whose confines Lucy fancies herself a "long-buried prisoner" (356). During the "Long Vacation" sequence, the school

literally becomes a mental asylum (another of Foucault's carcereal establishments) as Lucy, left in charge of a helpless cretin, moves toward total nervous collapse; imagining herself "*prisoned* with some strange tameless animal" (229), she finds herself as much inmate as keeper, possessed by her own mental demons. Even the pastoral scene of Lucy's convalescence, La Terrasse, where her soul "re-enter[s] her *prison*"—the body—"with pain" (237), is figured as another kind of enclosure: a "very safe *asylum*" (244; emphases added) is the unintentionally ambiguous phrase Mrs. Bretton uses to describe its womblike insularity. The imprisoning potential of these dwelling places, literal and figurative, is also expressed in a series of analogous images in which enclosure becomes a deliberate (if generally unsuccessful) means of keeping potentially disruptive emotions under lock and key. For example, having awakened to the "keen relish" of acting during Madame's birthday fête, Lucy immediately decides this longing "must be put by," and so she "fasten[s it] in with the lock of a resolution which"—so she claims—"neither Time nor Temptation has since picked" (211). Likewise, Lucy's object in going to confession is to pour out her "long pent-up pain" into a contained "vessel whence it could not be again diffused" (234); and of the treasured memory of Dr. John's unconscious assistance to her the night of her arrival in Villette, she thinks, "it was a pleasant thought, laid by in my own mind, and best kept there" (306).

13. The phrase "liberal subject" refers to conceptions of subjectivity predicated on the humanist myth of the essential self, whose autonomy, inwardness, and privacy are the origin of its very being.

14. Karen Lawrence, "The Cypher: Disclosure and Reticence in *Villette*," *Nineteenth-Century Literature* 42 (Winter 1988): 448–50, offers a superb analysis of Lucy's manipulation of her signifying functions and her use of rhetorical figures as "coverings."

15. Charlotte Brontë, "Farewell to Angria," in *Legends of Angria,* ed. Fanny Ratchford with William Clyde DeVane (New Haven, CT: Yale Univ. Press, 1933), p. 316; see the discussion of this piece in my introduction.

16. Lawrence, "The Cypher," p. 453. See also Brenda R. Silver, "The Reflecting Reader in *Villette*," in *The Voyage In: Fictions of Female Development,* ed. Elizabeth Abel, Marianne Hirsch, and Elizabeth Langland (Hanover, NH: Univ. of New England Press, 1983): 90–111, on Lucy's strategic reeducation of the reader.

17. The reticences characterizing Lucy's elliptical narration are abetted, furthermore, by the self-consciously teasing games she plays with the reader: "Cancel the whole of that, if you please, reader—" (117), she playfully enjoins us at one point; "But stop—I must not, from the faithful narrator, degenerate into partial eulogist" (272), she parodies her role as narrator at another. The general instability of the narrator/reader relation is mirrored in the tendency of the line separating Lucy's experiencing and narrating selves to blur indiscriminately. It is precisely this slippage that gives rise to the complementary inverse of the text's blanks and lacunae—those fissures or gaps through which the emotional subtext of Lucy's narrative unexpectedly and unpredictably erupts, daunting us, for once, with its *lack* of reticence: "Oh, my childhood! I had feelings; passive as I lived, little as I spoke, cold as I looked . . . I *could* feel" (175); "Oh!—O speak the truth, and drop that tone of false calm which outwears nature's endurance" (350). Tony Tanner offers a perceptive commentary on these self-reflexive narrative moments in his introduction to the Penguin edition, pp. 45–46.

18. In addition to these examples, the question of self-representation arises in numerous scenes in which Lucy encounters her image in mirrors, such as the moment when Ginerva and Lucy stand side by side before the looking glass in chapter 14, or the unexpected glimpse Lucy catches of herself in her pink dress at the concert hall in chapter 20:

"Thus for the first, and perhaps only time in my life, I enjoyed the 'giftie' of seeing myself as others see me. No need to dwell on the result. It brought a jar of discord, a pang of regret" (286).

19. This is the general thesis of John Maynard's chapter on the novel in *Charlotte Brontë and Sexuality* (Cambridge: Cambridge Univ. Press, 1984), pp. 164–211, which he calls "the epic of [Lucy's] initiation into sexual awareness" (164) and "sexual growth" (180). A differently inflected reading of repression as the mainstay of Lucy's ability to maintain "erotic faith" in face of the continual loss of love informs Robert Polhemus's account in *Erotic Faith: Being in Love from Jane Austen to D. H. Lawrence* (Chicago: Univ. of Chicago Press, 1990), pp. 108–36. Robert Kiely offers a reading of how Lucy transforms repression into work without necessarily "laying to rest" the ghost of repression in *Reverse Tradition: Postmodern Fictions and the Nineteenth-Century Novel* (Cambridge, MA: Harvard Univ. Press, 1993), pp. 214–34.

20. The analysis that follows of the psychosexual and autoerotic contours of this quest owes greatly to Ruthanna Hooke's superb insights in her seminar paper, "Keeping the Secret: Lucy Snowe's Narrative in *Villette*" (15 May 1986).

21. Teresa de Lauretis, *Alice Doesn't: Feminism, Semiotics, Cinema* (Bloomington: Indiana Univ. Press, 1984), pp. 106–24; the quotation is from p. 108.

22. Peter Brooks, *Reading for the Plot: Design and Intention in Narrative* (New York: Knopf, 1984), pp. 102–4.

23. Susan Winnett, "Coming Unstrung: Women, Men, Narrative, and (the) Principles of Pleasure," *PMLA* 105 (May 1990): 516.

24. Teresa de Lauretis, *Technologies of Gender* (Bloomington: Indiana Univ. Press, 1987), p. 10. The deconstructive and Lacanian implications of Brontë's representation of Lucy's identity as unstable and shifting are well illustrated in Christina Crosby's "Charlotte Brontë's Haunted Text," *Studies in English Literature* 24, no. 4 (Autumn 1984): 701–15. Lawrence notes, however, that Lucy's elusiveness should be differentiated from a Lacanian reading of absence or lack that "sees woman as unrepresentable"; rather, Brontë has chosen to present "the enigma of Lucy Snowe . . . as a complex, shifting nexus of meaning and deferral of meaning that, like the sign itself, never refers to an ultimate and stable identity" ("The Cypher," p. 455). In a similar vein, Nancy K. Miller notes that Lucy anticipates the Lacanian subject, in that as a "female writing subject" she "also resides elsewhere, in the 'field of language' that constitutes her otherness to herself"; see "Changing the Subject: Authorship, Writing, and the Reader," in *Feminist Studies/Critical Studies,* ed. Teresa de Lauretis (Bloomington: Indiana Univ. Press, 1986), p. 116.

25. My language here draws on the contrast between D. A. Miller's phrase, "place elsewhere" (76), and Lawrence's "elsewhere of meaning" ("The Cypher," p. 457).

26. For complementary critiques of Miller, see Robert Caserio, "Supreme Court Discourse vs. Homosexual Fiction," *South Atlantic Quarterly* 88 (Winter 1989): 267–99, and John Kucich, "Transgression in Trollope: Dishonesty and the Antibourgeois Elite," *English Literary History* 56, no. 3 (Fall 1989): 593–618. Caserio forcefully argues that Foucauldian analyses of power such as Miller's blur distinctions between fictional and nonfictional modes of narrative discourse. Less explicitly than Caserio but not the less emphatically, Kucich argues that the nineteenth-century novel does not unilaterally police or domesticate desire; rather, the genre, like bourgeois middle-class society, in fact gives expression to transgressive energies that it values and affirms: "It is easy to overlook the transgressive, antibourgeois elements" (595) of novelists like Trollope, Kucich states as he sets his theory in opposition to those Foucauldian interpretations that "superciliously" claim that the novel

is inevitably "in cahoots with the police" and a "purveyor of middle-class disciplinary norms" (593).

27. See Patricia Yaeger's reading of *Villette* in *Honey-Mad Women: Emancipatory Strategies in Women's Writing* (New York: Columbia Univ. Press, 1988), pp. 44–51, which details how Brontë's appropriation of Romantic poetic language—particularly the imagery of Keats' "Hyperion"—in the park episode creates a multivoicedness that attests to the possibilities, rather than constrictions, that exist in the play of language for the woman novelist.

CHAPTER TWO

1. D. H. Lawrence to A. W. McLeod (21 Dec. 1916), in *The Collected Letters of D. H. Lawrence*, 2 vols., ed. and intro. Harry T. Moore (New York: Viking Press, 1962), 1: 495.

2. Muriel Rukeyser, "The Birth of Venus" (1958), in *The Norton Anthology of Literature by Women: The Tradition in English*, ed. Sandra M. Gilbert and Susan Gubar (New York: Norton, 1985), pp. 1781–82.

3. James Joyce, *Ulysses*, ed. Hans Gabler (1922; rpt., New York: Vintage Books, 1986), "Sirens" chapter, p. 633.

4. Luce Irigaray, "The 'Mechanics' of Fluids," in *This Sex Which Is Not One*, trans. Catherine Porter (1979; rpt., Ithaca, NY: Cornell Univ. Press, 1985), pp. 106–7.

5. Sigmund Freud, *Dora: An Analysis of a Case of Hysteria*, ed. Phillip Reiff (written 1899, published 1905; rpt., New York: Collier Books, 1963), p. 67, and "The Dissection of the Psychical Personality," in *New Introductory Lectures on Psychoanalysis*, trans. and ed. James Strachey (1933; rpt., New York: Norton, 1964), p. 71, respectively. (See the introduction, note 8, for Freud's *Three Essays*, cited hereafter in the text.) Images of mental "dams," "collateral channels," and the "floods" of component instincts that threaten to "break through" the barriers raised by ego defenses punctuate Freud's discussions of the emergence of perverse sexuality in the psychoneuroses, the process of sublimation, and the presence of polymorphous sexuality in children, whose "mental dams" are less fully constructed, in the *Three Essays* (see esp. pp. 43–44, 57–58). Nearly identical wording to the passage in *Three Essays* (36) cited in my text occurs in *Dora:* "A stream of water which meets with an obstacle in the river-bed is dammed up and flows back into old channels which had formerly seemed fated to run dry" (68). The metaphor of blockage also occurs on p. 30, where Freud compares Dora's first, incomplete narrative of her sexual trauma to an "unnavigable river," whose "stream" has been "choked" and "divided" into misleading tributaries by masses of rock, shallows, and sandbanks. All further references to *Dora* are cited in the text.

6. D. H. Lawrence, *The Virgin and the Gipsy* (1930; rpt., New York: Vintage, 1984), pp. 173, 155. All further references to this work are cited in the text.

7. Kate Chopin, *The Awakening and Selected Stories* (1899; rpt., Harmondsworth, England: Penguin, 1984), p. 123; emphasis added. All further references to this edition are cited in the text.

8. Lutz Rossin, quoted in Klaus Theweleit, *Male Fantasies: Women, Floods, Bodies, History*, vol. 1, trans. Stephen Conway (1977; rpt., Minneapolis: Univ. of Minnesota Press, 1987), p. 231. Women's "crime," Theweleit adduces from his overview of Freikorps literature, is "that they excite the men too much" (180). All further references to Theweleit are cited in the text. One other critic who draws upon water imagery to interpret the ambivalences of modernist writing, and who thus incorporates Theweleit's interpretations of female floods into her analyses, is Marianne DeKoven, *Rich and Strange: Gender, History, Modernism* (Princeton, NJ: Princeton Univ. Press, 1991), pp. 33–37; her interesting choice of water imagery as a focus for her analyses, however, remains a primarily thematic and

figural one and does not, as this chapter attempts to do, link the fictional representation of such floods to the hydraulic models of turn-of-the-century sexology, to the channeling and damming metaphors of early Freudian psychology, or to the specific techniques whereby protomodernist narratives incorporate into their very forms a flow or drift that mirrors the psychic states of their awakening protagonists.

9. Gilles Deleuze and Félix Guattari, *Anti-Oedipus: Capitalism and Schizophrenia,* trans. Robert Hurley et al. (1972; rpt., Minneapolis: Univ. of Minnesota Press, 1983), p. 116. Theweleit is greatly influenced by Deleuze and Guattari, who reject Freudian theories of the civilized sublimation of desire in favor of a more radical model of instinct as continual flow.

10. Irigaray, "The 'Mechanics' of Fluids," pp. 116 and 106–7. Irigaray's italics have been omitted. All further references to Irigaray's essay are cited in the text.

11. N. Katherine Hayles, "Gender Encoding in Fluid Mechanics: Masculine Channels and Feminine Flows," *differences* 4, no. 2 (Summer 1992), pp. 19, 27, 31.

12. See Theweleit, *Male Fantasies,* pp. 264, 270–72. This is not to suggest that these fantasies of deterritorialization are not colonizing; in fact, by their obsessive focus on women's bodies, they participate in the *re*territorialization process.

13. William Action, *The Functions and Disorders of the Reproductive Organs* (1857), quoted in Gail Finney, *Women in Modern Drama: Freud, Feminism, and European Theater at the Turn of the Century* (Ithaca, NY: Cornell Univ. Press, 1989), pp. 3–4.

14. Chopin's comment, from an 1894 diary entry, is quoted in Per Seyerstad, *Kate Chopin, A Critical Biography* (Baton Rouge: Louisiana State Univ. Press, 1969), p. 84. The fact that Chopin is addressing unveiled "human" nature and Freud, unveiled "female" minds imaged as bodies, of course reveals the critical difference in their uses of this topos. On the gender politics involved in the nineteenth-century scientific and medical discourse in which "unveiling" is a trope for attaining knowledge and in which the unveiled female body becomes figure for both desired Nature and Truth, see Ludmilla Jordanova, *Sexual Visions: Images of Gender in Science and Medicine between the Eighteenth and Twentieth Centuries* (Madison: Univ. of Wisconsin Press, 1989), pp. 87–94.

15. My wording paraphrases Elizabeth Young's formulation—itself a riposte to the much quoted passage in *The History of Sexuality* (see the introduction, note 4) where Foucault speaks of the confession as a "ritual of discourse in which the speaking subject is also the subject of the statement" (61)—in her seminar paper "Sexual Stories in Freud and Lawrence" (March 1985).

16. Jeffrey Weeks, *Sex, Politics, and Society: The Regulation of Sexuality since 1800* (London and New York: Longman, 1981), p. 7.

17. This placement, I argue, occurs irrespective of actual dates of composition. While Freud's and Chopin's texts literally emerge at the turn of the century (Freud writes *Dora* in 1899, Chopin publishes *The Awakening* the same year), Lawrence's narrative, composed as a draft in the mid-1920s and published posthumously in 1930, psychologically and epistemologically situates itself in the transition from "Victorian" to "modern" epochs—a transition that, as Lawrence shows, is locally variable.

18. Foucault, *History of Sexuality,* pp. 79–80; Weeks, *Sex, Politics, and Society,* p. 6.

19. See, for example, Judith Butler's argument throughout *Gender Trouble: Feminism and the Subversion of Identity* (New York: Routledge, 1990) that such conceptions of "inner" cores or sexual essences are themselves constructions of gender, the fantasmatic production of signs inscribed on rather than within the body.

20. Weeks, *Sex, Politics, and Society,* p. 9. Hayles, in "Gender Encoding," also comments on the hydraulic imagery that Freud employs to describe desire, which constructs

"the libido essentially as a *flow that must be regulated*" (30) and which Hayles then links to Victorian assumptions about spermatic expenditure as the loss of a vital substance that must be carefully conserved, regulated, and "spent" wisely: "Encoded into this imagery are the imperatives not only of nineteenth-century thermodynamics, but also of the socially constructed experience of male sexuality, with its deep assumptions about equivalences between life force and seminal fluid. . . . An orgasm spent one way cannot be spent another, so the wise man husbands his resources and spends them where they count" (30–31).

21. Foucault, *History of Sexuality,* p. 104.

The Awakening

22. Wendy Martin, "Introduction," in *New Essays on The Awakening,* ed. Wendy Martin (New York: Cambridge Univ. Press, 1988), p. 21.

23. For one perspective on the turn-of-the-century cultural project of American man-making engendered by a national anxiety over the (supposed) enervation and degeneration of men issuing from a breakdown of gender distinctions and boundaries, see Mark Seltzer, "The Love-Master," in *Engendering Men: The Question of Male Feminist Criticism,* ed. Joseph A. Boone and Michael Cadden (New York: Routledge, 1990), pp. 140–58.

24. Metaphors of clothing and divestiture abound in the text; when Robert unexpectedly announces he is going to leave Grand Isle, Edna feels "that her whole existence was dulled, like a faded garment which seems to be no longer worth wearing" (95); leaving the traumatic scene of Adèle's childbirth at the end of the text, Edna feels "all the tearing emotion of the last few hours . . . fall away from her like a somber, uncomfortable garment, which she had but to loosen to be rid of" (172).

25. Barbara Claire Freeman notes that although "the ocean is *The Awakening*'s central character, the axis around which the narrative turns," very "few critics have discussed [its] role . . . an omission made all the more startling [by] Chopin's insistence on it," in *The Feminine Sublime: Gender and Excess in Women's Fiction* (Berkeley: Univ. of California Press, 1995), pp. 26–27, 31. Freeman argues that the ocean becomes Chopin's symbol of a female version of the sublime, whose radical affirmation of "flux and dispersion" rather than the polarization of opposites such as life and death owes more to Sappho's than Longinus's evocation of sublimity. For male critics since Longinus, Freeman suggests, the sublime evokes a "potentially uncontainable form of excess" that is summoned forth precisely in order for it to be contained and "ensure that the boundary between self and other will remain unblurred" (26), an observation that resonates interestingly with those of Theweleit and Hayles, and that, on a philosophical level, complements the argument I make in this chapter.

26. Since this novel's rediscovery in the fifties, criticism has typically reduced the text to starkly polar extremes, pigeonholing Edna either as a "rebel" against female norms *or* as a "victim" of her socialized role, judging her quest for independence and identity either as a (spiritual) "success" or (material) "failure," and classifying the novel within American literary forms either as an Emersonian romance of the soul *or* as a Darwinian tragedy of the biologically determined body (typifying the turn-of-the-century naturalist movement). Such dichotomous thinking, I argue, simplifies the deliberate complexity infusing Chopin's representation of the contradictions built into Edna's psyche and her cultural context. See Martin, "Introduction," pp. 11–14, for a summary of these critical viewpoints.

27. "Books of the Day," *Chicago Times-Herald* (1 June 1899): 9, reprinted in the Norton Critical Edition of *The Awakening,* ed. Margaret Culley (New York: Norton, 1976), p. 145.

28. Notable exceptions include Marianne DeKoven, who analyzes the novel at length as an example of modernist writing "under erasure" in *Rich and Strange,* pp. 139–48, and Michael T. Gilmore, "Revolt Against Nature: The Problematic Modernism of *The Awakening,*" in *New Essays,* ed. Martin, pp. 59–87. As Lewis Leary says of the novel's complex web of illusion, "Almost every incident or reference in *The Awakening* anticipates an incident or reference that follows it or will remind a reader of something that has happened before," in *Southern Excursions: Essays on Mark Twain and Others* (Baton Rouge: Louisiana State Univ. Press, 1971), p. 172.

29. It should be noted that Chopin does not recognize the possibility that such a notion of interior sexual authenticity may itself be a social construction; Michael T. Gilmore, in "Revolt Against Nature," makes the point that Chopin, like Edna, ultimately believes in an authentic "nature" (of self, of the world) on which truth is grounded. While this may be true, however, it does not automatically mean, as Gilmore also argues, that Chopin demonstrates "no inkling of the decentered, internally conflicted self made familiar in the twentieth century by Freud" (83)—indeed the following pages argue that the novel registers an acute sense of the divided consciousness hypothesized by Freud.

30. This "aimless" wandering recurs on several levels throughout the text. Thus, "let[ting] her mind wander," Edna comes to realize that "she herself—her *present* self" is profoundly different from "the *other* self" (88; emphases added) that the external world perceives. Likewise, letting her body lead her where it will, Edna comes to take pleasure in "wander[ing] alone into strange and unfamiliar places" (109)—byways that echo the forgotten, unused channels of libidinal activity into which, in Freud's metaphor, the reactivated component instincts pour.

31. For an analysis of the revolutionary political language of (American and women's) rights infiltrating Chopin's discourse, see Ivy Schweitzer, "Maternal Discourse and the Romance of Self-Possession in Kate Chopin's *The Awakening,*" *boundary 2* (Spring 1990): 158–86. The fact that Chopin originally titled the novel *A Solitary Soul* is indicative of its place within the American literary heritage of transcendentalism, self-reliance, individualism, and existential freedom.

32. Dorrit Cohn, in *Transparent Minds: Narrative Modes for Presenting Consciousness in Fiction* (Princeton, NJ: Princeton Univ. Press, 1978), pp. 11–12, uses the term *psychonarration* (as opposed to the more familiar *omniscient narration*) to pinpoint the most indirect novelistic method of rendering consciousness: the narrator's third-person, past-tense discourse about a character's consciousness. In an analysis of that realm of sensuousness that "exceeds the logic of realistic discourse" whose approach differs from my own, Jean Wyatt applies Julia Kristeva's theory of the semiotic or maternal register in language to Chopin's attempt to move the reader "beyond thought and language," into "an alternative language" of sound and sense, in *Reconstructing Desire: The Role of the Unconscious in Women's Reading and Writing* (Chapel Hill: Univ. of North Carolina Press, 1990), pp. 64, 68.

33. Stroking a cat is a symbol of female masturbation, as Freud indirectly reminds the readers of *Dora* when he defends the explicitness with which he addresses topics like female autoeroticism by announcing, in a deliberately lewd pun, "*J'appelle un chat un chat*" (65).

34. For an analysis of the tentativeness that Chopin interjects into the narrative through sentence-structure choice (particularly in the repetition of "as if" clauses), see Christina Giorcelli, "Edna's Wisdom: A Transitional and Numinous Merging," in *New Essays,* ed. Martin, pp. 120–21.

35. Judith Kegan Gardiner, "On Female Identity and Writing by Women," *Critical*

Inquiry 8, no. 2 (Winter 1981): 353; Susan Stanford Friedman, "Beyond White and Other: Relationality and Narratives of Race in Feminist Discourse," *Signs: A Journal of Women in Society and Culture* 21, no. 1 (Autumn 1995): 1–49. See also Elizabeth Abel, "(E)merging Identities: The Dynamics of Female Friendship in Contemporary Fiction by Women," *Signs: A Journal of Women in Society and Culture* 6 (1981): 413–35; Joan Lidoff, "Virginia Woolf's Feminine Sentences: The Mother-Daughter World of the Lighthouse," *Literature and Psychology* 32 (1986): 43–59; Marianne Hirsch, *The Mother/Daughter Plot: Narrative, Psychoanalysis, Feminism* (Bloomington: Indiana Univ. Press, 1989), pp. 162–89; Shirley Nelson Garner, Claire Kahane, and Madelon Sprengnether, eds., *The (M)other Tongue: Essays in Feminist Psychoanalytic Interpretation* (Ithaca, NY: Cornell Univ. Press, 1985); Nancy Chodorow, *The Reproduction of Mothering: Psychoanalysis and the Sociology of Gender* (Berkeley: Univ. of California Press, 1978); and Julia Kristeva, *Desire in Language: A Semiotic Approach to Literature and Art*, ed. Léon S. Roudiez, trans. Thomas Gora, Alice Jardine, and Léon S. Roudiez (1977; rpt., New York: Columbia Univ. Press, 1980).

36. See, for example, Seyersted's assertion in *Kate Chopin* (an account with otherwise strong feminist sympathies) that "it is Edna's three men [Robert, Arobin, Léonce] who serve as *real catalysts*," whereas the women are set forth as dualities or foils to her awakening (155, 154; emphasis added). One critic who refutes this stance is Elaine Showalter in "Tradition and the Individual Talent: *The Awakening* as a Solitary Book," in *New Essays*, ed. Martin, who writes, "Edna's awakening, moreover, begins not with a man, but with Adèle" (45), and relates this fact to the homosocial world of women's culture in the nineteenth century, "[which] in fact allowed much leeway for physical intimacy and touch" (36). On female homosocial worlds, see Carol Smith-Rosenberg, "The Female World of Love and Ritual: Relations between Women in Nineteenth-Century America" (1975), reprinted in her *Disorderly Conduct: Visions of Gender in Victorian America* (New York: Knopf, 1985), and Martha Vicinus, *Independent Women: Work and Community for Single Women, 1850–1920* (Chicago: Univ. of Chicago Press, 1985).

37. Sandra Gilbert, introduction to the Penguin Classics Edition, of *The Awakening* (see note 7 above), pp. 25–26.

38. The oxymoronic extremes tied together in the phrase "sensuous Madonna" epitomize the deconstructive element in Chopin's representation of Adèle; the phrase occurs, significantly, in a passage describing Edna's attempt to sketch—that is, to represent—Adèle notable for its headily eroticized language: "She had long wished *to try herself on* Madame Ratignolle. Never had that lady seemed *a more tempting subject* than at that moment, seated there like some *sensuous Madonna*" (55; emphases added).

39. The salient difference from the Freudian model is the nurturing rather than invasive position Adèle assumes as analyst to Edna's analysand. In yet another example of metaphors anticipating reality, this clothing metaphor—"loosening a . . . *mantle* of reserve"— is literalized as Edna "remove[s] her collar and open[s] her dress at the throat" (59). The erotic current between the two women is underlined as Edna takes Adèle's fan to fan "both herself and her companion" and as they ineffectually attempt to secure their fluttering skirts, hairpins, and hatpins from the erotically teasing sea breeze (59). The importance of men's absence ("In some unaccountable way they had escaped from Robert" [58]) in unleashing Edna's uninhibited flow of memory can be measured in what she now reveals to Adèle (60–63) about her childhood, as opposed to what she has earlier *withheld* in telling Robert about growing up "in the old Kentucky blue-grass country" (47).

40. The fact that it is Robert, himself enamored of Edna, who entreats Mlle. Reisz to

play for Edna ironically confirms the primacy of the women's bond; to borrow the terms that Terry Castle has developed to theorize lesbian desire, one might say that he serves as the dispensable (male) intermediary in a triangle whose structural function is to unite the two women. See Castle, "Sylvia Townsend Warner and the Counterplot of Lesbian Fiction," *Textual Practice* 4, no. 2 (Summer 1990): 213–35.

41. Wyatt, *Reconstructing Desire,* p. 73. Having "loosened" her hair as well as her clothing, Edna falls to sleep in a strikingly open pose that attests the ease she feels with her unfettered body: "She clasped her hands easily above her head, and it was thus she fell asleep" (84). The positive effects of this bodily awakening are confirmed a few scenes later by Dr. Mandelet's observation, when dining with the Pontelliers, that his hostess has metamorphosed into "a being . . . palpitant with *the forces of life*": "There was *no repression* in her glance or gesture. She reminded him of some beautiful, sleek animal *waking up* in the sun" (123; emphases added).

42. Thanks to Moira Wallace for this insight, in her untitled seminar paper on Chopin and Lawrence (1985).

43. See Sigmund Freud, "Female Sexuality" (1931), in *Standard Edition,* vol. 21, pp. 221–43; and "Femininity" (1933), reprinted in *New Introductory Lectures on Psychoanalysis,* trans. and ed. James Strachey (New York: Norton, 1964), pp. 194–211. The latter essay is an expanded version of the former.

44. Deleuze and Guattari, *Anti-Oedipus,* p. 67.

45. I quote Theweleit's summary of Deleuze and Guattari's argument (211, 255); see *Anti-Oedipus,* chaps. 1 and 2.

46. On Deleuze and Guattari's critique of Freud, see Theweleit's useful commentary, pp. 210–14. As Theweleit summarizes it, "The chief criticism leveled . . . against Freud is that he invariably saw as the unconscious itself what were *in fact representational forms of social repression. . . .* [Deleuze and Guattari] don't dispute the aptness of the names he gave to ideas he considered significant, such as 'incest' or 'castration.' Yet, by declaring these to be formations and modes of expression of the unconscious, Freud himself contributed to *the repression of the unconscious as a productive force* that explodes the framework of authority in every society" (214; emphases added).

47. Thorstein Veblen, *The Theory of the Leisure Class: An Economic History of Institutions* (1899; rpt., New York: The Modern Library, 1931), pp. 81–83.

48. An acute analysis of this dynamic appears in Elizabeth Ammons's chapter on Chopin in *Conflicting Stories: American Women Writers at the Turn of the Twentieth Century* (New York: Oxford Univ. Press, 1991), pp. 74–76. The Creole dimension of the New Orleans society into which the Protestant Edna has married, moreover, highlights the complicated ways in which ethnicity intersects with issues of class and sexuality in both facilitating and impeding her awakening; to cite one example, the sexual frankness accepted in Creole company society at first shocks, then draws Edna out; yet the chivalric flirtatiousness also condoned within its highly moralistic strictures turns out to betray Edna when Robert's flirtation comes to mean more to her than a mere form. If race is the "repressed" of the text, it returns with a vengeance at the end in the reappearances of the Mexican girl Mariequita, who also makes palpable Chopin's understated commentary on the difficult intersections of sexuality and ethnicity; for if Mariequita's blatant wearing of her sexuality in front of Robert and his brother Victor initially offends Edna because it so easily achieves the expressions she desires but finds unnerving, Mariequita's reappearance on the beach at the very end of the text to name the Anglo-Creole obsession with "infidelity" for what it is ("it

was the fashion to be in love with married people" [173]) underlines the fact that so-called adulterous desire is constructed as a specifically *upper-middle-class* "worry" in the world that Edna inhabits. DeKoven, in *Rich and Strange,* p. 145, also comments on race and class as the "suppressed" of the novel.

49. Cynthia Griffin Wolff, "Thanatos and Eros: Kate Chopin's *The Awakening,*" *American Quarterly* 25 (Oct. 1973): 449–71; reprinted in the Norton edition of *The Awakening,* cited here, pp. 207, 208, 213; emphases added.

50. Significantly, their friendship is characterized by constant chatter (no silencing of one by the other, as illustrated in the opening vignette where Edna is rudely wakened by Léonce), and the repeated image of reciprocal glances (illustrating the degree to which Robert and Edna initially function as equally desiring subjects).

51. Patricia Yaeger, "'A Language Which Nobody Understood': Emancipatory Strategies in *The Awakening,*" *Novel* 20, no. 3 (Spring 1987), p. 207; emphasis added. The "romantic stories" to which Yaeger refers are Continental plots of illicit because adulterous love like that of *Madame Bovary.* Interesting in this regard is Willa Cather's review of *The Awakening,* whose author she criticizes for being a "Creole Bovary"; both Emma and Edna, Cather grouses, belong to "a class . . . forever clamoring in our ears, that demands more romance out of life than God put into it." What Cather misses is that Chopin is self-consciously critiquing Bovarian passion even when Edna isn't. See Cather's review [signed "Sibert"], in "Books and Magazines," *Pittsburgh Leader* (8 July 1899), p. 6, reprinted in the Norton Critical Edition.

52. See René Girard, *Deceit, Desire, and the Novel,* trans. Yvonne Freccero (1961; rpt., Baltimore, MD: The Johns Hopkins Univ. Press, 1965).

53. Edna's behavior is characterized by a number of the classic signs of clinical depression. However, she emphatically does *not* suffer from any of the three nervous disorders—anorexia, hysteria, neurasthenia—constructed around "femininity" (as a way of controlling it) by the medico-psychiatric professions in the late nineteenth century; for definitions of these "female maladies," see Elaine Showalter, *The Female Malady: Women, Madness, and English Culture, 1830–1980* (1985; Harmondsworth, UK: Penguin, 1987), pp. 121–44.

54. In addition to the triangles formed by Mr. Pontellier-Edna-Robert and Robert-Edna-Arobin, there is Robert's sexy younger brother Victor, incarnated as the "graven image of Desire" (146) at the Coup d'Etat dinner, who variously mediates Edna's attraction to Robert and to Arobin.

55. Note how Edna progresses from being a "woman" who has "got in a habit of expressing myself" (165) to the shattered self who feels "her speech was voicing the incoherency of her thoughts" and who bemoans, "Oh! I don't know what I'm saying, Doctor" (171–72); the motif of tragically silenced speech is continued in the very last episode by the reference to Philomele, the name of the cook Edna asks to cook her dinner upon her return to Grand Isle—a "last supper" that remains unconsumed. Throughout the novel, Edna is plagued by the fear of inarticulateness, of the inability to translate inner emotions into verbal equivalents, particularly to male auditors. The night of the swim, for instance, she says to Robert, "A thousand emotions have swept through me to-night. I don't comprehend half of them. Don't mind what I'm saying; I'm just thinking aloud" (75). What Chopin's text, as opposed to Edna's discourse, attempts to capture and convey is precisely this process of "thinking aloud," of barely conscious thought translated into narrative form.

56. Yaeger, "'A Language Which Nobody Understood,'" p. 217.

57. Kate Chopin, review of Zola's *Lourdes,* quoted in Seyersted, *Kate Chopin,* p. 87.

The Virgin and the Gipsy

58. D. H. Lawrence, "Psychoanalysis and the Unconscious" (1921), in *Fantasia of the Unconscious and Psychoanalysis and the Unconscious* (Harmondsworth, England: Penguin 1977), pp. 202–3.

59. That is, Lawrence's fable of provincial English life in the 1920s self-consciously repeats, on the psychodramatic level, a prototypically "Victorian" scenario in which the dead hand of tradition that punishes Edna continues to resist the emancipation of postwar women's sexuality with unabated vigor. Yvette herself is represented as an emblem of postwar modernity, part of the younger lost generation who are frustrated "rebels" without a cause (31–32).

60. Compare Lawrence's wording to the passage in *The Awakening* in which Edna feels as if she is "being borne away from some anchorage which had held her fast, whose chains had been loosening—had snapped the night before . . . leaving her free to drift whithersoever she chose to set her sails" (81).

61. If both Chopin and Lawrence create modernist texts whose verbal textures seem especially close to the rhythms of the unconscious, it is in part because of an accidental congruence in their composition. "I am completely at the mercy of unconscious selection," Chopin remarked of her spontaneous writing method; once she put words to paper, she hardly ever revised. *The Virgin and the Gipsy,* quickly written in January 1926, was posthumously printed in 1930 from a manuscript lacking final revisions. As a result, the writing exudes a certain immediacy that places the reader in closer proximity than usual to Lawrence's process of "unconscious selection." Another similarity uniting these texts is the public hostility that both authors faced for choosing to write so intimately and frankly of female sexuality. The local censorship that greeted the publication of *The Awakening* reached the proportions of international scandal in the case of Lawrence, whose *Lady Chatterley's Lover,* the last novel published in his lifetime, faced sensational obscenity trials in Britain and America.

62. This authorial mystification of virginity comprises one of the clearest markers of gender separating Lawrence's writing and Chopin's; in *The Awakening* the female protagonist need not be a "virgin" to undergo an erotic awakening, just as Chopin deliberately demystifies the sex act itself as one singular event or threshold.

63. Other indications of the allegorical cast of Lawrence's fable include the names he gives his characters (the family surname "Saywell," the aptly labeled "Mater," the "Rector," "Eve-ette"), and the emphasis on "types," whether national, racial, or generational: Yvette and her sister are "so terribly English" (15) in their arrogance; their friends, rebels without a cause, epitomize the lost generation (31); the Gypsies are "pariahs" born outside "the pale" (142–43); Mrs. Eastwood is "the Jewess" (104). On the use of oppositions to give the story its fablelike aura, see Ashby Bland Crowder and Lynn O'Malley Crowder, "Mythic Intent in D. H. Lawrence's *The Virgin and the Gipsy,*" *South Atlantic Review* 49, no. 2 (May 1984): 61–66.

64. See D. H. Lawrence, "Fantasia of the Unconscious," in *Fantasia:* "But our deepest lower consciousness is blood-consciousness. . . . Sex is our deepest form of consciousness. It is utterly non-ideal, non-mental. It is pure blood-consciousness. . . . It is the consciousness of the night, *when the soul is almost asleep*" (173; emphasis added).

65. An incisive analysis of the "devouring mother" imago in Lawrence's writing appears in Judith Ruderman, *D. H. Lawrence and the Devouring Mother: The Search for a Patriarchal*

Ideal of Leadership (Durham, NC: Duke Univ. Press, 1984). While most psychoanalytic readings of Lawrence since the 1930s have tended to see a movement in Lawrence from an unresolved Oedipus complex evinced in the obsessive mother-love of the early work to a resolution of the complex in his embrace of the father-principle in the later novels, Ruderman argues that a continuing, unresolved, preoedipal conflict exists "beneath the Oedipal overlay" (8) and is manifested in the devouring mother figures that run throughout the canon. Lawrence's embrace of a protofascistic heroic "leadership" model in the late novels is intrinsically tied to these unresolved preoedipal fears of maternal domination and devouring, Ruderman convincingly argues (5–9). As Lawrence writes in *Education of the People*, "If we are to save the ultimate sanity of our children it is *down with mothers!*" (quoted in Ruderman, p. 29). Lawrence's representation of the Mater's gross appetites— she is a voracious eater who slobbers over her disgustingly bland food with relish—forms a telling contrast to Chopin's depiction of Edna's positive experience of orality and sensual delight in eating.

66. See Lawrence, "Fantasia of the Unconscious," pp. 125, 141–43. Lawrence's most famous prototype of overpowering mother-love occurs in *Sons and Lovers*. On Freudian oedipal patterns in Lawrence, see Daniel A. Weiss, *Oedipus in Nottingham: D. H. Lawrence* (Seattle, WA: Univ. of Seattle Press, 1962).

67. On the young girl's development, Freud writes, "Her love was directed to her *phallic* mother [Freud's emphasis]; with the discovery that her mother is castrated it becomes possible to drop her as an object, so that the motives for hostility, which have long been accumulating, gain the upper hand." See Sigmund Freud, "Femininity," in *New Introductory Lectures on Psychoanalysis,* trans. and ed. James Strachey (1933; rpt., New York: Norton, 1964), p. 112. All further references to this work are cited in the text.

68. See Luce Irigaray, *Speculum of the Other Woman,* trans. Gillian C. Gill (1974; Ithaca, NY: Cornell Univ. Press, 1985).

69. Jessica Benjamin, "Master and Slave: The Fantasy of Erotic Domination," in *Powers of Desire: The Politics of Sexuality,* ed. Ann Snitow, Christine Stansell, and Sharon Thompson (New York: Monthly Review Press, 1983), p. 286. All further references to Benjamin's work are cited in the text. Benjamin's essay is reprinted, in expanded form, in her *The Bonds of Love: Psychoanalysis, Feminism, and the Problem of Domination* (New York: Pantheon, 1988).

70. Lucille takes a commuting job in a nearby city, where her daily life remains intriguingly blank, a story Lawrence chooses *not* to tell.

71. Thanks to Debra Silverman for pointing out the masturbatory implications of this scene.

72. Several points are relevant here. First, this scenario reveals a telling difference between Freud and Lawrence's inscriptions of female psychosexual development. In Freud's theory the final bridge to normal femininity entails the girl's successful transference of her incestuous desire for the father to another man. But in Lawrence's dramatization of the struggle of parent and child, it is the repressive parent who harbors the destructively incestuous desires, not the innocent child (a pattern investigated in more depth in chapter 5's analysis of Christina Stead's *The Man Who Loved Children*). Second, if both these confrontations demonstrate, on the psychoanalytic level, the inevitability of oedipal conflict within the Freudian family romance, on the sociopolitical level they provide a classic example, right out of Lévi-Strauss, of the way in which patriarchy traditionally perpetuates itself through male exchanges of women as items of barter. As arranger of the narrative syntax whereby each episode effects a symbolic transfer of Yvette from the Rector's hands

to the Gypsy's arms, Lawrence forms a crucial link in the chain of barter being effected here. On such male barter in women as the structural determinant of patriarchy, see Claude Lévi-Strauss, *The Elementary Structures of Kinship* (Boston: Beacon, 1969), p. 115.

73. D. H. Lawrence, "The Two Principles," in *Phoenix II: Uncollected, Unpublished, and Other Prose Works by D. H. Lawrence,* ed. Warren Roberts and Harry T. Moore (New York: The Viking Press, 1968), p. 235. Lawrence begins this essay, first published in 1919, declaring that we need new terms to express the elemental connection between the ocean and human soul: "The sea that we dream of, the sea that fills us with hate or with bliss, is a primal influence upon us beyond the personal range" (227).

74. Among critics who see the flood as an equivalent of male ejaculation, orgasm, or the Gypsy's phallicism, see Crowder and Crowder ("[the Gypsy's] sexual power becomes one with the water's force"), "Mythic Intent," p. 63; G. B. Crump ("it is the flood, that elemental force incarnate . . . which seems to be the aggressor"), "Gopher Prairie or Papplewick?: *The Virgin and the Gipsy* as Film," *D. H. Lawrence Review* 4, no. 2 (Summer 1971): 152; and Donald Gutierrez ("[the Gypsy] is a symbolic extension of the libidinal energy represented by the flood"), *Lapsing Out: Embodiments of Death and Rebirth in the Last Writings of D. H. Lawrence* (Cranbury, NJ: Farleigh Dickinson Univ. Press, 1980), p. 65.

75. Hence Deirdre d'Albertis's suggestion that this treatment of the maternal object more than anything else "marks Lawrence's writing of desire as masculine. His is the text of uncompromising difference and individuation at the cost of the annihilation of the maternal Other," in her seminar paper, "Writing Desire: Sexual Awakening in Lawrence and Chopin" (6 March 1985), p. 4. Similarly, Ruderman notes, in *D. H. Lawrence and the Devouring Mother,* that "psychoanalysts agree that the child's fear of being destroyed by the mother leads to a rage to destroy her—to commit matricide," and in Lawrence's work from 1920 forward, the violence directed toward devouring mothers "reveals a modern-day Orestes committing what he thinks is justifiable homicide in an effort to return the patriarch to his rightful throne" (21). On male versus female differentiation, see Benjamin, "Erotic Domination."

76. Lawrence to E. M. Forster, (3 Feb. 1915), in *The Collected Letters of D. H. Lawrence* (Viking Press 1962), quoted in P. N. Furbank, *E. M. Forster: A Life* (New York and London, Harcourt Brace Jovanovich, 1977), 2: 8.

77. Much critical energy has been expended in attempting to determine whether or not the Virgin and the Gypsy actually *have* "sex" when the Gypsy crawls in bed with Yvette; such critics are quick to note that the swooning lyricism of the final paragraph concludes with nothing more definitive than the minds of the two would-be lovers lapsing into "unconscious[ness]," "pass[ing] away into sleep" (165). Literal representations of coitus aside, what is undeniable is the "sex-in-language" that occurs in this passage. From the terrible bodily "convulsion" that Yvette experiences as a "rupture," to the "fearful relief" that the Gypsy's clasp brings to her "heart . . . strained to bursting," Lawrence's imagery enacts a scene of hymenal defloration, in which all the descriptive erotic terminology takes on sexual connotations: "electric," "rippled," "shuddering," "tension," "abated," "revived," "roused," and so on. As for the movement of "their tortured, semiconscious minds" into "unconscious[ness]" and thence "sleep" in the last line of the chapter, one only needs to recall how often Lawrence uses states of sleep to symbolize the entrance into the subliminal realm of blood-consciousness; for real consummation (as opposed to mere orgasm) *only* happens on this level, beneath "conscious" knowing and hence outside the field of written representation. See Jeffrey Meyers, "'The Voice of the Water': Lawrence's 'The Virgin and the Gipsy,'" *English Miscellany* 21 (1970): 205, on the language's approximation of sexual union; and

Julian Moynahan, *The Deed of Life: The Novels and Tales of D. H. Lawrence* (Princeton, NJ: Princeton Univ. Press, 1963), p. 218, on the question of actual coitus.

78. Thanks to Ami Regier for this insight.

79. Compare this to my reading, in chapter 6, of the final volume of Lawrence Durrell's *Alexandria Quartet, Clea,* in which a perfect woman is also, ironically, literally (re)made in man's image.

Dora

80. Steven Marcus, "Freud and Dora: Story, History, Case History," in *Representations: Essays on Literature and Society* (New York: Random House, 1975). Marcus argues at length that Freud's "continuous innovations in formal structure" (264) in composing the case study resemble "a modern experimental novel" (263).

81. Charles Bernheimer provides a useful summary of the etymology of hysteria and the historical tradition linking it to female sexuality, beginning with Plato's theory that hysteria is caused by the wandering womb in the woman who doesn't fulfill her naturally reproductive function; see his "Introduction: Part One," in *In Dora's Case: Freud—Hysteria—Feminism,* ed. Charles Bernheimer and Claire Kahane (New York: Columbia Univ. Press, 1985).

82. Philip Reiff comments on the "group illness" (10) that characterizes this case in his introduction to the Collier edition of *Dora* cited here.

83. This obsession functions as a neurotic displacement of quite real health worries, given the mother's fear that the vaginal discharges and irritations from which she suffers may be the result of exposure to her husband's syphilis. For a new historicist reading that reveals the epidemic proportions of venereal disease in *fin de siècle* Germany, see the statistics Maria Ramas reports in "Freud's Dora, Dora's Hysteria," in *In Dora's Case,* ed. Bernheimer and Kahane, which cites studies indicating that 45 percent of middle-class clerks and merchants between 18 and 28 years of age had contracted syphilis, that 100 percent had been infected with gonorrhea, and that one in every five German men had syphilis, while gonorrhea "averaged more than one attack per man" (178–79, n. 12).

84. Dora's older brother appears to be the only immediate member of her family who manages to escape some sort of mental disturbance or neurosis (indeed, he became a leading figure in socialist politics in prewar Austria); his strategy for surviving the family crises and insuring his own mental health—general withdrawal from the family and the creation of a meaningful career for himself outside its grip—reminds me of the survival tactic of Yvette's older sister Lucille, whose withdrawal from the oedipal battles in which she and Yvette are first paired (so too the younger Dora has looked to her brother as a mirror of her aspirations and desires) is marked by her gradual removal from the text itself, as she goes on to establish a never-narrated life for herself as a secretary—that is, as an urban professional, a working woman—in London.

85. Kahane, "Introduction: Part Two," in *In Dora's Case,* ed. Bernheimer and Kahane, p. 21.

86. Marcus, "Freud and Dora," pp. 255–56. See Gayle Rubin, "The Traffic in Women: Notes on the 'Political Economy' of Sex," in *Toward an Anthropology of Women,* ed Rayna R. Reiter (New York: Monthly Review Press, 1975), pp. 157–210.

87. Among the many feminist readings of Dora's case, Ramas, in "Freud's Dora," offers perhaps the most thoroughgoing materialist account of the ideological assumptions underlying Dora's society as well as Freud's conception of female hysteria as a cornerstone of psychoanalytic theory.

88. Various critics have also examined these blind spots. On Freud's conflation of the sexual response/arousal of an adolescent girl and a mature woman, see Marcus, "Freud and Dora," p. 286. On the erasure of the mother, see Kahane, "Introduction: Part Two"; Toril Moi, "Representation of Patriarchy: Sexuality and Epistemology in Freud's Dora"; and Jerre Collins, J. Ray Green, Mary Lydon, Mark Sachner, and Eleanor Honig Skoller, "Questioning the Unconscious: The Dora Archive," in *In Dora's Case*, ed. Bernheimer and Kahane, pp. 27–28, 193, and 250, respectively. Of Freud's frequently noted overidentification with Herr K., see his appreciative evaluation of his ex-client's "still quite young" and "prepossessing appearance" (44); his assertion that Herr K.'s "proposal [is] neither tactless or offensive" (54)—an assertion unsubstantiated by any evidence and countered by Dora's testimony; and his empathetic reading of Herr K. as a man unfairly jilted without explanation (115, 130).

89. In "Enforcing Oedipus: Freud and Dora," in *In Dora's Case*, ed. Bernheimer and Kahane, Madelon Sprengnether also argues that Freud "go[es] so far as to provide Herr K. with an erection," a fantasy she sees originating with Freud (260). Marcus, too, in "Freud and Dora," notes that "this pivotal construction becomes henceforth the principal 'reality' of the case," one that "remains Freud's more than Dora's" (288).

90. Freud writes that, instead of the responsive "sexual excitement" which "would certainly have been felt by a healthy girl under such circumstances," Dora's feelings of disgust and revulsion mark her as "already entirely and completely hysterical" (44); such feelings, he argues, also explain her subconscious displacement of the unpleasurable genital sensations she experiences in Herr K.'s embrace to her thorax, the somatic site (the throat) to which her hysteria first attaches. Moreover, Freud, as if inspired to further heights of giddy excitement by Herr K.'s supposed erection, cannot let go of the subject in the following paragraphs. He notes that Dora dislikes walking past any group of men after the Herr K. incident for fear they too may be "in a state of sexual excitement" (45–46), and then he adds in a footnote that "the subject of erection solves some of the most interesting hysterical symptoms," evinced in the attention that "women pay to the outlines of men's genitals as seen through their clothing" (47). Either one has to wonder about the state of affairs in Vienna, where it seems the whole male populace is walking around displaying their erections, or suspect Freud's comments as a sign of his own rather lurid imagination and of the patriarchal blinders that limit his vision.

91. I naively thought I had discovered this logical slip until reading *In Dora's Case*, ed. Bernheimer and Kahane, where the point is reiterated by Sprengnether, p. 256, Moi, p. 190, Neil Hertz, "Dora's Secrets, Freud's Techniques," p. 228, and Lacan, "Intervention on Transference" (first published in 1951), p. 98.

92. Freud to Fleiss (14 Oct. 1900), quoted in Reiff, "Introduction" to *Dora* (see note 5 above), p. 7.

93. My points in this paragraph are indebted to the trenchant insights into Freud's authorial techniques in the seminar papers of Elizabeth Traynor, "Authorial Intrusion and the Mask of Objective Realism in *Dora: An Analysis of a Case of Hysteria*" (6 March 1985), and Eleanor Drey, "The Rhetoric of Power: Inscribing Authority in Freud's *Dora*" (7 March 1985). Many critics have commented on the novelistic qualities of Freud's narrative technique in the case study, some likening it to the strategies of nineteenth-century omniscient and all-controlling narration, others to fragmented modernist modes of narration. In either case, Freud himself was aware of—indeed quite anxious about—the propensity of his case studies to read *like* fiction, as evinced in his comments on Fräulein Elisabeth von R., his

first full-length analysis of a hysteric (1892–94): "It still strikes me as strange that the case histories I write should read like short stories and that, as one might say, they lack the serious stamp of science. . . . The fact is that the . . . detailed description of mental processes such as we are accustomed to find in the works of imaginative writers enables me, with the use of a few psychological formulas, to obtain at least some kind of insight into the course of that affection" (Freud, *Studies on Hysteria,* vol. 2 of *Standard Edition,* pp. 160–61).

94. Kahane, "Introduction: Part Two, " p. 20.

95. Among the feminist critics who take up the homosexual implications of Dora's desires at some length (although they often conflate lesbianism and preoedipal desire for the mother), see Ramas, "Freud's Dora"; Collins et al., "Questioning the Unconscious"; Kahane, "Introduction: Part Two"; and Susan Rubin Suleiman, "Nadja, Dora, Lol V. Stein: Women, Madness and Narrative," in *Discourse in Literature, the Arts, and Psychoanalysis,* ed. Shlomith Rimmon-Kenan (London: Methuen, 1987). Interesting critiques of Freud's readings of Dora's lesbian desire from a lesbian/queer theoretical perspective are offered in Judith Roof, *A Lure of Knowledge: Lesbian Sexuality and Theory* (New York: Columbia Univ. Press, 1991), pp. 174–215, and Heather Finley, "Queer Dora: Hysteria, Sexual Politics, and Lacan's 'Intervention on Transference,'" *GLQ: A Journal of Lesbian and Gay Studies* 1, no. 3 (1994): 323–47.

96. Freud immediately qualifies the statement that the dream "turns upon your mother" by setting the latter up, in the next sentence, merely as Dora's rival for the father's attention, and he is quick to remind Dora that Herr K. has also made a gift of such a case to the girl (87).

97. Freud links the word Dora uses for train station *(Bahnhof)* and the term *Vorhof*— a word, moreover, that is merely Freud's free association and that literally means "forecourt" but can also signify the labia, also known as nymphae (119–20).

98. Various feminist critics interpret this rapture as evidence of a preoedipal desire in Dora's dreaming unconscious that in turn expresses her wish to escape the law of the father. "It may be, therefore, that Dora's deepest desire is not identification with the mother (in the sense of the assumption of the mother's role) but fusion with the mother, a return to that 'desperate paradise' which is riven by entry into the Symbolic," write Collins et al., in "Questioning the Unconscious," pp. 249–50.

99. As previously noted, Freud begins the narrative of Dora's immediate family by dismissing the mother's influence on her daughter, who is reported "to look down on . . . and criticize her mercilessly" (35). Contrary to first impressions, however, Dora seems to communicate with her mother quite a bit, particularly on matters that threaten to expose the patriarchal nature of her social world. A realm of female homosociality is intimated throughout the incidental facts revealed by the analysis: it is her mother in whom Dora confides about Herr K.'s proposition (which Freud immediately dismisses as a communication meant to be passed along to the father; 41); she goes to her mother to ask why her father demands the children's gratitude to Frau K. for supposedly averting his suicide (48); it is to Dora's mother that the governess complains that the relationship between the former's husband and Frau K. is intolerable (52); Dora's sexual knowledge seems to come from her mother, this governess who shares her readings on sexual matters with Dora, and Frau K., in whose bedroom Dora has been wont to stay and share intimate discussions; the first dream turns on the mother's jewel-box (81); Dora continually identifies herself with various of her mother's physical ailments, especially those susceptible to a sexual etiology, to the point that Freud comments on "[this] persistence with which she held to this identification

[via illness] with her mother" (93–94); and, as just mentioned, the second dream originates in the mother's summons of Dora home.

100. Wilhelm Reich, *Reich Speaks of Freud,* ed. Mary Higgins and Chester M. Raphael (New York: Noonday Press, 1968), p. 61.

101. These four characteristics of hysteria include reticence, amnesia, paramnesia, and alternation of chronology. This point is also made in Collins et al., "Questioning the Unconscious," p. 244.

102. For an interesting analysis of the textual marginalization of these suppositions by placing them in the notes, see Sprengnether, "Enforcing Oedipus," pp. 269–70.

103. Also noting these "split" narratives is Suleiman, "Women, Madness, and Narrative," p. 130.

104. See Marcus, "Freud and Dora," p. 259.

105. Such a hypothesis corroborates Hertz's argument, in "Dora's Secrets," pp. 221–42, made from a different vantage point, about the imaginative identification that exists between Freud and Dora, which Hertz ties to Freud's fears of feminization. See also Marcus's comment in "Freud and Dora" on the delayed publication of the case, which suggests that although Dora had done with Freud, "[he] had still not done with Dora" (262).

106. To my knowledge no critics have remarked on the possibility that, indeed, Herr K. may have "had his way" with Dora at the lake. Although such pseudobiographical speculation—attempting to second-guess the reality of Dora's life, as if we possess the true "key" to understanding her psychosis—is the most obvious pitfall of much criticism of the case study, perhaps this note is an appropriate place to indulge such speculation, less to claim it as a "truth" than an overlooked possibility, which, if taken into consideration, would put a far different spin on many "facts" of the case. What if Herr K. *had* raped Dora during the "scene" on the lake, and this is the secret knowledge that Dora harbors within her psyche, unsuccessfully attempting to communicate it to others who are invested in only hearing other stories? Would not such a scenario, for instance, give an entirely new meaning to the hysterical symptoms of pregnancy that Freud attributes to Dora's wish to have born Herr K. a child? Such a hysterical manifestation would then be expressing a real if repressed fear, not simply a fantasy. It is telling that no one connected to Dora, much less her physician, has bothered to consider this possibility, despite Herr K.'s sexual relations with and seductions of other women, such as the abandoned governess Dora talks to at the lake resort.

107. Other fictions sharing similarities with the format and subject matter investigated in this chapter include Edith Wharton's *Summer* (1917), a quintessential awakening plot with a heroine who drifts through a libidinal haze as blindly as Edna and Yvette; Virginia Woolf's first novel, *The Voyage Out* (1915), in which the thresholds marking Rachel Vinrace's awakening to and repression of passion are consistently figured in terms of water imagery (the transit across the Atlantic; the river-bound quest into South American jungle; the metaphoric pool of water into which Rachel sinks during her loss of consciousness in her mysterious terminal illness associated with sexual knowledge); Gertrude Stein's "The Good Anna" and "Melanctha," from *Three Lives* (1909), stories of repression and sexuality, respectively, whose circling narrative rhythms render the texts' present-time narrations entirely fluid); Dorothy Richardson's *Pilgrimage* (1915–1938), whose continuous narrative of female sexual and textual awakening is often credited with inaugurating "stream-of-consciousness" practice in England; E. M. Forster's *A Room with a View* (1908), where the desired "view," that of the flowing Arno, goes hand in hand with the virginal Lucy Honeychurch's awakening to Mediterranean passion; D. H. Lawrence's flood-drenched *The Rain-*

bow (1915); and, in the genre of drama, Frank Wedekind's *Spring Awakening* (1891) and *Pandora's Box* (orig. 1895). George Eliot's classic *Mill on the Floss* (1860) provides, of course, the *locus classicus* among nineteenth-century realist novels linking water, women, and the floods of unruly desire.

108. Foucault, *History of Sexuality,* p. 81.

CHAPTER THREE

1. Virginia Woolf, *Mrs. Dalloway* (1925; rpt., New York and London: Harvest/HBJ, 1953), p. 85. This is part of Peter's dream of the solitary traveler. All further references to this work are cited in the text.

2. James Joyce, *Ulysses,* ed. Hans Gabler (1922; rpt., New York: Vintage Books, 1986), p. 126. All further references to this work are cited in the text.

3. Virginia Woolf, "Modern Fiction" (1925), in *Collected Essays,* 4 vols. (New York: Harcourt, Brace & World, 1967), 2: 106–7. All further references to this work are cited in the text. See also "Introduction," note 3.

4. Georg Lukács, *Realism in Our Time: Literature and the Class Struggle,* trans. John and Necke Mander (1956; rpt., New York: Harper and Row, 1964), pp. 33–34. I am grateful to Susan Stanford Friedman for sharing her book-in-progress, *History's Return: The Politics of Rupture and Repression in Modernism,* whose meticulous research led me to this and other helpful bibliographical references.

5. Brecht, "Against Georg Lukács," in Ernst Block et al. *Aesthetics and Politics,* with an afterword by Fredric Jameson (London: NLB, 1977), p. 82.

6. Peter Burra, rev. article, *Nineteenth Century* (Jan. 1936), reprinted in *Virginia Woolf: The Critical Heritage,* ed. Robin Majumdar and Allen McLautin (London: Routledge and Kegan Paul, 1975), pp. 321–22; emphasis added.

7. Virginia Woolf, "Modern Novels," unpublished ms. in the Berg Collection of the New York City Public Library. Quoted in Suzette A. Henke, "Virginia Woolf Reads James Joyce: The *Ulysses* Notebook," in *James Joyce: The Centennial Symposium,* ed. Morris Beja et al. (Urbana and Chicago: Univ. of Illinois Press, 1986), p. 39. See also Woolf's reviews of Dorothy Richardson in the *Times Literary Supplement,* 13 Feb. 1919, and 19 May 1923, where she critiques Richardson's attempt to capture the flow of sensations and impressions that remain on the surface, "without shedding quite as much light as we had hoped into the *hidden depths*"; quoted in *Virginia Woolf: Women and Writing,* ed. Michele Barrett (New York: Harcourt Brace Jovanovich, 1979), p. 191; emphasis added.

8. Arthur Power, *Conversations with James Joyce,* ed. Clive Hart (London: Millington, 1974), p. 54; emphasis added.

9. Djuna Barnes, "James Joyce," *Vanity Fair* 18 (1922): 65.

10. Similarly, Woolf uses the metaphor of a river to describe levels of consciousness in "A Sketch of the Past": "The past only comes back when the present runs so smoothly that it is like the sliding surface of a deep river. Then one sees through the surface to the depths"; see *Moments of Being: Unpublished Autobiographical Writings,* ed. Jeanne Schulkind (New York: Harcourt Brace Jovanovich, 1985), p. 122. The comparison to Joyce's metaphor is enlightening, for whereas in Joyce's figure the hidden tides of the unconscious flow in a direction opposite to the apparent flood, or conscious perception, in Woolf's rendition surface and depth are moving at the same pace and in the same direction, making possible the suspension of time that allows the perception, as if through a transparent medium, of the submerged depths of the deep past: consciousness and the unconscious become part of

the same inseparable flux. Elizabeth Abel uses the above passage from Woolf as the epigraph to the first chapter of her *Virginia Woolf and the Fictions of Psychoanalysis* (Chicago: Univ. of Chicago Press, 1989), p. 1.

11. Freud, "Repression" (1915), in *The Standard Edition of the Complete Psychological Works of Sigmund Freud,* trans. James Strachey (London: Hogarth Press, 1957), vol. 14, pp. 151, 154. The concept of the "return of the repressed" appears in Freud as early as "The Neuro-Psychoses of Defence" (1896).

12. Critics' recourse to the analogy of a "stream of consciousness" to describe the techniques whereby writers such as Joyce and Woolf attempt to evoke the flux of the mind in writing is, as I have warned in my introduction, potentially dangerous, as the all-too-loose applications of the term to widely disparate types of modernist writing demonstrate—applications that often fail to distinguish between uses of the term *stream* as description of technique, linguistic device, state of consciousness, aesthetic mode, and so forth.

13. Julia Kristeva, "Word, Dialogue, and Novel," in *Desire in Language: A Semiotic Approach to Literature and Art,* trans. Thomas Gora et al. (1977; rpt., New York: Columbia Univ. Press, 1980), p. 90; emphasis added. In addition to the technique of interior monologue, Kristeva also points an accusatory finger at "confessional mode, continuous psychological speech, [and] automatic writing" as guilty of the same humanistic gesture (90).

14. Judith Butler, *Gender Trouble: Feminism and the Subversion of Identity* (New York: Routledge, 1990), pp. 134, 136, 70, respectively. Butler continues, "In other words, acts, gestures, and desire produce the effect of an internal core or substance, but produce this *on the surface* of the body, through the play of signifying absences that suggest, but never reveal, the organizing principle of identity as a cause" (136).

15. As Habermas writes, "Modernity revolts against the normalizing functions of tradition: modernity lives on the experience of rebelling against all that is normative" ("Modernity versus Postmodernity," *New German Critique* 22 [Winter 1981]: 5).

16. For a fuller description, see "Working Proposition #5: The Return of the (Textually) Repressed," in my introduction. The concept is greatly indebted to Friedman's theorization of the "textual unconscious" as an interpretive hermeneutic in her book in progress, *History's Return,* especially chapter 2, "Reading the Political *within* Modernism."

Ulysses

17. Quoted in Barnes, "James Joyce," p. 65. See Patrick McGee, *Paperspace: Style as Ideology in Joyce's Ulysses* (Lincoln, Nebraska: Univ. of Nebraska Press, 1988), p. 2. This is McGee's paraphrase of Lacan's wording in "Joyce le symptôme," in *Joyce in Paris, 1902 . . . 1920 . . . 1940 . . . 1975,* 2 vols., ed. J. Aubert and Maria Jolas, (Paris: Editions du C.N.R.S., 1929) 1: 13–17. See also Lacan's comment, "I shall speak of Joyce, who has preoccupied me much this year, only to say that he is the simplest consequence of a refusal . . . of psycho-analysis, which, as a result, his work illustrates," in *The Four Fundamental Concepts of Psycho-Analysis,* ed. Jacques-Alain Miller, trans. Alan Sheridan (New York: Norton, 1978), p. ix.

18. Power, *Conversations with James Joyce,* p. 54.

19. Hélène Cixous, "At Circe's, or the Self-Opener," *boundary 2,* no. 3 (Winter 1975): 390, 388–89.

20. Karen Lawrence, *The Odyssey of Style in Ulysses* (Princeton, NJ: Princeton Univ. Press, 1981), p. 153. See also Dorrit Cohn's observation concerning "Circe" that the Freudian unconscious "can never be quoted directly" since its activities do not take verbal form; hence in this episode Joyce abandons "the realistic monologue technique in favor of a dis-

tinctly surrealistic dramatic phantasmagoria," in *Transparent Minds: Narrative Modes for Presenting Consciousness in Fiction* (Princeton, NJ: Princeton Univ. Press, 1978), p. 88.

21. The language in which these fantasies are expressed, moreover, is not specific to any one character's verbal ticks or thought patterns; rather, the words that compose "Circe" well up from the text's entire repertoire of figures and images—from, as it were, the dreaming unconscious of *Ulysses* itself. As Lawrence explains, "the 'dream of the text'" that makes up "Circe" "is not equivalent to the fantasies or dreams of the characters. . . . For the psychological boundaries of the characters' minds are wildly, extravagantly transgressed; . . . that is, the narrative memory of the book provides the resources for this extraordinary drama, often in violation of the actual memories and associations of the characters" (*Odyssey of Style*, 151–52).

22. See David Hayman, *'Ulysses,' The Mechanics of Meaning* (Englewood Cliffs, NJ: Prentice-Hall, 1970), pp. 76–77, and Lawrence, *Odyssey of Style*, p. 8

23. As Caroline Cowie puts it in a seminar paper, "Interpreting Circe" (April 1985), "It is surely more valid to say that fantasies are not prompted by external phenomena but latch on to them, as does the 'dreamwork' of the subconscious, selecting details from waking experience to express the patterns of pre-existing mental currents. 'My girl's a Yorkshire girl' does not prompt an access of guilt, but it allows a loophole for the pre-existing guilt to find its own release" (3).

24. As potentially offensive as this negative caricature of Bella-as-Bello is, I would argue that, as an emanation of Bloom's subconscious, it says more about his destructive feelings toward himself as a "womanly" man than about his (or Joyce's) attitude toward Bella as a "manlike" or destructive woman. Having internalized his male peers' derision of his behavior as effeminate, unmanly, and servile, he subconsciously fantasizes in this moment that a masculine-appearing woman such as Bella must be his opposite: domineering, castrating, shrewish. I develop this reading further in "A New Approach to Bloom as 'Womanly Man': The Mixed Middling's Progress in *Ulysses*," *James Joyce Quarterly* 20 (1982): 67–85; see esp. pp. 71–74. For more negative readings of the Bella/o sequence, see Elaine Unkeless, "Leopold Bloom as Womanly Man," *Modernist Studies: Literature and Culture* 2 (1976): 35–38, and Sandra M. Gilbert, "Costumes of the Mind: Transvestism as Metaphor in Modern Literature" (1980), reprinted in *Gender Studies: New Directions in Feminist Criticism,* ed. Judith Spector (Bowling Green, OH: Popular Press, 1986), pp. 73–74.

25. Joyce's more specific debt is to Richard von Krafft-Ebing, from whose *Psychopathia Sexualis* he culled much of his technical knowledge of male fetishism and masochism, as documented in Don Gifford and Robert J. Seideman, *Notes for Joyce: An Annotation of James Joyce's Ulysses* (New York: Dutton, 1974), pp. 410–15.

26. Cowie, "Interpreting Circe," p. 7.

27. Frances Restuccia, "Molly in Furs: Deleuzian/Masochian Masochism in the Writing of James Joyce," *Novel* 18, no. 2 (1985): 109.

28. Houses of prostitution, as Jane L. Pinchin pithily notes of Lawrence Durrell, "are places men go to play with one another." See Pinchin, "Durrell's Fatal Cleopatra," *Modern Fiction Studies* 28 (Summer 1982): 231, and the discussion of male homosociality in Durrell in chapter 6.

29. "Circe's" relentless textualization of sexuality and subsequent emptying out of any "real" sexual content also characterizes the innuendos that cluster around the floating signifier, "teapot," in the flirtatious but inconclusive dialogue of Bloom and Mrs. Breen: "BLOOM: I'm teapot with curiosity . . . ; MRS. BREEN: [*gushingly*] Tremendously teapot! London's teapot and I'm simply teapot all over me" (363). Later Bella/o will identify

the "teapot" with Bloom's male signifier—"Where's your curly teapot gone . . . cockyolly?" (441)—which, linguistically present ("*cock*-yolly") but reputedly anatomically absent ("where's [it] gone?"), becomes, like the empty or hollow "phallic design" on the wall, another displacement of the sexual.

30. See Sandra Gilbert and Susan Gubar, "Sexual Linguistics: Gender, Language, and Sexuality," *New Literary History* 16 (1985): 518–19, 534–35; and Karen Lawrence, "Compromising Letters: Joyce and Women," *Western Humanities Review* 42 (1988): 4. "Oxen of the Sun" proves an interesting case in point. Gilbert and Gubar argue that the episode "presents us with a wresting of patriarchal power from the mother tongue" (533) with its masterful simulation of the history of English literary styles imposed over the story of Mina Purefoy's lying-in. But Joyce's use of stylistic rhetoric in "Oxen," as Lawrence shows, may also be interpreted as critiquing the manner in which male discourse has historically attempted to use the fiat of the word, the patronym, to cover over its anxieties about female productivity; hence the relegation of Mina's delivery to off-stage action during the parodically inflated argument of the male medical students (which Joyce shows to be void of content or meaning), and hence the dizzying succession of literary styles that, as Lawrence argues, in their very errancy "subvert the integrity of the *pater* texts expropriated" (12). A similar gap between stylistic "prowess" and content characterizes the novel's major scene of male voyeurism and scopophilia, as Bloom spies on Gerty McDowell in "Nausicaa"; here, Joyce's "masterful" simulation of sentimental prose operates to deconstruct the hold that the gendered clichés of contemporary advertising and popular commodity culture exert on the sexual imaginations of Bloom and Gerty, as Thomas Karr Richards demonstrates in "Gerty MacDowell and the Irish Common Reader," *English Literary History* 52, no. 3 (Fall 1985): 755–76.

31. I am grateful to Carolyn Cowie's work ("Interpreting Circe," [7]) for bringing the orgasmic "explosiveness" of this passage to my attention.

32. Clive Hart, "The Sexual Perversions of Leopold Bloom," in *Ulysses Cinquante ans après: Temoignages Franco-anglais sur le Chef-d'Oeuvre de James Joyce,* ed. Louis Bonnerot (Paris: Didier, 1974), p. 131. I am reminded of my defense, in chapter 2, of Edna Pontellier's non-object-specific desires against Cynthia Wolff's charge that her sexuality is infantile because it is not genitally oriented.

33. McGee, *Paperspace,* p. 131.

34. See Cheryl Herr, "'One Good Turn Deserves Another': Theatrical Cross-Dressing in Joyce's 'Circe' Episode," *Journal of Modern Literature* 11, no. 2 (1984): 262–76, and "'Penelope' as Period Piece," *Novel* (Winter 1989): 130–42. In the former Herr conclusively shows how Joyce's familiarity with the transvestite tradition of popular pantomime influenced his depiction of Bloom's sexual disguises in "Circe." In the latter Herr notes that it was not unusual for a theatrical bill to include "selected scenes from classics" or favorite arias, which "were valued quite apart from their function in the works from which they were drawn—as tours de force that provided opportunities for an actor's talents to be measured and savored" (131). "Penelope" likewise "shows us a singer doing her most famous aria, a performer delivering the somewhat scandalous speech that made her notorious" (131).

35. For feminist critical perspectives on Molly (and Joyce's uses of Molly), see the essays in Richard Pearce, ed., *Molly Blooms: A Polylogue on "Penelope" and Cultural Studies* (Madison: Univ. of Wisconsin Press, 1994), and Suzette Henke and Elaine Unkeless, eds., *Women in Joyce* (Urbana: Univ. of Illinois Press, 1982); for a summary of the range of interpretations

that Molly's characterization has elicited, see Bonnie Kime Scott, *Joyce and Feminism* (Bloomington: Indiana Univ. Press, 1984), pp. 151–61.

36. I am thinking of Moira Wallace's superb, untitled seminar paper, written in April 1985, which has had a significant influence on my interpretation of "Penelope." Suzette Henke opens her book *James Joyce and the Politics of Desire* (New York: Routledge, 1990), with a similar question: "How can a feminist begin to approach the writings of James Joyce?" (1).

37. Joyce to Frank Budgen, 16 Aug. 1921, in *Selected Letters* (New York: Viking, 1975), p. 285. The various meanings of *clou* are glossed by Herr, "Period Piece," p. 130, and McGee, *Paperspace*, p. 171.

38. See Herr, "Period Piece," pp. 130–31, and Kimberly J. Devlin, "Pretending in 'Penelope': Masquerade, Mimicry, and Molly Bloom," in *Molly Blooms*, ed. Pearce, pp. 81, 88.

39. Devlin, "Pretending," p. 82.

40. Mary Anne Doane, "Film and the Masquerade: Theorizing the Female Spectator," *Screen* 23 (Sept.–Oct. 1982): 82.

41. Carol-Anne Tyler, "Female Impersonation," Ph.D. diss. Brown Univ. (1989): 21; quoted with permission of the author.

42. Devlin, "Pretending," p. 83.

43. Herr, "Period Piece," p. 134.

44. McGee, *Paperspace*, pp. 172, 181.

45. Butler, *Gender Trouble;* quotations are from pp. 24, 33, and 70, respectively.

46. Joyce, *Selected Letters*, p. 278.

47. Cohn, *Transparent Minds*, p. 218; emphases added. I am indebted to Moira Wallace for directing me to Cohn's argument.

48. As Cohn also notes, this self-sufficiency is reflected in the fact that Molly's thoughts are primarily *exclamatory* in syntax, which is "the self-sufficient, self-involved language gesture par excellence" (225).

49. Cohn, *Transparent Minds*, p. 230.

50. Wallace, p. 14; Gillet is quoted in Richard Ellman, *James Joyce* (1982 rev. ed.; New York: Oxford Univ. Press, 1959), p. 712.

51. Wallace, p. 12. Wallace offers a beautifully nuanced deconstruction of Joyce's reading of Molly's "yes," taking as her starting point the letter to Frank Budgen in which Joyce transforms the Faustian formula, "I am the spirit that always denies," into what he claims is its Penelopean analogue, "*Ich bin der [sic] Fleisch der stets bejaht*" ("I am the flesh that always says yes"). But the *text's* Molly, as Wallace argues, is "far closer to being the acting subject of *Faust* than she is to being the object of that subjectivity. Molly questions, denies, exploits, and interchanges men in a way that is definitely Faustian. . . . She can be seen as the constructor of an eternal masculine" (12). If Molly thus also says *no,* Wallace demonstrates how her literal *yes* is less a sign of female acquiescence than of the self-sufficiency implicit in the structure of autonomous monologue. For the Faustian reference, see *Letters of James Joyce*, ed. Gilbert Stuart (New York: Viking, 1965), 1: 170.

52. This self-affirmation on Molly's part is not without its problems or ambiguities. Molly may emerge as an acting subject in her reveries, but her subjectivity may still seem more congruent with male fantasies of femaleness than with contemporary theories of female psychosexual and ego development originating within feminist object-relations and Lacanian-feminist criticism. Not only is Molly's sense of identity conspicuously "non-

relational," but her relations with other women are almost uniformly competitive and denigrating, reflecting a traditionally male fantasy of women as "naturally" jealous of each other. And however liberating Molly's grammatical conflation of all the male objects of her lust to a metonymic series of interchangeable "he's," she still remains dependent on her reflection in their eyes to assure her of her worth. Even in the twist whereby Joyce's boastful "Jamesy" is submerged in references to female menstruation and domesticity, the ambiguities linger, to the extent that Molly's counterauthority resides in an appeal to the body— again, perhaps more of a man's fantasy of female subjectivity than a woman's evocation of her power.

53. Lawrence, "Compromising Letters," p. 3.

54. Joyce's versions of the dream are recounted in Ellman, *James Joyce,* p. 549, and in Herbert Gorman, *James Joyce* (New York: Rinehart, 1948), p. 283.

55. I borrow the phrase from Philip Herring's "The Bedsteadfastness of Molly Bloom," *Modern Fiction Studies* 15 (1969): 49–61.

Mrs. Dalloway

56. Virginia Woolf, *The Diary of Virginia Woolf,* 4 vols., ed. Anne Olivier Bell, with Andrew McNeillie (New York: Harcourt Brace Jovanovich, 1978), 26 Sept. 1920, 6 and 7 Sept. 1922; 2: 69, 199, 200, respectively. Other references to correspondence from this edition will be cited by date, volume, and page number in the text.

57. In addition to the 6 Sept. 1922 entry cited above, see the entries for 26 Jan. 1920, where Woolf speaks of "the damned egotistical self, which ruins Joyce and [Dorothy] Richardson" (2: 14) and the continuation of the 16 Aug. 1922 entry, where she labels Joyce "egotistic, insistent, raw, striking, & ultimately nauseating" (2: 189).

58. Woolf, "Modern Novels," unpublished notebook in the Berg Collection, New York Public Library, quoted by Henke, "Woolf Reads Joyce," p. 39; emphasis added.

59. Unsigned review, "A Novelist's Experiment," *Times Literary Supplement* (21 May 1925), reprinted in *Virginia Woolf: The Critical Heritage,* ed. Robin Majumdar and Allen McLaurin (London: Routledge and Kegan Paul, 1975), p. 160. The phrase "the very stream of life" is echoed by George Bullett to describe the novel's "incessant flux" in *Saturday Review* (30 May 1925): 558, reprinted in *Critical Heritage,* ed. Majumdar and McLaurin, p. 164.

60. In *Vanishing Subjects,* Judith Ryan links Woolf's concern with the interrelation of consciousness and perception to late-nineteenth-century psychological theories influenced by German empiricism and William James's pragmatism; for Ryan, the empiricist view that the self is coterminous with the perceptual field, erasing "the familiar distinction between subject and object" (9), underlies Woolf's challenge to conceptions of the contained self (191–98).

61. Maria Di Battista, "Joyce, Woolf, and the Modern Mind," in *Virginia Woolf: New Critical Essays,* ed. Patricia Clements and Isobel Grundy (New York: Barnes and Noble, 1983), p. 112; emphasis added.

62. Jennifer L. Kapuscik, "Female Identity and the 'Unwritten Novel': Virginia Woolf's Innovative Modernism," Senior Honors Thesis, Department of English, Harvard Univ. (1984), pp. 15–18. My analysis is greatly indebted to this student's fine work, especially her probing of the "unwritten novel" references as a key to unlocking Woolf's innovations in modernist form from a feminist perspective. The complement to the way Woolf positions the novelist as reader is her conception of readers as "partners in this business of writing books," in the December 1922 essay "Mr. Bennett and Mrs. Brown," in *Collected*

Essays, 4 vols. (London: Hogarth Press, 1966), 1: 336. Susan Sniader Lanser voices an opposing view of Woolf's manipulation of her authorial stance in *Fictions of Authority: Women Writers and Narrative Voice* (Ithaca, NY: Cornell Univ. Press, 1992), arguing that the forms Woolf devises to submerge the overt authorial voice are "subtly hegemonic themselves" (113).

63. Kapuscik, "Female Identity," p. 9.

64. Woolf first mentions her idea for a story named "Mrs. Dalloway in Bond Street" on 23 June 1922 (2: 178); two months later, 16 Aug. 1922, she juxtaposes her opinion that *Ulysses* is "an illiterate, underbred book" with the comment about "dredging" her mind and bringing up "buckets" for the Dalloway idea (2: 189); a month after finishing *Ulysses,* 14 Oct. 1922, she notes that the short story *"Mrs. Dalloway* has branched into a book" (2: 207).

65. Abel, *Fictions of Psychoanalysis,* p. xvi.

66. The importance of the preoedipal, Freud writes, "comes to us as a surprise, like the discovery, in another field, of the Minoan-Mycenean civilization behind the civilization of Greece." See Freud, "Female Sexuality" (1931), *Standard Edition* 21: 226 and Abel, *Fictions of Psychoanalysis,* p. 8.

67. Abel, *Fictions of Psychoanalysis,* pp. 5–20; the quotation is from p. 14.

68. M. E. Kelsey, "Virginia Woolf and the She-Condition," *Sewanee Review* (Oct.–Dec. 1931): 436. One need only recollect young James Ramsay wedged between his mother's knees, wielding a pair of scissors as he thinks murderous thoughts of his father in *To the Lighthouse,* to sense Woolf's awareness of key Freudian concepts ranging from oedipal individuation to libidinal repression.

69. Edwin Muir, "Virginia Woolf," *Nation and Atheneaum* (17 April 1926): 70–72, reprinted in Majumdar and McLaurin, eds., *Critical Heritage,* p. 182.

70. Sometimes these parentheses are used as devices to make way for the emergence of memory or hitherto repressed thoughts. More striking, however, is the frequency with which the quotidian events of everyday life—the traditional minutiae of "novelistic" reality—are displaced to a parenthesis, while thoughts of the past assume the foreground. Note, for example, the passage where Clarissa first begins to think of Peter Welsh and "scene after scene at Bourton" (8–9); in the midst of this upswelling of memory stands an entire paragraph in parentheses that describes, in typical novelistic terms, the present June day and passersby on the street.

71. J. Hillis Miller's chapter on *Mrs. Dalloway,* "Repetition as a Raising of the Dead," in *Fiction and Repetition: Seven English Novels* (Cambridge: Harvard Univ. Press, 1982), offers an eloquent reading of the ways in which Woolf creates a narrative voice, especially through techniques of indirect free discourse, that suffuses the novel with a "state of mind" that permeates every consciousness (176–202; the quotation is from p. 178).

72. In a 1926 essay on cinema (one year after the publication of *Mrs. Dalloway*), Woolf speculates on the ways in which the visual emphasis of this relatively new medium might be used to convey "thought processes" in "a shape more effectively than words" can do. When she notes how cinema's "picture-making power" has the "speed and slowness; dartlike directness and vaporous circumlocution," to achieve "the most fantastic contrasts . . . with a speed which the writer can only toil after in vain," she might well be describing the cinematic effects achieved in the airplane passage cited above. See "The Cinema," *Collected Essays* (1967), 2: 270–72.

73. Woolf's use of inanimate objects to create the illusion of seamless movement also draws on the novel's urban setting, for the street intersections and curbs at which characters

pause or pass other characters repeatedly function as "switch-points" where disparate narrative lines cross and separate without a discernible break. In such examples, the physical motion of the pedestrian works in conjunction with the stationary setting to effect the transition in scene or point of view. For more on such "switch-points" and their relation to modernist urban writing, see chapter 4.

74. Woolf recalls in "A Sketch of the Past" that such "scene making" is her "natural way of marking the past. Always a scene has arranged itself: representative; enduring. . . . Is this liability to scenes the origin of my writing impulse?" But, as Abel notes of this passage, the fictions that emerge from this distillation of the past into mental scenarios are as "suspect as [they are] gratifying," covering up much more than they reveal. See Woolf, "Sketch," p. 122, and Abel, *Fictions of Psychoanalysis,* p. 1–2.

75. In her diary on 15 Oct. 1923, Woolf records the fear that her title character may be "too stiff, too glittering & tinsely" (2: 272); on 18 June 1925 she recalls the feeling of having saved Clarissa from being "too tinselly" by "inventing her memories" (3: 32).

76. See the discussion of Kristeva in this chapter's introductory section.

77. Donna Haraway, "A Manifesto for Cyborgs: Science, Technology, and Socialist Feminism in the 1980s," in *Coming to Terms,* ed. Elizabeth Weed (New York: Routledge, 1989), p. 201.

78. Patricia Yaeger, "Towards a Female Sublime," in *Gender and Theory: Dialogues in Feminist Criticism,* ed. Linda S. Kauffman (Oxford: Basil Blackwell, 1989), p. 205.

79. Nancy K. Miller, "Emphasis Added: Plots and Plausibilities in Women's Fiction," *PMLA* 96 (1981): 36–48.

80. The images of scent and sound in the sentence immediately preceding the indented passage also contribute to its powerful appeal to the senses: "And whether it was pity [for other women], or their beauty, or that she was older, or some accident—like a faint scent, or a violin next door (so strange is the power of sounds at certain moments), she did undoubtedly then feel what men felt."

81. Many students approaching the text for the first time tend to read the image as androgynous or heterosexual, combining male (match) and female (crocus) iconography. The logic of the passage, however, indicates that the match is a clitoral rather than phallic image; to read it as a penis inserted into the crocus/vulva is to fall into the trap of reading the passage as Clarissa's imagining of "what men feel," rather as an expression, welling up from within, of what *she* feels.

82. The same, ultimately, is true of Woolf's representation of Clarissa's psyche and desires. "To dispute the psyche as *inner depth,*" Judith Butler notes in an important qualification to her deconstruction of the psychological rhetoric of interiority, "is not to refuse the psyche altogether." See Judith Butler, "Imitation and Gender Insubordination," in *Inside/ Out: Lesbian Theories, Gay Theories,* ed. Diana Fuss (New York: Routledge, 1991), p. 28; emphasis added.

83. I am grateful to Michael Bacchus for pointing out the applicability of the language of the closet to this scene.

84. The emphasis on the tactile rather than visual also recalls Freud's hypothesis that female sexuality is less scopically constructed than male sexuality, and the rhythm of ebb and flow interjected by the women's movements "up and down, up and down" the terrace also distinguishes this moment from the linearity that Woolf associates with maleness in *A Room of One's Own,* (1929; rpt., New York: Harvest/HBJ, 1957), pp. 90–95. Compare the image of the wrapped but radiating gift to that of the translucent envelope in Woolf's "Modern Fiction," another permeable container of illumination.

85. Given Theweleit's theory of male body armor discussed in chapter 2, the image of the wall that comes into Clarissa's mind all too aptly conveys Peter's compulsion to make his bodily presence a dam capable of halting any outpouring of female desire that excludes his participation.

86. The eroticized connection that Clarissa establishes with the "things" of her world has most often been noted in terms of her love of nature, but it also includes the electric thrill she receives from being part of modern urban consumer culture. Love of nature and urban consumption come together in Clarissa's sensuous raptures in buying cut flowers—that is, nature rendered an object of consumption with a price tag—during her morning walk. The fact that these raptures function as a displaced form of Clarissa's erotic feelings for Sally is implicit in the language used to register her impression of the flowers: "every flower seem[ed] to burn by itself, softly, purely in the misty beds" (18). Such an image not only echoes Woolf's metaphor for her narrative aims in the diary ("fire in the mist") but anticipates the radiant, covered-up warmth that images Sally's "gift" to Clarissa at Bourton, the kiss on the terrace.

87. Luce Irigaray, *This Sex Which Is Not One*, trans. Catherine Porter (1979; rpt., Ithaca, NY: Cornell Univ. Press, 1985) p. 29. Irigaray's celebration of the plurality of female sexuality and subjectivity often evokes Woolf's characterization of Clarissa as a plurality of expansive selves and desires contained in one subject; see, for instance, Irigaray's lyrical proclamation, "Woman always remains several, but she is kept from dispersion because the other is already within her and is autoerotically familiar to her." Female libidinal pleasures, Irigaray continues, form an "expanding universe to which no limits could be fixed and [yet] which would not be incoherent," a free play that Irigaray distinguishes from the Freudian understanding of infantile "polymorphous perversion," "in which the erogenous zones [of the child] . . . lie waiting to be regrouped under the primacy of the phallus" (31). In recent years, several critiques have been made of Irigaray's tendency to essentialize "woman" and reduce female textuality to female anatomy. Helpful in decoding the metaphorical from the morphological dimensions of Irigaray's argument is chapter 4 of Diana Fuss, *Essentially Speaking: Feminism, Nature, and Difference* (New York: Routledge, 1989), pp. 55–72.

88. Writing a bodily text whose language "touches (upon)" is precisely the act in which an early avatar of Clarissa Dalloway, making a cameo appearance in *The Voyage Out*, engages: "Thus established, Mrs. Dalloway began to write. A pen in her hands become a thing one caressed paper with" (49).

89. Abel, *Fictions of Psychoanalysis*, pp. 31, 33–34.

90. I am indebted to Carla Mazzio for making this brilliant connection between these opposing images of trees and the way they reveal the schisms underlying Clarissa's vision of life-affirming wholeness in an untitled graduate seminar essay (Fall 1989), p. 3.

91. Abel also focuses on this moment in *Fictions of Psychoanalysis*, but reads the scene quite differently, seeing it as a final stage in Clarissa's renunciation of the past, as Septimus's example forces her to choose between development (within a limited phallocentric plot that mandates the forfeiture of female intimacy) or death while embracing passion (40).

92. This unreported story, however, contains its own disturbing ambiguities. We know Clarissa and Peter will talk, since the final lines are filtered through Peter's viewpoint, but how about Clarissa and Sally? Is Sally still present when Clarissa appears before Peter? Is the omission of mention of Sally at this final moment further evidence of the textual repression of the lesbian/libidinal plot?

93. I have in mind the conception of the artist as the supreme authority in a fragmented world, a godlike figure who bestows meaning on chaos by creating totalizing textual worlds

that are complete unto themselves, and the privileging of textual difficulty as a counter to the encroaching anti-intellectualism of the masses and mass culture. See T. S. Eliot's famous "Ulysses, Order, and Myth" (1923), in *Selected Prose of T. S. Eliot,* ed. Frank Kermode (New York: Harcourt Brace Jovanovich/Farrar, Straus, and Giroux, 1975), and Astradur Eysteinsson's useful summary, *The Concept of Modernism* (Ithaca, NY: Cornell Univ. Press, 1990), pp. 8–18.

94. See Malcolm Bradbury, "The Cities of Modernism," pp. 96–104, and "London 1890–1920," pp. 172–90; James McFarlane, "Berlin and the Rise of Modernism 1886–96," pp. 105–19; Eric Homberger, "Chicago and New York: Two Versions of American Modernism," pp. 151–60, all in *Modernism, 1980–1930,* ed. Malcolm Bradbury and James McFarlane (Harmondsworth, England: Penguin, 1976).

CHAPTER FOUR

1. Countee Cullen, *On These I Stand: An Anthology of the Best Poems of Countee Cullen* (1927; rpt., New York: Harper and Row, 1947), p. 26. "Heritage" is dedicated to Harold Jackman, Cullen's longtime lover, in a volume of verse dedicated, interestingly enough, to Cullen's wife, the daughter of W. E. B. DuBois. For mentions of Cullen's lifelong relationship with Jackson, see Eric Garber, "A Spectacle in Color: The Lesbian and Gay Subculture of Jazz Age Harlem," in *Hidden from History: Reclaiming the Gay and Lesbian Past,* ed. Martin Duberman, Martha Vicinus, and George Chauncey Jr. (New York: Meridian, 1989), p. 327; and David Levering Lewis, *When Harlem Was in Vogue* (New York: Knopf, 1984), p. 76. I came across these lines in Blair Niles's *Strange Brother* (1931; rpt., London: GMP Publishers, 1991), p. 234, where they are (mis)quoted by the gay protagonist to express his personal credo of gay survival and angst. All further references to this work by Niles are cited in the text.

2. Charles Warren Stoddard, *For the Pleasure of His Company: A Tale of the Misty City* (1903; rpt., San Francisco, Gay Sunshine Press, 1987), p. 30. Originally titled *So Pleased to Have Met You,* Stoddard's tale of Bohemian life in turn-of-the-century San Francisco is, as his friend Rudyard Kipling noted, a "rummy, queer, original" story, comprised of three homoerotically shaded episodes whose formal "oddness" is echoed in its (in all senses) "queer" themes. See the introduction by Roger Austen, pp. 5–11.

3. "The appeal of 'queer theory,'" Michael Warner notes in an excellent synopsis of the movement's rise, "has outstripped anyone's sense of what exactly it means": see his "From Queer to Eternity: An Army of Theorists Cannot Fail," *Village Voice Literary Supplement* (June 1992): 18.

4. On the hold of this binary, see Eve Kosofsky Sedgwick, *Epistemology of the Closet* (Berkeley and Los Angeles: Univ. of California Press, 1990), pp. 67–90.

5. For Escoffier and Bérubé, the use of the term *queerness* (as opposed to *gayness*) signals the desire to include *all* "people who have been made to feel perverse, queer, odd, outcast, different, and deviant"; it "affirm[s] sameness by defining a common identity on the fringes." See Jeff Escoffier and Allan Berube, "Queer/Nation," *OUT/LOOK: National Lesbian and Gay Quarterly* 11 (Winter 1991): 14–16. My articulation of the combination of anti-assimilationist and antiseparatist politics is a paraphrase of Lisa Duggan, "Making It Perfectly Queer," *Socialist Review* 22 (1992): 11–31. On queer definitions, see also Alisha Solomon, "In Whose Face? A Gay Generation Is Not an Age Group," *Village Voice* (July 1991): 18–19, and Eve Kosofsky Sedgwick, "Queer and Now," in *Tendencies* (Durham, NC: Duke Univ. Press, 1993), pp. 1–20.

6. Ann Powers, "Queer in the Streets, Straight in the Sheets: Notes on Passing," *Village Voice* (June 1993): reprinted in *Utne Reader* (Nov.–Dec. 1993): 75.

7. Other fictions that might be examined within this paradigm include Stoddard's tale of gaily bohemian San Francisco, *For the Pleasure of His Company;* the glimpses of gay Harlem that appear in Wallace Thurman's *Infants of the Spring* (1932) and Claude McKay's *Home to Harlem* (1928); and those of Paris in Marcel Proust's *Sodome et Gomorrhe* (1921), Barnes's *Ladies Almanack* (1928), Janet Flanner's *Cubical City* (1926), André Gide's *The Counterfeiters* (1926), Jean Rhys's *The Left Bank* (1927) and *Good Morning Midnight* (1939), and various works by Colette. On Harlem, one might also think about Waldo Frank's *City Block* (1932) and Carl Van Vechten's *Nigger Heaven* (1926). Other metropolises whose bohemian/gay enclaves find their way into modernist writings include London's Bloomsbury and Weimer Berlin (Christopher Isherwood's *Berlin Stories* [1945]). J. S. Watson's and Melville Weber's 1933 avant-garde American film, *Lot in Sodom* (1933) provides a fascinating contemporaneous cinematic counterpart to these queer city narratives, displacing the "sins" associated with the modern metropolis to that earliest urban blight of biblical fame, Sodom.

8. Georg Simmel, "The Metropolis and Mental Life," in *Classic Essays in the Culture of Cities,* ed. Richard Sennett (New York: Appleton-Century-Crofts, 1969), pp. 47–60. Reprinted from *The Sociology of Georg Simmel,* ed. Kurt Wolff (New York: The Free Press, 1950).

9. Raymond Williams, "Metropolitan Perceptions and the Emergence of Modernism," *The Politics of Modernism* (London and New York: Verso, 1989), pp. 37–48; quotations are from pp. 43, 44, and 45 respectively.

10. Charles Henri Ford and Parker Tyler, *The Young and Evil* (New York: Sea Horse Book/Gay Presses of New York, 1988), p. 15. All further references to this work are cited in the text.

11. George Chauncey, *Gay New York: Gender, Urban Culture, and the Making of the Gay Male World, 1898–1940* (New York: Basic Books, 1994), pp. 1–29.

12. Here I have liberally adapted and collapsed the wording of Steven Watson in his excellent introduction to the Gay Presses of New York/Sea Horse edition of *The Young and Evil,* where he writes of the "universe of shifting relationships and labile sexuality" that constitutes the backdrop of this novel, which "doesn't present a strictly homosexual world, but one of polymorphous sexuality" (ix).

13. Sedgwick, *Tendencies,* p. 8. An early manifestation of this principle exists in Natalie Barney's composition of her salon on the Left Bank of Paris, which, while primarily composed of lesbians, also deliberately included various disenfranchised groups. As Sheri Benstock writes, "Although [Barney] organized a community of women in Paris (perhaps an effort to recreate Lesbos), she clearly saw the danger of forming separatist groups and made her salon an eclectic, international, and multisexual meeting place." See Benstock, *Women of the Left Bank: Paris, 1900–1940* (Austin, TX: Univ. of Texas Press, 1986), p. 12.

14. Intriguing in this regard is the conflation of textual and bodily "styles" underlying Parker Tyler's reminiscence of his and Charles Henri Ford's attempt to create their own "brand" of avant-garde literature in the late 1920s. Well known throughout the Village for his theatrical self-presentation and sartorial flamboyance, Tyler writes, "We were trying to create our own brand [of modernism]. What we didn't realize too consciously was that *we were* (I hope this isn't too much of a boast!) *modern poetry.*" Quoted in Watson, "Introduction," p. xx. The italics are Tyler's.

15. David Harvey, *The Condition of Postmodernity: An Enquiry into the Origins of Cultural Change* (Oxford: Basil Blackwell, 1989), p. 213. My observations are indebted to Harvey's sage positioning of Foucault in relation to theories of time, space, and modernity.

16. See Foucault, *The History of Sexuality*, pp. 96, 157, and *Discipline and Punish*, pp. 201–3.

17. Rosalind Krauss, "Grids," in *The Originality of the Avant-Garde and other Modernist Myths* (Cambridge, MA: The MIT Press, 1985), p. 9; the comment on the city comes from Krauss's "Grids, You Say," in *Grids: Format and Image in Twentieth-Century Art* (New York: The Pace Gallery, 1978), n.p.

18. On the European city model of the baroque axial network as "a strategy for the economical application of central power," and as a "way of using the city as an expression of central power and a strategy for maintaining visual magnificence and control within available means," see Kevin Lynch, *A Theory of Good City Form* (Cambridge, MA: MIT Press, 1981), pp. 280–84; quotations are from 281 and 283 respectively. My observations here are significantly shaped by discussions with Dale M. Wall.

19. See Lynch, *Good City Form*, p. 283.

20. On the most basic level, such pockets or sectors require the proximity of both commercial and residential entities appropriate to unmarried individuals living on their own (this would entail the study of the rise of gay-friendly institutions such as the boarding house and the cafeteria). Relevant here is Chauncey's work on the rise of an urban bachelor subculture in New York City. "Tellingly," Chauncey writes, "gay men tended to gather in the same neighborhoods where many of the city's other unmarried men and women clustered, since they offered the housing and commercial services suitable to the needs of a nonfamily population. Gay male residential and commercial enclaves developed in the Bowery, Greenwich Village, Times Square, and Harlem in large part because they were the city's major centers of furnished-room housing for single men. . . . Rooming houses and cafeterias served as meeting grounds for gay men, facilitating the constant interaction that made possible the development of a distinctive subculture" (*Gay New York,* p. 136). On a more theoretical level, such pockets or interstices are reminiscent of Aldo Rossi's hypothesis of the city "as an entity constituted of many parts which are complete in themselves . . . [and] which truly permits *freedom of choice*"; part of this "freedom of choice," tellingly, also lies in the fact that the so-called city of parts is also always in process, constituting what Rossi calls the "analogous city" whose "elements are preexisting . . . but whose true meaning is unforeseen at the beginning and unfolds only at the end of the process. Thus the meaning of the process is identified with the meaning of the city." See his *The Architecture of the City* (Cambridge, MA: MIT Press, 1982), pp. 96, 18.

21. Rossi, *Architecture of the City,* p. 65 n.

22. As Norma Evenson notes in *Paris: A Century of Change, 1878–1978* (New Haven, CT: Yale Univ. Press, 1979), pp. 65–71, Haussmann's plans in fact included a boulevard that would have bisected the Saint Germain and Latin Quarters parallel to the Seine and leveled much of their "ancient fabric" (it was blocked for complicated reasons that Evenson reports). Later attempts were made to revive the Haussmann plan, in part because of the association of the physical layout of the Latin Quarter with past political insurrection and present-day sexual sins. Note how the spatial conception of this "no-man's land" of hidden vice is appropriated by Radclyffe Hall in *The Well of Loneliness* (1928; rpt., New York: Anchor-Doubleday, 1956) to describe Stephen and Mary's entrance into the homosexual underworld of Paris: "So now they were launched up the stream that flows silent and deep

through all great cities, gliding on between precipitous borders, away and away into no-man's land" (356; emphases added).

23. The physical shape of Harlem's "insularity" is evoked in Rudolph Fisher's 1927 story, "Blades of Steel," which begins with a description of how the neighborhood's three main thoroughfares form, emblematically enough, "the letter *H,* with Lenox and Seventh Avenues running parallel northward, united a little above their midpoints by the east-and-west 135th Street. . . . These two highways, frontiers of the opposed extreme of dark-skinned social life [Lenox being more raucous, Seventh more high-toned], are separated by an intermediate any-man's land, across which is the heart and soul of black Harlem; it is common ground, the natural scene of unusual contacts, a region that disregards class. It neutralizes, equilibriates, binds, rescues union out of diversity." See Rudolph Fisher, quoted in *Voices from the Harlem Renaissance,* ed. Nathan Irvin Huggins (New York: Oxford Univ. Press, 1976), p. 110.

24. Lewis explains the title reference in *When Harlem Was in Vogue,* p. 186.

25. James Weldon Johnson, quoted in Huggins, ed., *Voices from the Harlem Renaissance,* p. 65.

26. Michel de Certeau, *The Practice of Everyday Life,* trans. Steven F. Rendall (Berkeley, CA: Univ. of California Press, 1984), pp. 97–98, 102; see de Certeau's refutation of Foucault's totalizing spaces on pp. xiv–xv, 45–49, 96, and passim.

27. Harvey, *Condition of Postmodernity,* p. 213. Harvey's summary of de Certeau's argument concludes, "Spaces can be more easily 'liberated' than Foucault imagines, precisely because social practices spatialize rather than becoming localized within some repressive grid of social control" (214).

28. The classic treatment of the rise of the *flâneur,* the detached observer of the city through which he strolls, is Walter Benjamin's *Charles Baudelaire: A Lyric Poet in the Era of High Capitalism* (London: New Left Books, 1973); the term originates in Baudelaire's essay, "Le Peintre de la vie moderne." On the subversive role of the female *flâneur,* see Deborah Epstein Nord, *Walking the Victorian Streets: Women, Representation, and the City* (Ithaca, NY: Cornell Univ. Press, 1995).

29. Ernest Hemingway, *A Moveable Feast* (New York: Macmillan, 1964), title page epigraph; emphasis added.

30. See Williams, "Metropolitan Perceptions," pp. 44–45, on the definition of the metropolis "beyond both city and nation in their older senses" and on the impact of the internationalism of the "imperial capital" on modernist "innovations": "The most important general element of the innovations in form is the fact of immigration to the metropolis, and it cannot too often be emphasized how many of the major innovators were, in this precise sense, immigrants," newly "liberated or breaking from their national and provincial cultures, placed in quite new relations to . . . other native languages or native visual traditions, encountering . . . a novel and dynamic common environment from which many of the older forms were obviously distinct" (45).

31. Wallace Thurman, *Infants of the Spring* (1932; Boston: Northeastern Univ. Press, 1992), p. 184.

32. Chauncey, *Gay New York,* p. 246; Lewis, *When Harlem Was in Vogue,* p. 157.

33. It is worth noting that Gwendolyn Brook's story, "Wedding Day," her contribution to the journal *Fire!!,* is set among blacks in the Montmartre district of jazz-age Paris. Cheryl A. Wall compares the attractions of these two urban locations in "Paris and Harlem: Two Culture Capitals," *Phylon* (March 1974): 64–73.

34. Summarizing his in-depth analysis of the various "public" spaces—restaurants and cafeterias, parks, the street, public bathrooms, and so on—that become sites of gay life in New York City, Chauncey writes that "gay men devised a variety of tactics that allowed them to move freely about the city, to appropriate for themselves spaces that were not marked as gay, and to construct a gay city in the midst of, yet invisible to, the dominant city" (*Gay New York*, 180). Normative heterosexual male life, by contrast, has increasingly been defined by the separation of the public and domestic realms since the mid-nineteenth century; one of the best sources on the rise of new standards of heterosexual masculinity in the nineteenth century is Ed Cohen, *Talk on the Wilde Side* (New York: Routledge, 1993).

35. Chauncey cites Tyler's correspondence on pp. 168–69 of *Gay New York*, and reports on the spectacle afforded by the Life Cafeteria on pp. 166–68.

36. Walter Benjamin, "Paris, Capital of the Nineteenth Century," in *Reflections* (New York: Harcourt Brace Jovanovich, 1978), pp. 146–47.

37. On the tradition of the rent party and buffet flat in Harlem, and their highly charged sexual—and often gay—atmosphere, see Garber, "Lesbian and Gay Subculture," pp. 318–31, esp. 321–23. On Barney's desire to form a Sapphic circle dedicated to love of beauty and sensuality, and on the particular attraction of Paris as a modern-day Isle of Lesbos, see Benstock, *Women of the Left Bank*, pp. 268–307; Karla Jay, *The Amazon and the Page: Natalie Clifford Barney and Renée Vivien* (Bloomington: Indiana Univ. Press, 1988); and George Wickes, *The Amazon of Letters: The Life and Loves of Natalie Barney* (London: Allen, 1977). On the gay activity prevalent in the YMCA and the public baths, see Chauncey, *Gay New York*, pp. 155–57 and 207–25 (chap. 8: "The Social World of the Baths").

38. Wayne Koestenbaum makes a similar point in his intelligent review of *Gay New York*, "Vagabond Blues," in the *Los Angeles Times Book Review* (Sunday, 7 Aug. 1994), pp. 2, 13. See also Chauncey's critique of the closet as the "spatial metaphor people typically use to characterize gay life before the advent of gay liberation," despite the fact that the metaphor was never used by gay people before the 1960s (*Gay New York*, p. 6; see p. 375 n. 9, for his comments on Sedgwick's *Epistemology of the Closet*.)

39. Such a reading sheds a different light on the commonplace of the modernist writer fighting the meaninglessness, chaos, and randomness of the fragmented post–World War I world by the creative act of willing into being self-contained, self-referential fictional orders; from a queer perspective, the self-referentiality and self-containment of the fictional world create an otherwise invisible gay reality.

40. See, for example, Terry Castle, *Masquerade and Civilization: The Carnivalesque in Eighteenth-Century English Culture and Fiction* (Stanford, CA: Stanford Univ. Press, 1986).

41. Evidence of the historical presence of specifically gay argot in use among urban homosexual subcultures reaches as far back as eighteenth-century London. In accounts of a series of raids on London's "molly houses" published in the 1726 *Select Trials*, informants testify not only to the suspicious sexual assignations going on in the back rooms of these sites of homosexual interaction but to the particular "dialect," or coded terms, that the men use to refer to their sexual activities. Cited in Ed Cohen, "Legislating the Norm: From Sodomy to Gross Indecency," in *Hidden from History*, ed. Duberman, Vicinus, and Chauncey, p. 183; for more on London's "molly house" subculture, which evocatively links urban sites, architectural space, and something close to twentieth-century "homosexual identity," see Alan Bray, *Homosexuality in Renaissance England* (London: Gay Men's Press, 1982), pp. 81–114. Jeffrey Weeks, in *Sex, Politics, and Society: The Regulation of Sexuality*

since 1800 (London and New York: Longman, 1981), also refers to the gay argot or "parlare," derived from theatrical and circus slang, that had become a part of late-nineteenth-century communication and modes of gossip among gay men, and he suggests that by this time there existed "a widespread and often international homosexual argot, suggesting a widely dispersed and organized subculture" (p. 111). For a compendium of homosexual argot in America in the years before the gay liberation movement, see Gershon Legman, "The Language of Homosexuality: An American Glossary," in *Sex Variants*, vol. 2, ed. George W. Henry (New York: Paul B. Hoeber, 1941).

42. See, respectively, Peter Brooks, *Reading for the Plot. Design and Intention in Narrative* (New York: Knopf, 1984), and Joseph A. Boone, *Tradition Counter Tradition: Love and the Form of Fiction* (Chicago: Univ. of Chicago Press, 1987).

"Smoke, Lilies, and Jade"

43. Like Nugent's "Smoke, Lilies, and Jade," Lewis Alexander's "Streets," quoted here in full, appeared in *Fire!! A Quarterly Devoted to the Younger Negro Artists* 1, no.1 (1926), p. 23.

44. For biographical information on Nugent, see Lewis, *When Harlem Was in Vogue*, pp. 196–97; Charles Michael Smith's interview-based article, "Bruce Nugent: Bohemian of the Harlem Renaissance," in *In the Life: A Black Anthology*, ed. Joseph Beam (Boston: Alyson Press, 1986), pp. 209–20; and Eric Garber, "Richard Bruce Nugent," entry in *Afro-American Writers from the Harlem Renaissance to 1940: Dictionary of Literary Biography*, ed. Trudier Harris, vol. 51 (Detroit, Gale Press, 1987): 213–21. All three report that Nugent moved from Washington, DC, to Manhattan at thirteen with his recently widowed mother, details which match the profile of the autobiographical character Alex, who moves to New York City at fourteen after his father's death. Lewis notes that Nugent supported himself in the city by becoming a bellhop and then "mascot" of Rudolph Valentino (the possibilities of which are mind-boggling). When Nugent decided he was an artist and therefore did not need to work, his mother sent him back to Washington in 1924 to mend his ways; in Washington, however, Nugent met Langston Hughes, with whom he returned to New York in 1925, just as the New Negro movement in the arts was being launched. Never closeted about his homosexuality, Nugent married in 1952, living with his wife in a deeply felt but nonphysical love relationship that, as Nugent explained to Smith, did not preclude his sleeping with men. Garber provides a list of Nugent's scant number of published works. A trove of several unpublished novels and stories, along with artwork, remain in the care of Nugent's executor in Hoboken, New Jersey, where Nugent died in 1987 at the age of eighty-one, one of the oldest survivors of the Harlem Renaissance.

45. Chauncey, *Gay New York*, p. 246. A sense of this density is conveyed by James Weldon Johnson's estimate, in *Black Manhattan*, that two square miles of Harlem had become home to two hundred thousand black people, "more to the square acre than any other place known on earth" (quoted in Huggins, ed., *Voices from the Harlem Renaissance*, p. 66). The factors leading to this influx included the negative impact of the economic depression of 1904–1905 on the newly developed residential properties north of Central Park, which were bought up by a handful of enterprising African-American businessmen who rented them to black tenants; the "great migration" of Southern blacks northward beginning at the turn of the century; and the advent of World War I, which attracted blacks to Manhattan to fill labor positions hitherto denied to minority populations. See Lewis, *When Harlem Was in Vogue*, chap. 2: "City of Refuge"; Nathan Irvin Huggins, "Harlem: Capital of the Black World," in *Harlem Renaissance* (New York: Oxford Univ. Press, 1971), chap. 1; and James

de Jongh, *Vicious Modernism: Black Harlem and the Literary Imagination* (Cambridge: Cambridge Univ. Press, 1990), chap. 1.

46. De Jongh, *Vicious Modernism,* p. 17.

47. Johnson, *Black Manhattan,* in Huggins, ed., *Voices from the Harlem Renaissance,* p. 66; Bontemps is quoted in Lewis, *When Harlem Was in Vogue,* p. 103.

48. De Jongh, *Vicious Modernism,* pp. 31, 28.

49. Rossi, *Architecture of the City,* p. 96; Thurman, *Infants of the Spring,* p. 222.

50. For a sampling of these gay fictional characters, see Thurman's *The Blacker the Berry* (1929) and *Infants of the Spring,* which includes a flamboyantly bisexual character, the decadent artist Paul Arbian (modeled on Bruce Nugent); McKay's *Home to Harlem,* which includes minor gay characters; Blair Niles's *Strange Brother,* which I discuss later in this chapter; and Nella Larsen's *Passing* (1929), which recent critics have read from a lesbian perspective. Some other noteworthy participants in Harlem gay life included Harold Jackman (Cullen's lover), Clinton Moore, Ma Rainey, Moms Mabley, Gladys Bentley, Alexander Gumby, and Josephine Baker; rumors of Zora Neale Hurston's bisexuality, which remain unproved, are commonplace among Hurston scholars. The most thorough account of Harlem's gay subculture, to which I am greatly indebted, is Eric Garber's "A Spectacle in Color: The Lesbian and Gay Subculture of Jazz Age Harlem," in *Hidden from History,* ed. Duberman, Vicinus, and Chauncey, pp. 318–31. A useful summary of the gay Harlem phenomenon appears in Neil Miller, *Out of the Past: Gay and Lesbian History, 1865 to the Present* (New York: Vintage-Random, 1995).

51. Garber, "Lesbian and Gay Subculture," pp. 321–24; the newspaper reference is quoted in Chauncey, *Gay New York,* p. 249.

52. Quoted in Chauncey, *Gay New York,* p. 252.

53. The official "party line," laid down by senior statesmen such as DuBois and Locke, sought to further the Negro cause by promoting the so-called Talented Tenth, the privileged, educated, black middle-class deemed capable of contributing to "high" culture and, conversely, by muting literary expressions that, by tapping into folk traditions, might feed white culture's stereotype of blacks as "primitive," instinctual, tied to the earth, and incapable of higher aspirations.

54. Bruce Nugent, "Smoke, Lilies, and Jade," reprinted in *Voices from the Harlem Renaissance,* ed. Nathan Huggins (New York: Oxford Univ. Press, 1976), p. 110. The story was published under the pseudonym Richard Bruce. All further page references are to this edition, and are cited in the text.

55. Such an association led to the uproar among Harlemites over Carl Van Vechten's *Nigger Heaven,* which could be read to imply that its pallid, middle-class lovers would have done better hearkening to the "tom-tom beat" of the primordial, which they, as members of a race that has (supposedly) escaped "overcivilization," were in a better position to appreciate. We will return to this problematic equation of the primitive and "natural" life force in the discussion of *Strange Brother.* It is important to note, however, that the "tom-tom beat" of the primordial that could be used to symbolize the black person's innate primitivism could also lend itself to an entirely different use in the hands of the New Negro writers for whom the image of Africa became a marker of a rich, sustaining heritage and a source of pride. Thus, Langston Hughes advocates the expression of "our individual dark-skinned selves without fear and shame," adding, "We know we are beautiful. And ugly too. The tom-tom cries and the tom-tom laughs," in his essay, "The Negro Artist and the Racial Mountain," *Nation,* 1926, reprinted in Huggins, ed., *Voices from the Harlem Renaissance,* p. 309.

56. Hughes, "The Negro Artist," p. 309.

57. Smith, "Bruce Nugent," (interview), in *In the Life,* ed. Beam, p. 214.

58. Smith notes in his interview in *In the Life* that Nugent's original intention was to use ellipses of differing lengths throughout the story to capture the lulls in speech and thought patterns, but the idea was nixed by the printers (214–15). Except for the extended ellipses at the end of paragraphs that generally indicate a transition between scenes, the only extended (nine point) ellipsis that occurs *within* a paragraph is used to mark the occasion when Alex and Beauty first make love, thereby accentuating the unspoken and, indeed, the unsayable.

59. There are four explicit references to Wilde in this short text: first, when Alex muses about his favorite writers, which include "Wilde . . . Freud . . ." (101); second, when he wonders if Wilde's parents badgered him about his artistic ambitions as much as his mother does him; third, when he wonders "was it Wilde who had said . . . a cigarette is the most perfect pleasure because it leaves one unsatisfied" (102), one of Lord Henry's sayings in *Picture of Dorian Gray;* fourth, when he uses lines from Wilde's *Salome* to articulate his desire to kiss Beauty: "Alex wondered why he always thought of that passage from Wilde's Salome . . . when he looked at Beauty's lips . . . I would kiss your lips . . . he *would* like to kiss Beauty's lips" (106–7). In addition, Wilde's influence is implicit in Alex's fantasy of striding the streets in a long black cape, then lying "back among strangely fashioned cushions and sip[ping] eastern wines" in a darkened room smelling of incense and dressed in a yellow silk shirt and black velvet trousers (104), in the text's numerous references to calla lilies (hence the title reference), and in Nugent's embedded citation of the famous trope of the "love that dare not speak its name" in the passage in which Alex admits he loves both Beauty and Melva: "He loved them both . . . there . . . he had thought it . . . actually dared to think it . . . but Beauty must never know" (106).

60. Another Wildean touch occurs on the last pages of *Infants,* in the campy dedication of the novel, *Wu Sing: The Geisha Man,* that Paul Arbian (the Nugent character) leaves behind after committing suicide: "To Huysmans' Des Esseintes and Oscar Wilde's Oscar Wilde / Ecstatic Spirits with whom I Cohabit / And whose golden spores of decadent pollen / I shall broadcast and fertilize" (284).

61. Quoted in Watson, "Introduction," xviii.

62. Arna Bontemps, quoted in Lewis, *When Harlem Was in Vogue,* p. 103; de Jongh, *Vicious Modernism,* p. 24. See Hughes's "Jazzonia" and "Lenox Avenue: Midnight," in the poem-series "The Weary Blues."

63. The repetition of the image "blue" to suggest multiple, simultaneous meanings illustrates a modernist understanding of the image: blueness indicates a mood (as in "feeling blue"); it evokes the jazz blues musical tradition; it becomes a poetical expression of the urban nightscape (as in the repeated description of the streets Alex walks as "the long blue narrow"); when associated with the rising smoke from Alex's cigarette, it symbolizes the imagination adrift; and, finally, I suspect it also encodes a specifically gay meaning that tropes on the French phrase, *l'amour blue,* a euphemism for "gay love."

64. I purposefully refrain from specifying Beauty's "racial" otherness. On the one hand, some critics have assumed Beauty is, in Lewis's phrase, a "Hispanic Adonis" (*When Harlem Was in Vogue,* p. 197)—which Garber hyperbolically recasts as "a stunning Latin Adonis" ("Lesbian and Gay Subculture," p. 330)—in part on the basis of some of Nugent's personal sexual preferences and in part on the basis of the fact that Beauty first addresses Alex in Spanish when he asks for a match. On the other hand, the adjective "white" is the one exclusively used by Alex to describe Beauty's skin tone. The most interesting point about

the Spanish address, I think, is not that it fixes Beauty as Hispanic but rather that Alex is totally flattered that he, Alex, is mistaken for a Spanish speaker ("Alex was glad he had been addressed in Spanish . . . to have been asked for a match in English . . . or to have been addressed in English at all . . . would have been blasphemy just then" [105]. In addition to *Alex's* desire to be seen as other, as exotic and erotic at once, his pleasure perhaps reflects his own ambiguous feelings about race: in his imagination he is passing during this sexually charged moment as "not-black" as well as "not-American." An intriguingly self-conscious and political twist on the interraciality of Nugent's story exists in Isaac Julien's 1989 film, *Looking for Langston,* which features a voice-over reading the love-making passages from "Smoke, Lilies, and Jade" as its male characters make love on scene; Julien, however, transforms the lovers into two unambiguously *black* men. The interpenetrations between Nugent's text and Julien's poetic evocation of the Harlem Renaissance could be investigated at length, starting with the fact that the film is dedicated to three gay black men who died in 1987: Nugent himself, James Baldwin (whose open gayness becomes a kind of substitute for Hughes's closetedness), and Joseph Beam, the editor of the volume *In the Life,* in which Nugent is interviewed.

65. The journal *Fire!!* takes its name from these lyrics, which are printed at the beginning of the issue: in prototypically modernist fashion, then, Nugent's story thus self-reflexively encodes its extratextual context and "origin."

Nightwood

66. Djuna Barnes, *Nightwood* (1936; rpt., New York: New Directions, 1961), pp. 116–17. All further references to this work are cited in the text.

67. Lewis, *When Harlem Was in Vogue,* p. 99. In such a formulation Harlem quite literally represents a space of transit between the bohemian Village and the expatriate artists' colony established in Paris.

68. Benstock, *Women of the Left Bank,* p. 46; Natalie Barney, *Souvenirs indiscrets* [*Indiscreet Memories*] (Paris: Flammarion, 1960), p. 21, quoted in Jay, *Amazon and the Page,* p. 8. On gay Paris, see, in addition to Benstock, Brassaï's photo-essay collection, *The Secret Paris of the 1930s,* trans. Richard Miller (1932; rpt., New York: Pantheon, 1976); and Bertha Harris, "The More Profound Nationality of Their Lesbianism: Lesbian Society in Paris in the 1920s," in *Amazon Expedition: A Lesbian Feminist Anthology,* ed. Phyllis Birkby et al. (Washington, NJ: Times Change Press, 1973), pp. 77–88. On the many books on the American expatriate presence in the Paris of this period, see the section of chapter 5 on Barnes in J. Gerald Kennedy, *Imagining Paris: Exile, Writing, and American Identity* (New Haven, CT: Yale Univ. Press, 1993), pp. 219–42; Hugh Ford, ed., *The Left Bank Revisited: Selections from the Paris Tribune 1917–1934* (University Park, PA: The Pennsylvania State Univ. Press, 1972); and Robert McAlmon, *Being Geniuses Together, 1920–1930* (San Francisco: North Point Press, 1984).

69. Djuna Barnes to Natalie Barney, 10 Sept. 1967, quoted in Phillip Herring, *Djuna: The Life and Works of Djuna Barnes* (New York: Viking, 1995), p. 348 n. 1; Herring's work is the new, definitive, and much needed authoritative biography of Barnes, replacing the often inaccurate, bafflingly organized Andrew Field biography, *Djuna: The Life and Times of Djuna Barnes* (New York: G. P. Putnam, 1983).

70. Marilyn Reizbaum, "A 'Modernism of Marginality': The Link between James Joyce and Djuna Barnes," in *New Alliances in Joyce Studies,* ed. Bonnie Kime Scott (Newark, DE: Univ. of Delaware Press, 1988), pp. 185–86.

71. Jane Marcus, "Laughing at Leviticus: *Nightwood* as Woman's Circus Epic," in *Si-*

lence and Power: A Reevaluation of Djuna Barnes, ed. Mary Lynn Broe (Carbondale, IL: Univ. of Southern Illinois Press, 1991), p. 223.

72. To cite just one example, Benstock's reading, in *Women of the Left Bank,* while attempting to be inclusive and incorporating much useful material, is ultimately hampered by the desire to read *into* the novel a "feminist" message consistent with the critic's feminist methodology: such a tactic leads Benstock to declare that the novel traces "Barnes's feminist discovery" (262) of how patriarchy has socially produced the state of alienation that women have internalized, resulting in the "nightwood" of depravity in which women experience their "difference," their sexuality, as other and alien. In this dichotomous vision of villains and martyrs, Robin's complex passivity becomes a manifestation of her victimization at the hands of patriarchy (with Nora playing the role of oppressor as patriarchy's agent), and the novel's representation of the *human* condition as a state of radical "estrangement" turns out to be an allegory of *woman's* estrangement from herself (258). While the subjects of women, women's sexuality, and women's bodies pervade Barnes's canon, to make her viewpoint on these issues so uniformly feminist in our contemporary sense overlooks the contradictory attitudes that equally pervade her writings and also limit our perception of other ways in which she probes categories of difference. The same straight-jacketing effect surfaces in readings that focus primarily on the novel as a "lesbian narrative," whether one of lesbian damnation, as in Catharine R. Stimpson's mention of *Nightwood* in "Zero Degree Deviancy: The Lesbian Novel in English," in *Writing and Sexual Difference,* ed. Elizabeth Abel (Chicago: Univ. of Chicago Press, 1982), or one of poststructuralist/feminist reclamation, as in Elizabeth A. Meese's chapter, "A Crisis of Style—Re:finding Djuna Barnes's *Nightwood,*" in *(Sem)Erotics: Theorizing Lesbian:Writing* (New York: New York Univ. Press, 1992), pp. 43–62, which backs the claim that "*Nightwood* is a lesbian novel" written in a kind of lesbian *écriture,* whose "crisis of style" is both "*Nightwood* and lesbianism" (56).

73. Philip Rahv review, 1937, *New Masses,* quoted in Jane Marcus, "Mousemeat: Contemporary Reviews of *Nightwood,*" in *Silence and Power,* ed. Broe, p. 200; the unsigned review in *Newstatesman and Nation,* 17 Oct. 1936, is also quoted in Marcus, "Mousemeat," who finds the tone "remarkably like Rebecca West" (197–99). Clifton Fadiman's review in the *New Yorker,* 13 March 1937, is quoted in Marcus, "Mousemeat," p. 203. Benstock's exaggerated claim that *Nightwood* has long served as a "cult guide to the homosexual underground nightworld of Paris" (*Women of the Left Bank,* p. 235) participates in this reading of the novel as a gay treatise. One is hard put, however, to imagine these cult followers making much progress in discovering the precise location of Paris's gay "underground" with this largely nonrealistic novel as their guide! Nearly contemporaneous works, including Hall's *The Well of Loneliness* (1928), Colette's *The Pure and Impure* (1931), and Lucy Delarue-Madrus's *The Angel and the Perverts* (1930) provide a more accurate road map to lesbian Paris.

74. See also Donna Gerstenberger's related claim that the text undoes all binaristic modes of categorization, in "The Radical Narrative of Djuna Barnes's *Nightwood,*" in *Breaking the Sequence: Women's Experimental Fiction,* ed. Ellen G. Friedman and Miriam Fuchs (Princeton, NJ: Princeton Univ. Press, 1989), p. 130.

75. Even though several of her footnotes point to openings for a "queer" rather than "lesbian" reading of the text, Carolyn Allen persistently refers to the novel as a "lesbian narrative" and a "narrative of lesbian erotics" in "The Erotics of Nora's Narrative in Djuna Barnes's *Nightwood,*" *Signs: Journal of Women in Culture and Society* 19 (Autumn 1993): 177–200, which argues that Barnes is revising Freud's theory of homosexuality as a kind of narcissism. Despite an offhanded acknowledgment of the role of contemporary queer poli-

tics in reviving an interest in bisexuality, Fran Michel's break with the "lesbian" designation for Barnes and her works only replaces the term with a construction of authorial "bisexuality," rather than a queering of sexuality or textuality, in "'I Just Loved Thelma': Djuna Barnes and the Construction of Bisexuality," *Review of Contemporary Fiction* 13, no. 3 (Fall 1993): 53–62.

76. The parallels that Barnes draws between the outcast or "estranged" status of homosexuals and Jews such as Felix—and their relation to Barnes's reading of Proust's similar analogue in *Cities of the Plain*—are thoroughly documented by Julie L. Abraham, "'Woman, Remember You': Djuna Barnes and History," in *Silence and Power,* ed. Broe, p. 256. Without using specifically queer terminology, critics such as Reizbaum ("James Joyce and Djuna Barnes," p. 181), and Marcus ("Laughing at Leviticus," p. 223), both evoke well the queer ambience of the world of otherness embodied in *Nightwood.* Within the text, O'Connor provides a roster of the outcasts who make up Barnes's textual universe when he speaks to Nora of the habitués of the city who, like "my Sodomites," "turn the day into night": "the young, the drug addict, the prolifigate, the drunken and that most memorable, the lover who watches all night long in fear and anguish" (94–95). A similar list occurs in Barnes's description of those who populate Nora's "pauper's" salon in America: "poets, radicals, beggars, artists, and people in love . . . Catholics, Protestants, Brahmins, dabblers in black magic and medicine" (50). Marcus makes an especially interesting case for the figure of the circus performer Nikka the Nigger as part of Barnes's attempt to align racial and sexual oppressions ("Laughing at Leviticus," pp. 223–24); this crossing of racial and homosexual oppression is also implicit in the fact that the chapter title "Go Down, Matthew" is a reference to the gospel spiritual, "Go down, Moses, let my people go," as Barnes confirmed in a 1959 letter. See Cheryl J. Plumb, ed., *Djuna Barnes, Nightwood: The Original Version and Related Drafts* (Normal, IL: Dalkey Archive Press, 1995), p. 226 n.

77. Reizbaum, "James Joyce and Djuna Barnes," p. 186.

78. Marilyn Reizbaum has explicated these Bakhtinian resonances in the novel in an unpublished essay, "The Carnivalesque in Djuna Barnes's *Nightwood* and Joyce's 'Nightworld': This Sex/Race Which Is Not One" (presented at the 1988 Joyce International Symposium in Venice, Italy).

79. Thanks to the recent publication by Cheryl J. Plumb of the original manuscript version of the novel, *Djuna Barnes, Nightwood: The Original Version,* we can now measure more accurately Barnes's unabashed frankness (and bawdiness) in representing both male and female homosexuality in various passages deleted by her publisher and T. S. Eliot for fears of censorship. Nearly all the longer omitted passages involve blatantly, often comical, homosexual yarns told by O'Connor; one involves his arrest by the vice squad and subsequent dismissal by a friendly judge (26–28—a scene that echoes the content of the "Cruise" chapter of *The Young and Evil*), and another the humorous tale of a "boy who has been queer all his hour" inadvertently routing the German enemy and thus winning the *croix de guerre* for battlefield "prowess" (95–96).

80. Gertrude Stein, *Paris France* (New York: Scribners, 1940), p. 11.

81. Andre Menabrea, "Les Enseignements du vieux Pont Neuf," *Urbanisme* 8–9 (Nov.–Dec. 1932): 226; quoted in Evenson, *Paris: A Century of Change,* p. 70. This diatribe was published in 1932, as scores of artists and expatriates were moving to the Left Bank in search of the very atmosphere that this commentator wishes to eradicate.

82. Ford's comments are made in the preface he wrote to a story collection by another Paris expatriate, Jean Rhys, titled *The Left Bank* (London: Jonathan Cape, 1927), p. 24, quoted in Benstock, *Women of the Left Bank,* p. 450.

83. Ned Rorem, letter to Broe, 23 Sept. 1984, in *Silence and Power,* ed., Broe, p. 206. Barnes, indeed, corroborates Rorem's impression in a 22 July 1936 letter written to her patron Emily Coleman: "I haunt the Place St. Sulpice now, because I've made it in my book into my life—as if my life had really been there," even though Thelma, Robin's prototype, "never put her foot, in reality, over [the] steps" to the Hôtel Récamier, "where, in my book, Robin lived" and which Barnes now "haunts." Quoted in Herring, *Djuna,* p. 217.

84. In the textual notes to *Nightwood: The Original Version,* p. 192, n. 40.11, Plumb notes that a phrase identifying Robin as an "orphan" was deleted by Emily Coleman.

85. Jacques Maritain, quoted in Louis F. Kannenstine, *The Art of Djuna Barnes: Duality and Damnation* (New York: New York Univ. Press, 1977), p. 89; Marcus, "Laughing at Leviticus," p. 224–25; Kannenstine, pp. 90–91.

86. See Watson, "Introduction," pp. xxviii and n. 47, xxxvi.

87. In her excellent chapter on Barnes, "The Learned Corruption of Language: *Nightwood*'s Failed Flirtation with Fascism," in *Sapphic Modernism and Fascist Politics* (forthcoming from Stanford Univ. Press), Erin Carlston makes a convincing case for relating Barnes's doctrine of the inorganic and abnormal to the decadent aesthetic privileging artifice over the natural: as in *fin de siècle* art, the figure of the lesbian becomes valuable precisely because her (assumed) nonprocreativity places her beyond loss, degeneration, and decay. My thanks to Carlston for giving me to permission to quote from her manuscript.

88. "The surface is the true object of desire—to linger there, exploring its baroque intricacies while avoiding inevitabilities, catastrophes associated with forays which bring on the future tense," writes Joan Retallack in "One Acts: Early Plays of Djuna Barnes," in *Silence and Power,* ed. Broe, p. 51. On the paucity of "plot-advancing events" in the novel, see Carolyn Allen, "'Dressing the Unknowable in the Garments of the Known': The Style of Djuna Barnes's *Nightwood,*" in *Women's Language and Style,* ed. Douglas Butturff and Edmund L. Epstein (Akron, OH: L&S Books, 1978), p. 108, who comments that "traditional plot development is of scant interest to Barnes . . . it operates as a pretext rather than context," and who notes that by the end of chapter 4 all the essential action of the novel has been completed.

89. Sharon Spencer, *Space, Time, and Structure in the Modern Novel* (New York: New York Univ. Press, 1971), p. 41, quoted in Kannenstine, *Art of Djuna Barnes,* p. 92. The first serious attempt to explicate the novel in spatial terms is by Joseph Frank, "Spatial Form in Modern Literature," *Sewannee Review* 53 (1945): 221–40, 433–56. See also A. Desmond Hawkin's comment, in his review of the novel in *New English Weekly* (29 April 1937), that the novel is a "relentless confession counterpointed with oracular pronouncement" in which all the action has *already occurred* and is now "relived in dialogue," as in the Renaissance drama of Webster: "We have a stream of superb sentences, of penetrating epigrams lighting up an essentially static scene"; quoted in Marcus, "Mousemeat," pp. 201–2.

90. Gerstenberger, "Radical Narrative," p. 133.

91. Attempts to describe the novel's overall structure often hinge on spatial metaphors. Readers often compare its form either to that of Dante's *Inferno,* with its circles of the damned, or, given its carnival imagery, to that of a three-ring circus, with its simultaneity and free play. What is striking about both analogies is the degree to which spatial concepts—Dante's circles, circus rings—take precedence over linear/temporal ones. Like a series of concentric circles, each chapter draws the reader closer and closer to the "still heart" of the novel, the forementioned cluster of chapters that replay the catastrophic severance of Robin and Nora from different angles.

92. All these queer narrative interventions, furthermore, have a profoundly and deliber-

ately alienating effect on the reader, for Barnes's linguistic, temporal, and spatial disjunctions tend to hold the reader, as previously mentioned, at a certain distance from the text. To borrow from Barnes's description of Hedvig's relation to Guido, we are always "moving toward" the novel "in recoil"—spurned by that which we impossibly seek to know. The reader remains as estranged, *vis à vis* the text as are its characters, *vis à vis* each other. Implicit in such distancing effects, of course, is Barnes's pose of authority or control over both her text and its readers; for what Barnes facetiously says about O'Connor's unstoppable, maddening, but hypnotic monologues could well be applied to herself as narrator: "Once [he] had his audience . . . nothing could stop him" (15). The position of the reader, moreover, is like that of the *flâneur/*cruiser, whose perspective is always limited to a partial view, a few tantalizing hints, rather than assuming full panoptic vision or control. Barnes thematizes this failure of scopic control throughout the novel, showing the ways in which the "surveillance" of the subject by other watching subjects is continually being circumvented. The Foucauldian implications of this tension are notably present in the "Night Watch" chapter, as Nora helplessly witnesses Robin's forays into the anonymity of the night (see 59–61). Nora's furtive attempts at surveillance—hence the chapter's title—only bring her visual confirmation of the betrayals she cannot afford to see. For more on surveillance and the genre of fiction, see chapter 2 of this book.

93. Kannenstine, *Art of Djuna Barnes,* pp. 21, 87. Along with "Bow Down" and "Nightwood," "Anatomy of [the] Night" was another of Barnes's working titles; T. S. Eliot was responsible for choosing "Nightwood" over "Anatomy," reports Herring in *Djuna,* p. 223.

94. Alfred Kazin's contrast of Barnes and Woolf appears in his review of *Nightwood* in the *New York Times Book Review* (7 March 1937), quoted in Marcus, "Mousemeat" (197); see also Kannenstine, *Art of Djuna Barnes,* pp. 105, 95. Noting that the novel, "like modernism itself, begins in Vienna in the 1880s," Marcus theorizes in "Leviticus" that the text forms a deliberate parody of psychoanalysis (222).

95. See similar Jungian concepts expressed in Eugene Jolas, *Language of Night* (The Hague: Servire Press, 1932), p. 47, quoted in Kannenstine, *Art of Djuna Barnes,* pp. 107–8; Kannenstine hypothesizes that the journal *transition,* under Eugene Jolas's editorship, was a likely conduit of such Jungian and surrealist topoi as the primitive, dreams, and the racial unconscious to Barnes. Note, for example, Jolas's comments in "Night-Mind and Day-Mind," *transition: An International Workshop for Orphic Creation* 21 (March 1932), that "any metaphysical experimentation that does not first investigate the night-side of life deprives itself of the necessary precondition of success" and that "to understand the very springs of the human psyche it is imperative to study the nocturnal manifestations of the spirit," which reveal themselves in, among other things, he continues, the "sexual aberrations" (222).

96. This is Jessica Benjamin's thesis in *The Bonds of Love: Psychoanalysis, Feminism, and the Problem of Domination* (New York: Pantheon, 1988).

97. Carlston, "Learned Corruption of Language," pp. 33–34.

98. Benjamin, *Bonds of Love,* p. 56.

99. Benjamin, *Bonds of Love,* pp. 75–77, 83.

100. Hence the passage likening Robin's absence to a "physical removal, insupportable and irreparable. As an amputated hand cannot be disowned because it is experiencing a futurity, of which the victim is its forebear, so Robin was an amputation that Nora could not renounce" (59).

101. Emblematic of this "truth" is the case of the oxymoronically named Frau Mann

(who also goes by the fabricated title the Duchess of Broadbent), a trapeze artist who "seemed to have a skin that was the pattern of her costume. . . . The stuff of her tights was no longer a covering, it was herself" (13); in a reversal of the western cultural myth that the self emanates from some inner core to the surface, which then becomes its expression, Frau Mann's surface is represented as having grown inward, "as the design runs through hard holiday candies" (13).

102. Marcus, "Laughing at Leviticus," pp. 225–27, 246–49. Herring notes that Barnes "was in love with all aspects of the theater," from her early work with the Provincetown Players to her attendance at the circus in Paris to her final published work, *The Antiphon* (179).

The Young and Evil

103. Steven Watson, "An Introduction," *The Young and Evil*, p. vii. Hailing from the South, Ford was a precocious artist who, as Watson recounts, determined at the tender age of seventeen that he was going to be famous within two years. Indeed by 1929 he had published a radical poetry magazine, *Blues*, with contributions he had audaciously solicited from William Carlos Williams, H. D., Alfred Kreymborg, James Farrell, Paul Bowles, and Erskine Caldwell. During his Paris years, Gertrude Stein and Djuna Barnes became his supporters. In 1932 Ford met the Russian artist Pavel Tchelitchew, who became his lover for the next twenty-three years, during which period Ford founded the prestigious art magazine, *View*, wrote dozens of volumes of surrealist-influenced poetry, and made the cult experimental film *Johnny Minotaur*. Watson credits Ford with doing most of the actual composing of the novel, often incorporating materials from Tyler's letters. The descendant of two presidents, Harrison Parker Tyler had been in New York six years when Ford arrived in the Village in 1930, having already established a local reputation as a poet and book reviewer. Throughout a long career, Tyler published numerous volumes of poetry, several biographies, and eight books of Freudian film criticism, including *Screening the Sexes* (1973), the first study of homosexuality in film. Watson's excellent introduction provides these and other biographical details on these two largely forgotten players in the international arts scene from the late 1920s to the 1950s. Charles Boultenhouse, Tyler's lover, reminisces at length about Tyler's literary influences in "Parker Tyler's Own Scandal," *Film Culture* 77 (Fall 1992): 10–23, including his correspondence with Ezra Pound on the subject of "bhoogery" (17). Ford's unpublished memoir, "I Will Be What I Am," and Parker Tyler's unpublished autobiography, "Acrobat in the Dark: A Metaphysical Biography," are both housed at the Harry Ransom Humanities Research Center at the University of Texas at Austin.

104. Indeed, when the novel was released in 1933 by Obelisk Press, the Paris-based operation of Jack Kahane—who also published Radclyffe Hall's *Well of Loneliness,* Henry Miller's *Tropic of Cancer,* and Anaïs Nin's *House of Incest*—it was instantly seized by English and American customs. See Watson, "Introduction," p. xxv.

105. Each had a shaping hand, moreover, in the other's work. Barnes read the manuscript that Ford had brought to Paris and commented favorably on it (she went on to write one of its promotional blurbs), and Ford helped her type the *Nightwood* manuscript as she was composing it in 1933 while she and Ford were sharing a house in Tangiers: hence certain of the idiosyncratic imagistic continuities—the Little Red Riding Hood motif; the doll as emblem of same-sex love; the turning of arrests for homosexual solicitation into a humorous fantasy of justice working to vindicate the gay victim because of the judge's own propensities. On the latter resemblance, compare chapter 14 ("Cruise") of *The Young and*

Evil to the anecdote of O'Connor deleted from the manuscript of *Nightwood* by T. S. Eliot (see note 79 of the preceding section). For the Barnes-Ford relationship, see chapter 8, "Charles Impossible Ford," in Herring, *Djuna,* pp. 171–84.

106. In Watson's words, "The homosexual community didn't distinguish itself as separate from the other marginal communities that dominated the Village" ("Introduction," p. xviii). Note, as well, Tyler's quip, already cited, that a "homosexual, if he was artistic and intellectual, was just another bohemian."

107. See Sedgwick, *Epistemology of the Closet,* pp. 82–86, Chauncey, *Gay New York,* pp. 8–9, 23, and Watson, "Introduction," p. ix.

108. In early-twentieth-century parlance, Gabriel and Louis's sexual positioning is similar to that of "trade," who, as Chauncey explains, were masculine-identified men who considered themselves "normal" despite the fact that they engaged in sex with other males—men who, because of their effeminacy, were known as "fairies." The custom, according to Chauncey, was for trade to pay for the services of the fairy; the ironic twist in this novel, however, is that Louis is being supported by his "fairy," Karel, a gender inversion which no doubt adds to the anxieties and defensiveness that prey on Louis and emerge in his combative attack on Karel ("What gave you the idea that I was queer?") as well as in his virulent name-calling (labeling Karel's type as "homos," as mere "approximations" of virile manhood; 143–45).

109. Mabel Dodge (Luhan) ran an influential literary salon in the Village in the 1910s and eventually ended up a devotee and patron of D. H. Lawrence at her artist's colony in Taos.

110. See Eve Kosofsky Sedgwick, "Queer Performativity: Henry James's *The Art of the Novel,"* and Judith Butler, "Critically Queer," both in *GLQ: A Journal of Lesbian and Gay Studies* 1, no. 1 (1993): 1–16, 17–32.

111. Both Ford and Tyler are quoted in Watson, who is drawing on interviews ("Introduction," pp. xx, viii).

112. For the colloquial use of *wolf* in gay vernacular, see Chauncey, *Gay New York,* p. 87. The perverse opening gambit of *The Young and Evil,* furthermore, anticipates the scene in *Nightwood* when Nora happens upon Matthew O'Connor in bed in drag and instantly flashes upon the wolf-disguised-as-grandmother in the Red Riding Hood fairy tale, which in turn leads Nora to recall the dream of her grandmother in bed, dressed in men's clothes and leering at her; I suspect Barnes may well be borrowing from Ford, whose manuscript she had read before writing *Nightwood.*

113. On the historicity of these balls, which attracted participants of all races and persuasions by the thousands, see Chauncey, *Gay New York,* pp. 257–63.

114. Bruce Rogers, "The Degenerates of Greenwich Village," *Current Psychology and Psychoanalysis* (Dec. 1936), 29 and following, quoted in Chauncey, *Gay New York,* p. 234.

115. The characters of *The Young and Evil* seem to live entirely in the present, devoid of the encumbrances of past or family (none of the surnames of the five main characters are reported). Only once each do Karel and Julian, at the ends of chapters 2 and 3 respectively, remember their childhoods, and the function of these stream-of-consciousness passages is quite explicitly to posit narratives of the origins of homosexual difference in childhood.

116. Quoted in Watson, "Introduction," p. vii, from unpublished papers in the Parker Tyler Archives at the University of Texas—Austin, in a mock (self) interview that Parker penned upon the 1969 reissue of the novel. Although "evil" taken in this sense signifies a heroic rejection of stifling convention, placing itself in a tradition that reaches from Baudelaire to Jean Genet, the novel also unconsciously attests to the degree to which free-floating

desire and anarchic libidinal impulses encourage behaviors that issue in a more concretely dangerous kind of "evil," namely, the sadistic abuses of power that characterize nearly all the sexual relationships represented in the novel, in which one character is always being forced to submit to the will of another.

117. The model of urban flow describes particularly well how the chapters of this novel interface with one another. As if "turning a corner" in moving from one chapter to the next, the pedestrian/reader is suddenly, unexpectedly, launched into a simultaneously existing but hitherto unglimpsed reality, a terrain at once contiguous with but completely unknown to the previously traversed textual space/city block.

118. Joseph Litvak, "Proustian Anachronisms: Sophistication, Naïveté, and Gay Narrativity," presented at Division of Prose Fiction meeting, "Remapping 'Gender and Narrative'" at the 1994 MLA meeting. Thanks to Litvak for allowing me to quote from this manuscript.

119. For example, chapter 4 ends with Julian, Karel, and a character named Vivian naked in bed after a game of strip poker; chapter 5 ends with Louis and the now unconscious Karel collapsed together in Julian's bed; chapter 10 climaxes with Julian, Mrs. Dodge, and Santiago going home together; chapter 12 varies the pattern by having Louis invite Gabriel to join him and Karel in bed (a gambit declined); and chapter 6 concludes with Julian fantasizing (as far as I can tell) a threesome among himself, as voyeuristic onlooker, a sailor, and girl. My point is not that these threesomes *literally* lead to a new pairing that then emerges as the next narrative thread—this is generally not the case—but rather that these threesomes, like the couplings and recouplings that interlink them, act as *structural switch-points,* on/off signals, allowing the *narrative itself* to take off in a new direction or on a new track.

120. In these regards, the two characters share much with their authors. Like Julian, Ford was known for his youthful good looks, attested to by countless photographs of him, often taken by famous photographers, striking self-consciously dashing poses. These narcissistically inflected photographs might be seen as "mirrors" in which their subject, Ford, catches himself in the act of practicing, modifying, and performing his identity as desirable gay man. As for Tyler, who like Karel cultivated a deliberate persona in Village society as a modern-day dandy in flamboyant dress and makeup, Watson writes, "His fame was as much a product of his theatrical self-presentation as it was of the words he wrote. He was never simply Parker Tyler, writer, but The Beautiful Poet Parker Tyler, a character in a drama of his own devising" ("Introduction," p. xv).

121. In Karel's hands, using makeup not only functions to disrupt gender binaries but also becomes a mode of severing western notions of fixed identity from the presumption of essence by using the body's surface, in Butlerian fashion, to construct protean possibilities of being: "His eyebrows . . . could be pencilled into almost any expression: Clara Bow, Joan Crawford, Norma Shearer, etc. He thought he would choose something obvious for tonight. Purity" (56).

122. This passage bears comparison to Barnes's evocation of the doll as an image of lesbian love. The doll that one woman gives another, Nora tells O'Connor, represents the child they cannot have (142); as a signifying surface whose human image belies the lack of an interior core, the doll is also evocative of postmodern formulations of identity embraced in queer criticism as an escape from the trap of fixed identity.

123. Lee Edelman, *Homographesis,* (New York and London: Routledge, 1994), pp. 199–200, 7, and xiv–xv. The project of "reading" homosexuality in order to secure the fixity of (hetero)sexuality is, as Edelman shows, ironically to compel "heterosexual masculinity to

engage in the self-subverting labor of reading and interpreting *itself*" (205), thereby stripping it of its privileged status as natural and self-evident.

124. This relentless textualization of the homosexual—and hence destabilization of all sexuality—is related to the constant interplay between discourses of art and sex pervading Julian's and Karel's bohemian world. "Sex it's a false landscape only art giving it full colors" (157), is one of the Wilde-like epigrams that make up the surreal swirl of overheard words at the drag ball; Karel, upon initiating an affair, proclaims he is "finding out . . . oh so much so that there is nothing now but the writing of it" (85); Theo is writing a play titled *Artists and Lovers;* during a political conversation a communist puts down art by arguing that "poetry [is] a secondary sexual characteristic" (99); Karel's high-toned speech on the artist's political liberty is juxtaposed with Julian's giving a blow job to Danny, "the kind that makes homosexuality worthwhile" (141); and in an example of typographical characters once again conveying sexual "meaning," Julian thinks of all the handsome men who stride throughout the city with "their trousers . . . adjusted over the exclamation point" (74–75)—an odd reminder of Freud's fantasy that Dora imagines that nearly all Viennese men are walking around with visible erections.

125. Kristin Ross, *The Emergence of Social Space: Rimbaud and the Paris Commune* (Minneapolis: Univ. of Minnesota Press, 1988), p. 45 (Ross's emphases).

Strange Brother

126. Walt Whitman, "I Dream'd in a Dream" (1860), from *Calamus,* in *Leaves of Grass,* ed. Harold Woolf Blodgett and Sculley Bradley (New York: Norton, 1965), p. 133. Mark Thornton, protagonist of *Strange Brother,* quotes from this passage twice, on pp. 78 and 311.

127. The phrase "the shadow world," suggesting a liminal space between light and dark, is related to the euphemisms "twilight men" and "twilight lovers" often used in the period to describe gay men's and women's "half" or "inbetween" lives. See André Tellier's novel of 1931, *Twilight Men* (New York: Greenberg, 1931), as well as the title that Lillian Faderman gives *Odd Girls and Twilight Lovers: A History of Lesbian Life in the Twentieth Century* (New York: Columbia Univ. Press, 1991).

128. Like her female protagonist in the novel, June Westbrook, Blair Niles was an avid explorer and ethnographer of the unknown, often turning her journalistic practice to the investigation of foreign cultures. Her writings are inflected throughout with an empathetic interest in issues of race; these include, among other titles, *Casual Wanderings in Equador* (1923), *Columbia, Land of Miracles* (1924), *Black Haiti* (1926), *Day of Immense Sun* (1936), *The James* (1939), and *Condemned to Devil's Island* (1928). See the chapter on Niles in David Blackmore's Ph.D. dissertation, "Masculinity, Anxiety, and Contemporary Discourses of Sexuality in United States Fiction between the Wars" (UCLA, 1995).

129. Kobena Mercer, "Skin Head Sex Thing: Racial Difference and the Homoerotic Imaginary," in *How Do I Look? Queer Film and Video,* ed. Bad Object-Choices (Seattle: Bay Press, 1991), p. 193.

130. Curiously, Mark expresses no interest in living in the Village, which he claims to Ira and Caleb has been "spoiled" by tourists, as he fears Harlem soon will be (30).

131. Originally published in 1931 by the New York publisher Horace Liveright, *Strange Brother* was widely reviewed, as Peter Burton reveals in his introduction to the Gay Modern Classics reprint (iv). In general the reviewers tended to dismiss the novel as a piece of special pleading, overlooking its solid fictional qualities—within a certain formula of fiction-writing, it is actually quite well crafted. The fact that Liveright turned down the

manuscript of Ford's and Tyler's *The Young and Evil,* quipping that despite its "brilliance," "I could not think of publishing it as a book—life is too short and the jails are unsatisfactory," but took a risk on *Strange Brother* says something about its more conspicuous "best seller" format and potential appeal: it may be about controversial subject matter, yet it aims not to offend but to woo the reader. See Watson, "Introduction," *The Young and Evil,* p. xxiv.

132. The echoes of Woolf's language in these passages suggest Niles's familiarity with Woolf's famous essay.

133. My observations on the relationship between museum culture and modernism are indebted to the insights of Alice Gambrell, who has suggested in conversation that the pastiche of literary borrowings underlying the famously fragmented structure of T. S. Eliot's "The Wasteland" operate as an extension of the ethnographical impulse fueling the museum aesthetic and its similar appropriation of other cultures.

134. Like many of the other gay protagonists analyzed in this chapter, Mark is an artist, and his sketches of New York City capture something of this entity of many parts: "Most of his recent work consisted of various impressions of New York life; the mass of skyscrapers . . . tenements . . . Hell Gate Bridge . . . studies of Italian boys and Harlem types" (72).

135. Nancy Cunard, "Harlem Reviewed" (1935), reprinted in Huggins, ed., *Voices from the Harlem Renaissance,* p. 125.

136. This projection of marginality onto Harlem, it should be noted, contrasts with the perception of Harlem held by its advocates and inhabitants, as indicated in the comments of James Weldon Johnson in *Black Manhattan,* cited in the introduction to this chapter. For its black residents, he writes, Harlem was not a "fringe" or "border" territory that one must "go out to," but existed as the "heart of Manhattan," vitally connected to its other parts. See Johnson, in Huggins, ed., *Voices from the Harlem Renaissance,* p. 65.

137. The racism in this association is most apparent in the primal imagery of "the jungle" that is repeatedly applied by the novel's white visitors (and sometimes by the authorial voice) to Harlem to describe its nightclub acts in chapter 1: June herself likens the appearance of the singer Sybil in chapter 2 to "the heart of Africa . . . the heart of darkness!" (41), and the narrative represents Sybil's voice as echoing "like a love-cry heard far off in some jungle night" (42). Despite her celebratory intentions, Niles's use of primitivist language to uphold the black race as more "natural" than the white race thus occasionally reveals the unconscious racism involved in the frequent modernist association of blackness with sex and primitive civilization.

138. The figure of Sybil is based on the real-life Gladys Bentley. Bentley, as Garber notes, was "a 250-pound, masculine, dark-skinned lesbian, who performed all night long in a white tuxedo and top hat" at Harry Hansberry's Clam House, "the most famous gay-oriented [Harlem] club of the era" and the prototype of Niles's Lobster Pot ("Lesbian and Gay Subculture," p. 324).

139. See Powers, "Queer in the Streets, Straight in the Sheets." As such, June participates in one of the "strategic self-othering[s]" that Kobena Mercer uses to defend the white artist Robert Mapplethorpe's representation of black male nudes; her "experienc[e] of marginality" locates her, as Mercer suggests of contemporary gay black artists, "at the interface between different traditions" ("Skin Head Sex Thing," pp. 207, 204).

140. June mentally pictures herself as Glory dressed in a scarlet negligee, "lying back . . . with her brown arms raised" and clasped behind her head, entirely relaxed as she awaits a lover's arrival (11). On the one hand these images reinforce the American cultural stereotype of the black woman as a hypersexualized body; on the other hand, the degree of identi-

fication that is transpiring in June's mind is rather remarkable, for she has absolutely no qualms picturing herself *as* the sexualized black woman. The crucial difference between June's gaze and that of the white male voyeur, of course, is that she identifies with the object that she is looking at rather than attempting to possess her as sexual chattel.

141. Interestingly, it is a text that leads to Mark's discovery of Harlem, for he happens upon the now-famous "Negro Negro" issue of the *Survey Graphic* (1925) shortly after arriving in the city.

142. David M. Halperin, *One Hundred Years of Homosexuality and Other Essays on Greek Love* (New York: Routledge, 1990), pp. 15–18.

143. See Foucault's famous articulation in *The History of Sexuality:* "The nineteenth-century homosexual became a personage, a past, a case-history, and a childhood. . . . The sodomite had been a temporary aberration; the homosexual was now a species" (p. 43).

144. Irwin's enlightened and admirable views on homosexuality are the product, Niles makes clear, of a Continental Jewish background and cultured upbringing—qualities that Niles intimates are sadly lacking in parochial and puritanical America (165–66).

145. See D. A. Miller, *"Anal Rope,"* in *Inside/Out: Lesbian Theories, Gay Theories* (New York: Routledge, 1991), pp. 124–25.

146. Edelman, *Homographesis,* pp. 6–7. See my discussion in the previous section on *The Young and Evil.*

147. Among the contemporary songs cited in the text are Adelaide Hall's respective 1926 and 1927 hits, "I Must Have That Man" and "Creole Love Song," as well as "She's Funny That Way," "Why Was I Born?" and "Oh Give Me Something to Remember You By."

148. Another example of this process of internalization are the lyrics to the song Glory sings in the Magnolia Club: "There's no use pretending . . . Love needs no defending" (17). June focuses on the second phrase as an expression of her desire to open her heart to Seth, whereas Mark fixes on the first phrase, which underscores for him the closeted life he must daily lead. Ira also quotes the line, "There's no use pretending," but for him it signifies the inescapable visibility of racial difference (28). "She's Funny That Way" is another evocative example of the adaptability of popular music to various subcultural contexts: sung by a man, it refers to a woman who's "crazy for me"; sung by Sybil, it becomes a lesbian anthem; if applied to June, it glosses her "faghag" tendencies to bond deeply with gay men—for June is indeed, "peculiar in that fashion," "strange in that manner," as the lyrics say (55).

149. Another site where this tension between inner and outer, the authentic and the constructed, manifests itself is in the representation of commodity culture's articulations of the "feminine," which is presented as an essence but most often turns out to be a staged performance of certain "types." June becomes an important filter for these expressions: at the newspaper where she works, she writes a column for the Women's Page, and she has a "woman's eye" for reading into other women's dress their class background and economic status. The degree to which such femininity turns out to be less instinctual than socially produced is underscored by the *hyperfemininity* of the drag queens June observes at the Harlem ball, who, June realizes with a shock, have transposed qualities from "the world of Nature"—that is, supposed traits of biological gender—"to that of Art": "We must look to it," June exclaims, "that they don't beat us at our own game!" She then adds, in a very telling gloss on the sense of defamiliarization she is experiencing as the drag queens parade in the competition for best costume, "They make us *see ourselves.* . . . Actually, it as though *I'd never seen a woman before!"* (212; emphasis added).

150. For equivalent dynamics in contemporary contexts, see Mercer, "Skin Head Sex

Thing," pp. 169–210, which examines Mapplethorpe's homoerotic focus on the black male nude, and bell hooks, "Is Paris Burning?" in *Black Looks: Race and Representation* (Boston: South End Press, 1992), which criticizes white filmmaker Jennie Livingston's focus on contemporary Harlem drag balls in *Paris Is Burning* (1992). Livingston's position *vis à vis* her subject matter is very similar to Blair Niles's. A fascinating essay could be constructed around these two texts, both of which feature white women creating ethnographic documentaries of gay "otherness" in "black" Harlem. Despite the obvious empathy that marks both projects, both novel and film tend to erase the whiteness of the observing gazes that problematizes their authorial positions. The very fact that the name of the bar where the vogue balls are occurring is named "*Paris* Is Burning" takes on added significance in light of this chapter's focus on the queer affiliations linking Harlem and Paris as interchangeable urban sites in the subcultural formation of racially mixed gay communities.

151. My terms here are extrapolated from Susan Stanford Friedman's attempt to resist and dissolve "the fixities of the white/other binary" by positing a concept of relational positionality in "Beyond White and Other," p. 17.

152. The use of black wisdom as a closural device is an intriguing modernist trope, one that Faulkner, for instance, draws on for the conclusion of *The Sound and the Fury* but revises, as we will see in the next chapter, at the end of *Absalom, Absalom!*

153. One might also interpret this return of the repressed as Niles's repressed: a symptom, that is, of her own unconscious violence against, or dis-ease with, the racial subject matter that she otherwise liberally embraces. Another destabilizing return of the (racially) repressed in terms of latent violence against the oppressor might also be seen in Beulah's consolation of June. Somehow, in her mistress's absence, Beulah has missed the news of Seth's death and has laid out on June's bed as a surprise gift to celebrate her return to New York a wedding nightgown hand-embroidered by Beulah's mother in Trinidad. Seeing the "native" wedding dress deals June a great blow, since it only underlines the lack of romance with Seth when he was alive and the sexual fulfillment which his death now renders forever impossible. Once the "gift" has reduced June to tears, Beulah steps in to volunteer her comforting "diagnosis" of impotence as the root of Seth's problem—yet another blow to poor June's peace of mind!

154. Wallace Thurman, *Infants of the Spring*, p. 220. Intriguingly, given the self-reflexive reference to Stein's lost generation in Thurman's novel, Dorothy West encodes the author's gay proclivities in her biographical salute to him, "Elephant's Dance: A Memoir of Wallace Thurman," *Black World* 20 (Nov. 1970): 77–85, by first mentioning the "queer assortment of the 'lost generation' of Blacks and whites" (80) and then "the queer assortment of queer people" (81) with whom Thurman liked surrounding himself—phrases which for my purposes perfectly condense the queer, racial, and artistic aspects that I am aligning with being part of a "lost generation" here.

CHAPTER FIVE

1. Virginia Woolf, *Three Guineas* (1938; rpt., San Diego, CA: Harvest/HBJ, 1966), p. 135. All further references to this work are cited in the text.

2. Gertrude Stein, *Everybody's Autobiography* (New York: Random House, 1937), p. 135.

3. See Roland Barthes, *The Pleasure of the Text*, trans. Richard Miller (New York: Hill and Wang, 1975), pp. 10, 47; Peter Brooks, *Reading for the Plot: Design and Intention in Narrative* (New York: Knopf, 1984), esp. ch. 3; Teresa de Lauretis, *Alice Doesn't: Feminism, Semiotics, Cinema* (Bloomington: Indiana Univ. Press, 1984), esp. ch. 5.

4. Susan Stanford Friedman, "Lyric Subversions of Narrative in Women's Writing: Virginia Woolf and the Tyranny of Plot," in *Reading Narrative: Form, Ethics, and Ideology,* ed. James Phelan (Columbus: Ohio State Univ. Press, 1989), pp. 162–85. In addition, see feminist explorations of narrative erotics in women's fiction in critics as wide-ranging as Susan Winnett, "Coming Unstrung: Women, Men, Narrative, and (the) Principles of Pleasure" *PMLA* 105 (May 1990): 505–18; Marianne Hirsch, *The Mother/Daughter Plot;* Elizabeth Abel, "(E)merging Identities: The Dynamics of Female Friendship in Contemporary Fiction by Women," *Signs: Journal of Women in Society and Culture* 6 (1981): 413–35; and Teresa de Lauretis, *The Practice of Love: Lesbian Sexuality and Perverse Desire* (Bloomington: Indiana Univ. Press, 1994).

5. Even if Stephen Dedalus ends *Portrait of the Artist as a Young Man* with a call to his "father artificer" as he embarks on his quest to forge the "conscience of [his] race," it is telling that this is a constructed father and an artistic mentor, not his literal father. The correlation between fatherhood, "race" conscience, and legal paternity (another of Stephen's obsessions in *Ulysses*) will assume significance later in my discussion.

6. Elizabeth Abel, *Virginia Woolf and the Fictions of Psychoanalysis* (Chicago: Univ. of Chicago Press, 1989), pp. 89–94, 103–7.

7. Stein, *Everybody's Autobiography,* pp. 133, 135.

8. Kathryne V. Lindberg, "Mass Circulation versus *The Masses:* Covering the Modern Magazine Scene," *boundary 2* 20, no. 2 (Summer 1993), pp. 75–78. Lindberg brilliantly uncovers how the *Saturday Evening Post's* preference for the German boxer Max Schmeling in its post-match coverage of his well-publicized fight with American Joe Louis in 1935 betrays the magazine's avowedly apolitical stance, given the fact that Schmeling was a personal friend of Hitler and Goebbels and seen as a representative of "Nazi Aryan pride" (67–73). As Lindberg sardonically notes, "African Americans, it seemed, posed a greater threat to the Post's staff and readers than did Hitler" (68).

9. Quoted in Robert H. Brinkmeyer Jr., "Faulkner and the Democratic Crisis," in *Faulkner and Ideology: Faulkner and Yoknapatawpha, 1992,* ed. Donald M. Kartiganer and Ann J. Abadie (Jackson, MS: Univ. of Mississippi Press, 1995), p. 83.

10. Laura Doyle, *Bordering on the Body: The Racial Matrix of Modern Fiction and Culture* (New York and Oxford: Oxford Univ. Press, 1994), pp. 14–18; the quotation is from p. 18.

11. Quoted in Magnus Hirschfield's *Racism* (1937), trans. and ed. Eden and Cedar Paul (New York: Kennikat Press, 1938), p. 298, and cited by Doyle in *Bordering on the Body,* p. 10.

12. Christina Stead, *The Man Who Loved Children* (1940; rpt., New York: Holt, Rinehart, and Winston, 1965), p. 50. All further references to this work are cited in the text. Stead makes clear the disturbing link between this vision of a "perfect" world and the very American transcendentalism of the vision of which Sam, as we will see, is a major proponent: hence, again we see a surprising link between a tenet of American democracy and fascistic policy.

13. William Faulkner, *Absalom, Absalom!* (1936; rpt., New York: Vintage, 1972), p. 19. All further references to this work are cited in the text. Punctuation changes and minor variants have been silently added in light of the corrected text (Vintage, 1986) directed by Noel Polk.

14. Brinkmeyer, "Democratic Crisis," p. 72. To my knowledge Brinkmeyer is the only Faulkner critic who has made an explicit analogy between Sutpen's actions in *Absalom, Absalom!* and "the popular conception of the fascist dictator" (91).

15. Walter Benjamin, "The Work of Art in an Age of Mechanical Reproduction" (1936), in *Illuminations,* ed. Hannah Arendt (New York: Schocken Books, 1969), pp. 241–42.

16. While I do not mean to collapse the differences between American and German racism, it is noteworthy that Hitler reinforces his diatribes against the contamination of Aryan purity by Jewish blood in *Mein Kampf* (1925–27; rpt., New York: Stanpole, 1939) by drawing analogies to the contamination of whiteness by the inferior Negro; in particular he notes that France is being "permeated more and more by negro blood," which "constitutes a lurking danger to the existence of the white race in Europe" by "poisoning" Europe in its very "heart" (605). See also the propagandistic illustrations, reproduced in Klaus Theweleit, *Male Fantasies: Women, Floods, Bodies, History,* vol. 1, trans. Stephen Conway (1977; rpt., Minneapolis: Univ. of Minnesota Press, 1987), pp. 94, 96, of the Allied threat in the form of a ravaging, apelike black soldier; the first, "Jumbo," protests the stationing of black French troops in Germany after 1918 by showing a naked, lascivious, giant black soldier gathering white Rhine maidens in his hands; the second, a World War II poster, depicts the Allied arrival of U.S. troops in Italy in the form of an apelike black soldier carting off the white, nude statue of Venus di Milo. Further references to Theweleit's work are cited in the text.

17. Luce Irigaray, *Speculum of the Other Woman,* trans. Gillian C. Gill (1974, rpt. Ithaca, NY: Cornell Univ. Press, 1985). Theweleit has written how many theorists of fascism err in supposing an absolute division between subject and object reigning in the fascist oppression of different others; rather, Theweleit argues, the libidinal investments of fascism actually eradicate the very boundaries of self and other (205–226), creating the fantasmatic fear of engulfment which the "dams" of masculine armor are constructed to stop; this is not unlike my hypothesis, following Irigaray, of a paternal narcissism that dissolves the boundaries of self and other in the name of the father.

18. Geoffrey Hartmann, following Kenneth Burke, notes the monological intensity of *Mein Kampf,* which uses the "absolute magnitude" of "one voice" to subsume all other voices, in *Criticism in the Wilderness: The Study of Literature Today* (New Haven, CT: Yale Univ. Press, 1980), p. 100.

19. See Hitler's open embrace and careful outlining of propaganda as an efficacious political tool in *Mein Kampf,* vol. 1, ch. 6, and vol. 2, ch. 11.

20. Theodor Adorno, "Freudian Theory and the Pattern of Fascist Propaganda" (1951), in *The Essential Frankfurt School Reader,* ed. Andrew Arato and Eike Gebhardt (New York: Urizen Books, 1978), pp. 132.

Absalom, Absalom!

21. William Faulkner to Malcolm Cowley (1945), in *Selected Letters of William Faulkner,* ed. Joseph Blotner (New York: Random House, 1974), p. 202, quoted in Brinkmeyer, "Democratic Crisis," p. 92. Faulkner is referring to his character Percy Grimes, the racist murderer of Joe Christmas in *Light in August* (1931).

22. Maxwell Geismar, *Writers in Crisis: The American Novel Between Two Wars* (Boston: Houghton Mifflin, 1942), pp. 179–80. The phrase "Gothic fascist" comes from Joseph Blotner, *Faulkner: A Biography* (New York: Random House, 1977), p. 166. Both are quoted in Brinkmeyer, "Democratic Crisis," pp. 72.

23. Brinkmeyer, "Democratic Crisis," p. 77.

24. W. J. Cash, *The Mind of the South* (1941; rpt., New York: Vintage, 1991), p. 134; Katherine DuPre Lumpkin, *The South in Progress* (New York: International Publishers,

1940), pp. 115–16; and Richard M. Weaver, "The South and the Revolution of Nihilism," in *The Southern Essays of Richard M. Weaver,* ed. George M. Curtis III and James J. Thompson Jr. (Indianapolis, IN: Liberty Press, 1987), p. 183, all quoted in Brinkmeyer, "Democratic Crisis," pp. 78–80.

25. Lawrence H. Schwartz, *Creating Faulkner's Reputation: The Politics of Modern Literary Criticism* (Knoxville: Univ. of Tennessee Press, 1988), cited in Brinkmeyer, "Democratic Crisis," p. 78.

26. Brinkmeyer, "Democratic Crisis," pp. 72–73. Brinkmeyer also notes Faulkner's attempts to enlist in World War II and letters to his nephew in which he declares his patriotic support of the war effort.

27. Sigmund Freud, *Group Psychology and the Analysis of the Ego,* quoted in Adorno, "Freudian Theory," p. 124.

28. Quentin's incestuous feelings for Caddy can be derived from an intertextual reading of *Absalom, Absalom!* with *The Sound and the Fury* (1929). See John T. Irwin's influential reading of the two novels as companion texts in *Doubling and Incest/Repetition and Revenge: A Speculative Reading of Faulkner* (Baltimore: The Johns Hopkins Univ. Press, 1975).

29. Adorno, "Freudian Theory," p. 123.

30. Brinkmeyer, "Democratic Crisis," p. 91.

31. Peter Brooks, in *Reading for the Plot,* also uses the phrase "compensatory plot" (300) to describe Sutpen's design. What I find fascinating about Brooks's excellent chapter on the novel is the degree to which his arguments, if taken one more step, could be used to deauthorize the maleness of the oedipal model his reading attempts to establish.

32. Brooks puts it well when he notes that "Sutpen attempts to write the history of the House of Sutpen prospectively, whereas history is evidently always retrospective. . . . [O]ne cannot postulate the authority and outcome of a genealogy in its origin" (*Reading for the Plot,* p. 301). Or, as one of my students, Deirdre d'Albertis, noted in a seminar paper, "'The Web of the Text': Narrative Strategies in Faulkner's *Absalom, Absalom!*" (1985), Sutpen is "doomed to fail" because one cannot demand "an end in the midst of [one's] middle. . . . The violation of time which enables Sutpen to impose narrative selection on his life can be sustained only in such moments of isolated telling, not in the organization of his own 'work in progress' or unfinished existence" (4).

33. Warwick Wadlington in *Reading Faulknerian Tragedy* (Ithaca, NY: Cornell Univ. Press, 1987) explicates this irony in terms of the performative aspects of the text's vocal registers. In attempting to enforce his design of an immortal house and name, Sutpen commits himself to "an impervious heroic voice" that depends upon "purist self-enclosure" and the violent suppression of "vocal reciprocity," "the collapse of cultural dialogue into monologue" (171–72); yet, as Wadlington persuasively argues, this "monological fiat" depends upon the very "dialogical practice it excludes, [for] Sutpen's immortality is sustained by others' mutually competing voices" (172), as the very presence of the various narrators, ceaselessly interchanging and putting into circulation the Sutpen myth—his only immortality—attests.

34. So Quentin imagines the effect of Henry's disappearance on Sutpen, for whom his legitimate namesake is "gone, vanished, more insuperable to him now than if the son were dead since now (if the son still lived) *his name would be different* and those to call him by it strangers, and whatever dragon's outcropping of Sutpen blood the son might sow . . . would therefore carry on the tradition . . . *under another name*" (181–82; emphases added).

35. Bon's worldly sophistication and sensuality, as filtered through Mr. Compson's

jaded *fin de siècle* projections, become "a little femininely flamboyant" (110), the seductive charm of an "indolent esoteric hothouse bloom" (97). Mr. Compson's repeated description of the student lounging around in flowered dressing gowns and "the outlandish and almost feminine garments of his sybaritic privacy" (96) also work to feminize Bon's sexuality.

36. Jessica Benjamin, "Master and Slave: The Fantasy of Erotic Domination," in *Powers of Desire: The Politics of Sexuality,* ed. Ann Snitow, Christine Stansell, and Sharon Thompson (New York: Monthly Review Press, 1983), pp. 281–99.

37. Irwin, *Doubling and Incest,* p. 43 (here Irwin is reading Freud through Otto Rank) and pp. 89 90.

38. Relevant in light of this chapter's focus is the attitude toward same-sex love in fascist Germany. The basis for antihomosexual regulations under the Third Reich was less driven by morality, Stuart Marshall argues, than by the eugenics imperative, since homosexuals failed to reproduce for the "good" of the race; at the same time, the Nazi cult of male "bonding in the service of the state" led to an aesthetization of homoeroticism not unlike the ideal of brotherly love that, as will be shown, at once characterizes and destroys the relationship of Henry and Charles Bon. See Stuart Marshall, "The Contemporary Political Use of Gay History: The Third Reich," in *How Do I Look? Queer Film and Video,* ed. Bad Object-Choices (Seattle: Bay Press, 1991), pp. 78–79.

39. See also Patricia Tobin's discussion of incest and narrative repetition in *Time and the Novel: The Genealogical Perspective* (Princeton, NJ: Princeton Univ. Press, 1978), pp. 107–32, and Brooks, *Reading for the Plot,* p. 109, on literary incest as the threat of a narrative "short circuit."

40. Eve Kosofsky Sedgwick, *Between Men: English Literature and Male Homosocial Desire* (New York: Columbia Univ. Press, 1985), pp. 1–5.

41. See 2 Sam. 13. Absalom, son of King David, kills his brother Ammon for raping their sister Tamar.

42. It should be added that within Faulkner's psychologically freighted scenario, this exposure to the homosocial paradigm may be primary in *female* development as well; for, unknown to Sutpen, Judith and Clytie also witness the scene and, unlike the sickened Henry, remain ominously unmoved.

43. The erotics of Quentin and Shreve's storytelling, echoing the homoerotics of the Henry and Bon story, are underlined not only by this language of marriage and love, but by the authorial narrator's repeated emphasis on the rosy pink—as if virginal—flesh of the two college boys as they lie in bed in the closed, intimate space of their dorm room at Harvard and create this "marriage of speaking and listening."

44. These masculine fears are well attested to by the characterization of Scarlett O'Hara in Margaret Mitchell's *Gone With the Wind* (1936), published the same year as Faulkner's novel, for Scarlett embodies the paradox of the Southern belle whose sexual agency, in comparison to the image of enervated postwar Southern manhood, is potentially castrating. The commercial failure of Faulkner's novel in comparison to Mitchell's success led him to quip, in sexist fashion, "I seem to be so out of touch with the Kotex Age here"; his statement is a quintessential expression of sexual anxiety turned authorial anxiety. For this reference I am grateful to Elizabeth Young's forthcoming essay, "The Rhett and the Black: Sex and Race in *Gone With the Wind.*"

45. The equation of gender and race implicit in Freud's characterization of female geography as a dark continent is echoed in Faulkner's text when Sutpen describes the island of Haiti, the place where he encounters female sexuality for the first time (in the form of

Eulalia Bon, with her shadowy racial heritage), as "a dark inscrutable continent from which the black blood, the black bones and flesh and thinking and remembering and hopes and desires, was ravished by violence" (250). I am grateful to Elizabeth Young for bringing this connection to light in her seminar paper, "Gender and Anxiety in William Faulkner's *Absalom, Absalom!*" (15 April 1985). Doyle's commentary in ch. 1 of *Bordering on the Body,* "Of Race and Woman: Eugenics, Motherhood, and Racial Patriarchy," and in ch. 8, "'To Get to a Place': Intercorporeality in *Beloved,*" are also illuminating in this context.

46. Wadlington, in *Reading Faulknerian Tragedy,* pp. 176–81, 191–94, also looks at the subversive role that daughters, especially Judith, play in unweaving Sutpen's paternal myth of self-enclosed "purity" by transmitting the stories suppressed by his monologic voice to future generations.

47. One recalls, for instance, that the "primal scene" unfolded at the end of chapter 1 has not only been witnessed by Henry; unknown to Sutpen, Judith has hidden in the barn loft with Clytie and, in contrast to Henry, remains disturbingly unmoved by the bloody spectacle. Similarly, it is Judith who thrills in Sutpen's demonlike, decorum-breaking carriage drives to Sunday church, going into fits when they are halted.

48. See d'Albertis's seminar paper, "'The Web of the Text,'" p. 5. It also appears that Rosa is the one who executes Judith's deathbed orders, and authors the "text" that marks Judith's stone: "Suffered the Indignities and Travails of this World 42 Years . . . Remember Vanity and Folly and Beware" (211).

49. In regard to Clytie's unsung importance to the plot, see Brooks' intriguing theory that Quentin does not learn of Bon's racial background from Henry (the common assumption) on the night of his trip to the old plantation with Rosa, but from his "reading" of Clytie's face, which "opens the possibility of other part-Negro Sutpen children and alerts the narrators (and readers) to the significant strain of miscegenation" (*Reading for the Plot,* p. 299). Although I find this hypothesis a bit too ingenuous, it does attest to the significance of *female* transmissions of knowledge in the making of this story.

50. On the subversive centrality of Rosa's narrative role, see Linda Kauffman, "A Lover's Discourse in *Absalom, Absalom!*" *Modern Fiction Studies* 29 (1983): 183–200; Robert Con Davis, "The Symbolic Father in Yoknapatawpha County," *The Journal of Narrative Technique* 10 (1980): 39–44; Wadlington, *Reading Faulknerian Tragedy,* pp. 183–85; and Minrose C. Gwin's two books, *Black and White Women in the Old South: The Peculiar Sisterhood in American Literature* (Knoxville: Univ. of Tennessee Press, 1985), p. 116, and *The Feminine and Faulkner: Reading (Beyond) Sexual Difference* (Knoxville: Univ. of Tennessee Press, 1990), p. 75.

51. Winnett, "Coming Unstrung," p. 516. What Winnett has to say about the communal genesis of legend in George Eliot's *Romola* as a counter to the intentions of oedipal plotting is equally applicable to the counternarratives established by the community of tellers in *Absalom, Absalom!:* "Legend tells a story that is over. Its significance has been established *not by its protagonist, but by the community whose retelling of the story has become the sole measure of [its] importance.* . . . The narrative significance of a life history lies ultimately in the hands (ears, mouths, pens) of others; however we attempt to shape this [plot] in terms of our sense of its retrospective significance, [the] retelling [of the tale] is always beyond our control" (515, 514; emphasis added).

52. I am indebted to Michele Whelan for making a similar point in class. Much of Irwin's argument in *Doubling and Incest,* pp. 68–76, has to do with Quentin's contradiction-ridden attempts to master his father through the fantasy of a reversal of generations.

53. Brooks, *Reading for the Plot,* p. 306.

The Man Who Loved Children

54. Sylvia Plath, "Daddy" (1966), *Modern Poems,* ed. Richard Ellman and Robert O'Clair (New York: Norton, 1973), pp. 459–61.

55. Marilou B. McLaughlin, "Sexual Politics in *The Man Who Loved Children,*" *Ball State University Forum* 21 (1980): 30. McLaughlin's statement echoes Randall Jarrell's well-known preface to the novel, in which he identifies it as a masterpiece on the order of *War and Peace* and *Remembrance of Things Past.*

56. Joan Lidoff, "Home Is Where the Heart Is," *Southerly* 38 (1978): 370; comments on R. D. Laing are on p. 364.

57. When his sister, Jo, expresses her worries about the influence of his agnosticism on the children ("when they grow up they will have nothing to believe in"), Sam responds, without skipping a beat, "*Now* they believe in their poor little dad": the implication is that he is God enough for them (112).

58. Psychoanalysis's split between the liberator-father and archaic mother, between paternal superego and maternal narcissism, as Jessica Benjamin has deftly demonstrated, falsifies the complexity of the psychological mechanisms influencing *all* the parties involved in Oedipal triangulation, parents as well as child. See Benjamin, "The Oedipal Riddle," in *The Bonds of Love,* pp. 133–81. Judith Kegan Gardiner makes a similar point about Sam's "maternal" narcissism in an essay I read after completing this section, "Male Narcissism, Capitalism, and the Daughter of *The Man Who Loved Children,*" in *Fathers and Daughters,* ed. Lynda E. Boose and Betty S. Flowers (Baltimore: Johns Hopkins Univ. Press, 1989), pp. 387–88.

59. Adorno, "Freudian Theory," p. 127.

60. This is narcissistic engulfment attempting to disguise itself as nurturance; Joan Lidoff puts it well when she notes in *Christina Stead* (New York: Ungar, 1982) that Sam "feed[s] off that which [he] pretends to feed" (26). Correlatively, Sam treats his children as receptacles to penetrate and fill at will: "Already he was beginning to slop over, drown them with his new knowledge, bubbling, gurgling, as he poured into them as quickly as possible all he had learned" (295).

61. Gardiner also makes this point in "Male Narcissism," p. 388.

62. Lidoff, "Home," p. 365.

63. This insight complements Henny's view that Sam is "try[ing] to talk [her] to death" (165). Indeed, in the marital war of words that the two wage, Sam's threat is "shut up or I'll shut you up" (142; see also 35 and 497–98).

64. Stead writes "long parts [of *The Man Who Loved Children*] in [Sam's] very own Sam language" (217), comments Margot Horne in "A Family Portrait: Christina Stead and *The Man Who Loved Children,*" *Dutch Quarterly Review of Anglo-American Letters* 2 (1981): 217.

65. McLaughlin, "Sexual Politics," p. 30.

66. Susan Sheridan notes the lack of marked authorial commentary in the novel in " *The Man Who Loved Children* and the Patriarchal Family Drama," in *Gender, Politics, and Fiction: Twentieth-Century Australian Women's Novels,* ed. Carole Ferrier (Univ. of Queensland Press, 1985), p. 139; McLaughlin, in "Sexual Politics," pp. 33, 36, explains the calculated risks that Stead takes in moving from indirect free discourse to authorial viewpoint; and Terry Sturm comments on the purposeful "disorientation of perspective" characteristic of Stead's method in "Christina Stead's New Realism: *The Man Who Loved Children* and *Cotter's England,*" in *Cunning Exiles: Studies of Modern Prose Writers,* ed. D. Anderson and S. Knight (Sydney: Angus and Robertson, 1974), p. 16.

67. See, for example, Dorothy Green's consternation with Stead's chronology in "*The Man Who Loved Children:* Storm in a Tea-Cup," in *The Australian Experience,* ed. W. S. Ramson (Canberra: Australian National Univ. Press, 1974), p. 178. Among other withheld or delayed information, offhanded comments reveal, long after the fact, that the house has remained unheated the whole winter that Sam is away and that Henny has not arranged a hospital delivery for Charles-Franklin's birth because Sam has not sent the money to cover the expenses.

68. Note, for example, the combination of the commonplace and the grotesque in the description of Sam "as large as life, like a great red and yellow apple bounding about," an image which perfectly condenses the American, Edenic, and Satanic references embedded in his characterization. This linguistic warping of reality is particularly evident in Henny's inspired descriptions of her downtown outings, where people look like dirty shrimps, are big as hippopotamuses, grin like sharks, and have hair "like a haystack in a fit": "all these wonderful creatures," the narrator continues, "who swarmed in the streets, stores, and restaurants of Washington, ogling, leering, pulling, pushing, stinking, overscented, screaming and boasting, turning pale at a black look from Henny, ducking and diving, dodging and returning, were the only creatures Henny ever saw" (8–9). Lidoff, in *Christina Stead,* notes that Stead's modernist use of language "casts words into new associations which, disjointed and dislocated, create painful new perceptions" and create "a psychology of fluidity" (22). McLaughlin, in "Sexual Politics," also comments on how Stead's "elaborate, even excessive" (36) language is often ambiguous in its location.

69. An entire essay could be written on the traumatizing effects that Sam's paternal law has on these two sensitive sons. The account of the twelve-hour marlin boil provides a particularly harrowing illustration of the way in which Sam lords his castrating power over his sons, engaging them in unequal competition to prove himself their superior. Speaking to Little-Sam in terms of sympathetic identification that merely disguise the sadism underlying his command, Sam orders the boy to shovel the putrifying marlin offal as an act of manly self-discipline—despite the fact that the boy cannot stop throwing up: "Little-Sam here is the dead spit of his old man, and he got to have a strong stomach: he got to stomach anything" (491). When Little-Sam continues to retch, Sam viciously flings marlin liquid all over the stunned boy. As a consequence Little-Sam lapses into complete muteness: and, soberingly, *we do not hear him utter a logical word the rest of the novel.* (I suspect Stead had Melville's chapter "The Try-Works" in *Moby-Dick* in mind when creating this scene, given the Ahab-like malevolence and hubris Sam here assumes; throughout the novel Stead makes numerous self-conscious allusions to American transcendental and democratic literature— Emerson, Thoreau, Whitman—to illuminate the ease with which American "patriotic" ideals can easily be bent to totalitarian oppression and dictatorship.) The case of Ernie evinces another dimension of oedipal conflict. Due to Sam's financial ineptitude, the boy has assumed the role of "husband" to Henny as her confidant in money-matters: "He alone knew, of all the children, that Daddy had realized on his life insurance, that there was no fire insurance, and that there was a second mortgage on the house" (392). Prematurely aged by the burden of this knowledge, Ernie becomes fixated—in a classic Freudian example of anality—with making, saving, and hiding money. It is grimly appropriate that Sam exerts his control over Ernie by making him throw away the scrap metal the boy has been hoarding to sell for money. Ernie's ballooning misery reaches a nightmarish, psychodramatic climax when he hangs himself in effigy—not even an adolescent, he is already determinedly suicidal. It is depressing to imagine the fates of Sam's sons outside the temporal parameters of the text.

70. The essentially sadistic view of male sexuality that Sam thus impresses upon Louie implies a corresponding ideal of female masochism, one in which his letters from Malaya attempt to school her. Wanting Louie to "grow up to be like her own sweet, womanly mother, a blessing to some man," Sam writes to her in perversely rapturous detail of Buddhist temple paintings that depict the slow torture and beheading of "women who wouldn't do what their husbands told them" (231, 239). "Women are the blessing of men," he later schools Louie, while simultaneously warning her of the venereal dangers that inevitably follow sexual indulgence (480). The double message is clear: a woman's future happiness as man's helpmate depends on the repression of her sexual agency.

71. One is reminded of Freud's rejection of his early "seduction theory" in favor of the oedipal complex, which, as we have seen, relocates the source of incestuous desire in the daughter's *fantasy* rather than in the father's *reality*. Christine Froula provides an interesting exegesis of the literary ramifications of this rejected theory in "The Daughter's Seduction: Sexual Violence and Literary History," *Signs* 11, no. 4 (1986): 653–57. On the relationship between patriarchally structured societies and the prevalence of father-daughter incest, see Judith Lewis Herman and Lisa Hirschman, "Father-Daughter Incest," *Signs* 2 (1977): 735–57.

72. Lidoff, *Christina Stead*, p. 21.

73. Sheridan also comments on the homosocial triangle formed by Henny, her father, and Sam in "Patriarchal Family Drama," p. 137.

74. From Henny's point of view her *only* power lies in carrying out a series of undercover thefts and piracies (recall Lucy Snowe's undercover operations); as the narrator informs us, she is one of that large race of embattled and embittered human beings who see life "as a series of piracies of all powers" (13). Chiseling away at Sam's dominant text from a position of advance-and-retreat on its margins, she resembles one of the *voleuses de langue* imagined by Claudine Herrmann in *Les voleuses de langue* (Paris: des femmes, 1976).

75. Constantly described in imagery of pieces and fragments, Henny is Freud's Dora grown up, the female hysteric whose neuroses are both internally and externally created. "A dirty cracked plate! that's just what I am!" (13), Henny declares in a telling evocation of her internalized feminine self-hatred. The sexual revulsion implicit in this image is tied to the one-dimensional role she has served within Sam's paternal plot as child-bearer, and the result is a self-loathing that she projects outward against Louie, whose pubescence is an all-too-visible reminder of her own dismal sexual destiny.

76. Sheridan, "Patriarchal Family Drama," p. 139.

77. Neither story, moreover, is an "innocent" fairy tale; both incorporate the physical and psychic violence surrounding the children and displace it into the realm of myth.

78. Sheridan, "Patriarchal Family Drama," p. 148.

79. Patricia Yaeger, *Honey-Mad Women: Emancipatory Strategies in Women's Writing* (New York: Columbia Univ. Press, 1988), pp. 6, 20.

80. Yaeger, *Honey-Mad Women*, p. 41.

81. That the "irresistible call of sex" tying mother and daughter together in a covert league is a formidable opponent to Sam's proclaimed authority is made clear in the brilliantly perverse metaphor Stead develops to describe Henny's and Louie's intuited alliance: "Against him, the intuitions of stepmother and stepdaughter came together and procreated, began to put on carnality, feel blood and form bone, and a heart and brain were coming to the offspring. This creature that was forming against the gay-hearted, generous, eloquent, goodfellow was bristly, foul, a hyena, hate of woman the house-jailed and child-chained against the keycarrier, childnamer, and riothaver" (36).

82. Significantly, Henny's last words before realizing what Louie is doing are "My womb is tearing . . . my insides are torn to pieces" (506), whereupon she seizes the teacup as if defiantly resolved to replace Louie's act of potential matricide with her own suicide. Henny's Medusa-like powers make one last appearance as Louie is "struck dumb" by her gaze, "unable to speak a word" (506), while the mother directs her final curse not at Louie but at Sam: "'My womb is torn to pieces with you . . . she's not to blame, she's got guts, she was going to do it. . . .' Sam looked at Henny with hatred. 'All right,' said Henny, 'damn you all!'" (506–7). Now it is Henny rather than Sam (see note 69 above) who assumes the Ahab-like position of ultimate defiance to the end, even to damnation.

83. In terms of Stead's next novel, Louie indeed successfully exits *The Man Who Loved Childen* to a new "textual" life, for, as Christopher Wallace-Crabbe has pointed out in conversation, *For Love Alone* (1944) takes up Louie's quest where its predecessor leaves off, with Louie resurrected in the figure of Teresa Hawkins, whose story begins with her physical and metaphorical journey across the world. Rudolf Bader, in "Christina Stead and the *Bildungsroman*," *World Literature Written in English* 23 (1984): 34–45, proposes a similar view of *For Love Alone* as a continuation of Louie's story.

84. I am indebted to David Wingrove for his superb insights in uncovering and developing this fascinating parallel in the seminar paper "Family, Gender, and Narrative in *The Man Who Loved Childen*" (24 April 1985), p. 7.

85. Sheridan, "Patriarchal Family Drama," p. 147. See Freud, "Femininity," pp. 104–7, 110–14.

86. De Lauretis, *Alice Doesn't*, pp. 112, 119, 108, 133 (emphases added).

87. De Lauretis, *Alice Doesn't*, p. 119.

88. De Lauretis, *Alice Doesn't*, p. 119.

89. De Lauretis, *Alice Doesn't*, pp. 121, 120.

CHAPTER SIX

1. Jonathan Dollimore, "The Cultural Politics of Perversion: Augustine, Shakespeare, Freud, and Foucault," *Textual Practice* 4, no. 2 (Summer 1990): 191.

2. Homi K. Bhabha, "The Other Question . . . Homi K. Bhabha Reconsiders the Stereotype and Colonial Discourse," *Screen* 24, no. 6 (1983): 33.

3. See Doris Lessing's introduction to *The Golden Notebook* (1962; New York: Bantam, 1981), viii–ix, which was added to the novel in 1971. All further page references to this edition are cited in the text.

4. The Lessing statistics are reported in the introduction to *Approaches to Teaching Lessing's The Golden Notebook,* ed. Carey Kaplan and Ellen Cronan Rose (New York: The Modern Language Association of America, 1989), p. 13, which also includes the quotation from Molly Hite's "*The Golden Notebook* in a Graduate Seminar on Contemporary Experimental Fiction," p. 89.

5. Claire Sprague, "*The Golden Notebook:* In Whose or What Great Tradition?" in *Teaching Lessing's The Golden Notebook,* ed. Kaplan and Rose, p. 79.

6. Relevant here are the theories of what has been called the antipsychiatric movement of the 1960s and 1970s, seventies, notably the psychopolitics of R. D. Laing and Otto Rank, whose emendations of Jung's concepts of the psyche and the collective unconscious attempt to account for the impact of contemporary ideology in creating mental disturbance and inner division. For the intersection of Jungian and Laingian psychology in Lessing, see note 60 in the following section on *The Golden Notebook*.

7. I have put the word *exterior* in quotation marks because several critics argue that

Anna's lover Saul may not have an objective existence at all, but exists *only* as a psychological projection given "life" in her diaries. See Linda Kauffman, *Special Delivery: Epistolary Modes in Modern Fiction* (Chicago: Univ. of Chicago Press, 1992), pp. 145–46, and Evelyn J. Hinz and John J. Teunissen, "The *Pietà* as Icon in *The Golden Notebook,*" *Contemporary Literature* 14 (Fall 1973): 459.

8. *Balthazar* (1958; rpt., New York: Pocket Edition, 1961), p. 185. The *Alexandria Quartet* was originally published by E. P. Dutton, in the following order: *Justine* (1957), *Balthazar* (1958), *Mountolive* (1959), *Clea* (1960). I cite from the Pocket edition (1961) throughout. Subsequent page references are included in the text, along with the first initial of the volume unless the context makes the citation clear.

9. On the mythic significance of Tiresias's androgyny, see Joseph Cambell, *The Mask of the Gods: Occidental Mythology* (New York: Viking, 1964), pp. 26–27, 171.

10. Androgynous symbols occur, for instance, in Durrell's use of the topos of incest to define the mirroring between his lovers, who replace the "symbolic lovers of the free Hellenic world [with] . . . something different, something subtly androgynous" (*J* 4) and in Anna's recurring dream of the leering, ambiguously sexed dwarf that she climactically realizes is both herself and Saul ("I was the malicious male-female dwarf figure . . . and Saul was my counterpart, male-female, my brother and my sister" [594]).

11. C. G. Jung, *Collected Works: The Development of Personality,* ed. Sir Herbert Read, Michael Fordham, and Gerhard Adler (Princeton, NJ: Princeton Univ. Press, 1954), 17: 198; emphasis added; quoted in Calvin S. Hall and Vernon J. Nordby, *A Primer of Jungian Psychology* (New York: Penguin/Mentor, 1973), p. 47. For a summary of Jung on the anima and animus archetype, see Hall and Nordby, pp. 46–48. Carolyn G. Heilbrun uses both Jung's and Joseph Campbell's work to support her arguments for the role androgyny has played in literature in *Toward a Recognition of Androgyny* (New York: Harper, 1973).

12. George Wickes, ed., *Lawrence Durrell—Henry Miller: A Private Correspondence* (New York: Dutton, 1963), pp. 4–5.

13. Edward Said, *Orientalism* (New York: Vintage, 1979), pp. 1, 190.

14. Bhabha, "The Other Question," p. 33.

15. Wickes, *Correspondence,* pp. 189–90; emphasis added.

16. Wickes, *Correspondence,* pp. 190, 195.

17. Wickes, *Correspondence,* p. 196; emphasis added.

18. For a groundbreaking contemporary critique of this ideology, see Simone de Beauvoir's *The Second Sex* (1952). De Beauvoir's work and Betty Friedan's *The Feminine Mystique* (1962) serve as appropriate bookends for the period I am describing, before the "official" advent of the women's liberation movement of the sixties.

19. Juliet Mitchell, *Women: The Longest Revolution* (1966), excerpt quoted in Betty Roszak and Theodore Roszak, eds., *Masculine/Feminine: Readings in Sexual Mythology and the Liberation of Women* (New York: Harper Colophon, 1969), p. 170. Importantly, Mitchell goes on to argue that this liberalization of sexual behavior does not necessarily constitute a "revolution," because it often works in tandem with "new forms of neocapitalist ideology and practice" which commoditize sexual freedom as a consumable pleasure.

20. See Paul Robinson's chapter on Kinsey in *The Modernization of Sex: Havelock Ellis, Alfred Kinsey, William Masters, and Virginia Johnson* (Ithaca, NY: Cornell Univ. Press, 1976), pp. 43 and following.

21. My thoughts here are informed by Janice Gore's study of hyperfemininity, "Boobs, Boys, and High Heels: Postfeminism and the Neofifties Aesthetics," written for a graduate seminar (Spring 1992).

22. Leo Braudy, "'No Body's Perfect': Method Acting and Fifties Culture," *Michigan Quarterly Review* 35, no. 1 (Winter 1996): 191–215.

23. Kauffman, *Special Delivery,* p. 143.

The Alexandria Quartet

24. See Joan Goulianos, "A Conversation with Lawrence Durrell about Art, Analysis, and Politics," *Modern Fiction Studies* 17 (1971): 164–65.

25. Durrell to Miller, Aug. 1935, and Miller to Durrell, 1 Sept. 1935, in Wickes, *Correspondence,* pp. 4–5. Durrell repeats the phrase "man-size" twice in his letter.

26. Wickes, *Correspondence,* p. 5.

27. Durrell to Miller, April 1937, in Wickes, *Correspondence,* p. 90.

28. Morton P. Levitt, "Art and Correspondences: Durrell, Miller, and *The Alexandria Quartet,*" *Modern Fiction Studies* 13 (1967): 302.

29. Durrell to Miller, Spring 1944, in Wickes, *Correspondence,* pp. 189, 190.

30. Wickes, *Correspondence,* p. 189–90; emphasis added.

31. Hence, when Durrell, reminiscing about the closing of the French brothels, laments the loss of some "marvellous encounters," he is *not* talking about encounters with their female clientele but those with the other male patrons, particularly his fellow artists: "I spent some fabulous hours with Henry Miller at the Sphinx," he remembers—hours "spent," we are meant to assume, in verbal rather than, as the archaic expression goes, the "criminal conversation" more commonly associated with *maisons closes.* See Lawrence Durrell, *The Big Supposer: A Dialogue with Marc Alyn,* trans. Francine Barker (1972; New York: Grove Press, 1974), p. 130. Jane L. Pinchin, in "Durrell's Fatal Cleopatra," *Modern Fiction Studies* 28, no. 2 (Summer 1982): pp. 229–36, offers an acute exegesis of the way in which women become pawns in what is an essentially homosocial world of male bonding; writing in 1982 before Sedgwick coined the term *homosocial,* Pinchin nonetheless comes to very similar conclusions as those advanced by Sedgwick.

32. As Darley aptly notes, the "politics of love" in Alexandria are caught up in another political agenda, "the slime of plot and counterplot" (*B* 12–13) most thoroughly revealed in *Mountolive.* Whereas the Coptic minority—who consider themselves the true descendants of Pharaonic Egypt—traditionally served the country as "the brains of Egypt," they have fallen from favor during the British colonial administration's support of the Moslem-led government. Nessim, a Christian Copt, marries Justine, an Egyptian Jew, in order to win over the trust of the Zionist revolutionaries plotting to overthrow Palestine; such a move, Nessim calculates, would improve the Coptic cause in Egypt by breaking up Arab unity. Pursewarden, who serves under Mountolive in the British embassy, also feels that the British support of the Arab-backed Egyptian government is a grave mistake because of the fanatical impulses behind the cause of Arab unity that could well lead to disintegration of British influence; he, like Nessim, believes the way to stabilize the situation in Egypt is to "[re]build Jewry into the power behind the scenes" (*M* 90). What is particularly interesting here is the way in which the overt opposition of colonial British presence and colonized Egypt is made more complex by the competing minority factions within Egypt that consider the Arab-led Egyptian majority to be the real oppressor. Mountolive's diplomatic mission is made even more delicate by the approaching war: at stake in what side Egypt might take in the coming conflagration is strategic control of the Suez, and there is concern that Arab nationalists are flirting with the fascist powers. The amount of influence that the British had in Egypt during the years covered by the fictional Mountolive's tenure, moreover, had recently been attenuated by the Anglo-Egyptian Treaty of 1936, which had abol-

ished the long-standing, highly influential British High Commission; by the time Durrell is writing the *Alexandria Quartet,* Egypt was emerging as a nonaligned power under the leadership of Nasser after the Egyptian Revolution of 1952. For historical details, see Anne Ricketson Zahlan, "The Destruction of the Imperial Self in Lawrence Durrell's *The Alexandria Quartet," Perspectives on Contemporary Literature* 12 (1986): 3–12, and Peter Mansfield, *The British in Egypt* (London: Weidenfeld and Nicholson, 1971).

33. Durrell, *The Black Book* (1938; rpt., New York: Dutton, 1963), pp. 234–35, quoted in Levitt, "Art and Correspondences," p. 303.

34. Lawrence Durrell, *A Key to Modern British Poetry,* pp. 3, 26, 29, quoted in Levitt, "Art and Correspondences," p. 310–11.

35. This self-reflexive commentary is only the tip of the iceberg. Pursewarden throughout pompously intones ideas about novel-writing in a post-Einsteinian age, proclaiming at one point that the relativity proposition lies behind all modern art (*B* 133); at another touting the idea of the "'*n*-dimensional' novel" trilogy, (*J* 224); and likening his mode of characterization to random aggregates of "quanta" (*B* 241).

36. These texts include Balthazar's revised manuscript of *Justine;* Arnauti's semifictional *Moeurs* (based on his affair with Justine); what Darley and Balthazar believe is Justine's diary (but turns out to be rejected pages of *Moeurs*); Nessim's folio documenting his descent into madness; excerpts from Pursewarden's journals; Clea's correspondence; and countless other "sliding panels."

37. Said, *Orientalism,* p. 188; Allen Edwardes and R. E. L. Masters, *The Cradle of Erotica* (New York: Julian, 1963), p. 175; and Sir Richard Burton, trans. and ed., *The Book of the Thousand Nights and a Night: A Plain and Literal Translation of the Arabian Nights Entertainments,* 10 vols. (London: Burton Club private edition, 1885–86), 10: 194.

38. Said, *Orientalism,* pp. 103, 187.

39. Gustave Flaubert to Brouilhet, 15 Jan. 1850, in *Flaubert in Egypt: A Sensibility on Tour,* trans. and ed. Francis Steegmuller (Chicago: Academy Chicago Publishers, 1979) [compilation of Flaubert's travel notes and letters], pp. 84–85; emphasis added. All further page references to this work are cited in the text. Flaubert's travel writings are filled with many more moments of excited homoerotic voyeurism and experimentation, which I examine at greater length in "Mappings of Male Desire in Durrell's *Alexandria Quartet," Displacing Homophobia,* spec. issue of *South Atlantic Quarterly* 88 (1989): 73–106, and "Vacation Cruises; or, The Homoerotics of Orientalism," *PMLA* 110 (Jan. 1995): 89–107.

40. Josephus, *Jewish Antiquities,* trans. Ralph Marcus (Cambridge, MA: Harvard Univ. Press [Loeb Classical Library], 1963), 8: 15–16; C. S. Sonnini, *Travels in Upper and Lower Egypt,* 3 vols., trans. Henry Hunter (London: Stockdale, 1807), 1: 251–52.

41. Compare Durrell's representation to Said's description of western visions of the Orient as "passive, seminal, feminine, even silent and supine" (*Orientalism,* p. 138).

42. Antonia Lant makes the valuable point that Alexandria is not just or simply the "other," because its historical position as conduit between East and West renders it *at once* familiar and foreign to its western visitors, in "The Curse of the Pharaoh; or, How Cinema Contracted Egyptomania," *October* 59 (1992): 86–112. The association between Alexandria and Cleopatra (whose love affair with Antony provides a classic meeting of "East" and "West") does not go unnoted by Durrell, who indicates that Justine is a "minor" modern-day "Cleo," whom "you can read all about in Shakespeare" (*J* 82).

43. My terminology here evokes Teresa de Lauretis's description in *Alice Doesn't: Feminism, Semiotics, Cinema* (Bloomington: Indiana Univ. Press, 1984)—also discussed in chapters 1 and 5—of narrative desire as an oedipal and male-gendered activity, in which

woman is doomed to serve as a marker or obstacle, like the Sphinx, in a story of heroic quest that is never her own (109).

44. As such, Durrell's representation of Justine forms a classic illustration of the phenomenon that Alice Jardine labels "gynesis," the philosophical setting-into-motion of the concept of Woman as a symbol of the postmodern crisis. See Jardine, *Gynesis: Configurations of Woman and Modernity* (Ithaca, NY: Cornell Univ. Press, 1985), pp. 33–34, 42. For more on Durrell's existentialism, see Chet Taylor, "Dissonance and Digression: The Ill-Fitting Fusion of Philosophy and Form in Lawrence Durrell's *Alexandria Quartet*," *Modern Fiction Studies* 17 (1971): 167–79.

45. I am greatly indebted to David Wingrove—whose superb seminar paper on the relation of erotic perception and narrative in Durrell, "Dance of the Black Dominos: Narrative and Sex-Roles in Durrell's *Balthazar*" (April 1985), inspired me to reread Durrell seriously—for uncovering, much as I detail in the following pages, the psychological significance of the homosexual doublings of Darley in Toto and Keats revealed by this photograph, as well to the roles that Scobie, Clea, and Narouz play in Darley's quest to alleviate his heterosexual anxieties.

46. Freud, *Three Essays,* pp. 13–14, 37–38.

47. Hindsight reveals that this scene has been briefly represented in *Justine,* where Darley describes entering a prostitute's lighted booth "to wait my turn" (166)—the same phrase used in *Balthazar*—but mistakes (or so we are now led to suppose) the male partner for the barber Mnemjian. Thus the recollection in *Balthazar* becomes an instance not merely of Darley's psychic repression but of the textually repressed, that which was "forgotten" in writing *Justine.*

48. David Wingrove, whose analysis of the Darley-Toto doubling is particularly acute, brought this imagistic connection to my attention. See Wingrove, "Narrative and Sex-Roles," pp. 13–14.

49. Wingrove, "Narrative and Sex-Roles," p. 14.

50. Alan Warren Friedman, *Lawrence Durrell and the Alexandria Quartet: Art for Love's Sake* (Norman: Univ. of Oklahoma Press, 1970), p. 148. Upon this "necessary sacrifice," Friedman continues, Darley "sheds his unmanly timidity" (149).

51. Pinchin also notes that Darley's role here represents an attempt at "revers[ing] the sexuality of birth," in "Durrell's Fatal Cleopatra," p. 235.

52. To view Clea as sexually incomplete until her seduction by a man overlooks the sexual experience she has earlier shared with Justine: only from a heterosexual viewpoint is she a "virgin" at the time of Amaril's seduction. As Pinchin wittily puts it, "Amaril and Darley, male doctor and writer . . . make a good woman of Clea . . . [by] curing her of her homosexuality and her virginity" (235).

The Golden Notebook

53. Kauffman, *Special Delivery,* p. 154.

54. Foucault, *History of Sexuality,* p. 43.

55. "Because the world is so chaotic art is irrelevant" (42), Anna declares to Molly when the latter chastises her for not writing.

56. Interview with Lessing reported in Robert Rubens, "Footnote to *The Golden Notebook,*" *The Queen's,* 21 Aug. 1962, p. 31, quoted in Michael Thorpe, *Doris Lessing's Africa* (London: Evans Brothers, 1978), p. 88.

57. For an excellent exposition of these similarities, see Mark Spilka, "Lessing and Lawrence: The Battle of the Sexes," *Contemporary Literature* 16, no. 2 (Spring 1975): 218–40.

In a letter to Roberta Rubenstein, dated 28 March 1977, Lessing acknowledges that Lawrence has been a major influence on her work. See Rubenstein, *The Novelistic Vision of Doris Lessing: Breaking the Forms of Consciousness* (Urbana: Univ. of Illinois Press, 1979), p. 124 n. 3.

58. Spilka notes in "Lessing and Lawrence" that Lessing's expression of the modern themes of "the fragmentation of society and of consciousness . . . follows the example of Joyce, Faulkner, and Woolf, in their use of multiple perspectives upon common strands of modern experience to convey its many-sidedness, and of the stream-of-consciousness techniques to express both alienation and the quest to get beyond it to some kind of . . . connectedness" (222). Rubenstein comments in *Novelistic Vision* on a specific instance of Lessing's manipulation of temporal sequence, "This arrangement breaks up chronology, reinforcing the layering of experience and the necessity for the reader to consider the simultaneity of events . . . from several perspectives as if at once" (90).

59. Much Lessing criticism has been dedicated to "decoding" the complexities of Lessing's puzzlelike, fragmented narrative structure, attempting to separate its representations of the "fictional" from the "facts" of Anna's experience—a process complicated by the revelation that the omnisciently narrated "Free Women" chapters, which the framing structure encourages the reader to accept as unmediated "fact," turn out to be another novel written by Anna. Among the numerous helpful analyses of Lessing's splintered form and multiplying viewpoints, see Rubenstein, *Novelistic Vision;* Kauffman, *Special Delivery;* Betsy Draine, *Substance Under Pressure: Artistic Coherence and Evolving Form in the Novels of Doris Lessing* (Madison: Univ. of Wisconsin Press, 1983); Molly Hite, "The Future in a Different Shape: Broken Form and Possibility in *The Golden Notebook,*" in *The Other Side of the Story: Structures and Strategies of Contemporary Feminist Narrative* (Ithaca, NY: Cornell Univ. Press, 1989), ch. 2, pp. 61–69; Patricinio P. Schweickart, "Reading a Wordless Statement: The Structure of Doris Lessing's *The Golden Notebook,*" *Modern Fiction Studies* 31, no. 2 (Summer 1985): 263–79; and Joseph Hynes, "The Construction of *The Golden Notebook,*" *The Iowa Review* 4, no. 3 (Summer 1973): 100–113.

60. Despite Lessing's reservations about certain aspects of psychoanalytic theory, the text abounds with references to psychotherapy, from the declaration that initiates the Blue Notebook upon Anna's return to England, "I think I shall go to a psycho-analyst" (232), to reports of her sessions with the Jungian analyst Mrs. Marks, her frequent use of the notebooks to record and interpret her dreams, the fact that her lover Michael (the prototype of Paul in the Yellow notebook) is a "witchdoctor" (Anna's word for psychoanalysts), and the states of hysteria, depression, schizophrenia, and altered consciousness that beset numerous characters. Lessing's knowledge of psychological theory and psychotherapy runs deep and wide; particularly relevant are the popularization of Jung and the "antipsychiatry" school of the 1950s and 1960s, touched upon in the introduction to this chapter (see note 6). Lessing was reading Jung seriously before writing *Martha Quest,* whom she cites throughout the *Children of Violence* series, as Draine notes in *Substance Under Pressure,* p. 44. A useful summary of the impact of Jungian concepts on Lessing's work appears in Rubenstein, *Novelistic Vision,* pp. 22–34, who also reports Lessing's dissatisfaction with Freudian theory (or, more accurately, the psychiatric establishment's conservative version of his theories being promulgated in the 1950s) for making the unconscious into, as she says in a 1969 interview, a "great dark marsh full of monsters" dialectically opposed to reason. She feels that Jung, in contrast, more usefully embraces the unconscious as the repository of those archetypal, complementary forces of light and dark that create human wholeness. See "Doris Lessing at Stony Brook: An Interview by Jonah Raskin," in *A Small*

NOTES TO PAGES 393–95

Personal Voice, ed. Paul Schlueter (New York: Knopf, 1974), p. 67, quoted in Rubenstein, *Novelistic Vision,* p. 23. While the influence of Jung can still be seen in Lessing's use of archetypes, dream material, and the interior quest motif in *The Golden Notebook,* she had also begun to question Jungian therapy by the late 1950s. Anna's satire of her Jungian therapist, Mrs. Marks, as "Mother Sugar" for sugar-coating the ills of contemporary society by referring every conflict to the primitive realm of myth and folklore makes clear this dissatisfaction. Around this period, Lessing's understanding of the psyche's relationship to the world was increasingly influenced by the philosophy of R. D. Laing, under whose supervision she experimented with hallucinogens to induce temporary psychotic states. Marion Vlastos summarizes the influence on Lessing's work of Laing's theories of the social origins of madness and schizophrenia in *The Divided Self* (1959) and *The Politics of Experience* (1967) in "Doris Lessing and R. D. Laing: Psychopolitics and Prophecy," *PMLA* 91(1976): 245–58. Kauffman's "schizoanalytic" reading of the novel in *Special Delivery* also relies on Laing's influence on Lessing. For Lessing's turn to Sufi philosophy in the 1970s as a more authentic predecessor to Jung's ideas, see Rubenstein, *Novelistic Vision,* pp. 230–31, and Draine, *Substance Under Pressure,* pp. 92–93.

61. Rubenstein, *Novelistic Vision,* pp. 99, 85.

62. Claire Sprague, "'Anna, Anna, I Am Anna': The Annas of Doris Lessing's *The Golden Notebook,*" in *The Anna Book: Searching for Anna in Literary History* (Westport, CT: Greenwood Press, 1992), p. 155.

63. Rubenstein, *Novelistic Vision,* p. 77.

64. Southern Rhodesia was settled by English entrepreneurs long before Britain stepped in to make it a Crown colony. In this role Britain attempted to mitigate the forces of apartheid, through policies aimed at moderating the worst of the segregationist policies of the white colonists, who themselves opposed British rule. In the 1950s, Southern Rhodesia formed a "Federation" with Northern Rhodesia and Nyasaland, which ushered in a period of prosperity, black economic advancement, and limited integration; this period was followed by a white backlash in the form of Ian Smith's explicitly apartheid Rhodesian Front party, which dissolved the Federation and declared the country's independence from Great Britain in 1965. A protracted racial and civil war followed, lasting until 1979, when Britain intervened to force the open elections that led to the election of Mugabe's socialist party and the declaration of Zimbabwe's independence in 1980. See Eve Bertelsen's summary in "*The Golden Notebook:* The African Background," in *Approaches to Teaching Lessing's The Golden Notebook,* ed. Kaplan and Rose, pp. 31–33; and, with special reference to Lessing's youth in Rhodesia, Michael Thorpe's account in *Lessing's Africa,* pp. 4–6. For two divergent readings of Lessing's complex relation to colonialism in her life and fiction, see Antony Beck, "Doris Lessing and the Colonial Experience," *The Journal of Commonwealth Literature* 19, no. 1 (1984): 64–73, which argues that her representation of colonialism "functions to conceal her fundamental commitment to the bedrock values she shares with the white settlers" (69), and Jenny Taylor, "Memory and Desire in *Going Home:* The Deconstruction of a Colonial Radical," *Critical Essays on Doris Lessing,* ed. Claire Sprague and Virginia Tiger (Boston: G. K. Hall, 1986), which reads Lessing's 1965 autobiography, *Going Home,* as a symptomatic "speaking of the unspoken that lies beneath Lessing's official fictional projection" (38). In both cases, note the shared assumption that the fiction contains a repressed content that hovers around the "problem" of colonialism and race.

65. Thorpe, *Lessing's Africa,* pp. 6, 7. The man Lessing married, Gottfried Lessing, also a Communist, was one of these refugees and the model for Willi Wulf in the novel.

66. Florence Howe, "A Conversation with Doris Lessing (1966)," in *Doris Lessing: Crit-*

ical Studies, ed. Annis Pratt and L. S. Dembo (Madison: Univ. of Wisconsin Press, 1974), p. 10; emphasis added.

67. On the slippery relationship between Anna and her fictional character Ella, see the passage in which Anna halts her continuing description of her plans for the *Shadow* novel to declare, "I, Anna, see Ella. Who is, of course, Anna. But that is the point, for she is not" (459). The same might be said of the relationship of the Anna of the notebooks to the "Anna" of "Free Women" (who is as much a fictionalized self-portrait as "Ella"), as well as to the unnamed, black female protagonist of *Frontiers,* who, as the lover of Paul's fictional prototype, "stands in" for Anna.

68. This sexual consummation, however, is entirely undercut as a swooning narrative climax when Paul meets a very unheroic death a few days later. Summoned to duty, he inadvertently walks into his airplane's moving propeller, and, in an instance of the "return of the repressed" that verges on parody, severs both legs "just below the crutch" (78), dying instantly. A symbolic castration of manhood if ever there were one, Paul's death casts a rather ironic light on the effects of his heterosexual initiation.

69. The chain of displacements at work goes something like this: George is in love with the cook's wife (white/black), the cook's wife is married to Jackson the cook (black/black), Jackson "loves" Jimmy (so Jimmy says) (black/white), Jimmy is in love with Paul (white/white), Paul makes love to Anna (white/white). Anna's surrogate in her novel, in this scheme, thus becomes the black woman, the most oppressed other who is also the most invisible character of this entire group.

70. See Spilka, "Lessing and Lawrence," p. 229.

71. Spilka comments that Lessing, in advocating the necessity of the heterosexual love act to achieve "true" orgasm, here "subscribes to one of the male myths of our day which Lawrence helped to create" (237).

72. This incident bears comparison to the scene in *Strange Brother* where Caleb tells June about going bird-hunting with his white masters back on the old plantation, which also facilitates a return of the racially/sexually repressed. See chapter 4.

73. Thorpe, in *Lessing's Africa,* pp. 92–93, also notes how this "perfect" match exposes Anna's romanticization of her material in her war novel.

74. This male ambivalence is revealed in the thoughts that immediately precede this expression of disgust, as Anna recalls Comrade Nelson's confession that "sometimes he looked at his wife's body and hated it for its femaleness. . . . Sometimes, he said, he saw his wife as a kind of spider, all clutching arms and legs around a central devouring mouth" (612). See also Lawrence's description of the Mater as the devouring toad in chapter 2.

75. See Elizabeth Abel's suggestion that the writing of female bonding in the novel performs a kind of *écriture féminine* or female writing that stresses the relational, nonverbal, and gestural, in "The Golden Notebook: 'Female Writing' and 'The Great Tradition,'" in *Critical Essays,* ed. Sprague and Tiger, pp. 102–4. True enough, Anna and Molly's relationship bears many resemblances, both explicit and implicit, to a mother-child relationship; but this seems to me a parental model rooted in a more traditionally oedipal sense of the need for separation and distance (hence the separation that follows their final kiss in the last line) rather than, in Chodorovian revisions of Freud's paradigm, the mirroring symbiosis that becomes a model for adult relationships between women.

76. Gilles Deleuze and Félix Guattari, *Anti-Oedipus: Capitalism and Schizophrenia,* trans. Robert Hurley et al. (1972; rpt., Minneapolis: Univ. of Minnesota Press, 1983), p. 170; also cited in Kauffman, *Special Delivery,* p. 157.

77. My terms here are indebted to Lee Edelman's analysis of the film *Laura* in *Homo-*

graphesis (New York and London: Routledge, 1994), pp. 192–241, in which he argues that the ultra-femme Laura represents "the other face" of Waldo Lydecker's effeminately gendered homosexuality. Lessing, in contrast, represents effeminate gay maleness (the Waldo position) as the other face of Anna's desired femininity (the Laura position).

78. Lessing's valorization of the irrational—in contradistinction to her understanding of doctrinaire Freudian psychoanalysis—shows the influence of the antipsychiatry movement contemporaneous with the writing of the novel, particularly the thought of Otto Rank, who writes in *Beyond Psychology* (New York: Dover, 1958), "We still have to learn, it seems, that life, in order to maintain itself, must revolt every so often against man's ceaseless attempts to master its irrational forces with his mind" (18). Quoted in Hinz and Teunissen, "The *Pietà* as Icon," p. 470.

79. Claire Sprague, for instance, writes in "Doubletalk and Doubles Talk in *The Golden Notebook*," *Papers on Language and Literature* 8, no. 2 (Spring 1982), that Anna must come to learn that the "principle of destruction" is really within herself and *not* a gendered principle: "But Anna perceives it as male and must unlearn that perception" (196). Draine, in *Substance Under Pressure*, asserts that Saul is "the first and indispensable factor in a series of conditions that lead [Anna] to . . . wisdom," a basically affirming mentor figure whose sadistic impulses Draine misrecognizes as merely "romantic egotism" (83–84); and Roberta Rubenstein in "Doris Lessing's *The Golden Notebook:* The Meaning of Its Shape," *American Imago* 32, no. 1 (Spring 1975), reads Saul's declaration, in one of Anna's dreams, that "I am going to hurt you. I enjoy it" (579) as Anna's projection onto Saul because she refuses to admit that she enjoys hurting herself (51–52). However true the latter point may be, it divorces Anna's internalized masochism from its source in the male abuse that she has experienced in daily life, not just in her dreams. In all these critiques, there is a failure to see the codependence between the psychological mechanism of *projection* (of inner emotions onto external representatives) and the equally operative psychic mechanism of *internalization* (the unconscious assimilation of externally imposed standards of behavior).

80. For one of the better Jungian readings of the novel, see Hinz and Teunissen, "The *Pietà* as Icon," who conclude that "during her period of madness, Anna does 'go back'; she descends to the lowest and most primal reaches of the collective unconscious. . . . We recognize immediately that [Jungian] theory provides the rationale for Lessing's technique in *The Golden Notebook*" (470, 468). At various moments in the text, indeed, Anna and Saul seem to become timeless archetypes, "two unknown quantities, two forces anonymous, without personality" (631) locked in eternal warfare. See also the night of dreams on pp. 603–4, in which Anna and Saul act out every archetypal gender role imaginable; Anna's declaration that "something has to be played out, some pattern worked through" (583); and her (premature) epiphany that "I had been delivered from disintegration because I could dream it" (600). On the other hand, as indicated in note 60 above, Anna is openly critical of her psychologist Mrs. Marks's method of archetypal dream interpretation for reducing every symptom to "the safety of myth" (470).

81. Gwen Bergner, "Who Is That Masked Woman? or, The Role of Gender in Fanon's *Black Skin, White Masks*," *PMLA* 101 (Jan. 1995): 78; Frantz Fanon, *Black Skin, White Masks* (1952; trans. 1967; New York: Grove, 1991), p. 110, quoted in Bergner.

AFTERWORD

1. E. M. Forster, *Aspects of the Novel* (New York: Harcourt, Brace, 1927), p. 126. Also quoted in Peter Brooks, *Reading for the Plot: Design and Intention in Narrative* (New York: Knopf, 1984), p. 5.

2. Jessica Benjamin, *Like Subjects, Love Objects: Essays on Recognition and Sexual Difference* (New Haven, CT: Yale Univ. Press, 1995), pp. 7, 4.

3. For a recent literary explication of the uses of intercorporeality in modern writing, see Laura Doyle, *Bordering on the Body: The Racial Matrix of Modern Fiction and Culture* (New York and Oxford: Oxford Univ. Press, 1994), pp. 8–9, 70–80, and chapter 8.

4. On the relation of Freud's analysis of the game of *fort* and *da* to narrative repetition and mastery, see Brooks, *Reading for the Plot,* pp. 97–98.

Index

Abel, Elizabeth, 177, 190, 195–96, 292, 450n. 10, 456n. 74, 457n. 91, 478n. 75, 493n. 75

Abraham, Julie L., 468n. 76

Absalom, Absalom! (Faulkner), 298–322; biblical archetype of, 311; black sons in, 315–16; black wisdom as closural device in, 477n. 152; demagoguery in, 297; and fascism, 294; historical grounding of, 295; on history as cyclical repetition, 294; mothers as absent in, 314–15; multiple narrators of, 300–303; narrative structure of, 302–3, 310; on overpass to love, 422; plot of the father in, 29–30, 290–91; primal scene in, 312, 481n. 42, 482n. 47; self-reflexivity and indeterminacy of, 296, 302–3, 322; setting of, 300; as Southern modernist gothic, 290, 338; sublimated homoeroticism in, 14, 310–12; wrestling spectacle in, 312, 481n. 42, 482n. 47

Action, William, 67–68, 436n. 13

Adorno, Theodor, 297, 305, 329, 430n. 50

agency, female, 10, 78, 95, 358

Alexander, Lewis, 220

Alexandria Quartet (Durrell), 364–88; central topic of, 364–65; as colonial narrative, 370; descent into the irrational in, 355, 356, 365; Egypt as setting for, 365, 373, 386–87; foreign otherness in, 358–59; inspiration for, 360; interior confrontations projected outward, 30; male homosexuality as threat in, 355, 359–61, 365, 372–73, 385; postmodern rejection of, 354; race and colonialism as issues in, 349–50; reception of, 353; relativity in viewpoint of, 364, 365, 367–73, 387, 489n. 35; spectrum of variant sexual prac-

tices, 371. *See also Balthazar; Clea; Justine; Mountolive*

Allen, Carolyn, 467n. 75

Ammons, Elizabeth, 440n. 48

Analysis of a Case of Hysteria (Freud). *See Dora*

androgyny, 357, 487nn. 10, 11

Antiphon (Barnes), 336

antipsychiatric movement, 486n. 6, 494n. 78

anxiety: all stories provoking, 297; crisis in modernist narrative, 10–11; in Freud's analysis of female sexuality, 121–27; homosexuality as scapegoat for, 360, 361; in Woolf and Joyce, 149–50

argot, gay, 219, 255–57, 462n. 41

Armstrong, Isobel, 9, 25, 428n. 25

Auerbach, Nina, 432n. 9

authority: anxieties of in Woolf and Joyce, 149–50; attempts to authorize female desire, 139; as contested in *Dora*, 133–36; crisis in modernist narrative, 10–11. *See also* narrative authority; sexual authority

autoeroticism. *See* female masturbation

awakening, sexual. *See* sexual awakening

Awakening, The (Chopin), 73–93; female erotic awakening plot of, 27–28; as fiction of interiority and sexuality, 5; formal innovations in, 75; Gilded Age context of, 84–85; Lawrence and Freud contrasted with, 72; modernity of, 70; narrative strategies of, 78–81, 143; ocean's centrality in, 437n. 25; as protomodernist, 85; water as metaphor in, 64

Bacchus, Michael, 456n. 83

Baker, Houston, 427n. 12

Baker, Josephine, 261, 464n. 50

Bakhtin, Mikhail: on dialogical quality of the